CALIFORNIA REAL ESTATE PRACTICE

First Edition

All content, suggestions, ideas, concepts and conclusions presented in this book are subject to local, state and federal law; court cases revisions or any revisions of the same. Great care has been taken to provide the most accurate, up-to-date material, however all topics may be subject to revisions both legal and otherwise. The reader is urged to consult legal counsel regarding any points of law. This publication is not intended to be used a substitute for competent legal or accounting advice.

TABLE OF CONTENTS

CHAPTER 10 — Title Insurance and Escrow

CHAPTER 11 — Property Management

CHAPTER 12 — Ethics

CHAPTER 13 — Real Estate Investment

CHAPTER 14 — Exchanges and Trade-In Programs

CHAPTER 15 — Business Sales and Other Brokerage Activities

THE REAL ESTATE PROFESSION

What you will learn in this Chapter

- The real estate profession

- Real estate marketplace

- Real estate economics

- Brokerage

- The right attitude

- Finding the right broker

- Continuing education

Test Your Knowledge

1. Real estate agents must have a good understanding of which of the following aspects of the industry?
    a. Appraisal
    b. Finance
    c. Property Management
    d. All of the above

2. Which is the best term to describe the economic condition of the real estate marketplace?
    a. Supply and demand economics
    b. Imperfect market
    c. Buyer's market
    d. Seller's market

3. Which term describes a property's decline in value because of external factors influencing a neighborhood?
    a. Economic obsolescence
    b. Diminishing returns
    c. Filtering down
    d. Economic life

4. The term brokerage means:
    a. A real estate office
    b. A loan office
    c. To bring people together
    d. A general real estate term used to describe offices where professionals work.

5. Which one of the following is not a question a real estate agent can ask himself or herself in looking for a positive attitude?
    a. Are you persistent?
    b. Are you willing to chance failure by trying?
    c. Are you happy with your current income?
    d. Are you a problem solver?

6. A successful agent will:
    a. Actively research all hiring brokers before making a decision about where to work.
    b. Maintain a positive outlook and attitude.
    c. Participate in all mandatory continuing education classes as well as any supplemental training provided by the broker.
    d. All of the above.

7. The late renewal period for a real estate licensee is:
    a. 90 days
    b. 1-year
    c. 2-years
    d. There is no late renewal period; all licensees must retake the state examination if they allow their license to expire.

INTRODUCTION

If a group of accountants, attorneys, architects, bankers, surveyors, insurance agents and title company representatives are all working together, what common thread binds them? In our situation it is the real estate industry, more specifically realtors. Each member of this group of professionals depends on the knowledge and expertise of real estate salespersons and brokers to make sure their portion of a property transaction goes smoothly, accurately and legally. More importantly, your client depends on you for understanding of each step in a very detailed process.

In this first chapter, you will learn what it means to be a real estate professional. Different aspects of real estate will be introduced and covered, above and beyond merely listing property. The relationships that can be established between professionals and clients will be examined, as well as the complex nature of the real estate marketplace and where you as a realtor fit into this mix. Additionally, we will cover different steps you can take to ensure success in this very dynamic and ever changing profession. To be successful as a real estate professional, you need to anticipate what the market will do, and stay one step ahead of the competition. In order to do this you must constantly educate yourself about new law changes concerning all aspects of the real estate industry - from sales, leasing, taxation, development and appraisal to setting challenging goals for yourself.

THE REAL ESTATE PROFESSION

The real estate profession is a very dynamic, multi-layered career that goes far beyond showing homes and filling out paperwork. A real estate professional must have an understanding of all the steps in the real estate process -- appraisal, financing, escrow, property management and sales. People can specialize in any of the areas of real estate; however, for our purposes we will focus mostly on sales. Above and beyond choosing a specialty in real estate, or a sales niche, a real estate professional must be a good communicator and listener, and patient with all types of people. After all, without clients, a real estate professional would not have a job, and the better you are at communicating with your clients, the better real estate agent you will be.

Remember
Besides being knowledgeable sales persons, real estate agents must possess a working knowledge of:
• Appraisal
• Finance
• Escrow
• Property Management

Real estate transactions can be an overwhelming experience for people, and it is important for you as the agent and expert to be able to handle all of your client's questions knowledgeably. For the first-time homebuyer the excitement and confusion of the process may seem very difficult or challenging. A good agent will make sure to communicate every step in the process, no matter how big or small. In circumstances surrounding a death of a loved one, property transfer may be emotionally difficult. The agent must be very patient and understanding. In other transactions, your client may be a busy professional or new to the community. Whatever the challenge, your client will depend on your expertise, and good communication will always be the key for good agent / client relationships.

Getting to know your client on a personal, yet professional, level will also make a property transfer go smoothly. The more information you possess regarding the client, the better, more quickly and accurately you can serve them. For example, a real estate sales agent most likely would not show a client homes with 2 bedrooms if the agent knew the client was married with four children and was actively seeking a larger home. This may seem overly simplistic; however there are many factors a real estate agent should know in order to best help the client find the perfect home or property for their specific needs.

As we have illustrated, being a real estate professional is much more than selling homes. While the property transaction is the ultimate goal, all the steps leading up the actual transfer will define how successful you will be.

THE REAL ESTATE MARKETPLACE

The real estate market is a very dynamic environment where numerous factors play a role in determining property prices at different times. From a strict economic standpoint, the law of supply and demand will dictate prices of homes based on the amount of housing available in a given area. When demand for housing is high, and the number of houses on the market is low, prices are driven up. When there is a large supply of houses on the market and demand is low, the prices generally will be lower. If the market were strictly driven by supply and demand, real estate economics would be a very simple topic to understand. Unfortunately, the real estate market is an imperfect market which means that the market conditions do not adhere to traditional supply and demand economics, thus our discussion on economics will be much more complex than simple supply and demand models. The economics of the real estate market will be discussed in more detail later.

Remember
The real estate market is an imperfect market, not closely adhering to traditional supply and demand economics.

Some might suggest that buyers set home prices. The volume of buyers determines the demand, and the price is set by how much a buyer is willing to pay for a property. On the other hand, most people are familiar with the common phrases "buyer's market" and "seller's market." No matter how you look at it, there is give and take on the part of both buyers and sellers. A buyer will determine what the most appropriate offer is, and the seller will decide if it is acceptable.

Because the real estate market is an imperfect market, prices for one property may be lesser or greater given the area, timing, personal emotions or other circumstances of the sale. Even similar properties may have a sharp contrast in price given different criteria. A 2000 square foot California Craftsman home in Los Angeles would most likely be more expensive than a similar home in Bakersfield. The homes may functionally and cosmetically be twins, but the location determines a price difference. Or, two similar homes in San Diego may have a sharp contrast in price depending on the neighborhood, time of year of the sale, or economic climate. The phrase "location, location, location" is often used in real estate to justify or explain why one property is markedly more expensive in comparison to another, whether the functionality or physical features of the home justify this price difference or not.

The following are some other reasons that the housing market is considered imperfect:

- Buyer and seller knowledge. This term is perhaps misleading. Real estate prices may become inflated or sell for under market value because the buyer and seller have misinformation on what property is worth or what it should sell for. A seller may be misinformed of the property values in a neighborhood and decide to sell his or her property for under market value. This will create a favorable scenario for the buyer. On the other hand, the homeowner may believe the properties in his or her neighborhood are worth much more than the actual market price. If a buyer purchases property at an inflated price, it is usually an uninformed buyer who has not done much research on home prices or the market for certain areas. Because of buyer's and seller's knowledge, or misinformation, an imperfect market may be created. When buyers and sellers are more educated about current real estate markets and prices, true market values will be better reflected in property transactions.

- Interest rates or term of the trust deed. Current interest rates can both positively and negatively affect the market. In times with high interest rates, fewer people will be willing to borrow money for large purchases like real estate because of large finance charges. The opposite is true when interest rates are low. People are very eager to purchase property and lock in a low rate of interest, reducing financing charges and mortgage payments.

- Emotion. Emotion plays a big part in determining the right house for each individual. Sometimes you may show the same client several houses that are similar, almost identical, but based on emotion or other external factors one will stand out as perfect while the others are simply not what the client is looking for. A nostalgic color, a certain tree growing on the property, or a completely unrelated event that happened earlier in the day may make a huge difference in the client's attitude and emotional mindset.

- Real estate agent error. Sometimes the variations in price from one property to another are due to mistakes made by the real estate agent. An inexperienced agent or an agent new to an area may not know the market well enough to suggest the right selling prices for property, and may underestimate or overestimate prices based on current market conditions. Occasionally, an agent may also act unethically in his or her own interest to obtain a listing. While this is rare, it is another factor creating an imperfect market.

- Stratified market. The market may be stratified based on the available supply of homes in specific price ranges and the amount of qualified buyers in that price range. For example, a market with many buyers looking for homes in the $200,000 - $300,000 price range where there few available homes will see prices driven up due demand outstripping supply. Conversely, a market with many homes for sale in the $500,000 - $600,000 range with few buyers will force the seller to accept a lower price for the property. Stratification will create an imperfect market based on simple supply and demand theories when coupled with price. A market with more buyers and fewer available properties is considered a "seller's market," as the property will usually sell for a premium. The opposite is true for a market situation where there are more properties than buyers. This is a "buyer's market," as the buyer can usually obtain property for under market value.

- Product differentiation. Unless the same person built identical homes on equally sized lots with the same design, décor and landscaping, no two homes are the same. Even homes that are similar will have differences setting them apart from the others. Square footage might vary; colors, architecture, design, landscaping or other added features or amenities such as a hot tub or swimming pool create differences between even very similar homes.

- "Will-sell" versus "must-sell" and "will-buy" versus "must-buy." Sellers and buyers can also influence variation in housing prices depending on the urgency of the sale. In a "will-sell" situation the seller has decided to place his or her house on the market, but is not in a rush to sell. In a scenario such as this, the seller usually will ask a premium for the house, above market value, and wait for a buyer to pay that amount. In a "must-sell" situation, the seller is under some sort of deadline to sell the home as soon as possible. In this scenario, the seller usually does not have the luxury of time, and will often let the home go for less than market value, or less than the listed price.

- Just as the "will-sell" versus "must-sell" situations create an imperfect market, so will the "will-buy" versus "must-buy" situation. In a "will-buy" scenario the buyer has a lot of time to find the perfect house at the perfect price. Perhaps he or she currently owns a home in the same town or development and is simply casually looking for a change, with no time pressure. On the opposite end of the spectrum is the "must-buy situation." In a "must-buy" scenario the buyer is under a time crunch and must find a home immediately. People relocating for a job to a new town or state who only have a few weeks to find a place to live and move are often faced with a "must-buy" situation. These people will usually pay more for a home than a buyer in a "will-buy" situation.

- Imperfect knowledge. In the real estate industry, increasing the supply of new homes takes a long time. A developer must purchase the land, and then obtain all the necessary permits and maps to develop it. After the development phase comes the construction and then sale of the properties. Because a developer will not know the future of the market or the economy, or what the competition might be doing, it is a gamble to move forward with a development and changes usually are not feasible due to time constraints. A developer's imperfect knowledge of what the future might hold contributes to an imperfect market.

Remember
Some reasons the real estate market is imperfect and does not follow conventional economics:

- Buyer and seller knowledge, or misinformation
- Interest rates, or the term of the trust deed
- Emotion
- Real estate error
- Product differentiation
- "Will-sell" versus "must-sell" and "will-buy" versus "must-buy" situations
- Imperfect knowledge
- Stratified market based on prices

An Overview

Real estate economics is similar to the principles of general economic studies. However, as we have seen, the real estate market is imperfect and will not always adhere to general economic principles. In both general economics and real estate economics, the concept of scarcity of goods and the demand for these goods applies. Because of the difficulty in forecasting what will happen with real estate markets, economists generally will not readily apply their principles to this aspect of economics. A substantial amount of our nation's wealth – estimated at nearly two-thirds – is contained in real estate. Additionally, after government employment, jobs dealing directly or indirectly with real estate make up the second largest industry in this country. You can see why the study of real estate economics is so important.

Keep in mind when studying real estate economics that the economic life of a building is usually much longer than most other investments. The useful life of a building can extend much further than the depreciation schedule used for tax purposes. The life of a building is generally determined by the quality of materials used when building it, the type of structure built, the location where it is built and the degree of maintenance and upkeep put into the building. Those buildings that were well designed and cared for will last for over a hundred years.

Another idea to keep in mind is that decisions made in real estate now will affect both the future market and future owners. The amount of care that goes into construction and quality of materials will determine how long the building will be in use, and the longer it is in use it the more potential it has to change owners. The older a building, the more it will appreciate in value. Additionally, well-placed buildings will appreciate the value of the land they occupy.

The real estate market is a very turbulent market with changes that affect the economy. Sometimes these factors work with each other; other times they are working against each other. In the event that the economy is healthy and people have a lot of money to invest, the real estate market will boom. Add onto this manageable interest rates and the market will be even better. In the event that there is a depression or many people are out of work, there real estate market is generally depressed and weak. Other factors influence the real estate market on a much more local scale. When a highway is redirected to bypass a small town, or a road is widened within a city property, values can either plummet or increase.

When advising clients on the direction of the market or the different prices they should offer or ask, you are expected not only to know the current market trends, but also to have an understanding of real estate economics in order to make educated suggestions. Obviously, real estate economics is a volatile concept, subject to change with no warning, but real estate agents who understand the markets and economics will be a in a much better position for success than those agents who don't have a firm grasp of the subject.

Real estate economics can be understood at four levels. The four levels are national, regional, city and neighborhood. When conducting an analysis of the real estate economy, one would first begin with analyzing the neighborhood level and work up from there. Many times the local economies will have huge effects on a small area, while having a very minute effect, if any, on the regional or national level.

Example
A small city has recently experienced the closing of a major manufacturing plant, the city's largest source of employment. With the closing of the plant, many of the city's residents found themselves without employment, and could not afford to pay their mortgages. In order to survive, many of the residents decided to relocate to other cities and towns for employment. The local economy of this particular city will experience a depression, reverberating into the housing market as well. The cities and towns offering the residents new jobs will also experience a change in their economy as new people move into the community, purchase homes and spend their money for goods and services. One city's economy will be devastated, while other economies will prosper, as a result of just one event. This, however, would not affect the national or even regional area of the economy.

Markets, Prices and the Law of Supply and Demand

What determines the price for a piece of property, or how much money a person may pay in rent from one region to the next? Why are rents higher in the middle of the city compared to the suburbs, or in smaller communities? Markets with perfect competition will see an equal amount of goods and services supplied to an equal amount of people demanding these services. Consumers in this situation will naturally opt to purchase the least costly goods to fit their specific needs. In an imperfect market, there are more sellers than buyers, or vice versa. People can't always depend on finding the lowest priced goods, as there will be many people trying to obtain the same product, driving the price up. When the market is imperfect, either the buyer or the seller is exercising some degree of control over the market by influencing the price for goods or services. In a market with perfect competition, the buyers and sellers exert no control over the market.

In a perfect, balanced market the law of supply and demand dominates the economic rules. Supply is the amount of goods or services available for consumers, and demand is the number of consumers demanding a specific product or good. In the real estate world, supply would obviously be the amount of real estate available in an area, and demand would be all potential buyers in an area. While real estate economics don't generally follow the traditional rules of supply and demand, it is important for you to understand what they are, when we can examine how this is relevant to real estate economics.

First, let's look at the law of demand. The law of demand states that when goods or services are offered at a lower price, more people will be interested in making a purchase. The opposite is true when the price for a good or service goes up in price; there are less people willing to pay for the product. When people are not able to afford a product, demand will drop. There are several relationships between demand and communities' demographics.

- An increase or decrease in income will affect demand. When income decreases, there will be lower demand for certain goods and services; when income increases, the demand for the same goods and services will increase.

- Advertising can have an effect relationship on demand. A well-written ad enticing the public to go out and purchase a specific good or service will increase demand. Additionally, advertising may alert consumers about goods and services in their area they did not know about, increasing awareness and potentially increasing demand.

- Population will change the demand for a product as well. An increase in population will increase demand for goods and services, while a population decline will decrease demand.

- When credit is easily obtained, demand for goods and services will increase, as people will be able to afford to purchase more. Less credit available in an area will reduce demand. This is especially true for high-dollar purchases such as real estate. When interest rates are low, and banks have more money to extend, demand will increase for qualified applicants.

- Consumers' wants and desires will affect demand. As desire for one product rises over another, certain goods will be in higher demand over rival goods. For example, as hybrid vehicles have become more efficient and affordable, there has been more demand for hybrid vehicles over traditional combustion engine vehicles.

Remember
- Income
- Advertising
- Population
- Credit
- Consumers' wants, needs or desires

The law of supply states that as sales for a particular product increase, manufacturers will increase the supply of that product. As sales for another item decrease, the manufacturer will supply less of that item.

Different factors contribute to the changes in supply. As demand increases or decreases, supply will reflect the consumer's change of interest or desires. As stated in the law of supply, once consumers begin purchasing more of one type of goods over another, more of the goods in higher demand will be produced. Less of the products with low demand will be produced. Another factor that can affect the level of supply is anticipation of future market trends, consumer wants or profits. If forecast models or predictions show a higher profit for one product over another, the supply of the product with a higher profit margin will increase. If profit margins are forecasted to decrease for a product, the manufacturer may cut supply of the particular item or service. Finally, changes in the production costs of a good can change the supply. As labor, raw materials, shipping costs and other price factors increase, and the item become less profitable, manufacturers, tend to decrease supply.

As we already know, the real estate market is an imperfect market, one where there are multiple factors creating less than free market conditions. Most real estate purchases require financing; financing is controlled in part by the government's actions with the Federal Reserve, which controls the money supply and interest rates. So even if we could talk strictly on a product supply and demand level, we must take into account these financing factors to understand real estate economics. Home and rent prices will influence demand; however, demand is meaningless unless the potential purchaser has adequate purchasing power backed up with the appropriate financing. A consumer with no purchasing power has no effect on supply, and one could argue is not a consumer at all since he or she is not actively participating in the market.

Economics deals with the concept of elasticity in supply and demand. Elasticity is the change in the consumer's reaction based on price. As the price is raised or lowered, whether the supply and demand are greatly affected or not affected at all depends on elasticity or inelasticity. Elasticity means that the demand or supply will be affected while inelasticity means that the supply and demand will not change much, if at all.

Remember
- Elasticity is the change in supply or demand in relation to price changes
- Supply or demand is elastic if a price change will dramatically change supply or demand of a product
- Supply or demand is inelastic when price changes have little effect on the supply or demand of a product

In terms of real estate, the total supply of land is inelastic. Occasionally, after a natural disaster such as a flood, hurricane, volcanic eruption or the depositing of sediment from a river, land can be formed, but as a general rule the supply of land remains constant or inelastic. On the other hand, the supply of land for specific uses is elastic. For example, if a city or town was growing at a remarkable rate, farmland adjacent to the town or city will become very valuable and farmers may be enticed to sell their land to developers planning new developments. The supply of land available for development will increase, while the supply of farmland in the area will decrease. Finally, the demand for real estate will almost always be elastic. With the number of homes on the market and the cost of homes, consumers will usually opt for the least expensive property. This will influence prices in the immediate, local market.

Remember
- Supply of land is inelastic
- Demand for land is elastic
- Supply of land for specific purposes is elastic

Real Estate Supply and Demand

When sellers think that market prices are increasing, they will hold onto their properties and wait for prices to increase to the optimum levels. This puts fewer properties on the market, creating low supply with higher demand. High demand for real estate with lower supply will increase prices. If sellers believe that market prices are decreasing, they will quickly put their properties on the market to sell while prices are high. This creates an abundance of supply for a lower demand; prices now begin falling to remain competitive with all the other houses on the market. If buyers believe prices are coming down, they will postpone their decision to purchase property until the prices have come down to a satisfactory level. This creates a surplus of houses on the market, again causing prices to fall to remain competitive. Consumers generally will act upon, or react to; information regarding the market and these actions will influence the prices of homes in a region or neighborhood.

The term "seller's market" generally indicates a high demand from many buyers, with a limited supply of homes on the market. This is good news for the sellers, as they can obtain a premium for their property and often obtain multiple bids. A "buyer's market" is the opposite. When there are many properties on the market and few buyers, sellers must price their home or property competitively with what the other sellers are doing. Additionally, sellers may be willing to take bids lower than their original asking price if there is a buyer interested in the property. In this market condition the buyers and sellers realize that if a property cannot be obtained at a desired price, there are other properties that may be obtainable at that same price.

The existence of buyer's and seller's markets directly correlates to inflationary and deflationary trends in real estate. When there are more properties available to a limited consumer base, a deflationary trend occurs. Real estate values tend to decline during deflation. In inflation there are more buyers than properties available, thus prices begin to rise. Deflation correlates to a buyer's market; however, if an area is experiencing a buyer's market, this does not always mean they are experiencing deflation. The same is true for inflation and a seller's market. One can happen independently of the other, but they are often related.

Remember
- A seller's market favors the sellers, with more buyers (demand) than sellers (supply) = higher prices
- A buyer's market favors the buyers with more sellers (supply) than buyers (demand) = lower prices
- Inflation occurs when there are fewer properties on the market than demand (more demand than supply)
- Deflation occurs when there are more properties on the market than demand (more supply than demand)

Real Estate Economic Principles and Theories

Assemblage occurs when two or more adjacent plots of land are put together to increase the value of the land. In developments, smaller plots are formed to build a single-family residence or other single unit building. These homes or units will sell for a premium; however, a developer can get more money out of a larger plot of land as it is more versatile and has more potential uses. For example, three smaller plots of land put together could become a condominium project, or apartment complex where the multiple units can sell or rent for more than a single family home occupying one-third the space. While assemblage would increase the value of land, there are times when it is not feasible to accumulate several plots together to develop. In a development, after the lots are sold, it is very difficult to purchase several adjacent lots, and often zoning laws and regulations will prevent developments other than residential or single family homes.

Economic life is the time period in which the property provides beneficial returns. At the point when a building has reached the end of its economic life, it is more beneficial financially to tear down the building than put money into repairs or renovations.

Economic obsolescence occurs when a property decreases in value due to negative external factors. The property itself may not be in bad condition, or even be very old, but if a negative factor moves into the neighborhood, it will drag down prices for all properties. For example, if you own a home next to a main road or highway and the highway is going to be replaced with a freeway, the value of your property will decrease because of the increased noise and possible congestion in the area.

Economy of scale is the concept that building more units spreads the cost over several units making each one cheaper for the producer, who will also see a higher profit from each unit. Building a 10-unit condominium would be more expensive per unit than building a 50-unit condominium complex as the materials would be cheaper to the more that are purchased, but the units would not be sold for any less. Similarly, building structure of two or more stories is more economical than building a one-story structure spread out over more land. The reason for this is because the multi-story structure will not require a larger foundation or roof for more square footage compared to a single-story structure. Economy of scale is an important concept to understand; however there comes a point where more units will not equal a lower cost per unit. The opposite is true in the concept of diminishing returns. There exists a threshold where creating more stories, units or buildings increases costs to the builder or contractor. For example, if a developer were building a high rise office building, at some point the cost of cranes, elevators and the logistics of getting materials and workers higher and higher becomes more expensive per unit than if the building were to have fewer floors.

The economics of subdividing seems to be in contrast to the assemblage principle; however, using the concept of economies of scale we can see that one larger plot of land subdivided into several smaller lots sold to buyers who intend on building a single family home will bring in more money than the one large plot of land. This is true for a development zoned for single-family use; however, it may not be true in other zoned areas.

Filtering down is the concept that property is passed down or sold to groups in a lower economic bracket. As new developments are built or old areas are redeveloped, people with more economic means tend to move to these new areas for larger or more elaborate housing. The existing homes or properties are often sold to buyers who cannot afford these new or "up-and-coming" areas.

The principles of first choice, change and competition will influence the amount of money a property will sell for. With the **principle of first choice** we see land being used for the "best and highest" use. This principle suggests that those people or businesses that want the land the most are willing to pay the highest amount of money for a property. A manufacturer who relies on rail transfer to transport goods from one place to another will pay a high premium to have property next to a railroad line to load and unload goods. A rancher would probably not pay the premium the manufacturer would pay because the railroad is not as important to raising cattle as it might be to ship goods. **The principle of competition** states that when one area of real estate or property use is making a lot of money, there will be people moving into that area to try to capitalize on the profits. For example, if a parking garage is built in an area with a high density of commuters or entertainment, the parking garage will be at capacity daily with the owner taking in a premium for the parking spaces. If more and more people invest money into parking structures there will be more vacancies in each garage, producing less money for the owner. If one garage owner decides to cut prices, the others must also cut prices to remain competitive in order to keep business. The **principle of change** tells us that land use is constantly changing. What once used to be agricultural land may now be split up and divided into a housing development. What once used to be industrial warehouses may now be developed into modern lofts and apartments.

Remember
- **Assemblage** is the combination of two or more adjacent plots of land
- **Economic obsolescence** is the decline of property value due to negative external factors
- **Economic life** is the time span a property is financially productive before it is cheaper to tear it down than renovate
- **Economy of scale** is the principle where building more units will decrease the cost per unit to build
- **Diminishing returns** states that at some threshold more units or larger buildings create a higher cost per unit
- **Economies of subdividing** states that smaller single family plots bring in more money than a larger undivided plot
- **Filtering down** states that as new developments are built, the wealthy will move, leaving their old residences for someone who can't afford the new development.
- **Principle of first choice** outlines the "highest and best use" theory of land
- **Principle of competition** states that competition will move into sectors of the real estate with high profit margins
- **Principle of change** states that land use is constantly changing from one use to another.

Real estate goes through cycles, just as business does. Business goes through a four-cycle stage of prosperity, recession, depression and recovery. Real estate experiences these cycles, but also experiences a life cycle described as development (when the value of properties are increasing,) maturity (when values are stable) and decline (when values of property are decreasing.) It is difficult to predict how long it takes real estate to go through the business cycle, or its own life cycle; however, economists have accepted two time frames for these cycles. The long real estate cycle takes 18 years for prosperity, recession, depression and recovery while the short real estate cycle takes just three to six years to experience the same cycle.

There are many factors that can contribute to a real estate cycle and its time span. Short-term real estate cycles are most influenced by the cost of borrowing money. When interest rates are high, fewer people are able to make large mortgage payments, while the opposite is true when rates are lowered. Besides interest rates, population increase or decline in an area plays a very important role in the real estate cycle, as does age, income levels, cost of building and local taxes.

The basic term "brokerage" means to bring people together. The act of forming a brokerage is the act of connecting people who are seeking a common end result. In real estate, brokerages are formed to connect buyers with sellers. In a brokerage, a real estate broker will secure listings from clients and seek out prospective buyers who may be interested in these listings. Brokers will hire salespeople to work under them, but will empower them to find interested buyers and sellers to bring into the brokerage.

In order to make a brokerage more efficient, and assist all clients in the best way possible, brokers and salespersons can use the Multiple Listing Service, or the MLS. It lists what properties are currently on the market – properties an agent may be able to show an interested buyer, but which are not necessarily a listing held by the brokerage.

A brokerage does much more than just securing listings and finding potential buyers for the listings. There are many functions that are performed in a brokerage, which can serve all different types of clients. A brokerage will employ agents, which can be both brokers and salespeople. Some of the functions performed by agents include:

- **Commercial, industrial and agricultural sales**. Agents specializing in commercial, industrial and agricultural sales generally move fewer properties per year compared to agents working with residential sales; however, the value of the properties is high, making up for the lower volume. Within each of these specializations, there are subspecialties that an agent can concentrate on. For example, a commercial property agent can specialize in warehouses or office buildings, while agents representing agricultural land can seek out producers who will farm the land, or developers who may subdivide the land and build houses.

- **Mobile home sales** are a separate entity apart from residential sales because of a few unique features associated with manufactured homes versus traditional homes built on a foundation. Mobile homes are manufactured and then moved to the site. The home is moved on its own chassis, meaning the structure is attached to wheels and is capable of being moved. Because of this, it must be registered with the department of motor vehicles before it can be moved. Only when the home is attached to a foundation with no intention to move it will the registration with the Department of Motor Vehicles no longer be necessary. The other major difference distinguishing mobile homes from residential homes is that the owner of the mobile home does not own the land on which the home sits - it is leased from another property owner. The only real estate agents who are allowed to sell mobile homes are licensed through the Department of Housing and Community Development.

- **Business opportunities** are a unique sales transaction as real property may or may not be transferred in the sale of a business. Sometimes the physical building where the business is located will be part of the transaction; however, if the space is leased, the building will not be part of the sale and the lease will be renegotiated in the new owner's name.

- **Residential income property sales** deal directly with multi-unit residential buildings such as apartment complexes, duplexes or other such units. Many agents representing single-family residential homes will also sell these types of properties.

- **Property management** is the business of being an onsite manager at a condominium or apartment complex where tenants rent units. The property manager will make sure each unit is leased out (if applicable) and make sure the property is taken care of by managing a staff. Property managers sometimes live on site, but not always.

- **Leasing agents**, which are not always a property manager, specialize in finding tenants to lease properties. This could be a commercial, industrial, agricultural or residential lease. The leasing agent will be paid according to the spaces he or she fills. Again, this is separate from a property manager, although a property manager sometimes does find tenants in addition to their other duties.

- **Lot sales** deal directly with the sale of land to developers looking to subdivide, or directly to a builder who is interested in building a home. The sizes of the lots vary from single lots to large parcels, which could be subdivided or sold whole.

- **Loan brokerage** is the process of bringing together investors looking to take on a trust deed and people interested in buying property who need to borrow money. Just as real estate brokers are in the business of bringing together parties to a transaction, so are loan brokers.

- **Mortgage loan agents** are lenders who arrange financing for potential borrowers. Many real estate agents are also loan agents. The amount of paperwork and administrative tasks that loan agents must do is similar to that of a real estate agent, so it is a natural and comfortable transition – or, sometimes, a dual position – for real estate professionals.

- **Real estate auction sales** are also an important area of real estate. Foreclosures, state sales and unclaimed properties are all disposed of through auctions. Many firms specialize in nothing but auctions and don't carry traditional listings.

- **Salaried assistants** choose to work as assistants to other licensed agents for a steady paycheck. Most agents typically work on a commission basis, with no guaranteed paycheck. Salaried assistants can avoid this uncertainty while still working in the real estate business.

- **Appraisal** is an important real estate career option for all agents to understand. Many real estate agents will have clients ask the agents opinions of a property's value to make an educated bid or to know how much to ask for a listed property. A licensed real estate agent will hold a separate appraisal license aside from a real estate license, but most people who currently do appraisals began their career as a licensed real estate agent, or hold concurrent licenses.

There are different types of relationships within a brokerage, which are important to examine. There are relationships between brokers and salespersons and brokers and clients, and broker-to-broker relationships.

In almost every brokerage firm, there are salespeople working alongside the brokers. Salespeople are essentially considered independent contractors. Brokers, however, must have a written contract with each salesperson working in the office, thus creating an employee-employer relationship. Salespeople are empowered by the broker to represent not only the firm, but also the broker, in all transactions. Conversely, for tax and compensation purposes, both brokers and salespersons are considered independent contractors. The Internal Revenue Service requires individuals to file their taxes as an independent contractor if they meet the following criteria:

- If the salesperson is licensed as a real estate agent;

- If there is a written contract that states the salesperson will be considered an independent contractor for tax purposes; or

- If compensation is based on sales and not based on the amount of hours worked.

Brokers are placed in a very difficult situation regarding the employment status of their sales staff. If a broker wishes to keep his or her salespeople as independent contractors, the broker must be careful not to exercise too much control over their activities, or the independent contractor status may be changed to employee status. If the salespeople are employees, then the broker must contribute to their social security accounts and withhold income taxes from their individual earnings. Even with a contract stating that the salespeople are independent contractors, the IRS will consider the salespeople to be employees if the broker exerts too much control. The following is a fast reference sheet to help determine if an individual is an employee or independent contractor.

Control factors	Employee	Independent Contractor
Is the worker required to comply with employer instructions regarding work, when it is to be completed, where and how?	Yes	No
Are there certain, set hours during which the worker's job must be completed?	Yes	No
Are written or oral reports required of the employee?	Yes	No
Is compensation given in one lump sum?	No	Yes
Does the worker make his or her services directly available to the general public without going through an employer?	No	Yes
Is there training required?	Yes	No
Is this job considered a full-time position?	Yes	No
Does the employer furnish tools and materials?	Yes	No
Will the worker directly hire, train, or supervise another person to perform work which he or she is responsible for?	No	Yes
Does the job need to be performed on the employer's property or at the employer's place of business?	Yes	No
Do tasks need to be performed in a certain order, as designated by the employer?	Yes	No
Is there a set salary, whether it is hourly, weekly or monthly?	Yes	No
Does the worker have to rent his or her own workspace?	No	Yes
Can a worker work for more than one firm at the same time?	No	Yes
Can the employer fire a worker?	Yes	No
Can the worker quit the job at any time no matter what stage a project is?	Yes	No
Does the employer pay businesses expenses?	Yes	No
Will the worker see a direct profit or loss as a result of his or her actions?	No	Yes

Regardless of a salesperson's status as an employee or independent contractor, the broker is responsible for the salesperson's actions. Salespeople directly represent a broker and must conduct business ethically and lawfully, or the broker's reputation will be hurt just as much as the salesperson's. Brokers will hold an employment agreement with the salesperson and may break that contract if the salesperson is not representing the broker to the expected standards.

The employment agreement between a salesperson and broker will define their relationship. Obligations and responsibilities will be outlined in this agreement so all parties know their duties in the brokerage. If the salesperson is considered an independent contractor, the broker does not have to withhold taxes from the salesperson's earnings, nor will the broker require set hours or other requirements characterizing the employer-employee relationship. Those salespersons that are considered employees must adhere to the wishes of the broker. This may include not only set hours, but also dress code, attendance at meetings, quotas, and any other requirements the broker determines are necessary. The broker must in turn withhold money for all taxes and pay unemployment compensation taxes, and may offer benefits to employees.

The relationship between brokers and clients is considered to be an independent contractor relationship. Brokers and clients, or principals, will enter into an agency agreement wherein the broker agrees to list the client's home and use due diligence to find a ready, willing and able buyer. This agency can be set up in many different ways, but is considered to be an employment contract.

Brokers can work with other brokers as cooperating brokers, a symbiotic relationship where two brokers may be working with one principal or client. The brokers generally agree to split any commission earned from the sale of the home. In a relationship such as this, there must be full disclosure to the client or principal so there is no confusion as to what is happening.

Where the salesperson's employment status has a blurred line between employee and independent contractor, the broker is almost always an independent contractor. Brokers are generally self-employed and don't have to follow the direction of a supervisor or manager. Brokers will work directly for the client, but still do not take any direction from the client. Brokers are only responsible for the final outcome of the process: to close a real estate transaction.

T H E   R I G H T   A T T I T U D E

Much of the sales environment is attitude driven. If you have a positive attitude, and are upbeat and helpful, people are more likely to rely on you, and place trust in your skills and talents. People with a negative attitude generally will not be very successful salespeople. When a person believes he or she is going to fail, failure is imminent. Also, a negative attitude is easily picked up by those around us. Your clients will not want to do business with someone with a "can't.do" attitude when they could be working with a very positive affirming individual. Remember, you are most likely not the only real estate agent in the neighborhood, and those displaying positive energies and producing results will be much busier than an agent with the negative attitude.

The successful real estate agent will surround himself or herself with successful people. Agents working in productive teams, or working in a positive environment, are more likely to succeed and display the positive attitude than agents in the opposite environment. Part of choosing the best brokerage to work for is finding out about the environment, the training, team building and other exercises or resources available to the agent to ensure success.

The following is a series of questions a salesperson should ask himself or herself on a regular basis to make sure he or she is projecting the right attitude when at work.

1. How do you overcome objections? Do you act or react? The active person will find a way to solve problems and move forward while the reactive person may complicate a situation with a negative response.

2. Are you persistent? When a client is looking for the perfect house, are you

INDEPENDENT CONTRACTOR AGREEMENT
(Between Broker and Associate-Licensee)

This Agreement, dated _____ is made between _____
_____ ("Broker") and
_____ ("Associate-Licensee").

In consideration of the covenants and representations contained in this Agreement, Broker and Associate-Licensee agree as follows:

1. **BROKER:** Broker represents that Broker is duly licensed as a real estate broker by the State of California, ☐ doing business as _____
   _____ (firm name), ☐ a sole proprietorship, ☐ a partnership, ☐ a corporation.
   Broker is a member of the _____
   Association(s) of REALTORS®, and a subscriber to the _____ multiple
   listing service(s). Broker shall keep Broker's license current during the term of this Agreement.

2. **ASSOCIATE-LICENSEE:** Associate-Licensee represents that, (a) he/she is duly licensed by the State of California as a ☐ real estate broker,
   ☐ real estate salesperson, and (b) he/she has not used any other names within the past five years, except _____
   _____ Associate-Licensee shall keep his/her license current during
   the term of this Agreement, including satisfying all applicable continuing education and provisional license requirements.

3. **INDEPENDENT CONTRACTOR RELATIONSHIP:**
   A. Broker and Associate-Licensee intend that, to the maximum extent permissible by law: (i) This Agreement does not constitute an employment agreement by either party; (ii) Broker and Associate-Licensee are independent contracting parties with respect to all services rendered under this Agreement; (iii) This Agreement shall not be construed as a partnership.
   B. Broker shall not: (i) restrict Associate-Licensee's activities to particular geographical areas or, (ii) dictate Associate-Licensee's activities with regard to hours, leads, open houses, opportunity or floor time, production, prospects, sales meetings, schedule, inventory, time off, vacation, or similar activities, except to the extent required by law.
   C. Associate-Licensee shall not be required to accept an assignment by Broker to service any particular current or prospective listing or parties.
   D. Except as required by law: (i) Associate-Licensee retains sole and absolute discretion and judgment in the methods, techniques, and procedures to be used in soliciting and obtaining listings, sales, exchanges, leases, rentals, or other transactions, and in carrying out Associate-Licensee's selling and soliciting activities, (ii) Associate-Licensee is under the control of Broker as to the results of Associate-Licensee's work only, and not as to the means by which those results are accomplished, (iii) Associate-Licensee has no authority to bind Broker by any promise or representation and (iv) Broker shall not be liable for any obligation or liability incurred by Associate-Licensee.
   E. Associate-Licensee's only remuneration shall be the compensation specified in paragraph 8.
   F. Associate-Licensee shall not be treated as an employee with respect to services performed as a real estate agent, for state and federal tax purposes.
   G. The fact the Broker may carry worker compensation insurance for Broker's own benefit and for the mutual benefit of Broker and licensees associated with Broker, including Associate-Licensee, shall not create an inference of employment.

4. **LICENSED ACTIVITY:** All listings of property, and all agreements, acts or actions for performance of licensed acts, which are taken or performed in connection with this Agreement, shall be taken and performed in the name of Broker. Associate-Licensee agrees to and does hereby contribute all right and title to such listings to Broker for the benefit and use of Broker, Associate-Licensee, and other licensees associated with Broker. Broker shall make available to Associate-Licensee, equally with other licensees associated with Broker, all current listings in Broker's office, except any listing which Broker may choose to place in the exclusive servicing of Associate-Licensee or one or more other specific licensees associated with Broker. Associate-Licensee shall provide and pay for all professional licenses, supplies, services, and other items required in connection with Associate-Licensee's activities under this Agreement, or any listing or transaction, without reimbursement from Broker except as required by law. Associate-Licensee shall work diligently and with his/her best efforts: (a) To sell, exchange, lease, or rent properties listed with Broker or other cooperating Brokers; (b) To solicit additional listings, clients, and customers; and (c) To otherwise promote the business of serving the public in real estate transactions to the end that Broker and Associate-Licensee may derive the greatest benefit possible, in accordance with law. Associate-Licensee shall not commit any unlawful act under federal, state or local law or regulation while conducting licensed activity. Associate-Licensee shall at all times be familiar, and comply, with all applicable federal, state and local laws, including, but not limited to, anti-discrimination laws and restrictions against the giving or accepting a fee, or other thing of value, for the referral of business to title companies, escrow companies, home inspection companies, pest control companies and other settlement service providers pursuant to the California Business and Professions Code and the Real Estate Settlement Procedures Acts (RESPA). Broker shall make available for Associate-Licensee's use, along with other licensees associated with Broker, the facilities of the real estate office operated by Broker at _____
   _____ and the facilities of any other office
   locations made available by Broker pursuant to this Agreement.

Broker and Associate-Licensee acknowledge receipt of copy of this page, which constitutes Page 1 of _____ Pages.
Broker's Initials (_____) (_____)   Associate-Licensee's Initials (_____) (_____)

INDEPENDENT CONTRACTOR AGREEMENT (ICA-11 PAGE 1 OF 3)

5. **PROPRIETARY INFORMATION AND FILES:** (a) All files and documents pertaining to listings, leads and transactions are the property of Broker and shall be delivered to Broker by Associate-Licensee immediately upon request or termination of their relationship under this Agreement. (b) Associate-Licensee acknowledges that Broker's method of conducting business is a protected trade secret. (c) Associate-Licensee shall not use to his/her own advantage, or the advantage of any other person, business, or entity, except as specifically agreed in writing, either during Associate-Licensee's association with Broker, or thereafter, any information gained for or from the business, or files of Broker.

6. **SUPERVISION:** Associate-Licensee, within 24 hours (or ☐ _____) after preparing, signing, or receiving same, shall submit to Broker, or Broker's designated licensee: (a) All documents which may have a material effect upon the rights and duties of principals in a transaction, (b) Any documents or other items connected with a transaction pursuant to this Agreement in the possession of or available to Associate-Licensee and, (c) All documents associated with any real estate transaction in which Associate-Licensee is a principal.

7. **TRUST FUNDS:** All trust funds shall be handled in compliance with the Business and Professions Code, and other applicable laws.

8. **COMPENSATION:**

   A. **TO BROKER:** Compensation shall be charged to parties who enter into listing or other agreements for services requiring a real estate license:
   ☐ as shown in "Exhibit A" attached, which is incorporated as a part of this Agreement by reference, or
   ☐ as follows: _____
   _____
   Any deviation which is not approved in writing in advance by Broker, shall be (1) deducted from Associate-Licensee's compensation, if lower than the amount or rate approved above; and, (2) subject to Broker approval, if higher than the amount approved above. Any permanent change in commission schedule shall be disseminated by Broker to Associate-Licensee.

   B. **TO ASSOCIATE-LICENSEE:** Associate-Licensee shall receive a share of compensation actually collected by Broker, on listings or other agreements for services requiring a real estate license, which are solicited and obtained by Associate-Licensee, and on transactions of which Associate-Licensee's activities are the procuring cause, as follows:
   ☐ as shown in "Exhibit B" attached, which is incorporated as a part of this Agreement by reference, or
   ☐ other: _____
   _____

   C. **PARTNERS, TEAMS, AND AGREEMENTS WITH OTHER ASSOCIATE-LICENSEES IN OFFICE:** If Associate-Licensee and one or more other Associate-Licensees affiliated with Broker participate on the same side (either listing or selling) of a transaction, the commission allocated to their combined activities shall be divided by Broker and paid to them according to their written agreement. Broker shall have the right to withhold total compensation if there is a dispute between associate-licensees, or if there is no written agreement, or if no written agreement has been provided to Broker.

   D. **EXPENSES AND OFFSETS:** If Broker elects to advance funds to pay expenses or liabilities of Associate-Licensee, or for an advance payment of, or draw upon, future compensation, Broker may deduct the full amount advanced from compensation payable to Associate-Licensee on any transaction without notice. If Associate-Licensee's compensation is subject to a lien, garnishment or other restriction on payment, Broker shall charge Associate-Licensee a fee for complying with such restriction.

   E. **PAYMENT:** (1) All compensation collected by Broker and due to Associate-Licensee shall be paid to Associate-Licensee, after deduction of expenses and offsets, immediately or as soon thereafter as practicable, except as otherwise provided in this Agreement, or a separate written agreement between Broker and Associate-Licensee. (2) Compensation shall not be paid to Associate-Licensee until both the transaction and file are complete. (3) Broker is under no obligation to pursue collection of compensation from any person or entity responsible for payment. Associate-Licensee does not have the independent right to pursue collection of compensation for activities which require a real estate license which were done in the name of Broker. (4) Expenses which are incurred in the attempt to collect compensation shall be paid by Broker and Associate-Licensee in the same proportion as set forth for the division of compensation (paragraph 8(B)). (5) If there is a known or pending claim against Broker or Associate-Licensee on transactions for which Associate-Licensee has not yet been paid, Broker may withhold from compensation due Associate-Licensee on that transaction amounts for which Associate-Licensee could be responsible under paragraph 14, until such claim is resolved. (6) Associate-Licensee shall not be entitled to any advance payment from Broker upon future compensation.

   F. **UPON OR AFTER TERMINATION:** If this Agreement is terminated while Associate-Licensee has listings or pending transactions that require further work normally rendered by Associate-Licensee, Broker shall make arrangements with another associate-licensee to perform the required work, or Broker shall perform the work him/herself. The licensee performing the work shall be reasonably compensated for completing work on those listings or transactions, and such reasonable compensation shall be deducted from Associate-Licensee's share of compensation. Except for such offset, Associate-Licensee shall receive the compensation due as specified above.

9. **TERMINATION OF RELATIONSHIP:** Broker or Associate-Licensee may terminate their relationship under this Agreement at any time, with or without cause. After termination, Associate-Licensee shall not solicit (a) prospective or existing clients or customers based upon company-generated leads obtained during the time Associate-Licensee was affiliated with Broker, or (b) any principal with existing contractual obligations to Broker, or (c) any principal with a contractual transactional obligation for which Broker is entitled to be compensated. Even after termination, this Agreement shall govern all disputes and claims between Broker and Associate-Licensee connected with their relationship under this Agreement, including obligations and liabilities arising from existing and completed listings, transactions, and services.

Broker and Associate-Licensee acknowledge receipt of copy of this page, which constitutes Page 2 of _____ Pages.
Broker's Initials (_____) (_____)   Associate-Licensee's Initials (_____) (_____)

REVISED 10/98

Page 2 of ___ Pages.

PRINT DATE

10. **DISPUTE RESOLUTION:**
   A. **Mediation:** Mediation is recommended as a method of resolving disputes arising out of this Agreement between Broker and Associate-Licensee.
   B. **Arbitration:** All disputes or claims between Associate-Licensee and other licensee(s) associated with Broker, or between Associate-Licensee and Broker, arising from or connected in any way with this Agreement, which cannot be adjusted between the parties involved, shall be submitted to the Association of REALTORS® of which all such disputing parties are members for arbitration pursuant to the provisions of its Bylaws, as may be amended from time to time, which are incorporated as a part of this Agreement by reference. If the Bylaws of the Association do not cover arbitration of the dispute, or if the Association declines jurisdiction over the dispute, then arbitration shall be pursuant to the rules of California law. The Federal Arbitration Act, Title 9, U.S. Code, Section 1, et seq., shall govern this Agreement.

11. **AUTOMOBILE:** Associate-Licensee shall maintain automobile insurance coverage for liability and property damage in the following amounts $_____/$_____. Broker shall be named as an additional insured party on Associate-Licensee's policies. A copy of the endorsement showing Broker as an additional insured shall be provided to Broker.

12. **PERSONAL ASSISTANTS:** Associate-Licensee may make use of a personal assistant, provided the following requirements are satisfied. Associate-Licensee shall have a written agreement with the personal assistant which establishes the terms and responsibilities of the parties to the employment agreement, including, but not limited to, compensation, supervision and compliance with applicable law. The agreement shall be subject to Broker's review and approval. Unless otherwise agreed, if the personal assistant has a real estate license, that license must be provided to the Broker. Both Associate-Licensee and personal assistant must sign any agreement that Broker has established for such purposes.

13. **OFFICE POLICY MANUAL:** If Broker's office policy manual, now or as modified in the future, conflicts with or differs from the terms of this Agreement, the terms of the office policy manual shall govern the relationship between Broker and Associate-Licensee.

14. **INDEMNITY AND HOLD HARMLESS:** Associate-Licensee agrees to indemnify, defend and hold Broker harmless from all claims, disputes, litigation, judgments, awards, costs and attorney's fees, arising from any action taken or omitted by Associate-Licensee, or others working through, or on behalf of Associate-Licensee in connection with services rendered. Any such claims or costs payable pursuant to this Agreement, are due as follows:
   ☐ Paid in full by Associate-Licensee, who hereby agrees to indemnify and hold harmless Broker for all such sums, or
   ☐ In the same ratio as the compensation split as it existed at the time the compensation was earned by Associate-Licensee
   ☐ Other: _____
   _____
   _____

   Payment from Associate-Licensee is due at the time Broker makes such payment and can be offset from any compensation due Associate-Licensee as above. Broker retains the authority to settle claims or disputes, whether or not Associate-Licensee consents to such settlement.

15. **ADDITIONAL PROVISIONS:** _____
   _____
   _____

16. **DEFINITIONS:** As used in this Agreement, the following terms have the meanings indicated:
   (A) "Listing" means an agreement with a property owner or other party to locate a buyer, exchange party, lessee, or other party to a transaction involving real property, a mobile home, or other property or transaction which may be brokered by a real estate licensee, or an agreement with a party to locate or negotiate for any such property or transaction.
   (B) "Compensation means compensation for acts requiring a real estate license, regardless of whether calculated as a percentage of transaction price, flat fee, hourly rate, or in any other manner.
   (C) "Transaction" means a sale, exchange, lease, or rental of real property, a business opportunity, or a manufactured home, which may lawfully be brokered by a real estate licensee.

17. **ATTORNEY FEES:** In any action, proceeding, or arbitration between Broker and Associate-Licensee arising from or related to this Agreement, the prevailing Broker or Associate-Licensee shall be entitled to reasonable attorney fees and costs.

18. **ENTIRE AGREEMENT; MODIFICATION:** All prior agreements between the parties concerning their relationship as Broker and Associate-Licensee are incorporated in this Agreement, which constitutes the entire contract. Its terms are intended by the parties as a final and complete expression of their agreement with respect to its subject matter, and may not be contradicted by evidence of any prior agreement or contemporaneous oral agreement. This Agreement may not be amended, modified, altered, or changed except by a further agreement in writing executed by Broker and Associate-Licensee.

Broker:	**Associate-Licensee:**
_____	_____
(Brokerage firm name)	(Signature)
By _____	_____
Its Broker/Office manager (circle one)	(Print name)
_____	_____
(Print name)	(Address)
_____	_____
(Address)	(City, State, Zip)
_____	_____
(City, State, Zip)	(Telephone) (Fax)
_____	
(Telephone) (Fax)	

REVISED 10/98

Page 3 of ___ Pages.

OFFICE USE ONLY
Reviewed by Broker
or Designee _____
Date _____

INDEPENDENT CONTRACTOR AGREEMENT (ICA-11 PAGE 3 OF 3)

on the ball, actively searching not only your brokerage's inventory, but also the local inventory on the MLS? Are you connecting with your clients on a regular basis to keep them informed of any developments?

3. Are you willing to chance failure by trying? Success only comes through learning, and making mistakes or failing provides an excellent opportunity to learn.

4. Are you excited about your job? A real estate agent who is upbeat and enthusiastic about his or her job will project positive energy others will feel.

5. Are you a problem solver? When a problem arises, do you work diligently to find the solution, or do you give up easily?

6. Are you confident in your abilities? Do you see yourself as a knowledgeable professional, with detailed information on each of your listings? Knowledge provides confidence.

7. Are you displaying positive actions and speech? A positive person not only thinks positively, but also shows it in his or her speech and actions.

8. Are you flexible in an ever-changing environment? A good agent will not fear change, but embrace the challenge.

F I N D I N G   T H E   R I G H T   B R O K E R

Just as important as any other factor for success is finding the right broker or brokerage for which to work. As a student of real estate, you will receive academic training, gaining the appropriate knowledge to pass a written exam, entitling you to become a licensed real estate agent. Outside of this training, you really will not get practical, hands-on training until you go to work. If you are new to the industry, it is important for you to find a brokerage that offers training, mentoring or a partner system where you can learn from more experienced agents. While real estate is sometimes seen as a competitive business between agents, working in teams or having a mentor will provide you invaluable experience for you and just might help an experienced agent to keep their skills fresh, or even learn something from you!

It is important for new licensees to do research on the firms in which they are interested. It is a very exciting time when find out you passed the licensing exam and you have a new career waiting, but every agent should approach the job hunt with cautious optimism. Accepting your first invitation to work for your first brokerage is not a good idea, unless the necessary research has been done to make sure this is a good fit. A blind job acceptance may quickly tarnish your outlook for the new career you have spent time and energy learning.

Agents should look for firms that specialize in the area of real estate that interests them most. An agent trained in residential property sales should probably try to find a brokerage specializing in this type of sales. The agent might not be as successful in industrial property or agricultural property transfers because of lack of training in these areas. A general brokerage is a good place for many agents as they can be exposed to many different types of property transfers and learn how to sell them. Who knows, an agent who thought he or she was most interested in commercial real estate might find industrial real estate more rewarding, more profitable and a better fit for his or her sales skills. It is important to recognize that all sales skills that are learned in one aspect of real estate can be easily applied to all areas of the business.

Compensation is another important area to discuss. There are different methods of compensation in brokerages; however, 100% commission is one method the real estate industry is probably most known for. In a 100% commission situation, the salesperson generally has to rent or pay a desk fee for a workspace in the broker's office. Any support staff must be paid for by the salesperson in addition to all supplies the agent may need. In situations where there is a commission split, the broker will generally supply more of these items for the office environment or workspace. There are also situations where there might be a commission split until a certain quota has been reached, and then the salesperson will receive 100% of the commission after that quota has been surpassed. Whatever the arrangement is between you and the broker, make sure you understand it up front so there are no surprises later.

To summarize, and speaking in general terms, it is important for a licensee to go to work for a broker who brings in development or training elements to the work atmosphere. A broker should provide a new agent with training. The proper training will aid a good salesperson to be a great salesperson and provide important knowledge of the industry. In addition to the training, it is good when the brokerage has its own trainer on staff, taking care of all the needs of the new agents, providing assistance and being a general resource. It is helpful to the new agent to have a broker with a good library full of resources not only for training, but for career development as well. The information can be in book form, audio or video. No matter the form of media, it is important for agents to have access to these resources. Working in a firm specializing in your area of expertise is important; it will allow you to use your skills and training to be your most successful. Also an office with successful, happy salespeople will offer good morale. Perhaps the most important factor is your own personal comfort. It is important to work in an environment where you feel confident and comfortable and are not intimidated or anxious about going into the office.

Remember
Some of the most important things to look for when seeking a broker to work for are:
- Training / trainer
- Resource library
- Specialized in your trained area
- Successful coworkers
- Comfortable environment

CONTINUING EDUCATION

All agents must remember to renew their licenses every four years. An agent's license will expire four years after the date it was issued, for those agents who hold permanent licenses. Agents with a conditional license are required to complete all necessary classes for the permanent license within 18 months of issuance of the conditional license. The California Department of Real Estate will send out a renewal form to the licensee's address 90 days in advance of the expiration.

Salesperson's First License Renewal
Salespersons who are renewing their original license for the first time are required to take 12 hours of continuing education. These 12 hours consist of four separate 3-hour classes approved through the department of real estate. The four specific classes are Ethics, Trust Fund Handling, Fair Housing and Agency.

Real Estate Broker's First License Renewal
Real estate brokers renewing an original license for the first time must complete 45 clock hours of DRE-approved continuing education consisting of:

- Four separate three-hour courses in the following subjects: Ethics, Agency, Trust Fund Handling, and Fair Housing;

- A minimum of 18 clock hours of consumer protection courses; and

- The remaining 15 clock hours related to either consumer service or consumer protection.

Salespersons and Brokers Renewing After the First Time

For subsequent renewals, all real estate brokers and salespersons must complete 45 clock hours of DRE-approved continuing education consisting of:

- One six-hour survey course that covers the four mandatory subjects (Ethics, Agency, Trust Fund Handling, and Fair Housing);

- At least 18 clock hours of consumer protection courses; and

- The remaining 21 clock hours in either consumer service or consumer protection courses.

You may submit your renewal application 90 days prior to your license expiration date. Your renewal is on time if your application is postmarked before midnight on your license expiration date. If you renew on time, Business and Professions Code Section 10156.2 permits you to continue operating under your existing license after its expiration date unless notified otherwise by the DRE. If your renewal is not on time you may renew it in the two-year late renewal period, but you are not allowed to perform any activities which require you to have a license. It is important that this is clearly understood. You have a two-year period in which you may renew your license without having to sit for the state examination again; however, this does not allow you to continue practicing as a real estate agent.

Remember
Continuing Education Requirements At-A-Glance
- First time sales renewals require 12 hours of training
- First time broker renewals require 45 hours of training
- All subsequent broker and salesperson license renewals require 45 hours of training

S U M M A R Y

Real estate is a dynamic industry requiring its professionals to be knowledgeable in many cross-functional areas in order to be successful. As an agent it is important for you to understand the many different specializations you could go into as an agent, the different specializations you can practice within the industry such as appraisal or property management, and the many factors that play into real estate economics. A well informed agent will be a successful agent, as he or she will be seen as an authority in the industry, and a professional that clients would like to work with – for what will most likely be the largest purchase a person will make in his or her life.

Being a well-rounded agent with knowledge in many of the cross-functional aspects of real estate will be a large factor in an agent's success, as will the agent's attitude.

Clients will not want to work with an agent who is pessimistic, grumpy, or unhappy with their job or working environment. Purchasing a home is a very exciting time for most clients – marking life changes, arriving at a financial goal, or simply upgrading to a larger property. An agent who mirrors the client's enthusiasm and energy will not only be appreciated, but also referred!

Additionally, an agent's success is largely associated with the broker he or she will be working for. A broker with good training and resources, happy agents, and a mentoring or team atmosphere will be just as important as the original training an agent went through to become licensed.

Finally, an agent needs to be aware of all continuing education requirements. A successful agent will not want to have his or her license become inactive because they forgot to renew it on time. That costs you money, clients and possibly your position at your broker's office. It is important to keep your contact information updated with the California Department of Real Estate so they can contact you when it is time to renew your license.

TERMS AND PHRASES

Agency – A special relationship of trust by which one person (agent) is authorized to conduct business, sign papers, or otherwise act on behalf of another person (principal).

Agent – One who represents another (called a principal) and has authority to act for the principal in business matters and in dealing with third parties. The relationship is referred to as an agency.

Appraisal – An estimate and opinion of value; an opinion or estimate of the fair market value of a property.

Assemblage – The same concept as Plottage, a process of increasing land's assessed value by joining two or more adjoining lots to create a larger plot of land.

Broker – An agent who earns income by arranging sales and other contracts. A real estate broker is an individual licensed by the state of California to arrange the sale or transfer of interests in real property for compensation.

Brokerage – The act of bringing people together for a mutually beneficial relationship or transaction.

Commission – (A) An agent's compensation for performing the duties of his or her agency agreement. In the real estate business, it is usually a percentage of the selling price or a percentage of the lease or rents. (B) A group of people officially authorized to perform certain duties or functions.

Diminishing Returns – At some threshold, building more units or larger buildings creates a higher cost per unit.

Economic Life – The remaining useful life of an improvement or structure; that period during which an improvement will yield a return on the investment.

Economic Obsolescence – A property's loss of value due to external causes such as zoning or a deteriorating neighborhood. It is also referred to as social obsolescence.

Economy of Scale – The principle where building more units will decrease the cost per unit to build.

Employee – A person working for another person in exchange for compensation.

Employer – A person who hires another person to perform a job in exchange for compensation. By law, the employer must also withhold taxes from the employee's wages and pay unemployment taxes for the employee.

Escrow – The deposit of instruments and funds with a third neutral party with instructions to carry out the provisions of an agreement or contract. A complete or perfect escrow is one in which everything has been deposited to enable carrying out the instructions. The neutral third party (stakeholder) who holds deeds or other documents pursuant to instructions for delivery upon completion or occurrence of certain conditions.

Filtering Down – As new developments are constructed, or more prestigious areas of town are developed, the wealthy will relocate to these areas, leaving their old homes for persons with lesser economic means.

Imperfect Market – A market where traditional principles of supply and demand do not apply.

Independent Contractor – A person who works for himself or herself with no direction from a manager, boss or supervisor. The independent contractor works on a performance basis, having a task to achieve and focusing on the end product without guidance on how to get there.

Must-Buy – A person who is under pressure from one source or another and must purchase a home regardless of whether the market is in their favor, or whether they are paying above market value for the home.

Must-Sell – A person who is under pressure from one source or another and must sell a home, no matter if he or she has to take a loss or sell the house for under market value.

100 Percent Commission – An situation where a real estate agent is receiving his or her entire compensation from commissions, and collecting his or her entire commission without sharing with a broker. Usually, in this situation the agent is required to rent a desk or space in the office and receives no administrative or financial support from the broker.

Principle of Change – Land use is constantly changing, i.e. from agricultural to commercial or residential.

Principle of Choice – Land will be used for the "highest and best" use, i.e. the most profitable and competitive use possible.

Principle of Competition – When one area of real estate or property use is making a lot of money, there will be people moving into that area to try to capitalize on the profits.

Stratified Marketplace – The market may be divided, or lopsided, based on the available supply of homes in specific price ranges and the number of qualified buyers in that price range

Subdividing – Smaller single-family plots bring in more money than a larger undivided plot.

Will-Buy – A buyer who is looking to buy a home, but has plenty of time to find the best deal for the most desirable home on the market that will fit his or her individual needs.

Will-Sell – A seller who is willing to sell his or her home if the right price was offered. This person does not have to sell and can take as much time as desired until satisfied with an offer.

CHAPTER QUIZ

1. Real estate agents must have a good understanding of which of the following aspects of the industry?
   a. Escrow
   b. Appraisal
   c. Finance
   d. All of the above

2. Which is the best term to describe the economic condition of the real estate market place?
   a. Supply and demand economics
   b. Imperfect market
   c. Buyers market
   d. Sellers market

3. A buyer looking for a new house, who is making sure to find the perfect home at the right price based on the home she grew up in, would be an example of which imperfect marketplace conditions?
   a. Emotion
   b. Differences between each home
   c. Will-buy
   d. Both A and C

4. A housing market where there are more homes for sale than interested buyers creates what?
   a. A stratified market
   b. A buyer's market
   c. Both A and C
   d. Neither A nor C

5. Which of the following is not one of the four levels of real estate economics?
   a. National
   b. Local
   c. City
   d. Regional

6. When goods are offered at a higher price, and fewer consumers purchase the goods or services, it is an example of what principle?
   a. Law of demand
   b. Law of supply
   c. Equilibrium
   d. Imperfect market

7. As consumers demand more of a specific product, what is the most logical action for the manufacturer to take?
    a. Increase prices of the product
    b. Decrease prices
    c. Increase supply
    d. None of the above

8. A trend where there are more homes on the market than people looking to buy is referred to as:
    a. Buyer's market and / or inflation
    b. Seller's market and / or inflation
    c. Seller's market and / or deflation
    d. Buyer's market and / or deflation

9. Which term describes a property's decline in value due to external forces influencing a neighborhood?
    a. Economic obsolescence
    b. Diminishing returns
    c. Filtering down
    d. Economic life

10. Which of the following is not a component of the business cycle?
    a. Recession
    b. Depression
    c. Interest rates
    d. Recovery

11. The term brokerage means:
    a. A real estate office
    b. A loan office
    c. To bring people together
    d. A general real estate term to describe where professionals work.

12. A person who takes applications for empty space for rent and oversees a staff would best be described as:
    a. Leasing agent
    b. Property manager
    c. Residential income property agent
    d. Salaried assistant

13. Which of the following is not a career path a real estate professional may choose?
    a. Appraisal
    b. Mobile home sales
    c. Salaried assistant
    d. Salaried broker

14. The Internal Revenue Service classifies professionals as independent contractors if they meet which of the following requirements?
    a. Work at a real estate brokerage
    b. Receive compensation based on sales made, not hours worked
    c. Both A and B
    d. Neither A nor B

15. All of the following control factors are characteristic of an independent contractor working environment except
   a. The worker has the right to quit a job at any time, regardless of whether or not the task is finished.
   b. A person may work for more than one firm at a time.
   c. The worker will receive compensation in one lump sum.
   d. The worker must rent his or her own office space.

16. Which one of the following is not a question a real estate agent can ask himself or herself in looking for a positive attitude?
   a. Are you persistent?
   b. Are you willing to chance failure by trying?
   c. Are you happy with your current income?
   d. Are you a problem solver?

17. A successful agent will:
   a. Actively research all hiring brokers before making a decision about where to work.
   b. Maintain a positive attitude.
   c. Participate in all mandatory continuing education training as well as any supplementary training sessions the broker may provide.
   d. All of the above.

18. Generally a salesperson working for a broker at 100% commission can rely on the broker for:
   a. A support staff
   b. Administrative materials
   c. A desk or space to rent
   d. None of the above

19. The late renewal period for a real estate licensee is:
   a. 90 days
   b. 1-year
   c. 2-years
   d. There is no late renewal period; all licensees must retake the state examination if they allow their license to expire.

20. First time broker renewals require _____ hours of training, while all subsequent broker renewals require _____ hours of training.
   a. 12, 45
   b. 45, 45
   c. 45, 90
   d. None of the above

2

MARKETING

What you will learn in this Chapter

- Prospecting
- Sources
- Methods of Prospecting
- Managing Contacts
- Referrals
- Advertising
- Media Vehicles
- Effectiveness of Advertising
- Legal Implications
- Budgets
- Promotion

Test Your Knowledge

1. Finding sellers or buyers is called?
    a. Marketing
    b. Prospecting
    c. Advertising
    d. None of the above

2. Which of the following is NOT a factor in choosing the most appropriate prospecting method?
    a. Potential commission to the agent
    b. Type of property
    c. Neighborhood characteristics
    d. Time period

3. As a successful agent, it is important for you to:
    a. File all contacts exclusively in electronic format for the most efficient way to manage data.
    b. Use only a Rolodex so you can take your contact information with you wherever you need, simply and easily.
    c. Wait for your clients to contact you when they are ready to make a transaction – you don't want to bother them until they are ready to make a move.
    d. None of the above.

4. After you gain a referral from a current client, what is one of the most important things to do?
    a. Wait for them to call you – you don't want them to feel like you are pressuring them into any decisions.
    b. Follow up with them via a phone call.
    c. Ask your client to talk to the referral on your behalf and get back to you.
    d. None of the above.

5. Which of the following is not represented in institutional advertising?
    a. The broker
    b. The salesperson
    c. The entire real estate firm
    d. An individual listing

6. Which of the following is not covered in the Civil Rights Act of 1968?
    a. Gender
    b. Religion
    c. Sexual orientation
    d. Familial status

7. Promotion is considered to be the same as:
    a. Advertising
    b. Prospecting
    c. Neither A nor B
    d. Both A and B

INTRODUCTION

Marketing is an all-encompassing term used to describe the promotional activities an agent will carry out in seeking out listings, buyers or prospecting and advertising. In this chapter you will be introduced to all the different concepts having to do with marketing. It is important to know the guidelines of what an agent can and cannot do to avoid violating any rules or misleading clients. Marketing is essential to any agent's success, and must be thoroughly understood so the agent can make sure he or she is always operating legally, ethically and under the rules of the California Department of Real Estate.

PROSPECTING

Simply stated, prospecting is the act of finding owners who want to sell their property and buyers who are looking to purchase property. You might be thinking that this sounds easy, or that the majority of your clients will actively seek you out in at the brokerage where you will be working, but the simple fact is that the most successful realtors do not sit back and wait for the business to come to them -- they actively seek listings and buyers for those listings. Prospecting is a combination of being completely aware of the industry around you so that you know trends, being persistent with any leads you have and making sure to follow up regularly, and having good time management skills so that you can actively pursue new leads and service existing customers.

Prospecting includes learning how to, and actively going after and obtaining listings. Additionally there is finding buyers for the listings you have obtained. Prospecting does not end when you obtain the listing: you then need to work just as hard, if not harder, to sell the property and move on to the next. Again, we will talk more in the next section regarding sources of potential buyers.

Remember
Prospecting is obtaining listings and then finding buyers for these listings.

SOURCES

There are almost unlimited sources of listings, if you know where to look. Agents who wait for the listings to come to them will not be real estate agents for very long, or will not be very successful. Those agents who know where to look and are persistent will benefit financially from their hard work. Additionally, finding buyers is a much more in-depth activity than simply hanging an open sign on the front of your firm's door.

Sources of Listings
There are the obvious leads, such as: seeking out "For Sale By Owner" ads and seeing if the owners would like representation; working with developers who are putting in new housing tract; using direct mail and posting flyers; or placing newspaper notices. These are all very effective ways to find new listings, but there are many, many other sources that usually go unnoticed. The following is a sample list of sources for obtaining listings. It is certainly not a complete list; it is up to you to be creative, and think of places that others may overlook. Sometimes people are willing to sell, but they just need one last push or the support from the right agent.

- Acquaintances, friends and relatives

- Ad Switchers and Buyers – In an ad switch situation a client may be approaching an agent to find a home. This client may possibly have a home to sell; it is up to the agent to find out if the buyer could also be a seller, and obtain the listing.

- Advertising, brochures, flyers, posters, Internet – Advertising in newspapers, telephone books, outdoor advertising or television commercials will get a lot of exposure.

- Apartment owners – Apartment owners or managers may know of residents who are living there temporarily until they buy a home, or may allow you to have a flyer in a commons area for tenants to see.

- Appraisers

- Bulletin boards – Anywhere possible

- Canvassing – Putting "Sold" signs out in front of properties you have sold, showing potential sellers you are a successful agent.

- Civic, church, professional or private activities / organizations – Any place where there will a group of people assembled (and you are allowed to promote your services) is a great place to reach multiple people for very little or no cost.

- Closed escrows – sending a notice of a sale to the neighbors in the community to announce your or your firm's activity in the area.

- Client referrals

- Cold calling

- Developers, builders or contractors – a good way to find clients is to go to the source of new, unsold construction.

- Door-to-door canvassing – visiting each of the homes in a neighborhood soliciting your services directly.

- Employee relocation services – offer your services to companies who are relocating employees from one office to another.

- Executors of estates

- Financial institutions – Clients looking to get approved for a home loan may not have an agent yet; your advertising in these places will catch them before they go somewhere else.

- For sale by owner – Looking at the ads in the paper under "for sale by owner" may be a good way to pick up a listing if the owner has been trying for a long time to sell the property by himself or herself.

- Foreclosures

- Letters and mailings – a good way to announce yourself to an entire community and make them aware of your services.

- Mortgage loan brokers / representatives

- Moving companies – This could be a great referral service for people moving on the spur of the moment who don't have much time to plan the sale of their home.

- Neighbors

- Open houses – People looking at a property you represent are potential buyers, and could also be potential sellers if they currently own their home.

- Previous clients – Follow up with previous clients to see if they are in need of your services, or remind them you are available when they need you.

- Publicity or news releases – Send a news release or announcement to the newspaper, or circulate it where you can, showing your community involvement, success and any awards you may have received. A successful person is always an attractive agent for those looking to sell.

- Real estate boards

- Savings and loan associations

- Sold signs – Placing a sold sign, if permitted, is a great way to show others in the neighborhood that you are a successful agent, capable of finding buyers for available properties.

- Telephone directory – You can't be found if you don't make yourself available.

- Window advertising – Hang a sign at your residence and office, let people know who you are, what you do and that you are available to help.

Sources of Buyers

Just as there are almost unlimited sources for obtaining listings if you really search hard, there is an equal number of buyers looking for properties. It is important to note, however, that an agent will most likely spend 1/2 or more of his or her time trying to obtain listings and doing necessary administrative duties. That leaves or less than 1/2 of their time to find qualified, serious buyers. The following is a sample of some of the places an agent can find a ready, willing and able buyer. You will notice that many of the same sources considered useful in finding listings will also be used to find buyers. So, given the time constraints you will be experiencing as a busy professional, it is important for you to be able to multi-task – it will prove fruitful for your success!

- Builders can be a great source for finding buyers, since a builder is strictly involved in the construction of homes; they are not real estate agents. Unless a builder holds a license as a real estate agent, they must refer all activities requiring a license to a licensed professional. A good relationship with a builder will yield referrals or clients. Additionally, if a client approaches a builder and discovers he or she cannot afford a new home, the builder may refer them to you as an agent to search for existing inventory already on the market, which may be a little less expensive than building new.

- Phone calling can be an effective way to introduce your services or inventory to prospective clients. It is important to call at specific times of the day, however. Morning and early evening tend to be the best times to reach the resident, and these are usually the least busy parts of their day. This is a very efficient way to cover an entire neighborhood or town directly from your office. Sometimes people have such busy schedules that they may be considering looking for a home, but simply don't have the time to seek out an agent and take the time to look at listings. If the agent comes to them, and presents them with homes they may be interested in, it makes the process much easier and convenient for the buyer, and gains you a new client!

- Owner ads and "for sale by owner" advertisements in the newspapers are a great place to potentially find new buyers. You already know the person is interested in selling his or her home (and you can even obtain a new listing if they are interested,) and now it is your job to see if they are trying to find a replacement home, and if they are currently being represented by an agent. These ads take the guesswork out of the agent's job, because you already know they are interested in at least one transaction; now you must offer your services.

- Door-to-door prospecting may seem like an old-fashioned way to find interested buyers, but it can be extremely effective considering that there is very little competition for this source of buyers. Although many communities have outlawed solicitation door-to-door, the places where it is allowed open up an untapped resource for the aggressive agent. Door-to-door prospecting is not just asking if a person is interested in purchasing a home, but also showing a willing participant the inventory that may be in the area, or inventory available through the agent's office. While success rates for door-to-door prospecting are fairly low, the lack of competition can make this lucrative for willing agents.

- Open houses can generate a lot of foot traffic into one specific home, allowing the agent to gather information on people who are potentially looking for similar properties, in a similar price range. While not every person who attends an open house is actually in the market, it is a great way to gather a name and phone number to follow up with at a later time.

- The people you meet on the street, in an elevator, in line at the bank and virtually everywhere may be prospects. Remember to always carry your business cards; that way if you engage someone in conversation at one of these places you can give him or her your card. You don't necessary have to tell the person that you are a real estate agent, but your card will. It may spark a conversation regarding real estate; they may have a friend, neighbor, relative or co-worker looking to purchase a home, which gives you a great lead to follow up on. It is important not to approach everyone you see with "Hi, my name is so-and-so and I am a real estate agent," but always have your card handy for chance encounters with new people.

- Former customers provide a great source of new business, whether the former customer is looking to purchase another home or they refer business to you. Some of the best advertising is by word of mouth from satisfied customers, allowing your good reputation to be passed onto their friends, family and neighbors. It is important for you to follow up with these former clients periodically. A good way to do this is to send out a greeting card once or twice a year, perhaps on the anniversary of when the customer first purchased his or her home from you.

- Additionally, besides customers you have already sold to, there are a lot of people you see around you every day that could be considered an influential source of leads or business. The mail carrier, a familiar store clerk, or even a delivery driver that you encounter on a weekly, if not daily, basis also interacts with many other people, some of whom might be in the market for a new home. They can be your eyes and ears for potential new business, passing on your good name to these potential clients.

- Membership in a community club, civic organization or church group is also a good way to find clients. Being an active member in one or more organizations will compel people to use your services to keep their business in their own circle of influence, or community. You can also advertise in these organizations' newsletters, bulletins or papers. It is a very easy way to reach a lot of new people, and have the opportunity to be active in your community at the same time.

- Hosting seminars introducing people to the possibility of home ownership is a good way to let people who currently rent or lease their dwelling know that they are closer to owning their own homes than they might think. You are able to reach a lot of people who may otherwise not think having their own place is possible. It is a good idea to collaborate with a mortgage lender or broker, an escrow officer and other real estate professionals to provide a well-rounded seminar, so that people understand not only the inventory available to them, but also financing options and the | general process they will have to go through to become a homeowner. In these seminars it is important not only to introduce the possibility of ownership, but also the advantages of ownership versus renting or leasing.

- Pay close attention to the events, or happenings within your community. Are there new members joining your community? Did someone recently get married? Is there anyone you know expecting a child? All of these events may prompt the purchase of a new home, or a larger home, or the sale of a home. It is important for you to understand that the business may be right in front of you, and your proactivity might snag a few new clients.

Remember
Potential sources of buyers include, but are not limited to:
- Builders
- Neighborhood / community phone campaigns
- Owner advertisements / newspaper classified ads
- Door-to-door prospecting
- Open houses
- Former clients
- People you meet every day, anywhere (it is a good idea to carry your business cards at all times)
- Civic, community or church groups
- Seminars
- Community activities, events

There are different methods for prospecting, and a good agent will recognize which method best suits him or her. It is important for the agent to find the right fit, producing the highest productivity for time invested. An inefficient method of prospecting, requiring a lot of time but producing minimal results, will keep an agent busy, but not very successful. Choosing the type of prospecting will depend on a number of factors. These factors include the type of property involved, the time period planned for, the neighborhood and property characteristics, and the types of prospects. Some of the neighborhood and property characteristics you need to examine are size of the property, number of bedrooms, location of the property, neighborhood changes such as single family homes or multiple family dwellings and any economic factors or changes the community is experiencing.

Remember
Factors in choosing a prospecting method include:
- Type of property
- Time period
- Neighborhood / property characteristics
- Types of prospects

Agents must recognize the different interests and motivations clients have when buying or selling property. No two clients will be the same. There will be differences in political, social, economic and philosophical viewpoints. You as an agent must be sensitive to these views, and tailor your work style and approach around these views. Additionally, you should take into account your own skills, personality and attributes, then choose a method of prospecting which will best match you and your clients' characteristics.

The different methods of prospecting include:

- Direct mail canvassing

- Personal letters

- Door-to-door canvassing

- Telephone canvassing

Direct Mail Canvassing
A direct mailing campaign needs to engage the recipient, or have a very clear, convincing "call to action" to be truly effective. Direct mail can reach many people in a very short amount of time, and if done effectively can produce real results.

Direct mail may be used to find buyers by enlisting the help of the neighborhood. Send out a mailer simply alerting the neighbors to the sale of a home in their neighborhood, telling them which home it is, giving a brief description, and requesting any referrals they might know of that are looking for homes in the same neighborhood, such as family, friends or co-workers. This is a great way to generate leads on a current listing. Additionally, the neighbors receiving the mailer may themselves be interested in moving into the available property if it is larger, has more amenities, or if it would fit their needs better than their current home. Often people would be willing to purchase a different home which would fit their needs better but want to stay in the same neighborhood.

Other mailers can announce a new neighbor to the community rather than announce an available property. This type of mailer will show a salesperson's success, and may be effective in getting other listings based on a good sales record.

There are some general rules to follow when conducting a direct mail campaign. These are really more like helpful hints than hard-and-fast rules, but they are important for you to understand to produce optimum results for your efforts.

- Use a number 10, plain white envelope without a window. This will make the mailer look more personalized. A lot of "junk" mail comes in pre processed window envelopes, so that the person or company doing the mailing did not have to address both the letter and the envelope. In addition to the plain white envelope, handwrite the recipient's address on the piece of mail; it shows effort and personalization on your part. This will take a little extra time, but is more effective in the long run.

- Test your mailers before doing a mass mailing. If the piece you are about to mail to hundreds of people is not effective, you will be wasting your time and money. Send the mailer to a small sample of people to gauge the response, and then decide if the mailer is going to be efficient and produce results.

- Make sure the mailer engages the reader within the first line or so. If the mailer is interesting, or catches the reader's attention, chances are they will keep reading. If the mailer is not exciting, the reader will likely toss the mail into the trash.

- Use a stamp on the outside of the envelope, rather than electronic or prepaid postage. Both electronic and prepaid postage make the mailer look like junk mail. A stamp will make the mailer look personalized.

- It is important for you to make your letter look personalized, but don't give it the appearance that it will be something different than what it actu- ally is. If you make it look like personal correspondence from a friend, it will be thrown away. If you make it look like an attempt to personally be contacted by a local business you have a much better chance the letter will be read.

- Using other mediums besides mail, such as faxing, is illegal. Make sure you don't blanket a target market with unsolicited faxes.

- Use follow-up calls after sending out your mailer. Don't rely on the recipi- ent to call you – make sure you put forth the effort.

Personal Letters
Personal letters are very similar to the direct mailing campaigns. It is important that this letter does not look or feel like a form letter, and it must be addressed specifically

to the recipient. Letters addressed to "Mr. or Mrs. Homeowner, Resident or Occupant" will not be as effective a letter addressed to Mr. Adam Jones. To be less formal, just use the person's name, with no title, such as Adam Jones. The personal letter needs to have a specific reason as well. This should not be a mass form letter being sent out to hundreds of people, but rather a very specific letter being sent to one or very few people. For example, you might target the residents of one single apartment complex highlighting the benefits of homeownership versus renting. You can point out to them that by renting, you are building another persons equity in property, but by buying you will be building your own equity in property.

The personal letter can be even more specifically targeted. If you have decided you want to take the "renter versus owner" approach, target those people whom you know have recently been promoted, married, expanded their family or have any other valid reason to move into a place of their own, besides building equity. The letter should get their attention, convince them to at least explore the opportunity, and perhaps even invite them to an open house where you can go into more detail in person about all the benefits of homeownership versus renting.

Each letter should include a "call to action," or a suggestion for the recipient to act or react. A phrase such as "call to reserve your spot today" or "call for more information" is appropriate at the end of the letter to initiate action from the recipient of the letter. It is important to note, however, that you should not rely on just this call to action, and a follow-up phone call would be appropriate. Make sure to keep very accurate records regarding who received letters from you, the message in the letter and who has responded so you are not calling people you have already called, or that have already responded to you.

Remember
Helpful hints with personal letters:
- Hand address the letters to specific individuals, don't use labels
- Don't use a form letter, use a customized letter specifically targeted to the recipient
- Include a call to action in the letter
- Use a follow-up phone call after the letter has been sent
- Set up a seminar or information session to further cover the information contained in the letter

Door-to-Door Canvassing
Not many agents do door-to-door canvassing; thus, it can be extremely effective to those agents who choose to utilize this method of prospecting. It is extremely targeted and specific, and a very efficient way to cover a large geographical area. Be careful, however -- some neighborhoods have ordinances outlawing door-to-door canvassing, or others may require a permit. Additionally, be sensitive to any posted signs at individual homes declining any solicitation.

The most useful trick to know about door-to-door canvassing is what time of day to contact the resident at home. Each residence will naturally have a different schedule from the next, but generally speaking a dual income family with children will most likely have one decision-making adult home in the early evenings, and on Saturday mornings. The best time to reach retired clients is between 9 A.M. and 11 A.M. and then again between 2 P.M. and 4 P.M. Be sensitive to meal times, and never do any canvassing after dark.

While door-to-door canvassing is very effective for those agents who choose to do it, there are many helpful pointers to make the experience more effective. The first we have already covered -- the appropriate times to target different clients. Secondly, when visiting people, make sure to smile when you talk, and be engaging. If it is possible, try to engage the potential client within 20 seconds of ringing the door. Don't be overly aggressive – stand back from the door after ringing the bell and bring only the necessary items to the door with you. These items include your business card, a tablet to write notes and a writing utensil. All other items can stay in your vehicle or back at the office, so that you don't intimidate the resident. It may be most effective to canvass the area after you have closed on a property in that neighborhood. It will show potential clients and residents you have good sales skills, and are well connected to move properties fast!

When approaching a home, it is important for you to follow four general steps to guide the conversation. The first step is to introduce yourself, give your broker affiliation, and if possible, use the resident's name. You can find the resident's name by using the telephone directory in reverse. Locate the address, and then find who lives there. Online directories are much faster than going through a phone book as it will electronically search the specific address you have identified.

The second step is to explain to the resident or potential client why you are calling on them. It is effective to engage them with a question such as: "Do you know of any friend or family member who is currently actively looking for a place to live?" This will invite them into a dialogue with you, allowing you to most thoroughly present your services, brokerage and available listings.

The third step, which is very similar to the second, is to ask the resident if they know of any person in the neighborhood who may be moving in the near future. For either step two or three, the question might apply to someone the homeowner knows, or perhaps the homeowner himself or herself. In any case, it is important not to push. If the residents offer helpful information to you regarding themselves or other people they know, it is important for you to make the appropriate notes and follow-up. If they simply are not interested or don't have the time to talk to you at the moment, you must respect their schedule and politely go on to your next stop.
The fourth and last step is to thank the owner. Regardless of any information gathered from the visit, you must thank the owner for his or her time. Additionally, and most importantly, before you leave, offer your business card to the homeowner.

As you can see, door-to-door canvassing works well for both obtaining listings and buyers. By gathering information from residents regarding their future plans, or the plans of their friends, neighbors or co-workers, you can start to build a very impressive database of potential clients.

Telephone Canvassing
Telephone canvassing is a bit more common than door-to-door canvassing for many reasons. Essentially, you are doing the exact same thing. The ideas of engaging the resident within 20 seconds, asking questions, and being sensitive to the time you call are key to your success. Telephone canvassing is considered more effective because it is faster. You are able to cover more residents faster than if you were going door to door. It is safer, as you will not need to worry about personal safety in the confines or your office, versus out in the neighborhoods. Unfortunately, it is much easier for the recipient of the call to hang up; people are less likely to slam the door in your face when you are physically there, but an anonymous phone call is much easier to termi-

nate. Additionally, people are usually more annoyed with a phone solicitation than they are with a personal visit. When phone canvassing, you need to make sure to have a very engaging or positive introduction to keep the resident on the phone. Without this, it is very easy for the person to simply say "No thank you," and hang up before you can get to the purpose of the call.

To keep the resident on the phone, make sure you utilize reverse directory tactics. You should have adequate knowledge of which neighborhood the person resides in, their address, the characteristics of the neighborhood and the pronunciation of their name. If you call someone and struggle to pronounce their name, they will immediately know it is an unsolicited call, and be very likely to hang up. Practice saying the name: if you are having a hard time with its pronunciation, ask another person how they would say it. Little things like this will make a big difference in the tone of the call.

To maintain a conversational flow, it is a good idea to have a script handy. Not a script you are reading for the first time, -- this creates a choppy, unrehearsed call – but a script you are very familiar with so that you make sure to touch upon all the important points of the call. In this script, make sure to introduce a real, interested family looking for a home in the resident's neighborhood. Engage them in the conversation by asking if they know of any neighbors who might be selling a home. Never make up an interested buyer; you never know, the recipient of the call may be interested in selling their home, and if you have just introduced a false buyer, you will lose credibility.

It is a good idea to call people who might be able to connect to the new family looking for a home. For example, if the family were actively involved in a community club or activity, you would begin by calling all the members of this activity or club. Let's say our new family, the Busbooms, are actively involved in Girl Scouts of America. You might contact the local Girl Scouts chapter in the community and call all the members, stating that the Busbooms are moving into the community, they are active members in Girl Scouts of America in their old community and are looking for a new home. The people you call will have an immediate connection, and be more willing to listen to you and ultimately help you than if there was no personal connection or link to themselves.

If the caller is interested in selling, it is a good idea to set up an appointment to view their home sooner than later. A good approach to make this appointment is to offer the resident an appraisal of the property. This will not be an official appraisal of value, but an estimate of what the home could sell for on the open market. This way, the resident will know how much they could charge for their home in the event they do decide to list it with you. When you are finished with your conversation, whether or not the person was able to help you, it is important to thank them for their time and any assistance they were able to provide you.

Remember
In phone canvassing it is important to:
- Engage the caller within the first 20 seconds
- Tell them about an actual interested buyer
- Use a script for optimum conversational flow
- Know their neighborhood, name and location of their home
- Contact people with similar interests or that might belong to a similar civic, community or church organization as the interested buyer
- Set up an appointment to view the home and offer an estimation of value to the potential client if they are interested
- Thank the caller for their time

During your prospecting, you will encounter many people, each with different needs. Obtaining information about a potential client is only the first step in successful prospecting. Now that you have information about your potential clients, you must devise a system to organize potential listings from buyers, current active clients, referrals or any other categories you think necessary. Information on clients or potential clients is practically useless if not properly organized and utilized.

There is no right or wrong way to organize your contacts. You can choose the best method for you, but make sure to use it! Some people prefer to write down their contacts and file them away into a Rolodex, file cabinet or some other filing system. Others use electronic devices such as a personal computer or PDA. Electronic methods of data storage are especially helpful, as you can flag certain dates or information on an individual file and be automatically alerted to that specific event. For example, if you like to send a personal greeting to existing clients on the anniversary of their home purchase, you can set up an electronic data file to alert you to these important dates. Or if you send out a holiday greeting, or any other greeting, an electronic filing source can be a very efficient way to find data quickly.

Make sure to be detailed with each of your entries. Note the type of client. Is the person a source for a listing, buyer, potential listing or potential buyer? Is he or she looking for a single-family residence, condo, income property or other type of property? Will this be his or her primary residence? Is this person selling because of a life event to which you should be sensitive? Is this a first-time buyer or seller? The more information you have regarding the client, the better you can serve them now and in the future.

Good, detailed record keeping is a very important step an agent can take to be successful. Having a briefcase or desk drawer full of business cards or names is useless unless they are properly managed and organized. Make the extra time and take the extra step to make sure a new contact does not slip through the cracks; each new contact may represent your next transaction. Make sure you follow up with your leads. Persistence keeps your name fresh in people's minds. When they are ready to act, you will be the person they think of.

Remember
- File your contacts in a simple system, readily useable
- Keep a detailed record of each client
- Follow up with your leads – make sure they know you are still interested in assisting them

R E F E R R A L S

Good service is essential for the successful real estate agent. Providing adequate service, or performing a job completely, is different than going the extra steps above and beyond what is expected. By giving more of your time, energy and talents, you will gain something very important -- referrals. A satisfied customer may say "Thanks," and might tell a few people about his or her experience with you. If you take it a few extra steps, do more than expected and do it well, and impress the client with your skills, then they are quite likely to pass this information on to their friends, relatives and co-workers. Hobart C. Brady mentions in his book, Real Estate is Wonderful, "Service is something gained, not given." When you give excellent service, beyond expectations, you gain trust, confidence and referrals from your clients. It is important to note, however, that the same is true if you do not perform to the standards or expectations of the client. An unhappy client will most likely tell friends, family and co-workers not to use you for any future property transfers.

Referrals are very important for your business. With all the prospecting you will be doing, paperwork, administrative work and showing homes, referrals are a very valuable source of qualified leads, which generally don't take much time to obtain. They don't take much time to obtain because you can ask your current client for any names or leads they may know of, expending very little time away from what you would have been doing anyway, which is helping out a current client.

Going above and beyond expectations can happen in numerous ways. A basic service that you can perform, which may or may not be noticed by the client, is to check the accuracy of the Preliminary Report on Title. By taking an extra few minutes to make sure all details are correct for taxes and assessments and checking for liens, encumbrances or any other items which may cause a clouded title, you will save your client a lot of headache at the end of the transaction. If this is not checked, and there is a problem with the transferability of the title, your client will not be very happy, and may decide to back out of the transfer. This seems like a very elementary detail to check, but some agents may not take the extra time to make sure everything is in order, and instead just trust that the transaction will not have any difficulties with the title. Another extra service item a real estate agent can do for the client is to aid in the financing portion of the transaction. Making forms available, being a liaison between the client and the financing company, explaining all forms and processes and aiding in closing will not only aid the client's understanding of the process, but also minimizes the client's own legwork. As a real estate agent, you can be part of the entire transaction process if you choose; your participation will ease any uncertainty the client may have.

Remember, you are the agent for your client, but that does not mean you can't be helpful to the other party involved. By being detail-oriented during the closing process, explaining all forms and inspections and orchestrating the timely completion of all work, you will gain the trust of the third party as well. Remember, you owe your client fiduciary responsibility, but you can also take one extra step and make sure the third party is informed of all processes, progress or any possible problems which may occur. By keeping each party informed, you will avoid misunderstandings and perhaps gain the confidence of the third party to the point that they may ask you for a business card, and possibly give you a referral, or their future business.

To break the referral process up into a step-by-step series of events that you can track for yourself, think of it as having four steps. First, plan your strategy. Second, think of all sources of referral information. The third step is to gain the trust and confidence of your client to obtain referrals, and finally, the last step is to follow up. Gaining referrals without following up is like buying all the ingredients for a gourmet meal, but not having a kitchen to prepare the food.

Plan Your Strategy
- Have a specific referral in mind. In conversation, if you remember that the client has a relative, friend or co-worker who is thinking of buying a home, this will be a good place to begin.

42

- When you ask for a lead, make sure to do it strategically; don't just come out of nowhere and ask. Perhaps after you have just done something for your client, you can then ask about that friend, relative or co-worker that they know is interested in purchasing property.

- Ask your client for helpful suggestions that may have helped them out during the transaction that maybe you did not think of, or areas in which you could have improved your services or availability.

- Most clients need to be educated on the specific types of referrals you are seeking. If you ask for referrals without letting them know the type of referrals you want, you may end up receiving referrals in a neighboring community you don't know much about and where you have to spend additional traveling time to get to your referral. This would take time away from your familiar base of clients and property.

- Clients generally don't freely offer referrals without your leading them. You can let them know you are looking for referrals in the area.

- People are usually happy to help, and often are flattered when asked. By asking for their help you will not only gain referrals, but also build a good rapport with your client.

Sources of Referral Information
- With permission, search any files your broker may have in the office.

- Offer your business card to people you know, and people you are meeting for the first time. You don't have to reserve your card for business transactions, but can offer it on or off the clock, when appropriate.

- Inquire about your clients' local neighbors, and whether any of them have plans to relocate or move in the future.

- Talk to friends. They may have valuable leads for you.

Gain Your Clients' Trust and Confidence
- If you have a good working relationship with your clients, some only need to be asked and they will gladly give you the names of people they know that you might be able to assist.

- Get your clients to talk about their specific needs, or what they are looking for. In these conversations, you may be able to ask them about other people they know -- perhaps where they gathered some of their ideas for their ideal property -- who are also looking to do a real estate transaction.

- Tell your clients that you appreciate their business, and ask if they know of anyone who you might be able to assist as well. This is subtle, and not as direct as asking for a referral, but sometimes more appropriate.

- Let your client know of any other services you can assist with. This might not be direct assistance from you, for example the financing of the property, but you can offer helpful suggestions and point them in the right general direction to answer their questions.

- Tell your client that the area, your brokerage, and your client base are growing at a phenomenal rate, and then ask to see if they know of any one you can assist.

- Go so far as to tell of a time where a previous client gave you a referral, how you were able to help that person and ask to see if your current client knows of anyone for whom you can do the same.

Follow Up

Following up with a client is the most important thing. Whether you are following up on a lead they gave you, following up on their own transaction, or simply touching base with an old client to see if they are still happy in their home, following up is the biggest key to success. If you allow a client to slip between the cracks, they will simply find another agent to work with. Follow these steps to make sure you are staying current with all clients and leads.

- Follow up on leads promptly; don't allow a lot of time to go by. If you do, they may change their minds about moving, may find another agent, or you may lose their confidence because you did not act fast enough.

- Place all potential leads in your client database to make sure you follow up in a timely and appropriate fashion.

- Thank your client if he or she passed along a referral. You may even tell them about a successful transaction from the referral, if appropriate.

A D V E R T I S I N G

Advertising is the single most important way to get a broker's inventory out to prospective buyers. Most people who look at advertisements for property are in the market, or are ready to purchase a home, land, business or income property. If you advertise and display a sample of what your broker has to offer, they may contact you directly and request to view one or more of the available properties, giving you an opportunity to show them other listings or find the appropriate property for them through the MLS. Prospecting is a very good way to find clients, but you are not necessarily contacting people in the market, actively looking to buy or sell.

Good advertising will help you accomplish many things. Remember, you are displaying a sample of the listings you have available to the interested public: you don't want to simply list your entire inventory. Give a good sample of the different types of properties you have, and let the advertising work for you. Advertising should expose your name to the general public while building a good reputation. This can be done by showing listings you have successfully sold or maybe even a testimonial from a happy client.

Advertising should stimulate activity in a market. This can be very specifically targeted to one neighborhood or one type of property, or be more general, spreading over an entire city or region. Remember, you are in control of what the ad will say, the media you will use and whom you target. Be specific -- the more specific the better. Skilled advertising also allows the agent to establish him or herself as the leader in a certain area. Highlight your successes and track record. It will show that you have the sales skills to successfully move open properties. Advertisements don't always have to show listings: they can show a listing, and then talk about your successes in the industry, or your firm's success in the community.

Remember
- Advertising allows you to showcase some of your inventory
- It allows you to establish yourself as an industry leader
- It will expose your name and good reputation to the general public
- Advertising can be very specific or general depending on your sales goals
- It lets you establish a good, aggressive track record
- Provides the opportunity to print testimonials

Advertising can serve several purposes. It can call attention to something, it can generate interest and it can provide additional information regarding a product or service. Whether we realize it or not, real estate advertising happens around us every day. Stop and think about the different places you have seen advertisements for a real estate agent, agency or listing. On the bus bench, on a taxicab, in the phone book, on a billboard, in the newspaper or newspaper inserts, magazines and Internet advertising – it is literally everywhere.

Real estate advertising can be divided into two categories; institutional, and specific or operational. Institutional advertising promotes the firm itself. Whether it is promoting the broker, salesperson or the brokerage, the purpose of this form of advertising is to promote a good image for the firm. It spreads the name of the firm and introduces the agents working there to the community. Specific or operational advertising is when a specific property is being advertised. This serves to create instant results.

Remember
- Institutional advertising promotes the firm, its agents and the general goodwill of the business.
- Specific or operational advertising promotes a specific listing, designed to create instant results.

Many real estate agents will use the AIDA approach to advertising. AIDA stands for attention, interest, desire and action.

In any effective ad, you first want to catch the viewer's **attention**. Headlines, type size, font type, wording, layout, color, sound, and graphics are a good way to grab a viewer's attention. Humor, when appropriate, is another useful tool to gain attention. Once you have the viewer's attention, they are most likely to read on to the body of your advertisement and receive the intended message.

A successful ad will create **interest** for the service or product being advertised. If the viewer finds the ad catchy, humorous or interesting, but it fails to convey the desired message, the ad is a failure. If the ad is all those things, and conveys the intended message and creates interest, then the ad is a success.

Now that you have grabbed the viewer's attention and created interest in the product being offered, you need to create a **desire** for them to want to own the product. Tell or show them why they need to obtain this product. Know your audience, and then make an appropriate appeal regarding why they need to purchase a home or trade up / down. You have successfully created desire when you appeal to the viewer's emotions and senses.

The final step in the AIDA approach is to get the viewer to act or take **action**. Obviously the advertisement itself is not going to sell a property, but the ad should get the viewer to call, email or visit your offices to learn more about the specific listing.

M E D I A   V E H I C L E S

There are many different media "vehicles" available to use when trying to get your message out. Media vehicles are simply another name for the type of media used. Examples of this would be newspapers, direct mail and billboards. When choosing the type of media you will use, you need to consider the budget, the type of people you are trying to reach, which type of media will reach them most efficiently, and what message you plan on conveying as determined by your marketing goals. By answering these questions, you can select the best form of advertising to achieve your goals.

Media Vehicles
- Newspapers
- Magazines
- Phone Directory / Yellow pages
- Special Interest Publications
- Radio
- TV
- Outdoor Advertising
- Bus, Car and Taxicab Advertising
- Personal Advertising
- Signs
- Direct Mail
- Newsletters / Clubs and Organizations
- Press Releases
- Specialty Gifts / Giveaways
- Internet
- Shopping Guides
- Window Displays
- Community Relations

Newspaper advertising is the most important form of advertising, especially for residential listings. This form of advertising composes about half the broker's marketing budget. The newspaper is one of the first places, if not the first place, a person will check for listings when he or she decides to open a home search. Newspaper advertising is composed of classified, display, classified-display, institutional and news releases.

Newspaper advertising can be as simple as including an ad in the classified section, or as elaborate as buying a multi-page insert with full photographs of available properties, pictures of agents, and contact information for the firm. Newspaper advertising is very diverse and reaches many people; however, depending on the newspaper you select to place your ad, newspaper advertising can be extremely selective, targeting a specific group of people. Advertising in a community newspaper is much more specific than you placing an advertisement in a major newspaper covering a multi-county area. When placing an ad in the classified section of the paper, the ad must contain the broker's name, phone number and Internet address. It is illegal to use blind ads in California, i.e., ads not containing this information.

Since classified advertising is the most popular form of advertising, you need to remember that your ad will be in direct competition with many, many other ads. You need to make your ad stand out and catch the reader's eye in order for it to be successful. A catchy headline, boldface type or posing a question to the reader are effective ways for your ad to be noticed, and hopefully read. Always include the contact information where the reader can get a hold of you. By law, you must put your broker's information in the ad, but if you neglect to put your own contact information and name in the advertisement, people will not be able to find you.

When writing or designing an ad, it is important for you to include a number of elements to make sure it gets noticed. First, select an appropriate font type and size. Second, make sure to list the positive or good attributes about the property. Third, use adjectives when describing the property. Find an attribute of the property or area, like "palm-lined street," or "sprawling gardens," and use it in the advertising. These words paint a picture in the readers' minds, and allow them to better visualize the property, and hopefully also visualize themselves living there.

Depending on the size of your firm, and whether you have any branch offices covering a large area, you may choose to utilize or avoid large papers. A large paper, such as the Los Angeles Times, is delivered to a multi-county region, reaching millions of people. Large brokerage firms may choose to place an ad in this type of paper if they have multiple offices around Southern California. If you work for a smaller, boutique office with one location, you may wish to steer clear of advertising in a large paper. For you, it would make sense to place an ad in a smaller, local paper with circulation primarily in your sales region.

Display advertising is the most costly form of newspaper advertising, and may be either institutional or operational. Generally, display advertising is very helpful in getting the good name of a firm out to the public, and the same ad can also include a listing of properties. Unless you work for a large real estate firm with its own marketing department, it is a good idea for many reasons to seek professional help in designing display advertisements. Because of the high cost of the ad itself, it is important for it to look professional. For the size, amount of information and circulation it will reach, it is important for the ad to follow the ADIA advertising principle. A professional can help make your ad stand out amongst all the others.

Magazine advertising is effective if the appropriate publication is selected. If you are trying to reach a very select group of people within a small area, advertising in a local or limited circulation magazine can be effective. You can create very impressive color ads which will be seen by your target audience, as dictated by your magazine selection. Choosing the wrong magazine, for instance, one with national circulation that is read by a wide variety of people will be a huge waste of resources. Choosing a local magazine serving one community or segment of a community would be a good choice. An institutional ad might be particularly effective.

Another type of magazine which would be appropriate for your advertisement would be a local homebuyer magazine. These magazines will reach all kinds of interested potential buyers. Usually, these magazines have a photo display of properties, and one of you with all the appropriate contact information. Neighborhood, region, rentals or high-end estates can further differentiate these local homebuyer magazines.

Phone Directory / Yellow pages It is imperative you have your name in the directory and perhaps in the yellow pages as well. This insures that you have the maximum exposure in the region that receives that particular phone book. You can also choose to buy a larger space in the yellow pages to stand out amongst the other agents displaying their names.

Special Interest Publications are particularly useful for commercial, industrial or land sales. You can target developers or business owners who subscribe to trade publications that may be interested in expanding their business or growing into new areas. An example of a special interest publication might be a farming magazine, listing ranches and farms for sale in the classified portion of the publication.

Radio advertising is an important form of advertising because of its reach. Radio advertising can be very selective based on the stations chosen to run the ad and the listener demographic. It is important to consult with a professional when making the decision to utilize radio advertising. Allow the professional to figure out the best times to broadcast the ad, the creative wording of the message, and which stations would be best suited for your target audience.

TV advertising, much like radio, is a costly form of advertising, and a professional should be consulted when making the decision to use this form of media. Generally, the only agents using television advertising are large firms with many locations covering a very large area. Additionally, you will see developers advertising a new development or resort where people can buy a permanent home, time-share or vacation property.

Television advertising can be effective because it appeals to multiple senses, whereas all the advertising vehicles up to this point only appealed to one sense. Television appeals to both hearing and sight, creating a more effective message.

Outdoor Advertising can take place practically anywhere. Billboards are usually the most common form of outdoor advertising, but they can be costly. Generally, an entire firm will take out an ad promoting the good will of their business, but on occasion you might see a team of agents buy the space and advertise themselves. Billboards generally are used for institutional advertising, as the viewer usually only has a few seconds to focus on the message.

Other forms of outdoor advertising may include advertisements at bus stops and park benches and signs on buildings or phone booths. Be creative -- think of places where people go every day or things people see daily, research the availability of the space, and place an attention-grabbing ad.

Bus, Car and Taxicab advertising is a good way to get your name out in your city or neighborhood. By buying space on the side of a bus or a placard on a taxi or using a magnetic sign on your own vehicle you can broadcast your name on familiar routes. Repetition of your name or picture may cause an interested buyer to think of you when they decide to make a property transaction.

Personal Advertising includes the materials you will hand out to clients and potential clients -- items such as business cards, nametags or other handouts you might give to people with your contact information.

Business cards are very important to hand out to people so that they have your contact information and can reach you when they need your services, or just to serve as a reminder that you are an agent. Because business cards are the norm in everyday business, you should think of a way to make your card stand out from others, perhaps with its coloration, material used, use of a graphic, or even a picture of yourself. It should also include phone numbers, office location, Internet address and your email address.

Nametags to be placed on your desk should not only have your name, but also any professional designations you might have. It you have taken the extra steps to be part of professional organizations; it is to your advantage to highlight these. It helps establish you as an authority or expert within the profession. The nametags should be readable from roughly six feet away.

Other personal advertising you might do includes electronic multimedia. You may want to hand out a CD-ROM in addition to your business card, containing all of your contact information, your picture and perhaps some sample listings you have. This is a great way to provide information regarding properties in color and with more detail than taking out an advertisement in other forms of media. Be careful -- you must make sure this CD-ROM remains up to date. You would not want to hand out this material to a potential client displaying available properties you have already sold. If you choose to utilize this form of personal advertising, you will need to make sure it is updated often.

Signs offer a very cheap and effective way for you to get your firm's name out to the general public. Placing a "For Sale sign in the front yard or in front of the unit of the property you represent is a good way for the neighbors and passers-by to see your name, your firm's name, and a contact number. To differentiate your sign, you may try using an attractive color scheme, a logo unique to you or your firm, or creative font types so the sign stands out. Being creative is important to being recognized and unique, but never lose the functional aspect of the sign; make sure it is clear and easy to read. You don't want to dilute its function by being overly creative.

Direct Mail can be a very effective way to generate a response from people. Direct mail will include a call to action, whether it is an invitation to an open house or seminar on home ownership, or as simple as urging the recipient to call for more information regarding an event you have planned. Direct mail is very selective; you choose what demographic will see your message. This can be targeted to new families moving into an area or families with newborns, or you can target any other significant event in a person's life to see if you can be of service.

Even though your direct mailer may have a call to action, it is important for you to follow up each mailing with a phone call. The phone call can remind them that they need to RSVP to an event, or it can be as simple as a courtesy call to see if they received the mailer.

There are different forms of direct mail you can utilize. Some examples of direct mailers are pamphlets, booklets, pictures, maps, letters, postcards or brochures. This form of advertising can be institutional and/or operational, depending on what message you are trying to convey.

Newsletters / Clubs and Organizations Offices and agents can utilize newsletters to send to clients or prospective clients informing them of properties recently acquired, or any news the clients may need to know regarding a possible property transaction. These newsletters are successful at blending both institutional and operational advertising in one message or document.

In addition to a newsletter from you or your firm, , some organizations of which you might be a member may publish a weekly, bi-weekly or monthly newsletter where you can run an ad or purchase space for a message. It is a good way to reach members within your own community circle, and let them know of the services you might be able to provide to them. This type of advertising tends to be institutional rather than operational.

Press Releases provide you a great way to receive free advertising. A well-written press release submitted to a newspaper will generally be printed, provided it is newsworthy. Examples of newsworthy events for which you might be able to create a press release include the opening of a new branch office in the community, the addition of new staff members, acquiring a listing to a famous or historical property, or simply the groundbreaking of a major development which will provide listings in the future. These press releases can be faxed to the newspaper or other news source in your community, along with a clear, glossy photograph, and at the editor's discretion may be published in the real estate section of the paper. This is a very good way to gain free institutional advertising in what would normally be a pricey media vehicle.

Specialty Gifts / Giveaways It is customary for agents to provide new customers with a giveaway. These giveaways are generally very simple. They are refrigerator magnets, tablets, pencils, pens, calendars, basic function calculators or any other such item that can have the agent's name, the firm's name and contact information. These are then used in everyday events, and seen by guests when they visit the new home. Generally, when a person buys a new property, there will be housewarming parties, dinner parties, or simple visits from friends, relatives and co-workers to see the new property. The giveaway items will be readily visible for any guests who might stop by.

Internet Firm web pages, internet advertisements or individual agent web pages used to be a rare item for an agent or firm, but now Internet activity represents a significant portion of contacts or leads for an agent or firm.

Internet sites allow the viewer to utilize the senses of sight and sound, and are also interactive. Agents can have a very simple web site with their photo, some sample listings and the contact information where they can be reached. Some agents also include a link to their firm's home page. Other agents can become very creative and interactive on their pages. They can feature Flash technology – which could include a virtual tour of some of the listings – music, interactive graphics or other unique images. Be careful; as with any other form of advertising, it is important not to lose your message or the importance of the page in fancy or flashy graphics or technology. Use the technology to enhance the user's experience; don't allow it to take away from the purpose of the site.

The agent can create a web page himself or herself, but these sites tend to be simple, basic or elementary. They will be adequate at communicating your idea, but usually don't stand out as much as they would if you utilized a professional web page designer. You can tell the designer what you want to include on the site, and then let them create it. Much like using an advertising agency to create your print, audio or video ads, it also is important to use a professional here. A little extra money spent upfront could equal a lot of business in the end.

Regarding content, it is up to the individual agents or firms what they wish to share online. From a design standpoint, the following is a list of elements or criteria a good web page should have.

- **Your contact information.** People need to know how to get ahold of you. Include all contact information you feel is necessary such as phone numbers, email addresses or the physical address of your firm or office.

- A **sample of your inventory**. This does not have to be an exhaustive list of your listings, but it should give a good sample of the different properties you have available, in all kinds of sizes, price ranges and communities. Photos are also a good element to work into the site, as well as interactivity with the photos. Offer a map feature as well, so that people not familiar with the area can see where the property is located.

- Give a little **biography** of yourself: how long you have been in real estate,

- maybe a testimonial from happy clients and a little about your firm. Use this as a chance to introduce yourself to a potential client.
- Work in **sound** to the page -- maybe a background song, audio testimonial or even your voice welcoming the potential client to your page.

- Other **services** you might be able to help with or links to other people who can aid the client in their property search such as loan brokers, escrow agents or inspection agencies.

Shopping Guides Some supermarkets provide home listings for their customers via a circular. This magazine or circular provides a good opportunity for a firm or agent to display a weekly sample of available listings, as well as contact information, thus covering both institutional and operational advertising.

Window Displays Is your office or firm located on a street with a lot of foot traffic? Do you have a good window up front that is not being utilized much? Try window displays as a way to display your contact information and some examples of available properties. The properties can have photos and a brief description, and you can show examples of sold properties and available properties to instill confidence to the viewer. This is a very inexpensive way to advertise, it literally only costs you the ink and paper you printed it on. This can be very effective if you are located in the right location.

Community Relations A good way to get your name out into the community is by being a sponsor for a local event. Find out if any local groups are doing an event, and see if they need a sponsor. Usually sponsors get recognized in all informational fliers and brochures, and then have a banner or sign visible the day of the event.

Additionally, you can volunteer to work the event, and come armed and ready with business cards. When done appropriately, this is a really good way to give back to your community and achieve some great institutional advertising.

EFFECTIVENESS OF ADVERTISING

It is important for brokers to keep track of the cost of each ad they place, the media used, and the results. In order to determine if advertising is justified, measurable results must be traced back to the advertising. It is important to set up a system to make a determination whether you will use that particular advertising media again or utilize the same ad again, or if you need to change the wording, graphics, color or other attributes of the ad.

Tracking the effectiveness of an ad does not have to require a complicated mathematical equation, or hours of compiling data. It can be a simple formula based on the cost of the ad divided by the number of sales the advertisement generated. In order to know if the sales were a direct result of an ad you placed, you should have a tracking number or other identifier on each of your advertisements. When a client contacts you regarding a property he or she saw in a particular advertisement, you can ask him or her what the "promotional code" is for that specific ad, and keep a log of all responses per ad.

Example:
Mark placed an ad in the community newspaper showing four of his listings. At the bottom of the ad, he made sure to mention the promotional code M789 regarding these specific listings. The community newspaper where Mark ran the ad has a circulation of 45,000, and the total cost of the ad was $300.

There were 36 responses to the ad (citing the promotional code M789), prompting 3 sales. To find out how much the advertisement cost per sale, we simply divide the cost of the ad by the number of sales.

> *$300 / 3 sales = $100*

Each sale represents $100 worth of advertisement costs.

Is the money spent per sale worth the cost? That will be determined when you see how much money went into selling the home, including your time, other expenses such as signs, and advertising expenses.

L E G A L   I M P L I C A T I O N S

There are several regulations and rules you must follow when placing advertisements. The Real Estate Commission, Federal Consumer Protection Act (or "Truth-in-Lending Act") and California Real Estate Law govern how and agent can advertise listings.

There are seven different sections within the California Real Estate Law regulating advertising.

Misleading Advertisement, or section 1023 A licensee may not advertise, print, display, publish distribute, televise, or broadcast false or misleading statements regarding rates and terms or conditions for making, purchasing, or negotiating loans or real property sales contracts, nor may a licensee permit others to do so.

Mobile-Home Advertising or Section 10131.7 . It is unlawful for any real estate licensee acting under authority of Section 10131.6 to do any of the following:

(a) To advertise or offer for sale in any manner any mobile home, unless it is either in place on a lot rented or leased for human habitation within an established mobile home park as defined in Section 18214 of the Health and Safety Code and the advertising or offering for sale is not contrary to any terms of a contract between the seller of the mobile home and the owner of the mobile home park, or is other wise located, pursuant to a local zoning ordinance or permit, on a lot where its presence has been authorized or its continued presence and that use would be authorized for a total and uninterrupted period of at least one year.

(b) To fail to withdraw any advertisement of a mobile home for sale, lease, or exchange within 48 hours after the real estate licensee's receipt of notice that the mobile home is no longer available for sale, lease, or exchange.

(c) To advertise or represent a mobile home as a new mobile home.

(d) To include as an added cost to the selling price of a mobile home, an amount for licensing, as prescribed by Section 10751 of the Revenue and Taxation Code, except where the buyer and seller agree to the proration of the license fees for the applicable license period, or transfer of title of the mobile home as a vehicle, which amount is not due to the state unless, prior to the sale, the amount has been paid by the licensee to the state in order to avoid penalties that would have accrued because of late payment of the fees.

(e) To make any representation that a mobile home is capable of being transported on California highways if the mobile home does not meet all of the equipment requirements applicable to mobile homes of Division 12 (commencing with Section 24000) of the Vehicle Code, or to fail to disclose any material fact respecting those equipment requirements.

(f) To advertise or otherwise represent, or knowingly to allow to be advertised or represented on the real estate licensee's behalf or at the real estate licensee's place of business, that no down payment is required in connection with the sale of a mobile home when down payment is in fact required and the buyer is advised or induced to finance the down payment by a loan in addition to any other loan financing the remainder of the purchase price of the mobile home.

(g) To fail or neglect properly to cause the endorsement, dating, and delivery (or fail to endorse, date, and deliver) of the certificate of ownership or certificate of title of the mobile home, and, when having possession, to fail to deliver the registration card to a transferee who is lawfully entitled to a transfer of registration. Except when the certificate of ownership or certificate of title is demanded in writing by a purchaser, the licensee shall satisfy the delivery requirement of this subdivision by submitting appropriate documents and fees to the Department of Housing and Community Development for transfer of registration in accordance with Chapter 8 (commencing with Section 18075) of Part 2 of Division 13 of the Health and Safety Code and rules and regulations promulgated thereunder.

Penalties for Unlicensed Person or Section 10139 Any person acting as a real estate broker or real estate salesperson without a license or who advertises using words indicating that he or she is a real estate broker without being so licensed shall be guilty of a public offense punishable by a fine not exceeding ten thousand dollars ($10,000), or by imprisonment in the county jail for a term not to exceed six months, or by both fine and imprisonment; or if a corporation, be punished by a fine not exceeding fifty thousand dollars ($50,000).

False Advertising or Section 10140 Every officer, agent or employee of any company, and every other person who knowingly authorizes, directs or aids in the publication, advertisement, distribution or circularization of any false statement or representation concerning any land or subdivision thereof, as defined in Chapter 1 (commencing at Section 11000) of Part 2 of this division, offered for sale or lease, or, if the land is owned by the State or Federal Government, which such person offers to assist another or others to file an application for the purchase or lease of, or to locate or enter upon, and every person who, with knowledge that any advertisement, pamphlet, prospectus or letter concerning any said land or subdivision, as defined in Chapter 1 (commencing at Section 11000) of Part 2 of this division, contains any written statement that is false or fraudulent, issues, circulates, publishes or distributes the same, or causes the same to be issued, circulated, published or distributed, or who, in any other respect, willfully violates or fails to comply with any of the provisions of this section, or who in any other respect willfully violates or fails, omits or neglects to obey, observe or comply with any order, permit, decision, demand or requirement of the commissioner under this section, is guilty of a public offense, and shall be punished by a fine not exceeding one thousand dollars ($1,000), or by imprisonment in a county jail not exceeding one year, or by both such fine and imprisonment, and, if a real estate licensee, he shall be held to trial by the commissioner for a suspension or revocation of his license, as provided in the provisions of this part relating to hearings. The district attorney of each county in this State shall prosecute all violations of the provisions of this section in respective counties in which the violations occur.

Disclosure of Name or Section 10140.5 Each advertisement or other statement which is published by a real estate broker or salesman offering to assist persons to file applications for the purchase or lease of, or to locate or enter upon, lands owned by the State or Federal Government shall, when published, indicate the name of the broker for whom it is published and state that he is licensed as a real estate broker by the State of California.

False Advertising or Section 10140.6 A real estate licensee shall not publish, circulate, distribute, nor cause to be published, circulated, or distributed in any newspaper or periodical, or by mail any matter pertaining to any activity for which a real estate license is required which does not contain a designation disclosing that he is performing acts for which a real estate license is required. The provisions of this section shall not apply to classified rental advertisements reciting the telephone number at the premises of the property offered for rent or the address of the property offered for rent.

Inducements, or Section 10236.1 No real estate licensee shall advertise to give or to offer to give to a prospective purchaser or lender any premium, gift or any other object of value as an inducement for making a loan, or purchasing a promissory note secured directly or collaterally by a lien on real property or a real property sales contract.

The **Real Estate Commissioner** has a set of regulations that every agent must follow, just the same, as they must follow the law. The Commissioner has two such regulations regarding advertising and advertising practices.

Electronic Communication – Advertising and Dissemination of Information on the Internet, Section 2770

(a) The following definitions shall apply for the purposes of this section:

　　(1) "Customer" means the person located within the State of California on whose behalf a service is provided or offered or to whom an advertisement is directed.

　　(2) "Services" means any activity for which a real estate license is required and which is offered or provided to a customer located within this state.

(b) Persons who advertise or disseminate information about services over the Internet, the World Wide Web, or similar electronic common carrier systems, will not be deemed to be engaged in the business, act in the capacity of, advertise or assume to act as a real estate broker within this state if any of the following apply:

　　(1) The advertisement or information involves a service but (A) is not directed to any particular person or customer located within the State of California, (B) is limited to general information about the services offered to customers or the public in general, and (C) includes the legend "The services referred to herein are not available to persons located within the State of California."

(2) The advertisement or information does not involve a service provided in connection with activity for which a real estate license is required.

REGULATIONS OF THE REAL ESTATE COMMISSIONER 306

(3) The advertisement or information is not being published, circulated or transmitted on behalf of another or others.

(c) A person who advertises or disseminates information with respect to providing a service is not required to have a real estate broker license if any of the following conditions apply:

(1) The person publishing, circulating or transmitting the advertisement or disseminating the information is acting within the exemptions from the definition of real estate broker contained in Sections 10133 or 10133.1. of the Code;

(2) The services provided do not include any of the acts within the meaning of Sections 10131, 10131.1, 10131.2, 10131.3, 10131.4, 10131.45 and 10131.6 of the Code.

(3) (A) Prior to any direct electronic communication or any response or contact with a specific customer there is in place, barriers or other imple- mented policies and procedures, designed to ensure that prior to the response or contact, the person making it is appropriately licensed under the Real Estate Law or qualifies for an exemption from real estate broker licensure; and, (B) There is a legend in all advertising and information disseminated about services offered indicating whether the person making the advertising or disseminating the information is a licensed California real estate broker. If the person is not a licensed California real estate broker, an additional legend shall be included which provides as follows: "The services are not available to persons located within the State of California."

Advertising – License Designation, Section 2770.1
Use of the terms broker, agent, Realtor, loan correspondent or the abbreviations bro., agt., or other similar terms or abbreviations, is deemed sufficient identification to fulfill the designation requirements of Section 10140.6 of the Business and Professions Code.

Civil Rights Act of 1968
Due to discrimination in real estate advertising campaigns, the Civil Rights Act of 1968 was passed. Discrimination based on sex, religion, race, color, handicap, national ori- gin and familial status is strictly prohibited. Brokers and agents must be very careful regarding their choice of words when writing advertising copy to make sure they don't inadvertently offend, or exclude a protected class from their offerings. Brokers and agents must think about the implications of what they are saying to all groups of peo- ple, and make sure what they are saying will not be found offensive or misinterpreted by the general public. Obviously, geographic location will dictate interpretations of cer- tain words, so the writer of the ad must be fully aware of his or her surroundings. It requires putting in a little extra effort in writing ads, but it does not eliminate the oppor- tunity to write a very good, attention-getting ad.

If any person feels as if they have been discriminated against regarding real estate advertising, they are to take their complaint to the Department of Housing and Urban

Development, or HUD. HUD is the agency responsible for enforcing the Civil Rights Act of 1968. Although HUD enforces the Civil Rights Act and are responsible for interpreting if any violation has occurred, they do not provide any assistance as to what is appropriate when writing ads. On January 9, 1995 HUD issued a memo describing what choices of wording are acceptable, and what choices are not. The following are the five main points covered in this memo.

1. **Race, color, national origin**. Real estate advertisements should state no discriminatory preference or limitation on account of race, color, or national origin. Use of words describing the housing, the current or potential residents, or the neighbors or neighborhood in racial or ethnic terms (i.e., white family home, no Irish) will create liability under this section. However, advertisements which are facially neutral will not create liability. Thus, complaints over use of phrases such as master bedroom, rare find, or desirable neighborhood should not be filed.

2. **Religion**. Advertisements should not contain an explicit preference, limitation or discrimination on account of religion (i.e., no Jews, Christian home). Advertisements which use the legal name of an entity which contains a religious reference (for example, Roselawn Catholic Home), or those which contain a religious symbol, (such as a cross), standing alone, may indicate a religious preference. However, if such an advertisement includes a disclaimer (such as the statement "This Home does not discriminate on the basis of race, color, religion, national origin, sex, handicap or familial status") it will not violate the Act. Advertisements containing descriptions of properties (apartment complex with chapel), or services (kosher meals available) do not on their face state a preference for persons likely to make use of those facilities, and are not violations of the Act. The use of secularized terms or symbols relating to religious holidays such as Santa Claus, Easter Bunny or St. Valentine's Day images, or phrases such as "Merry Christmas", "Happy Easter", or the like does not constitute a violation of the Act.

3. **Sex**. Advertisements for single-family dwellings or separate units in a multi-family dwelling should contain no explicit preference, limitation or discrimination based on sex. Use of the term master bedroom does not constitute a violation of either the sex discrimination provisions or the race discrimination provisions. Terms such as "mother-in-law suite" and "bachelor apartment" are commonly used as physical descriptions of housing units and do not violate the Act.

4. **Handicap**. Real estate advertisements should not contain explicit exclusions, limitations, or other indications of discrimination based on handicap (i.e., no wheelchairs). Advertisements containing descriptions of properties (great view, fourth-floor walk-up, walk-in closets), services or facilities (jogging trails), or neighborhoods (walk to bus stop) do not violate the Act. Advertisements describing the conduct required of residents ("non-smoking", "sober") do not violate the Act. Advertisements containing descriptions of accessibility features are lawful (wheelchair ramp).

5. **Familial status**. Advertisements may not state an explicit preference, limitation or discrimination based on familial status. Advertisements may not contain limitations on the number or ages of children, or state a preference for adults, couples or singles. Advertisements describing the properties (two bed-

room, cozy, family room), services and facilities (no bicycles allowed) or neighborhoods (quiet streets) are not facially discriminatory and do not violate the Act.

The Miami Valley Fair Housing Center, Inc. in Dayton, Ohio has come up with a list of words or phrases they feel are appropriate, words that may be interpreted one way or another and other words that are absolutely not acceptable. The following table highlights these words or phrases. Please be aware this is just a sample of words or phrases that could be interpreted acceptable by some and unacceptable by others. This is not an exhaustive list. The words universally acceptable do not appear on this list, so note that the acceptable column will not list the obviously accepted words or phrases.

Acceptable	Take caution in using	Not acceptable
Assistance animal(s)	Active	Able bodied
Assistance animals(s) only	Bachelor	Adult community
Close to	Board approval	Adult living
No college students	Catholic	Adult park
Convalescent home	Christian	Adults only
Convenient to	Curfew	African
Credit check required	Domestic quarters	Agile
Den	Exclusive	American Indians
No drug users	Executive	Asian
No drugs	Female roommate**	Bachelor Pad
Equal housing opportunity	Female(s) only**	Caucasian
Families welcome	55 and older community*	Chinese
Family room	Gender	Churches near
Fixer-upper	Jewish	Colored
Gated community	Landmark reference	Congregation
Great for families	Male roommate**	Couple
Golf course nearby	Men only**	Couples only
Guest house	Mature	Empty nesters
Handicap accessible	Membership	English only
"Ideal for …"	approval required	Ethnic references
Kids welcome	Mexican-American	Golden agers only
Membership available	Muslim	Healthy only
Mother in law apartment	Nanny's room	Hispanic
Neighborhood name	Near	Housing for older
Nice	No gays	persons / Seniors*
Non smokers	No lesbians	Indian
No seasonal workers	No pets	Integrated
No smoking	No section 8	Latino
Number of bedrooms	No smoking	Males only**
Number of sleeping areas	No students	Mature complex
Nursery	# of persons	Mature couple
Nursing home	Older persons	Mature individual
"Perfect for …"	Prestigious	Mature person(s)
Pets limited to assistance	Private	Mexican
animals	Quality neighborhood	Mormon Temple
Privacy	Retirees	Mosque
Private driveway	Retirement home	Must be employed
Private entrance	Safe neighborhood	Nationality
Private property		Newlyweds

Acceptable	Take caution in using	Not acceptable	
Private setting	School name or	# of children	No Supplemental
Public transportation	school district	No AIDS	Security
(near)	Secluded	No Alcoholics	Income
Quality construction	Secure	No Appalachian	(SSI)
Quiet	Senior adult	No Blacks	No tenant
Quiet neighborhood	community*	No Blind	description
References required	Senior citizen(s)*	No Chicano	No unemployed
Responsible	Senior housing*	No Children	No wheelchairs
Se habla espanol	Seniors*	No Crippled	One child
Seasonal rates	Sex or gender**	No Deaf	One person
Section 8 welcome /	Single man, woman*	No disabled	Oriental
accepted	Sixty-two and older	No families	Parish
Security provided	community*	No group homes	Physically fit
Single family home	Snowbirds*	No handicap	Preferred
Sober	Sophisticated	parking	community
Spanish speaking	Straight only	Not for	Puerto Rican
Square feet	Tranquil setting	Handicapped	Religious refer-
Student(s)	Two people	No Hindu	ences
Townhouse	Within walking	No HIV	Restricted
Traditional style	distance	No Hungarian	Senior discount
Verifiable income	Winter / summer	No impaired	Shrine
Winter rental rates	visitors*	No Irish	Single person
	Women only**	No Italian	Singles only
		No mentally	Spanish speak-
		handicapped	ing
		No mentally ill	Synagogue
		No migrant work-	near
		ers	Temple near
		No Negro	Traditional
		No Philippine or	neighborhood
		Filipinos	White
		No play area	Whites only
		No retarded	

*Permitted to be used only when complex or development qualifies as housing for older persons.

**Permitted to be used only when describing shared living areas or dwelling units used exclusively as dormitory facilities by educational institutions.

Truth-in-Lending Act / Regulation Z

The Truth-in-Lending Act, part of the Federal Consumer Credit Protection Act of 1968, serves to inform customers of all credit costs as a percentage and the total finance charges. It is a disclosure every lender must make to all clients with which they do business.

Truth-in-Lending applies to any amount of money financed requiring more than four installments, or to credit that is subject to finance charges. Whenever an ad includes the down payment amount, amount of payments, a repayment period or the total amount of finance charges, then the ad must also include all three of the following elements:

- The annual percentage rate, or APR

- The percentage or total amount required in the down payment

- The terms of repayment

All lenders who extend loans secured by a primary residence more than five times per year must supply the truth-in-lending disclosure showing all terms and facts of the loan.

Exemptions

There are certain exemptions where the lender does not have to follow the truth-in-lending procedures and disclosure. Loans made for businesses purposes, agricultural, personal property above $25,000, interest-free loans with four or less payments and construction purposes are all exempt. Additionally, a seller who is carrying back a note on the property being sold does not have to disclose the truth-in-lending requirements, provided the seller does not provide this service more than five times per year. A non-owner-occupied housing loan for an income property is also exempt since it is treated like a business.

Rescission Right

A borrower has the right to cancel any loan extended to him or her up to three days after the offer has been made. This right is extended to borrowers who are using their personal residence for security on the loan. The right of rescission is not extended to home purchase loans.

Bait-and-Switch Advertising

Occasionally brokers and agents will advertise a property for sale that is not available, or which has already sold, in order to get traffic into their firm in the hope that the client would become interested in some of the broker's other listings. This practice is not only illegal; it is considered a federal offense.

ADVERTISING BUDGET

As you can imagine, advertising is a very expensive part of the selling process. The trick to effective advertising is to know which media vehicle to use, the type of ad, creativeness and timing. In order to do all of this, there must be money budgeted for such expenses. A good broker will be able to allocate income dollars toward advertising, maximizing the return on each dollar. A listing not being advertised is not making money. The question is: How is a broker supposed to determine the optimization of financial resources? The best way to learn how to appropriately set an advertising budget is to determine how effective the current methods are.

Budgeting for advertising comes from a percentage of all commissions earned by the firm. Generally a real estate firm will budget 5-7% of each dollar brought into the firm on commissions, or 5-7 cents on every dollar. Outside of the 5-7% for commissions, there are other ways to determine an advertising budget. The following are other ways a broker may determine how much money he or she should spend on their total advertising budget.

- Use sales or profits from a previous period, representational of the firm's quarterly average earnings, and take a percentage of this figure.

- Take a percentage of the gross income.

- Use net commissions from a previous period, representational of the firm's quarterly average commissions, and take a percentage of this number.

- Estimate a certain dollar figure per month.

- Use the number of people on the sales staff, and make the budget based on a certain dollar figure per sales associate.

- Use a certain dollar figure per listing based on the listing's commission potential. Properties with a higher commission potential will have a larger budget than properties with a lower commission potential. More ads or more elaborate ads for a property with higher income potential will be seen by people looking for property, and may inspire them to call or visit your firm to see what other properties you have available. It is operational advertising for one property; however, it also serves as institutional advertising for the entire firm.

- A set dollar figure per month for the entire office, not based on number of associates or individual listings, but a fixed figure.

- An adjustable amount based on market conditions. You can choose to increase the budget when the market is good, getting more visibility amongst many buyers, or increase the budget when the market is slow, and have less competition with other firms.

- Fluctuate the budget based on the time of year or newness of the firm or for special sales. Increase the budged to get your name out or when you have many listings with high commission potential, and perhaps decrease the budget when the earning potential is not as high. It is important to base the advertising expenditure on the anticipated income it will generate. An exception to this rule is for new offices; it is important to advertise heavily at the inception of the office to promote your new firm.

- Keep the budget completely random based on the management's decisions. If it seems right to spend a lot in one month, allocate the money. If it makes the sales staff happy to spend more money in one month over another to get their listings visible to the public, spent the money then. Keep a tentative budget in mind, but you don't necessarily have to stick to it.

P R O M O T I O N

Promotion is another way to market your business. It is not the same as advertising; however, it serves much the same purpose as institutional advertising. Nor is it the same as prospecting; however, you will most likely gain new clients from your promotion efforts. Promotion is not the same as advertising or prospecting because promotion is something that you do at no cost. You get your name out to the community, but don't utilize the assistance of an advertising agency; nor do you have to spend the resources prospecting requires.

The way promotion works is by getting news coverage for participating in a worthwhile event. What events are happening in the community that you could be a part of? Fundraisers, cultural activities, volunteering opportunities, participation in local government, or being active in other community activities are all great ways for a broker to gain free press in a positive manner. When the press reports on an event, they generally name the volunteers, the board members, the person who raised the most money and so on and so forth. By donating your time and energy, you might possibly be written up in the paper, where they will name who you are and what organization you work for or belong to. Having your firm's name in print promotes the goodwill of the office in the community. Other events, that may not have a civic nature, would be your participation in opening a new branch office, developing a new subdivision, or expanding an existing office. These events would be seen as newsworthy by news sources, who will happily write free press regarding your firm's activities.

It is important for you to know how to write an effective press release. Often news sources may not know of your firm's the community involvement or news coming out of your firm. By being able to write an effective press release, and then submitting it to local news agencies, especially newspapers, you have more opportunities to have your events covered by the press. When the public reads stories written in the newspaper, they generally accept them as true. This is a great way to gain positive public opinion for your agency and gain new prospects at the same time. People often like to do business with an active member of the community rather than a person or firm who does not give back their time and energy.
Promotion is a wonderful way for you to gain valuable coverage in the newspaper or other media. It is important for a broker to know how to present stories effectively to these news sources. By leaning this important technique, you will not only gain coverage, but free coverage!

S U M M A R Y

In Section One, we discussed the notion of prospecting. Prospecting is the process by which you can gain new listings and buyers through direct contact with prospective clients, either in person or by correspondence. Some methods of prospecting include door-to-door canvassing, telephone canvassing, direct mail and open houses. While the physical activity of prospecting takes quite a bit of an agent's time, it is equally important for the agent to have a very detailed method of data management in place for the contacts he or she will be making. By keeping track of all the possible contacts and following up with these people, an agent can rapidly expand his or her business.

In Section Two, we learned about advertising and the importance of getting the attention of the community. Advertising can be institutional or operational. Institutional advertising basically promotes the goodwill of the real estate firm or agent himself or herself, while operational advertising calls the viewer's attention to available properties for sale. When possible, it is good practice to intermix institutional and operational advertising together.

When advertising, it is important to keep the AIDA approach in mind, gaining the reader's attention, interest, and desire, and causing an action. There are many different approaches and media vehicles to use when getting the advertising to the recipients. An agent or broker can use personal advertising, newspaper, television, radio, outdoor, and other media to get the message to the appropriate viewer.

In addition to understanding effective advertising, it is equally important for brokers and agents to understand the legal implications of advertising and budgetary planning for effective advertising. Good advertising strategies often fall to budget constraints. Good advertising copy may only speak to a few segments of the population while discriminating against others. It is important to choose your language very carefully, and then be creative.

Section Three talks about promotion and the practice of getting your firm in print for free. It is important for brokers and agents to participate in community activities, not only for the good press, but also for the goodwill it instills in the community. Additionally, it is important for all brokers and agents to understand how to write an effective press release. Often your firm will be participating in or creating newsworthy events that may not be noticed by the press. It is important to be able to convey this information in a well-written press release and then get it to the appropriate news source, which will most likely print the story.

T E R M S   A N D   P H R A S E S

AIDA advertising approach – A type of advertising which focuses on gaining the viewer's attention and interest, creating a desire for the product and then initiating an action.

Bait-and-switch advertising – The practice of advertising a property for sale, which either does not exist or has already been sold. This practice is a federal offense.

Blind Advertising – An advertisement that does not list the broker, the telephone number or office Internet page.

Business card – The card an agent can carry with him or her to hand out to potential clients. This card should contain the agent's contact information, a picture if possible, and some unique design or coloration to stand out amongst other business cards.

Car sign – A magnetic sign the agent can place on his or her car letting the public know who he or she is, and supplying contact information such as the firm's name or phone number.

CD-ROM Business cards – CD-ROMs an agent can hand out to clients with electronic sample listings, their photo, and contact information. This CD-ROM can be simple information, or it can be interactive with an audio component.

Classified advertising – The most important form of advertising for agents and brokers. This is advertising placed in the classified section of periodicals, usually the first place people look when beginning their search for property.

Civil Rights Act of 1968 – The Federal act making discrimination based on sex, religion, race, color, handicap, national origin and familial status strictly prohibited. The Department of Housing and Urban Development (HUD) is responsible for enforcing the act.

Company dollar – The money the firm takes in from the sale of a home.

Contact management – The process an agent goes through to organize, store and recall the names and information of potential clients they gain through prospecting. Contact management is a very important function, because it makes all subsequent follow-ups easy when looking for data.

Direct mail – Mail sent to targeted individuals with the hopes of gaining new clients. Direct mail is considered a form of prospecting, and can be used to invite people to seminars, or to encourage people to see the listings you have available.

Display advertising – The advertising method whereby an entire section or page of a newspaper is purchased for the purpose of institutional and operational advertising. The ad typically includes the photos of agents and the featured listing.

Door-to-door canvassing – The physical act of going door-to-door asking neighbors for any referrals they may have, or to see if they are interested in a property transfer.

Media – The different forms of mass communication where advertising can take place. Some examples of media would be newspapers, magazines, radio, television and outdoor advertising.

Name tag – The physical tag an agent can wear, identifying himself or herself as a real estate professional and displaying any professional designations the agent may have earned.

Networking – Utilizing your current contacts as a way to gain new clients; for example, asking an existing client if they know of anyone looking to move to the neighborhood, or if they know of anyone trying to sell their home.

Newsletters – A simple circular put out to highlight the business's activities and events. Newsletters can be used for interoffice-only news, or sent to clients to keep them aware of any interesting things that may affect them or someone they know.

Operational advertising – Advertising a specific property or properties in the hopes of finding interested buyers.

Outdoor advertising – Utilizing outdoor spaces such as billboards to post a message. Outdoor advertising generally is utilized only for institutional advertising.

Press release – An informational news memo that is written to highlight a past or future event to be submitted to a newspaper or news source. This memo is written by a member of the real estate firm, generally the broker, and then submitted to a news source for their consideration.

Prospecting – The act of finding homeowners who are interested in selling their homes, as well as finding interested buyers looking to purchase property.

Specialty gifts – Giveaways that an agent can hand out to prospective clients and current clients or send to past clients. They are generally simple but useful items such as calenders, pencils, pens, note pads or basic function calculators. These giveaways have the agent's name and contact information on them.

Telephone canvassing – Prospecting one area utilizing the reverse telephone directory to identify a potential client.

Truth-in-Lending Act – The federal act requiring loan term disclosures as well as advertising disclosures.

C H A P T E R   Q U I Z

1. Finding sellers or buyers is called:
   a. Marketing
   b. Prospecting
   c. Advertising
   d. None of the above

2. Of the following methods, Ad Switches, Canvassing, Advertising, Open Houses, For Sale Signs and Window Advertising, which of the following are considered viable sources to obtain listings?
    a. Ad Switches, Advertising, Open Houses and For Sale Signs
    b. Ad Switches, Advertising and Window Advertising
    c. Canvassing, Advertising, Open Houses and For Sale Signs
    d. All of the above

3. On average, how much time will an agent spend obtaining listings?
    a. 1/4
    b. 3/4
    c. 1/2
    d. None of the above

4. Which of the following is NOT a factor in choosing the most appropriate prospecting method?
    a. Potential commission to the agent
    b. Type of property
    c. Neighborhood characteristics
    d. Time period

5. Which of the following are different methods of prospecting?
    a. Direct mailing, newspaper advertising, open houses
    b. Door-to-door canvassing, open houses, personal letters
    c. Direct mail, telephone canvassing, door-to-door canvassing
    d. Personal letters, newspaper advertising, telephone canvassing

6. When conducting door-to-door canvassing it is important for you to remember to take with you:
    a. Business cards
    b. Briefcase
    c. Tablet and pencil
    d. Both A and C

7. In the event you are able to gain a listing from a phone canvassing conversation, why is it important for you to set up an appointment to view the home?
    a. So you know if you will make enough commission from the listing
    b. To make sure the home is up to your broker's standards
    c. To offer an estimation of value so the homeowner knows how much to ask for the home
    d. To make an official appraisal of value for tax purposes

8. Personal letters are generally:
    a. Addressed by hand
    b. Sent to a small number of recipients
    c. Have a call to action
    d. All of the above

9. As a successful agent, it is important for you to:
    a. File all contacts exclusively in electronic format for the most efficient way to manage data.
    b. Use only a Rolodex so you can take your contact information with you where ever you need, simply and easily.

c. Wait for your clients to contact you when they are ready to make a transaction – you don't want to bother them until they are ready to make a move.

d. None of the above

10. After you gain a referral from a current client, what is one of the most important things to do?

a. Wait for them to call you – you don't want to feel like you are pressuring them into any decisions.

b. Follow up with them via a phone call.

c. Ask your client to talk to them for on your behalf and get back to you.

d. None of the above

11. Which of the following is not represented in institutional advertising?

a. The broker

b. The salesperson

c. The entire real estate firm

d. An individual listing

12. Which of the following would be considered a form of outdoor advertising?

a. Billboards

b. Window signs

c. Bus sign / placard

d. All of the above

13. Which of the following are examples of direct mail?

a. Pamphlets, postcards and newsletters

b. Newsletters, brochures and postcards

c. Postcards, pamphlets and letters

d. Letters, newsletters and maps

14. What is a good way to track your advertisement's effectiveness?

a. Ask each respondent how he or she found your particular office.

b. Utilize a promotional code in the ad.

c. Use only one media vehicle per week, per advertisement, and assume that all responses are based on the current week's ad.

d. Both A and B

15. Which of the following is not covered in the Civil Rights Act of 1968?

a. Gender

b. Religion

c. Sexual Orientation

d. Familial Status

16. The practice of advertising a property which is not actually available is called:

a. Bait-and-switch advertising.

b. Rescission advertising.

c. Flip-flop advertising

d. Dummy advertising.

17. Promotion is considered the same as:

a. Advertising

b. Prospecting

c. Neither A nor B

d. Both A and B

18. Of the following words, which is the most acceptable word to use in an advertisement for a new condominium?
    a. Private
    b. Security provided
    c. Secure
    d. Restricted

19. Which of the following budgeting methods would most likely be used in a real estate firm?
    a. Use a certain dollar figure per listing based on its commission potential. Properties with a higher commission potential will have a larger budget than properties with a lower commission potential. More elaborate, or simply more ads based on a property with higher income potential will be seen by people looking for property, and may inspire them to call or visit your firm to see what other properties you have available. It is operation advertising for one property, however serves as institutional advertising for the entire firm.
    b. Take a percentage of the gross income.
    c. Use the number of people on the sales staff, and make the budget based on a certain dollar figure per sales associate.
    d. Any of the above would be acceptable depending on the specific firm.

20. What percentage of a firm's commissions is generally spent on promotion?
    a. 5 %
    b. 1 1/2 %
    c. 0 %
    d. 7 %

3

LISTING AGREEMENT

What you will learn in this Chapter

- Agency

- Listing Agreement

- Types of Listings

- Analysis of Exclusive Authorization and Right-to-Sell

- Valuation of the Listing

- Servicing the Listing

Test Your Knowledge

1. The listing agreement is:
   a. A binding contract
   b. An employment contract between the broker and seller
   c. A contract between the buyer and broker
   d. All of the above

2. An agency agreement where the broker is the only agent who will list the property is defined as:
   a. Open listing
   b. Nonexclusive listing
   c. Exclusive listing
   d. Net listing

3. After a listing agreement has expired, is the broker entitled to any commission from the sale of the property?
   a. Only if the broker provides the seller with the name of a prospective and eventual buyer within 3 days of the listing agreement's expiration.
   b. Only if the broker can produce evidence that he or she originally showed the property to the buyer during the life of the listing agreement, with the offer coming to the seller after the agreement's expiration.
   c. No, after the listing agreement has expired, the broker is not entitled to any commission.
   d. Both A and B

4. Conducting a competitive market analysis is appropriate for which type of property?
   a. Residential with 1-4 units
   b. Residential with more than 4 units
   c. Industrial
   d. Commercial

5. When servicing the listing, an agent will rely on his or her office for what type of support?
   a. 30-day letter
   b. Property inspections
   c. Open houses
   d. Soliciting neighbors for leads

6. The method of valuation most commonly used by agents when making an estimation of value is:
   a. Cost approach
   b. Competitive market analysis
   c. Income approach
   d. Certified appraisal

7. The most important thing an agent can do for a client while servicing a listing is:
   a. Ask the neighbors for leads
   b. Put a "For Sale" sign in the front yard
   c. Have clear communication regarding the progress and process
   d. Create good information sheets for distribution

In this chapter, you will learn about the listing agreement, or the contract a seller and broker will enter. There are different types of listing agreements, depending on what your client is comfortable with. These types will be discussed at length, so that you understand the differences between agreements. Additionally, you will be walked through how to properly fill out a listing agreement. Since this is the employment contract between you and the client, and your first opportunity to show how capable and professional you are, you will want to make sure to fill the agreement out completely and accurately. Mistakes here might cause your client to lose confidence in your ability.

In addition to the listing agreements, we will discuss valuation of the property. There are different ways to arrive at the market value for property, and it is necessary for you to understand how to accurately arrive at a listing price. Homeowners can hold you liable if they sell their home for less than it is actually worth.

Finally, we will end the chapter by discussing how to properly service the listing. This will keep your client up-to-date on the activity on his or her home from the beginning to the very end of escrow.

A G E N C Y

Before we can really analyze the different types of listings, we need to fully understand who is representing whom. What seems like a simple concept can sometimes become blurred and confusing. **Agency** is the authority to act for another person for a specific act, or certain period of time. An agent is the person who acts for another person, or principal. An agent owes his or her client fiduciary responsibility, but must also disclose all information to the third party in the transaction. These disclosures should not be misconstrued as advice, direction, representation or any other acts an agent would perform for the client.

As an agent, are you representing the buyer or seller, or are you in a dual agency situation where you are representing both parties? Clearly, defining "agency" will help alleviate any misunderstandings that may arise about representation.

The following table highlights the duties you as an agent owe to your client, the principal, and your responsibilities to the third party.

Agent's relationship to the principal (Fiduciary Relationship)	Agent's relationship to the third party (Truthful Relationship)
Honesty; all disclosures must be made	Honesty; all disclosures must be made
No secret profits may be made	Fair dealing
Integrity for all actions	Reasonable skill and care must be taken in every step of the process
Always obey all laws and regulations	Always operate in good faith
Utmost care must be taken in all steps of the process	
Loyalty to the principal before anyone else	

L I S T I N G   A G R E E M E N T S

The listing agreement is a binding, legal contract that will outline the broker's rights and duties to his or her principal. Essentially, the listing agreement is an employment contract between the broker and the principal, entitling the broker to receive a commission upon finding a ready, willing and able buyer who executes a purchase contract and goes through escrow.

Listing agreements can be set up between the broker and the seller, or the broker and a prospective buyer. The broker will enter into a listing agreement with the seller to find and secure a qualified buyer to purchase the property. Often, these listing agreements will have a time frame associated with them, depending on the type of agreement. More on the different types of agreements and time frames will be covered in the next section. A broker can enter into a buyer agency listing to locate a suitable property for the buyer to make an offer.

A listing binds the broker legally to his or her client. The broker is obligated to carry out all responsibilities covered in the contract before receiving any compensation or commission. When the listing agreement or contract is fully performed, then the broker is entitled to the agreed-upon commission.

Every listing agreement has a set of elements that must be present to create a valid, binding contract. The following is a list of these elements:

- First, and perhaps most importantly, the contract must be in writing. An oral contract is not binding, thus it is unenforceable. If a broker enters into an oral contract, performs all duties and closes the property, the seller legally does not have to pay the broker; or if the seller does pay the commission, he or she can determine a fair rate, and pay that amount rather than the commission amount agreed upon in the oral contract. If a broker wants to receive the set commission rate agreed upon, the listing agreement must be in writing in order to be binding.

- Every listing agreement must have competent parties, legally capable to enter into a contract.

- Each contract must have consideration. Consideration in a listing agreement means that the broker will use due diligence to find a ready, willing and able buyer. In exchange, the seller promises to pay the broker a commission upon the sale of the home. When both parties -- the broker and the seller – make a promise of consideration, this creates a bilateral contract. Consideration is any thing of value. Traditionally, brokers can be compensated monetarily; however, the principal may compensate the broker in any form of value they both agree upon.

- Every listing agreement must contain mutual offer and acceptance or consent. By signing the listing agreement, each party has given his or her consent.

- All contracts must contain lawful object.

Remember
Listings are considered valid contracts. All listings must:
- Be in writing
- Have competent parties
- Have a form of consideration, or mutual consideration
- Contain mutual offer and acceptance
- Contain lawful object

All listings belong to the broker. Salespersons cannot have their own listings. Salespersons may represent the broker on one of his or her listings, but the listing itself belongs to the broker. Additionally, listings are not transferable to another broker. If the broker or principal should die during the duration of a listing agreement, the agreement is cancelled.

T Y P E S   O F   L I S T I N G S

There are many different types of listings in California. These include open listings, exclusive-authorization-and-right-to-sell listings, exclusive-agency listings, net listings, option listings and exclusive authorizations to acquire real property listings. Each type of listing generally falls into one of two categories, exclusive or nonexclusive listings. Exclusive listings mean that the agent is the only person, besides the owner, who may sell the property. Even if the owner sells the property, the broker is entitled to a commission. No other agents can sell the property in question. Nonexclusive listings mean that other brokers may sell the property, and the broker procuring the ready, willing and able buyer will receive the commission. The basic purpose of a listing is to define the relationship between the broker and principal, including who is authorized to sell the property, and the commission the broker will earn upon producing a ready, willing and able buyer.

One final aspect of a listing is whether the agreement is unilateral or bilateral. A unilateral agreement is when only one party makes a promise. An example of this would be when a seller makes the promise to a broker that he or she will receive a commission, provided he or she is the one who procured the ready, willing and able buyer. A bilateral agreement is one in which both the principal and broker make promises to each other. The broker promises the principal that he or she will use due diligence in finding a buyer, or in finding a property. The principal in turn makes a promise that the broker will receive a commission upon producing a buyer, or finding the buyer the desired home.

Remember
There are six different types of listings used in California:
- Open listings
- Exclusive-agency listings
- Exclusive-authorization-and-right-to-sell listings
- Net listings
- Option listings
- Exclusive authorization to acquire real property listings

Remember
There are two categories listings can fall under:
- Exclusive
- Nonexclusive

Open Listings
Open listings are considered nonexclusive, unilateral contracts. A homeowner may give each of several different brokers an open listing on the same property in order to find a buyer. Because this is a nonexclusive listing, if the homeowner sells the property

himself or herself, he or she is not obligated to reward any broker with the commission. If a broker is the procuring cause for the sale, the seller must pay the agreed-upon commission.

There are no time constraints paced on open listings. This listing could stay open as long as the property is on the market. Unlike other listing types, no notice of sale is required upon the sale of the home. Any broker with an open listing should check the property's status before showing it to any interested clients. Open listings are not very popular amongst brokers. The broker incurs expenses on the property, such as advertising, but is not guaranteed to be the selling agent, thus there is no guaranteed commission.

Exclusive-Agency Listings

Exclusive-agency listings are listings where one broker has the sole right to list the property. The broker will not be in competition with other brokers to procure the ready, willing and able buyer. The homeowner, however, does retain the right to sell the property independently of the employed broker. If the broker finds the buyer, the broker receives his or her full commission. If the homeowner finds a buyer, the broker will not receive any commission. Essentially, the broker's only competition is the homeowner. Exclusive-agency listings are much more popular amongst brokers than open listings, but the broker is still not guaranteed a commission.

Exclusive-agency listings have a termination date, meaning the broker does not have exclusive rights to the listing for as long as it takes to find a buyer. The agreement will clearly state the date that the listing is terminated if a buyer has not been found. During the duration of the listing, the broker will typically post the property with the Multiple Listing Service, or MLS, to find a buyer within the time allowed per the listing agreement in order to receive a commission on the property.

Exclusive-Authorization-and-Right-to-Sell Listings

The exclusive-authorization-and-right-to-sell listing is the most common listing agreement that brokers will enter into. The agreement has a definite duration with a termination date. During the life of the listing, the broker is entitled to a commission on the property, no matter who sells it. If the seller finds a buyer, the broker will still make his or her commission. Essentially, the broker is not competing with anyone.

Exclusive-authorization-and-right-to-sell listings will often contain a safety clause. A safety clause entitles the broker to a commission after the listing has expired. The way the safety clause works is that the broker must keep an accurate record of all people he or she has shown the property to. If, after the listing agreement has expired, one of these people comes back and purchases the home, there will be proof that the broker was the initial procuring cause of the sale, entitling him or her to the commission.

If a seller offers a 90-day exclusive-authorization-and-right-to-sell listing to broker Smith, and then two weeks later decides to offer an open listing to broker Carr, who brings in a buyer and offer, both brokers are entitled to a commission. The exclusive-authorization-and-right-to-sell gives broker Smith the right to the commission, as well as broker Carr, as she was the procuring cause of the sale. Again, any broker who signs an exclusive-authorization-and-right-to-sell essentially is not competing with anyone for the commission; any broker who makes the sale is essentially working with the broker who has the listing.

Net Listings

A net listing is not a stand-alone listing, but rather, an addendum to one of the three we have already discussed. A net listing is an agreement where the broker will sell the property for a minimum price. Any amount made over that minimum asking price will be retained by the broker as commission.

Example:
Julie employs broker Alex to sell her home. She states the listing agreement will be an exclusive-authorization-and-right-to-sell net listing, and that the minimum price she would accept for the home is $300,000. Alex finds a buyer who offers $345,000 on the home. Alex's total commission is $45,000, as that is the amount received for the property over the set minimum asking price.

It is important that the broker discloses the net listing terms to both the buyer and seller so they can see where the commission is coming from. This disclosure must be in writing. This type of listing is very seldom used in California.

Option Listings

An option listing is when the broker has the option to purchase the property himself or herself. It is important for the broker to disclose all details to the principal. For example, if a broker is offered $50,000 over the asking price of the property, the broker may choose to purchase the property himself at the asking price, make the commission on the transaction, then turn around and sell the property to the original buyer for the $50,000 profit. The broker must disclose to the seller the higher bid, and let the seller decide which offer to accept.

Brokers must be very careful in a situation like this. If the broker had made the decision to hide the higher bid from the homeowner, go through with the transaction and then sell the property for a big profit, the broker's reputation would suffer. Option listings are legal provided all necessary disclosures are made to all parties.

Exclusive Authorization to Acquire Real Property Listings

The "exclusive authorization to acquire real property" form has been developed to define who represents the buyer in a transaction. Until this form was developed, any cooperating broker working with the buyer was considered a subagent of the listing broker. Thus, the cooperating broker was essentially an agent of the principal, not the buyer. The exclusive authorization to acquire real property is a buyer listing, or exclusive agency wherein the buyer could buy a home without an agent and not be obligated to pay a fee to an agent or it could be an open listing situation.

This form is similar to the exclusive-authorization-and-right-to-sell listing, but it gives the broker authority to act as the agent of the buyer, not the seller. The agent working with the buyer will be looking at the entire transaction or process from the buyer's point of view, protecting the buyer and making sure the buyer has representation. There is no shared loyalty to clients; fiduciary responsibility is totally given to the buyer. The agent must fully disclose all facts to the seller, just as the seller's broker must disclose all facts to the buyer.

In the exclusive authorization to acquire real property, the buyer sets forth the type of property – or certain parameters regarding the property – that he or she wishes to buy. The commission is negotiable, and paid for by the buyer. If the agent ends up acting as a double agent for both the buyer and the seller, the seller's potion of the commission will go towards the agreed-upon commission owed by the buyer. Any other commissions paid to the buyer's agent by any other parties will be applied toward the amount the buyer owes.

RESIDENTIAL LISTING AGREEMENT
(Exclusive Authorization and Right to Sell)
(C.A.R. Form LA, Revised 10/02)

CALIFORNIA ASSOCIATION OF REALTORS®

1. **EXCLUSIVE RIGHT TO SELL:** _____ ("Seller")
   hereby employs and grants _____ ("Broker")
   beginning (date) _____ and ending at 11:59 P.M. on (date) _____ ("Listing Period")
   the exclusive and irrevocable right to sell or exchange the real property in the City of _____,
   County of _____, California, described as: _____
   _____ ("Property").

2. **ITEMS EXCLUDED AND INCLUDED:** Unless otherwise specified in a real estate purchase agreement, all fixtures and fittings that are attached to the property are included, and personal property items are excluded, from the purchase price.
   ADDITIONAL ITEMS EXCLUDED: _____
   ADDITIONAL ITEMS INCLUDED: _____
   Seller intends that the above items be excluded or included in offering the Property for sale, but understands that: (i) the purchase agreement supersedes any intention expressed above and will ultimately determine which items are excluded and included in the sale; and (ii) Broker is not responsible and does not guarantee that the above exclusions and/or inclusions will be in the purchase agreement.

3. **LISTING PRICE AND TERMS:**
   A. The listing price shall be: _____ Dollars ($_____).
   B. Additional Terms: _____
   _____

4. **COMPENSATION TO BROKER:**
   Notice: The amount or rate of real estate commissions is not fixed by law. They are set by each Broker individually and may be negotiated between Seller and Broker (real estate commissions include all compensation and fees to Broker).
   A. Seller agrees to pay to Broker as compensation for services irrespective of agency relationship(s), either ☐ _____ percent of the listing price (or if a purchase agreement is entered into, of the purchase price), or ☐ $_____,
      AND _____, as follows:
      (1) If Broker, Seller, cooperating broker, or any other person procures a buyer(s) who offers to purchase the Property on the above price and terms, or on any price and terms acceptable to Seller during the Listing Period, or any extension.
      (2) If Seller, within _____ calendar days (a) after the end of the Listing Period or any extension, or (b) after any cancellation of this Agreement, unless otherwise agreed, enters into a contract to sell, convey, lease or otherwise transfer the Property to anyone ("Prospective Buyer") or that person's related entity: (i) who physically entered and was shown the Property during the Listing Period or any extension by Broker or a cooperating broker; or (ii) for whom Broker or any cooperating broker submitted to Seller a signed, written offer to acquire, lease, exchange or obtain an option on the Property. Seller, however, shall have no obligation to Broker under paragraph 4A(2) unless, not later than _____ calendar days after the end of the Listing Period or any extension or cancellation, Broker has given Seller a written notice of the names of such Prospective Buyers.
      (3) If, without Broker's prior written consent, the Property is withdrawn from sale, conveyed, leased, rented, otherwise transferred, or made unmarketable by a voluntary act of Seller during the Listing Period, or any extension.
   B. If completion of the sale is prevented by a party to the transaction other than Seller, then compensation due under paragraph 4A shall be payable only if and when Seller collects damages by suit, arbitration, settlement or otherwise, and then in an amount equal to the lesser of one-half of the damages recovered or the above compensation, after first deducting title and escrow expenses and the expenses of collection, if any.
   C. In addition, Seller agrees to pay Broker: _____
   D. (1) Broker is authorized to cooperate with and compensate brokers participating through the multiple listing service(s) ("MLS"): (i) in any manner; OR (ii) (if checked) by offering MLS brokers: either ☐ _____ percent of the purchase price, or ☐ $_____.
      (2) Broker is authorized to cooperate with and compensate brokers operating outside the MLS in any manner.
   E. Seller hereby irrevocably assigns to Broker the above compensation from Seller's funds and proceeds in escrow. Broker may submit this agreement, as instructions to compensate Broker pursuant to paragraph 4A, to any escrow regarding the Property involving Seller and a buyer, Prospective Buyer or other transferee.
   F. (1) Seller represents that Seller has not previously entered into a listing agreement with another broker regarding the Property, unless specified as follows: _____
      (2) Seller warrants that Seller has no obligation to pay compensation to any other broker regarding the Property unless the Property is transferred to any of the following individuals or entities: _____
      (3) If the Property is sold to anyone listed above during the time Seller is obligated to compensate another broker: (i) Broker is not entitled to compensation under this agreement; and (ii) Broker is not obligated to represent Seller in such transaction.

LA REVISED 10/02 (PAGE 1 OF 3)   Print Date

Seller acknowledges receipt of a copy of this page.
Seller's Initials (_____)(_____)

Reviewed by _____ Date _____

RESIDENTIAL LISTING AGREEMENT-EXCLUSIVE (LA PAGE 1 OF 3)

Property Address: _____ Date: _____

5. **OWNERSHIP, TITLE AND AUTHORITY:** Seller warrants that: (i) Seller is the owner of the Property; (ii) no other persons or entities have title to the Property; and (iii) Seller has the authority to both execute this agreement and sell the Property. Exceptions to ownership, title and authority are as follows: _____

6. **MULTIPLE LISTING SERVICE:** Information about this listing will (or ☐ will not) be provided to the MLS of Broker's selection. All terms of the transaction, including financing, if applicable, will be provided to the selected MLS for publication, dissemination and use by persons and entities on terms approved by the MLS. Seller authorizes Broker to comply with all applicable MLS rules. MLS rules allow MLS data to be made available by the MLS to additional Internet sites unless Broker gives the MLS instructions to the contrary.

7. **SELLER REPRESENTATIONS:** Seller represents that, unless otherwise specified in writing, Seller is unaware of: (i) any Notice of Default recorded against the Property; (ii) any delinquent amounts due under any loan secured by, or other obligation affecting, the Property; (iii) any bankruptcy, insolvency or similar proceeding affecting the Property; (iv) any litigation, arbitration, administrative action, government investigation or other pending or threatened action that affects or may affect the Property or Seller's ability to transfer it; and (v) any current, pending or proposed special assessments affecting the Property. Seller shall promptly notify Broker in writing if Seller becomes aware of any of these items during the Listing Period or any extension thereof.

8. **BROKER'S AND SELLER'S DUTIES:** Broker agrees to exercise reasonable effort and due diligence to achieve the purposes of this agreement. Unless Seller gives Broker written instructions to the contrary, Broker is authorized to order reports and disclosures as appropriate or necessary and advertise and market the Property by any method and in any medium selected by Broker, including MLS and the Internet, and, to the extent permitted by these media, control the dissemination of the information submitted to any medium. Seller agrees to consider offers presented by Broker, and to act in good faith to accomplish the sale of the Property by, among other things, making the Property available for showing at reasonable times and referring to Broker all inquiries of any party interested in the Property. Seller is responsible for determining at what price to list and sell the Property. Seller further agrees to indemnify, defend and hold Broker harmless from all claims, disputes, litigation, judgments and attorney fees arising from any incorrect information supplied by Seller, or from any material facts that Seller knows but fails to disclose.

9. **DEPOSIT:** Broker is authorized to accept and hold on Seller's behalf any deposits to be applied toward the purchase price.

10. **AGENCY RELATIONSHIPS:**

   A. **Disclosure:** If the Property includes residential property with one-to-four dwelling units, Seller shall receive a "Disclosure Regarding Agency Relationships" form prior to entering into this agreement.

   B. **Seller Representation:** Broker shall represent Seller in any resulting transaction, except as specified in paragraph 4F.

   C. **Possible Dual Agency With Buyer:** Depending upon the circumstances, it may be necessary or appropriate for Broker to act as an agent for both Seller and buyer, exchange party, or one or more additional parties ("Buyer"). Broker shall, as soon as practicable, disclose to Seller any election to act as a dual agent representing both Seller and Buyer. If a Buyer is procured directly by Broker or an associate licensee in Broker's firm, Seller hereby consents to Broker acting as a dual agent for Seller and such Buyer. In the event of an exchange, Seller hereby consents to Broker collecting compensation from additional parties for services rendered, provided there is disclosure to all parties of such agency and compensation. Seller understands and agrees that: (i) Broker, without the prior written consent of Seller, will not disclose to Buyer that Seller is willing to sell the Property at a price less than the listing price; (ii) Broker, without the prior written consent of Buyer, will not disclose to Seller that Buyer is willing to pay a price greater than the offered price; and (iii) except for (i) and (ii) above, a dual agent is obligated to disclose known facts materially affecting the value or desirability of the Property to both parties.

   D. **Other Sellers:** Seller understands that Broker may have or obtain listings on other properties, and that potential buyers may consider, make offers on, or purchase through Broker, property the same as or similar to Seller's Property. Seller consents to Broker's representation of sellers and buyers of other properties before, during and after the end of this agreement.

   E. **Confirmation:** If the Property includes residential property with one-to-four dwelling units, Broker shall confirm the agency relationship described above, or as modified, in writing, prior to or concurrent with Seller's execution of a purchase agreement.

11. **SECURITY AND INSURANCE:** Broker is not responsible for loss of or damage to personal or real property, or person, whether attributable to use of a keysafe/lockbox, a showing of the Property, or otherwise. Third parties, including, but not limited to, appraisers, inspectors, brokers and prospective buyers, may have access to, and take videos and photographs of, the interior of the Property. Seller agrees: (i) to take reasonable precautions to safeguard and protect valuables that might be accessible during showings of the Property; and (ii) to obtain insurance to protect against these risks. Broker does not maintain insurance to protect Seller.

12. **KEYSAFE/LOCKBOX:** A keysafe/lockbox is designed to hold a key to the Property to permit access to the Property by Broker, cooperating brokers, MLS participants, their authorized licensees and representatives, authorized inspectors, and accompanied prospective buyers. Broker, cooperating brokers, MLS and Associations/Boards of REALTORS® are not insurers against injury, theft, loss, vandalism or damage attributed to the use of a keysafe/lockbox. Seller does (or if checked ☐ does not) authorize Broker to install a keysafe/lockbox. If Seller does not occupy the Property, Seller shall be responsible for obtaining occupant(s)' written permission for use of a keysafe/lockbox.

13. **SIGN:** Seller does (or if checked ☐ does not) authorize Broker to install a FOR SALE/SOLD sign on the Property.

14. **EQUAL HOUSING OPPORTUNITY:** The Property is offered in compliance with federal, state and local anti-discrimination laws.

15. **ATTORNEY FEES:** In any action, proceeding or arbitration between Seller and Broker regarding the obligation to pay compensation under this agreement, the prevailing Seller or Broker shall be entitled to reasonable attorney fees and costs from the non-prevailing Seller or Broker, except as provided in paragraph 19A.

16. **ADDITIONAL TERMS:** _____
_____
_____

17. **MANAGEMENT APPROVAL:** If an associate licensee in Broker's office (salesperson or broker-associate) enters into this agreement on Broker's behalf, and Broker or Manager does not approve of its terms, Broker or Manager has the right to cancel this agreement, in writing, within 5 days after its execution.

18. **SUCCESSORS AND ASSIGNS:** This agreement shall be binding upon Seller and Seller's successors and assigns.

Seller acknowledges receipt of a copy of this page.
Seller's Initials (_____)(_____)

| Reviewed by _____ Date _____ |

LA REVISED 10/02 (PAGE 2 OF 3)

RESIDENTIAL LISTING AGREEMENT-EXCLUSIVE (LA PAGE 2 OF 3)

Property Address: _____ Date: _____

19. DISPUTE RESOLUTION:

A. **MEDIATION:** Seller and Broker agree to mediate any dispute or claim arising between them out of this agreement, or any resulting transaction, before resorting to arbitration or court action, subject to paragraph 19B(2) below. Paragraph 19B(2) below applies whether or not the arbitration provision is initialed. Mediation fees, if any, shall be divided equally among the parties involved. If, for any dispute or claim to which this paragraph applies, any party commences an action without first attempting to resolve the matter through mediation, or refuses to mediate after a request has been made, then that party shall not be entitled to recover attorney fees, even if they would otherwise be available to that party in any such action. THIS MEDIATION PROVISION APPLIES WHETHER OR NOT THE ARBITRATION PROVISION IS INITIALED.

B. **ARBITRATION OF DISPUTES:** (1) Seller and Broker agree that any dispute or claim in Law or equity arising between them regarding the obligation to pay compensation under this agreement, which is not settled through mediation, shall be decided by neutral, binding arbitration, including and subject to paragraph 19B(2) below. The arbitrator shall be a retired judge or justice, or an attorney with at least 5 years of residential real estate law experience, unless the parties mutually agree to a different arbitrator, who shall render an award in accordance with substantive California Law. The parties shall have the right to discovery in accordance with Code of Civil Procedure §1283.05. In all other respects, the arbitration shall be conducted in accordance with Title 9 of Part III of the California Code of Civil Procedure. Judgment upon the award of the arbitrator(s) may be entered in any court having jurisdiction. Interpretation of this agreement to arbitrate shall be governed by the Federal Arbitration Act.

(2) **EXCLUSIONS FROM MEDIATION AND ARBITRATION:** The following matters are excluded from mediation and arbitration hereunder: (i) a judicial or non-judicial foreclosure or other action or proceeding to enforce a deed of trust, mortgage, or installment land sale contract as defined in Civil Code §2985; (ii) an unlawful detainer action; (iii) the filing or enforcement of a mechanic's lien; and (iv) any matter that is within the jurisdiction of a probate, small claims, or bankruptcy court. The filing of a court action to enable the recording of a notice of pending action, for order of attachment, receivership, injunction, or other provisional remedies, shall not constitute a waiver of the mediation and arbitration provisions.

"NOTICE: BY INITIALING IN THE SPACE BELOW YOU ARE AGREEING TO HAVE ANY DISPUTE ARISING OUT OF THE MATTERS INCLUDED IN THE 'ARBITRATION OF DISPUTES' PROVISION DECIDED BY NEUTRAL ARBITRATION AS PROVIDED BY CALIFORNIA LAW AND YOU ARE GIVING UP ANY RIGHTS YOU MIGHT POSSESS TO HAVE THE DISPUTE LITIGATED IN A COURT OR JURY TRIAL. BY INITIALING IN THE SPACE BELOW YOU ARE GIVING UP YOUR JUDICIAL RIGHTS TO DISCOVERY AND APPEAL, UNLESS THOSE RIGHTS ARE SPECIFICALLY INCLUDED IN THE 'ARBITRATION OF DISPUTES' PROVISION. IF YOU REFUSE TO SUBMIT TO ARBITRATION AFTER AGREEING TO THIS PROVISION, YOU MAY BE COMPELLED TO ARBITRATE UNDER THE AUTHORITY OF THE CALIFORNIA CODE OF CIVIL PROCEDURE. YOUR AGREEMENT TO THIS ARBITRATION PROVISION IS VOLUNTARY."

"WE HAVE READ AND UNDERSTAND THE FOREGOING AND AGREE TO SUBMIT DISPUTES ARISING OUT OF THE MATTERS INCLUDED IN THE 'ARBITRATION OF DISPUTES' PROVISION TO NEUTRAL ARBITRATION."

Seller's Initials _____ / _____   Broker's Initials _____ / _____

20. ENTIRE CONTRACT: All prior discussions, negotiations and agreements between the parties concerning the subject matter of this agreement are superseded by this agreement, which constitutes the entire contract and a complete and exclusive expression of their agreement, and may not be contradicted by evidence of any prior agreement or contemporaneous oral agreement. If any provision of this agreement is held to be ineffective or invalid, the remaining provisions will nevertheless be given full force and effect. This agreement and any supplement, addendum or modification, including any photocopy or facsimile, may be executed in counterparts.

By signing below, Seller acknowledges that Seller has read, understands, accepts and has received a copy of this agreement.

Seller _____ Date _____
Address _____ City _____ State _____ Zip _____
Telephone _____ Fax _____ E-mail _____

Seller _____ Date _____
Address _____ City _____ State _____ Zip _____
Telephone _____ Fax _____ E-mail _____

Real Estate Broker (Firm) _____
By (Agent) _____ Date _____
Address _____ City _____ State _____ Zip _____
Telephone _____ Fax _____ E-mail _____

Published by the
California Association of REALTORS®

LA REVISED 10/02 (PAGE 3 OF 3)

Reviewed by _____ Date _____

RESIDENTIAL LISTING AGREEMENT-EXCLUSIVE (LA PAGE 3 OF 3)

EXCLUSIVE AUTHORIZATION TO ACQUIRE PROPERTY
BUYER BROKER COMPENSATION CONTRACT
(C.A.R. Form AAP, Revised 4/02)

1. **EXCLUSIVE RIGHT TO REPRESENT:** _____ ("Buyer")
grants _____ ("Broker")
beginning on (date) _____ and ending at (I) 11:59 p.m. on (date) _____ or (ii) completion of a resulting transaction, whichever occurs first ("Representation Period"), the exclusive and irrevocable right, on the terms specified in this Agreement, to represent Buyer in acquiring real property or a manufactured home. Broker agrees to exercise due diligence and reasonable efforts to fulfill the following authorizations and obligations. Broker will perform its obligations under this Agreement through the individual signing for Broker below, who is either Broker individually or an associate-licensee (an individual licensed as a real estate salesperson or broker who works under Broker's real estate license). Buyer agrees that Broker's duties are limited by the terms of this Agreement, including those limitations set forth in paragraphs 5 and 6.

2. **AGENCY RELATIONSHIPS:**
   A. **DISCLOSURE:** If the property described in paragraph 4 includes residential property with one-to-four dwelling units, Buyer acknowledges receipt of the "Disclosure Regarding Real Estate Agency Relationships" form prior to entering into this Agreement.
   B. **BUYER REPRESENTATION:** Broker will represent, as described in this Agreement, Buyer in any resulting transaction.
   C. **(1) POSSIBLE DUAL AGENCY WITH SELLER:** (C(1) APPLIES UNLESS C(2)(i) or (ii) is checked below.)
   Depending on the circumstances, it may be necessary or appropriate for Broker to act as an agent for both Buyer and a seller, exchange party, or one or more additional parties ("Seller"). Broker shall, as soon as practicable, disclose to Buyer any election to act as a dual agent representing both Buyer and Seller. If Buyer is shown property listed with Broker, Buyer consents to Broker becoming a dual agent representing both Buyer and Seller with respect to those properties. In event of dual agency, Buyer agrees that: **(a)** Broker, without the prior written consent of Buyer, will not disclose to Seller that the Buyer is willing to pay a price greater than the price offered; **(b)** Broker, without the prior written consent of Seller, will not disclose to Buyer that Seller is willing to sell property at a price less than the listing price; and **(c)** other than as set forth in (a) and (b) above, a dual agent is obligated to disclose known facts materially affecting the value or desirability of the Property to both parties.
   OR (2) SINGLE AGENCY ONLY: (APPLIES ONLY IF (i) or (ii) is checked below.)
   ☐ **(i) Broker's firm lists properties for sale:** Buyer understands that this election will prevent Broker from showing Buyer those properties that are listed with Broker's firm or from representing Buyer in connection with those properties. Buyer's acquisition of a property listed with Broker's firm shall not affect Broker's right to be compensated under paragraph 3. In any resulting transaction in which Seller's property is not listed with Broker's firm, Broker will be the exclusive agent of Buyer and not a dual agent also representing Seller.
   OR ☐ **(ii) Broker's firm DOES NOT list property:** Entire brokerage firm only represents buyers and does not list property. In any resulting transaction, Broker will be the exclusive agent of Buyer and not a dual agent also representing Seller.
   D. **OTHER POTENTIAL BUYERS:** Buyer understands that other potential buyers may, through Broker, consider, make offers on or acquire the same or similar properties as those Buyer is seeking to acquire. Buyer consents to Broker's representation of such other potential buyers before, during and after the Representation Period, or any extension thereof.
   E. **CONFIRMATION:** If the Property includes residential property with one-to-four dwelling units, Broker shall confirm the agency relationship described above, or as modified, in writing, prior to or coincident with Buyer's execution of a Property Contract.

3. **COMPENSATION TO BROKER:**
   NOTICE: The amount or rate of real estate commissions is not fixed by law. They are set by each Broker individually and may be negotiable between Buyer and Broker (real estate commissions include all compensation and fees to Broker).
   Buyer agrees to pay to Broker, irrespective of agency relationship(s), as follows:
   A. **AMOUNT OF COMPENSATION:** (Check (1), (2) or (3). Check only one.)
   ☐ **(1)** _____ percent of the acquisition price AND (if checked ☐) $ _____
   OR ☐ **(2)** $ _____
   OR ☐ **(3)** Pursuant to the compensation schedule attached as an addendum _____
   B. **BROKER RIGHT TO COMPENSATION:** Broker shall be entitled to the compensation provided for in paragraph 3A:
   (1) If Buyer enters into an agreement to acquire property described in paragraph 4, on those terms or any other terms acceptable to Buyer during the Representation Period, or any extension thereof.
   (2) If, within ____ **calendar days** after expiration of the Representation Period or any extension thereof, Buyer enters into an agreement to acquire property described in paragraph 4, which property Broker introduced to Buyer, or for which Broker acted on Buyer's behalf. The obligation to pay compensation pursuant to this paragraph shall arise only if, prior to or within **3 (or ☐ ____) calendar days** after expiration of this Agreement or any extension thereof, Broker gives Buyer a written notice of those properties which Broker introduced to Buyer, or for which Broker acted on Buyer's behalf.

AAP-11 REVISED 4/02 (PAGE 1 OF 4) Print Date

Buyer and Broker acknowledge receipt of a copy of this page.

Buyer's Initials (_____)(_____)
Broker's Initials (_____)(_____)

Reviewed by _____
Broker or Designee _____ Date _____

EXCLUSIVE AUTHORIZATION TO ACQUIRE PROPERTY (AAP-11 PAGE 1 OF 4)

Buyer: _____ Date: _____

C. **PAYMENT OF COMPENSATION:** Compensation is payable:
   (1) Upon completion of any resulting transaction, and if an escrow is used, through escrow.
   (2) If acquisition is prevented by default of Buyer, upon Buyer's default.
   (3) If acquisition is prevented by a party to the transaction other than Buyer, when Buyer collects damages by suit, settlement or otherwise. Compensation shall equal one-half of the damages recovered, not to exceed the compensation provided for in paragraph 3A, after first deducting the unreimbursed expenses of collection, if any.

D. **BUYER OBLIGATION TO PAY COMPENSATION:** Buyer is responsible for payment of compensation provided for in this Agreement. However, if anyone other than Buyer compensates Broker for services covered by this Agreement, that amount shall be credited toward Buyer's obligation to pay compensation. If the amount of compensation Broker receives from anyone other than Buyer exceeds Buyer's obligation, the excess amount shall be disclosed to Buyer and if allowed by law paid to Broker, or (if checked) ☐ credited to Buyer or ☐ other _____.

E. Buyer hereby irrevocably assigns to Broker the compensation provided for in paragraph 3A from Buyer's funds and proceeds in escrow. Buyer agrees to submit to escrow any funds needed to compensate Broker under this Agreement. Broker may submit this Agreement, as instructions to compensate Broker, to any escrow regarding Property involving Buyer and a seller or other transferor.

F. **"BUYER"** includes any person or entity, other than Broker, related to Buyer or who in any manner acts on Buyer's behalf to acquire property described in paragraph 4.

G. (1) Buyer has not previously entered into a representation agreement with another brokerage firm regarding property described in paragraph 4, unless specified as follows (name other brokerage firm here): _____
   (2) Buyer warrants that Buyer has no obligation to pay compensation to any other brokerage firm regarding property described in paragraph 4 unless Buyer acquires the following property(ies): _____.
   (3) If Buyer acquires a property specified in G(2) above during the time Buyer is obligated to compensate another broker, Broker is neither (i) entitled to compensation under this Agreement nor (ii) obligated to represent Buyer in such transaction.

4. **PROPERTY TO BE ACQUIRED:**
   Any purchase, lease or other acquisition of any real property or manufactured home described as follows:
   _____
   _____
   _____
   Price range: $ _____ to $ _____

5. **BROKER AUTHORIZATIONS AND OBLIGATIONS:**
   A. Buyer authorizes Broker to: (i) locate and present selected properties to Buyer, present offers authorized by Buyer, and assist Buyer in negotiating for acceptance of such offers; (ii) assist Buyer with the financing process, including obtaining loan pre-qualification; (iii) upon request, provide Buyer with a list of professionals or vendors who perform the services described in the attached Buyer's Inspection Advisory; (iv) order reports, and schedule and attend meetings and appointments with professionals chosen by Buyer; (v) provide guidance to help Buyer with the acquisition of property; and (vi) obtain a credit report on Buyer.
   B. For property transactions of which Broker is aware and not precluded from participating in by Buyer, Broker shall provide and review forms to create a property contract ("Property Contract") for the acquisition of a specific property ("Property"). With respect to such Property, Broker shall: (i) if the Property contains residential property with one-to-four dwelling units, conduct a reasonably competent and diligent on-site visual inspection of the accessible areas of the Property (excluding any common areas), and disclose to Buyer all facts materially affecting the value or desirability of such Property that are revealed by this inspection; (ii) deliver or communicate to Buyer any disclosures, materials or information received by, in the personal possession of or personally known to the individual signing for Broker below during the Representation Period; and (iii) facilitate the escrow process, including assisting Buyer in negotiating with Seller. Unless otherwise specified in writing, any information provided through Broker in the course of representing Buyer has not been and will not be verified by Broker. Broker's services are performed in compliance with federal, state and local antidiscrimination laws.

6. **SCOPE OF BROKER DUTY:**
   A. While Broker will perform the duties described in paragraph 5B, Broker recommends that Buyer select other professionals, as described in the attached Buyer's Inspection Advisory, to investigate the Property through inspections, investigations, tests, surveys, reports, studies and other available information ("Inspections") during the transaction. Buyer agrees that these Inspections, to the extent they exceed the obligations described in paragraph 5B, are not within the scope of Broker's agency duties. Broker informs Buyer that it is in Buyer's best interest to obtain such Inspections.
   B. Buyer acknowledges and agrees that Broker: (i) does not decide what price Buyer should pay or Seller should accept; (ii) does not guarantee the condition of the Property; (iii) does not guarantee the performance, adequacy or completeness of Inspections, services, products or repairs provided or made by Seller or others to Buyer or Seller; (iv) shall not be responsible for identifying defects that are not known to Broker and either (a) are not visually observable in reasonably accessible areas of the Property or (b) are in common areas; (v) shall not be responsible for identifying the location of boundary lines or other items affecting title; (vi) shall not be responsible for verifying square footage, representations of others or information contained in Inspection reports; (vii) shall not be responsible for providing legal or tax advice regarding any aspect of a transaction entered into by Buyer in the course of this representation; and (viii) shall not be responsible for providing other advice or information that exceeds the knowledge, education and experience required to perform real estate licensed activities. Buyer agrees to seek legal, tax, insurance, title and other desired assistance from appropriate professionals.

AAP-11 REVISED 4/02 (PAGE 2 OF 4) Print Date

Buyer and Broker acknowledge receipt of a copy of this page.

Buyer's Initials (_____)(_____)
Broker's Initials (_____)(_____)

Reviewed by _____
Broker or Designee _____ Date _____

EXCLUSIVE AUTHORIZATION TO ACQUIRE PROPERTY (AAP-11 PAGE 2 OF 4)

Buyer: _____ Date: _____

C. Broker owes no duty to inspect for common environmental hazards, earthquake weaknesses, or geologic and seismic hazards. If Buyer receives the booklets titled "Environmental Hazards: A Guide for Homeowners, Buyers, Landlords and Tenants," "The Homeowner's Guide to Earthquake Safety," or "The Commercial Property Owner's Guide to Earthquake Safety," the booklets are deemed adequate to inform buyer regarding the information contained in the booklets and, other than as specified in 5B above, Broker is not required to provide Buyer with additional information about the matters described in the booklets.

7. **BUYER OBLIGATIONS:**

A. Buyer agrees to timely view and consider properties selected by Broker and to negotiate in good faith to acquire a property. Buyer further agrees to act in good faith toward the completion of any Property Contract entered into in furtherance of this Agreement. Within 5 (or ☐ _____) calendar days from the execution of this Agreement, Buyer shall provide relevant personal and financial information to Broker to assure Buyer's ability to acquire property described in paragraph 4. If Buyer fails to provide such information, or if Buyer does not qualify financially to acquire property described in paragraph 4, then Broker may cancel this Agreement in writing. Buyer has an affirmative duty to take steps to protect him/herself, including discovery of the legal, practical and technical implications of discovered or disclosed facts, and investigation of information and facts which are known to Buyer or are within the diligent attention and observation of Buyer. Buyer is obligated to and agrees to read all documents provided to Buyer. Buyer agrees to seek desired assistance from appropriate professionals, selected by Buyer, such as those referenced in the attached Buyer's Inspection Advisory.

B. Buyer shall notify Broker in writing of any material issue to Buyer, such as, but not limited to, Buyer requests for information on, or concerns regarding, any particular area of interest or importance to Buyer ("Material Consideration").

C. Buyer agrees to (i) indemnify, defend and hold Broker harmless from all claims, disputes, litigation, judgments, costs and attorney fees arising from any incorrect information supplied by Buyer, or from any Material Consideration that Buyer fails to disclose in writing to Broker, and (ii) pay for reports, inspections and meetings arranged by Broker on Buyer's behalf.

D. Buyer is advised to read the attached Buyer's Inspection Advisory for a list of items and other concerns that typically warrant inspections or investigation by Buyer or other professionals.

8. **DISPUTE RESOLUTION:**

A. **MEDIATION:** Buyer and Broker agree to mediate any dispute or claim arising between them out of this Agreement, or any resulting transaction, before resorting to arbitration or court action, subject to paragraph 8B(2) below. Paragraph 8B(2) below applies whether or not the arbitration provision is initialed. Mediation fees, if any, shall be divided equally among the parties involved. If, for any dispute or claim to which this paragraph applies, any party commences an action without first attempting to resolve the matter through mediation, or refuses to mediate after a request has been made, then that party shall not be entitled to recover attorney fees even if they would otherwise be available to that party in any such action. THIS MEDIATION PROVISION APPLIES WHETHER OR NOT THE ARBITRATION PROVISION IS INITIALED.

B. **ARBITRATION OF DISPUTES:** (1) Buyer and Broker agree that any dispute or claim in law or equity arising between them regarding the obligation to pay compensation under this Agreement, which is not settled through mediation, shall be decided by neutral, binding arbitration, including and subject to paragraph 8B(2) below. The arbitrator shall be a retired judge or justice, or an attorney with at least five years of residential real estate law experience, unless the parties mutually agree to a different arbitrator, who shall render an award in accordance with substantive California law. In all other respects, the arbitration shall be conducted in accordance with Part III, Title 9 of the California Code of Civil Procedure. Judgment upon the award of the arbitrator(s) may be entered in any court having jurisdiction. The parties shall have the right to discovery in accordance with Code of Civil Procedure §1283.05.

(2) **EXCLUSIONS FROM MEDIATION AND ARBITRATION:** The following matters are excluded from mediation and arbitration hereunder: (i) a judicial or non-judicial foreclosure or other action or proceeding to enforce a deed of trust, mortgage, or installment land sale contract as defined in Civil Code §2985; (ii) an unlawful detainer action; (iii) the filing or enforcement of a mechanic's lien; (iv) any matter that is within the jurisdiction of a probate, small claims, or bankruptcy court; and (v) an action for bodily injury or wrongful death, or for any right of action to which Code of Civil Procedure §337.1 or §337.15 applies. The filing of a court action to enable the recording of a notice of pending action, for order of attachment, receivership, injunction, or other provisional remedies, shall not constitute a waiver of the mediation and arbitration provisions.

"NOTICE: BY INITIALING IN THE SPACE BELOW YOU ARE AGREEING TO HAVE ANY DISPUTE ARISING OUT OF THE MATTERS INCLUDED IN THE 'ARBITRATION OF DISPUTES' PROVISION DECIDED BY NEUTRAL ARBITRATION AS PROVIDED BY CALIFORNIA LAW AND YOU ARE GIVING UP ANY RIGHTS YOU MIGHT POSSESS TO HAVE THE DISPUTE LITIGATED IN A COURT OR JURY TRIAL. BY INITIALING IN THE SPACE BELOW YOU ARE GIVING UP YOUR JUDICIAL RIGHTS TO DISCOVERY AND APPEAL, UNLESS THOSE RIGHTS ARE SPECIFICALLY INCLUDED IN THE 'ARBITRATION OF DISPUTES' PROVISION. IF YOU REFUSE TO SUBMIT TO ARBITRATION AFTER AGREEING TO THIS PROVISION, YOU MAY BE COMPELLED TO ARBITRATE UNDER THE AUTHORITY OF THE CALIFORNIA CODE OF CIVIL PROCEDURE. YOUR AGREEMENT TO THIS ARBITRATION PROVISION IS VOLUNTARY."

"WE HAVE READ AND UNDERSTAND THE FOREGOING AND AGREE TO SUBMIT DISPUTES ARISING OUT OF THE MATTERS INCLUDED IN THE 'ARBITRATION OF DISPUTES' PROVISION TO NEUTRAL ARBITRATION."

| Buyer's Initials _____ / _____ | Broker's Initials _____ / _____ |

Buyer and Broker acknowledge receipt of a copy of this page.
Buyer's Initials (_____)(_____)
Broker's Initials (_____)(_____)

AAP-11 REVISED 4/02 (PAGE 3 OF 4) Print Date

Reviewed by _____ Date _____
Broker or Designee

EXCLUSIVE AUTHORIZATION TO ACQUIRE PROPERTY (AAP-11 PAGE 3 OF 4)

Buyer: _____ Date: _____

9. **TIME TO BRING LEGAL ACTION:** Legal action for breach of this Agreement, or any obligation arising therefrom, shall be brought no more than two years from the expiration of the Representation Period or from the date such cause of action may arise, whichever occurs first.

10. **OTHER TERMS AND CONDITIONS, including ATTACHED SUPPLEMENTS:** ☑ Buyer's Inspection Advisory (C.A.R. Form BIA-11)
_____
_____
_____
_____
_____

11. **ATTORNEY FEES:** In any action, proceeding or arbitration between Buyer and Broker regarding the obligation to pay compensation under this Agreement, the prevailing Buyer or Broker shall be entitled to reasonable attorney fees and costs, except as provided in paragraph 8A.

12. **ENTIRE CONTRACT:** All understandings between the parties are incorporated in this Agreement. Its terms are intended by the parties as a final, complete and exclusive expression of their agreement with respect to its subject matter, and may not be contradicted by evidence of any prior agreement or contemporaneous oral agreement. This Agreement may not be extended, amended, modified, altered or changed, except in writing signed by Buyer and Broker. In the event that any provision of this Agreement is held to be ineffective or invalid, the remaining provisions will nevertheless be given full force and effect. This Agreement and any supplement, addendum or modification, including any copy, whether by copier, facsimile, NCR or electronic, may be signed in two or more counterparts, all of which shall constitute one and the same writing.

Buyer acknowledges that Buyer has read, understands, accepts and has received a copy of this Agreement.

Buyer _____ Date _____
Address _____ City _____ State _____ Zip _____
Telephone _____ Fax _____ E-mail _____

Buyer _____ Date _____
Address _____ City _____ State _____ Zip _____
Telephone _____ Fax _____ E-mail _____

Real Estate Broker (Firm) _____
By (Agent) _____ Date _____
Address _____ City _____ State _____ Zip _____
Telephone _____ Fax _____ E-mail _____

EXCLUSIVE AUTHORIZATION TO ACQUIRE PROPERTY (AAP-11 PAGE 4 OF 4)

There will be many different contracts that must be filled out during a property transfer. The first form that you will be required to fill out, understand, and (usually) explain to the client is the listing agreement. It is very important that this form be filled out accurately, and that you understand exactly what it means; this way, you can convey accurately and confidently all information on this contract to the client. After all, this agreement is considered a legal contract, and if your client is signing his or her name to the document, they will want to know what all of it means!

The most important part of filling out the contract from the agent's perspective is accuracy and clarity. You don't want to have vague wording or unclear terms, leaving room for misinterpretation, misunderstandings or anything that might place your commission in jeopardy. Additionally, if you struggle with filling out the listing agreement, your client may not place a lot of trust or faith in your ability to sell their property. The following step-by-step analysis of both the exclusive-authorization-and-right-to-sell and exclusive authorization to acquire real property will aid your understanding of the forms. Please refer to the previous pages for examples of these forms.

Exclusive-authorization-and-right-to-sell
- Section 1, Exclusive-Right-To-Sell.
  In this first section, you will fill in the name of the seller and then the name of the broker who is taking the listing. If you are a salesperson, not the broker, you will need to write in your broker's name here. Following the name of the seller and broker, you will need to enter the beginning and end date for the listing. Listings generally last between three and six months; however, this is not a hard-and-fast rule. If you have a property you think will need more time to sell, or if the market is slow, you can ask for more time from the seller. Finally, you need to fill in the city, county and address of the property. In addition to the address, a property description may be appropriate such as the lot, block and tract numbers. This will serve to differentiate the property from any other properties in the close vicinity which may also be for sale.

- Section 2, Items Excluded and Included
  In this section you will fill out the items of real property that are excluded in the sale of the home. Additionally, you will want a complete list of personal property items the seller wishes to sell with the home. Some items of personal property that people generally sell with the home include appliances, recreational items such as a trampoline or hot tub, and furniture. Getting a very accurate list is important so that the buyer understands exactly what will stay in or with the home, and what items will not be there at closing.

- Section 3, Listing Price and Terms
  The listing price for the home and terms are included here. The terms of sale may be anything required by the owner to sell the property to an interested buyer. This may include financial arrangements, escrow length or any other similar terms determined by the seller.

- Section 4, Compensation to Broker
  You will notice at the beginning of section 4 that it is clearly stated in boldface type that the law does not regulate the commission a broker receives. The broker and seller decide upon the commission amount. This statement is required by law to be on every listing agreement for properties having 1-4 living units. Properties with more than 4 units will not be required to have this statement. Additionally, this section is quite lengthy, broken down into six subsections.

Subsection A describes the commission due upon the sale of the property. Because this is an exclusive-authorization-and-right-to-sell listing, subsection A also stipulates that the agreed-upon commission is due whether the broker produces a ready, willing and able buyer or the homeowner is the one who actually sells the property. This buyer must be found during the time period of the listing. If an offer comes in after the listing expires, the broker may still be eligible for his or her commission. Many listing agreements include a safety clause allowing this to happen. If a broker shows the home to a prospective buyer, but that buyer does not make an offer until after the listing agreement expires, the broker is still entitled to that commission. For this to occur, it is important for the broker to keep a detailed record of all people to whom he or she showed the property during the life of the listing agreement. Additionally, if the broker furnishes the homeowner with the name of a possible buyer within three days after the listing agreement expires, the broker is again eligible for the full commission.

Should the seller withdraw the listing, or rent, sell or make the property unavailable without the consent of the broker for any reason during the life of the agreement, the broker is still entitled to a full commission.

Subsection B outlines that if the sale of the property is not possible due to actions by any person other than the seller or broker, and the seller receives damages, the broker is entitled to a commission. This commission is to be equal to the lesser of either the original agreed-upon commission or half of the damages received by the seller.

Subsection C describes any other fees the broker may charge the seller. It is beginning to be common for the broker to charge the seller fees for various administration costs incurred by the broker. Some of these fees can come from MLS listings or transaction and documentation fees. Any additional fees charged by the broker above and beyond the commission must be stated in the listing agreement.

Subsection D allows the broker to cooperate with other brokers or agents and divide up the commission in any manner agreed upon by the cooperating agents.

Subsection E is an assignment of commission fees directly to the broker. These fees will not go into an escrow account where the seller has the power to change the allocation, but rather will go directly to the broker. This protects the broker or agent from having the commission returned to the seller for any reason.

Subsection F must clearly state whether the seller has entered into any other agreement with another broker, or whether another broker would be entitled to any commission from the sale of the property. If the seller has entered into a contract with another broker, it is understood that you will not be receiving any compensation, nor will you be responsible for representing the seller in the transaction.

- Section 5, Ownership, Title and Authority
  This section states that the sellers have the authority to sell the property and that they do not share title to the property with any other party, unless otherwise stated. It also states that the owners have the authority to sell the property.

- Section 6, Multiple-Listing Service
  This section allows the sellers to determine whether they want to have the property listed on the MLS. By marking the appropriate section, they either give their consent, or state that they do not want the property listed on the MLS. If the sellers decide to list their property, they must also be aware that all terms of the transaction will be listed as well.

- Section 7, Seller Representations
  The seller represents that the property is clear for sale, clean of any notices of default, delinquencies on the note, bankruptcy, insolvency, litigation, arbitration, administrative action, government investigation or other pending threatened actions that affect the seller's ability to transfer the property. If there is any problem with the property, it must be clearly stated in writing; if any problem arises after securing a listing agreement with the broker, the seller must immediately notify the broker of this problem in writing.

- Section 8, Broker's and Seller's Duties.
  The broker promises to use due diligence in finding qualified, ready, willing and able buyers interested in the property. The seller in turn promises to make the property available for showings, stands by the information submitted to the broker as truthful and factual, and will consider seriously any offers the broker brings forth. Additionally, the seller agrees to not hold the broker liable for any misrepresentations the seller made regarding the property in the event action is taken against the seller.

- Section 9, Deposit
  The broker is authorized to accept and hold any deposits made on the property on behalf of the seller.

- Section 10, Agency Relationships
  The broker discloses to the seller that he or she represents the seller, and owes the seller fiduciary responsibility. However, dual agency may occur if the broker finds a ready, able and willing buyer without representation. In this case, the broker would make all necessary disclosures, and be the representation for both the seller and the buyer. Additionally, the broker makes the seller aware that he or she may have other listings, or obtain other listings, during the span of the listing agreement. In this case, the broker would be showing interested parties all properties he or she represents that fit the interested parties' criteria.

- Section 11, Security and Insurance
  This section explains that the broker is not responsible for any lost, stolen or damaged property during open houses, or during the length of the listing. During the listing, not only will the broker need access to the property to show, but third parties such as inspectors or appraisers will also need to have access. The owner understands that he or she must take all necessary precautions to protect his or her property, and the seller is urged to take out the necessary insurance in the event there is loss or damage to the property.

- Section 12, Key Safe / Lockbox
  The seller has the option to allow the broker to install a lockbox to the property, giving the broker, cooperating brokers, agents, inspectors and all other interested parties with permission access to enter the property for the purpose of inspections or showings. If the seller elects to allow a lockbox, the seller understands that the broker and all other authorized parties are free of any responsibility for lost, stolen or destroyed items.

- Section 13, Sign
  This section of the agreement allows the seller to authorize a "For Sale" / "Sold" sign on the property. The seller can elect to not allow this signage on the property.

- Section 14, Equal Housing Opportunity
  The seller is made aware of federal, state and local anti-discriminatory laws. The seller is further made aware that they cannot reject an offer from a qualified buyer based on any discrimination that is prohibited under the anti-discriminatory laws.

- Section 15, Attorney's Fees
  This section helps to alleviate unnecessary lawsuits based on property transfer. Section 15 states that if there should be legal action brought by either the seller or broker, the person losing the law suit will be responsible for paying the attorneys' fees for both parties.

- Section 16, Additional Terms
  Any other terms specified by either the broker or the owner can be stated clearly in this space. Any terms here must comply with all federal, state and local laws.

- Section 17, Management Approval
  If any person authorized by the broker enters into a listing agreement with a seller, but the broker finds the terms to be unacceptable, the broker has the power to terminate the listing agreement within 5 days. Termination of the listing agreement must be in writing.

- Section 18, Successors and Assigns
  This section states that the contract with the broker is binding upon seller and seller's successors and assigns.

- Section 19, Dispute Resolution
  Subsection A states that the broker and seller will use mediation as an initial action to solve a dispute resulting from this agreement. If an acceptable solution cannot be achieved by mediation, then it is appropriate to move onto other methods of action.

  Subsection B states that by signing the listing agreement, each party agrees to neutral binding arbitration regarding any dispute they may have. By agreeing to neutral binding arbitration, each party is giving up their rights to take the dispute to court and litigate.

- Section 20, Entire Contract
  This section of the contract simply states that the agreement is as written, and any prior agreements or verbal statements cannot contradict the current agreement.

- Signatures
  The final item on the contract is for the seller and broker to sign the listing agreement, signifying they have read the contract, understand its contents and have each received a copy.

VALUATION OF THE LISTING

Agreeing upon a listing price with the seller is a very difficult and important step in determining how successful the sale of the property will be. Those listings priced too high will move slowly, if at all. Those listings that are underpriced will sell fast, but the homeowner will not realize the full economic potential of the property. Perhaps the most important discussion an agent will have with the client is determining at what price the home should be listed. Agents must help steer the clients in the right direction and guide them into the correct price range. Without the aid of the agent, a homeowner might not know what to ask for a property, or even what a fair price would be.

The listing price needs to be based on what the market will support, or market value. Market value can be described as the highest price a property will bring in open market conditions. This assumes there is a willing seller who will sell his or her home at that specific price, and a willing buyer who will buy the home at that price.

There are three different ways an agent can value a home. The most reliable way to find the value of a home is to compare it to other properties that have recently been sold. This is called **market data** or **competitive market analysis**. The **cost approach** calculates the cost to replace or reproduce an existing structure, less depreciation. The last approach, used for income properties is called the **income capitalization** approach. It is important to note that the competitive market analysis approach is the best approach to use, and the other two methods of valuation should only be used if there is no data to utilize for the competitive market analysis.

Competitive Market Analysis

Competitive market analysis is a tool that real estate agents can use when helping clients determine a fair listing price to ask for a home or property. The competitive market analysis gives the homeowner or property owner a good estimation of value based on what the market is currently asking for similar properties located in the same area. Additionally, it can give the agent, or client, a good view of what the market has been doing over a 6-month average -- have prices gone up or down, or remained the same? This is important when deciding on a listing price, so that the house is not only competitive with other similar homes in the area, but also so the client gets the maximum value of the house in the current market conditions.

In a competitive market analysis, the broker will search the selling prices of similar properties which have recently sold in the same area. These listings are generally searched up to 6 months prior to the current date. In addition to recent property transactions, an agent can research the asking price for similar homes currently on the market.

The Multiple Listing Service, or MLS, has made this process much faster. With the MLS, an agent can quickly perform specific searches of an area. Criteria such as location, amenities, lot size, number of bedrooms and bathrooms and square footage can be entered into the system, with the properties instantaneously shown. In addition to the MLS, escrow and title companies can provide an agent with data used to compile a competitive market analysis.

A competitive market analysis is not an official appraisal, and should not be treated as such. The purpose of the competitive market analysis is simply to give the homeowner an idea of the most competitive, fair and appropriate asking price in the current market conditions. Asking too much might mean the property will be overlooked by would-be buyers. Asking too little might move the property fast, but the property owner will not capitalize on the full potential of the home.

When conducting a competitive market analysis, it is important for the agent to obtain the most current information so that the client knows what the maximum asking price could be. If an agent fails to include the most recent data in his or her analysis, he or she could be held liable for any lost potential income from the sale.

A competitive market analysis is a good way to find the general market value of residential properties with 1-4 units and undeveloped land. It is not appropriate to use the competitive market analysis when finding the market value of commercial, industrial or income properties.

Remember
A competitive market analysis is appropriate for
- Residential properties with 1-4 units
- Undeveloped land.

When conducting a competitive market analysis, it is usually necessary to make adjustments between the property being evaluated and the comparative properties. For example, a home next to your client's home sold this week for $450,000. You know that your client's lot size is the same, and that there are the same number of bedrooms; however, the client's home has 3_ bathrooms, and the neighbors' home has 3 bathrooms. The neighboring house was remodeled before it was sold, while your client's home has not had any updating done in several years. Additionally, the neighbors' home has a pool, while the client's home does not. The necessary adjustments would be made in the following way:

Your client's property	Comparable property	Adjustment
3 bathrooms	3 bathrooms	+
Outdated interior style / appliances	Recent remodel	−
No pool	Pool	−

In making a price adjustment between what your client could ask for his or her house, compared to the neighbor's home, you would increase the asking price based on bathrooms; however, you must lower the asking price based on the lack of a swimming pool and the fact that the client's home needs an interior update. If the neighbors received $450,000 for their home, you know that your client's asking price should be less than that to remain competitive in the market.

As mentioned before, a six-month period is generally used when conducting a competitive market analysis. When searching properties that have been sold, this is referred to as **reported-sold-prior-six-months**. This is perhaps the most important data an agent can collect when conducting a competitive market analysis. It shows actual selling prices for properties, rather than current listing prices. The more recent the data, the better, as information from six months ago is not as reliable as three weeks ago. However, all data within the six-month time period will be helpful in determining a listing price.

Agents will also look for listings **on-market-now**. These listings show other like properties and their asking prices. These are not indicative of the actual selling prices, as the properties are still on the market as listings. However, this information gives the agent a good idea of what other homes are listing at, so that his or her client can remain competitive in the market, and not be overpriced. An overpriced home may eventually fall onto the **reported-expired-prior-six-months list**. These are the homes that were listed for sale within the last six months, but did not sell. Usually, when evaluating these listings, an agent will see that they were priced higher than similar competition. It is important when conducting competitive market analysis that the eventual listing price should remain true to the market conditions and the competition.

Cost Approach

There are certain times when competitive market analysis is simply not available due to lack of data on recent or past sales. An example of this would be houses offered for sale in a new development, where there are very few recently sold houses, if any, to compare the prices to. In this situation, the best method of valuation is the cost approach.

The cost approach estimates the current costs of replacing the existing structure. Any depreciation the structure has incurred must be subtracted from the cost of replacing it, and then this figure needs to be added to the value of the land. The final figure you arrive at will be the value of the property.

The cost approach is not as exact as competitive market analysis. All figures must be extremely accurate to arrive at a dependable final figure. Because of uncertainty in arriving at numbers, it is wise for the appraiser to attempt to find the value of the property using each of the three methods. Comparing the values for the property indicated by each one of the methods will help the appraiser determine the most accurate valuation for the property in question.

Income Approach

The income approach is not used for finding the value of a residential property; it is used when finding the value of an income property where the owner is not planning on making any of the living units his or her primary place of residence.

An appraiser will be attempting to find the present worth of future benefits associated with an income property, as determined by the net income generated from the property after all costs have been subtracted. There will be a rate of capitalization estimating future income, converted into present value.

Determining the capitalization rate will be the biggest challenge for the appraiser in determining value. There are several variables that go into determining this number. Some of the variables are the type of property, age of the property, market conditions, requirements of the investor, cost of money, market risks, income tax considerations and other variables. Generally speaking, the larger the risk associated with the investment, the larger the capitalization rate will be. On the other hand, for a safe investment, the capitalization rate will be small.

There are specific steps in determining value. First, the gross annual income must be determined. This number must be accurate, and adjusted for any vacancies. Next, all operational costs must be subtracted from the gross annual income. Thirdly, the capitalization rate is determined based on market conditions. Finally, the net income will be divided into the capitalization rate to determine the current estimated value of the property.

Appraisals

Real estate agents are allowed to make an educated estimate of the value of property for the purpose of determining what the house's listing price should be. By no means is this value considered an accurate or legal appraisal. Certified, licensed appraisers are the only people who can determine the official appraised value of a property for taxation or legal reasons. Any person offering a non-certified estimation of value on property, who then claims it to be certified, may be held liable for damages.

Staying attentive and in touch with the seller will keep the seller's confidence high in your actions and abilities during the life of the listing. Keeping the seller posted about any changes, progress or other details as they become available will let the seller know that you are doing everything in your power to find a suitable buyer.

It is wise for the broker to include the seller in the selling process. By telling the seller what he or she can do to aid the sale of the home, it not only helps you, but also empowers the seller to be an active participant in the selling process. Let the seller know what he or she can do during an open house to make their property more enticing to prospective buyers. Having the house clean may not be enough. The broker can advise the seller about different things they can do to make the house look more "put together," such as flower arrangements, candles, or other decorative touches to make the house stand out from others on the market.

Information is key in a broker's relationship with the seller. Close contact and a good relationship with the seller will allow the broker leverage when dealing with third parties. If an offer comes in and it is just under the listing price, a broker with a good relationship with the seller may be able to present the offer in a way the seller will accept. There are other areas where open and clear communication will be beneficial to the broker as well. In the case of commissions, it is important for the seller to understand just how much work a broker puts in. Once this is understood, the seller will be much more agreeable about paying the broker's commission. All too often, people think a broker only puts in a very small amount of time for a large commission check. When they understand all the effort that goes into selling, such as open houses, paperwork, advertising, and unscheduled meetings or showings, they will have a greater appreciation for all the effort it takes to sell a property.

Communication does not end with the seller. It is important for the broker to have consistent communication with all other agents who are involved with showing or selling the property. This will allow for important feedback regarding the property, the interest level in the property, and things that can be done to improve the desirability of the property. For example, if you are a broker, and you list one of your properties on the MLS, it is visible for virtually all members in the area to see and show to interested clients. If the property is being shown and potential buyers find that there is a problem with the plumbing, this is something the seller's broker needs to know and alert the sellers about. If the sellers were unaware of this problem, they may want to fix or disclose the problem.

There are several different steps in servicing a listing. The amount and frequency of these steps all depend on how long the property is on the market.

Initially, the most important step is obtaining the listing. This is accomplished when you visit the client for the first time and go over the different agency options, and all parties sign the contract. Once the contract is signed, it is sent to the multiple listing service, where the listing will be posted on the MLS site for all members to search or access.

After the listing is secured, the broker will place a lockbox on the outside of the home, giving all cooperating brokers access to the home. The lockbox is necessary because the broker cannot be available for all showings of the property. When a cooperating broker finds a client interested in the property, they don't have to make an appointment with the broker to view the property; they can simply go directly to the home and allow the client to view the property.

Next, the broker will, with permission, place the "For Sale" sign in the front of the property. The sign should include all required and necessary contact information. Some neighborhoods will not allow these kinds of signs; additionally, some sellers will not want to have a sign placed in the yard, so the broker must first obtain permission to do this.

Information sheets will be created, usually with a photo of the house or property and all pertinent statistical and logistical information regarding the home or property. This usually includes things such as number of bedrooms, bathrooms, living space, amenities, age and types of utilities, address, and information regarding area schools. These information sheets will be useful to hand out to interested buyers during open houses, to have on hand in the office for other agents to distribute to interested clients, and to take to other real estate firms for distribution.

The broker should make arrangements for the required inspections or provide all necessary information to the client to do this. This will tell the owner and broker if there are any problems with the property, and subsequently what must be fixed, updated or disclosed to the potential buyer.

The broker will now conduct a preliminary title report to reveal the condition of the title. Are there liens against the property due to failure to pay a contractor or taxes, or missed payments on the note? The title report will reveal these items. The preliminary title report will indicate how easy it will be to transfer the title from the current owner to the buyer, or if it is possible at all. In addition to the title report, the broker will obtain all existing loan information, the status on the current loan and new financing options for the potential buyers. Some properties may be financed through special programs, while others are not eligible for special programs and require traditional financing.

It is a good idea to send your client a thank-you note. This initial note is to thank them for offering their listing to you. A casual, friendly note saying "Thanks" will show your appreciation for their business, and will show them you will work hard to find a suitable buyer for the property.

The broker will now begin to host open houses. These are usually held on a Saturday to get as much exposure as possible. Immediately after the open house is over, the broker will compile any feedback received from potential buyers. This feedback is important, as it will aid you and your client in making good choices, or possibly suggest alterations to the property which will make it more desirable and easier to sell. The broker will also compile a list of contacts received at the open house. This list of contacts will provide a good database of people to contact down the road to see if they are still interested in the property. The broker will also present any offers received during the open house. These offers should be immediately presented to the seller for consideration. If a counteroffer needs to be written, this can be taken into consideration at this time.

An aggressive broker looking for good leads will also contact the neighbors in the area close to the property for sale. This will allow them to suggest whom they might like as a neighbor. They may have a friend, co-worker, or relative who is looking for a home in the area. This is a great method of prospecting, discussed in a previous chapter.

It is important to maintain continuous contact with the seller to inform him or her of the market activity, different sales in the area, the prices of those sale, and whether you would suggest doing anything different regarding the property. This could include lowering the price, increasing the price, hosting another open house, or taking other actions which might generate new interest in the property. It is also important for you to visit the property occasionally, in addition to being in contact with the seller via phone, email or mail.

At the 30-day interval, if the property is not sold yet, put together a summary of all the activity that has happened in the past 30 days. This summary should be delivered to the seller in the form of a letter, but the letter should come from the sales manager, managing broker or another person in a management position within the firm. It looks official, and as though the entire firm has taken an interest in the seller, the property and its status. List the efforts you have taken to sell the property. If you feel it is necessary at this time, also suggest some changes to the listing, or to the property itself, that might make the property more attractive to a buyer. This might include lowering the asking price, changing the terms of the listing (such as financing requirements), or extending the listing if the listing is a short-term listing. It could also include making small improvements to the property such as painting a room, doing some small-scale landscaping such as planting a flower garden in an empty spot in the yard, or similar projects such. After sending the letter, it is important for the agent to follow up with the homeowner to make sure he or she understands the recommendations and see if there is follow-through. If the property is not yet sold in 60 days, another letter should be sent. This is not to say that there will not be any other contact between the agent and client within this period; it is just a formality to keep the lines of communication open.

Remember

Steps in servicing the listing:

- Obtain the listing, agree upon the agency relationship, and sign all contracts.
- Provide the MLS with the listing.
- Place a lockbox on the property.
- With permission, place a "For Sale" sign on the property.
- Information sheets
- Inspections
- Preliminary title report
- Information on the existing note, and other necessary financial information regarding the property including new financing
- "Thank you" note to the seller
- Open house
- Ask neighbors for leads
- 30-day letter and status
- 60-day letter and status

S U M M A R Y

It is important to fully understand the entire process involved with listing agreements: obtaining them, understanding the different types of agreement and how to accurately write one, determining valuation, and servicing the listing. Clients expect professionalism and accuracy, and don't like mistakes.

We learned in this chapter what agency means, and what the different types of listing agreement are that you can enter into with a client. These include exclusive and non-exclusive agreements, and even an agency agreement between a broker and buyer where the broker is strictly the buyer's agent. In these different types of agency agreements, we saw that there are many different arrangements a broker can make with a client, from agreements where commission is assured regardless of who sells the property, to open listings where many brokers list the same property and look for buyers.

After learning about the different types of listing agreements, we then walked through how to fill out a listing step by step. It is imperative that you understand how to fill out these contracts accurately, as this is usually the first major task you will perform for your client. This form also outlines the commission you will receive upon finding a ready, willing and able buyer, so that the commission amount will be discussed at the time the form is being filled out and fully disclosed to the client.

In the state of California, agents are permitted to give their estimation of value for a property. The most widely used method among agents is the competitive market analysis. This is produced when an agent researches what other, similar homes have sold for within the same community or neighborhood. Sales for these homes are analyzed as far back as 6 months, and prices for current listings are also considered. This is the easiest way for agents to make a valuation. The cost approach, based on replacement costs, and the income approach for income properties, where current value is based on future benefits, are also used. However, these approaches are not used as often as the competitive market analysis. Additionally, the income approach for valuation is only used for income property, or those properties that will not serve as primary residences for the owner. Competitive market analysis is only used in estimating value for residences containing 1-4 units.

We ended the chapter by examining how to service a listing and what the different tasks are that you will need to do for your client. The most important idea to take away from this section is that you must have open and frequent communication with your client. Communicating everything about the process and progress will keep the client aware of what is going on and will keep you on task.

T E R M S   A N D   P H R A S E S

Adjustment – Making necessary changes to the asking price compared to similar houses recently sold in the area. One property may have more amenities, such as one more bathroom or other features justifying a higher asking price; in that event, the asking price for the subject property must be changed accordingly.

Agency – The relationship between the broker and client regarding a property listing. The agency agreement is a binding contract linking both parties for the duration of the listing agreement.

Binding Contract – A legal document stating that if one party violates the terms of the agreement, that party may be held liable for damages.

Capitalization Rate – The number, rate or percentage into which the net income is divided to find the present worth of future benefits.

Certified Appraisal – An appraisal of real property done by a certified, licensed appraiser.

Commission – An agent's compensation for performing the duties of his or her agency; in real estate practice, a percentage of the selling price of property or percentage of rental income.

Competitive Market Analysis – Obtaining and analyzing the sales prices of other similar properties in the same area as the property you are currently representing. Competitive market analysis may compare properties that have been sold up to 6months prior, as well as current listings.

Consideration – Anything of value given to induce entering into a contract; it may be money, personal services, or anything else having value.

Cost Approach – One of three methods used in the appraisal process. An analysis in which a value estimate of a property is derived by estimating the replacement cost of the improvements, deducting them from the estimated accrued depreciation, and then adding the market value of the land.

Depreciation – Loss of value in real property brought about by age, physical deterioration or functional or economic obsolescence. Broadly, a loss in value from any cause.

Employment Contract – A contract between the employer (client) and employee (broker) binding the two parties to one specific function, the sale of real property.

Exclusive-Agency Listing – A written instrument giving one agent the right to sell property for a specified time but reserving the right of the owner to sell the property himself or herself without the payment of commission.

Exclusive Authorization to Acquire Real Property Listing – The contract between a broker and buyer to find property that meets the buyer's specifications. The buyer will then pay the broker a commission for services rendered. With this type of listing, the broker is the agent of the buyer, not the seller.

Exclusive-Authorization-and-Right-to-Sell Listing – A written agreement between owner and agent giving the agent the right to collect a commission if the property is sold by anyone during the term of the agreement.

Exclusive Listing – A listing giving the broker the exclusive rights to sell the property and receive a commission for his or her time. No other brokers may have an agency agreement with the seller during the term of the agreement.

Income Approach – One of three methods used in the appraisal process. An analysis in which the estimated net income from the subject residence is used as a basis for estimating value. The estimated net income is divided by a capitalization rate.

Information Sheets – Fliers to be handed out at open houses or in the broker's firm or delivered to other firms regarding the specifics on a property: i.e., number of bedrooms, baths, type of utilities, lot size, amenities, local schools and other information regarding a listing.

Listing Agreement – An employment contract between principal and agent authorizing the agent to perform services for the principal involving the latter's property; listing contracts are entered into for the purpose of securing persons to buy, lease or rent property. Employment of an agent by a prospective purchaser or lessee to locate property for purchase or lease may be considered a listing.

Lockbox –A secured box or storage device housing a key, allowing cooperating brokers access to the property for showings when the listing agent is not available.

Multiple Listing Service – A listing, usually an exclusive right to sell, taken by a member of an organization composed of real estate brokers, with the provision that all members will have the opportunity to find an interested client; a cooperative listing.

Non-Exclusive Listing – A listing agreement wherein other brokers may enter into an agency agreement with the seller. The broker or broker's agent actually making the sale will earn the commission, while all other brokers will not receive any compensation.

Valuation – Estimated worth or price. The act of valuing by appraisal.

C H A P T E R   Q U I Z

1. Agency is:
   a. The office where your real estate broker works.
   b. The relationship between you and your real estate agent.
   c. The authority to act on another's behalf for a specific period of time.
   d. The relationship between the buyer and seller.

2. The listing agreement is:
   a. A binding contract
   b. An employment contract between the broker and seller
   c. A contract between the buyer and broker
   d. All of the above

3. Which of the following is not an element in a valid listing agreement?
   a. Consideration
   b. Competent parties
   c. Written contracts
   d. Due diligence

4. An agency agreement wherein the broker is the only agent who will list the property is defined as:
   a. Open listing
   b. Nonexclusive
   c. Exclusive
   d. Net listing

5. What is the most common type of listing agreement a broker will enter into?
   a. Exclusive-authorization-and-right-to-sell
   b. Net
   c. Open
   d. Exclusive-agency

6. A listing where the broker is the only agent representing the property, but will only get paid if he, and not the property owner, sells the house is called:
   a. Net
   b. Exclusive-agency
   c. Exclusive-authorization-and-right-to-sell
   d. Option

7. After a listing agreement has expired, is the broker entitled to any commission from the sale of the property?
- a. If the broker provides the seller with the name of a prospective and eventual buyer within 3 days of the listing agreement's expiration.
- b. If the broker can produce evidence that he or she originally showed the property to the buyer during the life of the listing agreement, with the offer coming to the seller after the agreement's expiration.
- c. No, after the listing agreement has expired, the broker is not entitled to any commission.
- d. Both A and B

8. How long do exclusive-authorization-and-right-to-sell listings generally last?
- a. 1-3 months
- b. 3-6 months
- c. 6-9 months
- d. 9 months – 1 year

9. Conducting a competitive market analysis is appropriate for which type of property?
- a. Residential with 1-4 units
- b. Residential with more than 4 units
- c. Industrial
- d. Commercial

10. What is the furthest back in time that an agent will typically research when doing a competitive market analysis?
- a. 1 month
- b. 3 months
- c. 6 months
- d. 1 year

11. The most useful information used in a competitive market analysis comes from which of the following reports?
- a. On-market-now
- b. Reported-sold-prior-six-months
- c. Reported-expired-prior-six-moths
- d. Professional appraisal

12. Which one of the following is not a method used by agents to find the value of property?
- a. Income capitalization
- b. Competitive market analysis
- c. Cost
- d. Original listing

13. When servicing the listing, an agent will rely on his or her office for what type of support?
- a. 30-day letter
- b. Property inspections
- c. Open houses
- d. Soliciting neighbors for leads

14. After an open house, an agent should take what steps?
- a. Compile all names and contact information gathered into a database to call at a later time.

b. Compile a list of any suggestions or feedback regarding the property that you received during the open house.
c. Both A and B
d. Neither A nor B

15. In an agent's relationship with a third party, the agent is responsible for which of the following actions?
    a. Full disclosure
    b. Fair dealing
    c. Good faith
    d. All of the above

16. In an non-exclusive listing arrangement the broker:
    a. Gets a commission no matter who sells the property
    b. The homeowner is not allowed to sell the property, only the broker or an agent of the broker
    c. The listings are only valid for 30 days
    d. The homeowner may employ several different brokers to sell the property

17. An agent or broker may make which of the following suggestions to a homeowner in order to sell a property that has been on the market for a long time?
    a. Lower the asking price
    b. Make some cosmetic improvements to the inside of the house such as paint ing, or replace the carpet
    c. Do some simple landscaping to improve "curb appeal"
    d. All of the above

18. The method of valuation most commonly used by agents when making an estimation of value is:
    a. Cost approach
    b. Competitive market analysis
    c. Income approach
    d. Certified appraisal

19. The most important thing an agent can do for a client while servicing a listing is:
    a. Ask the neighbors for leads
    b. Put a "For Sale" sign in the front yard
    c. Have clear communication regarding the process and progress
    d. Create good information sheets for distribution.

20. Capitalization rate, net income and operating expenses are most likely factored into what form of valuation?
    a. Cost approach
    b. Competitive market analysis
    c. Income approach
    d. Certified appraisal

THE BUYER

What you will learn in this Chapter

- Setting the Appointment

- The First Meeting

- Showing the Property

- Retaining Potential Buyers as Clients

- Answering and Overcoming Objections

- Obtaining the Offer

Test Your Knowledge

1. Floor time refers to:
   a. The time an agent spends conducting an open house.
   b. The time an agent spends during a transaction filling out paperwork and making sure all documents have been delivered to the appropriate parties.
   c. The time an agent spends in the office answering incoming phone calls.
   d. None of the above.

2. An offer made by a buyer to a seller may be:
   a. Accepted
   b. Rejected
   c. Returned with a counteroffer
   d. Any of the above

3. Which of the following is a good tactic to use when showing homes?
   a. Explain to the buyer what each room could be used for, allowing him or her to visualize utilizing the living space.
   b. Highlight benefits of certain features which may be of specific interest to the buyer.
   c. Simply tell the buyer the specifics regarding the house, with a quick tour to keep the process moving forward, allowing the buyer to see as many properties as possible.
   d. Both A and B.

4. When showing a "call first" property, when is it appropriate to show the home without calling first?
   a. Never
   b. On weekends
   c. After the home has been on the market for at least 30 days
   d. If the listing is one of your own

5. If an agent knows of a problem or an issue with a home, he or she should:
   a. Ignore the issue; it might prevent the buyers from making an offer.
   b. Privately inform the sellers there is an issue, and make sure they take care of it.
   c. Not show that aspect of the home.
   d. Inform the buyers of the issue immediately and have a dialogue regarding what they think about the issue and how to overcome it.

6. An agent should see a buyer's objection as:
   a. An opportunity to show the buyer other properties that may be more suited to his or her needs
   b. An opportunity to answer more questions or expose more of the home's selling points
   c. Hesitation and uncertainty, suggesting to the agent they seek different representation
   d. Hesitation and uncertainty, suggesting to the agent they are not ready to make a purchase of this magnitude at this time.

7. Which of the following is not an approach an agent can use to get the buyer to make an offer?
   a. Minor Point Approach
   b. Negative Yes Approach
   c. Deal Breaker Approach
   d. Scratch Pad Approach

This chapter will walk you through the process of setting up appointments with buyers to look at properties you have for sale, all the way to taking an offer and a deposit on the property.

The first appointment is generally initiated from some form of advertisement you have placed regarding available properties. People will contact you after seeing an advertisement for a property that they are potentially interested in seeing. From there, you need to aggressively take control of the process of meeting with the buyers and setting up appointments to see properties, gain their trust and keep them as your own clients (provided they are not working with another broker), and help answer any objections they may have regarding the buying process.

This may seem like a very easy process from start to finish, with the potential buyer initiating the first meeting, but as you will learn there are many factors that go into obtaining and keeping a buyer. You will learn how to approach interested parties based on their response from an advertisement or a "For Sale" sign. You will learn how to convert an inquiry into a meeting, rather than having just a quick fleeting phone conversation where you give out the address of a property you may have. You will learn how to retain clients after the initial contact, whether the initial contact is a phone call, face-to-face meeting, chance meeting at an open house or other form of contact. It is important for you to understand how to do this: you don't want to connect with a potential buyer and tell them about properties they are very interested in and then have them go to another agent for the transaction. One way to retain clients is to be very informative and helpful in the initial meeting. Having a detailed knowledge of your properties and a good grasp of all steps in the property transfer process will allow you to gain the trust and confidence of potential buyers.

Being able to service your buyers is also very important. After your initial meeting, you will know more about their needs and what type of home would best fit those needs. You will want to take all the information you gather regarding the buyer, and find homes that will fit the buyer's needs and qualifications. You would not want to show a 5 bedroom, $1,100,000 property to a buyer who can only qualify for a $700,000 property. This only wastes your time and theirs, perhaps causing them to seek out different representation.

We will discuss some of the objections a buyer may have, and how you can discuss these objections with the client and move through them to an appropriate solution. Sometimes the objections a client might have are based on first-time home buying jitters, or the fact that they are upgrading from a smaller payment to a larger one, even if they can afford it. Finally, we will look at how to obtain an offer and deposit on a property.

S E T T I N G   T H E   A P P O I N T M E N T

Most inquires you will receive regarding property will be from your advertising. Remember that advertising comes in several forms, and is carried in different media vehicles. These inquiry calls may be in response to a full-page color ad you are running that highlights several properties, or from a window poster showing just one property. They could be calls from people who saw your personal advertising in the phone book, or calls regarding a property for sale from someone who saw your number on the "For Sale" sign. These inquiries will usually be in the form of a phone call. On occasion, you may receive an email from a person who visited your website, or a walk-in client to your office, but by and large most of the initial inquires will be phone calls. This gives you a great opportunity to set up an appointment with the caller to meet face-to-face and to discuss his or her needs. At the very least, if the caller is reluctant to set up an appointment with you, it is still important to obtain the caller's name and number so that you can contact him or her with more information regarding the property.

As an agent, you will be performing multiple tasks during the day, with time spent in the office just as important as time spent meeting with clients, showing homes or doing other out of the office work. While in the office, you have the opportunity to have floor time. Floor time is time during which incoming calls to the firm can be transferred to your line. These calls are generally from potential buyers responding to an advertisement. These buyers usually don't have representation yet, and this is most likely the first contact they have made with any broker or agent. This is a great opportunity for you to establish a rapport with the potential buyer, who may be a potential client! Since advertising is expensive, any time there is a response to any form of advertising, it is important that you are able to schedule a meeting with the potential buyer to further discuss his or her needs. Advertising is considered successful when these calls come into the office, and now it is up to you not to let a good sales opportunity slip away.

Remember
- **Floor time** is the time you spend in the office when incoming calls can be transferred to your line. These incoming calls are from people responding to one of the firm's advertisements.

It is important for you to have a current list of available properties – both your own listings and the other listings in the firm. When you take calls during floor time, you can utilize these lists as backup or **switch property** in the event the caller finds out something about the advertised property they don't like. Switch property is a property within 20% of the asking price of an advertised property.

Let's say that you are putting in floor time, and are receiving incoming calls from potential clients. You receive a call from a couple that is interested in a home your firm has advertised. The couple has two small children, with another on the way. They need to buy a larger home to accommodate their growing family. The advertised property looks good to them, as it has 5 bedrooms, with plenty of square footage for the growing household. You begin discussing the property with the callers, and upon finding out it has a pool, they decide it is not for them. They are afraid that a pool presents too much of a risk for small children. You quickly refer to your current listings on your desk, and find several switch properties, none of which have pools, which may work for the couple. You tell them you have several properties within the same price range, in the neighborhood where they are looking, and they agree to meet with you. Situations such as this are why having a copy of the most current listings is so important. You may have lost the opportunity to set up a meeting with the couple if you had not been able to tell them you had other, similar homes, with the one important difference of having no pool.

Remember
- Switch property is property within 20% of the asking price of the advertised property about which a caller is inquiring.

Often people will respond to an advertisement or "For Sale" sign without knowing what the price of the property is. Or they might respond knowing it is out of their price range, but they do not indicate to you what their budget is. It is important for you to inquire about a buyer's budget before getting too far into the process. It saves your time and theirs. Knowing a budget also gives you the opportunity to find a switch property that is similar in design and located in the same neighborhood, but priced less, making it feasible for the caller. Approach the subject delicately, however; you won't want to offend the caller, or assume he or she cannot afford the property. Simply let the caller know you have a few questions to ask regarding his or her budget and the type of property he or she is looking for. Or, if the caller has already told you the type of property he or she is looking for, ask what the budget is for this purchase. Asking direct, straightforward questions will avoid misunderstandings and save time for both parties.

It is important for you to recognize the amount of information you can gather just by knowing what prompted the call. If the caller is calling in regard to an advertisement, you know that the caller likes the general dimensions the home has to offer, such as the number of bedrooms or bathrooms or the square footage. You can use this information when finding switch property. When a caller is referring to a "For Sale" sign, you know he or she likes the neighborhood and the general style of the home. If a caller is calling regarding a Spanish style home, you would not want to use a ranch or colonial home as switch properties. Additionally, it is important for you to keep a map of the city, community or neighborhood that you service. Have all your listings marked on the map so that you know exactly which area the caller is referring to, and you can see which listings are in the area that you might be able to use as switch properties. If the home they liked the look of will not work, hopefully there is a similar home in the same neighborhood that might fulfill the client's needs.

Remember
When finding switch properties, it is a good idea to have the following resources in your office, available at a glance:
- A current copy of your listings as well as the firm's listings
- A map of the area you service, with addresses marked for each available listing represented by you and your firm.

Besides receiving calls regarding properties in advertisements and properties with "For Sale" signs, you will potentially receive calls from people responding to an Internet site. This site could be your personal site or the firm's site. The caller may have been attracted to one or more properties, researched their locations, liked the general style, equipment and amenities, and may want to know more or even set up an appointment. These calls are the easiest calls from which to get an appointment or meeting. The caller knows more about the property from its Internet description than a caller who has only seen an advertisement or a "For Sale" sign would know. While all three are certainly viable and valuable leads, a phone call prompted by an Internet site might be the easiest for you to convert into a meeting, and ultimately a sale. Additionally, your Internet site will be able to reach far more people than your local advertisements or "For Sale" signs can. People in other cities, states or countries relocating to your region have the opportunity to view your site and conduct research, while the other forms of prospecting may not be seen by them. Again, Internet inquires almost always end in an appointment being set, because of the amount of information the caller already knows about the property. Additionally, the appointment is usually set for that specific property rather than a switch property; however, it never hurts to have a backup plan.

The following is a list of important steps or helpful hints when taking calls from potential buyers:

- Seek out more information than you offer. You don't want to give out all the information regarding a property and receive nothing about the buyer in return. The buyer may simply be interested in knowing the price, and upon finding out the price of the property, they might seek out representation from another broker and work toward making an offer on your property. Getting information from the caller also will help in finding switch properties that might suit the caller's needs better than the home he or she is calling about. A good rule of thumb is to offer only a few more details than what was given in the ad. This will increase your chances of setting up an appointment with the caller.

- Get the caller's name and contact information. In the event that you don't have all the necessary information in front of you regarding the property in question, or other similar properties, you can do some quick research and call the person back with the information.

- Answer a question with a question. This will aid you in learning more about the client's needs. If the caller asks if the home has a pool, ask if a pool is a deal breaker, or just a nice amenity to have.

- Find out the type of properties the buyer is interested in, and his or her reasons for buying a property.

- Keep the call short. It is better to meet face-to face to find out more about the client and his or her needs than to have lengthy phone conversations.

- End the conversation with the appointment. Ask the caller what the best time and place to meet might be. If you ask if the person wants to meet with you, you might get a "No"; if you ask when and where to meet, the caller will most likely set up an appointment.

- When setting up the appointment, include a mention of switch properties; this will entice the caller to show up for the appointment, knowing that if the target home does not satisfy his or her buying objectives, perhaps another one will.

- Set up the meeting with the potential client. This can either be at your office or you at the caller's current place of residence. It is better for the clients to come to your office, as you can more easily show them other available homes, or even do a search of the MLS with their criteria, producing all options in the desired area.

Some questions you might ask a caller responding to an ad, "For Sale" sign or Internet site would be:

- Do you currently own your own house?

- Do you plan on selling your house?

- Where is your current home located?

- When do you need your new home?

- How large is your family?

- (besides the area they are calling about) What other areas are you interested in?

- What is your price range or budget for a new home?

For callers responding directly to an advertisement, after asking them the appropriate questions, you would then want to offer a few meeting times for the same day or the next day. This does not give them the choice of whether they want to meet or not, but when they will meet you and where. If you have set your appointment up for the following day, make sure to call the prospective clients in the morning to remind them of your meeting, and tell them of a few similar properties in the area that they might also be interested in seeing. This will get them excited not only to see the property they are already interested in, but others that they have not seen yet. Additionally, offering switch properties will give them more incentive to show up to the appointment. DO NOT offer to show switch properties if you don't actually have anything in the area just to entice them to the meeting. This is not ethical, and your client will certainly see through the lie.

Make sure the prospective buyers know where they will be meeting you. Are you going to meet at your office, or will you go to them? It is always more desirable to meet at your office, as you have the resources there to show them more switch properties, or different properties altogether. You can immediately search the MLS for properties in the areas where they want to live. When meeting with a prospective client at his or her home, make sure you bring plenty of materials regarding the home in question, and also regarding switch properties in the same neighborhood.

The sample questions listed are a good way to direct the initial phone conversation with a prospective client. You can see from the questions that you will be getting information on the client, his or her needs, and his or her specific wants. You will not be offering much information regarding the subject property that they don't already know, but you will be taking an interest in them, which they will readily recognize. It is important to keep the initial phone conversation short, and always end with an appointment. Make sure this appointment is clear, and that each party knows when and where the appointment will take place.

Engage the client, or empower him or her to help you. If a caller is calling you regarding an advertisement, chances are that the caller has done the same with other ads. In order for you to stop the caller from proceeding with other phone calls after yours, empower him or her to help you. Ask the caller to circle or highlight all the properties he or she is interested in, and tell the caller that you will be able to research those properties and provide more information on them at your meting. This will give the caller further incentive to set up a meeting with you, and keep him or her off the phone initiating contact with other agents.

Reluctant Callers
Sometimes callers are not interested in giving out any information on the telephone, and simply want to know the address of the property. It is important for you not to push, but do offer your time to show the property. Let the caller know of any newly posted listings in the area that he or she might also be interested in learning about or even seeing, and let the caller know you would be available to show these properties at his or her leisure. Be sincere, never pushy or fake. If the caller feels you are truly trying to help, he or she will be more likely to make an appointment to meet with you.

If the caller will not give out his or her name, you can obtain it by asking for other information, ultimately leading to a name. The caller will feel more comfortable giving you a name once he or she discovers that you are trying to help or provide a service, rather than just collecting names to call later. For example, you can offer to put together a packet of information on the home, and send it to the caller via mail. You will be doing a service, and by offering to mail it to the caller, you will have to have his or her name and address. Another way to get a name is to offer to do a little additional research on the advertised home, and other like properties in the area, and call the person back. When you offer to gain more information on the specific house, and then call back with the information the caller was looking for, he or she is more likely to offer a name and number for the callback.

An alternative approach to obtaining information from callers would be to use the Internet. Many people have access to the Internet, and use it when conducting searches for everything from buying new cars, to finding reviews of restaurants or movies, to searching available properties. Use this to your advantage. If a hesitant caller calls regarding a property and does not want to give out a name or phone number or any contact information, offer to email pictures, information or other details on the property. Some people prefer to use email because it is convenient; others prefer it because it is more anonymous.

If the caller is firm about not setting up an appointment at this time, and all he or she wants to do is view the property, get a name and phone number and then give the caller the property's address. This allows the caller to do a drive by and see from curbside what the property looks like. Call back in a day or so, and see what he or she thought. Again, ask if he or she would like to set up an appointment and see the inside of the home. Viewing the outside may have made the caller more interested in the property, or may have turned him or her off completely. If the caller is turned off, offer to show other, similarly priced properties.

There are many ways to get a potential client's contact information or even to get an appointment. The most important thing to remember is to be sincere. If you are sincerely trying to help the person, he or she will sense that and allow you to help. Be persistent, but not pushy. Follow up with inquiries through email, phone calls or mail, and always do what you have promised. Remember that happy clients tend to refer business back to you, while unhappy clients tend to share their bad experiences with friends, family and co-workers who might be in the market for a new home.

Remember

Tips on how to gain information on a reluctant caller:
- Offer to put together an information packet on the desired property and mail it out
- Offer to research the property more thoroughly and call back with details
- Give the caller the address of the property, and offer a callback to get his or her impressions and/or offer a showing of the property
- Offer to email information directly to the caller regarding the property

An alternate source of information on each caller can be found at www.callsource.com. This service will not only give the names of people you gather off your caller ID, but also financial information, family data and current residence. This is a good way to research missed calls found on your caller ID system, or research the reluctant callers who might not want to supply you with any personal information. It is important to use this information wisely, and only as the potential client is comfortable in revealing his or her identity.

Your first meeting with a potential client gives you the chance to make a good impression upon him or her. If you come across as genuine, sincere and capable of helping your client find the perfect property, he or she will gain confidence in your abilities. Initially, you can do little things to help build the client's confidence level in you. Remembering your potential client's name is very important. Use whatever methods work best for you, but make sure to use and remember his or her name. Another small thing you can do it so make sure you are pronouncing the name correctly. If it is a difficult name to pronounce, ask the potential client how to correctly pronounce it, and make sure you are saying it correctly. These simple, seemingly insignificant steps will make quite a difference in the long run.

When potential clients come to visit you for the first time, you will want to begin with the qualifying process. Most offices have a qualifying room, where a client can relax while an in-house mortgage specialist determines what the potential client can afford. This process should take about an hour, leaving you, the agent, plenty of time to explain to the buyer the different steps you will be taking in the process of finding the perfect property for his or her needs.

During this first meeting, if the client is a first-time home buyer, you will want to explain the steps in the process so that he or she understands them. The steps to explain are as follows:

Listing Agreement
The owner will list the property, for which you will either be the listing agent, or have access to view properties listed for sale on the MLS, which is how you will search properties for the buyer.

Marketing
The agent will advertise the property, which is perhaps what brought the potential buyer into your office.

Deposit Receipt
When an offer is made, the purchase contract is commonly referred to as the deposit receipt.

Acceptance
Acceptance is when the seller reviews the buyer's offer and decides to agree to the terms and the offer that has been extended. The seller has the opportunity to offer the buyer a counter-offer at this time.

Escrow
Once the seller and buyer agree upon all terms of the purchase contract, escrow is opened. Escrow is when the deposit has been received and placed in a trust account, inspections are made and all necessary funds have been deposited and disbursed.

Financing
When escrow is opened, the loan qualification of the buyer takes place. Once all documents are processed, the money for the property is deposited into escrow.

Title Search
When escrow is opened, the title is searched to make sure it is clear and capable of being transferred to another party. Any liens, encumbrances or other clouds on the title must be cleared if the property is to be transferred to another party.

Ancillary Activities

Inspections, repairs, improvements, insurance policies and other activities such as this must be done during escrow to collect all necessary documentation to prepare for the closing of escrow.

Final Settlement

When escrow is ready to be closed, all prorations are made regarding insurance, taxes or other prepaid monies. Funds are disbursed to all appropriate parties and all final instruments are recorded, such as the grant deed.

> **Remember**
> The steps you need to make sure the buyer understands about the buying process are as follows:
> - Listing agreement
> - Marketing
> - Deposit receipt
> - Acceptance
> - Escrow
> - Financing
> - Title Search
> - Ancillary Activities
> - Final Settlement

Often, clients will choose a property or be interested in properties that are out of their budget. The qualifying process will help an agent understand any limitations or parameters that must be worked around. Once a prospective client has been qualified for a specific amount, you can move forward in the meeting and work toward finding the right property to fit the client's needs and budget.

During the qualifying session, it is important for you to discuss the needs of your potential client so you know how best to proceed in finding the right property. If the client is responding to an advertisement, find out what about the advertised home caught his or her eye, what features are absolutely required, and which features would be nice to have, but are not deal breakers. By knowing what the client's requirements are, you will know what type of properties to search in the event that the desired property will not work for some reason.

The buyer qualifying process is a three-step process:

- What are the potential client's needs and interests? What is required in the client's search for a new home, and what is simply desired?

- What is the buyer's financial status? How much money will he or she be qualified to borrow? What is the buyer's budget in respect to a monthly payment? How much money does he or she have saved up for a down payment? What type of financing can the buyer qualify for? Is he or she qualified for any special programs that could increase the amount available to spend?

Prospective Buyer Confidential Information Sheet

Name(s) _____

Phone number_____ Fax number_____

e-mail_____

Address_____

Size of Family_____

Names and Ages of all dependents living with you_____

Initial contact made to the firm was prompted by (Advertisement, "For Sale" sign, Internet,

referral, other) _____

Present address_____

How long at the current address?_____ Do you presently own your home?_____

If yes, must you sell it before you buy another home?_____

Is your home listed for sale? _____ With what agency?_____

How long has your house been on the market?_____

Your reason for buying a new home?_____

What features are you looking in your new home? _____

_____

What features do you absolutely do not want?_____

_____

Why?_____

Please list any hobbies or special interests_____

_____

_____

Have you qualified or been turned down for a home loan within the past year?_____

If you qualified for a loan, what was the name of the firm, and the loan amount?_____

_____

- What is the buyer's reason for buying a new home? Is this a first-time home buyer? Is this an upgrade to a larger home for a growing family? Is the buyer relocating from another city or town?

By asking a lot of questions, you will show the potential buyer that you are interested in him or her and his or her needs, and, ultimately, finding the perfect property. This will help gain the person's confidence and trust, moving closer to an agency relationship and converting the potential buyer into a client.

A qualification form is a helpful tool that many agents will use so that no information regarding the potential buyer is forgotten or lost. It also serves as a good reminder to the agent about what information they should gather from the potential client. The form tells you the needs of the buyers -- why they are buying a home. By no means is this process over after the form is filled out; the qualifying process is an ongoing process that continues right up until an offer has been extended. After showing homes and receiving feedback, you can tailor the form as you understand more of the buyer's likes, dislikes and style. The buyer may change his or her mind through the process after seeing different styles, and decide that he or she would like a completely different house than originally thought. Needs, wants, reactions, and types of properties should all be recorded and updated as new properties are shown. The following is an example of what one of these forms might look like.

Qualifying Financially

The more you know regarding loan types, programs and qualifications, the better you can serve your potential clients. A person who may not have been eligible for a traditional loan may be eligible for a FHA or VA loan. It is your job to know the requirements of special programs, who is eligible, and the logistical concerns a buyer may have such as down payment requirements, penalties or other concerns.

A buyer's housing-cost-to-income ratio is referred to by lenders as the front-end qualification. Gross income is used when figuring front-end qualification and the qualification is usually set at 28%. This means that the buyer's housing costs cannot exceed 28% of his or her total gross income. A simple equation to figure this ratio is:

Total monthly housing payment / Total gross monthly income =/< 28%

A lender will also look at a person's long-term debt when considering him or her for a loan. This consideration is called back-end qualification. A good ratio estimation is generally 36%. This means that a person's ratio of long-term debt to gross income cannot exceed 36%. Debt that is considered long-term debt consists of things such as a car note, credit car bills, or other long term notes such as another mortgage. A simple equation to figure this ratio is:

Total long-term debt / Total gross monthly income =/< 36%

The following charts show the maximum monthly amount a buyer could spend on a home, or the maximum monthly amount he or she can owe in long-term debt, to achieve the 28% and 36% numbers respectively. More regarding qualifying ratios and charts will be covered in the finance chapter.

Total Gross Annual Income ($)	Maximum Monthly Mortgage Payment ($)
20,000	467
30,000	700
40,000	933
50,000	1,167
60,000	1,400
70,000	1,633
80,000	1,867
90,000	2,100
100,000	2,333
130,000	3,033
150,000	3,500
200,000	4,667

Total Gross Annual Income ($)	Maximum Monthly Credit Debt ($)
20,000	600
30,000	700
40,000	1,200
50,000	1,500
60,000	1,800
70,000	2,100
80,000	2,400
90,000	2,700
100,000	3,000
130,000	3,900
150,000	4,600
200,000	6,000

A self-employed individual will usually have to produce two years of income tax returns in the qualification process. Because this individual is self-employed, stated income, or the person's own account of how much money he or she earns annually, will have to be cross-checked with his or her income tax statements so that the bank can finance a loan. A self-employed buyer must be very careful when declaring income, making sure it matches the income tax returns. It is usually more difficult for a self-employed person to secure a loan. In order to avoid difficulties in securing a loan, a self-employed person might consider looking for properties that are seller-financed, or being willing to pay a higher interest rate to secure the loan.

Additionally, during the financial qualifying process, you need to discuss the down payment with the buyer. Down payments will vary depending on the type of financing, the type of loan and any special programs the buyer may qualify for. Buyers choosing to pay for prime mortgage insurance will have a reduced down payment. There are some programs where a buyer can receive 100% financing with no down payment. It is wise to have the buyer discuss their needs with a mortgage professional.

Prequalifying
It is a good idea to prequalify all buyers before spending time showing them properties. A prequalification will help determine what your client's budget will be. If you fail to do this, you risk wasting your time and the buyer's time and entering into a purchase contract that cannot be executed.

Lender Prequalification Form

HERITAGE FINANCIAL SERVICES

LOAN PROSPECT WORKSHEET

Borrower: _____ Date: _____

Co-Borrower: _____ Loan Consultant: _____

Mailing Address: _____ Telephone #: _____

_____ Telephone #: _____

Originating Source: ( ) Phone ( ) RE Agent _____ ( ) Other _____

PROPERTY INFORMATION

Property Address: _____ Owner Occupied ( )

Non Owner Occupied ( )

Property Type: ( ) Single Family Residence ( ) 2-4 Units (# of Units _____)

( ) PUD ( ) Condo # of Units in Project _____ Year Built _____

# of Units Owner Occupied _____ Conversion Y or N

PURCHASE	REFINANCE
Sales Price: $_____	Estimated Value: $_____
Loan Amount: $_____	Loan Amount: $_____
Secondary Financing: $_____	Loan to Value: _____ %
Down Payment: $_____	Existing Liens: $_____ (1)
Source of Down Payment: _____	$_____ (2)
	$_____ (3)
Loan to Value: _____ % Combined LTV %: _____ %	Date Purchased: _____
Realtor: _____	Purpose of Refinance: _____
Firm: _____	_____
Telephone #: _____	_____

QUALIFYING INFORMATION

MONTHLY INCOME

	BORROWER	CO-BORROWER
Base:	$_____	$_____
Overtime:	_____	_____
Commission:	_____	_____
Bonus:	_____	_____
Other:	_____	_____
Other:	_____	_____
TOTAL:	$_____	
TOTAL COMBINED:	(A) $_____	

RATIOS

B÷A=Housing Ratio _____

B+C÷A=Debt Ratio _____

PROPOSED MONTHLY HOUSING DEBT

Payment (P & I):	$_____
Est. Property Taxes:	_____
Est. Property Insur.:	_____
Homeowners Dues:	_____
Mo. PMI:	_____
Other:	_____
TOTAL:	(B) _____

MONTHLY OBLIGATIONS

Revolving Debts:	$_____
Installment Debts:	_____
Auto Payment:	_____
Other:	_____
Other:	_____
TOTAL:	(C) $_____

LOAN PROGRAM QUOTED

Program: _____ Term: _____ Fees: _____ % + $_____

Initial Rate: _____ % Pay Rate: _____ % Spread: _____ % Cap: _____ %

Notes: _____

_____

_____

Mentally, prequalifying changes the buyer's mindset from "just looking" to "buying." Before a buyer is prequalified, he or she is simply house hunting, or looking to see what is on the market. Once the buyer is prequalified, the process is now mentally shifted into a purchase process. Additionally if you take the time to prequalify a buyer, they are likely to be committed to use you as their agent, and not consult another firm, or agency.

While you and the buyer are waiting for the loan qualification to be returned, you can cover other important aspects of the transaction. Purchase contracts can vary from office to office. While your client is waiting for a loan qualification to be returned, you can give him or her a copy of the purchase contract and let him or her examine it. Make sure the client understands all aspects of the document, and explain any uncertainties he or she may have.

If the buyer finds a home he or she likes, and the buyer is interested in making an offer, usually an **earnest money** deposit is placed. Make sure the buyer understands that this will be held, uncashed, until the buyer accepts the purchase offer. Once the purchase offer is accepted, this money will then be deposited into escrow.

If you have not discussed agency with the buyer, it is important to do so at this time. Before you invest a lot of time helping out the prospective buyer, you should make it clear where both parties stand on an agency agreement. Disclose any obligations you might have, including other agency agreements with the seller. If the buyer is interested in a property your firm does not represent, discuss the exclusive buyer's representation and obtain a buyer's listing.

After you have established an agency agreement with the buyer, and he or she is ready to begin looking at properties, and perhaps even make an offer, make sure to let him or her know what happens after the offer is made. One of three possible scenarios may happen. The sellers may accept the offer as written. If this is the case, escrow will be opened, the earnest money will be deposited into escrow, and the process of collecting all necessary documentation will occur, leading to the closing. The sellers may counteroffer, or negotiate a new offer or terms to the contract. This may include asking for more money, adding or taking away one or more items of personal property that were to be included in the transaction, or any other change to the purchase offer extended to the other party. Finally, the sellers may reject the buyer's offer, returning the earnest money deposit, uncashed.

Remember
After an offer is made by the buyer to the seller it may:
- Be accepted
- Be negotiated with a counteroffer
- Be rejected

Now, after spending some time with the buyer, and asking a significant amount of questions, you are ready to find the right home for your client. Use all the resources you have at your disposal to look for the house that fits the client's requirements in size, style, location and amenities, and then create an information packet for the client showing the different options he or she has. If the client likes some of the places you have selected, then proceed to showing the properties that fit his or her interests best.

Use what you know from your conversations with the buyer, as well as the information sheet the buyer has filled out, to conduct very detailed searches. Upon finding properties that you feel would be a good match, contact the seller, get more information and then set up an appointment that will work for both the buyer and seller. Make sure to find properties that not only match the buyer's needs, but also his or her interests or wants. There is a big difference between what a person needs and what he or she wants or is interested in. For your clients interested in gardening, a home with a lot of yard space or gardens might make the difference between a sale and no sale. The gardens might not be what your client's family needs space-wise, but it plays into their interests, making the property that much more desirable.

Most importantly, listen to your client. Really get to know what he or she is looking for, not only what he or she needs. Don't inject any of your personal ideas or opinions on a property; what you like and what your client likes may be two different things. Where you might see a rundown home, the client might see a great opportunity to fix up an old place to his or her specific wants.

S H O W I N G   T H E   P R O P E R T Y

Showing property is much more than just taking the buyer over to a property for sale and letting him or her walk through the property. Showing property requires you to be knowledgeable about all aspects of the home, especially those that are not readily seen by the eye, such as the type of plumbing, age of the water heater or roof, or other details such as this. It also means you should know neighborhood details such as school boundaries, recreational, entertainment and shopping facilities in the area, public transportation routes, and other items of interest that will help make the home look even more attractive than just explaining the home's features would.

Show your clients properties in their budget. You will be wasting their time by showing properties out of their price range, and perhaps making the affordable houses look less attractive. Additionally, make sure you are showing properties that appeal to the buyer. Don't show a home just because it is your listing, and you want the seller to be impressed with your work. Again, it will be wasting the buyer's time, and ultimately yours.

If a home you wish to show is currently occupied, make sure to call the owner and arrange for a showing. Give the owner plenty of time to tidy up, or to make arrangements to be out for the afternoon or showing period. Perhaps you could select homes to see immediately that are unoccupied, and have lockboxes where you can see the house with minimal or no notice, and plan to show the occupied properties with advance notice.

Remember
- Always make an advance appointment to show a home that is still owner-occupied.
- Vacant houses, with lockboxes, can be shown with little or no notice.

There are a few different approaches to deciding how many houses should be shown in one day. It depends on your client. If you have a local client, showing 3 or 4 homes in one day allows the client to digest what he or she has seen and critique the homes positively or negatively. If the client finds a property he or she likes, he or she will have the opportunity to make an offer; if the client has not found a property that interests him or her, ask for feedback about what the client liked and did not like, then restructure your house hunting accordingly. If you have out-of-town clients visiting for a limited amount of time, you might want to show many properties in one day to allow them to see many properties, and then make a decision regarding the property on which they might want to make an offer. A big factor in deciding how many properties to show will be your client. Make sure to be catering to the client's needs, time constraints and energy level.

Some agents like to strategically show the "best" house first, last or at a very specific time for optimal comparison or appeal to the client. If the "best" house is selected based on the buyer's information sheet and through your interaction with the buyer, this might work out well for you. If the "best" house was selected on your preferences, this tactic might not work, and may even backfire, with your client realizing you are not listening to what he or she is are looking for, and questioning whether you are the best agent for him or her.

When you are showing the properties, the neighborhood has the first opportunity to make an impression. The buyers will see other homes, attractions, recreational or entertainment venues in route to the property. Sell the neighborhood. Point out points of interest that you know your client will go for, based on what you know about him or her. Carefully plan your route, choosing the most scenic, visually desirable path from the entry point of the neighborhood to the property. Does the buyer have young children? You may want to drive past the school so they can see the proximity of the school to the house. Is the buyer a golfer? Is there a public or private course located in or near the new property? Drive past it. You can use this tactic for any other interests the neighborhood may hold for the buyer. By getting the buyer interested in the neighborhood first, and then the home second, they are more likely to want to make an offer.

Create the right mood. If the property you are looking at is owner-occupied, you can have the owner go the extra step by catering to the season. By this I mean having the fireplace going in winter, with a seasonal warm drink such as hot chocolate at the ready. If you are showing the home in the spring, having fresh-cut flowers inside with the windows open creates a nice, fresh, "spring" sort of mood; in the summer, have cool refreshment available, with the home's air conditioning going for maximum comfort.

When arriving at the property, park on the opposite side of the street to give your clients a good visual of the property. Wait a few seconds for them to take it in, and then enter the home. Let the buyer explore the home. Follow the buyer, and ask questions provoking the buyer to think about what could go where, and to begin visualizing living in the property.

Engage the entire party looking at the home. If you are showing a home to a family, ask the young child which bedroom he or she likes best, or if he or she would like to build a tree house in the back yard. With a buyer that you know likes to cook gourmet meals, ask what the first meal is that he or she plans on cooking in his or her new kitchen, and so on and so forth. Make the buyer visualize owning the home, beyond just showing them the property. Ask the buyer or buyers how they would utilize each of the rooms. Don't assume a second bedroom will be a bedroom. Perhaps the buyer visualizes an art studio, exercise room, library or office. Ask them what they see when they walk into a room, or ask them about the placement of furniture in obvious rooms such as the dining room, living room or master bedroom. Again, this helps the buyer to visualize living in the home, versus just looking at property.

Each home will have features which will be easy to highlight. But avoid highlighting the features; rather, sell the benefit of the feature. A large great-room or family room with high ceilings is a feature of a home; the benefit would be having an ideal space to entertain guests, or an ideal room for oversized furniture. A large deck is a feature; the benefit is that it could accommodate a spa or hot tub, or provide a really nice space for a barbeque and outdoor parties. It is important to remember not to generalize a benefit. What one buyer sees as a feature/benefit combination may not be recognized by another buyer. Don't assume, and make sure to always put the buyer's needs, wants and interests first.

Remember
Highlight the benefits of a homes specific features; don't just point out features. When choosing specific features, find the benefit that best suits your client's profile, interests or needs. Don't assume a feature will have a specific benefit to the buyer just because you see it as a benefit, but always tailor your showing to your client's specific profile.

After each showing, get feedback form the buyer. What were his or her likes or dislikes regarding the house? What is the buyer's reaction about the neighborhood and immediate surroundings? Use this feedback when selecting other properties to show the buyer.

When showing property, remember to respect the home and current owners. They may or may not be present, but they are still the owners of the property. If you follow these steps, you will make sure to remain respectful and professional in treating another's house.

- Do not allow anyone in your party to enter the home while smoking, and certainly do not allow smoking in the home at any time during the showing.

- Some homes have restrictions or guidelines regarding showing. Make sure to follow these preset conditions and guidelines, such as acceptable hours when it will be made available.

- If another agent is showing the property upon your arrival, allow the other agent to finish before you proceed with your client.

- If a property is listed as a "call first" property, make sure you call the owner before bringing a buyer to see the property. It is never acceptable to just knock on the door and ask to show the home with your buyer present when there is a "call first" stipulation.

- Always leave the home in the exact condition you found it. This includes the arrangement of furniture, positioning of blinds or drapes, or other factors such as making sure doors are secure and locked when you leave.

- Do not make negative comments about the home while inside. The owner may be within earshot, causing them embarrassment.

- If there is a problem with the home, notify the listing office immediately if the listing is not yours.

- Remember to leave your business card at each home you show, regardless if the owner is home or not.

- When calling another office, always identify yourself and your office affiliation.

Use comparisons between properties. If you are visiting multiple properties in the same day, compare one property's kitchen cabinets to another's, and ask the buyer which ones he or she prefers. This will help you understand more about what the buyer is looking for. Comparisons take buyer's feedback one step further. Rather than just asking if the buyer liked a property, you can have him or her compare two or three properties so you fully understand his or her interests and dislikes.

Real estate agents commonly use **tie-downs** to further engage their client. By using phrases like "isn't it," "can't it," or "don't you," you will encourage feedback from the client. Rather than making a statement which the buyer may not respond to, you make a statement and then ask for feedback. If you know your client likes being outdoors and has an interest in gardening, you can show him or her a yard, and make a tie-down statement such as "This yard is perfect for a flower garden, isn't it?" This will engage your client in not only responding, but also thinking of possibilities of alterations he or she might be interested in making.

Some final showing tips include:

- Begin and end the tour of a home in the most interesting, captivating or nicest room of the house. Make sure this is not to your subjective taste, but to your client's.

- Allow the buyers some privacy to walk around and quietly discuss the house.

- Stand along the walls of smaller rooms, it will give the impression the room is larger than if you are standing in the center.

- Buyers generally follow your lead. Remember this when entering a room; they generally follow where you walk, rather than spreading out on their own. Lead them to the best vantage point to view the space.

- Do not assume that your likes and dislikes of a home will mirror the buyer's likes and dislikes.

- Answer questions the client may have at the property, and overcome any concerns immediately; don't wait for later.

- Use any friends the buyer has brought along as an ally; don't try to undermine their opinions or make comments contrary to theirs.

- Highlight a few very eye-catching features to leave a lasting impression with the buyer.

- Show the rooms in a specific order, leaving the most desired room for last, based on your client's needs and wants.

- Engage kids: let them feel part of the process, or utilize them as helpers when appropriate.

- Use simple language.

RETAINING POTENTIAL BUYERS AS CLIENTS

After spending time on the initial visit with a potential client, and showing them a few properties, it is time to discuss an agency relationship. This is generally done back in your office. If the potential buyer sees a property he or she likes, and decides to place an offer on the property, and you are the agent writing and presenting the offer to the seller, you will make the commission from this sale. If the buyer did not see anything he or she liked, but wants to continue to search for a home, you can offer your services to the buyer as an exclusive agent.

Sometimes it is awkward to approach the buyer with this offer. A suggested method is to be very sincere and up-front with the buyer. Offer your exclusive services to find a property quickly, efficiently and to his or her specifications. Let the buyer know that you will not make him or her chase around looking at property in which he or she would not be interested. Assure the buyer that you are willing to put the time into this home search until the right property has been found. Do not make promises you cannot keep, however. If you have eight other clients you are currently trying to find homes for, let the buyer know you are working with eight other clients. Let the buyer know this can be a good opportunity, as one client's idea of the wrong home may be another's dream house. You have the opportunity to be doing multiple searches and multiple showings. Sometimes a negative can be quickly turned into a positive.

If you have gone above and beyond the call of duty, most likely the buyer will agree to work with you. Just make sure you remain honest, never make promises you know cannot be achieved, and keep the lines of communication open at all times.

ANSWERING AND OVERCOMING OBJECTIONS

How an agent overcomes objections may make the difference between making a sale and going back to the drawing board to come up with more properties for the buyer to consider. Objections are not necessarily a bad thing; when a buyer objects to a property that is a good indication he or she is interested, but wants more information regarding one aspect of the property or another. A concern is not always negative. For example, a buyer looking at a condominium may have concerns or objections to the placement of a wall creating two small rooms, and may want to remove the wall to open up both rooms. He or she may ask the whether the condominium board would allow such reconstruction in the unit. This shows that the buyer is genuinely interested, but wants to know the property's limitations before moving forward.

As an informed agent, you will know that buyers will inspect a house that they plan on purchasing with a sharp eye and a critical approach. When something does not seem right, they will comment or ask questions. Buyers will want to know the condition of the foundation, roof, plumbing, and major appliances. In addition to the condition of these items, the buyer will usually ask their age. Is the neighborhood safe, are the schools good, and are there conveniences within close distances such as banks, churches, stores, restaurants and shopping? It is important for the agent to anticipate these questions, any objections that may arise from the questions and how to handle the situation. Agents should always act, not react.

Make sure that the buyer, if an offer is made and accepted, is comfortable with the home, and knows everything there is to know about the property; this includes mandatory and non-mandatory disclosures, useful information and other helpful pointers. A buyer, who was rushed into making an offer, may begin to second-guess whether the property is right for him or her, and eventually take himself or herself out of escrow.

An important tactic when showing a home is to call problems to the buyer's attention before he or she discovers them. This shows you are looking out for the buyer's best interest. The buyer will recognize the issue, and a dialogue can determine how to best overcome the problem.

Objections can be classified into five categories; procrastination, price, insecurity, location, and prejudice or personal bias.

Procrastination

A buyer telling you that he or she wants to think it over could be saying he or she is not completely sold on the property. This might indicate the buyer has more questions that have not been asked, or questions that have gone unanswered. A good response from the agent at this point would be to agree with the buyer that this is a very big decision and that it is one that should not be entered into without a good amount of thought, but then to offer more information on the house that might answer questions the buyer did not know he or she had, or provide information that will close the deal. It may be worth the agent's time to go over the entire property again with the buyer, seeking out where they are unclear, unsure or not completely sold on the property, and then tackle objections from there.

Sometimes a buyer's hesitation does not have anything to do with the property itself, but with other external factors. If the buyer is concerned it is not the right time to buy property, you can tell him or her, and then statistically show, that real estate has historically been increasing through all time periods and market conditions. They may need to understand the tax benefits, the freedom of ownership or other financial aspects of owning versus renting.

Price

If a buyer states that the price is too high, or that he or she cannot afford the payment, even after obtaining pre-approval, you can use the competitive market approach to show the buyer that the house is priced at or below the level of other similar houses. This will give the buyer a good basis for comparison. Stress the benefits of the property, highlight the desirable features the buyer is looking for, and remind the buyer that prices usually only go up.

If the monthly payment is too high for the buyer, you as an agent may be able to go back to the mortgage specialist and see about finding a better rate, a special program the buyer might qualify for, or a completely different lending institution that might have a more attractive loan program. This will aid in lowering the monthly payment, making the home feasible for the buyers.

Insecurity

When a buyer tells you that he or she is afraid of getting tied down into a long term commitment, or that he or she is not comfortable with knowing that he or she may be losing out by purchasing now, you can remind the buyer that he or she can resell at any time, and most likely resell for a profit. This will help entice the buyer into making a move, and calming time issue fears he or she may have.

Location

If a buyer loves the property, but is not keen on the location, or is concerned with the community a good agent can highlight the benefits to overcome concerns. For example, if the property is in an "up and coming" transitional neighborhood, the agent can tell the buyer of recent investment in the area, property values increasing, and plans for new and improved commerce in the area. This will almost assure an increase in the value of property, with positive, big changes taking place in the community down the road.

Prejudice or Personal Bias

An individual's preferences regarding the physical characteristics of the property are another factor in a buyer's objection. "I prefer a house with..." or "I wanted ..." are common phrases an agent may hear. A good salesperson will be able to overcome these objections by highlighting the obvious advantages of the home. Small rooms create efficient energy bills. For every objection a buyer may have regarding the home, there are certainly multiple selling points being overlooked.

Remember

The five classifications of objections are:
- procrastination,
- price,
- insecurity,
- location
- prejudice or personal bias.

OBTAINING THE OFFER

Buyers generally don't come right out and say they are interested in making on offer; they generally must be asked, or you as the agent must initiate this conversation. But how do you know when your client is ready to make the offer? The following techniques will help you determine if your client is ready to make an offer, and how to approach the topic.

Expression Approach

If the buyers are exchanging very positive, excitement-filled glances while going through the property, this may be a good indication to the agent that the buyers are interested in the property. You can also pick up on their conversation and their excitement about the proximity of the property to desired areas of the community or neighborhood. If the buyer makes a comment such as how nice it would be to live so close to the elementary school, you can respond with "Yes, and you can be living here in 30 days." Ask the buyers if they are ready to make an offer, and to keep their excitement level high, mention that you will request a short escrow, making the property theirs sooner than anticipated.

Question Approach

If the buyer is asking you questions such as "What type of loans could we qualify for?" "How soon could we move in?" "How long does escrow usually take?" "Will the sellers be including any of the furniture?" or "How much will this house cost in annual taxes?" or other questions such as these, it is a good indication that the buyer is ready to make an offer. You should respond to these questions with a question. "Which furniture would you like the sellers to include?" would be an appropriate response, followed by asking the buyer if he or she is ready to make an offer.

Self-Sale Approach

When buyers begin assigning rooms for specific functions, or begin visualizing how they will use the space, you can move toward the purchase offer contract. This is a good indication that they are ready to make a move.

Minor Point Approach

Springing the purchase contract on the buyer suddenly may scare him or her, and cause further hesitation to make an offer. If you have the contract out the entire time, walking through minor points and asking detailed questions on these points, filling in the responses will make the buyer more comfortable about making an offer. Questions such as length of escrow, items of personal property you would like the seller to include, or other "showing" details included on the purchase contract will already be familiar when it is time to complete the entire document. When you get to each question on the contract when filling it out, confirm with the buyer from your previous questioning and his or her answer.

Scratch Pad Approach

The scratch pad approach engages the buyers to actively work out figures with you, to understand the technicalities of the process. The buyers can see what the home looks like on paper in terms of cost per month. Different loan types can be worked out, with you highlighting the advantages of different financing methods. Once the buyers become comfortable with understanding the financing, you can ask them if they are ready to make an offer based on the figures you worked out. More than one offer can be worked out on paper, so that they can see the difference between payments.

Fatal Alternative Approach

Probe the buyers to see if they like the general features of the house. Perhaps compare it to another property, having them confirm that they like the home they are currently touring. From there you can ask more solid questions, such as how they want to take title to the property. Offer different options such as joint tenancy or some other way. If the buyers respond that they prefer one way over another, you can assume the buyers are ready to make an offer on the property, and ask.

Affirmative Yes Approach

Ask the buyers questions you know will be answered with a positive yes. An example of this would be: "This house has plenty of space for your growing family, doesn't it?" Continue asking these types of questions, and then at the end ask them if they are ready to make an offer. After responding "Yes" to all your questions, they can't help but want to make an offer on the property after admitting to themselves how ideal it is.

Negative Yes Approach

If the buyer is not ready to make an offer, you can ask him or her a series of questions about what the point of disagreement is. Is it the house, neighborhood, me as the agent, or my firm? As they say no to each question, you can narrow down why the buyer is hesitant to make the offer. Discover why the buyer has not made the offer yet, and then sell him or her on the points you may have missed, ending in a change of mind and an offer.

After obtaining the offer, you can proceed toward getting the earnest money deposit and taking the offer to the listing agent; or, if you are the listing agent, submitting the offer to the sellers to see if it is acceptable to them.

S U M M A R Y

In this chapter, you were exposed to the buyer and their characteristics, everything from the initial contact all the way through the purchase contract and offer. You can see that the buyer has a lot going on when he or she is looking for a home, and needs your expertise and guidance, even if he or she doesn't realize it. You need to make "just looking" buyers into homeowners.

You know it is important to set up an appointment with the potential buyer as soon as possible to begin learning about his or her needs and wants. Giving too much information on the phone regarding a property might jeopardize getting a meeting with the potential buyer. We learned that the best way to answer questions is by asking a question, learning more about what the buyer is looking for in a home.

We learned we must prequalify the buyer at the first meeting, and gather important information from him or her to aid in finding the best home for his or her specific needs. The qualification process usually takes an hour, long enough for you to explain the home hunting process in detail, and gather the information necessary to get you started.

After qualification, you are ready to start looking at homes. By showing the buyer homes that match his or her profile, you will be utilizing your time most efficiently. Asking a buyer to compare homes to each other helps you get a picture of what he or she likes best, and what features he or she is not as interested in. During the showing you want to engage the buyer, his or her family and anyone else that comes with the buyer, helping make the decision. This will make the buyer feel like he or she is not just being shown a home, and will help them start visualizing themselves living in the house, a key point in getting the buyer to make an offer.

Once the buyers have seen the home and all fears or objections have been raised, answered and understood, it is time for you to ask the buyers if they are ready to make an offer. You will know they are ready by their reaction to the home and interaction with each other. Approach the subject carefully, and ease them through the process so they don't become nervous or hesitant.

Communication with the buyer and learning about and listening to the buyer are three very important steps when helping him or her find a home. If the buyer feels you are sincere and you are honestly working for their best interests, you will form a good relationship of trust, and ultimately find the right property, for which an offer will be extended.

TERMS AND PHRASES

Back-End Qualification – A ratio of a buyer's long-term debt obligations to their total gross income.

Call-first – A common guideline or specification for agents when they show houses. This rule simply means the agent must call the owner before showing, either to make an appointment or give the owner advance notice before bringing a buyer to look at the property.

Counteroffer – An offer made to the seller or buyer after an original offer was made. The original offer as written was not acceptable, but was further negotiated rather than simply rejected.

Deal Breaker – A phrase used by people when describing what features a property must have to determine if they would consider buying the property.

Callsource.com – An online resource listing individuals' names, phone numbers, and information regarding a person's residence, financial status and family data.

Floor Time – The designated time when an agent will receive incoming calls from prospective clients calling regarding advertisements, "For Sale" signs or Internet sites advertising your properties.

Front-End Qualification – A ratio of a buyer's housing costs to his or her gross income.

Long-Term Debt – Debt such as a car note, credit card bills, and other mortgages or long term loans.

Prequalify – A preliminary qualifying process, to get an idea of the amount of money a person will be able to spend on a home.

Stated Income - An individual's own account of how much money he or she makes annually.

Switch Property – A property that is similar and priced within 10% of another property in which a client is interested.

Tie-Downs – Finishing a statement or comment with a question to get the buyer's feedback. Phrases such as "isn't it," "can it," "won't it" and so on are examples of tiedowns.

C H A P T E R   Q U I Z

1. Floor time refers to:
   a. The time an agent spends conducting an open house.
   b. The time an agent spends during a transaction filling out paperwork and making sure all documents have been delivered to the appropriate parties.
   c. The time an agent spends in the office answering incoming phone calls.
   d. None of the above

2. Where are the most appropriate places for the first appointment to take place?)
   a. Your office or the potential client's house
   b. Your office or the property in question
   c. The potential client's house or the property in question
   d. Your office or a public meeting area

3. Which of the following methods is not an appropriate method to gain information regarding a reluctant caller?
   a. Offer to research a property and call back with more details.
   b. Look up the caller on callsource.com while they are on the phone with you and begin using their personal information during the call.
   c. Offer to mail an information packet directly to them with more information and pictures of the property in question.
   d. Offer to email photos and more information to the prospective client, with additional information on switch properties.

4. During the qualifying process, what information should you learn from the buyer?
   a. The client's needs and reasons for the purchase
   b. The client's financial status
   c. Both A and B
   d. Neither A nor B

5. Which of the following is considered long-term debt?
   a. Car note
   b. Credit card balances
   c. Student loans
   d. All of the above

6. An earnest money deposit is:
   a. Deposited into the broker's trust account until the sellers have accepted the buyers offer.
   b. Held uncashed by the broker until the sellers have accepted the offer.

     c. Held uncashed by the sellers until they have made a decision to accept or reject the offer.

     d. Immediately deposited into escrow.

7. An offer made by a buyer to a seller may be:
     a. Accepted
     b. Rejected
     c. Returned with a counteroffer
     d. Any of the above

8. Which of the following is a good tactic to use when showing homes?
     a. Explain to the buyer what each room could be used for, allowing him or her to visualize utilizing the living space.
     b. Highlight benefits of certain features which may be of specific interest to the buyer.
     c. Simply tell the buyer the specifics regarding the house, with a quick tour to keep the process moving forward, allowing the buyer to see as many properties as possible.
     d. Both A and B

9. Which of the following should you NEVER do when showing a property?
     a. Begin showing the home to your client even if another agent is inside: as long as you are not in the same space or room, there is no problem
     b. Ask your client to extinguish any cigarette, cigar or pipe
     c. Leave your business card for the owner
     d. All of the above

10. When gaining feedback from a client, which of the following methods are most helpful?
     a. Using tie-downs
     b. Asking the client's opinion of the property just shown
     c. Asking the client to compare more than one property
     d. All of the above

11. Which of the following is NOT a good idea to do when showing a home?
     a. Allow children to be part of the process by engaging them in the conversation or utilizing them as helpers.
     b. Allow the buyers privacy to discuss their thoughts.
     c. Interject your thoughts on the home, both positive and negative, while in the house.
     d. Solve any issues the buyer may have during the showing.

12. When showing a "call first" property, when is it appropriate to show the home without calling first?
     a. Never
     b. On weekends
     c. After the home has been on the market for at least 30 days
     d. If the listing is one of your own

13. Self-employed people usually
     a. Have an easier time securing a loan because they can vouch for their own incomes
     b. Have a harder time securing a loan because they are relying on stated income or must produce 2 years of tax returns

c. Will usually have a lower interest rate

d. None of the above

14. An agent should see a buyer's objection as:
    a. An opportunity to show the buyer other properties that may be more suited to his or her needs
    b. An opportunity to answer more questions or expose more of the home's selling points
    c. Hesitation and uncertainty, suggesting to the agent they seek different representation
    d. Hesitation and uncertainty, suggesting to the agent they are not ready to make a purchase of this magnitude at this time.

15. If an agent knows of a problem or issue with a home, he or she should:
    a. Ignore the issue; it might prevent the buyers from making an offer.
    b. Privately inform the sellers there is an issue, and make sure they take care of it.
    c. Not show that aspect of the home.
    d. Inform the buyers of the issue immediately and have a dialogue regarding what they think about the issue and how to overcome it.

16. Which of the following is not a category into which objections can be classified?
    a. Procrastination
    b. Price
    c. Zoning
    d. Bias

17. Buyers afraid of being tied down into a long-term commitment best demonstrate which category of objection?
    a. Personal bias
    b. Insecurity
    c. Prejudice
    d. Price

18. Which of the following is not an approach an agent can use to get the buyer to make an offer?
    a. Minor Point Approach
    b. Negative Yes Approach
    c. Deal Breaker Approach
    d. Scratch Pad Approach

19. The process in which a buyer begins assigning rooms to certain functions, or visualizing how he or she might use the space is an indication he or she is ready to make an offer. This approach is referred to as:
    a. Self Sale Approach
    b. Affirmative Yes Approach
    c. Question Approach
    d. Minor Point Approach

20. Systematically eliminating a buyer's objections regarding a property or the home buying process is called:
    a. Question Approach
    b. Negative Yes Approach
    c. Minor Point Approach
    d. Fatal Alternative Approach

5

DISCLOSURES

What you will learn in this Chapter

- Disclosure
- Agency Disclosure
- Real Estate Transfer Disclosure
- Fiduciary Responsibility and Disclosure
- Natural Hazards Disclosure
- Agent's Inspection Disclosure
- Environmental Hazards Disclosure
- Disclosure of Death or AIDS
- Subdivision Disclosure
- Common Interest Subdivision
- Financing Disclosure
- Mello-Roos Bond Disclosure
- Other Disclosures
- Right of Rescission
- California Association of REALTORS®
  Disclosure Chart

1. An agent unknowingly using an old or retired disclosure form:
   a. Is held liable for any damages the situation may cause
   b. Is not held liable for any damages
   c. May NOT be sued in a court of law
   d. Can substitute a similar, nationally focused form

2. When must agency disclosure take place?
   a. Prior to signing the deposit receipt
   b. As soon as possible
   c. Prior to accepting an offer
   d. None of the above

3. An agent is exempt from making a personal site inspection on a residential property with 1-4 units when:
   a. The property is being sold because of foreclosure
   b. The property is being transferred between spouses or blood relatives
   c. The property being sold requires a public report
   d. All of the above

4. Which booklet can a broker give to a buyer concerning lead-based paint and its hazards?
   a. Protect Your Family from Lead In Your Home
   b. Environmental Hazards: a Guide for Homeowners, Buyers, Landlords and Tenants
   c. Neither A nor B
   d. Both A and B

5. A conditional public report allows a developer to:
   a. Take deposits and reservations on property, but no contracts may be signed
   b. Enter into a contractual agreement with a buyer, but the developer cannot close escrow until the final public report has been issued
   c. Operate unrestricted with buyers for six months, the length of a valid conditional public report
   d. None of the above

6. Lenders are required to provide a potential borrower with a statement of why the borrower's loan application or credit application has been denied under which act?
   a. Holden Act
   b. Truth-in-Lending Act
   c. Regulation Z
   d. Equal Credit Opportunity Act

7. Which of the following is considered a mandatory disclosure?
   a. Commissions
   b. Sales Price
   c. Common Interest Subdivision
   d. All of the above

This chapter is designed to give you all the necessary information regarding disclosure, and how to protect yourself as an agent during a transaction from lawsuits arising from disclosure or the lack thereof. It is important for you to understand all requirements outlined in this chapter thoroughly. By arming yourself with knowledge about what disclosures are mandatory and what other disclosures you can make, you will protect yourself from misunderstandings and litigation.

We will examine both agent and lender disclosures. All disclosures required by law are discussed, as well as other disclosure obligations that might not be mandatory by law, but are still important to pass along to your client. Full disclosure may seem like unnecessary paperwork and might seem threatening or difficult to explain to a client, but in the end it serves to protect the interests of both the buyer and the seller, not to mention you.

D I S C L O S U R E

Disclosure is simply the act of giving your client or the third party all required information regarding a property, transaction, or financial aspects of the real estate transfer. Usually these disclosures are written forms that you present to the client or third party so they can be referred to later if he or she has questions, but you should also verbally explain to him or her the disclosure when presenting the form. The client or third party will acknowledge that he or she has been presented the information, and understands the information, by signing a form. Disclosure is rather simple; it just creates additional steps in the property transfer that an agent must remember to cover.

Full disclosure is the simple act of giving notice of all material facts related to a property transaction. The material facts include any fact that might influence the buyer's or seller's decision to go through with a property transfer. Parties responsible in full disclosure include the broker or real estate agent, lender or mortgage broker, and the principal. The principal is responsible for disclosing any defects in the property which might not be visible but which could make a difference in the property transfer. Full disclosure will protect the buyer, agent, and lender, establish trust amongst all people involved in the property transfer, and satisfy the law. Disclosure is required on all residential properties containing 1-4 units.

Remember
- Full disclosure means giving notice of all material facts related to the property transaction.

In the past, real estate transactions operated under the rule "buyer beware" or caveat emptor. This rule has been around for hundreds of years; however, in our ever-changing society, the California Legislature, the courts and the Department of Real Estate are increasingly adopting disclosures. Not only are these government or regulatory agencies adopting disclosures, but also they are making their way into law.

Remember
- Before disclosure, property transactions operated under the rule of caveat emptor, "buyer beware."

Disclosure has typically been part of real estate law, but never really enforced by California law or the Department of Real Estate. Additionally, many agents did not fully understand disclosure, or how to conduct the disclosures appropriately. Because of this, the courts began seeing numerous lawsuits regarding the lack of disclosure. Now, agents need to be aware of how disclosure works, what the mandatory disclosures are, and how to conduct themselves appropriately to avoid costly lawsuits and time away from servicing their listings.

California state law, as well as Department of Real Estate regulations, now enforce disclosure in property transfers. This enforcement is an effort to help reduce the number of lawsuits surrounding disclosure. While these laws are intended to protect the agents, they have led to a lot of extra paperwork for the agents. An agent now must present the client with all mandatory disclosures, discuss and explain the forms, and receive written confirmation from the client that he or she has seen and understands the forms.

Disclosures you present to your client tend to be of a very general nature. The disclosure information discussed in this chapter is representational of these types of disclosures. If you need to present a more in-depth disclosure to your client or third party, you will want to consult an attorney to draw up the appropriate documents and papers to present. If there is ever a question of whether to disclose information regarding the property, transaction or any other aspect of the real estate transfer, always err on the side of caution; it will potentially avoid a lengthy, costly lawsuit.

Amongst all the disclosures that an agent may make, some are mandated. The mandated disclosures are those that are required by law. Simply stated, a mandated disclosure is a material fact obligated by law to be disclosed to the appropriate party in the transaction. The information regarding these disclosures must be delivered to all parties involved, as required by the Department of Real Estate or state law. "Information," in this case, means any facts, data or figures that might influence a person's decision regarding a property.

Care must be taken when preparing all necessary disclosure forms for each property transfer. Forms may be updated over time, or other forms may seem to be very close to national disclosure forms. The agent must at all times be using the most up-to-date forms, and correct forms for each disclosure. If the agent uses a national form thinking the disclosure is close enough to what he or she must disclose, problems may arise, leaving the agent liable for any damages. This goes for outdated forms as well; any misunderstandings or damages caused by outdated forms may leave the agent liable.

A G E N C Y   D I S C L O S U R E

Agency disclosure pertains to whom the agent is representing. Sometimes there can be a misunderstanding about who the agent represents, or whether the agent is representing both the client and the seller. In that case, it becomes tricky, because the agent owes the principal fiduciary responsibility, essentially leaving the buyer without representation. Because of this, agency disclosure is required, so each party is aware of their representation, or the lack thereof. Civil Code Sections 2373-2382 outline agency relationships. The agency disclosure form defines agency as "[A] person acting under provisions of this title in a real property transaction, including a person who is licensed as a real estate broker under Chapter 3 of Part 1 of Division 4 of the Business & Professions Code, and under whose license a listing is executed or an offer to purchase is extended." To simplify, "agency" is the broker acting on behalf of the client in real property transactions.

Disclosing an agency relationship is a three-step process. The three steps in the process are **disclose**, **elect** and **confirm**.

Disclose

The agency disclosure form is filled out, and acknowledged by the agent and the client with signatures. Like most other disclosures, this must be in writing; it cannot be implied or verbal. At this time, the agent can explain to his or her client the different types of agency representing the buyer, seller or dual agency, and the type of agency the client is entering into.

Elect

In this stage of disclosure, the agent and client decide what type of agency agreement will be used. This step does not require any signatures, but there must be a meaningful conversation so that each party understands fully the arrangement.

Confirm

Confirmation is when each party signs the agency disclosure form, agreeing upon and acknowledging all details, especially the agency they elect to enter into, decided in the second step. A confirmation statement or form is signed and given to both parties. This confirmation statement or form can sometimes be part of the purchase contract, or it can be a stand-alone document. It is up to the broker to make sure all necessary disclosures have been made regarding the agency relationship, especially in a dual agency situation where each party must be clear regarding how the dual agency will work, fiduciary responsibilities, and any other disclosures that the agent might need to make regarding the agency.

Lastly, but not included in the three steps of agency disclosure, it is a good idea for the seller's agent to inform the buyer of the agency agreement. The buyer may or may not have an agent for representation, but it is a good idea to let the buyer know the agreement between the seller and agent. This disclosure keeps each party informed of who is representing whom; in the event there may have been questions.

> **Remember**
> The three steps in agency disclosure are:
> - Disclose
> - Elect
> - Confirm

When an agent is representing only the buyer or seller, this is referred to as a **single agency**, in which the agent is representing only a single client. When the same agent is representing both the buyer and the seller, it is referred to as **dual agency**. It is very important for a broker in a dual agency capacity to be very careful. It is easy for conflicts of interest to arise in this situation. Clear disclosure and communication will help keep both parties very aware of what is happening, but still it is imperative for the broker to be careful. Because of misunderstandings which may occur, many brokers choose to act as single agents only, reducing the likelihood of problems down the road.

In agency disclosure, the term agent takes on a different meaning than usual. "Agent" is casually used in conversation, and usually means a real estate professional, whether that person is a broker or salesperson. In the contractual sense, "agent" is the broker entering into the agency agreement with the principal. Each real estate office or firm has one agent, and that is the broker. The broker will enter into the agency agreement with the principal, and then empower licensees or salespersons working for him or her to represent the broker in dealing with the client. The salespersons are sometimes referred to as **subagents** of the broker.

There can be several different agents in a real estate transaction, or different designations of agents in the transaction. An agent representing the seller is called the **seller's agent**. An agent representing the buyer is referred to as the **buyer's agent**. The agent taking the listing is the **listing agent**, and the agent who brings in a ready, willing and able buyer is the **selling agent**. If a broker is acting as a **dual agent**, it is possible for him or her to fit all of the agency titles. If there are cooperating brokers working on the sale of the property, just one term may define one broker's efforts. It is important to understand the differences between all of these terms.

Agency can be either **implied** or **express**. A formal announcement of agency is not necessary for an agency relationship to be created or formed. Continuous contact between a licensee and client can create an implied agency; certain phrases or words used in conversation between a licensee and client can create an agency as well. If a licensee tells a client he or she can find the exact type of house that the client is looking for, this implies an agency relationship, whether a formal contract has been signed or not. The clients may assume that the licensee is their real estate agent, and if there should be any disagreements or damages caused by this implied agency, the licensee may be held liable. Express agency is established through signing of a listing agreement. As we learned in the previous chapter, this is a legal, binding contract linking the client and broker. Once the agency agreement has been established, whether it is implied or express, the broker or licensee owes the client fiduciary responsibility. This means that the broker or licensee must be working with the client's best interests and wishes in mind, not for their own personal gain.

It is important for you to understand that there is only one agent in each real estate firm. This does not mean one agent per office, but one per firm. Let's say you work for a very large real estate firm with offices in multiple cities, and this firm has one agent. The firm may have multiple brokers, but only one agent. This one agent is the person that will enter into contracts with the principal. If the agent takes a listing in Palm Springs, where the firm has an office location, and another office location in San Diego finds an interested buyer, this becomes a dual agency situation, because just one agent represents the entire firm. Full disclosure in this situation is very important, so everyone understands where the representation will be coming from, and that it is a dual agency situation.

Conversely, usually large real estate firms allow for independently owned franchise offices. In an event such as this, each office will have its own broker, and each broker is the agent for that specific franchise. If the real estate firm XYZ allows for franchised offices, each office will have its own broker, or agent. When XYZ Real Estate's franchise office in San Francisco enters into an agency agreement with a seller, and XYZ Real Estate's franchise office in Sacramento finds the broker, this is not considered a dual agency situation. XYZ San Francisco has its own agent, and XYZ Sacramento has a separate agent, making the two franchise offices independent of one another in every way except sharing the same name.

Different real estate offices have requirements or timelines that must be followed regarding when agency disclosure must take place, but the Department of Real Estate mandates that the disclosure should be as soon as possible. However, the three steps of the disclosure process don't necessary have to happen at the same time.

Disclosure summary for listing agents:

Disclosure step	Who	When	How
Disclosure	Provide disclosure form to the seller	Prior to entering into the listing agreement	Keep a signed copy of the form for your file
Elect	Tell seller whether you are seller's agent or dual agent	As soon as practical or possible (DRE mandate)	Orally or in writing
Confirm	Confirm with seller whether you are seller's agent or dual agent	Prior to coincident with seller's execution of deposit receipt.	In the deposit receipt or another document in writing by seller and listing agent.

Disclosure summary for agents selling their own listings:

Disclosure step	Who	When	How
Disclosure	Provide disclosure form to the buyer	As soon as possible before the buyer executes an offer	Keep a signed copy of the form for your file
Elect	Tell both the buyer and the seller whether you are the seller's agent, or a dual agent	As soon possible	Orally or in writing
Confirm	Confirm with the buyer and seller whether you are seller's agent or dual agent	Prior to or at the same time as the buyer's and seller's execution of the deposit receipt	In the deposit receipt or another document in writing by buyer, seller and listing agent.

Disclosure summary for selling agents:

Disclosure step	Who	When	How
Disclosure	Provide the buyer with the disclosure form	As soon as possible before the buyer makes an offer	Keep a signed copy of the disclosure for your files, obtain a signed copy directly from the seller or through the listing agent, or provide a copy of the agreement via certified mail to the seller
Elect	Tell both the buyer and the seller if you are the buyer's agent, seller's agent or a dual agent	As soon possible	Orally or in writing
Confirm	Confirm with the buyer and seller whether you are the seller's agent, buyer's agent or a dual agent	Prior to coincident with buyer's and seller's execution of the deposit receipt	In the deposit receipt or another writing by the buyer, seller and listing agent

DISCLOSURE REGARDING REAL ESTATE AGENCY RELATIONSHIPS
(As required by the Civil Code)
(C.A.R. Form AD, Revised 10/04)

CALIFORNIA ASSOCIATION OF REALTORS®

When you enter into a discussion with a real estate agent regarding a real estate transaction, you should from the outset understand what type of agency relationship or representation you wish to have with the agent in the transaction.

SELLER'S AGENT

A Seller's agent under a listing agreement with the Seller acts as the agent for the Seller only. A Seller's agent or a subagent of that agent has the following affirmative obligations:
To the Seller:
A Fiduciary duty of utmost care, integrity, honesty, and loyalty in dealings with the Seller.
To the Buyer and the Seller:
(a) Diligent exercise of reasonable skill and care in performance of the agent's duties.
(b) A duty of honest and fair dealing and good faith.
(c) A duty to disclose all facts known to the agent materially affecting the value or desirability of the property that are not known to, or within the diligent attention and observation of, the parties.

An agent is not obligated to reveal to either party any confidential information obtained from the other party that does not involve the affirmative duties set forth above.

BUYER'S AGENT

A selling agent can, with a Buyer's consent, agree to act as agent for the Buyer only. In these situations, the agent is not the Seller's agent, even if by agreement the agent may receive compensation for services rendered, either in full or in part from the Seller. An agent acting only for a Buyer has the following affirmative obligations:
To the Buyer:
A fiduciary duty of utmost care, integrity, honesty, and loyalty in dealings with the Buyer.
To the Buyer and the Seller:
(a) Diligent exercise of reasonable skill and care in performance of the agent's duties.
(b) A duty of honest and fair dealing and good faith.
(c) A duty to disclose all facts known to the agent materially affecting the value or desirability of the property that are not known to, or within the diligent attention and observation of, the parties.

An agent is not obligated to reveal to either party any confidential information obtained from the other party that does not involve the affirmative duties set forth above.

AGENT REPRESENTING BOTH SELLER AND BUYER

A real estate agent, either acting directly or through one or more associate licensees, can legally be the agent of both the Seller and the Buyer in a transaction, but only with the knowledge and consent of both the Seller and the Buyer.

In a dual agency situation, the agent has the following affirmative obligations to both the Seller and the Buyer:
(a) A fiduciary duty of utmost care, integrity, honesty and loyalty in the dealings with either the Seller or the Buyer.
(b) Other duties to the Seller and the Buyer as stated above in their respective sections.

In representing both Seller and Buyer, the agent may not, without the express permission of the respective party, disclose to the other party that the Seller will accept a price less than the listing price or that the Buyer will pay a price greater than the price offered.

The above duties of the agent in a real estate transaction do not relieve a Seller or Buyer from the responsibility to protect his or her own interests. You should carefully read all agreements to assure that they adequately express your understanding of the transaction. A real estate agent is a person qualified to advise about real estate. If legal or tax advice is desired, consult a competent professional.

Throughout your real property transaction you may receive more than one disclosure form, depending upon the number of agents assisting in the transaction. The law requires each agent with whom you have more than a casual relationship to present you with this disclosure form. You should read its contents each time it is presented to you, considering the relationship between you and the real estate agent in your specific transaction.

This disclosure form includes the provisions of Sections 2079.13 to 2079.24, inclusive, of the Civil Code set forth on the reverse hereof. Read it carefully.

I/WE ACKNOWLEDGE RECEIPT OF A COPY OF THIS DISCLOSURE AND THE PORTIONS OF THE CIVIL CODE PRINTED ON THE BACK (OR A SEPARATE PAGE).

BUYER/SELLER _____ Date _____ Time _____ AM/PM

BUYER/SELLER _____ Date _____ Time _____ AM/PM

AGENT _____ By _____ Date _____
(Please Print)   (Associate-Licensee or Broker Signature)

THIS FORM SHALL BE PROVIDED AND ACKNOWLEDGED AS FOLLOWS (Civil Code § 2079.14):
• When the listing brokerage company also represents Buyer, the Listing Agent shall have one AD form signed by Seller and one signed by Buyer.
• When Buyer and Seller are represented by different brokerage companies, the Listing Agent shall have one AD form signed by Seller and the Buyer's Agent shall have one AD form signed by Buyer and one AD form signed by Seller.

The copyright laws of the United States (Title 17 U.S. Code) forbid the unauthorized reproduction of this form, or any portion thereof, by photocopy machine or any other means, including facsimile or computerized formats. Copyright © 1991-2004, CALIFORNIA ASSOCIATION OF REALTORS®, INC. ALL RIGHTS RESERVED.
THIS FORM HAS BEEN APPROVED BY THE CALIFORNIA ASSOCIATION OF REALTORS® (C.A.R.). NO REPRESENTATION IS MADE AS TO THE LEGAL VALIDITY OR ADEQUACY OF ANY PROVISION IN ANY SPECIFIC TRANSACTION. A REAL ESTATE BROKER IS THE PERSON QUALIFIED TO ADVISE ON REAL ESTATE TRANSACTIONS. IF YOU DESIRE LEGAL OR TAX ADVICE, CONSULT AN APPROPRIATE PROFESSIONAL.
This form is available for use by the entire real estate industry. It is not intended to identify the user as a REALTOR®. REALTOR® is a registered collective membership mark which may be used only by members of the NATIONAL ASSOCIATION OF REALTORS® who subscribe to its Code of Ethics.

Published and Distributed by:
REAL ESTATE BUSINESS SERVICES, INC.
a subsidiary of the California Association of REALTORS®
525 South Virgil Avenue, Los Angeles, California 90020

Reviewed by _____ Date _____

EQUAL HOUSING OPPORTUNITY

AD REVISED 10/04 (PAGE 1 OF 1) PRINT DATE

DISCLOSURE REGARDING REAL ESTATE AGENCY RELATIONSHIPS (AD PAGE 1 OF 1)

132

California Civil Code 1.102-1.102.14 states that any residential property with four living units or fewer is entitled to a real estate transfer disclosure statement. This disclosure will come from the seller. "Transfer" refers to any property sale, exchange, option, lease, or other real property transaction.

The real estate transfer disclosure will inform any buyer of property about the condition of the property. This will apply to both defects and problems that are readily seen, and problems or conditions that may not be immediately seen. Three distinct subjects are discussed in this form. The first is items in the home and whether they are functional or problematic. The second is a list of any significant defects in the home. Lastly, the disclosure must include any improvements or alterations made to the property. This section will also highlight any concerns with neighbors or the neighborhood.

The buyer must receive a copy of this disclosure. The seller's agent is responsible for delivering this copy to the buyer; however, if it is a dual agency situation, the one and only agent will make sure the buyer receives the form. In the event the seller did not fill out a real estate transfer disclosure form, the buyer must be alerted in writing to his or her right to such a statement.

As with many other disclosures, the real estate transfer disclosure must be delivered as soon as possible and most certainly before the execution of an offer to purchase the property. If this disclosure is not delivered to the buyer within three days, the buyer has the right to opt out of the purchase contract. If the buyer does decide to cancel the contract, there must be a written notice of termination and it must be delivered to the seller or the seller's agent.

FIDUCIARY RESPONSIBILITY AND DISCLOSURE

An agent owes his or her principal fiduciary responsibility. This means that the agent will look out for the client's best interests in all property transfer dealings. With fiduciary responsibility, an agent will place the principal's interests above his or her own. Additionally, all loyalty is given to the client. When dealing with a third party, all necessary disclosures must be made and the agent must conduct himself or herself ethically and fairly. As long as there is fair dealing with the third party, and the third party understands that the licensee is acting as an agent of the other party, fiduciary responsibility will not be violated. Disclosures must be made to the third party before he or she makes an offer. Full disclosure is always required, even if it means the third party won't make an offer on the property; the third party is entitled to all facts before writing an offer.

Dual agency creates a unique situation where the agent must be very careful to not favor one principal over another. If one principal is benefiting while the other is suffering from these actions, fiduciary responsibility has been broken. Open communication and full disclosure is a must to avoid any problems, resulting in damages or lawsuits in which the agent could possibly be held liable.

One of the main duties in fiduciary responsibility that an agent must perform for the principal is full disclosure of all material facts discovered by the agent that would be important to the principal when making any decision regarding a property. This could mean warning the principal of possible problems with the property, or problems in getting into a lease or option, or any offer that might have red flags. Material facts could also include market conditions, value and other financial concerns.

**CALIFORNIA
ASSOCIATION
OF REALTORS®**

REAL ESTATE TRANSFER DISCLOSURE STATEMENT
(CALIFORNIA CIVIL CODE §1102, ET SEQ.)
(C.A.R. Form TDS, Revised 10/03)

THIS DISCLOSURE STATEMENT CONCERNS THE REAL PROPERTY SITUATED IN THE CITY OF _____, COUNTY OF _____, STATE OF CALIFORNIA, DESCRIBED AS _____.

THIS STATEMENT IS A DISCLOSURE OF THE CONDITION OF THE ABOVE DESCRIBED PROPERTY IN COMPLIANCE WITH SECTION 1102 OF THE CIVIL CODE AS OF (date) _____. IT IS NOT A WARRANTY OF ANY KIND BY THE SELLER(S) OR ANY AGENT(S) REPRESENTING ANY PRINCIPAL(S) IN THIS TRANSACTION, AND IS NOT A SUBSTITUTE FOR ANY INSPECTIONS OR WARRANTIES THE PRINCIPAL(S) MAY WISH TO OBTAIN.

I. COORDINATION WITH OTHER DISCLOSURE FORMS

This Real Estate Transfer Disclosure Statement is made pursuant to Section 1102 of the Civil Code. Other statutes require disclosures, depending upon the details of the particular real estate transaction (for example: special study zone and purchase-money liens on residential property).

Substituted Disclosures: The following disclosures and other disclosures required by law, including the Natural Hazard Disclosure Report/Statement that may include airport annoyances, earthquake, fire, flood, or special assessment information, have or will be made in connection with this real estate transfer, and are intended to satisfy the disclosure obligations on this form, where the subject matter is the same:

☐ Inspection reports completed pursuant to the contract of sale or receipt for deposit.
☐ Additional inspection reports or disclosures: _____

II. SELLER'S INFORMATION

The Seller discloses the following information with the knowledge that even though this is not a warranty, prospective Buyers may rely on this information in deciding whether and on what terms to purchase the subject property. Seller hereby authorizes any agent(s) representing any principal(s) in this transaction to provide a copy of this statement to any person or entity in connection with any actual or anticipated sale of the property.

THE FOLLOWING ARE REPRESENTATIONS MADE BY THE SELLER(S) AND ARE NOT THE REPRESENTATIONS OF THE AGENT(S), IF ANY. THIS INFORMATION IS A DISCLOSURE AND IS NOT INTENDED TO BE PART OF ANY CONTRACT BETWEEN THE BUYER AND SELLER.

Seller ☐ is ☐ is not occupying the property.

A. The subject property has the items checked below (read across):

☐ Range	☐ Oven	☐ Microwave
☐ Dishwasher	☐ Trash Compactor	☐ Garbage Disposal
☐ Washer/Dryer Hookups		☐ Rain Gutters
☐ Burglar Alarms	☐ Smoke Detector(s)	☐ Fire Alarm
☐ TV Antenna	☐ Satellite Dish	☐ Intercom
☐ Central Heating	☐ Central Air Conditioning	☐ Evaporator Cooler(s)
☐ Wall/Window Air Conditioning	☐ Sprinklers	☐ Public Sewer System
☐ Septic Tank	☐ Sump Pump	☐ Water Softener
☐ Patio/Decking	☐ Built-in Barbecue	☐ Gazebo
☐ Sauna		
☐ Hot Tub	☐ Pool	☐ Spa
☐ Locking Safety Cover*	☐ Child Resistant Barrier*	☐ Locking Safety Cover*
☐ Security Gate(s)	☐ Automatic Garage Door Opener(s)	☐ Number Remote Controls ___
Garage: ☐ Attached	☐ Not Attached	☐ Carport
Pool/Spa Heater: ☐ Gas	☐ Solar	☐ Electric
Water Heater: ☐ Gas	☐ Water Heater Anchored, Braced, or Strapped	
Water Supply: ☐ City	☐ Well	☐ Private Utility or
Gas Supply: ☐ Utility	☐ Bottled	☐ Other _____
☐ Window Screens	☐ Window Security Bars ☐ Quick Release Mechanism on Bedroom Windows*	

Exhaust Fan(s) in _____ 220 Volt Wiring in _____ Fireplace(s) in _____
☐ Gas Starter _____ ☐ Roof(s): Type: _____ Age: _____ (approx.)
☐ Other: _____

Are there, to the best of your (Seller's) knowledge, any of the above that are not in operating condition? ☐ Yes ☐ No. If yes, then describe. (Attach additional sheets if necessary): _____

(*see footnote on page 2)

TDS REVISED 10/03 (PAGE 1 OF 3) Print Date

Buyer's Initials (_____)(_____)
Seller's Initials (_____)(_____)

Reviewed by _____ Date _____

EQUAL HOUSING OPPORTUNITY

REAL ESTATE TRANSFER DISCLOSURE STATEMENT (TDS PAGE 1 OF 3)

Property Address: _____ Date: _____

B. Are you (Seller) aware of any significant defects/malfunctions in any of the following? ☐ Yes ☐ No. If yes, check appropriate space(s) below.

☐ Interior Walls ☐ Ceilings ☐ Floors ☐ Exterior Walls ☐ Insulation ☐ Roof(s) ☐ Windows ☐ Doors ☐ Foundation ☐ Slab(s) ☐ Driveways ☐ Sidewalks ☐ Walls/Fences ☐ Electrical Systems ☐ Plumbing/Sewers/Septics ☐ Other Structural Components

(Describe: _____
_____
_____)

If any of the above is checked, explain. (Attach additional sheets if necessary.): _____
_____
_____
_____

*This garage door opener or child resistant pool barrier may not be in compliance with the safety standards relating to automatic reversing devices as set forth in Chapter 12.5 (commencing with Section 19890) of Part 3 of Division 13 of, or with the pool safety standards of Article 2.5 (commencing with Section 115920) of Chapter 5 of Part 10 of Division 104 of, the Health and Safety Code. The water heater may not be anchored, braced, or strapped in accordance with Section 19211 of the Health and Safety Code. Window security bars may not have quick release mechanisms in compliance with the 1995 edition of the California Building Standards Code.

C. Are you (Seller) aware of any of the following:

1. Substances, materials, or products which may be an environmental hazard such as, but not limited to, asbestos, formaldehyde, radon gas, lead-based paint, mold, fuel or chemical storage tanks, and contaminated soil or water on the subject property .... ☐ Yes ☐ No
2. Features of the property shared in common with adjoining landowners, such as walls, fences, and driveways, whose use or responsibility for maintenance may have an effect on the subject property .... ☐ Yes ☐ No
3. Any encroachments, easements or similar matters that may affect your interest in the subject property .... ☐ Yes ☐ No
4. Room additions, structural modifications, or other alterations or repairs made without necessary permits .... ☐ Yes ☐ No
5. Room additions, structural modifications, or other alterations or repairs not in compliance with building codes ... ☐ Yes ☐ No
6. Fill (compacted or otherwise) on the property or any portion thereof .... ☐ Yes ☐ No
7. Any settling from any cause, or slippage, sliding, or other soil problems .... ☐ Yes ☐ No
8. Flooding, drainage or grading problems .... ☐ Yes ☐ No
9. Major damage to the property or any of the structures from fire, earthquake, floods, or landslides .... ☐ Yes ☐ No
10. Any zoning violations, nonconforming uses, violations of "setback" requirements .... ☐ Yes ☐ No
11. Neighborhood noise problems or other nuisances .... ☐ Yes ☐ No
12. CC&R's or other deed restrictions or obligations .... ☐ Yes ☐ No
13. Homeowners' Association which has any authority over the subject property .... ☐ Yes ☐ No
14. Any "common area" (facilities such as pools, tennis courts, walkways, or other areas co-owned in undivided interest with others) .... ☐ Yes ☐ No
15. Any notices of abatement or citations against the property .... ☐ Yes ☐ No
16. Any lawsuits by or against the Seller threatening to or affecting this real property, including any lawsuits alleging a defect or deficiency in this real property or "common areas" (facilities such as pools, tennis courts, walkways, or other areas co-owned in undivided interest with others) .... ☐ Yes ☐ No

If the answer to any of these is yes, explain. (Attach additional sheets if necessary.): _____
_____
_____
_____
_____

Seller certifies that the information herein is true and correct to the best of the Seller's knowledge as of the date signed by the Seller.

Seller_____ Date _____

Seller_____ Date _____

Buyer's Initials (_____)(_____)
Reviewed by _____ Date _____

Property Address: _____ Date: _____

III. AGENT'S INSPECTION DISCLOSURE
(To be completed only if the Seller is represented by an agent in this transaction.)

THE UNDERSIGNED, BASED ON THE ABOVE INQUIRY OF THE SELLER(S) AS TO THE CONDITION OF THE PROPERTY AND BASED ON A REASONABLY COMPETENT AND DILIGENT VISUAL INSPECTION OF THE ACCESSIBLE AREAS OF THE PROPERTY IN CONJUNCTION WITH THAT INQUIRY, STATES THE FOLLOWING:

☐ Agent notes no items for disclosure.

☐ Agent notes the following items: _____

_____

_____

_____

Agent (Broker Representing Seller) _____ By _____ Date _____
(Please Print)   (Associate Licensee or Broker Signature)

IV. AGENT'S INSPECTION DISCLOSURE
(To be completed only if the agent who has obtained the offer is other than the agent above.)

THE UNDERSIGNED, BASED ON A REASONABLY COMPETENT AND DILIGENT VISUAL INSPECTION OF THE ACCESSIBLE AREAS OF THE PROPERTY, STATES THE FOLLOWING:

☐ Agent notes no items for disclosure.

☐ Agent notes the following items: _____

_____

_____

_____

Agent (Broker Obtaining the Offer) _____ By _____ Date _____
(Please Print)   (Associate Licensee or Broker Signature)

V. BUYER(S) AND SELLER(S) MAY WISH TO OBTAIN PROFESSIONAL ADVICE AND/OR INSPECTIONS OF THE PROPERTY AND TO PROVIDE FOR APPROPRIATE PROVISIONS IN A CONTRACT BETWEEN BUYER AND SELLER(S) WITH RESPECT TO ANY ADVICE/INSPECTIONS/DEFECTS.

I/WE ACKNOWLEDGE RECEIPT OF A COPY OF THIS STATEMENT.

Seller _____ Date _____ Buyer _____ Date _____

Seller _____ Date _____ Buyer _____ Date _____

Agent (Broker Representing Seller) _____ By _____ Date _____
(Please Print)   (Associate Licensee or Broker Signature)

Agent (Broker Obtaining the Offer) _____ By _____ Date _____
(Please Print)   (Associate Licensee or Broker Signature)

SECTION 1102.3 OF THE CIVIL CODE PROVIDES A BUYER WITH THE RIGHT TO RESCIND A PURCHASE CONTRACT FOR AT LEAST THREE DAYS AFTER THE DELIVERY OF THIS DISCLOSURE IF DELIVERY OCCURS AFTER THE SIGNING OF AN OFFER TO PURCHASE. IF YOU WISH TO RESCIND THE CONTRACT, YOU MUST ACT WITHIN THE PRESCRIBED PERIOD.

A REAL ESTATE BROKER IS QUALIFIED TO ADVISE ON REAL ESTATE. IF YOU DESIRE LEGAL ADVICE, CONSULT YOUR ATTORNEY.

SURE TRAC
The System for Success®

Published by the
California Association of REALTORS®

TDS REVISED 10/03 (PAGE 3 OF 3)

Reviewed by _____ Date _____

REAL ESTATE TRANSFER DISCLOSURE STATEMENT (TDS PAGE 3 OF 3)

Agents must also respect their clients' wishes regarding boundaries, criteria or other requests made that the agent must follow. In other words, the agent must obey the wishes of the client. As long as the principal is directing the agent in a lawful direction, it is the duty of the agent to conduct business as directed by the principal.

All information regarding the principal that has been gathered by the agent is to be held in the strictest of confidence. Unless the principal has given permission to the agent, the agent is not to share any of this information with any third party. During the course of the agency relationship, an agent may receive sensitive financial, personal or other information that the principal will not want revealed to others. Sensitive information like this, prematurely given to the third party, may affect the asking price of the property, or the likelihood of the third party accepting any offer from the principal.

NATURAL HAZARDS DISCLOSURE

Houses sold in California that were built before 1960 must disclose any known earthquake weakness. Additionally, sellers of income properties built before 1975 must provide the buyer with a copy of the Commercial Property Owner's Guide to Earthquake Safety. If the property is exempt, the Commercial Property Owner's Guide to Earthquake Safety is not required.

Houses sold in California require the earthquake safety disclosure statement to be filled out by both the buyer and the seller. This form is simply referred to as the residential earthquake hazards report. The document contains seven questions regarding the security or safety of the property in the event of an earthquake. If there are any uncertainties regarding how to answer these questions, a good reference to consult for explanation is the Homeowner's Guide to Earthquake Safety published by the California Seismic Safety Commission. This guide will help people understand and identify any problematic areas on their property which may be hazardous in the event of an earthquake. The following is a list of the seven questions, and where you can find more information on how to answer them in the Homeowner's Guide to Earthquake Safety.

1. Is the water heater braced, strapped or anchored to resist falling during an earthquake? Information on what a braced water heater is, and how to brace one, can be found on page 6. A properly braced water heater is attached to the wall with metal strips so it will not tip over in an earthquake.

2. Is the house anchored or bolted to the foundation? Bolting requirements can be found on page 7. Houses are required to be bolted to the foundation. If the house has a crawl space, you can check to see. You should be able to see bolts every 4 – 6 feet, attached at the sill.

3. If the house has cripple walls, are the exterior walls braced? Have the concrete piers and posts been strengthened? Cripple walls are covered on pages 8 and 9. A cripple wall creates the crawl space under the house. It is a wood wall on the top of the foundation.

4. If the exterior foundation, or part of it, is made of unreinforced masonry, has it been strengthened? Information on unreinforced masonry can be found on page 10. Masonry walls are made of either brick or stone. Bricks or stone blocks that are hollow without steel rods are unreinforced.

5. For hillside houses, are the exterior tall foundation walls braced, and have they been built to resist earthquakes or strengthened? Information and

requirements can be found on page 11 on bracing and strengthening. It is a good idea to consult an engineer to determine if the walls need strengthening.

6. If the exterior walls of the house, or part of them, are made of unreinforced masonry, have they been strengthened? Page 12 will discuss exterior wall strengthening. To find out if your exterior walls have been strengthened, you can consult with the building department to check your plans, or have a professional testing service test for steel in the walls.

7. If the house has a living area over the garage, was the wall around the garage door opening either built to resist earthquakes or has it been strengthened? Page 13 discusses this bracing. If there is plywood around the garage door opening, or if the door opening is in line with the rest of the house, it is probably braced.

In addition to disclosing earthquake hazards, natural hazards must also be disclosed in the Natural Hazards Disclosure Statement. The following hazards are covered, or disclosed, on this statement:

- **Earthquake fault zones**. Sellers must disclose to the buyer if the property is located in a fault zone, as indicated by a map.

- **Seismic hazard zone**. Sellers must disclose to the buyer if the property being purchased is located in a seismic hazard zone, or one where a massive earthquake could occur, creating landslides and very strong shaking. If a seller is unsure if the property is located in such a hazard zone, he or she can check public postings of these zones located at the following offices: County Recorder, County Assessor and County Planning Agency.

- **State fire responsibility area**. In certain areas, the state sets protection requirements that residents must follow, such as keeping overgrowth and brush clear. In these areas, the state is also responsible for fighting any fire that should break out. If the seller is aware that the property sits within the state fire responsibility area, this disclosure must be made at the time of sale. If the buyer wants to know, and the seller is not sure, maps can be consulted at the following offices: County Recorder, County Assessor and County Planning Agency.

- **Very high fire hazard zones**. This is another area where the state has set protection requirements. Property owners must make sure they follow all guidelines to protect themselves from the potential of dangerous wildfires.

- **Wildland area that may contain substantial fire risks and hazards**. The state is not required to provide fire protection in wildland areas; this service is provided by the Department of Forestry. It is important for the seller to disclose this fact so the buyer does not misunderstand who will be providing fire protection in the event of a wildfire. Maps showing wildland areas covered by the Department of Forestry can be found posted in the office of the Country Recorder, Assessor and Planning Agency.

- **Special flood hazard areas**. The Federal Emergency Management Agency has published maps indicating where the risk for flooding could occur. If the property for sale is located in this area, it is up to the seller's agent to disclose this fact, if it is known. The Federal Emergency Management Agency also posts these maps in the County Recorder, Assessor and Planning offices.

RESIDENTIAL EARTHQUAKE HAZARDS REPORT

Refer to Section 8897 *et seq.*, California Government Code

Name	Assessor's Parcel No.
Street Address	Year Built
City and County	Zip Code

Answer these questions to the best of your knowledge. If you do not have actual knowledge as to whether the weakness exists or not, answer "Don't Know." If your house does not have the feature, answer "Doesn't Apply." The page numbers in the right-hand column indicate where in this guide you can find information on each of these features.

	Yes	No	Doesn't Apply	Don't Know	See Page
1. Is the water heater braced, strapped, or anchored to resist falling during an earthquake?	☐	☐	☐	☐	6
2. Is the house anchored or bolted to the foundation?	☐	☐	☐	☐	7
3. If the house has cripple walls:					
° Are the exterior cripple walls braced?	☐	☐	☐	☐	8
° If the exterior foundation consists of unconnected concrete piers and posts, have they been strengthened?	☐	☐	☐	☐	9
4. If the exterior foundation, or part of it, is made of unreinforced masonry, has it been strengthened?	☐	☐	☐	☐	10
5. If the house is built on a hillside, answer the following:					
° Are the exterior tall foundation walls braced?	☐	☐	☐	☐	11
° Were the tall posts or columns either built to resist earthquakes or have they been strengthened?	☐	☐	☐	☐	11
6. If the exterior walls of the house, or part of them, are made of unreinforced masonry, have they been strengthened?	☐	☐	☐	☐	12
7. If the house has a living area over the garage, was the wall around the garage door opening either built to resist earthquakes or has it been strengthened?	☐	☐	☐	☐	13

If any of the questions are answered "No," the house is likely to have an earthquake weakness. Questions answered "Don't Know" may indicate a need for further evaluation. If you corrected one or more of these weaknesses, describe the work on a separate page.

As Seller of the property described herein, I have answered the questions above to the best of my knowledge in an effort to fully disclose any potential earthquake weaknesses it may have.

EXECUTED BY

_____   _____   _____
(Seller)   (Seller)   Date

I acknowledge receipt of this form, completed and signed by the Seller. I understand that if the Seller has answered "No" to one or more questions, or if Seller has indicated a lack of knowledge, there may be one or more earthquake weaknesses in this house.

_____   _____   _____
(Buyer)   (Buyer)   Date

This earthquake disclosure is made in addition to the standard real estate transfer disclosure statement also required by law.

Keep your copy of this form for future reference.

NATURAL HAZARD DISCLOSURE STATEMENT

This statement applies to the following property: _____

The transferor and his or her agent(s) disclose the following information with the knowledge that even though this is not a warranty, prospective transferees may rely on this information in deciding whether and on what terms to purchase the subject property. Transferor hereby authorizes any agent(s) representing any principal(s) in this action to provide a copy of this statement to any person or entity in connection with any actual or anticipated sale of the property.

The following are representations made by the transferor and his or her agent(s) based on their knowledge and maps drawn by the state and federal governments. This information is a disclosure and is not intended to be part of any contract between the transferee and transferor.

THIS REAL PROPERTY LIES WITHIN THE FOLLOWING HAZARDOUS AREA(S): (Check the answer which applies.)

A SPECIAL FLOOD HAZARD AREA (Any type Zone "A" or "V") designated by the Federal Emergency Management Agency.

Yes _____   No _____   Do not know and information not available from local jurisdiction _____

AN AREA OF POTENTIAL FLOODING shown on a dam failure inundation map pursuant to Section 8589.5 of the Government Code.

Yes _____   No _____   Do not know and information not available from local jurisdiction _____

A VERY HIGH FIRE HAZARD SEVERITY ZONE pursuant to Section 51178 or 51179 of the Government Code. The owner of this property is subject to the maintenance requirements of Section 51182 of the Government Code.

Yes _____   No _____

A WILDLAND AREA THAT MAY CONTAIN SUBSTANTIAL FOREST FIRE RISKS AND HAZARDS pursuant to Section 4125 of the Public Resources Code. The owner of this property is subject to the maintenance requirements of Section 4291 of the Public Resources Code. Additionally, it is not the state's responsibility to provide fire protection services to any building or structure located within the wildlands unless the Department of Forestry and Fire Protection has entered into a cooperative agreement with a local agency for those purposes pursuant to Section 4142 of the Public Resources Code.

Yes _____   No _____

AN EARTHQUAKE FAULT ZONE pursuant to Section 2622 of the Public Resources Code.

Yes _____   No _____

A SEISMIC HAZARD ZONE pursuant to Section 2696 of the Public Resources Code.

Yes (Landslide Zone) _____

Yes (Liquefaction Zone) _____   No _____   Map not yet released by state _____

THESE HAZARDS MAY LIMIT YOUR ABILITY TO DEVELOP THE REAL PROPERTY, TO OBTAIN INSURANCE, OR TO RECEIVE ASSISTANCE AFTER A DISASTER.

THE MAPS ON WHICH THESE DISCLOSURES ARE BASED ESTIMATE WHERE NATURAL HAZARDS EXIST. THEY ARE NOT DEFINITIVE INDICATORS OF WHETHER OR NOT A PROPERTY WILL BE AFFECTED BY A NATURAL DISASTER. TRANSFEREE(S) AND TRANSFEROR(S) MAY WISH TO OBTAIN PROFESSIONAL ADVICE REGARDING THOSE HAZARDS AND OTHER HAZARDS THAT MAY AFFECT THE PROPERTY.

> The information in this box is not part of the statutory form.
> ☐ (If checked) The representations made in this form are based upon information provided by an independent third-party report provided as a substituted disclosure pursuant to California Civil Code §1102.4. Neither the seller nor the seller's agent (1) has independently verified the information contained in this form and the report or (2) is personally aware of any errors or inaccuracies in the information contained on this form.

Transferor represents that the information herein is true and correct to the best of the transferor's knowledge as of the date signed by the transferor.

Signature of Transferor _____ Date _____

Agent represents that the information herein is true and correct to the best of the agent's knowledge as of the date signed by the agent.

Signature of Agent _____ Date _____

Signature of Agent _____ Date _____

Transferee represents that he or she has read and understands this document.

Signature of Transferee _____ Date _____

THIS FORM HAS BEEN APPROVED BY THE CALIFORNIA ASSOCIATION OF REALTORS® (C.A.R.). NO REPRESENTATION IS MADE AS TO THE LEGAL VALIDITY OR ADEQUACY OF ANY PROVISION IN ANY SPECIFIC TRANSACTION. A REAL ESTATE BROKER IS THE PERSON QUALIFIED TO ADVISE ON REAL ESTATE TRANSACTIONS. IF YOU DESIRE LEGAL OR TAX ADVICE, CONSULT AN APPROPRIATE PROFESSIONAL.

This form is available for use by the entire real estate industry. It is not intended to identify the user as a REALTOR®. REALTOR® is a registered collective membership mark which may be used only by members of the NATIONAL ASSOCIATION OF REALTORS® who subscribe to its Code of Ethics.

The copyright laws of the United States (Title 17 U.S. Code) forbid the unauthorized reproduction of this form, or any portion thereof, by photocopy machine or any other means, including facsimile or computerized formats. Copyright © 1998-1999, CALIFORNIA ASSOCIATION OF REALTORS®, INC. ALL RIGHTS RESERVED.

Published and Distributed by:
REAL ESTATE BUSINESS SERVICES, INC.
a subsidiary of the CALIFORNIA ASSOCIATION OF REALTORS®
525 South Virgil Avenue, Los Angeles, California 90020

PRINT DATE

Page ___ of ___ Pages.
REVISED 10/99

OFFICE USE ONLY
Reviewed by Broker
or Designee _____
Date _____

FORM NHD-11

- **Areas of potential flooding**. This area is a potential flood hazard in the event a dam should fail. Disclosure may be made by the seller or the seller's agent, or can be researched on maps contained in the County Recorder, Assessor and Planning offices.

AGENT'S INSPECTION DISCLOSURE

When an agent takes a listing on a residential property with 1-4 units, he or she is required to make a personal visual inspection of the property to determine the condition of all aspects of the property. When doing the inspection, it is a good idea to fill out the transfer disclosure statement. This will help protect the agent from any damages caused for problems not disclosed which could have easily been identified by an agent on his or her visual inspection of the property. If an agent does not make the inspection and fill out the transfer disclosure statement, he or she may be held liable for damages up to two years after the sale. There are exemptions from this disclosure. These exemptions include property transfers:

- Requiring a public report

- Pursuant to a court order

- By foreclosure

- By a fiduciary

- From one co-owner to another

- Between spouses or direct blood relatives

- Between spouses in connection with a divorce

- By the state controller

- As a result of failure to pay property taxes

- To or from any government, which includes exchanges.

While the above situations do not require disclosure, it is a good idea to conduct a visual inspection and fill out a property disclosure statement anyway. This will leave no room for doubt or blame for any problems should any occur.

Remember
- It is always a good idea to conduct an inspection and fill out the transfer disclosure statement, even when one is not required.

The longer you are an agent, the more familiar you will be with what to check and how to check it. The following is a list of things to inspect when conducting your visual inspection of property.

Structure
Structure problems or structure failure may be caused by several factors. Poor materials, insects and pests, environment, faulty design or simply deterioration due to age can cause problems to the structure of the home. When making your inspection pay close attention to the following:

- Uneven floors, or floors that slope

- Cracks in the foundations, at the corners of walls, or around openings, or other cracks in structural walls, beams, and columns both on the inside and outside of the house.

- An uneven roof ridgeline.

- Bulges in the floor or walls.

- Caved in or squeaky floors indicating excessive deflection of girders and joists.

- Ill-fitting doors.

- Unstable structural components.

Mold

All property transfers must disclose the presence or evidence of mold. If the property is damp, or has had problems in the past with a leaky roof, it is a good idea to have the property tested for mold. If mold is found, it must be disclosed, or eradicated. Mold could be a very serious situation, as some people have severe allergies, and even life threatening conditions, resulting from mold. If you are unsure if there is mold present, you may make a recommendation to the buyer that he or she should check for mold based on your suspicion.

Water Problems

Water can cause serious problems to a house. The source of the water could come from either inside or outside, but any evidence of water leakage or damage must be disclosed, as it could cause mold. Some of the potential red flag signs to look for include:

- Warped or rotten wood

- Water spots or stains on the ceiling

- Rust, mold or mildew

- Roof problems such as leaks or other defects

- Paint problems such as peeling or other deterioration

- Tile damage

Insect Infestation

There are many insects that can cause damage to a home, and many of these insects can go undetected as they leave few visible signs that they are present until it is too late. Two of the worst offenders in the insect world are termites and carpenter ants. These insects will attack internally, behind walls in the main structural components of the house, causing them to weaken. An agent can look for the following signs to identify the presence of insects, particularly termites and carpenter ants:

- Mud "tubes" made from soil and wood shavings

- Wood shavings around wooden components

Material Deterioration

Material deterioration can occur from different factors such as pests, climate, poor building materials or substandard construction practices. Deterioration of materials in a structure can lead to rot, mold and decomposition of materials. Some signs of deterioration a real estate agent can look for when conducting an inspection are:

- Erosion of concrete, mortar or other masonry materials

- Decay or warping of wood

- Warping, rotting or cracking around windows and doors

There are many physical factors in a house that indicate there may be a problem. For example, as mentioned earlier, stains on the ceiling are an indication there may be issues with the roof, or that there is a water leak somewhere internally. Windows and doors that stick, or close hard are an indication that there could potentially be a problem with warping or deteriorating wood. Uneven floors, resawn doorjambs and any evidence of masonry erosion are all good indications there may be a problem the agent must look further into, and subsequently disclose.

To protect themselves, real estate agents generally use three techniques in home inspection. It is important to note, however, that even when using any or all of the following three methods of inspection, it is still the agent's responsibility to conduct an inspection of his or her own and disclose any problems.

- Have the seller supply the buyer with the pest inspection report.

- Have the buyer pay for a professional to inspect the home, examine the property and verify any defects on the transfer disclosure statement, and search for any defects not listed on the statement.

- Encourage the buyer to purchase a home protection plan that will cover any of the defects outlined in the plan for a set duration, usually one year.

During the agent's inspection of the property, it is important that he or she learns as much about the property, neighborhood, community and surrounding area as possible, and disclose any facts he or she thinks the buyer or seller might find important in making the decision. Some of these facts could include living in a flood zone or being in the flight path of an airport.

ENVIRONMENTAL HAZARDS DISCLOSURE

California has mandated that any environmental hazards affecting the property in any way be disclosed. If the seller is unaware of any hazards affecting his or her property, he or she must fill out a statement that he or she is unaware of any hazards, but that a hazard may exist unbeknownst to him or her. By making this statement, in the event there is an environmental hazard the seller will be released of any liability.

The booklet Environmental Hazards: a Guide for Homeowners, Buyers, Landlords and Tenants has been created for reference to see what possible hazards exist. The seller and the seller's agent are not required to give the buyer any additional information regarding environmental hazards, unless the seller or the seller's agent is aware of a specific environmental hazard that has the potential to affect the property.

Sick Building Syndrome

Sick building syndrome or SBS is a condition that is caused by the air quality in buildings. Most modern high-rises, expansive commercial buildings or other large buildings rely on fresh air being brought in through the ventilation system. When a building is experiencing SBS, the people using the space may experience fatigue, dizziness, nausea, headaches, eye, nose and throat infections, cough, itchy or dry skin or have sensitivity to odors.

A single specific cause or solution has not been identified for sick building syndrome. Poor ventilation or dirty air ducts could be a problem, and cleaning the ducts or increasing the output to those areas experiencing SBS is one possible solution. Regardless of the causes or solution for this condition, it is important for the agent to disclose SBS to any potential tenant.

Military Ordnance Location

If the seller or seller's agent is aware that the property is within one mile of a former military training ground which had contained explosives or other hazardous materials, this fact must be disclosed. If a buyer finds out that the property is within one mile of an old military training facility, he or she has the right to back out of the contract.

Lead-Based Paint

Properties built before 1978 have the potential to contain lead-based paint, which is hazardous if ingested. Agents must supply the buyer of a property built before 1978 the booklet Protect Your Family from Lead in Your Home written by the Federal Environmental Protection Agency. In addition to this booklet, the California booklet Environmental Hazards: A Guide for Homeowners, Buyers, Landlords and Tenants can also be given to the buyer covering lead-based hazards.

Any records, reports or known information regarding lead-based paint and its hazards must be supplied to prospective buyers or tenants. Owners must disclose to the agent whether the hazard exists in their property, and this information must then be disclosed to the potential buyers.

Hazardous Substances Released

Buyers and tenants must be informed of hazardous waste disposal on or near their property. Health and Safety code Section 25359.7(a) requires that this disclosure be made if there is evidence of hazardous waste disposal or if there is reasonable cause to believe there may have been dumping on the property at one time.

Tenants must notify landlords of any substances they know to exist or have released themselves. Any tenant not notifying the landlord of hazardous dumping will be in default under the terms of the lease.

Water Contamination

Any information an agent might have regarding water contamination in a community well or contamination around a property with a private well must be disclosed to the buyer. California has experienced contamination of some of its water sources through industrial, agricultural and military operations. This contamination can cause possible health risks serious enough to be identified by the Environmental Protection Agency.

Environmental Hazards Booklet

The Department of Real Estate and the Department of Health Services have prepared a booklet for homeowners and buyers. This booklet is distributed by the California Association of RELATORS® for use by real estate agents to fully disclose environmental issues to prospective buyers. The booklet contains a form inside the back cover stating the buyers have received the booklet. The buyers should tear out and sign the form, and it should be retained in the broker's file.

Under the mandated disclosure of environmental hazards, it is important for brokers to have copies of these tear-out sheets in their files. Sales agents should make photocopies of these sheets and keep them in their personal escrow files.

The booklet is divided into six sections:
1. Asbestos
2. Formaldehyde
3. Lead
4. Radon
5. Hazardous Waste
6. Household Hazardous Waste

The appendixes contain:
1. A list of Federal and State Agencies
2. A Glossary of Terms

All agents should familiarize themselves with this booklet.

Environmental Hazards Client Card

TO WHOM IT MAY CONCERN:

I have received a copy of "Environmental Hazards: A Guide for Homeowners and Buyers" from the Broker(s) in this transaction.

Date:	(Signature)
Time:	(Printed Name)
Date:	(Signature)
Time:	(Printed Name)

An agent should disclose deaths which have happened on the property within the past three years. A natural death need not be disclosed; however, other deaths such as homicide, suicide or accidental death should be disclosed. After three years, this disclosure is not necessary.

Death resulting from AIDS or AIDS-related complications is not necessary to disclose. The fact that an individual previously living in the property had been infected with AIDS is also not a necessary disclosure.

Besides suicide or murder, other events may stigmatize the property. Stigmatized property is property that is considered undesirable for reasons that are not physical or environmental. Properties once used by cult leaders, used in satanic rituals, or where molestations took place could all be considered stigmatized property. A good rule of thumb is to disclose any information you know regarding the property. If a court case should ever occur because of information discovered after-the-fact, the agent can always protect himself or herself through disclosure and honesty at the very beginning of the transaction.

When a property is close to a licensed care facility containing six or fewer people, that fact is not required to be disclosed. This is per Opinion 95-907 of the California Attorney General. Those care facilities housing more than six occupants must be disclosed to the buyer.

Remember
- Non-natural deaths such as suicide or murder must be disclosed if they occurred within 3 years from the date of sale
- Natural death, or a death related to AIDS, is not required to be disclosed..

S U B D I V I S I O N   D I S C L O S U R E

There are certain disclosures that apply only to subdivisions, and the protection of purchasers in these new areas. It would be easy for a developer to make fraudulent statements to make the development look enticing to a buyer, only to have the buyer discover after all the contracts have been signed that statements made regarding the property, land, or subdivision were false.

California uses the Subdivided Lands Law to protect buyers from fraud. Under the Subdivided Lands Law, a public report must be provided to buyers before they sign a contract. The public report is considered the disclosure for the property, and will accurately describe the property and subdivision. Any buyer in a new subdivision receiving a public report must sign a statement acknowledging that he or she has received the report.

The public report must be reviewed and approved by the California Real Estate Commissioner before it can be provided to any buyer. This report discloses information regarding the identity of the subdivider, the location of the subdivision, size of the property, use restrictions, unusual costs, taxes, assessments and other findings regarding the property. This report is considered valid for up to five years from its original date of issuance.

The Real Estate Commissioner may issue a preliminary public report, which is valid for one year. A preliminary public report will allow a developer to accept a deposit and reservation from any interested buyers, but the buyer is not obligated to enter into any contract until the final public report is issued.

There is a conditional public report that may be issued allowing the subdeveloper to enter into a binding contract with a buyer. This contract will be legal and binding, but escrow cannot close until the final public report is issued. The conditional report is valid for six months, and may be renewed one time for an additional six months. If the purchaser is not happy with the final report because of any changes made from the conditional report, he or she may be released from any contractual agreements, and he or she is entitled to a full refund of any deposit monies.

Remember

There are three types of reports:

- Preliminary public report allowing subdividers to take deposit monies and reservations on property, but no contracts are signed.
- Conditional pubic report allowing subdividers to enter into a contract, but cannot close escrow until the final public report is issued.
- Public report disclosing all information about the subdivision. This allows the developer to sign and execute contracts with buyers.

COMMON INTEREST SUBDIVISION

A common interest subdivision is a community where the owner will have his or her separate unit, apartment or space and share interest in the common areas of the project. Condominiums, cooperatives, community apartment projects and planned unit developments all fall under this type of subdivision. Generally, owners can do what they want to their units as long as it is allowed by the homeowners' association, or the governing body for the subdivision. The homeowners' association also governs the common areas of the community.

When a unit in a common interest subdivision is sold, the buyer must be given a copy of Common Interest Development General Information. Additionally, developers or sellers must give the buyer a copy of the covenants, conditions and restrictions, bylaws, and articles of incorporation, plus an owners' association financial statement including all current assessments and costs.

If there is a conflict between a developer and the homeowners' association that escalates into legal action, construction defects must be listed, if any, and a copy of this report must be given to any potential buyer. If there are defects, corrections must be described along with the estimated work date and time of completion. All defects or status of defect in addition to any legal action must be given to a potential buyer, as this may affect the buyer's decision in executing the purchase contract.

The interstate Land Sales Full Disclosure Act requires disclosures for interstate sale of unimproved lots for subdivisions of 25 or more lots. The disclosures that must be made include soil conditions, title, available utilities, location, facilities and any charges associated with the subdivision. Like other subdivision laws, this is intended to prevent fraud.

In the event a developer converts apartments into privately owned condominium units, a public hearing must be held to inform all tenants of this opportunity to purchase their units. This may seem like common sense, but it prevents the developer from privately selling the units out from underneath the current tenants, while giving the current tenants opportunity to stay by purchasing their unit.

FINANCING DISCLOSURE

Brokers as well as lenders are responsible for all disclosures relating to financing and the options available to buyers.

Mortgage Loan Disclosure Statement

If a real estate broker, rather than a mortgage broker, negotiates a loan on behalf of borrowers or lenders, the broker must deliver a mortgage loan disclosure statement (MLDS) to the borrower(s) within three business days of receiving the borrower's written loan application.

Borrower's Right to Copy of Appraisal

The borrower is entitled to a copy of the appraisal report if the borrower paid for the appraisal. It is the lender's responsibility to notify the borrower of this right.

Real Estate Settlement Procedures Act

The Real Estate Settlement Procedures Act (RESPA) applies to all residential properties containing 1-4 living units. The lender is responsible for furnishing the applicant with a good faith estimate of all closing costs, as well as a booklet prepared by the Department of Housing and Urban Development providing information regarding federally backed loans. The lender must supply the borrower with this information within three days of the loan application.

The borrower has the right to view the settlement on or before the date of settlement, and can actually request a copy of it one day prior to the date of settlement.

Under RESPA, the broker is allowed to have a business arrangement with other service providers where one or both parties stand to make a financial gain. If there is an agreement between the broker and another service provider, this must be fully disclosed to the borrower, and the borrower must be given the opportunity to utilize any other provider of his or her choice. Service providers could include a title company or escrow agent.

Seller Financing Disclosure

Any sellers who plan on carrying back a note on financing the property they are selling must disclose this fact to the buyer. This disclosure applies to residential properties having between 1 – 4 living units.

Seller financing, sometimes called "creative financing," happens when the seller carries back a second or third trust deed on the property that he or she just sold. Because of unethical transactions and high dollar losses, Civil Code 2956-2967 was enacted, requiring any seller carrying back a loan to provide the buyer with the seller financing addendum and disclosure.

Disclosure must be made by the arranger of credit, and is required before the note can be executed. The seller, buyer, and the person arranging credit must sign the disclosure, with each party receiving a copy of the disclosure. The person responsible for arranging credit must keep the disclosure on file for three years.

If there is more than one arranger of credit, the arranger who obtains the purchase offer must make the disclosure. This person could be the selling broker or the broker who is arranging the sale of the property. Besides the selling broker or broker arranging the sale of the property, a real estate licensee or an attorney may also make this disclosure, as long as the agreement is in writing. It will be the selling agent's responsibility to make sure this disclosure is made.

Besides making the seller's financing disclosure when the seller carries back a trust deed, disclosure must also be made when the seller extends credit to the buyer. This credit can be in the form of a deferred payment, where the seller will accept payment for the property at a later time. This is acceptable as long as all applicable finance charges are applied to any arrangement where more than four payments will be made.

It is important for you to understand what exactly must be disclosed with this form. The following is a list of all items that must be disclosed:

- The amount of the note, where the funds are coming from, the purpose for the money, and when the buyer receives cash from the proceeds of the transaction.

- Who is responsible for paying off an all-inclusive trust deed if the lender asks for an accelerated payoff.

- All terms of the note including length, number of payments, when the payment is due, and the amount of the note.

- That the deed of trust securing the note be recorded to avoid any future complications or problems.

- All current liens on the property and the status of the note.

- Buyer's credit score, job status, and other important background information on the buyer regarding his or her ability to repay the note.

- If the note is not fully amortized, it will have to be refinanced at maturity. If a balloon payment is used, the seller must notify the buyer between 60-150 days that the payment is approaching.

- A request for Notice of Default to be filed and recorded to protect the seller in the event other, senior loans are defaulted.

- Title insurance policy will be obtained and furnished to both the buyer and seller.

- Negative amortization and deferred interest, if applicable, must be explained to the buyer.

- Notice to the seller must be given to update property tax payment status.

- Notice to the seller in the event casualty insurance has been paid out due to an incident on the property.

Blanket Encumbrance Disclosure
There may be an underlying blanket encumbrance that affects more than one property. If such an encumbrance exists, the buyer must be made aware of this fact. The buyer's funds should be protected unless the property can be released from the blanket encumbrance. The borrower is required to sign the disclosure acknowledging that he

This is an addendum to the ☐ California Residential Purchase Agreement, ☐ Counter Offer, or ☐ Other _____
_____, ("Agreement"), dated _____

On property known as _____ ("Property"),

between _____ ("Buyer"),

and _____ ("Seller").

Seller agrees to extend credit to Buyer as follows:

1. **PRINCIPAL; INTEREST; PAYMENT; MATURITY TERMS:** ☐ Principal amount $_____ interest at _____%
   per annum, payable approximately $_____ per ☐ month, ☐ year, or ☐ other _____
   remaining principal balance due in _____ years.

2. **LOAN APPLICATION; CREDIT REPORT:** Within 5 (or ☐ _____) Days After Acceptance: (a) Buyer shall provide Seller a completed loan application on a form acceptable to Seller (such as a FNMA/FHLMC Uniform Residential Loan Application for residential one to four unit properties); and (b) Buyer authorizes Seller and/or Agent to obtain, at Buyer's expense, a copy of Buyer's credit report. Buyer shall provide any supporting documentation reasonably requested by Seller. Seller, after first giving Buyer a Notice to Buyer to Perform, may cancel this Agreement in writing and authorize return of Buyer's deposit if Buyer fails to provide such documents within that time, or if Seller disapproves any above item within 5 (or ☐ _____) Days After receipt of each item.

3. **CREDIT DOCUMENTS:** This extension of credit by Seller will be evidenced by: ☐ Note and deed of trust; ☐ All-inclusive note and deed of trust; ☐ Installment land sale contract; ☐ Lease/option (when parties intend transfer of equitable title); OR ☐ Other (specify) _____

THE FOLLOWING TERMS APPLY ONLY IF CHECKED. SELLER IS ADVISED TO READ ALL TERMS, EVEN THOSE NOT CHECKED, TO UNDERSTAND WHAT IS OR IS NOT INCLUDED, AND, IF NOT INCLUDED, THE CONSEQUENCES THEREOF.

4. ☐ **LATE CHARGE:** If any payment is not made within _____ Days after it is due, a late charge of either $_____, or _____% of the installment due, may be charged to Buyer. NOTE: On single family residences that Buyer intends to occupy, California Civil Code §2954.4(a) limits the late charge to no more than 6% of the total installment payment due and requires a grace period of no less than 10 days.

5. ☐ **BALLOON PAYMENT:** The extension of credit will provide for a balloon payment, in the amount of $_____ plus any accrued interest, which is due on _____ (date).

6. ☐ **PREPAYMENT:** If all or part of this extension of credit is paid early, Seller may charge a prepayment penalty as follows (if applicable): _____. Caution: California Civil Code §2954.9 contains limitations on prepayment penalties for residential one to four unit properties.

7. ☐ **DUE ON SALE:** If any interest in the Property is sold or otherwise transferred, Seller has the option to require immediate payment of the entire unpaid principal balance, plus any accrued interest.

8.* ☐ **REQUEST FOR COPY OF NOTICE OF DEFAULT:** A request for a copy of Notice of Default as defined in California Civil Code §2924b will be recorded. If Not, Seller is advised to consider recording a Request for Notice of Default.

9.* ☐ **REQUEST FOR NOTICE OF DELINQUENCY:** A request for Notice of Delinquency as defined in California Civil Code §2924e, to be signed and paid for by Buyer, will be made to senior lienholders. If not, Seller is advised to consider making a Request for Notice of Delinquency. Seller is advised to check with senior lienholders to verify whether they will honor this request.

10.*☐ **TAX SERVICE:**
   A. If property taxes on the Property become delinquent, tax service will be arranged to report to Seller. If not, Seller is advised to consider retaining a tax service, or to otherwise determine that property taxes are paid.
   B. ☐ Buyer, ☐ Seller, shall be responsible for the initial and continued retention of, and payment for, such tax service.

11. ☐ **TITLE INSURANCE:** Title insurance coverage will be provided to both Seller and Buyer insuring their respective interests in the Property. If not, Buyer and Seller are advised to consider securing such title insurance coverage.

12. ☐ **HAZARD INSURANCE:**
   A. The parties' escrow holder or insurance carrier will be directed to include a loss payee endorsement, adding Seller to the Property insurance policy. If not, Seller is advised to secure such an endorsement, or acquire a separate insurance policy.
   B. Property insurance does not include earthquake or flood insurance coverage, unless checked:
      ☐ Earthquake insurance will be obtained; ☐ Flood insurance will be obtained.

13. ☐ **PROCEEDS TO BUYER:** Buyer will receive cash proceeds at the close of the sale transaction. The amount received will be approximately $_____ from _____ (indicate source of proceeds). Buyer represents that the purpose of such disbursement is as follows: _____

14. ☐ **NEGATIVE AMORTIZATION; DEFERRED INTEREST:** Negative amortization results when Buyer's periodic payments are less than the amount of interest earned on the obligation. Deferred interest also results when the obligation does not require periodic payments for a period of time. In either case, interest is not payable as it accrues. This accrued interest will have to be paid by Buyer at a later time, and may result in Buyer owing more on the obligation than at its origination. The credit being extended to Buyer by Seller will provide for negative amortization or deferred interest as indicated below. (Check A, B, or C. CHECK ONE ONLY.)
   ☐ A. All negative amortization or deferred interest shall be added to the principal _____ (e.g., annually, monthly, etc.), and thereafter shall bear interest at the rate specified in the credit documents (compound interest);
   OR ☐ B. All deferred interest shall be due and payable, along with principal, at maturity;
   OR ☐ C. Other _____

*(For Paragraphs 8-10) In order to receive timely and continued notification, Seller is advised to record appropriate notices and/or to notify appropriate parties of any change in Seller's address.

SFA REVISED 10/02 (PAGE 1 OF 3) Print Date

Buyer's Initials (_____)(_____)

Seller's Initials (_____)(_____)

Reviewed by _____ Date _____

SELLER FINANCING ADDENDUM AND DISCLOSURE (SFA PAGE 1 OF 3)

Property Address: _____ Date: _____

15. ☐ **ALL-INCLUSIVE DEED OF TRUST; INSTALLMENT LAND SALE CONTRACT:** This transaction involves the use of an all-inclusive (or wraparound) deed of trust or an installment land sale contract. That deed of trust or contract shall provide as follows:
A. In the event of an acceleration of any senior encumbrance, the responsibility for payment, or for legal defense is: _____
_____ ; OR ☐ Is not specified in the credit or security documents.
B. In the event of the prepayment of a senior encumbrance, the responsibilities and rights of Buyer and Seller regarding refinancing, prepayment penalties, and any prepayment discounts are: _____ ;
OR ☐ **Are not specified in the documents evidencing credit.**
C. Buyer will make periodic payments to _____ (Seller, collection agent, or any neutral third party), who will be responsible for disbursing payments to the payee(s) on the senior encumbrance(s) and to Seller. NOTE: The Parties are advised to designate a neutral third party for these purposes.

16. ☐ **TAX IDENTIFICATION NUMBERS:** Buyer and Seller shall each provide to each other their Social Security Numbers or Taxpayer Identification Numbers.

17. ☐ **OTHER CREDIT TERMS:** _____

18. ☐ **RECORDING:** The documents evidencing credit (paragraph 3) will be recorded with the county recorder where the Property is located. If not, Buyer and Seller are advised that their respective interests in the Property may be jeopardized by intervening liens, judgments, encumbrances, or subsequent transfers.

19. ☐ **JUNIOR FINANCING:** There will be additional financing, secured by the Property, junior to this Seller financing. Explain: _____

20. **SENIOR LOANS AND ENCUMBRANCES:** The following information is provided on loans and/or encumbrances that will be senior to Seller financing. NOTE: The following are estimates, unless otherwise marked with an asterisk (*). If checked: ☐ A separate sheet with information on additional senior loans/encumbrances is attached

		1st	2nd
A. Original Balance	$		$
B. Current Balance		$	$
C. Periodic Payment (e.g. $100/month)	$		$ /
Including Impounds of:			$ /
D. Interest Rate (per annum)		%	%
E. Fixed or Variable Rate:			
If Variable Rate: Lifetime Cap (Ceiling)			
Indicator (Underlying Index)			
Margins			
F. Maturity Date			
G. Amount of Balloon Payment	$		$
H. Date Balloon Payment Due			
I. Potential for Negative Amortization? (Yes, No, or Unknown)			
J. Due on Sale? (Yes, No, or Unknown)			
K. Pre-payment penalty? (Yes, No, or Unknown)			
L. Are payments current? (Yes, No, or Unknown)			

21. **BUYER'S CREDITWORTHINESS:** (CHECK EITHER A OR B. Do not check both) In addition to the loan application, credit report and other information requested under paragraph 2:
A. ☐ No other disclosure concerning Buyer's creditworthiness has been made to Seller;
OR B. ☐ The following representations concerning Buyer's creditworthiness are made by Buyer(s) to Seller:

Borrower _____	Co-Borrower _____
1. Occupation _____	1. Occupation _____
2. Employer _____	2. Employer _____
3. Length of Employment _____	3. Length of Employment _____
4. Monthly Gross Income _____	4. Monthly Gross Income _____
5. Other _____	5. Other _____

22. **ADDED, DELETED OR SUBSTITUTED BUYERS:** The addition, deletion or substitution of any person or entity under this Agreement or to title prior to close of escrow shall require Seller's written consent. Seller may grant or withhold consent in Seller's sole discretion. Any additional or substituted person or entity shall, if requested by Seller, submit to Seller the same documentation as required for the original named Buyer. Seller and/or Brokers may obtain a credit report, at Buyer's expense, on any such person or entity.

Buyer's Initials (_____)(_____)
Seller's Initials (_____)(_____)

SFA REVISED 10/02 (PAGE 2 OF 3)

Reviewed by _____ Date _____

SELLER FINANCING ADDENDUM AND DISCLOSURE (SFA PAGE 2 OF 3)

Property Address: _____ Date: _____

23. CAUTION:

   A. If the Seller financing requires a balloon payment, Seller shall give Buyer written notice, according to the terms of Civil Code §2966, at least 90 and not more than 150 days before the balloon payment is due if the transaction is for the purchase of a dwelling for not more than four families.

   B. If any obligation secured by the Property calls for a balloon payment, Seller and Buyer are aware that refinancing of the balloon payment at maturity may be difficult or impossible, depending on conditions in the conventional mortgage marketplace at that time. There are no assurances that new financing or a loan extension will be available when the balloon prepayment, or any prepayment, is due.

   C. If any of the existing or proposed loans or extensions of credit would require refinancing as a result of a lack of full amortization, such refinancing might be difficult or impossible in the conventional mortgage marketplace.

   D. In the event of default by Buyer (1) Seller may have to reinstate and/or make monthly payments on any and all senior encumbrances (including real property taxes) in order to protect Seller's secured interest; (2) Seller's rights are generally limited to foreclosure on the Property, pursuant to California Code of Civil Procedure §580b; and (3) the Property may lack sufficient equity to protect Seller's interests if the Property decreases in value.

If this three-page Addendum and Disclosure is used in a transaction for the purchase of a dwelling for not more than four families, it shall be prepared by an Arranger of Credit as defined in California Civil Code §2957(a). (The Arranger of Credit is usually the agent who obtained the offer.)

Arranger of Credit - (Print Firm Name) _____ By _____ Date _____

Address _____ City _____ State _____ Zip _____

Phone _____ Fax _____

BUYER AND SELLER ACKNOWLEDGE AND AGREE THAT BROKERS: (A) WILL NOT PROVIDE LEGAL OR TAX ADVICE; (B) WILL NOT PROVIDE OTHER ADVICE OR INFORMATION THAT EXCEEDS THE KNOWLEDGE, EDUCATION AND EXPERIENCE REQUIRED TO OBTAIN A REAL ESTATE LICENSE; OR (C) HAVE NOT AND WILL NOT VERIFY ANY INFORMATION PROVIDED BY EITHER BUYER OR SELLER. BUYER AND SELLER AGREE THAT THEY WILL SEEK LEGAL, TAX AND OTHER DESIRED ASSISTANCE FROM APPROPRIATE PROFESSIONALS. BUYER AND SELLER ACKNOWLEDGE THAT THE INFORMATION EACH HAS PROVIDED TO THE ARRANGER OF CREDIT FOR INCLUSION IN THIS DISCLOSURE FORM IS ACCURATE. BUYER AND SELLER FURTHER ACKNOWLEDGE THAT EACH HAS RECEIVED A COMPLETED COPY OF THIS DISCLOSURE FORM.

Buyer _____ Date _____
         (signature)

Address _____ City _____ State _____ Zip _____

Phone _____ Fax _____ E-mail _____

Buyer _____ Date _____
         (signature)

Address _____ City _____ State _____ Zip _____

Phone _____ Fax _____ E-mail _____

Seller _____ Date _____
         (signature)

Address _____ City _____ State _____ Zip _____

Phone _____ Fax _____ E-mail _____

Seller _____ Date _____
         (signature)

Address _____ City _____ State _____ Zip _____

Phone _____ Fax _____ E-mail _____

THIS FORM HAS BEEN APPROVED BY THE CALIFORNIA ASSOCIATION OF REALTORS® (C.A.R.). NO REPRESENTATION IS MADE AS TO THE LEGAL VALIDITY OR ADEQUACY OF ANY PROVISION IN ANY SPECIFIC TRANSACTION. A REAL ESTATE BROKER IS THE PERSON QUALIFIED TO ADVISE ON REAL ESTATE TRANSACTIONS. IF YOU DESIRE LEGAL OR TAX ADVICE, CONSULT AN APPROPRIATE PROFESSIONAL.

This form is available for use by the entire real estate industry. It is not intended to identify the user as a REALTOR®. REALTOR® is a registered collective membership mark which may be used only by members of the NATIONAL ASSOCIATION OF REALTORS® who subscribe to its Code of Ethics.

SURE TRAC — The System for Success™
Published by the
California Association of REALTORS®

Reviewed by _____ Date _____

SFA REVISED 10/02 (PAGE 3 OF 3)

SELLER FINANCING ADDENDUM AND DISCLOSURE (SFA PAGE 3 OF 3)

or she understands that he or she might lose financial interests even if all payments are current on the note.

Lender/Purchaser Disclosure
Private lenders who lend money through a broker must make this disclosure. The broker must provide a statement outlining loan terms, status, information regarding the property used to secure the loan, and encumbrances.

Adjustable-Rate Loan Disclosure
All lenders offering adjustable-rate residential mortgages must provide borrowers with a copy of the Federal Reserve publication Consumer Handbook on Adjustable-Rate Mortgages.

Notice of Transfer of Loan Servicing
All lenders on loans secured by residential property (1-4 units only) must notify the borrower when the collection service is transferred from one agency to another.

Elder Abuse Disclosure
The California Elder Abuse Law requires any agent; escrow, real estate loan and other individuals who might witness the financial abuse of an elderly person's assets.

Holden Act Disclosure
The Holden Act, also known as the Housing Financial Discrimination Act, requires borrowers to be notified of the prohibition against discriminatory practices by lenders and the rights that borrowers have under the law.

Truth-in-Lending Act Disclosure
The Truth-in-Lending Act, also called Regulation Z, requires the disclosure of finance charges in advertising. Additionally, full credit disclosure to the borrower is required.

Equal Credit Opportunity Act Disclosure
The equal credit opportunity act, also known as notice of adverse action, requires lenders to supply a borrower with a statement as to why a credit application or loan application was denied. This statement is required to be supplied to a borrower within 30 days from his or her application.

Lender Compensation Disclosure
Any time a broker receives compensation from a client's loan; this fact must be disclosed to all parties involved. This is different from referral fees, which are strictly prohibited in California.

MELLO-ROOS BOND DISCLOSURE

Mello-Roos bonds are used to relieve the developer of high costs on streets, sewers and other public items. The bonds are a municipal bond purchased by the homeowner, shifting expenses from one person, the developer, to multiple people, or each of the homeowners living in the development.

Agents must disclose to potential buyers their property is subject to a Mello-Roos levy for sale or lease for more than five years. If the buyer is not made aware of this, he or she has a three day right of rescission.

OTHER DISCLOSURES

Buyer State Tax Withholding
Buyers are required to withhold 3 1/3 percent of the sales price on the house for state

income tax. It is your job as an agent to inform the buyer of this requirement.

Commissions
All real estate commissions are negotiable. California does not have a minimum or maximum on the amount a broker can charge for services. This amount must be disclosed to the person paying for the commission.

Sales Price
Within one month after escrow has closed, the broker is responsible for informing both the buyer and seller of the final sales price.

Importance of Home Inspection Notice
All borrowers of residential homes financed through FHA financing, or HUD properties with 1-4 units, must sign a home inspection notice called The Importance of a Home Inspection.

Megan's Law
Megan's Law requires agents to supply people buying or leasing residential property with 1-4 units with a notice with information regarding registered sex offenders and how to find this information.

Water Heater Bracing
All sellers of real property, regardless of what type or how many units, must certify that water heater bracing has been properly installed.

Energy Conservation Retrofit and Thermal Insulation Disclosures
Some communities require energy retrofitting as a condition of sale. All requirements and statutes must be disclosed to the buyer regarding energy retrofitting by the seller or seller's agent.

Smoke Detector Notice
All buyers of single family residences must receive a copy of a smoke detector disclosure statement saying that the property is in compliance with current California regulations regarding smoke detectors.

Structural Pest Control Inspection and Certification Reports
Not all lenders or real estate purchase contracts require a pest control inspection; however, if one is performed, a copy must be furnished to the buyer.

Foreign Investment Real Property Tax Act
Any foreign seller of property in California must inform potential buyers of the required IRS withholding of 10 percent of the gross sales price.

Window Security Bars
If a home is equipped with window security bars, the Real Estate Transfer Disclosure Statement must disclose the bars, and any safety release mechanism they contain.

Notice Regarding Advisability of Title Insurance
When no title insurance is issued through escrow, the buyer must be notified, and then informed of how to obtain title insurance.

RIGHT OF RESCISSION

The right of rescission gives a buyer the chance to back out of the contract without penalty. There are a number of rescission rights in each transaction that must be disclosed to the buyer. If the buyer is not informed of these rights, the time within which

CALIFORNIA ASSOCIATION OF REALTORS®

California Real Estate Law
Disclosure Chart

Member Legal Services
January 22, 2002 (Revised)

Tel 213.739.8282
Fax 213.480.7724
www.car.org

SUBJECT	DISCLOSURE TRIGGER	DISCLOSURE REQUIREMENT (Brief Summary) FORM	C.A.R. INFORMATION SOURCE LAW CITATION
Agent's Real Property Inspection	Sale[2] of all residential real property of 1-4 units (No exemptions except for never-occupied properties where a public report is required or properties exempted from a public report pursuant to Business & Professions Code § 11010.4)	A real estate licensee must conduct a reasonably competent and diligent visual inspection of the property; this inspection duty does not include areas which are reasonably and normally inaccessible, off the site, or public records or permits concerning the title or use of the property; this inspection duty includes only the unit for sale and not the common areas of a condo or other common interest development. There is no requirement that the inspection report be in writing; however, it is recommended that all licensees put it in writing.	Q&A, "Complying With The Real Estate Transfer Disclosure Statement Law And The Broker's Duty To Inspect Residential Real Property."
1	Also applies to Manufactured Homes (as defined in H&S § 18007, which includes personal property Mobilehomes)	C.A.R. Form TDS-11(or for mobilehomes and manufactured housing, C.A.R. Form MHTDS-11) may be used. If the seller is exempt from the TDS, then C.A.R. Form AID-11 may be used by the agent.	Cal. Civ. Code §§ 2079 – 2079.6

SUBJECT	DISCLOSURE TRIGGER	DISCLOSURE REQUIREMENT (Brief Summary) FORM	C.A.R. INFORMATION SOURCE LAW CITATION
Commercial or Industrial Zone Location 2	Transfer[3] or exchange of residential real property of 1-4 units.	The seller of real property subject to the TDS law must disclose "actual knowledge" that the property is affected by or zoned to allow an industrial use of property (manufacturing, commercial, or airport use) as soon as possible before transfer of title. C.A.R. Form TDS-11 may be used.	Cal. Civ. Code § 1102.17; Cal. Code Civ. Proc. § 731a
Death and/or AIDS 3	Sale, lease, or rental of all real property.	The transferor/agent has no liability for not disclosing the fact of any death which occurred more than 3 years prior to the date the transferee offers to buy, lease, or rent the property. Any death which has occurred within a 3-year period should be disclosed if deemed to be "material." Affliction with AIDS or death from AIDS, no matter when it occurred, need not be voluntarily disclosed. However, neither a seller nor seller's agent may make an intentional misrepresentation in response to a direct question concerning deaths on the property.	Q&A, "Disclosure of Aids and Death: The Legislative Solution." Cal. Civ. Code § 1710.2.
"Drug Lab" – Illegal Controlled Substances Contamination 4	Transfer[4] or exchange of residential real property of 1-4 units and lease of any residential dwelling unit. Same exemptions as for the Transfer Disclosure Statement.	In the event that toxic contamination by an illegal controlled substance has occurred on a property and upon receipt of a notice from the Dept. of Toxic Substances Control (DTSC) or other agency—or if the seller has actual knowledge of the toxic contamination—the seller must disclose this information to the buyer by checking item II.C.1 of the TDS form and attaching the DTSC notice, there is one. In the case of rental property, the landlord must give a prospective tenant written notice of the toxic contamination. Providing the tenant with a copy of the DTSC notice will suffice if there is such a notice. C.A.R. Form TDS-11 may be used.	Cal. Civ. Code §§ 1102.18, 1940.7.5
Earthquake Fault Zones[5] 5	Sale of all real property which does contain or will eventually contain a structure for human occupany and which is located in an earthquake fault zone (special studies zone) as indicated on maps created by the California Division of Mines and Geology.[6] Also applies to Manufactured Homes (as defined in H&S § 18007, which includes personal property Mobilehomes)	The seller's agent or the seller without an agent must disclose to the buyer the fact that the property is in an earthquake fault zone (special studies zone), if maps are available at the county assessor's, county recorder's, or county planning commission office, or if the seller or seller's agent has actual knowledge that the property is in the zone. If the map is not of sufficient accuracy or scale to determine whether the property is in the zone, then either the agent indicates "yes" that the property is in the zone or the agent may write "no" that the property is not in this zone, but then a report prepared by an expert verifying that fact must be attached to the form NHD-11. If a TDS is required in the transaction, either C.A.R. Form NHD-11, "Natural Hazard Disclosure Statement," or an updated Local Option disclosure form must be used to make this disclosure.	Q&A, "Earthquake and Flood Hazard Disclosures." Q&A, "Natural Hazard Disclosure Statement." Cal. Pub. Res. Code §§ 2621 et seq.; Cal. Civ. Code § 1103

3

SUBJECT	DISCLOSURE TRIGGER	DISCLOSURE REQUIREMENT (Brief Summary) FORM	C.A.R. INFORMATION SOURCE LAW CITATION
Earthquake Hazards – Homeowner's Guide	**Mandatory delivery:** Transfer of residential real property of 1-4 units, manufactured homes, and mobilehomes, of conventional light frame construction, and built prior to January 1, 1960, if not exempt (almost same exemptions as for the Transfer Disclosure Statement[7]). Additional exemption if the buyer agrees, in writing, to demolish the property within one year from date of transfer. **Voluntary delivery:** Transfer[8] of any real property.	**Mandatory delivery:** The licensee must give the transferor the booklet "The Homeowner's Guide to Earthquake Safety"[9] and the transferor must give this booklet to the transferee. Known structural deficiencies must be disclosed by the transferor to the transferee and the form in the booklet entitled "Residential Earthquake Hazards Report" may be used to make this disclosure. **Voluntary delivery:** If the Guide is delivered to the transferee, then the transferor or broker is not required to provide additional information concerning general earthquake hazards. Known earthquake hazards must be disclosed whether delivery is mandatory or voluntary.	Q&A, "Earthquake and Flood Hazard Disclosures." Cal. Bus. & Prof. Code § 10149; Cal. Gov't Code §§ 8897.1, 8897.2, 8897.5. Cal. Civ. Code § 2079.8.
Earthquake Hazards – Commercial Guide	**Mandatory delivery:** Sale, transfer, or exchange of any real property or manufactured home or mobilehome if built of precast concrete or reinforced/unreinforced masonry with wood frame floors or roofs and built before January 1, 1975, located within a county or city, if not exempt. Same exemptions as for Homeowner's Guide. **Voluntary delivery:** Transfer[10] of any real property.	**Mandatory delivery:** The transferor/transferor's agent must give the transferee a copy of "The Commercial Property Owner's Guide to Earthquake Safety."[11] **Voluntary delivery:** If the Guide is delivered to the transferee, then the transferor or broker is not required to provide additional information concerning general earthquake hazards. Known earthquake hazards must be disclosed whether delivery is mandatory or voluntary.	Q&A, "Earthquake and Flood Hazard Disclosures." Cal. Bus. & Prof. Code § 10147, Cal. Gov't Code §§ 8875.6, 8875.9, 8893.2, 8893.3. Cal. Civ. Code § 2079.9.

6

7

4

SUBJECT	DISCLOSURE TRIGGER	DISCLOSURE REQUIREMENT (Brief Summary) FORM	C.A.R. INFORMATION SOURCE LAW CITATION
Flood Hazard Areas (federal law) 8	Sale or lease of <u>all</u> improved real estate or mobilehomes located in flood hazard areas as indicated on maps published by the Federal Emergency Management Agency.[12]	The seller/lessor should disclose to buyer/lessee the fact that the property is located in such an area.[13] C.A.R. Form TDS-11 may be used (or for mobilehomes and manufactured housing, C.A.R. Form MHTDS-11).	Q&A, "Earthquake and Flood Hazard Disclosures." 42 U.S.C. §§ 4001 <u>et</u> <u>seq</u>., § 4104a.
"Special Flood Hazard Area" (state law)	Sale of real property located in Zone "A" or "V" as designated by FEMA and if the seller or the seller's agent has actual knowledge <u>or</u> a list has been compiled <u>by parcel</u> and the notice posted at a local county recorder, assessor and planning agency. Also applies to Manufactured Homes (as defined in H&S § 18007, which includes personal property Mobilehomes)	The seller's <u>agent</u> or the seller without an agent must disclose to the buyer if the property is in this Special Flood Hazard Area, if a parcel list has been prepared by the county and a notice identifying the location of the list is available at the county assessor's, county recorder's or county planning commission office, or if the seller or seller's agent has actual knowledge that the property is in an area. If a TDS is required in the transaction, either C.A.R. Form NHD-11, "Natural Hazard Disclosure Statement" or an updated Local Option disclosure form must be used to make this disclosure.	Q&A, "Natural Hazard Disclosure Statement." Cal. Civ. Code § 1103, Cal. Gov't Code § 8589.3
"Area of Potential Flooding" (in the event of dam or reservoir failure) (state law) 10	Sale of all real property if the seller or the seller's agent has actual knowledge <u>or</u> a list has been compiled <u>by parcel</u> and the notice posted at a local county recorder, assessor and planning agency. Also applies to Manufactured Homes (as defined in H&S § 18007, which includes personal property Mobilehomes)	The seller's <u>agent</u> or the seller without an agent must disclose to the buyer <u>if the property is</u> in this Area of Potential Flooding as designated on an inundation map, if a parcel list has been prepared by the county and a notice identifying the location of the list is available at the county assessor's, county recorder's or county planning commission office, or if the seller or seller's agent has actual knowledge that the property is in an area. If a TDS is required in the transaction, either C.A.R. Form NHD-11, "Natural Hazard Disclosure Statement" or an updated Local Option disclosure form must be used to make this disclosure.	Q&A, "Natural Hazard Disclosure Statement." Cal. Gov't Code §§ 8589.4, 8589.5; Cal. Civ. Code § 1103

5

SUBJECT	DISCLOSURE TRIGGER	DISCLOSURE REQUIREMENT (Brief Summary) FORM	C.A.R. INFORMATION SOURCE LAW CITATION
Flood Disaster Insurance (federal law) (Applicable for any flood disaster[14] declared after September 23, 1994) 11	Any transfer[15] of personal (e.g., mobilehomes), residential, or commercial property where the owner received federal flood disaster assistance conditioned on the owner subsequently obtaining and maintaining flood insurance.	The transferor must notify the transferee in writing on a document "evidencing the transfer of ownership of the property" about the requirement to obtain and maintain flood insurance in accordance with applicable Federal law. [Currently, there are no regulations detailing this requirement.] Failure to notify the transferee means that in the event the transferee fails to maintain the required flood insurance and the property is damaged by a flood disaster requiring Federal disaster relief, the transferor will be required to reimburse the Federal government. The law is unclear as to what document(s) should contain this notice. C.A.R. Forms RPA-14 and NHD-11 may be acceptable, but technically are not documents which "evidence the transfer of ownership." Clearly, a grant deed is such a document.	Legal Brief, "Federal Flood Insurance Disclosure." 42 U.S.C. § 5154a.
Home Energy Ratings 12	Transfer[16] or exchange of all real property. Also applies to Manufactured Homes (as defined in H&S § 18007, which includes personal property Mobilehomes)	If a home energy ratings booklet to be developed by the State of California is delivered to the transferee, then a seller or broker is not required to provide additional information concerning the existence of a statewide home energy rating program. NEITHER THIS PROGRAM NOR THE BOOKLET IS AVAILABLE AT THIS TIME.	Cal. Civ. Code § 2079.10; Cal. Pub. Res. Code §§ 25402.9, 25942.
Home Environmental Hazards 13	Transfer[17] or exchange of all real property. Also applies to Manufactured Homes (as defined in H&S § 18007, which includes personal property Mobilehomes)	If a consumer information booklet[18] is delivered to the transferee, then a seller or broker is not required to provide additional information concerning common environmental hazards. Although highly recommended, delivery is voluntary. However, known hazards on the property must be disclosed to the transferee.	Q&A, "Due Diligence and Disclosure of Environmental Hazards in Real Estate Transactions." Q&A, "Information Resources for Environmental Hazards." Cal. Civ. Code § 2079.7.
Home Inspection Notice (FHA/HUD) 14	Sale of residential real property of 1-4 units, including mobilehomes on a permanent foundation, which involve FHA loans or HUD-owned properties.	For all properties regardless of when they were built, the borrower must sign the notice entitled, "The Importance of a Home Inspection." C.A.R. Form HID-11 may be used for this purpose.	Q&A, "FHA Lead-Based Paint Disclosure Form and New FHA Inspection Disclosure Form," Legal Brief, "FHA Inspection Disclosure Form. " HUD Mortgagee Letter 96-10.

6

SUBJECT	DISCLOSURE TRIGGER	DISCLOSURE REQUIREMENT (Brief Summary) FORM	C.A.R. INFORMATION SOURCE LAW CITATION
Lead Hazard Pamphlet 15	Sale or lease of all residential property, built before 1978, except as indicated below. Mobilehomes are also subject to this law. Exemptions: · foreclosure or trustee's sale transfer (REO properties and deed in lieu of foreclosure are NOT exempt!) · zero-bedroom dwelling (loft, efficiency unit, dorm, or studio) · short-term rental (100 or fewer days) · housing for elderly or handicapped (unless children live there) · rental housing certified free of lead paint	The seller/lessor must provide the buyer/lessee with a lead hazard information pamphlet, disclose the presence of any known lead-based paint and provide a statement signed by the buyer that the buyer has read the warning statement, has received the pamphlet, and has a 10-day opportunity to inspect before becoming obligated under the contract. The purchaser (not lessee) is permitted a 10-day period to conduct an inspection unless the parties mutually agree upon a different time period. The agent, on behalf of the seller/lessor, must ensure compliance with the requirements of this law. C.A.R. pamphlet, "Protect Your Family From Lead in Your Home," and C.A.R. form FLD-11 satisfy these requirements (except for sales of HUD properties—HUD forms required). The C.A.R. revised home environmental hazards booklet may be used in lieu of the pamphlet mentioned above.	Q&A, "Federal Lead-Based Paint Hazards Disclosure." Residential Lead-Based Paint Hazard Reduction Act of 1992, 42 U.S.C.S. § 4852d.
Megan's Law Disclosure 16	Sale[19] or lease/rental of all residential real property of 1-4 units (No exemptions except for never-occupied properties where a public report is required or properties exempted from a public report pursuant to Business & Professions Code § 11010.4)	Every lease or rental agreement and every sales contract is required to include a statutorily-defined notice regarding the existence of public access to database information regarding sex offenders. The following C.A.R. forms contain this statutory notice: LR-14, LR-14-S, RIPA-14, RPA-14	Q&A, "Megan's Law: Notifying the Public About Registered Sex Offenders." Cal. Civ. Code § 2079.10a
Mello-Roos District or Any Other Bond Assessment 17	Transfer[20] or exchange of residential real property of 1-4 units subject to a continuing lien securing the levy of special taxes pursuant to the Mello-Roos Community Facilities Act. Same exemptions as for the Transfer Disclosure Statement except that new subdivisions are not exempt.	The transferor must make a good faith effort to obtain a disclosure notice concerning the special tax or assessment from each local agency that levies a special tax or assessment and deliver the notice(s) to the prospective transferee. The disclosure notice also provides a 3 or 5-day right of rescission to the transferee. There is no affirmative duty by an agent to discover a special tax or district or assessment not actually known to the agent.	Q&A, "Mello-Roos District Disclosure Requirements." Cal. Civ. Code § 1102.6b; Cal. Gov't Code Sections §§ 53340.2, 53341.5, 53754.

SUBJECT	DISCLOSURE TRIGGER	DISCLOSURE REQUIREMENT (Brief Summary) FORM	C.A.R. INFORMATION SOURCE LAW CITATION
Military Ordnance Location 18	Transfer[21] or exchange of residential real property of 1-4 units and lease of <u>any</u> residential dwelling unit. Same exemptions as for the Transfer Disclosure Statement.	Disclosure is required when the transferor/lessor has actual knowledge that a former military ordnance location (military training grounds which may contain explosives) is within one mile of the property. The transferor/lessor must disclose in writing to the transferee/lessee, that these former federal or state military ordnance locations may contain potentially explosive munitions. The transferee has a 3 or 5-day right of rescission. C.A.R. Form TDS-11 may be used.	Cal. Civ. Code §§ 1102.15, 1940.7.
Mold (Toxic) (no new disclosure duties upon transfer until after the DHS establishes guidelines) 19	Sale, lease, rental, or other transfer of any commercial, industrial or residential property	There are no <u>current</u> <u>disclosure</u> requirements until after the Dept. of Health Services (DHS) develops permissible exposure limits for molds and a consumer booklet. The TDS has been modified to include the word "mold" in paragraph II.C.1. As always, any transferor must disclose <u>actual knowledge</u> of toxic mold on the property.	Q&A, "Mold and Its Impact on Real Estate Transactions." Legal Update (November 19, 2001) Cal. Health & Safety Code §§ 26100 *et seq.*, §§ 26140, 26141, 26147, 26148
Seismic Hazard Zones 20	Sale of <u>all</u> real property which does contain or will eventually contain a structure for human habitation and which is located in a seismic hazard zone as indicated on maps created by the California Division of Mines and Geology. Also applies to Manufactured Homes (as defined in H&S § 18007, which includes personal property Mobilehomes)	The seller's <u>agent</u> or the seller without an agent must disclose to the buyer the fact that the property is in a seismic hazard zone if maps are available at the county assessor's, county recorder's, or county planning commission office, or if the seller or seller's agent has actual knowledge that the property is in the zone. If the map is not of sufficient accuracy or scale to determine whether the property is in the zone, then either the agent indicates "yes" that the property is in the zone or the agent may write "no" that the property is <u>not</u> in this zone, but then a report prepared by an expert verifying that fact must be attached to the form NHD-11. If a TDS is required in the transaction, either C.A.R. Form NHD-11, "Natural Hazard Disclosure Statement" or an updated Local Option disclosure form must be used to make this disclosure.	Q&A, "Earthquake and Flood Hazard Disclosures," Legal Brief, "Seismic Hazard Zone Maps," Q&A, "Natural Hazard Disclosure Statement." Cal. Pub. Res. Code § 2690 <u>et seq.</u>, § 2694; Cal. Civ. Code § 1103

SUBJECT	DISCLOSURE TRIGGER	DISCLOSURE REQUIREMENT (Brief Summary) FORM	C.A.R. INFORMATION SOURCE LAW CITATION
Smoke Detector Compliance 21	All existing dwelling units must have a smoke detector centrally located outside each sleeping area (bedroom or group of bedrooms). In addition, new construction (with a permit after August 14, 1992) must have a hard-wired smoke detector in each bedroom. Any additions, modifications, or repairs (after August 14, 1992) exceeding $1,000 for which a permit is required will also trigger the requirement of a smoke detector in each bedroom. (These may be battery operated.)	The seller of a single family home must provide the buyer with a written statement indicating that the property is in compliance with current California law. Same exemptions from compliance and disclosure as for the Transfer Disclosure Statement but only for single family homes and factory-built housing, not other types of dwellings. Transfers to or from any governmental entity, and transfers by a beneficiary or mortgagee after foreclosure sale or trustee's sale or transfers by deed in lieu of foreclosure, which are exempt under the TDS law, are not exempt from this law. LOCAL LAW MAY BE MORE RESTRICTIVE! Check with the local City or County Department of Building and Safety. C.A.R. Form SDS-11 may be used.	C.A.R. Memorandum, "Important Smoke Detector Update." Cal. Health & Safety Code §§ 13113.7, 13113.8, 18029.6.
State Responsibility Areas (Fire Hazard Areas) 22	Sale of any real property located in a designated state responsibility area (generally a "wildland area") where the state not local or federal govt. has the primary financial responsibility for fire prevention. The California Department of Forestry provides maps to the county assessor of each affected county.[22] Also applies to Manufactured Homes (as defined in H&S § 18007, which includes personal property Mobilehomes)	The seller must disclose to the buyer the fact that the property is located in this zone, the risk of fire, state-imposed additional duties such as maintaining fire breaks, and the fact that the state may not provide fire protection services. The disclosure must be made if maps are available at the county assessor's, county recorder's or county planning commission office, or if the seller has actual knowledge that the property is in the zone. If the map is not of sufficient accuracy or scale to determine whether the property is in this Area, then either the agent indicates "yes" that the property is in this Area or the agent may write "no" that the property is not in this Area, but then a report prepared by an expert verifying that fact must be attached to the form NHD-11. If a TDS is required in the transaction, either C.A.R. Form NHD-11, "Natural Hazard Disclosure Statement" or an updated Local Option disclosure form must be used to make this disclosure.	Q&A, "Natural Hazard Disclosure Statement." Cal. Pub. Res. Code §§ 4125, 4136; Cal. Civ. Code § 1103
"Very High Fire Hazard Severity Zone" 23	Sale of any real property. Also applies to Manufactured Homes (as defined in H&S § 18007, which includes personal property Mobilehomes)	The seller must disclose the fact that the property is located within this zone and whether it is subject to the requirements of Gov't Code Section 51182 (e.g., clear brush, maintain fire breaks). The disclosure must be made if maps are available at the county assessor's, county recorder's or county planning commission office, or if the seller has actual knowledge that the property is in the zone. If the map is not of sufficient accuracy or scale to determine whether the property is in this zone, then either the agent indicates "yes" that the property is in this zone or the agent may write "no" that the property is not in this zone, but then a report prepared by an expert verifying that fact must be attached to the form NHD-11. If a TDS is required in the transaction, either C.A.R. Form NHD-11, "Natural Hazard Disclosure Statement" or an updated Local Option disclosure form must be used to make this disclosure.	Q&A, "Natural Hazard Disclosure Statement." Cal. Gov't Code §§ 51178, 51183.5; Cal. Civ. Code § 1103

9

SUBJECT	DISCLOSURE TRIGGER	DISCLOSURE REQUIREMENT (Brief Summary) FORM	C.A.R. INFORMATION SOURCE LAW CITATION
Subdivided Lands Law 24	Sale, leasing, or financing of new developments (condos, PUDs) or conversions consisting of 5 or more lots, parcels, or interests. However, a transfer of a single property to 5 or more unrelated people (unless exempt) may also trigger this law. There are exemptions too numerous to discuss in this chart.	The owner, subdivider, or agent, prior to the execution of the purchase contract or lease, must give the buyer/lessee a copy of the final public report (FPR), preliminary public report (PPR), or the conditional public report (CPR) issued by the DRE. No offers may be solicited until the DRE has issued one of these three reports. If the DRE has issued a CPR or PPR, then offers may be solicited, but close of escrow is contingent upon issuance of the FPR. Contracts entered into pursuant to a PPR may be rescinded by either party; contracts entered into pursuant to a CPR are contingent upon satisfaction of certain specified conditions.	Q&A, "Subdivided Lands Law," Q&A, "Subdivision Applicability Chart." Cal. Bus. & Prof. Code § 11018.1. Cal. Bus. & Prof. Code § 11018.12; Cal. Code Regs., tit. 10, § 2795. See generally, Cal. Bus. & Prof. Code §§ 11000 et seq.; Cal. Code Regs., tit. 10, §§ 2790 et seq.
Subdivision Map Act 25	Any division of real property into 2 or more lots or parcels for the purpose of sale, lease, or financing. There are exemptions too numerous to discuss in this chart.	The owner/subdivider must record either a tentative and final map, or a parcel map (depending on the type of subdivision). Escrow on the transfer cannot close until the appropriate map has been recorded.	Q&A, "Subdivision Applicability Chart." Cal. Gov't Code §§ 66426, 66428. See generally, Cal. Gov't Code §§ 66410 et seq.
Water Heater Bracing 26	All properties with water heaters. Legislative intent suggests this law applies only to residential properties, but the language of the statute does not limit the requirement to residential properties.	All owners of new or replacement water heaters and all owners of existing residential water heaters must brace, anchor or strap water heaters to resist falling or horizontal displacement due to earthquake motion. The seller of real property must certify in writing to a prospective purchaser that he has complied with this section and applicable local code requirements. This certification may be done in existing transactional documents, including but not limited to, the Homeowner's Guide to Earthquake Safety, a real estate purchase contract, a transfer disclosure statement, or a local option disclosure of compliance. C.A.R. Form WHS-11 may be used.	Q&A, "Water Heater Bracing and Disclosure Requirements." Cal. Health & Safety Code § 19211.

The information contained herein is believed accurate as of January 22, 2002. It is intended to provide general answers to general questions and is not intended as a substitute for individual legal advice. Advice in specific situations may differ depending upon a wide variety of factors. Therefore, readers with specific legal questions should seek the advice of an attorney.

ENDNOTES

[1] This chart is current as of January 22, 2002 and all laws are currently effective unless otherwise noted. Although this chart summarizes disclosure requirements in the transfer of real property, agents should be aware that the seller/transferor, as well as the agent, is required to disclose all known information affecting the property which may be deemed "material." In addition, it is imperative to check local disclosure requirements. Local law may be more stringent than state law in certain areas or there may be additional disclosures required.

[2] This provision also applies to leases with an option to purchase, ground leases of land improved with 1-4 residential units, and real property installment sales contracts. Cal. Civ. Code § 2079.1.

[3] "Transfer" for the purposes of this law means transfer by sale, lease with option to purchase, purchase option, ground lease coupled with improvements, installment land sale contract, or transfer of a residential stock cooperative. Cal. Civ. Code § 1102.

[4] Same as number 3 above.

[5] These zones were formerly called, "Special Studies Zones." Some maps may still refer to the old name.

[6] The maps may be purchased from BPS Reprographics by calling (415) 512-6550 with the names of the required maps. Special Publication 42 indicates the names of the maps of the Earthquake Fault Zones. This publication is available from the California Division of Mines and Geology by calling (916) 445-5716.

[7] Transfers which can be made without a public report pursuant to Section 11010.4 of the Business and Professions Code are exempt from a TDS but not from the Homeowner's Guide.

[8] "Transfer" for purposes of this law means transfer by sale, lease with option to purchase, purchase option, ground lease coupled with improvements, or installment land sale contract.

[9] This Guide is available from CAR and/or local Boards/Associations.

[10] Same as number 7 above.

[11] This Guide is available from CAR and/or local Boards/Associations.

[12] The maps may be purchased from FEMA by calling (800) 358-9616

[13]. Federal law actually imposes the duty on a federal lender to notify the purchaser/lessee, in writing, "or obtain satisfactory assurances that the seller or lessor has notified the purchaser or lessee," of special flood hazards in advance of the signing of the purchase agreement. In any event, this information may be deemed a material fact and, thus, should probably be disclosed by the seller/lessor.

[14] "Flood disaster area" means an area so designated by the U.S. Secretary of Agriculture or an area the President has declared to be a disaster or emergency as a result of flood conditions.

[15] Same as number 3 above.

[16] Same as number 7 above.

[17] Same as number 7 above.

[18] The consumer information booklet entitled "Environmental Hazards, A Guide for Homeowners and Buyers" is available from C.A.R. and/or local Boards/Associations.

[19] This provision also applies to leases with an option to purchase, ground leases of land improved with 1-4 residential units, and real property installment sales contracts. Cal. Civ. Code § 2079.1.

[20] Same as number 3 above.

[21] Same as number 3 above.

[22] The Department of Forestry's telephone number is (916) 653-5121.

rescission is allowed is extended.

Time-share buyers have rescission rights up to three days after signing the contract. This rescission time has been given to buyers because of the various sales tactics used by developers which may confuse a buyer or cause him or her to enter into a contract prematurely.

Mello-Roos disclosure must be made to a buyer so that the buyer knows of any levy that may be attached to property he or she is considering. Failure to disclose the fact that the property is in a Mello-Roos district will give the buyer a three- to-five-day right of rescission.

The Truth-in-Lending Act requires disclosure to the buyer that if he or she uses property to secure a loan, he or she has until midnight on the third business day after the loan is completed to back out of the contract.

An undivided interest subdivision is one in which owners are tenants-in-common with other owners, but don't have an exclusive possessory interest in a particular unit or space. Campgrounds are a good example of this. Anyone entering into an undivided interest subdivision has a three-day right of rescission following the day the agreement is signed.

Homeowners have the right of rescission when selling their equity interest in a residence in foreclosure. The right to rescind extends to midnight on the fifth business day following the sales agreement, or 8:00 A.M. on the day of the sale, whichever comes first.

The Interstate Land Sales Full Disclosure Act calls for a property statement on developments of 25 or more unimproved lots, no larger than five acres each, that are sold in interstate commerce. Any purchaser of this type of lot has a seven-day right of rescission.

CALIFORNIA ASSOCIATION OF REALTORS® DISCLOSURE CHART

To help real estate agents remember the numerous disclosures they must make, the California Association of REALTORS® has created the California Real Estate Law Disclosure Chart. This should be used as a check list of disclosures to make sure you have not missed any required or important disclosures. Remember, by making disclosures, both required and non-required, you will protect yourself in the event that a misunderstanding escalates into a court case.

S U M M A R Y

Disclosure, while required by law, may seem on the surface to be unnecessary steps in a property transfer, but in the long run it serves to protect all parties involved in the transaction. As you can see from this chapter, there are many different disclosures that must be made for a lawful transaction.

Keeping a detailed file on each of your clients and storing all signed disclosure sheets in this file will serve you well if you ever need to produce evidence that the disclosure was made and that the client acknowledged receiving the information regarding the property.

Keeping a copy of the California Real Estate Law Disclosure Chart handy can serve as a checklist to help you to make sure all disclosures have been made. When in doubt, disclose. If there is an item not listed on the disclosure chart which you feel might be an issue, disclose this information to all parties anyway. It is always safer to err on the side of caution when conducting a property transfer.

Disclosures are designed to protect you in the event a lawsuit arises from a property transaction. Take the extra steps and make sure to fully disclose all facts; it will benefit you in the long run.

TERMS AND PHRASES

Agency Disclosure – Making sure all parties involved in a transaction understand who each agent represents.

Agent's Inspection Disclosure – A personal visual inspection of the property made by the agent to determine the condition of all aspects of the property. When doing the inspection, it is a good idea to fill out the transfer disclosure statement.

AIDS Disclosure – It is not required to disclose if a seller or person who used to occupy a property had AIDS or died from AIDS or an AIDS-related complications. Additionally, any other natural death is not a required disclosure. All other deaths on the property within three years from the sale must be disclosed.

Buyer's Agent – The agent representing only the buyer in a property transaction.

Caveat Emptor – The old phrase or adage meaning "buyer beware." Caveat Emptor applies to real estate transactions; however, with disclosure the buyer is protected from fraud.

Common Interest Subdivision – A community where each owner will have his or her separate unit, apartment or space, and share interest in the common areas of the project. Condominiums, cooperatives, community apartment projects and planned unit developments all fall under this type of subdivision.

Conditional Public Report – A temporary description of property and the subdivision where the property is located. This report is valid for six months, and can be renewed one time. A conditional report allows a developer to enter into a contractual agreement with a buyer, but escrow cannot close until the final public report has been released.

Confirm – The process by which each party will sign the agency disclosure form, agreeing and acknowledging all details, especially the agency they elect to enter into.

Disclosure - The act of telling your client or the third party all required information regarding a property, transaction or financial aspect of the real estate transfer.

Dual Agency – A situation where the broker will represent both the buyer and seller in the same transaction.

Earthquake Safety Disclosure – The form that poses seven questions regarding a property to help a buyer understand its relative safety in the event an earthquake should hit.

Elect - The agent and client decide what type of agency agreement will be used.

Environmental Hazards Disclosure – Telling a buyer of any environmental hazards they know or suspect may exist on the property, or nearby areas.

Fiduciary Responsibility - The agent will look out for the client's best interests in all property transfer dealings, putting the client's needs and wants ahead of his or her own, and remaining loyal in all dealings to the client.

Fire Hazard Areas – A region or area specifically identified and mapped out by the state and the Department of Forestry as being prone to possible elevated fire danger.

Flood Hazard Areas – A region or area specifically identified and mapped out by the Federal Emergency Management Agency as being prone to possible flooding.

Good Faith Estimate – An estimate of all closing costs given to the buyer.

Hazardous Waste Disclosure - Buyers and tenants must be informed of hazardous waste disposal on or near their property. Health and Safety code Section 25359.7(a) requires that this disclosure be made if there is evidence of hazardous waste disposal or if there is reasonable cause to believe there may have been dumping on the property at one time.

Home Inspection Notice - All borrowers on residential homes financed through FHA financing, or on HUD properties with 1-4 units, must sign a home inspection notice called The Importance of a Home Inspection.

Mello-Roos Bonds – Municipal-type bonds that homeowners assume to help transfer costs for public works projects such as streets and sewers from the developer to the homeowners.

Military Ordnance Location - If the seller or seller's agent is aware that the property is within one mile of a former military training ground which had contained explosives or other hazardous materials, this fact must be disclosed.

Preliminary Public Report – An initial public report regarding details of a property and development allowing a developer to take deposits and reservations on properties. Preliminary reports do not allow the developer to enter into any contracts.

Public Report – An official report regarding details of a property and development, allowing all real estate contracts to close through escrow.

Real Estate Transfer Disclosure Statement – A statement to inform any buyer of property about the condition of that property. This will cover both defects and problems that are readily seen, and problems or conditions that may not be immediately seen.

Red Flag – Any event, occurrence or obvious problem with a property causing a buyer to question the property. An example of a red flag would be uneven floors, indicating a structural problem.

Rescission Rights – The rights of a buyer to back out of a contract for non-disclosure, or other facts making the property less desirable than originally thought.

Seller's Agent – An agent representing only the seller in a property transaction.

Seller Financing Addendum and Disclosure - Sellers who plan on carrying back a note on financing the property they are selling must disclose this fact to the buyer. The person arranging the financing is responsible for making this disclosure.

Sick Building Syndrome (SBS) - A condition that is caused by the air quality in buildings. Most modern high-rises, expansive commercial buildings, or other large buildings rely on fresh air being brought in through the ventilation system. When a building is experiencing SBS, the people using the space may experience fatigue, dizziness, nausea, headaches, eye, nose and throat infections, cough, itchy or dry skin, or have sensitivity to odors.

Smoke Detector Disclosure – A statement saying that the property is in compliance with current California regulations regarding smoke detectors.

Stigmatized Property – Tainted property because of an event or previous owner. A house involved in a murder, crime or satanic worship would be an example of this type of property.

C H A P T E R   Q U I Z

1. Caveat emptor is:
    a. Full disclosure
    b. Buyer beware
    c. A mandatory disclosure on property regarding title
    d. None of the above

2. An agent unknowingly using an old or retired disclosure form:
    a. Is held liable for any damages the situation may cause
    b. Is not held liable for any damages
    c. May NOT be sued in a court of law
    d. Can substitute a similar, nationally focused form

3. When must agency disclosure take place?
    a. Prior to signing the deposit receipt
    b. As soon as possible
    c. Prior to accepting an offer
    d. None of the above

4. What are the three steps in agency disclosure?
    a. Elect, Disclose, Determine
    b. Disclose, Determine, Confirm
    c. Disclose, Elect, Confirm
    d. Elect, Confirm, Determine

5. Which of the following items is not discussed on the real estate transfer disclosure statement?
    a. Neighborhood or neighbor concerns
    b. Significant defects in the home
    c. School district information
    d. Problematic concerns with any amenities in the home

6. Fiduciary responsibility includes all of the following EXCEPT:
    a. Full disclosure of all material facts
    b. Loyalty

c. Withholding problems from any third party

d. Following through with the client's wishes or direction as long as it is lawful

7. Which of the following is not considered a natural hazard and is not disclosed in a property transaction?
   a. Wind
   b. Fire
   c. Flood
   d. Earthquake

8. An agent is exempt from making a personal site inspection on a residential property with 1-4 units when:
   a. The property is being sold because of foreclosure
   b. The property is being transferred between spouses or blood relatives
   c. The property being sold requires a public report
   d. All of the above

9. When an agent makes an inspection disclosure, he or she must disclose any evidence of problems with:
   a. Age of the appliances
   b. Mold
   c. Soil compaction
   d. None of the above

10. Which booklet can a broker give to a buyer concerning lead-based paint and its hazards?
    a. Protect Your Family from Lead In Your Home
    b. Environmental Hazards: a Guide for Homeowners, Buyers, Landlords and Tenants
    c. Neither A nor B
    d. Both A and B

11. A disclosure must be made that a property is located near a licensed care facility when:
    a. There are six or fewer residents in the care facility
    b. There are more than six residents in the care facility
    c. This disclosure never has to be made
    d. This disclosure must always be made

12. All of the following are considered environmental hazards that must be disclosed except:
    a. Sick Building Syndrome
    b. Military Ordnance Location
    c. AIDS
    d. Lead-based paint

13. Which of the following must be disclosed regarding death on a property?
    a. If the homeowner died of AIDS or AIDS-related causes
    b. If the homeowner died of natural causes
    c. If there was a suicide on the property 5 years before
    d. If there was a murder on the property 2 years before

14. A conditional public report allows a developer to:
    a. Take deposits and reservations on property, but no contracts may be signed.

b. Enter into a contractual agreement with a buyer, but escrow cannot be closed until the final public report has been issued.

c. Operate unrestrictedly with buyers for six months, the length of a valid conditional public report.

d. None of the above.

15. A public report regarding a subdivision will reveal:
   a. The identity of the developer
   b. The size of the property in question
   c. Use restrictions of the property
   d. All of the above

16. All of the following are considered common interest subdivisions except:
   a. Condominiums
   b. Cooperatives
   c. Duplexes
   d. Community apartment projects

17. Bonds sold to help shift the cost of streets, sewers or other developmental items in a subdivision to the homeowners are called:
   a. Mello-Roos bonds
   b. New development bonds
   c. Common interest bonds
   d. Subdivision bonds

18. The right of rescission allows the buyer of property:
   a. An unlimited amount of time to change his or her mind and back out of a purchase contract.
   b. A small window of time, usually three to seven days, to back out of a purchase contract.
   c. An extended window of time to back out of a purchase contract if all the necessary disclosures are not made.
   d. Both B and C.

19. Lenders are required to provide a potential borrower with a statement of why the borrower's loan application or credit application has been denied under which act?
   a. Holden Act
   b. Truth-in-Lending Act
   c. Regulation Z
   d. Equal Credit Opportunity Act

20. Which of the following is considered a mandatory disclosure?
   a. Commissions
   b. Sales Price
   c. Common Interest Subdivision
   d. All of the above

CHAPTER

THE PURCHASE
AGREEMENT

What you will learn in this Chapter

- Analysis of the Purchase Agreement

- Filling out the Purchase Agreement

- Estimated Buyer's Costs

- Special Provisions

- Presenting the Sellers with the Offer

- Counteroffer

1. Which of the following is true about the deposit receipt?
  a. It is also called a purchase agreement
  b. All California brokerage firms use one uniform version of the form
  c. It acts as the escrow instructions
  d. Both A and C

2. Which of the following payment methods would be acceptable as a deposit on property?
  a. Cash
  b. Non-monetary consideration
  c. Promissory note
  d. All of the above are acceptable

3. Liquidated damages specify the amount of money a seller will receive should the buyer do what?
  a. Fail to qualify for funding
  b. Request to keep some of the seller's personal property as part of the sale of the home
  c. Default on the contract
  d. Any of the above

4. A seller's personal property:
  a. Is never part of the deposit receipt; it can be negotiated in a separate agreement or transaction
  b. Is never part of the deposit receipt, and it is considered rude to request that the seller leave any of his or her belongings for the buyer in the transaction
  c. Can be negotiated amongst the buyer and seller, and then included in the deposit receipt
  d. Always stays with the home if it was specifically purchased for the house

5. Which of the following is not considered a special provision to the deposit receipt?
  a. "As is" clause
  b. Irrevocable order
  c. Unordinary vesting
  d. Uncashed checks

6. Which of the following is not a step in the formal presentation of an offer to your client?
  a. Review all appropriate documents
  b. Prepare counteroffer form
  c. Set up the interview
  d. Overcome objections

7. In a counteroffer situation, what part of the original purchase offer will be rewritten and attached to the original offer?
  a. The entire document
  b. The first page
  c. The second page
  d. The third page

The purchase agreement, or purchase offer, is not only the buyer's official offer to the seller, but it will also be the guideline for the escrow instructions. If the seller accepts the buyer's monetary offer, but would like to negotiate a few other terms, a counteroffer will be made. If the buyer agrees to this counteroffer, the parties sign the purchase agreement, and escrow will be opened, following the instructions as notated by the purchase agreement.

It is very important for you as the agent to understand how to fill out this agreement accurately and efficiently. You need to take extra care to fill it out clearly and concisely so it is easily understood, but also accurately, so it will not be misinterpreted. A mistake here and the sellers may reject the offer. Or a mistake on the counteroffer may cause the offer to be invalid, or create a situation down the road where the mistake is uncovered, and the deal fails. Additionally, you have gained the trust and confidence of your client up to this point by your professionalism and knowledge of all aspects of the property transaction; it is important to keep this confidence as you take your buyer into escrow. One mistake and hesitation may set in, causing you to lose the client and your commission.

In this chapter, you will learn all about the purchase agreement, what it looks like, and a detailed step-by-step process on how to fill it out. From there, you will be presented special provisions that you may have to deal with during the process of making an offer. Lastly, you will learn how to present the sellers with the offer and what to do in a counteroffer situation.

A N A L Y S I S   O F   T H E   P U R C H A S E   A G R E E M E N T

The deposit receipt, or purchase agreement, is perhaps the most important document in the real estate transaction. It is vital for you as the agent to fill it out accurately, as the information you convey from the buyer to the seller will determine if the seller accepts or rejects the offer. The purchase agreement will also be used as the escrow instructions. Mistakes in this contract could cause problems not only immediately, but if unnoticed, could also cause problems for you later.

The term "deposit receipt" might suggest it is simply a receipt for money, when in fact it is a legal, binding contract. The deposit receipt serves many functions. It is a receipt for money, the formal offer to purchase property, a binding contract and the instructions for escrow.

Remember
The deposit receipt functions as
- Receipt for money
- Formal offer to purchase property
- Binding contract
- Escrow instruction

Currently there isn't a uniform deposit receipt form that all agents use. Each firm has its own version of a deposit receipt or purchase contract. Each of these forms is based on the California Association of Realtors® Real Estate Purchase Contract and Receipt for Deposit. A firm can elect to use this CAR standardized form, or have some variation of the form.

Each purchase contract is a preprinted form, with blanks to be filled out by the buyer or the buyer's agent. On all forms, any handwritten words will supersede printed words in the event of a contradiction. Additionally, if the agent or buyer is filling out the form using a typewriter or on a scanned version on a computer, the typewritten instructions or words will supersede the standard information on the form. Specific instructions will override general instructions should a conflict arise.

Care should be taken to make sure all blanks are correctly filled out on the contract. The intentions of the buyer need to be very clear, as this is the final offer to be given to the seller. Anything marked down on this form is considered final. The contract should be filled out with simple words and terms, easily understood by anyone who should read the contract, and not just by a real estate professional or attorney.

The deposit receipt itself can be used to check to make sure the document is completely filled out. Cross out or delete any material printed on the form that is not applicable, or inaccurate. Any printed changes made to the text of the document should be initialed and dated to confirm the changes. Once you are completely finished, review the entire document with the client to make sure his or her intent is being correctly conveyed by what is written on the purchase agreement. If questions arise, or there is any uncertainty regarding the contract or how to fill out any of the sections, a more experienced professional should be contacted to make sure everything is filled out accurately.

Everyone involved in the property transaction will refer to the contract as the permanent set of instructions. It will be viewed by clients, brokers, attorneys, escrow holders and lenders. The contract will dictate to these professionals how they will conduct all aspects of the property transfer. It is the blueprint for all activity. You can see why it is so important to fill out this contract correctly.

FILING   OUT   THE   PURCHASE   AGREEMENT

Location and Date
The first thing to be filled out on a deposit receipt is the location and date where the contract is executed, and where the buyers have signed the contract. This is not necessarily where the property is located. Let's say for example that you purchase property in San Diego, but your realtor's office is located in La Jolla; the first line of the deposit receipt will read La Jolla, not San Diego. The reason for this is that if there is a

CALIFORNIA ASSOCIATION OF REALTORS®

CALIFORNIA
RESIDENTIAL PURCHASE AGREEMENT
AND JOINT ESCROW INSTRUCTIONS
For Use With Single Family Residential Property — Attached or Detached
(C.A.R. Form RPA-CA, Revised 10/02)

Date _____ at _____, California.
1. **OFFER:**
   A. **THIS IS AN OFFER FROM** _____ ("Buyer").
   B. **THE REAL PROPERTY TO BE ACQUIRED** is described as _____
      _____, Assessor's Parcel No. _____, situated in
      _____, County of _____, California, ("Property").
   C. **THE PURCHASE PRICE** offered is _____
      _____ Dollars $ _____.
   D. **CLOSE OF ESCROW** shall occur on _____ (date)(or ☐ _____ Days After Acceptance).
2. **FINANCE TERMS:** Obtaining the loans below **is a contingency** of this Agreement unless: (i) either 2K or 2L is checked below; or
   (ii) otherwise agreed in writing. Buyer shall act diligently and in good faith to obtain the designated loans. Obtaining deposit, down
   payment and closing costs **is not a contingency.** Buyer represents that funds will be good when deposited with Escrow Holder.
   A. **INITIAL DEPOSIT:** Buyer has given a deposit in the amount of ....$ _____
      to the agent submitting the offer (or to ☐ _____), by personal check
      (or ☐ _____), made payable to _____,
      which shall be held uncashed until Acceptance and then deposited within 3 business days after
      Acceptance (or ☐ _____), with
      Escrow Holder, (or ☐ into Broker's trust account).
   B. **INCREASED DEPOSIT:** Buyer shall deposit with Escrow Holder an increased deposit in the amount of ...$ _____
      within _____ Days After Acceptance, or ☐ _____.
   C. **FIRST LOAN IN THE AMOUNT OF** ....$ _____
      (1) NEW First Deed of Trust in favor of lender, encumbering the Property, securing a note payable at
          maximum interest of _____% fixed rate, or _____% initial adjustable rate with a maximum
          interest rate of _____%, balance due in _____ years, amortized over _____ years. Buyer
          shall pay loan fees/points not to exceed _____. (These terms apply whether the designated loan
          is conventional, FHA or VA.)
      (2) ☐ FHA ☐ VA: (The following terms only apply to the FHA or VA loan that is checked.)
          Seller shall pay _____% discount points. Seller shall pay other fees not allowed to be paid by
          Buyer, ☐ not to exceed $_____. Seller shall pay the cost of lender required Repairs
          (including those for wood destroying pest) not otherwise provided for in this Agreement, ☐ not to
          exceed $_____. (Actual loan amount may increase if mortgage insurance premiums,
          funding fees or closing costs are financed.)
   D. **ADDITIONAL FINANCING TERMS:** ☐ Seller financing, (C.A.R. Form SFA); ☐ secondary financing, ...$ _____
      (C.A.R. Form PAA, paragraph 4A); ☐ assumed financing (C.A.R. Form PAA, paragraph 4B)
      _____
      _____
   E. **BALANCE OF PURCHASE PRICE** (not including costs of obtaining loans and other closing costs) in the amount of ...$ _____
      to be deposited with Escrow Holder within sufficient time to close escrow.
   F. **PURCHASE PRICE (TOTAL):** ....$ _____
   G. **LOAN APPLICATIONS:** Within 7 (or ☐ _____) Days After Acceptance, Buyer shall provide Seller a letter from lender or
      mortgage loan broker stating that, based on a review of Buyer's written application and credit report, Buyer is prequalified or
      preapproved for the NEW loan specified in 2C above.
   H. **VERIFICATION OF DOWN PAYMENT AND CLOSING COSTS:** Buyer (or Buyer's lender or loan broker pursuant to 2G) shall, within
      7 (or ☐ _____) Days After Acceptance, provide Seller written verification of Buyer's down payment and closing costs.
   I. **LOAN CONTINGENCY REMOVAL:** (i) Within 17 (or ☐ _____) Days After Acceptance, Buyer shall, as specified in paragraph
      14, remove the loan contingency or cancel this Agreement; OR (ii) (if checked) ☐ the loan contingency shall remain in effect
      until the designated loans are funded.
   J. **APPRAISAL CONTINGENCY AND REMOVAL:** This Agreement is (OR, if checked, ☐ is NOT) contingent upon the Property
      appraising at no less than the specified purchase price. If there is a loan contingency, at the time the loan contingency is
      removed (or, if checked, ☐ within 17 (or _____) Days After Acceptance), Buyer shall, as specified in paragraph 14B(3), remove
      the appraisal contingency or cancel this Agreement. If there is no loan contingency, Buyer shall, as specified in paragraph
      14B(3), remove the appraisal contingency within 17 (or _____) Days After Acceptance.
   K. ☐ **NO LOAN CONTINGENCY** (If checked): Obtaining any loan in paragraphs 2C, 2D or elsewhere in this Agreement is NOT
      a contingency of this Agreement. If Buyer does not obtain the loan and as a result Buyer does not purchase the Property, Seller
      may be entitled to Buyer's deposit or other legal remedies.
   L. ☐ **ALL CASH OFFER** (If checked): No loan is needed to purchase the Property. Buyer shall, within 7 (or ☐ _____) Days After Acceptance,
      provide Seller written verification of sufficient funds to close this transaction.
3. **CLOSING AND OCCUPANCY:**
   A. Buyer intends (or ☐ does not intend) to occupy the Property as Buyer's primary residence.
   B. **Seller-occupied or vacant property:** Occupancy shall be delivered to Buyer at _____ AM/PM, ☐ on the date of Close Of
      Escrow; ☐ on _____; or ☐ no later than _____ Days After Close Of Escrow. (C.A.R. Form PAA, paragraph 2.) If
      transfer of title and occupancy do not occur at the same time, Buyer and Seller are advised to: (i) enter into a written occupancy
      agreement; and (ii) consult with their insurance and legal advisors.

Buyer's Initials (_____)(_____)
Seller's Initials (_____)(_____)

Reviewed by	Date

RPA-CA REVISED 10/02 (PAGE 1 OF 8) Print Date RPC Feb 05

Property Address: _____ Date: _____

C. **Tenant-occupied property: (i) Property shall be vacant** at least **5 (or ☐ _____) Days** Prior to Close Of Escrow, unless otherwise agreed in writing. **Note to Seller: If you are unable to deliver Property vacant in accordance with rent control and other applicable Law, you may be in breach of this Agreement.**

OR **(ii)** (if checked) ☐ **Tenant to remain in possession.** The attached addendum is incorporated into this Agreement (C.A.R. Form PAA, paragraph 3.);

OR **(iii)** (if checked) ☐ **This Agreement is contingent** upon Buyer and Seller entering into a written agreement regarding occupancy of the Property within the time specified in paragraph 14B(1). If no written agreement is reached within this time, either Buyer or Seller may cancel this Agreement in writing.

D. At Close Of Escrow, Seller assigns to Buyer any assignable warranty rights for items included in the sale and shall provide any available Copies of such warranties. Brokers cannot and will not determine the assignability of any warranties.

E. At Close Of Escrow, unless otherwise agreed in writing, Seller shall provide keys and/or means to operate all locks, mailboxes, security systems, alarms and garage door openers. If Property is a condominium or located in a common interest subdivision, Buyer may be required to pay a deposit to the Homeowners' Association ("HOA") to obtain keys to accessible HOA facilities.

4. **ALLOCATION OF COSTS** (If checked): Unless otherwise specified here, this paragraph only determines who is to pay for the report, inspection, test or service mentioned. If not specified here or elsewhere in this Agreement, the determination of who is to pay for any work recommended or identified by any such report, inspection, test or service shall be by the method specified in paragraph 14B(2).

A. **WOOD DESTROYING PEST INSPECTION:**
   (1) ☐ Buyer ☐ Seller shall pay for an inspection and report for wood destroying pests and organisms ("Report") which shall be prepared by _____, a registered structural pest control company. The Report shall cover the accessible areas of the main building and attached structures and, if checked: ☐ detached garages and carports, ☐ detached decks, ☐ the following other structures or areas _____ _____. The Report shall not include roof coverings. If Property is a condominium or located in a common interest subdivision, the Report shall include only the separate interest and any exclusive-use areas being transferred and shall not include common areas, unless otherwise agreed. Water tests of shower pans on upper level units may not be performed without consent of the owners of property below the shower.

OR (2) ☐ (If checked) The attached addendum (C.A.R. Form WPA) regarding wood destroying pest inspection and allocation of cost is incorporated into this Agreement.

B. **OTHER INSPECTIONS AND REPORTS:**
   (1) ☐ Buyer ☐ Seller shall pay to have septic or private sewage disposal systems inspected _____.
   (2) ☐ Buyer ☐ Seller shall pay to have domestic wells tested for water potability and productivity _____.
   (3) ☐ Buyer ☐ Seller shall pay for a natural hazard zone disclosure report prepared by _____.
   (4) ☐ Buyer ☐ Seller shall pay for the following inspection or report _____.
   (5) ☐ Buyer ☐ Seller shall pay for the following inspection or report _____.

C. **GOVERNMENT REQUIREMENTS AND RETROFIT:**
   (1) ☐ Buyer ☐ Seller shall pay for smoke detector installation and/or water heater bracing, if required by Law. Prior to Close Of Escrow, Seller shall provide Buyer a written statement of compliance in accordance with state and local Law, unless exempt.
   (2) ☐ Buyer ☐ Seller shall pay the cost of compliance with any other minimum mandatory government retrofit standards, inspections and reports if required as a condition of closing escrow under any Law. _____.

D. **ESCROW AND TITLE:**
   (1) ☐ Buyer ☐ Seller shall pay escrow fee _____.
       Escrow Holder shall be _____.
   (2) ☐ Buyer ☐ Seller shall pay for **owner's** title insurance policy specified in paragraph 12E _____.
       Owner's title policy to be issued by _____.
       (Buyer shall pay for any title insurance policy insuring Buyer's **lender,** unless otherwise agreed in writing.)

E. **OTHER COSTS:**
   (1) ☐ Buyer ☐ Seller shall pay County transfer tax or transfer fee _____.
   (2) ☐ Buyer ☐ Seller shall pay City transfer tax or transfer fee _____.
   (3) ☐ Buyer ☐ Seller shall pay HOA transfer fee _____.
   (4) ☐ Buyer ☐ Seller shall pay HOA document preparation fees _____.
   (5) ☐ Buyer ☐ Seller shall pay the cost, not to exceed $ _____, of a one-year home warranty plan, issued by _____ with the following optional coverage: _____.
   (6) ☐ Buyer ☐ Seller shall pay for _____.
   (7) ☐ Buyer ☐ Seller shall pay for _____.

5. **STATUTORY DISCLOSURES (INCLUDING LEAD-BASED PAINT HAZARD DISCLOSURES) AND CANCELLATION RIGHTS:**

A. (1) Seller shall, within the time specified in paragraph 14A, deliver to Buyer, if required by Law: (i) Federal Lead-Based Paint Disclosures and pamphlet ("Lead Disclosures"); and (ii) disclosures or notices required by sections 1102 et. seq. and 1103 et. seq. of the California Civil Code ("Statutory Disclosures"). Statutory Disclosures include, but are not limited to, a Real Estate Transfer Disclosure Statement ("TDS"), Natural Hazard Disclosure Statement ("NHD"), notice or actual knowledge of release of illegal controlled substance, notice of special tax and/or assessments, notice of special tax and/or assessments, or, if allowed, substantially equivalent notice regarding the Mello-Roos Community Facilities Act and Improvement Bond Act of 1915) and, if Seller has actual knowledge, an industrial use and military ordnance location disclosure (C.A.R. Form SSD).
   (2) Buyer shall, within the time specified in paragraph 14B(1), return Signed Copies of the Statutory and Lead Disclosures to Seller.
   (3) In the event Seller, prior to Close Of Escrow, becomes aware of adverse conditions materially affecting the Property, or any material inaccuracy in disclosures, information or representations previously provided to Buyer of which Buyer is otherwise unaware, Seller shall promptly provide a subsequent or amended disclosure or notice, in writing, covering those items. However, a subsequent or amended disclosure shall not be required for conditions and material inaccuracies disclosed in reports ordered and paid for by Buyer.

Buyer's Initials (_____)(_____)
Seller's Initials (_____)(_____)

RPA-CA REVISED 10/02 (PAGE 2 OF 8)

Reviewed by _____ Date _____

(4) If any disclosure or notice specified in 5A(1), or subsequent or amended disclosure or notice is delivered to Buyer after the offer is Signed, Buyer shall have the right to cancel this Agreement within **3 Days** After delivery in person, or **5 Days** After delivery by deposit in the mail, by giving written notice of cancellation to Seller or Seller's agent. (Lead Disclosures sent by mail must be sent certified mail or better.)

(5) Note to Buyer and Seller: Waiver of Statutory and Lead Disclosures is prohibited by Law.

B. NATURAL AND ENVIRONMENTAL HAZARDS: Within the time specified in paragraph 14A, Seller shall, if required by Law: **(i)** deliver to Buyer earthquake guides (and questionnaire) and environmental hazards booklet; **(ii)** even if exempt from the obligation to provide a NHD, disclose if the Property is located in a Special Flood Hazard Area; Potential Flooding (Inundation) Area; Very High Fire Hazard Zone; State Fire Responsibility Area; Earthquake Fault Zone; Seismic Hazard Zone; and **(iii)** disclose any other zone as required by Law and provide any other information required for those zones.

C. DATA BASE DISCLOSURE: NOTICE: The California Department of Justice, sheriff's departments, police departments serving jurisdictions of 200,000 or more and many other local law enforcement authorities maintain for public access a data base of the locations of persons required to register pursuant to paragraph (1) of subdivision (a) of Section 290.4 of the Penal Code. The data base is updated on a quarterly basis and a source of information about the presence of these individuals in any neighborhood. The Department of Justice also maintains a Sex Offender Identification Line through which inquiries about individuals may be made. This is a "900" telephone service. Callers must have specific information about individuals they are checking. Information regarding neighborhoods is not available through the "900" telephone service.

6. CONDOMINIUM/PLANNED UNIT DEVELOPMENT DISCLOSURES:

A. SELLER HAS: 7 (or ☐ _____) Days After Acceptance to disclose to Buyer whether the Property is a condominium, or is located in a planned unit development or other common interest subdivision (C.A.R. Form SSD).

B. If the Property is a condominium or is located in a planned unit development or other common interest subdivision, Seller has **3 (or ☐ _____) Days** After Acceptance to request from the HOA (C.A.R. Form HOA): **(i)** Copies of any documents required by Law; **(ii)** disclosure of any pending or anticipated claim or litigation by or against the HOA; **(iii)** a statement containing the location and number of designated parking and storage spaces; **(iv)** Copies of the most recent 12 months of HOA minutes for regular and special meetings; and **(v)** the names and contact information of all HOAs governing the Property (collectively, "CI Disclosures"). Seller shall itemize and deliver to Buyer all CI Disclosures received from the HOA and any CI Disclosures in Seller's possession. Buyer's approval of CI Disclosures is a contingency of this Agreement as specified in paragraph 14B(3).

7. CONDITIONS AFFECTING PROPERTY:

A. Unless otherwise agreed: **(i) the Property is sold (a) in its PRESENT physical condition as of the date of Acceptance and (b) subject to Buyer's Investigation rights; (ii)** the Property, including pool, spa, landscaping and grounds, is to be maintained in substantially the same condition as on the date of Acceptance; and **(iii)** all debris and personal property not included in the sale shall be removed by Close Of Escrow.

B. SELLER SHALL, within the time specified in paragraph 14A, DISCLOSE KNOWN MATERIAL FACTS AND DEFECTS affecting the Property, including known insurance claims within the past five years, AND MAKE OTHER DISCLOSURES REQUIRED BY LAW (C.A.R. Form SSD).

C. NOTE TO BUYER: You are strongly advised to conduct investigations of the entire Property in order to determine its present condition since Seller may not be aware of all defects affecting the Property or other factors that you consider important. Property improvements may not be built according to code, in compliance with current Law, or have had permits issued.

D. NOTE TO SELLER: Buyer has the right to inspect the Property and, as specified in paragraph 14B, based upon information discovered in those inspections: (i) cancel this Agreement; or (ii) request that you make Repairs or take other action.

8. ITEMS INCLUDED AND EXCLUDED:

A. NOTE TO BUYER AND SELLER: Items listed as included or excluded in the MLS, flyers or marketing materials are **not** included in the purchase price or excluded from the sale unless specified in 8B or C.

B. ITEMS INCLUDED IN SALE:

(1) All EXISTING fixtures and fittings that are attached to the Property;

(2) Existing electrical, mechanical, lighting, plumbing and heating fixtures, ceiling fans, fireplace inserts, gas logs and grates, solar systems, built-in appliances, window and door screens, awnings, shutters, window coverings, attached floor coverings, television antennas, satellite dishes, private integrated telephone systems, air coolers/conditioners, pool/spa equipment, garage door openers/remote controls, mailbox, in-ground landscaping, trees/shrubs, water softeners, water purifiers, security systems/alarms; and

(3) The following items: _____
_____

(4) Seller represents that all items included in the purchase price, unless otherwise specified, are owned by Seller.

(5) All items included shall be transferred free of liens and without Seller warranty.

C. ITEMS EXCLUDED FROM SALE: _____
_____

9. BUYER'S INVESTIGATION OF PROPERTY AND MATTERS AFFECTING PROPERTY:

A. Buyer's acceptance of the condition of, and any other matter affecting the Property, is a contingency of this Agreement as specified in this paragraph and paragraph 14B. Within the time specified in paragraph 14B(1), Buyer shall have the right, at Buyer's expense unless otherwise agreed, to conduct inspections, investigations, tests, surveys and other studies ("Buyer Investigations"), including, but not limited to, the right to: **(i)** inspect for lead-based paint and other lead-based paint hazards; **(ii)** inspect for wood destroying pests and organisms; **(iii)** review the registered sex offender database; **(iv)** confirm the insurability of Buyer and the Property; and **(v)** satisfy Buyer as to any matter specified in the attached Buyer's Inspection Advisory (C.A.R. Form BIA). Without Seller's prior written consent, Buyer shall neither make nor cause to be made: **(i)** invasive or destructive Buyer Investigations; or **(ii)** inspections by any governmental building or zoning inspector or government employee, unless required by Law.

B. Buyer shall complete Buyer Investigations and, as specified in paragraph 14B, remove the contingency or cancel this Agreement. Buyer shall give Seller, at no cost, complete Copies of all Buyer Investigation reports obtained by Buyer. Seller shall make the Property available for all Buyer Investigations. Seller shall have water, gas, electricity and all operable pilot lights on for Buyer's Investigations and through the date possession is made available to Buyer.

Buyer's Initials (_____)(_____)
Seller's Initials (_____)(_____)

Reviewed by _____ Date _____

10. REPAIRS: Repairs shall be completed prior to final verification of condition unless otherwise agreed in writing. Repairs to be performed at Seller's expense may be performed by Seller or through others, provided that the work complies with applicable Law, including governmental permit, inspection and approval requirements. Repairs shall be performed in a good, skillful manner with materials of quality and appearance comparable to existing materials. It is understood that exact restoration of appearance or cosmetic items following all Repairs may not be possible. Seller shall: (i) obtain receipts for Repairs performed by others; (ii) prepare a written statement indicating the Repairs performed by Seller and the date of such Repairs; and (iii) provide Copies of receipts and statements to Buyer prior to final verification of condition.

11. BUYER INDEMNITY AND SELLER PROTECTION FOR ENTRY UPON PROPERTY: Buyer shall: (i) keep the Property free and clear of liens; (ii) Repair all damage arising from Buyer Investigations; and (iii) indemnify and hold Seller harmless from all resulting liability, claims, demands, damages and costs. Buyer shall carry, or Buyer shall require anyone acting on Buyer's behalf to carry, policies of liability, workers' compensation and other applicable insurance, defending and protecting Seller from liability for any injuries to persons or property occurring during any Buyer Investigations or work done on the Property at Buyer's direction prior to Close Of Escrow. Seller is advised that certain protections may be afforded Seller by recording a "Notice of Non-responsibility" (C.A.R. Form NNR) for Buyer Investigations and work done on the Property at Buyer's direction. Buyer's obligations under this paragraph shall survive the termination of this Agreement.

12. TITLE AND VESTING:
  A. Within the time specified in paragraph 14, Buyer shall be provided a current preliminary (title) report, which is only an offer by the title insurer to issue a policy of title insurance and may not contain every item affecting title. Buyer's review of the preliminary report and any other matters which may affect title are a contingency of this Agreement as specified in paragraph 14B.
  B. Title is taken in its present condition subject to all encumbrances, easements, covenants, conditions, restrictions, rights and other matters, whether of record or not, as of the date of Acceptance except: (i) monetary liens of record unless Buyer is assuming those obligations or taking the Property subject to those obligations; and (ii) those matters which Seller has agreed to remove in writing.
  C. Within the time specified in paragraph 14A, Seller has a duty to disclose to Buyer all matters known to Seller affecting title, whether of record or not.
  D. At Close Of Escrow, Buyer shall receive a grant deed conveying title (or, for stock cooperative or long-term lease, an assignment of stock certificate or of Seller's leasehold interest), including oil, mineral and water rights if currently owned by Seller. Title shall vest as designated in Buyer's supplemental escrow instructions. THE MANNER OF TAKING TITLE MAY HAVE SIGNIFICANT LEGAL AND TAX CONSEQUENCES. CONSULT AN APPROPRIATE PROFESSIONAL.
  E. Buyer shall receive a CLTA/ALTA Homeowner's Policy of Title Insurance. A title company, at Buyer's request, can provide information about the availability, desirability, coverage, and cost of various title insurance coverages and endorsements. If Buyer desires title coverage other than that required by this paragraph, Buyer shall instruct Escrow Holder in writing and pay any increase in cost.

13. SALE OF BUYER'S PROPERTY:
  A. This Agreement is NOT contingent upon the sale of any property owned by Buyer.
  OR B. ☐ (If checked): The attached addendum (C.A.R. Form COP) regarding the contingency for the sale of property owned by Buyer is incorporated into this Agreement.

14. TIME PERIODS; REMOVAL OF CONTINGENCIES; CANCELLATION RIGHTS: The following time periods may only be extended, altered, modified or changed by mutual written agreement. Any removal of contingencies or cancellation under this paragraph must be in writing (C.A.R. Form CR).
  A. **SELLER HAS: 7 (or ☐ _____) Days** After Acceptance to deliver to Buyer all reports, disclosures and information for which Seller is responsible under paragraphs 4, 5A and B, 6A, 7B and 12.
  B. (1) **BUYER HAS: 17 (or ☐ _____) Days** After Acceptance, unless otherwise agreed in writing, to:
      (i) complete all Buyer Investigations; approve all disclosures, reports and other applicable information, which Buyer receives from Seller; and approve all matters affecting the Property (including lead-based paint and lead-based paint hazards as well as other information specified in paragraph 5 and insurability of Buyer and the Property); and
      (ii) return to Seller Signed Copies of Statutory and Lead Disclosures delivered by Seller in accordance with paragraph 5A.
    (2) Within the time specified in 14B(1), Buyer may request that Seller make repairs or take any other action regarding the Property (C.A.R. Form RR). Seller has no obligation to agree to or respond to Buyer's requests.
    (3) By the end of the time specified in 14B(1) (or 2I for loan contingency or 2J for appraisal contingency), Buyer shall, in writing, remove the applicable contingency (C.A.R. Form CR) or cancel this Agreement. However, if (i) government-mandated inspections/ reports required as a condition of closing; or (ii) Common Interest Disclosures pursuant to paragraph 6B are not made within the time specified in 14A, then Buyer has 5 (or ☐ _____) Days After receipt of any such items, or the time specified in 14B(1), whichever is later, to remove the applicable contingency or cancel this Agreement in writing.
  C. **CONTINUATION OF CONTINGENCY OR CONTRACTUAL OBLIGATION; SELLER RIGHT TO CANCEL:**
    (1) **Seller right to Cancel; Buyer Contingencies:** Seller, after first giving Buyer a Notice to Buyer to Perform (as specified below), may cancel this Agreement in writing and authorize return of Buyer's deposit if, by the time specified in this Agreement, Buyer does not remove in writing the applicable contingency or cancel this Agreement. Once all contingencies have been removed, failure of either Buyer or Seller to close escrow on time may be a breach of this Agreement.
    (2) **Continuation of Contingency:** Even after the expiration of the time specified in 14B, Buyer retains the right to make requests to Seller, remove in writing the applicable contingency or cancel this Agreement until Seller cancels pursuant to 14C(1). Once Seller receives Buyer's written removal of all contingencies, Seller may not cancel this Agreement pursuant to 14C(1).
    (3) **Seller right to Cancel; Buyer Contract Obligations:** Seller, after first giving Buyer a Notice to Buyer to Perform (as specified below), may cancel this Agreement in writing and authorize return of Buyer's deposit for any of the following reasons: (i) if Buyer fails to deposit funds as required by 2A or 2B; (ii) if the funds deposited pursuant to 2A or 2B are not good when deposited; (iii) if Buyer fails to provide a letter as required by 2G; (iv) if Buyer fails to provide verification as required by 2H or 2L; (v) if Seller reasonably disapproves of the verification provided by 2H or 2L; (vi) if Buyer fails to return Statutory and Lead Disclosures as required by paragraph 5A(2); or (vii) if Buyer fails to sign or initial a separate liquidated damage form for an increased deposit as required by paragraph 16. **Seller is not required to give Buyer a Notice to Perform regarding Close of Escrow.**
    (4) **Notice To Buyer To Perform:** The Notice to Buyer to Perform (C.A.R. Form NBP) shall: (i) be in writing; (ii) be signed by Seller; and (iii) give Buyer at least 24 (or ☐ _____) hours (or until the time specified in the applicable paragraph, whichever occurs last) to take the applicable action. A Notice to Buyer to Perform may not be given any earlier than 2 Days Prior to the expiration of the applicable time for Buyer to remove a contingency or cancel this Agreement or meet a 14C(3) obligation.

Buyer's Initials (_____)(_____)
Seller's Initials (_____)(_____)

Reviewed by _____ Date _____

EQUAL HOUSING OPPORTUNITY

D. EFFECT OF BUYER'S REMOVAL OF CONTINGENCIES : If Buyer removes, in writing, any contingency or cancellation rights, unless otherwise specified in a separate written agreement between Buyer and Seller, Buyer shall conclusively be deemed to have: **(i)** completed all Buyer Investigations, and review of reports and other applicable information and disclosures pertaining to that contingency or cancellation right; **(ii)** elected to proceed with the transaction; and **(iii)** assumed all liability, responsibility and expense for Repairs or corrections pertaining to that contingency or cancellation right, or for inability to obtain financing.

E. EFFECT OF CANCELLATION ON DEPOSITS: If Buyer or Seller gives written notice of cancellation pursuant to rights duly exercised under the terms of this Agreement, Buyer and Seller agree to Sign mutual instructions to cancel the sale and escrow and release deposits to the party entitled to the funds, less fees and costs incurred by that party. Fees and costs may be payable to service providers and vendors for services and products provided during escrow. **Release of funds will require mutual Signed release instructions from Buyer and Seller, judicial decision or arbitration award. A party may be subject to a civil penalty of up to $1,000 for refusal to sign such instructions if no good faith dispute exists as to who is entitled to the deposited funds (Civil Code §1057.3).**

15. FINAL VERIFICATION OF CONDITION: Buyer shall have the right to make a final inspection of the Property within **5 (or _____) Days** Prior to Close Of Escrow, NOT AS A CONTINGENCY OF THE SALE, but solely to confirm: **(i)** the Property is maintained pursuant to paragraph 7A; **(ii)** Repairs have been completed as agreed; and **(iii)** Seller has complied with Seller's other obligations under this Agreement.

16. LIQUIDATED DAMAGES: If Buyer fails to complete this purchase because of Buyer's default, Seller shall retain, as liquidated damages, the deposit actually paid. If the Property is a dwelling with no more than four units, one of which Buyer intends to occupy, then the amount retained shall be no more than 3% of the purchase price. Any excess shall be returned to Buyer. Release of funds will require mutual, Signed release instructions from both Buyer and Seller, judicial decision or arbitration award.
BUYER AND SELLER SHALL SIGN A SEPARATE LIQUIDATED DAMAGES PROVISION FOR ANY INCREASED DEPOSIT. (C.A.R. FORM RID)

Buyer's Initials _____/_____	Seller's Initials _____/_____

17. DISPUTE RESOLUTION:

A. MEDIATION: Buyer and Seller agree to mediate any dispute or claim arising between them out of this Agreement, or any resulting transaction, before resorting to arbitration or court action. Paragraphs 17B(2) and (3) below apply whether or not the Arbitration provision is initialed. Mediation fees, if any, shall be divided equally among the parties involved. If, for any dispute or claim to which this paragraph applies, any party commences an action without first attempting to resolve the matter through mediation, or refuses to mediate after a request has been made, then that party shall not be entitled to recover attorney fees, even if they would otherwise be available to that party in any such action. THIS MEDIATION PROVISION APPLIES WHETHER OR NOT THE ARBITRATION PROVISION IS INITIALED.

B. ARBITRATION OF DISPUTES: (1) Buyer and Seller agree that any dispute or claim in Law or equity arising between them out of this Agreement or any resulting transaction, which is not settled through mediation, shall be decided by neutral, binding arbitration, including and subject to paragraphs 17B(2) and (3) below. The arbitrator shall be a retired judge or justice, or an attorney with at least 5 years of residential real estate Law experience, unless the parties mutually agree to a different arbitrator, who shall render an award in accordance with substantive California Law. The parties shall have the right to discovery in accordance with California Code of Civil Procedure §1283.05. In all other respects, the arbitration shall be conducted in accordance with Title 9 of Part III of the California Code of Civil Procedure. Judgment upon the award of the arbitrator(s) may be entered into any court having jurisdiction. Interpretation of this agreement to arbitrate shall be governed by the Federal Arbitration Act.

(2) EXCLUSIONS FROM MEDIATION AND ARBITRATION: The following matters are excluded from mediation and arbitration: (i) a judicial or non-judicial foreclosure or other action or proceeding to enforce a deed of trust, mortgage or installment land sale contract as defined in California Civil Code §2985; (ii) an unlawful detainer action; (iii) the filing or enforcement of a mechanic's lien; and (iv) any matter that is within the jurisdiction of a probate, small claims or bankruptcy court. The filing of a court action to enable the recording of a notice of pending action, for order of attachment, receivership, injunction, or other provisional remedies, shall not constitute a waiver of the mediation and arbitration provisions.

(3) BROKERS: Buyer and Seller agree to mediate and arbitrate disputes or claims involving either or both Brokers, consistent with 17A and B, provided either or both Brokers shall have agreed to such mediation or arbitration prior to, or within a reasonable time after, the dispute or claim is presented to Brokers. Any election by either or both Brokers to participate in mediation or arbitration shall not result in Brokers being deemed parties to the Agreement.

"NOTICE: BY INITIALING IN THE SPACE BELOW YOU ARE AGREEING TO HAVE ANY DISPUTE ARISING OUT OF THE MATTERS INCLUDED IN THE 'ARBITRATION OF DISPUTES' PROVISION DECIDED BY NEUTRAL ARBITRATION AS PROVIDED BY CALIFORNIA LAW AND YOU ARE GIVING UP ANY RIGHTS YOU MIGHT POSSESS TO HAVE THE DISPUTE LITIGATED IN A COURT OR JURY TRIAL. BY INITIALING IN THE SPACE BELOW YOU ARE GIVING UP YOUR JUDICIAL RIGHTS TO DISCOVERY AND APPEAL, UNLESS THOSE RIGHTS ARE SPECIFICALLY INCLUDED IN THE 'ARBITRATION OF DISPUTES' PROVISION. IF YOU REFUSE TO SUBMIT TO ARBITRATION AFTER AGREEING TO THIS PROVISION, YOU MAY BE COMPELLED TO ARBITRATE UNDER THE AUTHORITY OF THE CALIFORNIA CODE OF CIVIL PROCEDURE. YOUR AGREEMENT TO THIS ARBITRATION PROVISION IS VOLUNTARY."

"WE HAVE READ AND UNDERSTAND THE FOREGOING AND AGREE TO SUBMIT DISPUTES ARISING OUT OF THE MATTERS INCLUDED IN THE 'ARBITRATION OF DISPUTES' PROVISION TO NEUTRAL ARBITRATION."

Buyer's Initials _____/_____	Seller's Initials _____/_____

Buyer's Initials (_____)(_____)
Seller's Initials (_____)(_____)

Reviewed by _____ Date _____

RPA-CA REVISED 10/02 (PAGE 5 OF 8)

18. **PRORATIONS OF PROPERTY TAXES AND OTHER ITEMS:** Unless otherwise agreed in writing, the following items shall be PAID CURRENT and prorated between Buyer and Seller as of Close Of Escrow: real property taxes and assessments, interest, rents, HOA regular, special, and emergency dues and assessments imposed prior to Close Of Escrow, premiums on insurance assumed by Buyer, payments on bonds and assessments assumed by Buyer, and payments on Mello-Roos and other Special Assessment District bonds and assessments that are now a lien. The following items shall be assumed by Buyer WITHOUT CREDIT toward the purchase price: prorated payments on Mello-Roos and other Special Assessment District bonds and assessments and HOA special assessments that are now a lien but not yet due. Property will be reassessed upon change of ownership. Any supplemental tax bills shall be paid as follows: **(i)** for periods after Close Of Escrow, by Buyer; and **(ii)** for periods prior to Close Of Escrow, by Seller. TAX BILLS ISSUED AFTER CLOSE OF ESCROW SHALL BE HANDLED DIRECTLY BETWEEN BUYER AND SELLER. Prorations shall be made based on a 30-day month.

19. **WITHHOLDING TAXES:** Seller and Buyer agree to execute any instrument, affidavit, statement or instruction reasonably necessary to comply with federal (FIRPTA) and California withholding Law, if required (C.A.R. Forms AS and AB).

20. **MULTIPLE LISTING SERVICE ("MLS"):** Brokers are authorized to report to the MLS a pending sale and, upon Close Of Escrow, the terms of this transaction to be published and disseminated to persons and entities authorized to use the information on terms approved by the MLS.

21. **EQUAL HOUSING OPPORTUNITY:** The Property is sold in compliance with federal, state and local anti-discrimination Laws.

22. **ATTORNEY FEES:** In any action, proceeding, or arbitration between Buyer and Seller arising out of this Agreement, the prevailing Buyer or Seller shall be entitled to reasonable attorney fees and costs from the non-prevailing Buyer or Seller, except as provided in paragraph 17A.

23. **SELECTION OF SERVICE PROVIDERS:** If Brokers refer Buyer or Seller to persons, vendors, or service or product providers ("Providers"), Brokers do not guarantee the performance of any Providers. Buyer and Seller may select ANY Providers of their own choosing.

24. **TIME OF ESSENCE; ENTIRE CONTRACT; CHANGES:** Time is of the essence. All understandings between the parties are incorporated in this Agreement. Its terms are intended by the parties as a final, complete and exclusive expression of their Agreement with respect to its subject matter, and may not be contradicted by evidence of any prior agreement or contemporaneous oral agreement. If any provision of this Agreement is held to be ineffective or invalid, the remaining provisions will nevertheless be given full force and effect. **Neither this Agreement nor any provision in it may be extended, amended, modified, altered or changed, except in writing Signed by Buyer and Seller.**

25. **OTHER TERMS AND CONDITIONS,** including attached supplements:
    A. ☑ Buyer's Inspection Advisory (C.A.R. Form BIA)
    B. ☐ Purchase Agreement Addendum (C.A.R. Form PAA paragraph numbers: _____)
    C. ☐ Statewide Buyer and Seller Advisory (C.A.R. Form SBSA)
    D. _____

26. **DEFINITIONS:** As used in this Agreement:
    A. **"Acceptance"** means the time the offer or final counter offer is accepted in writing by a party and is delivered to and personally received by the other party or that party's authorized agent in accordance with the terms of this offer or a final counter offer.
    B. **"Agreement"** means the terms and conditions of this accepted California Residential Purchase Agreement and any accepted counter offers and addenda.
    C. **"C.A.R. Form"** means the specific form referenced or another comparable form agreed to by the parties.
    D. **"Close Of Escrow"** means the date the grant deed, or other evidence of transfer of title, is recorded. If the scheduled close of escrow falls on a Saturday, Sunday or legal holiday, then close of escrow shall be the next business day after the scheduled close of escrow date.
    E. **"Copy"** means copy by any means including photocopy, NCR, facsimile and electronic.
    F. **"Days"** means calendar days, unless otherwise required by Law.
    G. **"Days After"** means the specified number of calendar days after the occurrence of the event specified, not counting the calendar date on which the specified event occurs, and ending at 11:59PM on the final day.
    H. **"Days Prior"** means the specified number of calendar days before the occurrence of the event specified, not counting the calendar date on which the specified event is scheduled to occur.
    I. **"Electronic Copy"** or **"Electronic Signature"** means, as applicable, an electronic copy or signature complying with California Law. Buyer and Seller agree that electronic means will not be used by either party to modify or alter the content or integrity of this Agreement without the knowledge and consent of the other.
    J. **"Law"** means any law, code, statute, ordinance, regulation, rule or order, which is adopted by a controlling city, county, state or federal legislative, judicial or executive body or agency.
    K. **"Notice to Buyer to Perform"** means a document (C.A.R. Form NBP), which shall be in writing and Signed by Seller and shall give Buyer at least 24 hours **(or as otherwise specified in paragraph 14C(4))** to remove a contingency or perform as applicable.
    L. **"Repairs"** means any repairs (including pest control), alterations, replacements, modifications or retrofitting of the Property provided for under this Agreement.
    M. **"Signed"** means either a handwritten or electronic signature on an original document, Copy or any counterpart.
    N. **Singular and Plural** terms each include the other, when appropriate.

Buyer's Initials (_____)(_____)
Seller's Initials (_____)(_____)

RPA-CA REVISED 10/02 (PAGE 6 OF 8)

Reviewed by _____ Date _____

EQUAL HOUSING OPPORTUNITY

Property Address: _____ Date: _____

27. AGENCY:

A. DISCLOSURE: Buyer and Seller each acknowledge prior receipt of C.A.R. Form AD "Disclosure Regarding Real Estate Agency Relationships."

B. POTENTIALLY COMPETING BUYERS AND SELLERS: Buyer and Seller each acknowledge receipt of a disclosure of the possibility of multiple representation by the Broker representing that principal. This disclosure may be part of a listing agreement, buyer-broker agreement or separate document (C.A.R. Form DA). Buyer understands that Broker representing Buyer may also represent other potential buyers, who may consider, make offers on or ultimately acquire the Property. Seller understands that Broker representing Seller may also represent other sellers with competing properties of interest to this Buyer.

C. CONFIRMATION: The following agency relationships are hereby confirmed for this transaction:
Listing Agent _____ (Print Firm Name) is the agent of (check one): ☐ the Seller exclusively; or ☐ both the Buyer and Seller.
Selling Agent _____ (Print Firm Name) (if not same as Listing Agent) is the agent of (check one): ☐ the Buyer exclusively; or ☐ the Seller exclusively; or ☐ both the Buyer and Seller. Real Estate Brokers are not parties to the Agreement between Buyer and Seller.

28. JOINT ESCROW INSTRUCTIONS TO ESCROW HOLDER:

A. **The following paragraphs, or applicable portions thereof, of this Agreement constitute the joint escrow instructions of Buyer and Seller to Escrow Holder,** which Escrow Holder is to use along with any related counter offers and addenda, and any additional mutual instructions to close the escrow: 1, 2, 4, 12, 13B, 14E, 18, 19, 24, 25B and C, 26, 28, 29, 32A, 33 and paragraph D of the section titled Real Estate Brokers on page 8. If a Copy of the separate compensation agreement(s) provided for in paragraph 29 or 32A, or paragraph D of the section titled Real Estate Brokers on page 8 is deposited with Escrow Holder by Broker, Escrow Holder shall accept such agreement(s) and pay out from Buyer's or Seller's funds, or both, as applicable, the Broker's compensation provided for in such agreement(s). The terms and conditions of this Agreement not set forth in the specified paragraphs are additional matters for the information of Escrow Holder, but about which Escrow Holder need not be concerned. Buyer and Seller will receive Escrow Holder's general provisions directly from Escrow Holder and will execute such provisions upon Escrow Holder's request. To the extent the general provisions are inconsistent or conflict with this Agreement, the general provisions will control as to the duties and obligations of Escrow Holder only. Buyer and Seller will execute additional instructions, documents and forms provided by Escrow Holder that are reasonably necessary to close the escrow.

B. A Copy of this Agreement shall be delivered to Escrow Holder within **3** business days after Acceptance (or ☐ _____). Buyer and Seller authorize Escrow Holder to accept and rely on Copies and Signatures as defined in this Agreement as originals, to open escrow and for other purposes of escrow. The validity of this Agreement as between Buyer and Seller is not affected by whether or when Escrow Holder Signs this Agreement.

C. Brokers are a party to the escrow for the sole purpose of compensation pursuant to paragraphs 29, 32A and paragraph D of the section titled Real Estate Brokers on page 8. Buyer and Seller irrevocably assign to Brokers compensation specified in paragraphs 29 and 32A, respectively, and irrevocably instruct Escrow Holder to disburse those funds to Brokers at Close Of Escrow or pursuant to any other mutually executed cancellation agreement. Compensation instructions can be amended or revoked only with the written consent of Brokers. Escrow Holder shall immediately notify Brokers: **(i)** if Buyer's initial or any additional deposit is not made pursuant to this Agreement, or is not good at time of deposit with Escrow Holder; or **(ii)** if Buyer and Seller instruct Escrow Holder to cancel escrow.

D. A Copy of any amendment that affects any paragraph of this Agreement for which Escrow Holder is responsible shall be delivered to Escrow Holder within **2** business days after mutual execution of the amendment.

29. BROKER COMPENSATION FROM BUYER:
If applicable, upon Close Of Escrow, **Buyer** agrees to pay compensation to Broker as specified in a separate written agreement between Buyer and Broker.

30. TERMS AND CONDITIONS OF OFFER:

This is an offer to purchase the Property on the above terms and conditions. All paragraphs with spaces for initials by Buyer and Seller are incorporated in this Agreement only if initialed by all parties. If at least one but not all parties initial, a counter offer is required until agreement is reached. Seller has the right to continue to offer the Property for sale and to accept any other offer at any time prior to notification of Acceptance. Buyer has read and acknowledges receipt of a Copy of the offer and agrees to the above confirmation of agency relationships. If this offer is accepted and Buyer subsequently defaults, Buyer may be responsible for payment of Brokers' compensation. This Agreement and any supplement, addendum or modification, including any Copy, may be Signed in two or more counterparts, all of which shall constitute one and the same writing.

Buyer's Initials (_____)(_____)
Seller's Initials (_____)(_____)

Reviewed by _____ Date _____

Property Address: _____ Date: _____

31. EXPIRATION OF OFFER: This offer shall be deemed revoked and the deposit shall be returned unless the offer is Signed by Seller and a Copy of the Signed offer is personally received by Buyer, or by _____ who is authorized to receive it by 5:00 PM on the third calendar day after this offer is signed by Buyer (or, if checked, ☐ by _____ (date), at _____ AM/PM.

Date _____ Date _____

BUYER _____ BUYER _____

_____ _____
(Print name) **(Print name)**

_____
(Address)

32. BROKER COMPENSATION FROM SELLER:
   A. Upon Close Of Escrow, **Seller** agrees to pay compensation to Broker as specified in a separate written agreement between Seller and Broker.
   B. If escrow does not close, compensation is payable as specified in that separate written agreement.

33. ACCEPTANCE OF OFFER: Seller warrants that Seller is the owner of the Property, or has the authority to execute this Agreement. Seller accepts the above offer, agrees to sell the Property on the above terms and conditions, and agrees to the above confirmation of agency relationships. Seller has read and acknowledges receipt of a Copy of this Agreement, and authorizes Broker to deliver a Signed Copy to Buyer.
   ☐ (If checked) **SUBJECT TO ATTACHED COUNTER OFFER, DATED** _____.

Date _____ Date _____

SELLER _____ SELLER _____

_____ _____
(Print name) **(Print name)**

_____
(Address)

(___/___) **CONFIRMATION OF ACCEPTANCE:** A Copy of Signed Acceptance was personally received by Buyer or Buyer's authorized
(Initials) agent on (date) _____ at _____ AM/PM. **A binding Agreement is created when a Copy of Signed Acceptance is personally received by Buyer or Buyer's authorized agent whether or not confirmed in this document. Completion of this confirmation is not legally required in order to create a binding Agreement;** it is solely intended to evidence the date that Confirmation of Acceptance has occurred.

REAL ESTATE BROKERS:
A. Real Estate Brokers are not parties to the Agreement between Buyer and Seller.
B. Agency relationships are confirmed as stated in paragraph 27.
C. If specified in paragraph 2A, Agent who submitted the offer for Buyer acknowledges receipt of deposit.
D. **COOPERATING BROKER COMPENSATION:** Listing Broker agrees to pay Cooperating Broker (**Selling Firm**) and Cooperating Broker agrees to accept, out of Listing Broker's proceeds in escrow: **(i)** the amount specified in the MLS, provided Cooperating Broker is a Participant of the MLS in which the Property is offered for sale or a reciprocal MLS; or **(ii)** ☐ (if checked) the amount specified in a separate written agreement (C.A.R. Form CBC) between Listing Broker and Cooperating Broker.

Real Estate Broker (Selling Firm) _____
By _____ Date _____
Address _____ City _____ State _____ Zip _____
Telephone _____ Fax _____ E-mail _____

Real Estate Broker (Listing Firm) _____
By _____ Date _____
Address _____ City _____ State _____ Zip _____
Telephone _____ Fax _____ E-mail _____

ESCROW HOLDER ACKNOWLEDGMENT:
Escrow Holder acknowledges receipt of a Copy of this Agreement, (if checked, ☐ a deposit in the amount of $ _____),
counter offer numbers _____ and _____, and agrees to act as Escrow Holder subject to paragraph 28 of this Agreement, any supplemental escrow instructions and the terms of Escrow Holder's general provisions.

Escrow Holder is advised that the date of Confirmation of Acceptance of the Agreement as between Buyer and Seller is _____

Escrow Holder _____ Escrow # _____
By _____ Date _____
Address _____
Phone/Fax/E-mail _____
Escrow Holder is licensed by the California Department of ☐ Corporations, ☐ Insurance, ☐ Real Estate. License # _____

(___/___) **REJECTION OF OFFER:** No counter offer is being made. This offer was reviewed and rejected by Seller on
(Seller's Initials) _____ **(Date)**

The System for Success®

Published and Distributed by:
REAL ESTATE BUSINESS SERVICES, INC.
a subsidiary of the California Association of REALTORS®
525 South Virgil Avenue, Los Angeles, California 90020

Reviewed by _____ Date _____

182

problem arising later in the property transaction, the location where the deposit receipt is filled out determines the jurisdiction or district where litigation will take place to solve the dispute.

The date of the offer is placed just after the name of the city where the contract is signed. The date establishes a time frame for acceptance of the contract by the sellers. This date is not necessarily the same as the one on page four of the contract, where the buyers place their signature.

Remember
- The location to be filled out on the contract is not where the property is located; it is the location where the contract is completed.

1. Offer

Buyers
The buyers need to make sure they correctly and carefully spell their names in the designated place. In the event that there is litigation regarding this contract, accurate identification of the buyers is essential.

It is important to note that only the person making the offer to purchase the property is listed here. Even if more than one person plans on taking title to the property, only the person making the offer is listed.

Property Description
An accurate description of the property must accompany the deposit receipt so all parties are fully aware of which property is in question. This may sound like an unnecessary step, as both parties should indisputably know which property they are selling and buying, but this step is taken in the event that there should be a dispute in the future. A legal description will allow any person involved in dispute resolution or litigation to clearly understand which property is in question.

An acceptable property description for most urban properties would be a full street address. Other properties may need to be described using metes and bounds or by the block and lot numbers associated with them. Most newer properties can have a land description that refers to a recorded map, or to a preliminary title report. Properties located outside of an urban area are described based on the most recent survey of the land.

It is very important to have an accurate description. When transcribing the legal description from one instrument onto another, there will be a chance an error may occur. For short or simple property descriptions, transcribing the description from an original recorded instrument to the deposit receipt is simple and relatively error-free. For longer descriptions, it may be better to photocopy the property description from an original recorded instrument and attach it to the deposit receipt. This will avoid any errors that may happen when transposing the material from one document to another.

Price
The next portion to fill out asks for the purchase price of the home, or the offer that the buyer is extending to the seller. The offer must be written out both in words and as

a numeric value. This is to make sure the offer is clearly understandable in the event the numbers are not clearly written. In the event that there is a dispute between the two values, the value expressed in words will be the official value.

2. Financing

The financing section of the deposit receipt is a contingency clause. The purchase is contingent on the buyer being able to secure financing for the property. If the buyer fails to secure financing, the contract becomes void, freeing the buyer from any responsibility. If the buyer makes the offer, and does not present the offer contingent upon financing, the buyer may be held liable for the contract whether he or she can obtain the financing or not.

A. Initial Deposits. Usually an agent will encourage his or her client to put down a large deposit. The larger the deposit, the more interested a hesitant seller might be in accepting the offer. Large deposits also usually mean the buyer is serious, and will most likely follow through with the transactions. This is not to say that a buyer offering a smaller deposit, or who can only afford a small deposit, is any less willing to follow through with the transaction. As an agent, you must present all offers to the seller regardless of the size of the deposit.

The deposit is spelled out in words, and then written in numerals. The reason the amount is entered twice is to make sure there was no error or misunderstanding by either party about the amount of the deposit.

Immediately following the amount of the deposit is the specification of the type of payment the buyer intends on using to make the deposit. There are boxes provided on the form to be checked indicating which form of payment will be used. These payment options are cash, personal check, cashier's check, money order, promissory note, certified check, irrevocable order, or non-monetary goods. A space is provided on the deposit receipt to indicate the form of non-monetary consideration to be used as deposit. As long as the consideration is acceptable to the sellers, it may be used. If a buyer uses a postdated check, this must be pointed out to, and approved by, the sellers.

Remember
There are eight methods a buyer may use when placing a deposit on property. They are:
- Cash
- Personal check
- Cashier's check
- Money order
- Promissory note
- Certified check
- Irrevocable order
- Non-monetary goods or consideration

After a deposit is made, the money or consideration belongs to the buyers making the offer until that offer is accepted by the sellers. The deposit is placed into a broker's trust account or into escrow unless otherwise stated by the buyers. The deposit may also be given directly to the seller if specified by the buyer. Once the offer is accepted the deposit no longer belongs to the buyer, but to the seller.

On occasion, the buyer may also make out the deposit check directly to the broker, instructing the broker to hold the funds for a specific amount of time up until, or even after, the offer has been accepted by the sellers. This is perfectly acceptable. The broker must enter the amount into his or her trust fund records, and then hold the check in a safe place where it can be located easily and quickly. When the offer is presented to the seller, the disclosure must be made that the deposit is being held, uncashed. This should also be stated on the deposit receipt. There is a possibility that the check may never be honored; the seller must be aware of this possibility. As an agent or broker, you must make sure to handle the disclosure of the uncashed deposit carefully, store it in a safe, accessible place, and make all necessary notations in the trust fund records. If the agent or broker has taken all these necessary steps, he or she will be protected from any disciplinary or legal action the seller or real estate commission may take in the event the check is not honored. If an agent or broker does not take all necessary steps, and make all necessary disclosures, it is possible for him or her to be held liable for this money, and be subject to disciplinary action.

B. If the buyer elects to increase the deposit toward the purchase price, he or she can fill out this section. If the buyer does not choose to increase the deposit, this section does not need to be filled out.

C. Buyers securing a new first loan must complete this section, including all details of the loan including loan fees and discount points associated with the loan. Buyers taking over an existing loan need not complete this section. The monthly payment, interest rate, and repayment schedule listed on the deposit receipt must accurately match the actual terms of the loan. If the terms written on the deposit receipt and the actual terms do not match, the contract may come unenforceable. In the event the terms do not match, both parties can agree to the changes, and acknowledge this fact on the document. To protect the buyers, the deposit receipt may contain a clause stating the maximum monthly payment, loan amount, and payment schedule, so as to not get the buyer in over his or her head. If the terms of the loan exceed these maximum amounts, the contract may become void.

The deposit receipt may also have a clause protecting the seller, outlining a time limitation on how long the buyer has to obtain financing. If the buyer can not secure financing by the specified time, the contract may become void, with the deposit being returned to the buyer.

H. The down payment is to be paid into escrow by a certain date. Escrow must then wait for the check to clear. If a cashier's check or certified check is used, this will allow escrow to close faster.

3. Closing and Occupancy
The buyer will indicate in this section if he or she plans on making the property his or her primary residence. The reason for specifying whether or not the property is a primary residence is because the liquidated damages law makes a distinction between a primary residence and a non-primary residence.

Generally, lenders will make smaller loans for property that will not be owner-occupied. Depending on the buyer's intentions, and the type of property, the seller might want to make sure the buyer can secure the necessary funding to complete the transaction before getting too far into the process.

Possession. As indicated by its name, possession determines when the buyer will take control of the property. This date is negotiable between the buyer and seller; however, it is good practice to have this date be the same as the closing date to avoid problems or issues between the two parties.

In the event that the seller will remain in possession of the property after closing, it is imperative that an "occupancy agreement after sale" is drawn up. This will state that the seller is not a tenant. The buyer can be compensated financially for the seller's holdover in the property, with all necessary prorations made.

4D. Escrow Period

This section of the deposit receipt will name the chosen escrow holder or company the parties have agreed upon. This section also outlines the time frame for escrow. This time frame is based on when the offer was accepted by the seller. Generally there is a time requirement as to when the documents must be delivered after acceptance. Once accepted, escrow opens, and will be open for the predetermined amount of time. The length of time escrow will last will be determined by the buyer and seller.

There is a space provided to specify who will pay for the different escrow fees and services. Again, this is not predetermined; it is something the buyer and seller will work out amongst each other, through their agents.

5. Statutory Disclosures and Cancellation Rights

This section states whether the buyer has received the mandatory disclosure statements, or whether the seller still needs to provide this to the buyer. If the seller needs to supply these documents, a time frame is given within which the seller has to provide it.

8. Items Included and Excluded

This section lists all personal property that is free of liens or conditions, to be left in the property at the time of sale. This is negotiable between the buyer and seller. If the buyer really likes a particular piece of furniture or other item of personal property, and the seller agrees to leave it, it will be recorded in this section. Items such as appliances should be referred to by make and model and include the serial number. This is to protect the buyer from the seller replacing the appliances with a different model or type. When there is a lot of personal property to be included, an attached sheet may be used to list all items to be left for the buyer.

Attached fixtures to be left should be listed here, with an attached sheet in the event there are more than the space allows. Fixtures are permanently installed property such as a garage door opener. There is also a space here to list any fixtures that will not be part of the purchase price of the home.

12. Title and Vesting

Title. It is important for a buyer making an offer on property to have a copy of the preliminary title report. Many times, the buyer has not received this document, and will make an offer subject to inspection of this document. It is important to see this, because if there is a cloud on the title or if there are liens, there might be a problem with the property transfer. This portion of the deposit receipt is referred to as the "condition of title" clause.

The broker should begin a title search or learn as much as he or she can about the title of a property when he or she takes the listing. Additionally, agents should not sell property subject to easements, restrictions, covenants, and conditions of record without knowing what they are. Having a buyer sign a form subject to these conditions may interfere with the buyer's intentions for the property, causing problems. A buyer should never be asked to make an endorsement of any restrictions that he or she has not read.

Buyers should receive a copy of the preliminary title report as soon as possible upon acceptance of the offer. The buyer will then have the opportunity to inspect the title report, and make any objections he or she may have. The buyer only has a specific amount of time to make these objections, however. Once the buyer has voiced an objection, the seller has a specific time frame in which he or she must correct the problem. Buyers should acknowledge by signature that they have received and read the title report. This will protect the sellers from arbitrary or false objections in the future. If the seller is not able to address the buyer's objections to the title, the buyer is able to cancel the purchase agreement. Additionally, the clause allowing the buyer to review and make objections to the title also specifies who will pay for the title report. The responsible party will vary from county to county, but if the buyer has to pay for the title report, and then decides to cancel the offer, he or she is also responsible for paying for cancellation fees. It is important to note here that if title insurance has been purchased, the title report will be free.

The responsible party for title insurance is also negotiable. The cost may be paid for by one party, or divided up between the buyer and seller. It is important for the buyer and seller to agree on who pays this amount, and fill in the appropriate party on the deposit receipt. If it is left blank, the responsible party will be determined by local custom. Customarily, in Northern California the buyer pays for the title insurance while the seller pays for it in Southern California. The policy issued will be a standard coverage California Land Title Association policy. If either party wishes to have an extended policy, he or she must request it at the appropriate part of the contract.

In the event that the seller does not deliver the title to the property, the buyers may cancel their offer and receive their full deposit back.

Vesting. How the buyer or buyers take title will be listed here. It is important for the licensee not to make any suggestions on how the title will read; it should be completely up to the buyers. The reason for this is that there are legal and tax consequences involved in how a buyer takes title to property. If the buyer is seeking advice on how to proceed, an attorney should be consulted. The licensee can and should, however, explain the different ways title may be taken. If the buyer or buyers have not determined how they will take title to the property, the licensee should put "instructions to follow" in the space provided.

16. Liquidated Damages and 17. Dispute Resolution
Liquidated damages are damages in an ascertained amount that may be recovered in a lawsuit. If both parties leave this section blank, they are signifying that they have chosen to forgo the possibility of liquidating damages. The paragraph reads as follows:

If Buyer fails to complete said purchase as herein provided by reason of any default of Buyer, Seller shall be released from obligation to sell the property to Buyer and may proceed against Buyer upon any claim or remedy which he may have in law or equity; provided, however, that by placing their initials here Buyer: ( ) Seller: ( ) agree that Seller shall retain the deposit as liquidated damages. If the described property is a dwelling with no more than four units, one of which the Buyer intends to occupy as his residence, Seller shall retain as liquidated damages the deposit actually paid on an amount therefrom, not more than 3% of the purchase price and promptly return any excess to Buyer.

If the buyer defaults on his or her obligation to purchase the property, the seller has the option to sue for specific performance, or prove the actual damages that he or she has suffered. If the parties initial the boxes in the paragraph, the seller can retain up to 3 percent of the sales price of the property if the buyer defaults. This deposit becomes a substitution for actual damages.

The clause sets different standards for residential and nonresidential properties. Residential property is defined as a property with no more than four living units, where the buyer plans on living on one of those units as his or her primary place of residence. The appropriate box must be checked by the licensee signifying that the buyer plans on making the property his or her primary residence. Should there be an increased deposit requirement to satisfy liquidated damages, a new liquidated damages provision satisfying the requirements of the law must be separately signed by each party.

For residential property, 3 percent of the purchase price of the property is to be paid in cash or check, unless the buyer can establish that such an amount is unreasonable. Because the amount of money the seller can retain in the event the buyer defaults is only 3 percent, regardless of the deposit amount, it is up the seller to prove that the deposit is unreasonable. If the contract allows the seller to retain more than 3%, then it is up to the seller to prove the reasonableness of the excess deposit. In the event that the increased deposit, along with the original deposit amount, is to be used as liquidated damages, the box and spaces in paragraph 1B should be filled out.

The seller of nonresidential property can to retain the deposit as liquidated damages, unless the buyer establishes that the provision was unreasonable under the circumstances existing at the time the contract was made.

When the buyer and seller choose not to initial the boxes agreeing to a specific amount of liquidated damages, and the buyer defaults, the seller can take any action he or she decides. This may be suing for actual damages, proceeding with a specific performance suit, or letting the buyer off with no penalty and no loss of deposit. By initialing the boxes the parties both agree to predetermine a damages amount as a substitute for actual damages.

It is important for you to understand liquidated damages very clearly. It is your responsibility to explain the process to your client, as well as to protect their interests and those of the other party.

This portion of the deposit receipt informs both parties of their right to arbitration in the event that there should be a dispute regarding the deposit. All arbitration is to be handled in accordance with the rules of the American Arbitration Association. The provisions of Code of Civil Procedure Section 1283.05 shall be applicable in such arbitration.

18. Prorations of Property Taxes and Other Items
This clause determines by what date the property taxes, insurance, interest, principal loan, sewer fees, maintenance contracts, FHA insurance premiums, impound accounts, leasehold payments, easements, license fees, liens and other payments will

be prorated. The proration date is not the same for all transactions. It may be the close of escrow, date the title is recorded, date the buyer takes possession, or any other date the buyer and seller agree upon. It is important to note it on the deposit receipt.

Many communities will have assessments for different projects which will become liens on property after it has gone to bond. If property is sold with the knowledge of an assessment, but it is one that has not gone to bond yet, the buyer must be told of all terms of the assessment. It is not fair for the buyer to agree blindly to an assessment and not know the terms.

Proper research must be done to find any current assessment liens on the property, and to see if all payments are current. Assessments attach to property, not to the owners. If the sellers are behind on their payments, these will automatically become the obligation of the buyer. Buyers must make sure the seller is current with these payments, or that they have made arrangements to make the appropriate payments, so that the buyer is not stuck with additional fees and financial obligations. In the event that there are no assessments on the property, this area will be left blank.

19. Withholding Taxes
In the event the property being sold is owned by a foreign investor, there will be back-up withholding tax to cover any obligations the seller may have. The section goes on to explain what the regulations are for withholding.

22. Attorney's Fees
This clause entitles the prevailing party in a lawsuit reasonable attorney's fees and costs.

24. Time is of the Essence; Entire Contract; Changes
The "time is of the essence" clause dictates that all parties are to perform all necessary functions by the time specified in the contract. Each party is given an adequate, fair amount of time to perform all duties in the contract in order to discover any objections or obstacles which might prevent closing. If any of the dates need to be altered, or any timetables changed, this is possible if both parties agree to the change, and initial the change made to the contract.

25. Supplements
Any items attached to the deposit receipt need to be checked and notated here. An example of some supplements are the Interim Occupancy Agreement (CAR Form IOA-11), Residential Lease Agreement after Sale (CAR Form RLAS-11), and VA and FHA Amendments (CAR Form VA / FHA-11).

In addition to the supplemental forms, other agreements or supplemental information to be added here might include personal property that will remain in the home, disclosure statements that must be made, or other information. Space is provided to write in these inclusions.

Supplements are the last item included on the first page of the deposit receipt. Both parties will receive a copy of this first page, and must sign it in acknowledgement. The buyer will sign when the offer is prepared, and the seller will sign when the acceptance on the last page is signed. Under the Real Estate Commissioner's Regulation 2902, the agent or broker must make a copy of this document available to every party signing the contract. The copy must be supplied at the time of signing.

30. Terms and Conditions of Offer

Additional terms and conditions can be the inspections or reports that are required by the lender, seller, buyer, or any other entity of the property transfer. Both parties are to initial the inspections that are to take place, indicating that uninitialed inspections are not necessary or required for this property transaction.

Any inspections or requirements not covered in the preprinted section can be added in this area, or attached at the end of the contract on a separate sheet of paper.

31. Expiration of Offer

This paragraph officially establishes that the deposit receipt is the buyer's offer to purchase the property. This section gives a time frame with in which the seller may accept the offer, and if the seller has not accepted the offer in this time period, it is considered void. Additionally, this section lists who the acceptance, if accepted, can be delivered to other than the buyer. Acceptance will come in the form of the seller's signature on the last page of the document.

Acceptance. The acceptance portion of the contract not only acknowledges that the seller agrees to sell the property to the buyer with all the listed terms and conditions, but that the seller also agrees to pay the broker the commission, and provides for attorney's fees and costs in the event the seller and broker should have a dispute over the commission. All cooperating brokers will be listed, and the exact amount of the commission will be spelled out both numerically and in words. Again, should there be a dispute over the two values; the one spelled out in letters will be the official amount. The broker should sign the contract where indicated, creating a bilateral contract between the seller and broker, assuring the broker commission will be paid.

In the event that the seller receives damages from the buyer due to default of the contract, the acceptance clause calls for the broker to receive not less than one-half of the damages the seller recovers, and not more than the commission that the seller has agreed to pay.

If the property in question is a residential property, and the buyer and seller agreed to liquidated damages in the deposit receipt of 3% of the sales price of the home, the broker may elect, with the court's permission, to take the entire deposit as commission fees. Typically, the broker will make more than 3% commission on a house, and if the courts decide the broker is entitled to his or her commission, he or she can rightfully take the entire deposit, leaving the seller with nothing.

CALIFORNIA
ASSOCIATION
OF REALTORS®

INTERIM OCCUPANCY AGREEMENT
Buyer in Possession Prior to Close of Escrow

(C.A.R. Form IOA, Revised 4/03)

_____ ("Seller/Landlord")
and _____ ("Buyer/Tenant")
have entered into a purchase agreement for the real property described below. Close of escrow for the purchase agreement is scheduled
to occur on _____ (date). Seller, as Landlord, and Buyer, as Tenant, agree as follows:

1. **PROPERTY:**
    A. Landlord rents to Tenant and Tenant rents from Landlord, the real property and improvements described as: _____
        _____ ("Premises").
    B. The Premises are for the sole use as a personal residence by the following named persons only: _____
        _____
    C. The personal property listed in the purchase agreement, maintained pursuant to paragraph 11, is included.

2. **TERM:** The term begins on (date) _____ ("Commencement Date") and shall terminate
    at _____ ☐ AM/☐ PM on the earliest of: **(a)** the date scheduled for close of escrow of the purchase agreement as specified above,
    or as modified in writing; or **(b)** mutual cancellation of the purchase agreement. Tenant shall vacate the Premises upon termination
    of this Agreement, unless **(i)** landlord and tenant have signed a new agreement, **(ii)** mandated by local rent control law, or **(iii)**
    Landlord accepts Rent from Tenant (other than past due Rent), in which case a month-to-month tenancy shall be created which either
    party may terminate pursuant to California Civil Code § 1946.1. Rent shall be at a rate agreed to by Landlord and Tenant, or as
    allowed by law. All other terms and conditions of this Agreement shall remain in full force and effect.

3. **RENT:** "Rent" shall mean all monetary obligations of Tenant to Landlord under the terms of this Agreement, except security deposit.
    A. Tenant agrees to pay $ _____ per month for the term of this Agreement.
    B. Rent is payable in advance on the 1st (or ☐ _____) day of each calendar week, and is delinquent on the next day; or ☐ in full at
        close of escrow; or ☐ _____.
    C. **PAYMENT:** The Rent shall be paid by ☐ cash, ☐ personal check, ☐ money order, ☐ cashier check, ☐ through escrow (per
        escrow instructions), ☐ other _____ to (name) _____
        (phone)_____ at (address) _____
        (or at any other location specified by Landlord in writing to Tenant) between the hours of _____ and _____ on the following
        days: _____. If any payment is returned for non-sufficient
        funds ("NSF") or other reason then all future Rent shall be paid by ☐ cash, ☐ money order, ☐ cashier check.

4. **SECURITY DEPOSIT:**
    A. Tenant agrees to pay $ _____ as a security deposit. Security deposit will be
        ☐ transferred to and held by Seller; ☐ held in Seller's Broker's trust account; or ☐ held in escrow (per escrow instructions).
    B. **(1)** If the tenancy is terminated due to the close of escrow by Buyer under the purchase agreement, the full amount of the security
        deposit, less any deductions below, shall be credited to Buyer's down payment on the purchase (or, if checked ☐ returned to
        Buyer from Seller's proceeds in escrow). If required by Seller for closing, Seller shall place the security deposit into escrow
        prior to the signing of loan documents by Buyer.
        (2) All or any portion of the security deposit may be used as reasonably necessary to: **(i)** cure Tenant's default in payment of Rent
        (which includes Late Charges, NSF fees or other sums due); **(ii)** repair damage, excluding ordinary wear and tear, caused by Tenant
        or by a guest or licensee of Tenant; **(iii)** clean Premises, if necessary, upon termination of the tenancy; and **(iv)** replace or return
        personal property or appurtenances. **SECURITY DEPOSIT SHALL NOT BE USED BY TENANT IN LIEU OF PAYMENT OF
        LAST MONTH'S RENT.** If all or any portion of the security deposit is used during the tenancy, Tenant agrees to reinstate
        the total security deposit within 5 days after written notice is delivered to Tenant.
        (3) Within three weeks after Tenant vacates the Premises, Landlord shall: furnish Tenant an itemized statement indicating
        the amount of any security deposit received and the basis for its disposition; and return any remaining portion of the
        security deposit to Tenant.
    C. Except when escrow closes, security deposit will not be returned until all Tenants have vacated the Premises. Any security
        deposit returned by check shall be made out to all Tenants named on this Agreement, or as subsequently modified.
    D. No interest will be paid on security deposit unless required by local ordinance.
    E. If the security deposit is held by Seller, Tenant agrees not to hold Broker responsible for its return. If the security deposit is held in
        Seller's Broker's trust account, and Broker's authority is terminated before expiration of this Agreement, and security deposit is
        released to someone other than Tenant, then Broker shall notify Tenant, in writing, where and to whom security deposit has been
        released. Once Tenant has been provided such notice, Tenant agrees not to hold Broker responsible for the security deposit.

5. **MOVE-IN COSTS RECEIVED/DUE:** Move-in funds made payable to _____ shall be
    paid by ☐ cash, ☐ personal check, ☐ money order, ☐ cashier check, ☐ through escrow (per escrow instructions).

Category	Total Due	Payment Received	Balance Due	Date Due
Rent from _____ to _____ (date)				
*Security Deposit				
Other _____				
Other _____				
Total				

*The maximum amount Landlord may receive as security deposit, however designated, cannot exceed two months' Rent for
unfurnished premises, or three months' Rent for furnished premises.

IOA REVISED 4/03 (PAGE 1 OF 6) Print Date

Tenant's Initials (_____)(_____)
Landlord's Initials (_____)(_____)

Reviewed by _____ Date _____

EQUAL HOUSING
OPPORTUNITY

6. LATE CHARGE; RETURNED CHECKS:

A. Tenant acknowledges either late payment of Rent or issuance of a returned check may cause Landlord to incur costs and expenses, the exact amounts of which are extremely difficult and impractical to determine. These costs may include, but are not limited to, processing, enforcement and accounting expenses, and late charges imposed on Landlord. If any installment of Rent due from Tenant is not received by Landlord within 5 (or ☐ _____) calendar days after the date due, or if a check is returned, Tenant shall pay to Landlord, respectively, an additional sum of $ _____ or _____ % of the Rent due as a Late Charge and $25.00 as a NSF fee for the first returned check and $35.00 as a NSF fee for each additional returned check, either or both of which shall be deemed additional Rent.

B. Landlord and Tenant agree these charges represent a fair and reasonable estimate of the costs Landlord may incur by reason of Tenant's late or NSF payment. Any Late Charge or NSF fee due shall be paid with the current installment of Rent. Landlord's acceptance of any Late Charge or NSF fee shall not constitute a waiver as to any default of Tenant. Landlord's right to collect a Late Charge or NSF fee shall not be deemed an extension of the date Rent is due under paragraph 3 or prevent Landlord from exercising any other rights and remedies under this Agreement and as provided by law.

7. PARKING: (Check A or B)

☐ A. Parking is permitted as follows: _____
_____
The right to parking ☐ is ☐ is not included in the Rent charged pursuant to paragraph 3. If not included in the Rent, the parking rent shall be an additional $ _____ per month. Parking space(s) are to be used for parking properly licensed and operable motor vehicles, except for trailers, boats, campers, buses or trucks (other than pick-up trucks). Tenant shall park in assigned space(s) only. Parking space(s) are to be kept clean. Vehicles leaking oil, gas or other motor vehicle fluids shall not be parked on the Premises. Mechanical work or storage of inoperable vehicles is not permitted in parking space(s) or elsewhere on the Premises.

OR ☐ B. Parking is not permitted on the Premises.

8. STORAGE: (Check A or B)

☐ A. Storage is permitted as follows:
The right to storage space ☐ is ☐ is not included in the Rent charged pursuant to paragraph 3. If not included in the Rent, storage space fee shall be an additional $ _____ per month. Tenant shall store only personal property Tenant owns, and shall not store property claimed by another or in which another has any right, title or interest. Tenant shall not store any improperly packaged food or perishable goods, flammable materials, explosives, hazardous waste or other inherently dangerous material, or illegal substances.

OR ☐ B. Storage is not permitted on the Premises.

9. UTILITIES: Tenant agrees to pay for all utilities and services, and the following charges: _____
except _____, which shall be paid for by Landlord. If any utilities are not separately metered, Tenant shall pay Tenant's proportional share, as reasonably determined and directed by Landlord. If utilities are separately metered, Tenant shall place utilities in Tenant's name as of the Commencement Date. Landlord is only responsible for installing and maintaining one usable telephone jack and one telephone line to the Premises. Tenant shall pay any cost for conversion from existing utilities service provider.

10. CONDITION OF PREMISES: Tenant has examined Premises, all furniture, furnishings, appliances, landscaping, if any, and fixtures, including smoke detector(s).
(Check all that apply:)

☐ A. Tenant acknowledges these items are clean and in operable condition, with the following exceptions: _____
_____

☐ B. Tenant's acknowledgment of the condition of these items is contained in an attached statement of condition (C.A.R. Form MIMO).

☐ C. Tenant will provide Landlord a list of items that are damaged or not in operable condition within 3 (or ☐ _____) days after Commencement Date, not as a contingency of the Agreement but rather as an acknowledgment of the condition of the Premises.

☐ D. Other: _____.

11. MAINTENANCE:

A. Tenant shall properly use, operate and safeguard Premises, including if applicable, any landscaping, furniture, furnishings and appliances, and all mechanical, electrical, gas and plumbing fixtures, and keep them and the Premises clean, sanitary and well ventilated. Tenant shall be responsible for checking and maintaining all smoke detectors and any additional phone lines beyond the one line and jack that Landlord shall provide and maintain. Tenant shall immediately notify Landlord, in writing, of any problem, malfunction or damage. Tenant shall be charged for all repairs or replacements caused by Tenant, pets, guests or licensees of Tenant, excluding ordinary wear and tear. Tenant shall be charged for all damage to Premises as a result of failure to report a problem in a timely manner. Tenant shall be charged for repair of drain blockages or stoppages, unless caused by defective plumbing parts or tree roots invading sewer lines.

B. ☐ Landlord ☐ Tenant shall water the garden, landscaping, trees and shrubs, except: _____
_____

C. ☐ Landlord ☐ Tenant shall maintain the garden, landscaping, trees and shrubs, except: _____

D. ☐ Landlord ☐ Tenant shall maintain _____

E. Tenant's failure to maintain any item for which Tenant is responsible shall give Landlord the right to hire someone to perform such maintenance and charge Tenant to cover the cost of such maintenance.

F. The following items of personal property are included in the Premises without warranty and Landlord will not maintain, repair or replace them: _____

Tenant's Initials (_____)(_____)
Landlord's Initials (_____)(_____)

Reviewed by _____ Date _____

INTERIM OCCUPANCY AGREEMENT (IOA PAGE 2 OF 6)

12. **NEIGHBORHOOD CONDITIONS:** Tenant is advised to satisfy him or herself as to neighborhood or area conditions, including schools, proximity and adequacy of law enforcement, crime statistics, proximity of registered felons or offenders, fire protection, other governmental services, availability, adequacy and cost of any speed-wired, wireless internet connections or other telecommunications or other technology services and installations, proximity to commercial, industrial or agricultural activities, existing and proposed transportation, construction and development that may affect noise, view, or traffic, airport noise, noise or odor from any source, wild and domestic animals, other nuisances, hazards, or circumstances, cemeteries, facilities and condition of common areas, conditions and influences of significance to certain cultures and/or religions, and personal needs, requirements and preferences of Tenant.

13. **PETS:** Unless otherwise provided in California Civil Code § 54.2, no animal or pet shall be kept on or about the Premises without Landlord's prior written consent, except: _____.

14. **RULES;REGULATIONS:**
   A. Tenant agrees to comply with all Landlord rules and regulations that are at any time posted on the Premises or delivered to Tenant. Tenant shall not and shall ensure that guests and licensees of Tenant shall not, disturb, annoy, endanger or interfere with other tenants of the building or neighbors, or use the Premises for any unlawful purposes, including, but not limited to, using, manufacturing, selling, storing, or transporting illicit drugs or other contraband, or violate any law or ordinance, or commit a waste or nuisance on or about the Premises.
   B. (If applicable, check one:)
      ☐ (1) Landlord shall provide Tenant with a copy of the rules and regulations within _____ days or _____.
      OR ☐ (2) Tenant has been provided with, and acknowledges receipt of, a copy of the rules and regulations.

15. ☐ (If checked) **CONDOMINIUM;PLANNED UNIT DEVELOPMENT:**
   A. The Premises is a unit in a condominium, planned unit, development or other common interest subdivision governed by a homeowners' association ("HOA"). The name of the HOA is _____. Tenant agrees to comply with all HOA covenants, conditions and restrictions, bylaws, rules and regulations and decisions. Tenant shall reimburse Landlord for any fines or charges imposed by HOA or other authorities, due to any violation by Tenant, or the guests or licensees of Tenant.
   B. (Check one:)
      ☐ (1) Landlord shall provide Tenant with a copy of HOA rules and regulations within _____ days or _____.
      OR ☐ (2) Tenant has been provided with, and acknowledges receipt of, a copy of the HOA rules and regulations.

16. **ALTERATIONS;REPAIRS:** Unless otherwise specified by law or paragraph 27C or pursuant to the purchase agreement, without Landlord's prior written consent, Tenant shall not make any repairs, alterations or improvements in or about the Premises including: painting, wallpapering, adding or changing locks, installing antenna or satellite dish(es), placing signs, displays or exhibits, or using screws, fastening devices, large nails or adhesive materials; (ii) Landlord shall not be responsible for the costs of alterations or improvements made by Tenant; (iii) Tenant shall not deduct from Rent the costs of any repairs, alterations or improvements; and (iv) any deduction made by Tenant shall be considered unpaid Rent. Tenant shall immediately notify Landlord if Tenant, individually or by or through others, commences any work on the Premises. Tenant shall be charged for any costs Landlord incurs to post and record a Notice of NonResponsibility. Upon completion of any such work, Tenant shall notify Landlord. Tenant shall be charged for any costs Landlord incurs to post and record a Notice of Completion relating to any such work. Tenant agrees to indemnify, defend and hold harmless Landlord for any mechanic's lien attaching to the Premises or other claim resulting from any work ordered by Tenant.

17. **KEYS;LOCKS:**
   A. Tenant acknowledges receipt of (or Tenant will receive ☐ prior to the Commencement Date, or ☐ _____):
      ☐ _____ key(s) to Premises,   ☐ _____ remote control device(s) for garage door/gate opener(s),
      ☐ _____ key(s) to mailbox,   ☐ _____
      ☐ _____ key(s) to common area(s), ☐ _____
   B. Tenant acknowledges that locks to the Premises ☐ have, ☐ have not, been re-keyed.
   C. If Tenant re-keys existing locks or opening devices, Tenant shall immediately deliver copies of all keys to Landlord. Tenant shall pay all costs and charges related to loss of any keys or opening devices. Tenant may not remove locks, even if installed by Tenant.

18. **ENTRY:**
   A. Tenant shall make Premises available to Landlord or Landlord's representative for the purpose of entering to make necessary or agreed repairs, decorations, alterations, or improvements, or to supply necessary or agreed services, or to show Premises to prospective or actual purchasers, tenants, mortgagees, lenders, appraisers, or contractors.
   B. Landlord and Tenant agree that 24-hour written notice shall be reasonable and sufficient notice. However, if the purpose of the entry is to: (i) show the Premises to actual or prospective purchasers, the notice may be given orally provided Tenant has been notified in writing within 120 days preceding the oral notice that the Premises are for sale and that oral notice may be given to show the Premises; or (ii) conduct an inspection of the Premises prior to the Tenant moving out, 48-hour written notice is required unless the Tenant waives the right to such notice; or (iii) enter in case of an emergency, Landlord or Landlord's representative may enter Premises at any time without prior notice.
   C. ☐ (If checked) Tenant authorizes the use of a keysafe/lockbox to allow entry into the Premises and agrees to sign a keysafe/lockbox addendum (C.A.R. Form KLA).

19. **SIGNS:** Tenant authorizes Landlord to place FOR SALE/LEASE signs on the Premises.

20. **ASSIGNMENT;SUBLETTING:** Tenant shall not sublet all or any part of Premises, or assign or transfer the Agreement or any interest herein, without Landlord's prior written consent. Unless such consent is obtained, any assignment, transfer or subletting of Premises or the Agreement or tenancy, by voluntary act of Tenant, operation of law or otherwise, shall be null and void and, at the option of Landlord, terminate the Agreement. Any proposed assignee, transferee or sublessee shall submit to Landlord an application and credit information for Landlord's approval and, if approved, sign a separate written agreement with Landlord and Tenant. Landlord's consent to any one assignment, transfer or sublease, shall not be construed as consent to any subsequent assignment, transfer or sublease and does not release Tenant of Tenant's obligations under the Agreement.

21. **JOINT AND INDIVIDUAL OBLIGATIONS:** If there is more than one Tenant, each one shall be individually and completely responsible for the performance of all obligations of Tenant under the Agreement, jointly with every other Tenant, and individually, whether or not in possession.

Tenant's Initials (_____)(_____)
Landlord's Initials (_____)(_____)

Reviewed by _____ Date _____

22. ☐ **LEAD-BASED PAINT (If Checked):** Premises was constructed prior to 1978. In accordance with federal law, Landlord gives and Tenant acknowledges receipt of the disclosures on the attached form (C.A.R. Form FLD) and a federally approved lead pamphlet.

23. ☐ **MILITARY ORDNANCE DISCLOSURE:** (If applicable and known to Landlord) Premises is located within one mile of an area once used for military training, and may contain potentially explosive munitions.

24. ☐ **PERIODIC PEST CONTROL:** Landlord has entered into a contract for periodic pest control treatment of the Premises and shall give Tenant a copy of the notice originally given to Landlord by the pest control company.

25. **DATABASE DISCLOSURE:** The California Department of Justice, sheriff's departments, police departments serving jurisdictions of 200,000 or more, and many other local law enforcement authorities maintain for public access a database of the locations of persons required to register pursuant to paragraph (1) of subdivision (a) of Section 290.4 of the Penal Code. The database is updated on a quarterly basis and a source of information about the presence of these individuals in any neighborhood. The Department of Justice also maintains a Sex Offender Identification Line through which inquiries about individuals may be made. This is a "900" telephone service. Callers must have specific information about the individuals they are checking. Information regarding neighborhoods is not available through the "900" telephone service.

26. **POSSESSION:** If Landlord is unable to deliver possession of Premises on Commencement Date, such Date shall be extended to the date on which possession is made available to Tenant. If Landlord is unable to deliver possession within 5 (or ☐ _____) calendar days after agreed Commencement Date, Tenant may terminate the Agreement by giving written notice to Landlord, and shall be refunded all Rent and security deposit paid. Possession is deemed terminated when Tenant has returned all keys to the Premises to Landlord. ☐ Tenant is already in possession of the Premises.

27. **TENANT'S OBLIGATIONS UPON VACATING PREMISES:** If the tenancy is terminated due to any reason other than close of escrow by Buyer under the purchase agreement, upon termination of the Agreement:
   A. Tenant shall: (i) give Landlord all copies of all keys or opening devices to Premises, including any common areas; (ii) vacate and surrender Premises to Landlord, empty of all persons; (iii) vacate any/all parking and/or storage space; (iv) clean and deliver Premises, as specified in paragraph C below, to Landlord in the same condition as referenced in paragraph 10; (v) remove all debris; (vi) give written notice to Landlord of Tenant's forwarding address; and (vii) _____.
   B. All alterations/improvements made by or caused to be made by Tenant, with or without Landlord's consent, become the property of Landlord upon termination. Landlord may charge Tenant for restoration of the Premises to the condition it was in prior to any alterations/improvements.
   C. **Right to Pre-Move Out Inspection and Repairs as follows:** (i) After giving or receiving notice of termination of a tenancy (C.A.R. Form NTT), or before the end of a lease, Tenant has the right to request that an inspection of the Premises take place prior to termination of the lease or rental (C.A.R. Form NRI). If Tenant requests such an inspection, Tenant shall be given an opportunity to remedy identified deficiencies prior to termination, consistent with the terms of the Agreement. (ii) Any repairs or alterations made to the Premises as a result of this inspection (collectively, "Repairs") shall be made at Tenant's expense. Repairs may be performed by Tenant or through others, who have adequate insurance and licenses and are approved by Landlord. The work shall comply with applicable law, including governmental permit, inspection and approval requirements. Repairs shall be performed in a good, skillful manner with materials of quality and appearance comparable to existing materials. It is understood that exact restoration of appearance or cosmetic items following all Repairs may not be possible. (iii) Tenant shall: (a) obtain receipts for Repairs performed by others; (b) prepare a written statement indicating the Repairs performed by Tenant and the date of such Repairs; and (c) provide copies of receipts and statements to Landlord prior to termination.

28. **BREACH OF CONTRACT;EARLY TERMINATION:** In addition to any obligations established by paragraph 27, in event of termination by Tenant prior to completion of the original term of the Agreement, Tenant shall also be responsible for lost Rent, rental commissions, advertising expenses and painting costs necessary to ready Premises for re-rental. Landlord may withhold any such amounts from Tenant's security deposit.

29. **TEMPORARY RELOCATION:** Subject to local law, Tenant agrees, upon demand of Landlord, to temporarily vacate Premises for a reasonable period, to allow for fumigation (or other methods) to control wood-destroying pests or organisms, or other repairs to Premises. Tenant agrees to comply with all instructions and requirements necessary to prepare Premises to accommodate pest control, fumigation or other work, including bagging or storage of food and medicine, and removal of perishables and valuables. Tenant shall only be entitled to a credit of Rent equal to the per diem Rent for the period of time Tenant is required to vacate Premises.

30. **DAMAGE TO PREMISES:** If, by no fault of Tenant, Premises are totally or partially damaged or destroyed by fire, earthquake, accident or other casualty that render Premises totally or partially uninhabitable, either Landlord or Tenant may terminate the Agreement by giving the other written notice. Rent shall be abated as of the date Premises become totally or partially uninhabitable. The abated amount shall be the current monthly Rent prorated on a 30-day period. If the Agreement is not terminated, Landlord shall promptly repair the damage, and Rent shall be reduced based on the extent to which the damage interferes with Tenant's reasonable use of Premises. If damage occurs as a result of an act of Tenant or Tenant's guests, only Landlord shall have the right of termination, and no reduction in Rent shall be made.

31. **INSURANCE:** Tenant's or guest's personal property and vehicles are not insured by Landlord, manager or, if applicable, HOA, against loss or damage due to fire, theft, vandalism, rain, water, criminal or negligent acts of others, or any other cause. **Tenant is advised to carry Tenant's own insurance (renter's insurance) to protect Tenant from any such loss or damage.** Tenant shall comply with any requirement imposed on Tenant by Landlord's insurer to avoid: (i) an increase in Landlord's insurance premium (or Tenant shall pay for the increase in premium); or (ii) loss of insurance.

32. **WATERBEDS:** Tenant shall not use or have waterbeds on the Premises unless: (i) Tenant obtains a valid waterbed insurance policy; (ii) Tenant increases the security deposit in an amount equal to one-half of one month's Rent; and (iii) the bed conforms to the floor load capacity of Premises.

Tenant's Initials (_____)(_____)
Landlord's Initials (_____)(_____)

IOA REVISED 4/03 (PAGE 4 OF 6)

Reviewed by _____ Date _____

33. WAIVER: The waiver of any breach shall not be construed as a continuing waiver of the same or any subsequent breach.

34. NOTICE: Notices may be served at the following address, or at any other location subsequently designated:
Landlord: _____ Tenant: _____
_____ _____
_____ _____

35. TENANT ESTOPPEL CERTIFICATE: Tenant shall execute and return a tenant estoppel certificate delivered to Tenant by Landlord or Landlord's agent within 3 days after its receipt. Failure to comply with this requirement shall be deemed Tenant's acknowledgment that the tenant estoppel certificate is true and correct, and may be relied upon by a lender or purchaser.

36. TENANT REPRESENTATIONS; CREDIT: Tenant warrants that all statements in Tenant's rental application are accurate. Tenant authorizes Landlord and Broker(s) to obtain Tenant's credit report periodically during the tenancy in connection with modification or enforcement of the Agreement. Landlord may cancel the Agreement: (i) before occupancy begins; (ii) upon disapproval of the credit report(s); or (iii) at any time, upon discovering that information in Tenant's application is false. A negative credit report reflecting on Tenant's record may be submitted to a credit reporting agency if Tenant fails to fulfill the terms of payment and other obligations under the Agreement.

37. MEDIATION:
A. Consistent with paragraphs B and C below, Landlord and Tenant agree to mediate any dispute or claim arising between them out of the Agreement, or any resulting transaction, before resorting to court action. Mediation fees, if any, shall be divided equally among the parties involved. If, for any dispute or claim to which this paragraph applies, any party commences an action without first attempting to resolve the matter through mediation, or refuses to mediate after a request has been made, then that party shall not be entitled to recover attorney fees, even if they would otherwise be available to that party in any such action.
B. The following matters are excluded from mediation: (i) an unlawful detainer action; (ii) the filing or enforcement of a mechanic's lien; and (iii) any matter within the jurisdiction of a probate, small claims or bankruptcy court. The filing of a court action to enable the recording of a notice of pending action, for order of attachment, receivership, injunction, or other provisional remedies, shall not constitute a waiver of the mediation provision.
C. Landlord and Tenant agree to mediate disputes or claims involving Listing Agent, Leasing Agent or property manager ("Broker"), provided Broker shall have agreed to such mediation prior to, or within a reasonable time after, the dispute or claim is presented to such Broker. Any election by Broker to participate in mediation shall not result in Broker being deemed a party to the Agreement.

38. ATTORNEY FEES: In any action or proceeding arising out of the Agreement, the prevailing party between Landlord and Tenant shall be entitled to reasonable attorney fees and costs, except as provided in paragraph 37A.

39. C.A.R. FORM: C.A.R. Form means the specific form referenced.

40. OTHER TERMS AND CONDITIONS; SUPPLEMENTS: _____
_____
The following ATTACHED supplements are incorporated in the Agreement: ☐ Keysafe/Lockbox Addendum (C.A.R. Form KLA);
☐ Interpreter/Translator Agreement (C.A.R. Form ITA); ☐ Lead-Based Paint and Lead-Based Paint Hazards Disclosure (C.A.R. Form FLD)

41. TIME OF ESSENCE; ENTIRE CONTRACT; CHANGES: Time is of the essence. All understandings between the parties are incorporated in the Agreement. Its terms are intended by the parties as a final, complete and exclusive expression of their Agreement with respect to its subject matter, and may not be contradicted by evidence of any prior agreement or contemporaneous oral agreement. If any provision of the Agreement is held to be ineffective or invalid, the remaining provisions will nevertheless be given full force and effect. Neither the Agreement nor any provision in it may be extended, amended, modified, altered or changed except in writing. The Agreement and any supplement, addendum or modification, including any copy, may be signed in two or more counterparts, all of which shall constitute one and the same writing.

42. AGENCY:
A. **CONFIRMATION:** The following agency relationship(s) are hereby confirmed for this transaction:
Listing Agent: (Agent representing the Seller in the purchase agreement)
(Print firm name) _____
is the agent of (check one): ☐ the Landlord exclusively; or ☐ both the Landlord and Tenant.
Selling Agent: (Agent representing the Buyer in the purchase agreement)
(Print firm name) _____
(If not same as Listing Agent) is the agent of (check one): ☐ the Tenant exclusively; or ☐ the Landlord exclusively; or ☐ both the Tenant and Landlord.
B. **DISCLOSURE:** ☐ (If checked): The term of this lease exceeds one year. A disclosure regarding real estate agency relationships (C.A.R. Form AD) has been provided to Landlord and Tenant, who each acknowledge its receipt.

Tenant's Initials (_____)(_____)
Landlord's Initials (_____)(_____)

Reviewed by _____ Date _____

Premises: _____ Date: _____

43. ☐ **INTERPRETER/TRANSLATOR:** The terms of the Agreement have been interpreted/translated for Tenant into the following language: _____. Landlord and Tenant acknowledge receipt of the attached interpretation/translation agreement, (C.A.R. Form ITA).

44. **FOREIGN LANGUAGE NEGOTIATION:** If the Agreement has been negotiated primarily in Spanish, Tenant shall be provided a Spanish language translation of the Agreement pursuant to the California Civil Code.

45. **RECEIPT:** If specified in paragraph 5, Landlord or Broker, acknowledges receipt of move-in funds.

Landlord and Tenant acknowledge and agree Brokers: **(a)** do not guarantee the condition of the Premises; **(b)** cannot verify representations made by others; **(c)** cannot provide legal or tax advice; **(d)** will not provide other advice or information that exceeds the knowledge, education or experience required to obtain a real estate license. Furthermore, Brokers: **(e)** do not decide what rental rate a Tenant should pay or Landlord should accept; and **(f)** do not decide upon the length or other terms of tenancy. Landlord and Tenant agree they will seek legal, tax, insurance and other desired assistance from appropriate professionals.

Tenant/Buyer _____ Date _____
Address _____ City _____ State ____ Zip ____
Telephone _____ Fax _____ E-mail _____

Tenant/Buyer _____ Date _____
Address _____ City _____ State ____ Zip ____
Telephone _____ Fax _____ E-mail _____

Landlord /Seller _____ Date _____
Landlord /Seller _____ Date _____
Landlord Address _____ City _____ State ____ Zip ____
Telephone _____ Fax _____ E-mail _____

REAL ESTATE BROKERS:
A. Brokers are not a party to the Agreement between Landlord and Tenant.
B. Agency relationships are confirmed as above.

Real Estate Broker _____
(Agent representing the Buyer in the purchase agreement)
By (Agent) _____ Date _____
Address _____ City _____ State ____ Zip ____
Telephone _____ Fax _____ E-mail _____

Real Estate Broker _____
(Agent representing the Seller in the purchase agreement)
By (Agent) _____ Date _____
Address _____ City _____ State ____ Zip ____
Telephone _____ Fax _____ E-mail _____

Published by the
California Association of REALTORS®

IOA REVISED 4/03 (PAGE 6 OF 6)

Reviewed by _____ Date _____

INTERIM OCCUPANCY AGREEMENT (IOA PAGE 6 OF 6)

CALIFORNIA
ASSOCIATION
OF REALTORS®

RESIDENTIAL LEASE AFTER SALE
Seller in Possession After Close of Escrow
(Intended for possession of 30 or more days)
(C.A.R. Form RLAS, Revised 4/03)

_____ ("Buyer/Landlord")
and _____ ("Seller/Tenant")
have entered into a purchase agreement for the real property described below. Close of escrow for the purchase agreement is scheduled to occur
on (date) _____. Buyer, as Landlord, and Seller, as Tenant, agree as follows:

1. **PROPERTY:**
   A. Landlord rents to Tenant and Tenant rents from Landlord, the real property and improvements described as: _____
   _____ ("Premises").
   B. The Premises are for the sole use as a personal residence by the following named persons **only:** _____
   _____
   C. The personal property listed in the purchase agreement, maintained pursuant to paragraph 11, is included.

2. **TERM:** The term begins on the date that escrow closes on the purchase and sale agreement ("Commencement Date"), and shall
   terminate on (date) _____ at _____ ☐ AM/ ☐ PM. Tenant shall vacate the
   Premises upon termination of this Agreement, unless **(i)** Landlord and Tenant have signed a new agreement, **(ii)** mandated by local
   rent control law, or **(iii)** Landlord accepts Rent from Tenant (other than past due Rent), in which case a month-to-month tenancy
   shall be created which either party may terminate pursuant to California Civil Code §1946.1. Rent shall be at a rate agreed to by
   Landlord and Tenant, or as allowed by law. All other terms and conditions of this Agreement shall remain in full force and effect.

3. **RENT:** "Rent" shall mean all monetary obligations of Tenant to Landlord under the terms of the Agreement, except security deposit.
   A. Tenant agrees to pay, per month, ☐ Buyer's PITI, or ☐ $ _____ for the term of the Agreement.
   B. Rent is payable in advance on the **1st (or** ☐ _____ **) day** of each calendar month, and is delinquent on the next day.
   C. If Commencement Date falls on any day other than the day Rent is payable under 3B and Tenant has paid one full month's Rent
   in advance of Commencement Date, Rent for the second calendar month shall be prorated based on a 30-day period.
   D. **PAYMENT:** Rent shall be paid by ☐ cash, ☐ personal check, ☐ money order, ☐ cashier check, ☐ through escrow (see paragraph 5
   below), ☐ other _____, to (name) _____ (phone)
   _____ at (address) _____, (or at any
   other location specified by Landlord in writing to Tenant) between the hours of _____ and _____ on the following days
   _____. If any payment is returned for non-sufficient funds ("NSF") or
   other reason then all future Rent shall be paid by ☐ cash, ☐ money order, ☐ cashier check.

4. **SECURITY DEPOSIT:**
   A. Tenant agrees to pay $ _____ as a security deposit. Security deposit will be paid
   by ☐ cash, ☐ personal check, ☐ money order, ☐ cashier check, ☐ through escrow (see paragraph 5 below), ☐ other
   _____. Security deposit will be ☐ transferred to and held by Buyer, or ☐ held in Buyer's Broker's trust
   account. (Note: The maximum amount that Landlord may receive as security deposit cannot exceed two months' Rent for
   unfurnished Premises, or three months' Rent for furnished Premises.)
   B. All or any portion of the security deposit may be used, as reasonably necessary, to: **(1)** cure Tenant's default in payment of Rent, which
   includes Late Charges, NSF fees, or other sums due; **(2)** repair damage, excluding ordinary wear and tear, caused by Tenant or by a
   guest or licensee of Tenant; **(3)** clean Premises, if necessary, upon termination of tenancy; and **(4)** replace or return personal property
   or appurtenances. **SECURITY DEPOSIT SHALL NOT BE USED BY TENANT IN LIEU OF PAYMENT OF LAST MONTH'S
   RENT.** If all or any portion of the security deposit is used during tenancy, Tenant agrees to reinstate the total security deposit
   within five days after written notice is delivered to Tenant. Within three weeks after Tenant vacates the Premises, Landlord shall:
   (1) furnish Tenant an itemized statement indicating the amount of any security deposit received and the basis for its disposition;
   and **(2)** return any remaining portion of the security deposit to Tenant.
   C. **Security deposit will not be returned until all Tenants have vacated the Premises. Any security deposit returned by
   check shall be made out to all Tenants named on the Agreement, or as subsequently modified.**
   D. No interest will be paid on security deposit unless required by local ordinance.
   E. If the security deposit is held by Landlord, Tenant agrees not to hold Broker responsible for its return. If the security deposit is held
   in Landlord's Broker's trust account, **and** Broker's authority is terminated before expiration of this Agreement, **and** security deposits
   are released to someone other than Tenant, **then** Broker shall notify Tenant, in writing, where and to whom security deposit has
   been released. Once Tenant has been provided such notice, Tenant agrees not to hold Broker responsible for the security deposit.

5. **ESCROW PAYMENT:** (Check all that apply) ☐ Security deposit, ☐ First month's Rent, ☐ Rent for the entire lease term (if lease term is at
   least 6 months), ☐ Other, per escrow instructions, shall be paid out of Seller's proceeds from the escrow for the purchase of the Premises.

6. **LATE CHARGE; RETURNED CHECKS:**
   A. Tenant acknowledges either late payment of Rent or issuance of a returned check (NSF) may cause Landlord to incur costs
   and expenses, the exact amounts of which are extremely difficult and impractical to determine. These costs may include, but
   are not limited to, processing, enforcement and accounting expenses, and late charges imposed on Landlord. If any installment
   of Rent due from Tenant is not received by Landlord within 5 (or ☐ _____) **calendar days** after date due, or if a check is
   returned, Tenant shall pay to Landlord, respectively, an additional sum of $ _____ or _____ % of the Rent due as a
   Late Charge and $25.00 as a NSF fee for the first returned check and $35.00 as a NSF fee for each additional returned check,
   either or both of which shall be deemed additional Rent.
   B. Landlord and Tenant agree these charges represent a fair and reasonable estimate of the costs Landlord may incur by reason
   of Tenant's late or NSF payment. Any Late Charge or NSF fee due shall be paid with the current installment of Rent. Landlord's
   acceptance of any Late Charge or NSF fee shall not constitute a waiver as to any default of Tenant. Landlord's right to collect
   a Late Charge or NSF fee shall not be deemed an extension of the date Rent is due under paragraph 3, or prevent Landlord
   from exercising any other rights and remedies under the Agreement, and as provided by law.

Tenant's Initials (_____)(_____)
Landlord's Initials (_____)(_____)

Reviewed by _____ Date _____

EQUAL HOUSING
OPPORTUNITY

RLAS REVISED 4/03 (PAGE 1 OF 5) Print Date BDC Aug 03

197

Everything in the purchase contract before the acceptance clause is the buyer's offer and the receipt for the buyer's deposit. It is not a purchase contract until the seller actually signs the document acknowledging acceptance of the offer.

Broker's Consent. When the broker signs the contract, he or she is giving his or her consent to comply with all regulations under Section 2725 of the Regulations of the Real Estate Commissioner, consents to divide any commission earned amongst cooperating brokers, and consents to provide adequate supervision over any salesperson working on the property transaction.

E S T I M A T E D B U Y E R ' S C O S T S

When completing the deposit receipt, it is important for you as an agent to formulate the **estimated buyer's costs**. This figure represents the amount of money the buyer must advance for the completion of the property transfer. It can include expenses such as paying for inspections, reports like the preliminary title report, title insurance and any other fees associated with escrow. The broker should also provide a realistic estimate of the buyer's total monthly payment, based on the offer he or she has made. An exact figure is next to impossible to quote for the buyer, as different lenders and escrow companies will have different fees or programs available to buyers, but a realistic estimate of costs will help to put the buyer's mind at ease. Don't underestimate this figure; if the buyer begins to rely on your estimated figure, and then finds out the amount of money owed for both closing costs and monthly payments is larger than you anticipated, you may have a very upset buyer on your hands.

Remember
- Be realistic and honest in all cost estimations you give to the buyer, and don't underestimate. An unpleasant financial surprise may anger the buyer and cause problems in the property transfer.

S P E C I A L P R O V I S I O N S

The deposit receipt is a fairly simple instrument for any real estate agent to negotiate, fill out, and explain to a buyer and seller. The contract is intended to be used on simple property transactions where a real estate professional will have no problems in filling out all forms, guiding the buyer and seller through the entire process, and seeing the transaction through to closing. For more complicated transfers, additional forms will be required, and even a real estate professional might consider consulting a legal professional to make sure all forms and contracts are filled out accurately and lawfully. Real estate agents should never give out legal advice. An agent is qualified to explain options to their clients, but should not suggest how a client should act. When special circumstances do arise, other trained professionals such as an attorney or tax specialist should be consulted for their expertise and guidance.

Irrevocable order
Purchasers have the option to give an irrevocable order, also called an "Assignment of Funds", in account of a deposit in escrow. This will transfer money that will come out of an escrow pending the sale of the purchasers' property. The irrevocable order is a relatively easy form to understand, but you as an agent must clearly understand its legal significance. When a buyer signs the irrevocable order, he or she agrees that he or

she cannot alter or cancel the irrevocable or unconditional order to transfer the proceeds from the first escrow into the second. If and when a buyer takes the option of an irrevocable order, this fact must be disclosed to the seller. The reason for this is that when an irrevocable order has been made, there is a strong possibility that the first escrow may fall through. If this should happen the sale will be lost, as well as any money from a deposit. All agents must make the seller aware of these possibilities when and if the situation should occur. Even the buyer's agent, who has fiduciary responsibility to the buyer, must tell the seller about the risks associated with an irrevocable order in order to abide by the commissioner's regulations. An agent failing to do so may be held responsible for damages.

Selling Without a Listing
If a broker sells a property for which he or she does not have a listing, the homeowner is not obligated to pay a commission. A sale without a listing may occur when the broker or salesperson knows of a person selling his or her house, but who is not interested in a formal listing. Another situation in which a home may be sold without a listing is one where the homeowner and broker enter into an oral listing, which does not bind the seller to pay the broker a commission. The issue here is – how can an agent assure that he or she will receive a commission?

Without a formal, written listing agreement, the agent can assure a full commission via the clause in the deposit receipt that states that when the sellers accept the offer, they are also agreeing to pay the agent the agreed-upon commission. This commission can be any amount the seller and agent have agreed upon; there is no set limit or lawful amount. The amount must be clearly written on the deposit receipt so that there is no debate regarding the money. In the acceptance portion of the deposit receipt, the words "selling broker has the right to sell" should be added, followed by the seller's signature. No matter what phrase or sentence is used, it should be abundantly clear to anyone interpreting the document that the sellers have agreed to pay a commission. The sellers will then sign the document after the added phrase or sentence obligating them to pay the commission. To make sure it is understood who is to receive the commission, the names of all cooperating brokers can also be added to the deposit receipt.

Agreement to Occupy Prior to the Close of Escrow
The seller may agree to allow the buyer to move into the property before the close of escrow. In this event, there should be a form attached to the deposit receipt outlining the specific instructions or agreement. There are problems that can arise from allowing the buyer to move into the home early, and this form serves as a way to avoid an unpleasant situation. This form will make sure the buyer cannot back out of the contract after living in the home simply because it is not what they wanted. A buyer may rescind if there is a problem with the title, a problem with financing, or another major issue, but not because they decide they don't like it after living there a few weeks. Additionally, the form prevents a landlord-tenant relationship between the buyer and seller.

Promissory Note Deposit
The promissory note deposit is a form filled out in lieu of a cash deposit, promising the seller cash for the note at a later predetermined time. The form allows for three common predetermined time frames as listed in brackets or a space for the person filling out the form to write in a custom time period. This time is to follow the five-day period for acceptance.

This option can be taken by buyers who may not have the funds available on the date they made an offer. Buyers may not have anticipated making an offer on property and therefore will need to move money from one account to another in order to make such a deposit, or other buyers would rather let their money stay in a certain account, drawing interest, until they know that their offer has been accepted. A seller agreeing to accept an offer with a promissory note deposit will take his or her property off the market, and not entertain any other offers.

As Is

"As is" means a buyer purchases a home in its current condition, regardless of any defects. This is a risky option for a seller, as legally they cannot sell a property known to have harmful defects. A buyer may inspect the property during his or her initial and subsequent visits to the home and witness physical defects such as carpet wear and tear, damage to the kitchen cabinets, or other minor problems. These items are not considered harmful defects which would cause the seller to be responsible for repair. "Patent defects" or imperfections don't pose the possibility of serious harm to the buyer, but "latent defects" do. Defects not visible or not obvious to an untrained professional would be considered latent defects. An example of this would be faulty wiring, installed without a permit. This poses a fire hazard. A seller cannot sell the home "as is" when he or she knows there are problems such as this. If the buyer challenged the seller legally, the buyer would most likely win.

As an agent, you must show the buyer all the "as is" conditions. This means you must point out what is broken, defective or otherwise problematic on the property. This will serve as the buyer's warning of all patent and latent imperfections. If the buyer chooses to continue and negotiate and make an offer, he or she does so at their own risk, knowing all defects, and knowing that the property is being sold "as is." It will be up to the buyer to make all necessary corrections or repairs. If a lawsuit should be filed, the agent will be protected from any wrong if he or she discloses all "as is" defects. If the broker does not fully disclose all the problems, he or she may be held liable for damages. The idea of caveat emptor or "let the buyer beware" is now being replaced with the notion of caveat vendor– the seller must beware. The buyer cannot be expected to be aware of issues that have not been disclosed.

"Subject To" Financing

In the deposit receipt, under section H of financing, the buyers are instructed to apply for financing as soon as possible. This will prevent the buyers from dragging their feet and procrastinating, delaying the approval of the loan, and ultimately delaying the close of escrow. Generally, the deposit receipt will give a cutoff date by which the buyer must apply for financing.

"Subject to" financing creates a clause in the deposit receipt that states the property is going to be purchased subject to the buyer securing financing. If the buyer is not able to secure financing, he or she will not be held responsible for the terms of the contract. If the buyer is able to secure financing, but not the amount specified in the deposit receipt, the contract is still considered unenforceable unless both the buyer and seller agree to the new conditions set forth by the financing, acknowledged by their signatures or initials.

Uncashed Checks

Occasionally a broker is given a check by the buyer and asked not to cash the check until the offer is accepted by the seller. The broker is allowed to do this, but disclosures must be made. The deposit receipt should have a phrase or sentence added in clear language to indicate the broker is holding the buyer's deposit check upon the seller's approval of the offer. This can be indicated in the deposit receipt under the financing section E. It is important for this disclosure to be made; if the broker does not make this disclosure, he or she may be violating the fiduciary relationship with the seller. The seller must give approval for the broker to hold the deposit, upon being informed of the buyer's request.

The broker must keep a record of receiving the check. In addition to making the appropriate record entry, the broker must also note the name of the escrow company where the check is being held, the instructions of the buyer who wrote the check, and the date the check was given to escrow.

> **Remember**
> • As an agent, you cannot negotiate the holding of a check; you can only disclose the buyer's intention or request to the seller, and then move forward according to the seller's instructions of acceptance, counteroffer or rejection of the buyer's offer.

Licensee Acting as a Principal

When a licensee or agent is interested in purchasing a property that he or she represents full disclosure must be made to the seller. The agent must not use an "arm's length" transaction, one where negotiations filter through a third party unknown to the sellers. If an agent utilizes a third party agent to purchase property, it is considered a breach of the fiduciary responsibility owed to the seller.

Agents have access to information regarding the condition and fair sales price of property to which a regular buyer may not have access. The buyer will then base his or her offer on this information, which may or may not be accepted by the seller. Above all, the most important thing to remember is full disclosure.

PRESENTING THE SELLERS WITH THE OFFER

The last major step in the process is for the agent to "sell" the seller on the buyer's offer. A considerable amount of work has been done by the agent up to this point, from finding and securing the listing and advertising the listing to entice potential buyers to look at the property, to finally securing the buyer and obtaining an offer on the property. It would be a shame to have put in all this work, only to have the seller reject the offer and go back to trying to find an appropriate buyer for the property.

Listing price is the main hurdle in the seller's initial inclination to accept or reject the offer. A buyer can avoid major problems during this process by getting the seller to ask a reasonable price for the property. If the property is reasonably priced, there will be no shortage of interested parties, as long as the property matches what they are looking for. Buyers usually try to negotiate the price to get a bargain. Depending on the number of offers, or the real estate market at the time, the seller may have to entertain offers for less than he or she is asking. Typically, an offer will come in for less than the seller has asked which leaves you the agent with the tremendous task of convincing the seller to accept the offer. You want to keep the seller's best interests in mind, however, not just thinking of your own commission on the sale, and you must only convince the seller the offer is a good one if it is in fact good. It is your job to present all offers to the sellers, but don't push an offer you know is subpar.

When you present the offer to the seller, there are a number of steps you may choose to follow. There is no one right or wrong way to present an offer; only you will know your client's personality and what makes him or her tick. If a formal presentation is required, the following steps are very helpful; if you are on a more personal level with your client, and don't have to give such a formal presentation, you can edit or tailor your presentation as necessary.

The first step is to call your client to an appointment. Naturally, the first thing your client might ask is how much the offer was made for. You want to avoid giving this information over the phone. A good response might be to inform the client that you simply cannot negotiate an offer over the phone, that there are many components that will go into it, and that you will go over all the specifics in the meeting. If you are concerned with answering this question, you might have one of the support staff in the office make the call for you. They will not have any information to give, and can truthfully and simply answer the buyer's questioning with "I don't know." You might even want to set up an appointment with the sellers before you receive an actual offer. An appropriate way to approach this is to call the seller and inform them you are about to take an offer on their property, or even avoid saying "their property" and just say you are about to take an offer on the advertised price. The advertised price of the property may be less than the asking price, getting the sellers prepared for an offer price closer to the advertised price than the asking price. No matter how you prepare the seller, the initial step is to get an appointment with him or her to cover all aspects of the offer.

The next step you will want to take is to review all documents related to the offer. Be prepared when you meet with the sellers, and be able to anticipate any questions they may have regarding the offer. The more familiar with the offer you are, the easier the meeting with the sellers will be. In addition to anticipating the possible questions your clients might have, you should also anticipate the possible objections they might have. A good way to counteract these objections is to tell them about the buyer's hesitations or concerns regarding the property, and his or her excitement about the property. Additionally, you can do a review of a current competitive market analysis to illustrate the validity of the buyer's offer.

If you are not the original listing agent, you will want to consult with the original listing agent and go over the offer. This may or may not be a requirement of the listing agreement, but it will certainly help when approaching the seller. The original listing agent may wish to accompany you in presenting the offer to the seller, and could be effective in communicating to the sellers. As the original contact and employed agent of the seller, the original listing agent can be a good asset, as the seller will trust his or her guidance and opinions.

The next step is to meet with the seller. This is when you will present the offer and terms of the contract. The meeting should take place with all owners of the property and obviously with all the sellers as well. There could be a difference. If an elderly widow wishes to sell her property but is not confident in conducting the business herself, she may ask a close relative, attorney, or even a friend to sell the home for her. He or she will be the person making the negotiations and will filter the information back to the owner for approval, or if the seller is authorized to make all decisions, the owner will be notified when the property is sold, and the process is over.

During the meeting, copies of the offer should be given to all sellers. The agent can then walk each person through the contract item by item, with each person able to follow along and ask questions as they arise. How you conduct this is up to you; some agents will allow the sellers some time to review the entire document, while others will begin by covering minor points and getting an agreement on small items, moving on to the larger items toward the end of the meeting. By getting the seller to agree on personal property items such as carpets, drapes or appliances, small repairs, or other contractual items, you will be setting the stage for acceptance of the entire contract. Discussion of price should be the last item of business, getting agreement on all items up to that point, or negotiation on the items in the event the seller chooses to counteroffer. It is a good idea to humanize the process so the seller knows a little about the buyer. If the seller feels he or she knows about the buyer, he or she might be more inclined to accept an offer a few thousand dollars less than asked for.

Overcoming objections will be the fifth and final step in the formal presentation process. The most common objection will be the matter of price. Should the buyer offer less then the original asking price, is will be up to you to get the sellers to accept this lesser amount. There are ways you can present the price to make it seem more attractive than negative. One of the things you can highlight is the savings on commission. The seller will pay less commission on a smaller offer versus the original asking price. Find out the exact savings and highlight this. Additionally, highlight other items or other areas where the seller will save money with the smaller offer. Suddenly the smaller offer will not seem as bad. If the sellers decide to refuse the offer, the extra time it will take to sell the property may cost the seller more money, or cause delay in finding and paying for a replacement property. In the event that the agent cannot get the seller to accept the offer as written, move onto a counteroffer as an alternative to rejecting the offer entirely.

Remember
Presenting an offer to your client may involve the following formal steps:

1. Set up an appointment
2. Review all appropriate documents
3. Consult the original listing agent
4. Present the offer
5. Overcome objections

C O U N T E R O F F E R

If you are not able to get the seller to accept the offer as written, you should encourage the seller to make a counteroffer. This should be explained to the buyer so that the buyer is aware of a possible counteroffer. If the buyer chooses to make an offer smaller then the amount the seller has asked for, you as an agent should prepare the buyer for a possible counter and let him or her know how hard you will work to persuade the seller to accept the offer as written, or at least get the seller to make a counter, versus having the seller reject the offer altogether.

The counteroffer is a separate form to be attached to the original purchase offer. All changes or items to be included in the counteroffer should be clearly itemized. They should be easy to read and clear, with no room for interpretation.

When presenting the counteroffer to the buyer, it is advantageous to highlight the items on the original contract that the seller agreed to. If there was a very important item the buyer really wanted to happen, and the seller agreed to it, talk about that first. If the buyer really wanted to keep the living room furniture and the seller agreed, let the buyer know the good news. Lead into the changes with the positive aspects of the contract.

Date _____, at _____, California.
This is a counter offer to the: ☐ California Residential Purchase Agreement, ☐ Counter Offer, or ☐ Other _____ ("Offer"),
dated _____, on property known as _____ ("Property"),
between _____ ("Buyer") and _____ ("Seller").

1. **TERMS:** The terms and conditions of the above referenced document are **accepted subject to the following:**
   A. Paragraphs in the Offer that require initials by all parties, but are not initialed by all parties, are excluded from the final agreement unless specifically referenced for inclusion in paragraph 1C of this or another Counter Offer.
   B. Unless otherwise agreed in writing, down payment and loan amount(s) will be adjusted in the same proportion as in the original Offer.
   C. _____
      _____
      _____
      _____
      _____
      _____
      _____
      _____
   D. The following attached supplements are incorporated in this Counter Offer: ☐ Addendum No. _____
      ☐ _____ ☐ _____

2. **RIGHT TO ACCEPT OTHER OFFERS:** Seller has the right to continue to offer the Property for sale or for other transaction, and to accept any other offer at any time prior to notification of acceptance, as described in paragraph 3. If this is a Seller Counter Offer, Seller's acceptance of another offer prior to Buyer's acceptance and communication of notification of this Counter Offer, shall revoke this Counter Offer.

3. **EXPIRATION:** This Counter Offer shall be deemed revoked and the deposits, if any, shall be returned unless this Counter Offer is Signed by the Buyer or Seller to whom it is sent and a Copy of the Signed Counter Offer is personally received by the person making this Counter Offer or _____,
   who is authorized to receive it, by 5:00 PM on the third Day After this Counter Offer is made or, (if checked)
   by ☐ _____ (date), at _____ This Counter Offer may be executed in counterparts.

4. ☐ **(If checked:) MULTIPLE COUNTER OFFER:** Seller is making a Counter Offer(s) to another prospective buyer(s) on terms that may or may not be the same as in this Counter Offer. Acceptance of this Counter Offer by Buyer shall **not** be binding unless and until it is subsequently re-Signed by Seller in paragraph 7 below and a Copy of the Counter Offer Signed in paragraph 7 is personally received by Buyer or by _____ who is authorized to receive it. Prior to the completion of all of these events, Buyer and Seller shall have no duties or obligations for the purchase or sale of the Property.

5. **OFFER: BUYER OR SELLER MAKES THIS COUNTER OFFER ON THE TERMS ABOVE AND ACKNOWLEDGES RECEIPT OF A COPY.**
   _____ Date _____

6. **ACCEPTANCE: I/WE** accept the above Counter Offer (If checked ☐ **SUBJECT TO THE ATTACHED COUNTER OFFER**) and acknowledge receipt of a Copy.
   _____ Date _____ Time _____ AM/PM
   _____ Date _____ Time _____ AM/PM

7. ┌──┐
   MULTIPLE COUNTER OFFER SIGNATURE LINE: By signing below, Seller accepts this Multiple Counter Offer.
   NOTE TO SELLER: Do NOT sign in this box until after Buyer signs in paragraph 6. (Paragraph 7 applies only if paragraph 4 is checked.)
   _____ Date _____ Time _____ AM/PM
   _____ Date _____ Time _____ AM/PM
   └──┘

8. (_____/_____) (Initials) **Confirmation of Acceptance:** A Copy of Signed Acceptance was personally received by the maker of the Counter Offer, or that person's authorized agent as specified in paragraph 3 (or, if this is a Multiple Counter Offer, the Buyer or Buyer's authorized agent as specified in paragraph 4) on (date) _____, at _____ AM/PM. A binding Agreement is created when a Copy of Signed Acceptance is personally received by the the maker of the Counter Offer, or that person's authorized agent (or, if this is a Multiple Counter Offer, the Buyer or Buyer's authorized agent) whether or not confirmed in this document. Completion of this confirmation is not legally required in order to create a binding Agreement; it is solely intended to evidence the date that Confirmation of Acceptance has occurred.

SURE TRAC The System for Success™

Published by the
California Association of REALTORS®

CO REVISED 10/02 (PAGE 1 OF 1)   **Print Date**

Reviewed by _____ Date _____

EQUAL HOUSING OPPORTUNITY

COUNTER OFFER (CO PAGE 1 OF 1)

Since you did a competitive market analysis when preparing to present the offer to the seller, use this information to show that the counteroffer is fair, and within what the market is demanding for similar properties. Let the buyer know the price or new terms the seller has proposed, and move on to getting the buyer to agree to the new terms. If the buyer agrees, you have officially closed the deal; if the buyer makes any changes, it will go back to the seller for approval. This process could go back and forth more than one time, with each party agreeing to any changes by initialing or signing next to the change, until all items have been agreed upon. At this point, the negotiations are over, the offer is signed and accepted, and escrow is opened. It is important to let the originator of the counteroffer know immediately upon the other party's acceptance to any of the changes. Until the acceptance has been conveyed to the originator, either party may withdraw from the contract. The final accepted contract should contain all signatures and initials next to all changes, and then it should be copied and distributed to all parties involved.

S U M M A R Y

This chapter walked you through how to accurately fill out the deposit receipt, and its components. The deposit receipt itself as a document is relatively simple to understand and straightforward; however, as an agent, you are encouraged to consult other professionals if there should be a question on how to accurately fill out any portion of the contract. Additionally, we discussed the irregular or special provisions of the contract which may require outside assistance to make sure you have legally filled out all documents and maintained your fiduciary responsibility while protecting yourself in the process, in the event that there should be legal action on the contract. Finally, we closed the chapter with a discussion of how to present the offer to the seller, and how to handle a counteroffer situation should the sellers not accept the original contract.

The main thing to remember from this chapter is that all documents must always be clearly and accurately filled out. Full disclosure, fiduciary responsibility and other items are also very important and should be remembered; however, filling out the document accurately will make the offer process much more smooth than it would be if it has to be amended and initialed for every mistake or misunderstanding. If you have a question regarding the deposit receipt, the best thing to do is ask for clarity or guidance.

T E R M S   A N D   P H R A S E S

CAR – The abbreviation for the California Association of Realtors®

Caveat Emptor – A phrase meaning "let the buyer beware". This used to be universally applied to the buyer in a real estate transaction, meaning the buyer had to be aware of any defects or problems, leaving the seller free of any responsibility.

Caveat Vendor – A phrase meaning "it is the seller who must be aware." This notion has replaced "caveat emptor," leaving the seller responsible for disclosure and for making all necessary repairs to a property.

Consideration – Any form of payment, monetary or not, given in exchange for something else.

Deposit Receipt – The form or document used when accepting earnest money to bind an offer for property by a buyer; when filled out properly and executed by both parties, it may result in a binding contract. This term can be used synonymously with the purchase contract.

Irrevocable Order – The transfer of funds into escrow

Latent Defects – Harmful defects in a property which may cause unforeseen harm to the buyer. These defects may or may not be visible to the untrained eye.

Liquidated Damages – Damages in an ascertained amount that may be recovered in a lawsuit.

Patent Defects – Defects in a property, which are not considered harmful. These defects may or may not be visible to the untrained eye.

Purchase Contract – Also called the purchase agreement, it is a written offer accompanied with a deposit (earnest money deposit) made when a buyer would like to make an offer on property.

Specific Performance – An action to compel performance of an agreement, such an agreement for the sale of property.

Subordination Agreement – An agreement under which a prior lien is made inferior to an otherwise junior lien; changes the order of priority.

Vesting – Transfer of title to property.

C H A P T E R   Q U I Z

1. Which of the following is true regarding the deposit receipt?
    a. It is also called the purchase agreement
    b. All California brokerage firms use one uniform version of the form
    c. It acts as the escrow instructions
    d. Both A and C

2. Which of the following is NOT a function of the deposit receipt?
    a. Formal offer to purchase property
    b. Binding contract
    c. Negotiable instrument
    d. Escrow instructions

3. On a purchase agreement, what form of writing takes precedence over any/all others?
    a. Printed writing already on the form
    b. Typewritten instructions in blank areas
    c. Handwritten instructions in blank areas, or over crossed out areas
    d. None of the above

4. Which of the following payment methods would be acceptable as a deposit on property?
    a. Cash
    b. Non-monetary consideration
    c. Promissory note
    d. All of the above are acceptable

5. Who is listed on the deposit receipt as "buyers"?
    a. Everyone taking title to the property

b. Only the person making the offer

c. The person making the offer and the financial institution granting the promissory note on the property

d. All people taking title to the property, and the financial institution granting the promissory note on the property.

6. An acceptable property description may be presented in which of the following ways?
   a. Street address
   b. Metes and Bounds
   c. Block and lot
   d. Any of the above

7. A financing contingency clause allows the buyer to back out of the contract if
   a. He or she cannot secure financing
   b. He or she finds a property he or she likes better
   c. He or she decides not to move from his or her current home
   d. None of the above: once the contract is signed, it is permanent

8. When does escrow open?
   a. When the escrow instructions are delivered to the escrow agent or company
   b. When the seller accepts the buyer's offer
   c. 15 days after the escrow instructions are received by the escrow agent of the escrow company
   d. None of the above

9. Liquidated damages specify the amount of money a seller will receive if the buyer should do what?
   a. Not qualify for funding
   b. Request to keep some of the seller's personal property as part of the sale of the home
   c. Default on the contract
   d. Any of the above

10. A seller's personal property:
    a. Is never part of the deposit receipt; it can be negotiated in a separate agreement or transaction.
    b. Is never part of the deposit receipt, and it is considered rude to request that the seller leave any of his or her belongings for the buyer in the transaction.
    c. Can be negotiated amongst the buyer and seller, and then included in the deposit receipt.
    d. Always stays with the home if it was specifically purchased for the house.

11. Fixtures are treated as:
    a. Personal property, and can be negotiated to stay with the property.
    b. Real property, are not negotiable, and will always be part of the property transaction.
    c. Neither real nor personal property: they are considered an attachment to the property and no negotiations are necessary. They automatically go with the sale of the home.
    d. None of the above.

12. Liens against the property are the responsibility of:
    a. The seller always
    b. The buyer

c. The person in possession of the property: the liens never attach to one specific person, only property and its owner at the time

d. None of the above

13. Which of the following is not considered a special provision to the deposit receipt?
   a. "As is" clause
   b. Irrevocable order
   c. Unordinary vesting
   d. Uncashed checks

14. A home may contain latent and patent defects. Of the two types of defects, which poses serious harm to the buyer?
   a. Latent
   b. Patent
   c. Both A and B
   d. Neither A nor B

15. A buyer offering a deposit with the request to hold the deposit check uncashed will negotiate with the:
   a. Licensee as to the time frame during which the check may be held.
   b. Seller, to see if he or she will accept this as part of the deposit receipt; if not, the seller may counteroffer with terms of his or her own.
   c. Neither the licensee nor the seller, this is not negotiable. The seller either accepts the offer as written with all disclosures of conditions, or rejects it.
   d. None of the above.

16. What is the major hurdle in getting the seller to accept an offer on property?
   a. Personal property negotiations.
   b. Buyer's request for the seller to repair small defects or make renovations.
   c. Buyer's request for the seller to pay inspection costs.
   d. Price.

17. Which of the following is not a step in the formal presentation of an offer to your client?
   a. Review all appropriate documents
   b. Prepare counteroffer form
   c. Set up the interview
   d. Overcome objections

18. Who should participate in the meeting when you present the seller with the buyer's offer?
   a. The listing agent
   b. All sellers
   c. All owners
   d. All of the above

19. In a counteroffer situation, what part of the original purchase offer will be attached to the counteroffer?
   a. The entire document
   b. The first page
   c. The second page
   d. The third page

20. When presenting a counteroffer to the buyer, what tactics are helpful to get him or her to agree to the new terms?
    a. Offer a competitive market analysis to show that the proposed price is fair
    b. Highlight the portions of the original offer that the seller accepted
    c. Highlight accepted terms of the original offer that were especially important to the buyer, such as items of personal property to be included in the contract, or a short escrow.
    d. All of the above

7

ACCURATELY CREATING A GOOD PURCHASE AGREEMENT

What you will learn in this Chapter

- Preparation

- Financing Terms and Conditions

- Language for Nonfinancial Terms and Conditions

- Special Considerations for Income and Business Properties

- Other Considerations

Test Your Knowledge

1. A good purchase agreement is:
   a. Very specific, with no room for interpretation.
   b. General, with a few specifications but room for interpretation to make changes as necessary.
   c. Vague, leaving the ability for either party to alter the contract as he or she sees fit.
   d. None of the above.

2. An All Inclusive Trust Deed (AITD) is also called:
   a. Second trust deed
   b. Junior Trust Deed
   c. Wrap around loan
   d. Both A and B

3. "Subject to," as used in a purchase agreement, most nearly means:
   a. Conditional to the seller's acceptance of the contract
   b. Conditional to the buyer's ability to secure financing
   c. Conditional to the seller's ability to produce a clear and transferable title
   d. All of the above

4. Who must carry flood insurance?
   a. All buyers who have financed any part of a property.
   b. All buyers who have financed any part of a property located in a special flood hazard zone.
   c. Only those properties built before 1983 located in a special flood hazard zone.
   d. Only those properties built before 1978 located in a special flood hazard zone.

5. A special studies zone refers to what geological condition or natural occurrence?
   a. Earthquake fault displacement
   b. High fire zone
   c. Flood zone
   d. Land located on top of a natural resource such as natural gas or oil

6. A transfer disclosure statement is required when selling what type of property?
   a. All privately owned residential properties.
   b. All residential property containing one to four living units.
   c. Residential property consisting of detached, single family homes only.
   d. On all properties: commercial, residential, agricultural and industrial.

7. A broker earns a commission when:
   a. He or she finds a ready, willing and able buyer
   b. He or she he has brought the buyer and seller together and enabled them to enter into a binding contract
   c. He or she has taken a listing agreement on a property
   d. When escrow closes

INTRODUCTION

In the previous chapter, you were walked through a purchase contract or deposit receipt, and how to accurately fill it out. In addition, you were exposed to special provisions, which may arise, causing you to consult a professional to fill out the special sections legally and accurately.

In this chapter, you will be exposed to certain sections of the purchase agreement in more depth, and you will learn how to fill them out so that the contract is not only enforceable, but clear and easy to understand. Buyers and sellers get nervous or worried when they see a lot of "legal-speak", with terms, phrases and wording they may not understand. Being able to fill out the purchase agreement clearly and accurately, so that all parties involved can easily understand the contract, is difficult. You as an agent should spend a considerable amount of time making sure you understand this, and can master the art of drawing up a good purchase contract.

PREPARATION

There are many reasons for preparing a good purchase contract. The following are just five of those reasons:

Reputation. A good reputation will spread by word of mouth to other professionals in the real estate industry and to potential clients. When this good word of mouth spreads to other agents, they will be more likely to work with you, while word of mouth to clients means more potential sales!

Client. You have a fiduciary responsibility to your client, and one of the best ways to demonstrate this is by carefully and accurately writing the contract. A mistake here will cause the deal to fall through.

Professional competency. A licensee showing he or she is very knowledgeable and competent in all aspects of the real estate process, especially the purchase contract, will gain confidence from his or her broker. When the contract is written very clear and accurate, it will stand any legal test that might be brought up.

Legal competency. A licensee will be challenged and tested on their ability to draw up complete contracts. Again, mistakes here may terminate the deal.

Time considerations. Time is usually a sensitive consideration in a property transaction. An agent must be able to write a contract that will be accurate and clear to all parties in a very expedient manner. This will aid in the general speed and excitement of the transaction.

It is important to be as complete and specific as possible when filling out the purchase contract. If the contract is written such that it could be interpreted more than one way by more than one person, there is a possibility that it could fall out of escrow. The entire agreement between the parties must be reflected, which benefits all parties to the transaction. The terms should be realistic and easily attain-able. Inserting language such as "not to exceed" will reduce confusion and the element of surprise. Finally, a skilled licensee will consult a checklist, such as the Purchase Agreement Checklist shown later in this chapter, to assure that nothing is missed in the agreement.

Remember

- A skilled licensee will usually consult a checklist while filling out the purchase agreement to make sure that he or she has accurately and specifically filled out all portions of the contract.

FINANCING TERMS AND CONDITIONS

The following steps are specific to writing the terms and conditions of financing for different financing types.

All Cash

1. Cash down payment to be $ _____ including the above deposit.

2. Buyer to deposit an additional $ _____ in escrow as part of purchase price (upon removal of contingencies on or before ten days from date here of; upon obtaining new loan commitment; upon signing of escrow instructions; etc.).

New First Trust Deed

1. Subject to buyer obtaining at his expense a new first loan of approximately
   $ _____
   with interest not to exceed _____% per annum, payable in not less than _____ years.

2. Any difference in the approximate new loan shall be adjusted by cash or second trust deed.

In quoting the number of points a seller may have to pay on an FHA or VA loan, disclose such factors which may enter into the transaction to raise the points: the appraisal may be lower than expected, there may be required work calling for building permit fees and the like, and there may even be an increase in the points structure due to market changes.

Assumption of an Existing Loan

Buyer shall assume, or take over, the existing first or second trust deed of record of approximately $ _____ payable $ _____ per month, including _____% interest.

Cal-Vet

This purchase is subject to buyer obtaining new Cal-Vet financing of not less than seller to carry back $ _____ at _____% interest per annum, payable $_____ per month; with the balance of purchase price to be paid in cash. Both the buyer and seller will be expected to pay their own, normal closing costs.

New Trust Deed

1.   Buyer to execute a note payable to the seller secured by a first trust deed (or second, third and any subsequent trust deed) in the amount of $ _____, or more, payable per month, including _____% interest per annum on the unpaid balance, all to be due in (?) years.

2. Buyer is to execute a note payable to the seller secured by a first trust deed (or second, third and any subsequent trust deed) for the balance of the purchase price, less the down payment, and new or existing loan payable at 1% (or more) of original amount per month, including _____% interest per annum on the unpaid balance, all due in _____ years.

"Subject To" Existing Loan

1. The buyer shall purchase "subject to" the existing first or second trust deed of record of approximately $ _____ payable $ _____ per month, including _____% interest.

   Any difference in the lender's statement will be adjusted by cash or in the second trust deed.

All Inclusive Trust Deed (A.I.T.D)

An All Inclusive Trust Deed, also called a wraparound mortgage, is a junior financing instrument that wraps around the existing loans, yet is subject to them in order of priority. In the event of default, the trust deed recorded first will be paid first, and so forth.

The proper way to word the provisions for such financing in the purchase contract is as follows:

$ _____ down payment including the deposit. The buyer is to execute a promissory note in favor of the seller secured by an all-inclusive deed of trust in the amount of $ _____ payable at $ _____ per month including principal and interest at the rate of _____ % per annum. Impounds should be paid as well, whenever applicable.

Land Contract

A land contract note shall be payable:

1. Interest only at the rate of _____% per year in the sale tax year, payable as monthly or quarterly installments, or to be paid all at one specific date.

2. Commencing on January 1st, or any other determined date, 1% of the original principal amount (or more) per month, including _____% interest on the unpaid balance continuing until the balance is paid in full, or for 60 months from close of escrow at which time the entire balance shall be due and payable.

3. In addition thereto, the buyer shall make a principal reduction payment of $_____ on January 1, 20xx.

RECORDING REQUESTED BY

AND WHEN RECORDED MAIL TO:

NAME

STREET
ADDRESS

CITY,
STATE
ZIP

SPACE ABOVE THIS LINE FOR RECORDER'S USE

THIS FORM FURNISHED BY PROVIDENT TITLE COMPANY

Title Order No. _____
Escrow or Loan No. _____

LONG FORM ALL-INCLUSIVE DEED OF TRUST
AND ASSIGNMENT OF RENTS

This All-Inclusive Deed of Trust, made this _____ day of, _____ between
_____
_____

herein called Trustor, whose address is _____
(number and street)   (city)   (state)   (zip)

PROVIDENT TITLE COMPANY, A California corporation, herein called Trustee, and _____
_____
_____ herein called Beneficiary.

Witnesseth: That Trustor Irrevocably Grants, Transfers and Assigns to Trustee in Trust, With Power of Sale, that property in _____
_____ County, California described as:

TOGETHER WITH the rents, issues and profits thereof, SUBJECT, HOWEVER, to the right, power and authority hereinafter given to and conferred upon Beneficiary to collect and apply such rents, issues and profits.

For the Purpose of Securing:

1. Performance of each agreement of Trustor herein contained. 2. Payment of the indebtedness evidenced by one all-inclusive purchase money promissory note of even date herewith, and any extension or renewal thereof, in the principal sum of $ _____ executed by Trustor in favor of Beneficiary or order.

Underlying Obligations:

This is an all inclusive purchase money deed of trust, securing an all-inclusive purchase money promissory note in the original principal amount of _____
Dollars ($_____) (the "Note") which includes within such amount the unpaid balance of the following:
(a) A promissory note in the original principal sum of _____ Dollars
($_____) in favor of _____ as
Payee, secured by a deed of trust recorded _____, 19 ___, as Document No. _____, in Book _____, Page _____
Official Records of _____ County,   California, and
(b) A promissory note in the original principal sum of _____ Dollars
($_____) in favor of _____
as Payee, secured by a deed of trust recorded _____, 19 ___, as Document No. _____, in Book_____, Page
_____, Official Records of _____ County, California.
(The Promissory Notes secured by such deeds of trust are hereinafter called the "Underlying Notes").

To Protect the Security of This Deed of Trust, Trustor Agrees:

(1) To keep said property in good condition and repair; not to remove or demolish any building thereon; to complete or restore promptly and in good and workmanlike manner any building which may be constructed, damaged or destroyed thereon and to pay when due all claims for labor performed and materials furnished therefor; to comply with all laws affecting said property or requiring any alterations or improvements to be made thereon; not to commit or permit waste thereof; not to commit, suffer or permit any act upon said property in violation of law; to cultivate, irrigate, fertilize, fumigate, prune and do all other acts which from the character or use of said property may be reasonably necessary, the specific enumerations herein not excluding the general.

(2) To provide, maintain and deliver to Beneficiary fire, vandalism and malicious mischief insurance satisfactory to and with loss payable to Beneficiary. The amount collected under any fire or other insurance policy may be applied by Beneficiary upon any indebtedness secured hereby and in such order as Beneficiary may determine, or at option of Beneficiary the entire amount so collected or any part thereof may be released to Trustor.

Such application or release shall not cure or waive any default or notice of default hereunder or invalidate any act done pursuant to such notice. The provisions hereof are subject to the mutual agreements of the parties as below set forth.

(3) To appear in and defend any action or proceeding purporting to affect the security hereof or the rights or powers of Beneficiary or Trustee; and to pay all costs and expenses, including cost of evidence of title and attorney's fees in a reasonable sum, in any such action or proceeding in which Beneficiary or Trustee may appear, and in any suit brought by Beneficiary to foreclose this Deed of Trust.

(4) To pay; at least ten days before delinquency all taxes and assessments affecting said property, including assessments on appurtenant water stock; subject to the mutual agreements of the parties as below set forth, to pay when due, all incumbrances, charges and liens, with interest, on said property or any part thereof, which appear to be prior or superior hereto; all costs, fees and expenses of this Trust.

0-13

Should Trustor fail to make any payment or to do any act as herein provided, then Beneficiary or Trustee, but without obligation so to do and without notice to or demand upon Trustor and without releasing Trustor from any obligation hereof, may: make or do the same in such manner and to such extent as either may deem necessary to protect the security hereof, Beneficiary or Trustee being authorized to enter upon said property for such purposes; appear in and defend any action or proceeding purporting to affect the security hereof or the rights or powers of Beneficiary or Trustee; pay, purchase, contest or compromise any incumbrance, charge or lien which in the judgment of either appears to be prior or superior hereto; and, in exercising any such powers, pay necessary expenses, employ counsel and pay his reasonable fees.

(5) To pay immediately and without demand all sums so expended by Beneficiary or Trustee, with interest from date of expenditure at the amount allowed by law in effect at the date hereof, and to pay for any statement provided for by law in effect at the date hereof regarding the obligation secured hereby any amount demanded by the Beneficiary not to exceed the maximum allowed by law at the time when said statement is demanded.

(6) That any award of damages in connection with any condemnation for public use of or injury to said property or any part thereof is hereby assigned and shall be paid to Beneficiary who may apply or release such moneys received by him in the same manner and with the same effect as above provided for disposition of proceeds of fire or other insurance. The provisions hereof are subject to the mutual agreements of the parties as below set forth.

(7) That by accepting payment of any sum secured hereby after its due date, Beneficiary does not waive his right either to require prompt payment when due of all other sums so secured or to declare default for failure so to pay.

(8) That at any time or from time to time, without liability therefor and without notice, upon written request of Beneficiary and presentation of this Deed and said note for endorsement, and without affecting the personal liability of any person for payment of the indebtedness secured hereby, Trustee may: reconvey any part of said property; consent to the making of any map or plat thereof; join in granting any easement thereon; or join in any extension agreement or any agreement subordinating the lien or charge hereof.

(9) That upon written request of the Beneficiary stating that all sums secured hereby have been paid, and upon surrender of this Deed and said note to Trustee for cancellation and retention and upon payment of its fees, Trustee shall reconvey, without warranty, the property then held hereunder. The recitals in such reconveyance of any matters or facts shall be conclusive proof of the truthfulness thereof. The guarantee in such reconveyance may be described as "the person or persons legally entitled thereto." Five years after issuance of such full reconveyance, Trustee may destroy said note and this Deed unless directed in such request to retain them).

(10) That as additional security, Trustor hereby gives to and confers upon Beneficiary the right, power and authority, during the continuance of these Trusts, to collect the rents, issues and profits of said property, reserving unto Trustor the right, prior to any default by Trustor in payment of any indebtedness secured hereby or in performance of any agreement hereunder, to collect and retain such rents, issues and profits as they become due and payable. Upon any such default, Beneficiary may at any time without notice, either in person, by agent, or by a receiver to be appointed by a court, and without regard to the adequacy of any security for the indebtedness hereby secured, enter upon and take possession of said property or any part thereof, in his own name sue for or otherwise collect such rents, issues and profits, including those past due and unpaid, and apply the same, less costs and expenses of operation and collection, including reasonable attorney's fees, upon any indebtedness secured hereby, and in such order as Beneficiary may determine. The entering upon and taking possession of said property, the collection of such rents, issues and profits and the application thereof as aforesaid, shall not cure or waive any default or notice of default hereunder or invalidate any act done pursuant to such notice.

(11) That upon default by Trustor in payment of any indebtedness secured hereby or in performance of any agreement hereunder, Beneficiary may declare all sums secured hereby immediately due and payable by delivery to Trustee of written declaration of default and demand for sale and of written notice of default and of election to cause to be sold said property, which notice Trustee shall cause to be filed for record. Beneficiary also shall deposit with Trustee this Deed, said note and all documents evidencing expenditures secured hereby.

After the lapse of such time as may then be required by law following the recordation of said notice of default, and notice of sale having been given as then required by law, Trustee, without demand on Trustor, shall sell said property at the time and place fixed by it in said notice of sale, either as a whole or in separate parcels, and in such order as it may be determined, at public auction to the highest bidder for cash in lawful money of the United States, payable at time of sale. Trustee may postpone sale of all or any portion of said property by public announcement at such time and place of sale, and from time to time thereafter may postpone such sale by public announcement at the time fixed by the preceding postponement. Trustee shall deliver to such purchaser its deed conveying the property so sold, but without any covenant or warranty, express or implied. The recitals in such deed or any matters or facts shall be conclusive proof of the truthfulness thereof. Any person, including Trustor, Trustee, or Beneficiary as hereinafter defined, may purchase at such sale.

After deducting all costs, fees and expenses of Trustee and of this Trust, including cost of evidence of title in connection with sale, Trustee shall apply the proceeds of sale to payment of: all sums expended under the terms hereof, not then repaid, with accrued interest at the amount allowed by law in effect at the date hereof; all other sums then secured hereby; and the remainder, if any, to the person or persons legally entitled thereto.

(12) Beneficiary, or any successor in ownership of any indebtedness secured hereby, may from time to time, by instrument in writing, substitute a successor or successors to any Trustee named herein or acting hereunder, which instrument, executed by the Beneficiary and duly acknowledged and recorded in the office of the recorder of the county or counties where said property is situated, shall be conclusive proof of proper substitution of such successor Trustee or Trustees, who shall, without conveyance from the Trustee predecessor, succeed to all its title, estate, powers and duties. Said instrument must contain the name of the original Trustor, Trustee and Beneficiary hereunder, the book and page where this Deed is recorded and the name and address of the new Trustee.

(13) That this Deed applies to, inures to the benefit of, and binds all parties hereto, their heirs, legatees, devisees, administrators, executors, successors and assigns. The term Beneficiary shall mean the owner and holder, including pledgees, of the note secured hereby, whether or not named as Beneficiary herein. In this Deed, whenever the context so requires, the masculine gender includes the feminine and/or neuter, and the singular includes the plural.

(14) That Trustee accepts this Trust when this Deed, duly executed and acknowledged, is made a public record as provided by law. Trustee is not obligated to notify any party hereto of pending sale under any other Deed of Trust or of any action or proceeding in which Trustor, Beneficiary or Trustee shall be a party unless brought by Trustee.

The Undersigned Trustor requests that a copy of any Notice of Default and of any Notice of Sale hereunder be mailed to him at his address hereinbefore set forth.

Trustor and Beneficiary Mutually Agree:

(A) By Beneficiary's acceptance of this All-Inclusive Purchase Money Deed of Trust, Beneficiary covenants and agrees that provided Trustor is not delinquent or in default under the terms of the Note secured hereby, Beneficiary shall pay all installments of principal and interest which shall hereafter become due pursuant to the provisions of the Underlying Note(s) as and when the same become due and payable. In the event Trustor shall be delinquent or in default under the terms of the Note secured hereby, Beneficiary shall not be obligated to make any payments required by the terms of the Underlying Note(s) until such delinquency or default is cured. In the event Beneficiary fails to timely pay any installment of principal or interest on the Underlying Note(s) at the time when Trustor is not delinquent or in default under the terms of the Note secured hereby, Trustor may, at Trustor's option make such payments directly to the holder of such Underlying Note(s), in which event Trustor shall be entitled to a credit against the next installment(s) of principal and interest due under the terms of the Note secured hereby equal to the amount so paid and including, without limitation, any penalty, charges and expenses paid by Trustor to the holder of the Underlying Note(s) on account of Beneficiary's failing to make such payment. The obligation of Beneficiary hereunder shall terminate upon the earliest of (i) foreclosure of the lien of this All-Inclusive Purchase Money Deed of Trust, or (ii) cancellation of the Note secured hereby and reconveyance of this All-Inclusive Purchase Money Deed of Trust.

Should Trustor be delinquent or in default under the terms of the Note secured hereby and if Beneficiary consequently incurs any penalties, charges, or other expenses on account of the Underlying Note(s) during the period of such delinquency or default, the amount of such penalties, charges and expenses shall be immediately added to the principal amount of the Note secured hereby and shall be immediately payable by Trustor to Beneficiary.

If at any time the unpaid balance of the Note secured hereby, accrued interest thereon, and all other sums due pursuant to the terms thereof and all sums advanced by beneficiary pursuant to the terms of this Deed of Trust, is equal to or less than the unpaid principal balance of the Underlying Note(s) and accrued interest thereon, the Note secured hereby, at the option of Beneficiary, shall be cancelled and said property shall be reconveyed from the lien of this Deed of Trust.

(B) Trustor and Beneficiary agree that in the event the proceeds of any condemnation award or settlement in lieu thereof, or the proceeds of any casualty insurance covering destructible improvements located upon said property, are applied by the holder of the Underlying Note(s) in reduction of the unpaid principal amount thereof, the unpaid balance of the Note secured hereby shall be reduced by an equivalent amount which shall be deemed applied to the last sums due under the Note.

(C) At such times as the Note secured hereby becomes all due and payable, the amount of principal and interest than payable to Beneficiary thereunder shall be reduced by the then unpaid balance of principal and interest due on the Underlying Note(s).

(D) Any demand hereunder delivered by Beneficiary to Trustee for the foreclosure of the lien of this Deed of Trust may be not more than the sum of the following amounts:

(i) The difference between the then unpaid balance of principal and interest on the Note secured hereby and the then unpaid balance of principal and interest on the Underlying Note(s); plus

(ii) The aggregate of all amounts theretofore paid by Beneficiary pursuant to the terms of this Deed of Trust prior to the date of such foreclosure sale, for taxes and assessments, insurance premiums, delinquency charges, foreclosure costs, and any other sums advanced by Beneficiary pursuant to the terms of this Deed of Trust, to the extent the same were not previously repaid by Trustor to Beneficiary; plus

(iii) The costs of foreclosure hereunder; plus attorneys fees and costs incurred by Beneficiary in enforcing this Deed of Trust or the Note secured hereby as permitted by law.

(E) Notwithstanding any provision to the contrary herein contained, in the event of a Trustee's sale in furtherance of the foreclosure of this Deed of Trust, the balance then due on the Note secured hereby, for the purpose of Beneficiary's demand, shall be reduced, as aforesaid, by the unpaid balance, if any, of principal and interest then due on the Underlying Note(s), satisfactory evidence of which unpaid balances must be submitted to Trustee prior to such sale. The Trustee may rely on any statements received from Beneficiary in this regard and such statements shall be deemed binding and conclusive as between Beneficiary and Trustor, on the one hand, and the Trustee, on the other hand, to the extent of such reliance.

Signature of Trustor

_____

_____   _____

Signature of Beneficiary

_____

_____   _____

STAPLE APPROPRIATE ACKNOWLEDGEMENTS HERE

(THIS DEED OF TRUST IS APPROPRIATE FOR USE ONLY IN CERTAIN TRANSACTIONS. PRIOR TO THE EXECUTION OF THIS DEED OF TRUST, THE PARTIES SHOULD CONSULT THEIR ATTORNEYS WITH RESPECT TO ITS SUITABILITY FOR THEIR PURPOSE.)

Title Order No. _____   Escrow or Loan No. _____

Long Form All-Inclusive Purchase Money Deed of Trust With Power of Sale

Provident Title Company
AS TRUSTEE

———— DO NOT RECORD ————

FOR RECONVEYANCE OR FORECLOSURE SEND TO THE NEAREST
OFFICE OF PROVIDENT TITLE COMPANY

REQUEST FOR FULL RECONVEYANCE

To be used only when note has been paid.

Dated _____

TO PROVIDENT TITLE COMPANY, Trustee:

The Undersigned is the legal owner and holder of all indebtedness secured by the within Deed of Trust. All sums secured by said Deed of Trust have been fully paid and satisfied, and you are hereby requested and directed, on payment to you of any sums owing to you under the terms of said Deed of Trust, to cancel all evidences of indebtedness secured by said Deed of Trust, delivered to you herewith together with the said Deed of Trust, and to reconvey, without warranty, to the parties designated by the terms of said Deed of Trust, the estate now held by you under the same.

MAIL RECONVEYANCE TO:

_____

_____

_____   (By) _____

_____   (By) _____

Do not lose or destroy this Deed of Trust OR THE NOTE which it secures.
Both must be delivered to the Trustee for cancellation before reconveyance will be made.

Alienation

1. The trust deed shall contain an alienation clause.

2. If buyer conveys or transfers title, the entire balance of this note and trust deed shall become due and payable should the beneficiary disapprove of the new buyer.

Prepayment Penalty Clause

The prepayment penalty clause is to be used only where the payments are not to be "or more", meaning the buyer or person holding the note is not allowed to make a larger payment than the required amount due. This prevents the property from being paid off early, allowing the financial institution to make its entire amount of interest due on the note.

1. Privilege is reserved of making partial payments of $_____ or any multiples thereof on said principal sum on any payment date before maturity without penalty.

2. Privilege is reserved of paying this note in full upon any interest payment date after one year (or any time specified) and before maturity upon giving the holder thereof _____ day's written notice of intention to pay this note.

3. Privilege is reserved of paying this note in full at any time.

4. Privilege is reserved of paying in full at any time up to one year from date hereof by payment of principal, accrued interest and _____ day's unearned interest.

5. After _____ year(s) from date hereof, privilege is reserved of paying this note in full without penalty of any kind.

FHA and VA Loans

There are certain specific notice provisions available from lenders or escrow companies that are mandatory in FHA and VA sales contracts. The simplest way of handling this requirement is to attach a form with the required text to the contract. Some offices have printed forms for these clauses. Terms of payment clauses for FHA and VA financing can be written as follows:

BUYER TO OBTAIN FHA 203B OWNER-OCCUPANT LOAN:

$_____ as loan proceeds, conditioned upon buyer's ability to obtain a first loan secured by subject property in that amount, to be insured by FHA for _____ years, payable at approximately $_____per month, including interest at _____ percent per annum, including FHA mortgage insurance, taxes, fire, and other hazard insurance. Buyer to pay 1 percent of loan origination fee, initial reserve, and normal closing cost. The seller is to pay no more than xx points and to comply with FHA requirements for structural pest control certification and repairs if any. (Buyer / Seller) _____to pay for FHA appraisal.

BUYER TO OBTAIN VA LOAN:

$_____ as loan proceeds, subject to the buyer's ability to obtain a first loan secured by subject property in that amount to be guaranteed by the Veterans Administration for _____ years, payable at approximately $_____ per month, including interest at _____ percent per annum, and taxes, fire and other hazard insurance.

The seller is to furnish the VA appraisal and pay all normal closing costs, all escrow fees, and points as required by lender.

Adjustable Interest Rate:

$_____ as loan proceeds, subject to the buyer's ability to obtain from _____(an institutional lender) an "adjustable interest rate" loan in that amount secured by subject property, payable at $_____ monthly including principal and interest at close of escrow at the rate of _____% per annum. Buyer to pay loan setup charges not to exceed xx points.

Subordination

The trust deed shall contain a clause that must be approved by the title company and lender, providing that said trust deed shall be subordinated to a new institutional loan not exceeding $_____ for not less than _____ years, bearing not more than xx% interest per annum.

Free and Clear

The seller agrees to deliver subject property free and clear of all encumbrances, including payoff penalty, if any, liens, bonds, and assessments of record or pending assessments, except as noted herein.

Impound Account

1. Buyer to reimburse seller the amount held by lender as impound account.

2. Seller to transfer impound account to buyer with no reimbursement.

Partial Release Clause

1. The deed of trust is to contain a release clause providing that upon payment of $_____ plus accrued interest on said amount the beneficiary shall execute a partial reconveyance of the property, or a portion of the property, to be released from deed of trust covering same.

2. So long as the trustor shall not be in default concerning the covenants contained herein or with respect to the payments due on the promissory note secured hereby, a partial reconveyance may be had and will be given on parcels of not less than xx square feet, or parcels containing not less than _____ front footage of the property hereinbefore described from the lien or charge hereof upon payment of an amount to apply on the principal of said note; based on the rate of $_____ for each square foot or front footage.

Purchase Agreement Checklist
Are all the terms clear and complete?
If creating a deed of trust payable to the seller, have you considered;

- A down payment sufficient to a secure second?
- Name of beneficiary as "additional insured" on the fire policy?
- Term, if due before normal maturity?
- Request for Notice of Default on first Trust Deed?
- Payment greater than 1 percent of face value per month?
- "Due on sale" clause?
- Buyer's credit?
- The interest rate?
- Are there any changes to the normal closing costs for the buyer or seller?
- If a structural pest control inspection is necessary, is the certification completed with limitation for expenditures by the seller, if required?
- Which party will pay for the appraisal?
- What other repairs must be completed, and which party will pay for these repairs?
- What personal property will be included or excluded?
- Has a provision been made for the rental of the property if possesion is not granted on escrow?
- What other certifications must be obtained? Who will pay for these inspections?
- Has there been any written disclosure of any deficiency affecting the property or structure which might adversely affect the use or enjoyment of the property or structure?
- Do both the buyer and the seller completely understand all costs they will incur, the payments they must make and any estimated net revenue to be received from this transaction?

LANGUAGE FOR NONFINANCIAL TERMS AND CONDITIONS

Purchase Option

This option made this _____ day of _____ by and between_____ , hereinafter called the "seller," and_____, hereinafter called the "buyer." In consideration of the sum of $_____ paid by the buyer to the seller, the receipt of which is hereby acknowledged, the seller hereby grants to the buyer the exclusive option to purchase the following described property.

Said option may be exercised at any time prior to 5:00 P.M., Pacific Standard Time by delivering written notice of exercise of this option addressed to seller at

Said written notice shall be deemed delivered to seller within___ hours of the depositing thereof postage-prepaid, certified mail, at any U.S. Post Office in the State of California.

The purchase price shall be $_____payable as follows:

Within two business days from the day of delivery of notice of exercise of this option to the seller, the buyer shall open an escrow at any escrow company on the following terms and conditions and the seller and buyer shall immediately execute same:

1. The escrow terms shall be for ____days.

2. At the opening of escrow, the buyer shall deposit therein $___ as a deposit on the accounts of the purchase price.
3. The seller shall furnish and pay for a policy of title insurance, showing title vested in the buyer free and clear of bonds, liens, assessments, and encumbrances of record except as noted herein.
4. The seller and buyer shall pay their usual escrow costs and fees.

5. Possession shall be given to the buyer at close of escrow.

6. Taxes, insurance premiums, interest, and rents, if any, shall be prorated to the close of escrow. Security deposits, if any, shall be given to the buyer at close of escrow.

Should the buyer exercise the option to purchase the subject property provided for herein, the seller agrees to pay a real estate commission to the brokerage in the sum of $ _____.

Preliminary Title Report
This escrow is contingent upon the buyer's approval of C.C. & R's and preliminary title report within _____days of the buyer's receipt of same. Escrow holder is authorized and instructed to order preliminary title report and C.C. & R's immediately. Upon receipt of same, the escrow holder shall forward to the buyer the preliminary title report and copy of C.C. & R's via registered mail with return receipt requested. In the event buyer has not advised escrow holder of his disapproval of same within _____days of his receipt of same, this contingency is null and void. The buyer shall pay all cancellation costs of this escrow.

Right to Exchange
1. Should the seller desire to exchange the subject property, the buyer agrees to cooperate and purchase subject property from the seller's assignee.

2. The seller intends to enter into a tax-deferred exchange of the seller's property. If prior to the date set for close of escrow, the seller locates property which the seller desires to acquire, the buyer agrees to do all acts reasonably necessary to assist in obtaining said property to be exchanged for the subject property, provided that the buyer's liability is not increased above the purchase price herein provided. If the seller does not locate such property prior to close of escrow, both parties shall proceed with the sale herein provided for.

Release Clause
If the seller accepts a second offer, the buyer shall, within ___hours of notice hereof, remove all contingencies or this agreement shall be void. Said notice is to be given through registered mail.

Counteroffers

If the seller makes a counteroffer involving only minor changes, write it on the front of the deposit receipt and have the seller initial the changes and sign at the bottom of the offer. Make sure the counteroffer contains a time for acceptance. If the counteroffer is more involved, write the counteroffer on the counteroffer form. Fill in the commission amount on the front side of the deposit receipt. For example:

Counteroffer

The offer on the reverse side is accepted subject to the following changes:

1. Sales price to be $ _____

2. Down payment to be $ _____

This counteroffer expires _____ days from date hereof.

Dated _____

The above counteroffer is accepted.

Dated _____

Seller_____

Seller_____

Buyer_____

Buyer_____

A third option is to write a new deposit receipt and have the seller sign it.

Inspection, Equipment and Appliances

The seller agrees that at the time occupancy of the property is delivered, the heating, sewer, plumbing, and electrical systems, including the water heater and any built-in appliances and equipment, as well as all outside locks and window hardware, shall be in good working order, that the grounds shall be maintained and free of debris and that there shall be no broken shower or window glass, with the exception of the following:

If in the reasonable opinion of a qualified technician any of the above conditions need to be repaired or corrected, the buyer shall furnish seller a copy of said technician's inspection report within 3 business days from date occupancy is delivered.

In the event the seller fails to make the repairs and or corrections in accordance with said report within 5 business days from receipt of said report, the seller herewith authorizes the escrow holder to disburse to the buyer against bills for such repairs and/or corrections a total sum not to exceed $ _____.
The seller agrees to leave said sum in escrow to be disbursed to the buyer or returned to the seller not later than 8 business days from date of occupancy.

Sale and Leaseback

1. The seller agrees to execute the attached lease in favor of the buyer and deposit same into escrow.

2. The seller agrees to lease property for _____ years at
$_____per month.

General Inspection

1. The buyer has inspected the property and is purchasing the same "as is."

2. Subject to the buyer's right to inspect and disapprove the property in writing within_____ hours from time of acceptance.

Roof Inspection

The buyer may choose to have the roof inspected by a licensed general or roofing contractor. If in the reasonable opinion of such contractor the roof is in need of repair, the buyer shall furnish the seller a copy of the inspection report within 15 days from acceptance.

In the event the seller fails to notify buyer within 5 days of receipt of said report that seller agrees to make such repairs, the buyer may terminate all rights and obligations of the parties hereunder.

Consent of an Attorney

The offer is pending upon the seller's attorney's approval.

Structural Alterations

All structural additions, alterations, and replacements of the dwelling completed during the seller's ownership were completed under an appropriate construction permit or other authority in accordance with an ordinance or regulation, EXCEPT:

NOTE: This is a requirement for all residential property up to four units. The seller must disclose in writing to the buyer before transfer of title in the case of a sale or exchange, or prior to the execution of the contract where the transfer is by a real property sales contract, or land contract. Otherwise, the seller will be liable for actual damages sustained by a transferee.

Covenants, Conditions and Restrictions (C.C. & R's)

1. Subject to the buyer's right to disapprove of C.C. & R's within _____ hours receipt thereof.

2. Subject to the buyer's right to disapprove within   hours receipt thereof C.C. & R's that affect the buyer's right to use the property (to construct an apartment house; to build commercial stores or an industrial building; to use for industrial, commercial, or multiple residential purposes; etc.).

Termite Report

A standard termite provision is provided in the preprinted portion of most deposit receipt forms.

1. The seller is to furnish a recent termite report, by a state-licensed pest control operator, showing on the property no visible signs of infestation, fungi, or dry rot in any accessible area.

2. The seller shall furnish at his or her expense a current termite report to be ordered by the broker showing the accessible portions of the building to be free of visible evidence of infestation caused by wood-destroying insects, fungi, and or dry rot. Seller shall pay for all corrective work recommended, but not for preventative work.

Warranty

The seller agrees to furnish buyer a Home Maintenance Warranty, to be paid for by to become effective _____ immediately upon date of closing

_____ on _____ for a period of _____.

Said warranty to be issued by

_____

a home maintenance warranty company in accordance with its terms and conditions. Said warranty to be delivered to the buyer upon date of closing.

Soil Report

Subject to the buyer's right to disapprove, a soil report to be obtained and paid for by the buyer within _____days from date of acceptance. The buyer shall be given the right to enter property for such purpose.

Building Code

1. The seller warrants that there are no building code violations.

2. The seller has no current or prior or current knowledge of any building code violation.

SPECIAL CONSIDERATIONS FOR INCOME AND BUSINESS PROPERTIES

Rental Statement

1. The seller shall execute a rental statement within _____hours and deliver the rental statement to the broker showing all income to be as represented.

2. Subject to the buyer's right to inspect and disapprove rent statement within _____ hour's receipt thereof.

Zone Change

1. Subject to the buyer obtaining at his own expense _____ zoning. Seller agrees to sign all papers necessary to effectuate this zone change. Buyer to apply for said zoning within _____ days after acceptance of this offer.

2. Close of escrow to be _____days after all the appropriate agencies approve the subject property as _____ zone.

Leases

1. The buyer is purchasing property subject to the existing leases, which shall be assigned to him or her by the seller.

2. Subject to the buyer's right to inspect and disapprove leases within hours receipt thereof.

3. Seller shall continue to lease vacancies during the escrow period.

4. Any leases negotiated during the escrow period shall be subject to the approval of buyer.

Possession

1. Possession of property to be delivered to the buyer at close of escrow or on (enter appropriate date here)

_____

2. As a memorandum of understanding between the parties hereto, and with which the undersigned the broker is not to be concerned, possession of subject property will be given to the buyer at close of escrow or on

_____

3. The seller is to deliver the property free of tenancies at the close of escrow, allowing for the buyer to have full use.

Insulation Disclosure

Full disclosure is now required by the Federal Trade Commission of insulation performance on all new homes prior to sale. Whenever a new home is sold, the brokers who represent the sellers should be advised of the following:

1. All sales contract forms must be amended to include sufficient space for insulation data.

2. Insulation data must include type, thickness, and R-value.

3. The insulation data will be made available by the insulation manufacturer or home builder (a further requirement of the FTC rule) and such data may be relied on by the seller and his or her agent, the broker.

4. The data should be included on forms when listings on new homes are submitted to various multiple listing services.

Suggested language for the sales contract might be as follows:

Insulation will be installed in the home as follows:

1. Exterior walls will be insulated with a given insulation to certain thickness in inches which, according to the manufacturer, will yield an R-value of insulation.

2. Interior walls will be insulated with (state type of insulation) to a thickness of (state thickness of insulation) inches which, according to the manufacturer, will yield an R-value of _____.

Advance Rents

Advance rents, any security deposits and cleaning fees, if any, shall be assigned to the buyer and adjusted in cash, or trust deed to the seller.

Personal Property

1. The seller shall furnish an inventory and bill of sale for all personal property included in purchase price.

2. The seller shall issue bill of sale for the following personal property included in the sales price:

_____

_____

3. The seller shall furnish an inventory and bill of sale for all personal property included in purchase price. Buyer shall have the right to disapprove of same within _____ hours receipt thereof.

Maintenance

1. The seller agrees to maintain the building in good condition and repair during the escrow period.

2. During escrow period, the seller agrees to pay all escrow charges.

Title

1. Subject to the seller acquiring a clear title to the property.

2. The buyer reserves right to vest title in a corporation, limited partnership, or any other entity he or she determines.

3. Should title vest other than in the buyer, the seller reserves right to approve vestee.

Sale of Other Property

This agreement is conditioned upon the close of escrow number _____ with _____ Escrow Company, under an agreement dated _____ 20__, with _____(name of buyer) pertaining to the property described as _____(insert address here) Said escrow is set for closing not later than ___,20__. If this condition is not satisfied, the buyer may, at the buyer's election, by notice in writing to the seller, waive this condition or cancel this agreement. If no such notice of cancellation is given within _____days of the date set herein for close of escrow, this condition shall be deemed waived.

Income and Expense Statement

1. The seller shall execute an income and expense statement within _____ hours after accepting the offer and deliver this statement to the broker showing verifiable revenue and expenses as of the date of acceptance.

2. Subject to the buyer's right to inspect and disapprove the income and expense statement within _____hours receipt thereof.

Approvals

The buyer shall disapprove leases; rents; personal property inventory; revenue and expense statement within _____hours of receipt thereof or they shall be deemed approved.

Illegal Rents

1. The seller represents that structures such as guest house; patio; room addition; converted garage were built with a permit and are legal structures.

2. The seller does not represent structures or building as being legal rental units; guest house, etc. and it is understood by all parties concerned the buyer is purchasing subject property "as is."

OTHER CONSIDERATIONS

Flood Insurance

You must carry flood insurance if your property has a loan secured by real property and if the property is located in an area designated by the Federal Insurance Administration (FIA) as having special flood hazards, where flood insurance is available for sale in such areas under the National Flood Insurance Program. It is necessary to carry a policy equal to the amount of the outstanding balance on the loan for the property. If the loan on the property exceeds the maximum coverage available in the area, the maximum coverage is sufficient.

All real estate professionals must be familiar with the National Flood Insurance Program established by the National Flood Insurance Act and expanded by the Federal Disaster Protection Act. It is imperative to be able to share this information with clients so keep them safe and informed. This program provides subsidies to homeowners living in flood zone areas. In order to take advantage of this federal program, the community where the property is located must have qualified for such subsidies. A home lies in a special flood hazard area if there is a 1 percent chance the property will be flooded within one year, or a strong possibility the property will be flooded once every 100 years.

Remember
- A special flood hazard zone is defined as an area where there is a 1 percent chance of flooding in one year, and very likely to be flooded once every 100 years.

Flood insurance is offered under two different programs. The first program called the regular program, of flood insurance is available up to a maximum of $185,000 on the dwelling and $60,000 on the belongings within the home. The second program, or the emergency program, the maximum coverage available is $35,000 for a single-family dwelling and $10,000 for any belongings within the home.

The responsibility of the lending institution to disclose this information to the borrower. It is not unreasonable to believe that courts of law will hold that the unavailability of federally related financing of insurance for flood-prone areas is a latent defect which an owner him - or herself is bound to disclose to a prospective purchaser at the time of negotiating a contract to sell the real property. If the owner is responsible for disclosure, a real estate licensee acting as agent of the owner in the transaction will be equally responsible with the owner to make appropriate disclosures. Additionally, the licensee may have an independent duty by reason of his experience and expertise to advise the prospective seller concerning the flood insurance program and the ramifications of a community having qualified or failed to qualify for participation in the program.

The property owner must have obtained the appropriate amount of flood insurance in order to close on property located in a flood zone. The premiums for this insurance policy will be collected from the owner at the same time as the monthly payment for the note on the property.

Special Studies Zones Act
There are two very important provisions from the Alquist-Priollo Special Studies Zones Act affecting all licensees concerning the issue of earthquake fault displacement:

1. If a property being sold is within an area designated as a "special studies zone," the broker or seller (if no broker) must disclose the fact that the property is located within such a zone to the buyer.

Special Studies Zone and Flood Hazard Disclosure.

SPECIAL STUDIES ZONE AND FLOOD HAZARD DISCLOSURE
CALIFORNIA ASSOCIATION OF REALTORS® STANDARD FORM

This Addendum is attached as Page _____ of _____ Pages to the Real Estate Purchase Contract and Receipt for Deposit
dated _____ 19_____ in which _____

_____
is referred to as Buyer and _____

_____ is referred to as Seller.

SPECIAL STUDIES ZONE DISCLOSURE

The property which is the subject of the contract is situated in a Special Study Zone as designated under Sections 2621-2625, inclusive, of the California Public Resources Code; and, as such, the construction or development on this property of any structure for human occupancy may be subject to the findings of a geologic report prepared by a geologist registered in the State of California, unless such report is waived by the city or county under the terms of that act. No representations on the subject are made by Seller or Agent, and the Buyer should make his/her own inquiry or investigation.

Note: California Public Resources Code #2621.5 excludes structures in existence prior to May 4, 1975;
California Public Resources Code #2621.6 excludes wood frame dwellings not exceeding two (2) stories in height and mobilhomes over eight (8) feet in width;
California Public Resources Code #2621.7 excludes conversion of existing apartment houses into condominiums;
California Public Resources Code #2621.8 excludes alterations and additions under 50% of value of structure from the Special Studies Zone Act.

Buyer is allowed _____ days from date of Seller's acceptance to make further inquiries at appropriate governmental agencies concerning the use of the subject property under the terms of the Special Study Zone Act and local building, zoning, fire, health and safety codes. When such inquiries disclose conditions or information unsatisfactory to the Buyer, Buyer may cancel this agreement. If notice in writing has not been delivered within such time, this condition shall be deemed waived.

Receipt of a copy is hereby acknowledged.

DATED: _____, 19_____   BUYER: _____

Receipt of a copy is hereby acknowledged

DATED: _____, 19_____   SELLER: _____

_____

FLOOD HAZARD ZONE DISCLOSURE

The property which is the subject of the contract is situated in a "Flood Zone" as set forth on H.U.D. "Special Flood Zone Area Map". The law requires that as a condition of obtaining financing on most properties located in a "Flood Zone", Banks, Savings and Loan Associations, and some insurance lenders will require that H.U.D. flood insurance be carried where the property or its attachments are security for the loan.

This requirement is mandated by the H.U.D. National Insurance Program, which requirement became effective March 1, 1976. The purpose of the program is to provide flood insurance to property at a reasonable cost.

The extent of coverage available in your area and the cost of this coverage may vary, and for further information you should consult your lender or insurance carrier. No representation or recommendation is made by the Seller and the Brokers in this transaction or their agents or employees, as to the legal effect, interpretation, or economic consequences of the National Flood Insurance Program and related legislation.

Receipt of a copy is hereby acknowledged.

DATED: _____, 19_____   BUYER: _____

Receipt of a copy is hereby acknowledged

DATED: _____, 19_____   SELLER: _____

_____

NO REPRESENTATION IS MADE AS TO THE LEGAL VALIDITY OF ANY PROVISION OR THE ADEQUACY OF ANY PROVISION IN ANY SPECIFIC TRANSACTION. A REAL ESTATE BROKER IS THE PERSON QUALIFIED TO ADVISE ON REAL ESTATE. IF YOU DESIRE LEGAL ADVICE CONSULT YOUR ATTORNEY.

To order, contact—California Association of Realtors®
525 S. Virgil Ave., Los Angeles, California 90020
Copyright © 1977, California Association of Realtors® (Revised 1978)   FORM SSD-FHD-11   T-L5-FG

2. If a property is within a "special studies zone" and new construction or development is anticipated, a geologic report defining any hazard of surface fault ruptures is required (unless waived) by the agency issuing building permits.

It is not a requirement of geologic reports in referring to new construction when:

- No occupancy on developed land;
- The development has single-family wood-frame dwellings not exceeding two stories in height, unless the construction is part of development of four or more such dwellings;
- For mobile homes;
- If previous geologic reports have been made or if the report was waived for any reason;
- For condominium conversions;
- For alterations or additions to existing structures which do not exceed 50 percent of the value of existing structures.

You must disclose this fact if a property you are representing is within a special studies zone. Disclosure can be done on the listing agreement, deposit receipt, or escrow instructions, but preferably on all three.

Remember

If property is listed within a special studies zone, it should be disclosed on any one of the following, preferably all of them:

- Escrow Instructions
- Deposit Receipt
- Listing Agreement

The Alquist Priollo Act strictly deals with earthquake faults and where they lie. It certainly does not mean it is the only disclosure required regarding geologic hazards or warnings. Make sure to check with the city where property is located for additional disclosures and procedures to operate under all local laws.

Full disclosure is required by law of all licensees. Using the CAR form "Special Studies Zone and Flood Hazard Disclosure" easily makes this specific disclosure. The deposit receipt form will have an area where the agent can check signifying the property is in this special zone. If the agent checks this portion of the contract, the agent must also make sure the buyers read and sign the disclosure, then provide a copy to them. Many agents check off this portion of the deposit receipt agreement and then fail to deliver the addendum, which is considered illegal.

If a property is exempt from geologic report, but it is located within a special studies zone, this fact must be disclosed. There are maps available from the city or county planning director for you to determine whether a property is within a special studies zone. To inquire about local government policies and regulations, or to consult (or obtain) copies of specific special studies zones maps, contact the planning director of each county or city.

Soft Prices

The listing agent always has a fiduciary duty to the owner of the property. Additionally the listing agent is required by law to make all mandatory disclosures to a potential purchaser of the property. If an agent knows of a defect with the property, it must be disclosed to the buyer. Usually the cooperating agent is considered to be a subagent of the seller and therefore bound to the same fiduciary obligation to the seller as the listing agent. The fiduciary obligation carries with it a duty to act in the best interests of the seller in all respects, and full disclosure to the buyer. Therefore, neither the listing nor the selling agent should suggest to a prospective purchaser any terms or conditions that would be less favorable to the seller than the terms set forth in the listing agreement. In the event the seller has granted his or her agent power of attorney, or if the seller has specifically given the agent permission to act in this way, then the agent may suggest to a prospective purchaser different terms or conditions that may not be as favorable as the original terms.

Remember
- The listing agent is the seller's agent and owes fiduciary responsibility to the seller. Any subagents or cooperating agents are also considered an agent of the seller, and thus are obligated to give the seller full fiduciary responsibility.

Best Prevailing Rate

It is a common practice for agents to write contracts based on contingencies. These contingencies make assumptions or have requirements of the buyer that must be met in order for the contract to be valid. One of these contingencies is that the buyer qualify for the best financing prevailing rate. This must be clearly explained to both the buyer and seller, so there are no surprises or so that neither party get upset and pull out of the contract due to misunderstanding. If the buyer feels as if he or she did not receive the best rate possible, then he or she could pull out of the contract, upsetting the seller.

Should a contract state the buyer must qualify for the best prevailing rate, it should also be specific as to what financing terms are acceptable. Simply stating "best prevailing rate" is vague, and could be interpreted differently by different people. Specific financing terms in the purchase agreement prevent any confusion over what the best prevailing rate might be. These terms include the minimum principal amount to be obtained, the minimum term of the loan, the maximum interest rate, and the maximum loan charges. It is up to the buyer to make the effort to find a financing institution to meet these terms. Any restriction on the maximum amount or rate of interest is important in determining the extent to which the buyer may be entitled to reject a loan on the basis of the interest offered.

Sometimes term "prevailing rate of interest" accurately represents the intent of the parties who are in agreement as to the meaning of the financing terms and the consequences of its use. A licensee must fulfill their obligation to accurately and carefully prepare the agreement to express their clients intentions and take all necessary precautions to avoid creating an ambiguous document, one that might be considered void or rejected by one or both parties.

Because of the nature of the market there is a diversity of interest rates because the market at a given time is subject to frequent and wide fluctuation. The use of a "prevailing rate" standard may create confusion and lead to dispute over such questions as what group of lenders and what market area are to be considered in making up a representative sample whether a specific point in time or an extended period of time is to be considered, and whether the single most frequently charged rate among all lenders, or the range of rates as charged by a majority of most lenders, is to be considered as prevailing. If the purchase contract is prepared by a salesperson acting as an agent for seller, any ambiguities not otherwise resolved are likely to be interpreted against the seller in court. The type of the prospective loan may be significant in at least partially defining the market to be considered in applying a "prevailing rate" standard. For example, a loan to be assumed at least makes reference to a specific loan and lender. Taking "subject to" an existing loan concentrates on the sources available to finance the balance of the purchase price. A variable rate loan concerns the initial rate offered for such loans. The type of the loan under certain terms may even provide a reasonably clear definition of the term "prevailing."

In the event interest rates increase, the maximum interest rate written into the purchase contract may be higher than the prevailing rate. Should the buyer insists on the use of a "prevailing rate" standard, there should at least be clear agreement on what is meant by "prevailing rate." Additionally, the way this rate is to be determined should also be clear and agreed upon. A stated maximum should be given should that be the intention of the buyer. If there is a problem with the buyer obtaining a loan with the specific terms and stated maximum after a diligent good faith effort, the questions with respect to the seller's agent are likely to be whether the seller was aware of the consequences of the upward rise in rates and whether the seller desires to renegotiate.

Sometimes using stated interest rate maximum is better than using a "prevailing rate" standard, as a way to avoid problems. Additionally defining all terms used in the contract is imperative so they cannot be left open for interpretation, but will be clearly understood by all parties looking at the contract.

Broker Responsibility for Information Furnished by Owner

An agent must, without exception, disclose all material facts to the customer or third party. Even if instructed not to disclose these material facts by the principal, the agent is legally responsible for full disclosure. Material facts regarding a property include information regarding the structure or defects in the property. An agent may be held responsible for any misrepresentation made regarding the property.

Civil Code Section 1710.2. Material Facts Provision:
A material fact can be anything that affects the value or desirability of the subject property. Because this is such a broad definition, the legislature and courts have created their own interpretations of what the prospective purchaser must know about a property. Of course, conspicuous physical defects must be revealed; but, it is not always easy to determine what other facts must be revealed. It is not necessary, for instance, to reveal a death on the premises if it occurred more than three years before an offer to purchase or lease the property is made. Nevertheless, the agent handling such a property may not make a misrepresentation if asked a direct question by the buyer, which might reveal the fact of death. The agent, however, need not reveal that an occupant of the property was afflicted with, or died from, AIDS.

An agent has a duty to act with honesty and fairness when dealing with all third parties. Accidentally blurring the truth, or blatantly misrepresenting a property is a violation of the law. Agents must be very careful not to misrepresent any material facts to third parties; as the agent is liable in such cases and may have to pay monetary damages to the third party or place their license in jeopardy as a result of their misconduct. An agent is protected, however, from any misrepresentation made by the principal. For example, if a principal does not tell the agent that there is a leak in the roof, and the agent then does not disclose this to the customer, the agent cannot be held responsible for the principal's misrepresentation.

There are three types of misrepresentation: innocent misrepresentation, negligent misrepresentation and fraudulent misrepresentation.

- Innocent misrepresentations are statements made regarding property that are not known to be false at the time they are made. Agents are not held liable for misrepresentations of this nature, though the injured party may elect to cancel the purchase contract.

- Negligent misrepresentations are statements made with no material facts to back them up. For example, an agent may tell a prospective buyer that the roof was newly installed five years ago when he or she has no real knowledge of the age of the roof. In such cases, an agent may be held liable for such statements.

- Fraudulent misrepresentations are false statements made by the agent despite the fact that the truth is known.

Puffing is also a form of misrepresentation to which an agent must be careful not to fall prey. An agent may make a false statement regarding a property if he or she believes it will aid in selling the property. An agent may be held responsible for any damages caused as a result of these statements.

An 'as is' clause in a contract does not eliminate the broker's responsibility of disclosure to the buyer. Even if a contract contains an 'as is' clause the broker must disclose all material facts to the buyer(s) just as if there were no 'as is' clause in place. The broker may be held liable for damages suffered due to a withholding of facts regarding the property.

The court case of *Easton v. Strassburger* (1984) expanded the agent's duty of full disclosure to third parties. This case dealt with a home built over a landfill. The agent noticed that there were uneven floors on the property. The verdict in this case not only made it mandatory for an agent to disclose any defects in the property that they could visually identify; it also required sellers to disclose to the agent any defects that could not be identified through a casual visual inspection. As a result of this case, agents are now required to make a competent inspection of a property and disclose their findings to all third parties.

When advertising property, **agents** must be careful not to make statements, which may lead customers to believe that the agent's opinions are fact. For example, an agent whose advertisement for homes in a new neighborhood claims the neighborhood is in the best school district in the city must be able to back up this claim with raw data (such as standardized test scores comparing the performance of students in its own and other school districts). If there is no data present to back up such claims, an agent may be held liable for his or her statements.

Real Estate Transfer Disclosure Statement.

REAL ESTATE TRANSFER DISCLOSURE STATEMENT
(CALIFORNIA CIVIL CODE 1102, ET SEQ.)
CALIFORNIA ASSOCIATION OF REALTORS® (CAR) STANDARD FORM

THIS DISCLOSURE STATEMENT CONCERNS THE REAL PROPERTY SITUATED IN THE CITY OF _____
_____, COUNTY OF _____, STATE OF CALIFORNIA
DESCRIBED AS _____
THIS STATEMENT IS A DISCLOSURE OF THE CONDITION OF THE ABOVE DESCRIBED PROPERTY IN COMPLIANCE
WITH SECTION 1102 OF THE CIVIL CODE AS OF _____, 19____. IT IS NOT A WARRANTY
OF ANY KIND BY THE SELLER(S) OR ANY AGENT(S) REPRESENTING ANY PRINCIPAL(S) IN THIS TRANSACTION,
AND IS NOT A SUBSTITUTE FOR ANY INSPECTIONS OR WARRANTIES THE PRINCIPAL(S) MAY WISH TO OBTAIN.

I
COORDINATION WITH OTHER DISCLOSURE FORMS

This Real Estate Transfer Disclosure Statement is made pursuant to Section 1102 of the Civil Code. Other statutes require disclosures,
depending upon the details of the particular real estate transaction (for example: special study zone and purchase—money liens on
residential property).

Substituted Disclosures: The following disclosures have or will be made in connection with this real estate transfer, and are intended to
satisfy the disclosure obligations on this form, where the subject matter is the same: _____
_____
_____

(list all substituted disclosure forms to be used in connection with this transaction)

II
SELLER'S INFORMATION

The Seller discloses the following information with the knowledge that even though this is not a warranty, prospective Buyers may rely on this
information in deciding whether and on what terms to purchase the subject property. Seller hereby authorizes any agent(s) representing any
principal(s) in this transaction to provide a copy of this statement to any person or entity in connection with any actual or anticipated sale of the
property.

THE FOLLOWING ARE REPRESENTATIONS MADE BY THE SELLER(S) AND ARE NOT THE REPRESENTATIONS OF
THE AGENT(S), IF ANY. THIS INFORMATION IS A DISCLOSURE AND IS NOT INTENDED TO BE PART OF ANY
CONTRACT BETWEEN THE BUYER AND SELLER.

Seller ☐ is ☐ is not occupying the property.

A. The subject property has the items checked below (read across):

☐ Range	☐ Oven	☐ Microwave
☐ Dishwasher	☐ Trash Compactor	☐ Garbage Disposal
☐ Washer/Dryer Hookups	☐ Window Screens	☐ Rain Gutters
☐ Burglar Alarms	☐ Smoke Detector(s)	☐ Fire Alarm
☐ T.V. Antenna	☐ Satellite Dish	☐ Intercom
☐ Central Heating	☐ Central Air Conditioning	☐ Evaporator Cooler(s)
☐ Wall/Window Air Conditioning	☐ Sprinklers	☐ Public Sewer System
☐ Septic Tank	☐ Sump Pump	☐ Water Softener
☐ Patio/Decking	☐ Built-in Barbeque	☐ Gazebo
☐ Sauna	☐ Pool	☐ Spa ☐ Hot Tub
☐ Security Gate(s)	☐ Garage Door Opener(s)	☐ Number of Remote Controls _____
Garage: ☐ Attached	☐ Not Attached	☐ Carport
Pool/Spa Heater: ☐ Gas	☐ Solar	☐ Electric
Water Heater: ☐ Gas	☐ Solar	☐ Electric
Water Supply: ☐ City	☐ Well	☐ Private Utility ☐ Other _____
Gas Supply: ☐ Utility	☐ Bottled	

Exhaust Fan(s) in _____ 220 Volt Wiring in _____
Fireplace(s) in _____ ☐ Gas Starter
☐ Roof(s): Type: _____ Age: _____ (approx.)
☐ Other: _____
Are there, to the best of your (Seller's) knowledge, any of the above that are not in operating condition? ☐ Yes ☐ No If yes, then describe.
(Attach additional sheets if necessary.): _____
_____
_____

B. Are you (Seller) aware of any significant defects/malfunctions in any of the following? ☐ Yes ☐ No If yes, check
appropriate space(s) below.
☐ Interior Walls ☐ Ceilings ☐ Floors ☐ Exterior Walls ☐ Insulation ☐ Roof(s) ☐ Windows ☐ Doors ☐ Foundation ☐ Slab(s)
☐ Driveways ☐ Sidewalks ☐ Walls/Fences ☐ Electrical Systems ☐ Plumbing/Sewers/Septics ☐ Other Structural Components
(Describe: _____
_____)

If any of the above is checked, explain. (Attach additional sheets if necessary.): _____
_____
_____

Buyer and Seller acknowledge receipt of a copy of this page, which constitutes Page 1 of 2 Pages.
Buyer's Initials (_____) (_____) Seller's Initials (_____) (_____)

Subject Property Address _____

C. Are you (Seller) aware of any of the following:

1. Features of the property shared in common with adjoining landowners, such as walls, fences, and driveways, whose use or responsibility for maintenance may have an effect on the subject property. .... ☐ Yes ☐ No
2. Any encroachments, easements or similar matters that may affect your interest in the subject property. .... ☐ Yes ☐ No
3. Room additions, structural modifications, or other alterations or repairs made without necessary permits. .... ☐ Yes ☐ No
4. Room additions, structural modifications, or other alterations or repairs not in compliance with building codes. ...... ☐ Yes ☐ No
5. Landfill (compacted or otherwise) on the property or any portion thereof. .... ☐ Yes ☐ No
6. Any settling from any cause, or slippage, sliding, or other soil problems. .... ☐ Yes ☐ No
7. Flooding, drainage or grading problems. .... ☐ Yes ☐ No
8. Major damage to the property or any of the structures from fire, earthquake, floods, or landslides. .... ☐ Yes ☐ No
9. Any zoning violations, non-conforming uses, violations of "setback" requirements. .... ☐ Yes ☐ No
10. Neighborhood noise problems or other nuisances. .... ☐ Yes ☐ No
11. CC&R's or other deed restrictions or obligations. .... ☐ Yes ☐ No
12. Homeowners' Association which has any authority over the subject property. .... ☐ Yes ☐ No
13. Any "common area" (facilities such as pools, tennis courts, walkways, or other areas co-owned in undivided interest with others). .... ☐ Yes ☐ No
14. Any notices of abatement or citations against the property. .... ☐ Yes ☐ No
15. Any lawsuits against the seller threatening to or affecting this real property. .... ☐ Yes ☐ No

If the answer to any of these is yes, explain. (Attach additional sheets if necessary.): _____

_____

_____

Seller certifies that the information herein is true and correct to the best of the Seller's knowledge as of the date signed by the Seller.

Seller _____ Date _____

Seller _____ Date _____

III
AGENT'S INSPECTION DISCLOSURE

(To be completed only if the seller is represented by an agent in this transaction.)
THE UNDERSIGNED, BASED ON THE ABOVE INQUIRY OF THE SELLER(S) AS TO THE CONDITION OF THE PROPERTY AND BASED ON A REASONABLY COMPETENT AND DILIGENT VISUAL INSPECTION OF THE ACCESSIBLE AREAS OF THE PROPERTY IN CONJUNCTION WITH THAT INQUIRY, STATES THE FOLLOWING:

_____

_____

Agent (Broker
Representing Seller) _____ By _____ Date _____
           (Please Print)   (Associate Licensee or Broker-Signature)

IV
AGENT'S INSPECTION DISCLOSURE

(To be completed only if the agent who has obtained the offer is other than the agent above.)
THE UNDERSIGNED, BASED ON A REASONABLY COMPETENT AND DILIGENT VISUAL INSPECTION OF THE ACCESSIBLE AREAS OF THE PROPERTY, STATES THE FOLLOWING:

_____

_____

Agent (Broker
obtaining the Offer) _____ By _____ Date _____
           (Please Print)   (Associate Licensee or Broker-Signature)

V

BUYER(S) AND SELLER(S) MAY WISH TO OBTAIN PROFESSIONAL ADVICE AND/OR INSPECTIONS OF THE PROPERTY AND TO PROVIDE FOR APPROPRIATE PROVISIONS IN A CONTRACT BETWEEN BUYER AND SELLER(S) WITH RESPECT TO ANY ADVICE/INSPECTIONS/DEFECTS.

I/WE ACKNOWLEDGE RECEIPT OF A COPY OF THIS STATEMENT.

Seller _____ Date _____ Buyer _____ Date _____

Seller _____ Date _____ Buyer _____ Date _____

Agent (Broker
Representing Seller) _____ By _____ Date _____
           (Please Print)   (Associate Licensee or Broker-Signature)

Agent (Broker
obtaining the Offer) _____ By _____ Date _____
           (Please Print)   (Associate Licensee or Broker-Signature)

A REAL ESTATE BROKER IS QUALIFIED TO ADVISE ON REAL ESTATE. IF YOU DESIRE LEGAL ADVICE, CONSULT YOUR ATTORNEY.

┌─────── OFFICE USE ONLY ───────┐
│ Reviewed by Broker or Designee _____ │
│ Date _____ │
└───────────────────────────────┘
SF-Feb 87

BROKER'S COPY

235

Agents are not only responsible for their own misrepresentation; they are also responsible for any misrepresentations made by their principal. The principal is responsible for his or her own actions, the acts of an agent or subagent on behalf of the principal, and torts committed by an agent who is an employee of the principal. Principles utilizing an independent contractor, however, are not held responsible for the actions of the contractor.

A recovery account was set up in California to aid those victims of fraud or misrepresentation in real estate. The account is designed for those who cannot collect from a licensee after a court judgment. The recovered account allows individuals to collect up to $20,000 per transaction and $100,000 per licensee. The money for the recovery fund comes from license fees collected from each licensee's license fee (currently 5% of the total fee) is placed in the recovery account for damage restitution. Recovery against a licensee will result in immediate suspension of his or her license. The license is reinstated when the licensee repays the recovery account in full (plus any interest that may have accrued).

Remember
- Five percent of every licensee's license fee is placed in a recovery account designed to protect individuals from fraud or misrepresentation.

One way an agent can protect him or herself is by using a transfer disclosure statement. Transfer disclosure statements are prescribed in the California Civil Code 1102, and they are forms used to disclose facts regarding the property.

Beginning January 1, 1987 the California State Legislature required all sellers of property consisting of one to four units to supply the buyer with a real estate transfer disclosure statement. This statement tells the exactly buyer what the seller knows about the condition of a property. All current defects or potential problems that could affect the value of the property (as well as the future value of the property) must be mentioned in the transfer disclosure statement. This statement must be given to all potential buyers before an offer is presented. Otherwise, the buyer has the right to rescind the offer within three business days.

Usury
Usury is when a person claims a rate of interest greater than that permitted by law. Generally the law allows 10%.

Regarding the sale or property, there are no prohibitions against usury in California. As a result, a seller of real property who takes back a secured promissory note as a deferred payment of part of the purchase price is not in violation of the prohibition against usury, even if the promissory note bears interest at more than the statutory maxi-mum rate, which until Proposition 2 in 1979 had been 10 percent.

Proposition 2 retains the 10 percent maximum for loans for personal, family, or household purposes, but does not limit real estate. For real estate, the usury limit is 10% or the prevailing annual rate charged by member banks of the Federal Reserve Bank of San Francisco plus 5%, which ever is greater. However, loans made or arranged by licensed California real estate brokers and secured by real property are exempt from the constitutional limitations. All of this just means that a licensee may charge whatever borrowers are willing to pay.

As long as the seller does not transfer the note and deed of trust to a third party at the close of escrow, the transaction does not violate any usury provisions in California Law. Invariably, this type of transaction is not characterized as a "loan or forbearance of any money," which would subject it to the usury statutes. Rather, the transaction is characterized as a "sale" not subject to the usury provisions. The California Supreme Court has attempted to define the distinction between a "sale" and a "loan":

A sale is the transfer of the property or any other items for a price. The transfer of the property is the thing sold for a price is the essence of the transaction. The transfer is that of the general or absolute interest in property as distinguished from a special property interest. A loan, on the other hand, is the delivery of a sum of money to another under a contract to return at some future time an equivalent amount with or without an additional sum agreed upon for its use;

Sales transactions in real property where the seller gives the buyer the purchase money promissory notes are governed under usury laws. It is considered usurious if the effective rate of interest exceeds the statutory maximum percent per year.

A prearranged discounted sale of a purchase money promissory note may be considered by a court of law to be a loan subject to the legal restrictions on interest. The prearranged transfer of the note could be interpreted as a loan because the third party is in effect financing the purchase of the real property. That is, the seller receives cash, and the third party will be deemed to have loaned the money to the buyer to finance the purchase. If, however, there was no prearrangement for financing of the transaction by a third party, the law of usury presumably would not apply, and there would be no legal limit on the interest rate that the seller could charge to the buyer.

To avoid problems with the usury laws, avoid situations in which the seller of real property takes back a purchase money note and deed of trust with an interest rate in excess of the statutory maximum and where: 1) it is prearranged before the sale is consummated for a third party to take over the note and deed of trust executed in favor of the seller; or 2) it looks as if it is prearranged by a transfer of the purchase money note and deed of trust from seller to a third party soon after the close of escrow.

Disclosures
Full disclosure is required in all aspects of the real estate transaction. This includes the lenders right to accelerate the loan. Sometimes this is called calling the loan, or when the lender demands payment in full on a loan. The real estate transfer disclosure statement will have an example format for this disclosure.

"As Is" Sale
Selling a property "as is" is when property is transferred to the buyer with no express warranty or guarantee. The seller basically waives all responsibility to make repairs or correct any problems. Sometimes this is referred to as caveat emptor or A Latin phrase meaning " let the buyer beware"; the legal maxim stating that the buyer must examine the goods or property and buy at his or her own risk.

An 'as is' clause in a contract does not eliminate the broker's responsibility of disclosure to the buyer. Even if a contract contains an 'as is' clause the broker must disclose all material facts to the buyer(s) just as if there were no 'as is' clause in place. The broker may be held liable for damages suffered due to a withholding of facts regarding the property.

The court case of *Easton v. Strassburger* (1984) expanded the agent's duty of full disclosure to third parties. This case dealt with a home built over a landfill. The agent noticed that there were uneven floors on the property. The verdict in this case not only made it mandatory for an agent to disclose any defects in the property that they could visually identify; it also required sellers to disclose to the agent any defects that could not be identified through a casual visual inspection. As a result of this case, agents are now required to make a competent inspection of a property and disclose their findings to all third parties.

A purchaser inspecting an improved real property, such as a residence, is certainly expected to have information about the property, which a reasonable inspection would disclose. However, hidden structural imperfections known only to the seller and/or the seller's agent that are not disclosed to the purchaser, such as a problematic roof that looks new but leaks during heavy rains, , an owner-built den constructed without a permit and not according to code, or recurring plumbing problems, pose a different question.

Proving that Compensation is Earned
The principal owes a commission to the broker when:

1. The broker initiates a valid binding contract upon terms and conditions agreeable to the principal. If the seller and buyer later rescind, the broker still earns a commission based on the listing contract

2. The broker is the procuring cause, or the person who initiated the sale

3. They produce a ready, willing and able buyer for the property, as described in the listing

"Ready and willing" means that the buyer is willing to enter into a binding purchase contract. "Able" means that the buyer is financially able to purchase the property.

Once an agent has fulfilled the contractual obligations of a listing, he or she is entitled to the agreed-upon commission. Fulfilling these obligations means finding a ready, willing and able buyer who meets all of the seller's requirements. In addition a written offer, signed by both parties, must be produced.

In a situation where there are many different brokers showing potential customers the same property, the agent receiving compensation must be the broker who procured the sale of the home. The procuring broker is the one who presented the qualified buyer to the seller and wrote the accepted offer.

Commissions are usually paid as a percentage of the selling price of the property. This also applies to rental properties where the commission is a percentage of the rental fee for those properties compensating the manager in this way. Commissions are earned when the agent both procures a ready, willing and able buyer who meets all the qualifications set forth by the seller as well as when the seller has accepted a purchase contract. This includes all counter offers or changes to the original purchase contract. All negotiations must be complete and acceptable to the seller.

In an agency agreement, if the seller decides to cancel the agency, he or she is allowed, but may be held liable for any or all of the agent's commission. If the seller maintains an open listing and a broker other than the listing broker procures the sale of the home, the procuring broker, rather than the listing agent, will receive a commission.

If the listing broker utilizes an exclusive authorization and right-to-sell listing agreement, that broker will make a commission regardless of which agent actually sells the home. Brokers generally work with each other in the sale of homes. If there are two brokers

A principle owes his or her agent the duty of care. This means that the principal may not sabotage the agent in securing a ready, willing and able buyer for the property. For instance, the principal may not make a private deal with the person the agent has secured to buy the property (cutting the agent out of the process). When a broker produces a buyer who meets all of the seller's terms, a commission is earned by the broker.

Commissions are not set by law. Rather, commissions are a negotiable amount agreed upon by the listing agent and the principal. California does not regulate the maximum or minimum amount a broker may charge a principal. Instead, it is left to the individual agent to decide.

Remember
- If a broker finds a ready, willing and able buyer, and then the seller insists on filling out all the paperwork him or herself, accepting an offer from the buyer, this is considered a consummated contract, as the seller accepted a buyer's bid. If the seller makes a mistake on the paperwork, causing the deal to fall apart, the broker is still entitled to a commission.

Due-on-Sale Clauses
The **due-on-sale or alienation clause** demands that the entire amount of the note be paid in the event that a property owner transfers ownership to another individual. A lender will typically do this to protect themselves from unqualified borrowers assuming the original loan, thus protecting the lender's interest from default.

"Due-on" provisions originally were intended to enable a lender from someone with bad credit assuming the loan, or one who was unable to pay the monthly payments on the note. Recently, however, many lenders have used the clause merely to impose higher interest rates on a prospective purchaser interested in taking over the seller's existing trust deed obligation. This has effectively prevented sellers from offering prospective buyers the opportunity to assume the seller's existing loan at typically lower interest rates as an incentive to purchase. Consequently, the "due-on" clause, originally intended as a means of protecting a lender's security interest, has evolved into a device for maximizing a lender's interest income.

S U M M A R Y

Being able to write a good, clear and legal purchase agreement is not as easy as it might seem. The purchase agreement, or deposit receipt, is a preprinted form that you will obtain from your broker and is relatively simple to follow and understand. A skilled licensee will utilize a checklist to make sure he or she has addressed all areas of the contract, consulting with another professional or attorney for unusual situations. This chapter covered in depth both financing requirements and nonfinancial portions of the purchase agreement. It is important for you to understand these sections and clauses, as your client will most likely need instruction on what they mean and information on all possible options that he or she has with each clause. Remember, you are not there to give advice or tell them how they should fill out a specific section, but you are there to inform them of all their options. What seems like a lot of technical forms and simple blanks to fill out can be challenging and require your careful attention to detail.

T E R M S   A N D   P H R A S E S

Acceleration Clause – The right of a lender to call the entire amount due on a note under a given circumstance.

Alienation – Also called a "due-on-sale" clause, it is a provision allowing a lender to require that any remaining balance of principal and interest on a loan be paid immediately upon the sale, transfer, conveyance, or further encumbrance of the property.

All Inclusive Trust Deed (AITD) – Also called a wrap around loan, the AITD is a junior financing instrument that wraps around the existing loans, yet is subject to them in order of priority. In the event of default, the trust deed recorded first will be paid first, and so forth.

Alquist Priollo – A legislative act making disclosure of property in special study zones mandatory, to let a potential buyer know if the property lies on earthquake fault lines.

"As Is" – A seller's statement that he or she is selling a home in its current condition and takes no responsibility for any improvements or repairs.

Best Prevailing Rate – The term means that the purchase contract is contingent upon the buyer finding the best rate of interest.

Caveat Emptor – "Let the buyer beware

Compensation – The payment a real estate agent will receive for procuring a ready, willing and able buyer, who makes an accepted offer on property. Compensation can also be referred to as commission.

Due on sale – A clause in a loan requiring full payment of the note in the event the property is sold.

Prepayment Penalty – The penalty incurred when paying off a loan, specifically a home loan, early.

Procuring Cause - The cause originating from a series of events that, without a break in continuity, results in the prime object of an agent's employment producing a final buyer.

"Subject To" – A phrase usually associated with the purchase agreement or deposit receipt, meaning the contract is valid and enforceable if certain conditions happen, such as the buyer being approved for a loan, or the seller being able to produce a clear and transferable title to the property.

Trust Deed – Similar to a mortgage, a trust deed is a legal document by which a borrower pledges certain real property or collateral as a guarantee for the repayment of a loan.

Usury – Claiming a rate of interest on a loan greater than that permitted by law.

1. A good purchase agreement is:
    a. Very specific, with no room for interpretation.
    b. General, with a few specifications but room for interpretation to make changes as necessary.
    c. Vague, leaving the ability for either party to alter the contract as he or she sees fit.
    d. None of the above.

2. An All Inclusive Trust Deed (AITD) is also called:
    a. Second trust deed
    b. Junior trust deed
    c. Wrap around loan
    d. Both A and B

3. Legal competency means:
    a. The ability of a licensee to understand and pass the law portion of the state real estate exam.
    b. The ability of a licensee to draw up a good, valid contract and the wherewithal to explain this contract to the client.
    c. The ability of a licensee to testify in court in the event a contract should be disputed.
    d. All of the above

4. A licensee will usually consult what source when filling out a simple purchase agreement form?
    a. An attorney to make sure everything is legal and correct.
    b. His or her broker for verification everything is correct as written.
    c. The California Association of Realtors® to make sure all local laws are being followed as well as state laws.
    d. A checklist to make sure nothing has been overlooked.

5. "Subject to" as used in a purchase agreement most nearly means:
    a. Conditional on the seller's acceptance of the contract.
    b. Conditional on the buyer's ability to secure financing
    c. Conditional on the seller's ability to produce a clear and transferable title
    d. All of the above

6. The prepayment penalty clause states:
    a. There will be no penalty for paying the monthly payment due at the beginning of the month instead of the end of the month.
    b. There will be no penalty for a late payment.
    c. There will be no penalty for making a larger payment than required.
    d. There will be no penalty for making a smaller payment than required.

7. The buyer can vest title as:
    a. A corporation
    b. A limited partnership
    c. Joint tenancy
    d. All of the above

8. Who must carry flood insurance?
   a. All buyers who have financed any part of a property.
   b. All buyers who have financed any part of a property located in a special floods hazard zone.
   c. Only those properties built before 1983 located in a special flood hazard zone.
   d. Only those properties built before 1978 located in a special flood hazard zone.

9. A special flood zone exists when there is:
   a. A 1% chance the land will be flooded each year.
   b. A strong chance the land will be flooded once every 100 years.
   c. Both A and B
   d. Neither A nor B

10. Who is responsible for disclosing to the buyer that the property they are interested in is located in a special studies zone?
    a. Seller
    b. Agent
    c. Lending institution
    d. Both A and B

11. A special studies zone refers to what geological condition or natural occurrence?
    a. Earthquake fault displacement
    b. High fire zone
    c. Flood zone
    d. Land located on top of a natural resource such as natural gas or oil.

12. Both the real estate agent and any cooperating brokers working on selling the property have a fiduciary responsibility to which party?
    a. Seller
    b. Buyer
    c. Both A and B
    d. Neither A nor B

13. Purchase agreements are usually contingent upon:
    a. The buyer finding a loan with a predetermined maximum interest rate or less.
    b. The buyer finding a loan with a predetermined maximum monthly payment or less.
    c. The buyer finding a loan with a predetermined maximum loan charge or less.
    d. All of the above.

14. A property being sold "as is" requires:
    a. No disclosure of any conditions or problems of which the seller is aware.
    b. Only disclosure on visible problems, but no disclosure necessary on conditions or problems not visible without a property inspection.
    c. Disclosure on all conditions and problems.
    d. Full inspections performed, and all reports delivered to the appropriate parties.

15. A transfer disclosure statement is required when selling what type of property?
    a. All privately owned residential properties.
    b. All residential property containing one to four living units.
    c. Residential property consisting of detached, single family homes only.
    d. On commercial property.

16. Requiring payment in full on any outstanding balance of a loan for a property being sold is called:
    a. Alquist Priollo
    b. Caveat Emptor
    c. Alienation
    d. All Inclusive Trust Deed

17. Property located within a special studies zone must be disclosed on which of the following documents?
    a. Listing agreement
    b. Deposit receipt
    c. Escrow instructions
    d. All of the above

18. "Due on sale" clauses do what?
    a. Protect a lender's interests
    b. Maximize the lenders interest income
    c. Cause the seller to loose money
    d. Both A and B

19. The cause originating from a series of events that, without break in continuity, results in the prime object of an agent's employment producing a final buyer is called:
    a. Procuring clause
    b. "Subject to" clause
    c. Alienation clause
    d. As is clause

20. A broker will have earned a commission when:
    a. He or she finds a ready, willing and able buyer
    b. He or she he has brought the buyer and seller together and enabled them to enter into a binding contract
    c. He or she has taken a listing agreement on a property
    d. When escrow closes

REAL ESTATE FINANCING

What you will learn in this Chapter

- Funding
- The Mortgage Money Market
- Conforming Loans
- Conventional Loans
- Other Types of Loans
- Interest Rates
- Financing
- Finance Regulation

Test Your Knowledge

1. A loan generated from the Government National Mortgage Association (GNMA) or Ginnie Mae is considered to be:
    a. Primary financing
    b. Secondary financing
    c. First trust deed
    d. None of the above

2. Conforming loans:
    a. Meet all Fannie Mae or Freddie Mac underwriting standards
    b. Are not assumable
    c. May be written for 15 or 30 years
    d. All of the above are correct

3. Commercial banks, savings associations, and life insurance companies are examples of which type of lender?
    a. Institutional lenders
    b. Commercial lenders
    c. Residential lenders
    d. Non-institutional lenders

4. What is the maximum commission a loan broker could make on a 5 year first trust deed under $30,000?
    a. 3%
    b. 5%
    c. 10%
    d. 15%

5. Shorter processing time, less red tape and more flexibility describes which type of loan?
    a. Government backed loan
    b. Conventional loan
    c. Commercial loan
    d. Institutional loan

6. A loan where the interest rate changes periodically, usually in relation to an index, with payments going up or down accordingly is called:
    a. Fixed rate.
    b. All inclusive trust deed
    c. Adjustable rate mortgage
    d. Piggyback note

7. Qualifying the borrower usually involves the three "C's". Which of the following is correct?
    a. Character
    b. Capacity
    c. Collateral
    d. All of the above are correct

INTRODUCTION

Home ownership is one of the largest (if not the largest) investments a person can make. Since few people can afford to purchase a home with cash, the vast majority of homeowners are currently paying off a mortgage (or trust deed, as it is called in California). So it is important for you, the real estate agent, to understand how financing works and provide advice to your clients accordingly. By knowing what programs are available to your client and providing the client with advice and guidance to speak with a mortgage broker, you can help homeownership become a more realistic goal than he or she may have thought possible.

In this chapter, we will learn about real estate financing and how it operates. We will look at the different programs and options people have when financing a home, and how those financing options function. Real estate finance has evolved far beyond obtaining a loan at a local bank; yet, it is still often just as simple as that. Pay close attention to terms or concepts to which you are introduced, as most ideas in real estate finance are related to each other in some fashion.

FUNDING

Most people will rely on some sort of financing to make their dreams a reality. Because our money market is a dynamic environment, constantly changing, the amount of money available will not always be the same, nor will the same sources of funding be available for all people.

Almost all of us are familiar with the terms "trust deeds" and "mortgages." The majority of homebuyers rely on financing their homes through trust deeds and mortgages, sometimes simply referred to as long-term financing. Trust deeds, which are primarily used in California, can be funded from many different sources. These sources include commercial banks, credit unions, savings associations and mortgage companies to name a few. Regardless of the source of the funds they will all fall into two categories direct or indirect financing. Direct financing occurs when the funds to purchase a home come directly from the individual or company lending out their own money. This is money they have saved up that is not borrowed from any other source. Indirect financing comes from lending institutions, like a bank, that uses other people's money. A bank typically lends out the money that is deposited into savings accounts.

Your clients will typically have questions regarding funding, and the more you know about the current money market, the more information you can pass along to the clients. This knowledge on the current markets will help make you look more authoritative regarding the entire real estate process and help your clients select the best loan and financial source for his or her purchase.

THE MORTGAGE MARKET

The mortgage market consists of the primary and secondary mortgage markets. Under each of the primary and secondary markets there are subdivisions. These subdivisions determine where the money comes from and the type of lenders that provide funds for consumers. As mentioned briefly earlier in the chapter, the main source of money for real estate loans comes from individual savings accounts held in banks and savings institutions.

Primary Mortgage Market

In the primary mortgage market, lenders make loans directly to the consumer. These are purchase money loans made in the form of a trust deed for the lender to purchase property. Both institutional and non-institutional lenders can make these purchase money loans in the primary money market.

Primary Mortgage Market:
- Made up of institutional and non-institutional lenders
- Loans are made directly to the consumers
- Provides purchase money loans in the form of a trust deed.

Institutional Lenders

Institutional lenders are conventional lenders and are perhaps the financial institutions we first think of when we need to borrow money for a home. Institutional lenders include savings banks, commercial banks, mutual savings banks, credit unions and insurance companies. These lenders obtain money for loans by using the money of depositors who maintain a savings account in their institution. The lenders then may loan that money to those who wish to borrow funds for a property purchase (or any other purchase, for that matter). The process by which the financial institution takes the depositors' money and transfer it to borrowers is called **intermediation**.

Institutional lenders include:
- Savings Banks
- Commercial Banks
- Mutual Savings Banks
- Credit Unions
- Insurance Companies

Savings banks are financial institutions that use money in an individual's savings account to make loans in the form of trust deeds. Because savings banks consist primarily of savings accounts held by private individuals and because most mortgages are made from personal savings accounts, savings banks are the main source for home loans. Savings banks are made up of both state- and federally-chartered institutions, and make it very simple for people to place excess money into a savings account to earn interest.

Commercial banks are the most versatile of all lenders. They make home loans, equity loans, business loans and other short-term loans. Commercial banks make quite a few construction loans, as they are short term and are paid off as soon as the property is sold. Commercial banks also lend money for traditional trust deeds, though not on the same scale as savings banks.

Mutual savings banks allow the depositors to share in the profits of the entire bank once all formal expenses, reserves and contributions to the surplus have been made. This means that the depositors will not only make money from the money they have deposited in the bank, but they will also draw interest on all funds the bank handles, once all bank obligations have been met. Mutual savings banks are uncommon in California.

Credit unions were developed as financial cooperatives by and for members who hold the same occupation (e.g., educators). These cooperatives offer their members some benefits that a traditional bank or savings institution cannot offer, such as higher paid interest rates on deposits and lower interest rates on loans.

Insurance companies are not thought of as traditional lenders when it comes to real estate, yet they are able to provide funds for the purchase of property. Insurance companies will not generally provide a home loan to an individual, but they provide large-scale loans to developers who are building several properties at a time or commercial properties that require a high dollar investment. Additionally, insurance companies participate in the secondary mortgage market. This means they will buy or sell government issued loans. This information will be examined later in this chapter.

Non-Institutional Lenders
Non-institutional lenders are a separate group, different from institutional lenders. When we think of obtaining a loan for property, we typically think of one or more of the traditional lenders. Non-institutional lenders (with the exception of mortgage companies) do not usually come to mind. Some non-institutional lenders we will study are mortgage companies, non-financial institutions and private individuals.

Non-Institutional Lenders:
- Mortgage Companies
- Non-Financial Lenders
- Private Individuals

The process by which **mortgage companies** lend may be a bit confusing for consumers who are trying to secure a real property loan. Does a mortgage company make the loan itself? Do they just do the legwork for the buyer, to find the best options from a number of available lenders? In actuality, a mortgage company may do both. Some mortgage companies actually use their own money to extend purchase loans in the form of trust deeds. These companies are considered **mortgage banks**. Other companies, called **mortgage brokers**, help borrowers find a lender who satisfies their needs. Usually when a mortgage bank makes a loan to a borrower, this loan is eventually sold to an investor. Again, this is not as clear as a traditional bank, which makes loans to borrowers who, in turn, make payments to the bank for the term of the loan.

When a mortgage company does not use their own money, but uses funding from a commercial bank with the intentions to sell the loan to an investor, the mortgage company is **warehousing the mortgage**. By doing this, the mortgage company will make a profit, and use those profits to make additional loans. The mortgage company then sells those loans to investors, as well.

Because of the nature of the mortgage company being a warehousing entity, they usually secure loans made by a government institution. These loan types are generally FHA or VA loans. The advantage in making such loans is that they are easily sold in the secondary mortgage market. Mortgage companies also seek conventional loans, which have advance purchase commitments. Clearly, the biggest role of the mortgage companies is to originate, service, then sell the loans, moving on to the next client as soon as possible.

Mortgage Companies:
- Make mortgages using their own money, and then sell those mortgages to investors
- Act as an intermediary between lenders and borrowers
- Usually secure conventional or VA loans so they can be easily sold into the secondary mortgage market

There are procedures that must be followed to insure that loans made by a mortgage broker are ultimately sold in the secondary mortgage market. In order for loans to be sold in the secondary mortgage market, the applicant must follow the following procedures:

- A loan application must be filled out by the customer

- A credit report of the loan applicant must be ordered

- The property involved must be appraised

- The full application package must be presented to the lender. The full package includes: the application form; the borrower's financial statement; property appraisal report; and a copy of the sales agreement

- The investor decides whether or not to accept the application

- Approval, if accepted, will then be sent to the mortgage company

- Loan funds are sent to escrow once all conditions of the loan are met

- After closing, all documents are sold to the interested investor, while the mortgage broker will continue to service the loan. This means that the borrower of funds will send payments directly to the mortgage broker. The mortgage broker keeps track of the loan status for the life of the loan.

Non-financial institutions include people or organizations that are not part of a traditional lending institution, but have money to invest. Non-financial institutions include: universities; pension funds; title companies; and, trust departments of banks, or mortgage investment companies.

As we saw in the previous chapter on real estate finance, **private individuals** sometimes finance the home they are selling to the buyer. A private investor can also go through a mortgage broker, who will find a borrower in need of funds. This type of loan is usually a short-term loan. This is one way for a private individual to provide money to borrowers, while gaining a large return on their investment. However, there is another method for gaining a larger return on investment. Individuals can form a Real Estate Investment Trust (REIT) where each person contributes a small amount of money to a larger, collective pool. This creates a large resource of funds. A REIT requires 100 investors or more.

Real estate mortgage brokers are limited to the amount of commission they can charge for loans. The allowable commission is based on whether the loan is a first trust deed or second trust deed, as well as the number of years for which the loan is set up. The box below describes the commission amounts that mortgage brokers are allowed to charge for each type of loan.

Real Property Loan Law:

First Trust Deed:
- Trust deeds of less than $30,000 fall under the loan law
- For loans lasting less than 3 years, the maximum amount of commission that may be charged is 5%
- For loans lasting 3 years or more, the maximum amount of commission that may be charged is 10%

Second Trust Deed:
- Trust deeds of less than $20,000 fall under the loan law
- For loans lasting less than 2 years, the maximum amount of commission that may be charged is 5%
- For loans lasting at least 2 years, but less than 3 years, the maximum amount of commission that may be charged is 10%
- For loans lasting 3 years or more, the maximum amount of commission that maybe charged is 15%

It is important to note that for first trust deeds of $30,000 or more and second trust deeds of $20,000 or more; there is no commission cap. In other words, mortgage brokers may charge as much as they want for these loans.

Secondary Mortgage Market

The initial lender of a real estate loan may be in full contact with the borrower issuing periodic statements of payments made, principal paid, balance remaining and other correspondence deemed necessary. Though the original lender may still be in contact with the borrower, there is a good chance that the original lender has sold the loan to another investor. Even if the lender has sold the promissory note, he or she will continue to service the loan until it has been paid in full.

The sale of real estate promissory notes makes up the secondary mortgage market. This provides investors with an additional opportunity to invest money in the secondary mortgage market, when they may have otherwise sought out different investment opportunities. In this section, we will review the federal agencies involved in the largest portion of the secondary mortgage market. These agencies are the Federal National Mortgage Association (Fannie Mae), Government National Mortgage Association (Ginnie Mae), Federal Home Loan Mortgage Corporation (Freddie Mac), and the Office of Federal Housing Enterprise Oversight (OFHEO).

Secondary Mortgage Market:
- Federal National Mortgage Association (Fannie Mae)
- Government National Mortgage Association (Ginnie Mae)
- Federal Home Loan Mortgage Corporation (Freddie Mac)
- Office of Federal Housing Enterprise Oversight (OFHEO)

Fannie Mae (www.fanniemae.com) was created in 1938, to serve as a secondary market for FHA-insured and VA-guaranteed loans. In later years, Fannie Mae's authority was expanded to allow them to offer conventional loans, as well. Fannie Mae currently buys properties financed through FHA, VA, graduated payment mortgages, adjustable-rate mortgages and conventional fixed rate first (and some second) mortgages for properties consisting of 1-4 units.

Loans meeting Fannie Mae's criteria are **conforming loans.** The dollar amount is limited to $333,700 per single-family residences; though higher limits exist for states outside of California.

Fannie Mae buys a group of mortgages from a lender in exchange for mortgage-backed securities that represent an undivided interest in the group of loans. The lender may choose to keep these loans, or sell them into the secondary mortgage market. Fannie Mae guarantees the payment of both interest and principal of these loans to the holder of the note, whether the note holder is the original lender or an investor.

In 1968, Fannie Mae was divided into a corporation owned by private investors called Ginnie Mae. Fannie Mae today issues its own stock and obtains its capital from its functions of buying, selling and investing.

Ginnie Mae (www.hud.gov/funcgnma) offers people high-yielding, risk-free, guaranteed securities. Ginnie Mae does not buy securities as Fannie Mae does. Rather, it guarantees securities already issued by FHA-approved home lenders. Investors who purchase the FHA loans in the secondary mortgage market are guaranteed to receive their investment back including interest (less any fees charged by Ginnie Mae). This means that if an investor purchases a loan, and the borrower is late on a payment, Ginnie Mae will make the payment to the investor who holds the note. This assures the investor that he or she will always be paid on time.

Freddie Mac (www.freddiemac.com) was created in 1970, due to a shortage of mortgage funds available to consumers. Freddie Mac will buy loans and then sell them into the secondary mortgage market to provide additional funds for borrowers and investors. Freddie Mac is restricted to the same $333,700 as Fannie Mae. Freddie Mac also issues stock to the general public, much like Fannie Mae.

The Office of Federal Housing Enterprise Oversight (OFHEO) (www.ofheo.gov) makes legislative recommendations designed to enhance Fannie Mae and Freddie Mac programs. OFHEO conducts audits of Fannie Mae and Freddie Mac, in which the OFHEO can make recommendations to the legislature when these programs are under consideration.

Overview

Fannie Mae:
- Issues stock to general public
- Issues mortgage-backed securities

Ginnie Mae:
- Guarantees securities issued by FHA-approved lenders

Freddie Mac:
- Issues stock to general public
- Buys and sells conventional loans

Office of Federal Housing Enterprise Oversight:
- Conducts audits of Fannie Mae and Freddie Mac
- Makes legislative recommendations

Participation of Real Estate Brokers

There are different levels of participation a broker may engage in real estate lending. A real estate broker may be a mortgage banker, a hard moneymaker or arranger of loans and a third-party originator of loans.

The broker who participates as a third-party originator will prepare documents for his or her customer, then submit these loan documents to a lender. The broker does not make any determination whether or not the customer receives the financing, but is pivotal in facilitating and aiding in the completion of the application for the client.

Real Estate Investment Trusts

A real estate investment trust (REIT) is a collaboration between a group of investors. Several investors will get together to form one REIT, contribute funds to raise venture capital and use this money to invest in real estate. It takes a minimum of 100 people to create a REIT.

> **Remember**
> Mortgage lenders can be divided into two groups:
> - Institutional lenders – commercial banks, savings associations and life insurance companies.
> - Non-institutional lenders – mortgage companies, mortgage loan brokers, credit unions, pension funds, real estate investment trusts and seller carryback financing.

C O N F O R M I N G   L O A N S

Now that you are familiar with the secondary mortgage market, the idea of selling loans should not be a difficult concept to grasp. Lenders have the opportunity after making a loan to keep that loan to themselves or within the lending institution that made the loan, or the lender may choose to sell the loan in the secondary market. If a lender keeps a loan (does not sell it in the secondary mortgage market) it is referred to as a portfolio loan. Additionally, if the lender chooses to sell the loan, it is logically called a non-portfolio.

Loans that are eligible to be bought and sold in the secondary mortgage market are called conforming loans. These loans must meet the standards set by Fannie Mae and Freddie Mac. Some of the standards include:

- A loan written for 15 or 30-years

- A loan that is not assumable

- Loans with specific down payment requirements

- Maximum loan amounts – presently it is $359,650 on a single family home (this amount is subject to change frequently, please make sure to check with the current allowable maximum loan amount.)

Loans that are eligible to be sold on the secondary mortgage market typically have lower interest rates than loans not eligible. This is due to the strict standards set forth by organizations such as Fannie Mae and Freddie Mac.

> **Remember**
> - Loans that a financial institution keeps are called portfolio loans.
> - Loans that a financial institution sells are called non-portfolio loans.

Real estate financing is not a black and white function of the home buying experience. There are many options, which might confuse a client who does not know what the best loan would be for him or her. It is your job to help direct your client in the most appropriate direction for his or her needs. Having a good working relationship with a professional in the mortgage industry is also good, as you can refer more complicated questions to that person.

Conventional loans are defined as a loan that is not backed by the government. These loans provide the consumer with more flexibility and require less approval or processing time. Those people who need to obtain a larger loan, or a loan above the monetary limits of most government backed loans, must choose the conventional loan if they want to finance a more expensive property. Generally conventional loans also have more variety in funding choices. These choices will be explained to you later in this section.

Government backed loans, by contrast, are more rigid. They are, however, ideal for some people. These loans usually require a very small down payment, lower than a conventional loan. Government backed loans do not require private mortgage insurance as this will be included in the specific mortgage program. Those who qualify for these programs may find it fits their financial situation better than a conventional loan.

Federal Participation in Real Estate Finance
Most people try diligently to save enough money to someday purchase a home. For some, this task is easy, because they can quickly save the down payment and qualify for a necessary loan. For others, it is difficult to save the down payment, pay their existing bills, and maintain a sufficient credit rating to be considered for a loan. For some, obtaining manageable financing is simply out of reach, even if they have a decent income. For people who find that purchasing a home is simply out of their reach, the government has set up two federal agencies that participate in real estate financing. These agencies make it possible for people to purchase a home using government-backed loans. The two federal agencies are the Federal Housing Administration (FHA) and the Veterans Administration (VA). In addition to these federal programs, California has a state program called the California Farm and Home Purchase Program, or Cal-Vet.

Federal Agencies:
- Federal Housing Administration (or FHA)
- Veterans Administration (or VA)

State Agency:
- California Farm and Home Purchase Program (or Cal-Vet)

Federal Housing Administration
The Federal Housing Administration (www.hud.gov) was created to insure loans made by approved lending institutions (such as banks or mortgage companies). The loans made must follow all FHA guidelines. If they do, the loans will be insured against default in the event that the borrower is unable to pay the note. In the event of default, the FHA will pay cash to the lender up to the established limit of the insurance. In addition, the lender may foreclose on the borrower. This is a way for lenders to ensure that they will recoup their investment in the case of default, beyond just a foreclosure sale.

The FHA has been around since 1934, rewriting the history of real estate finance.

MORTGAGE LOAN DISCLOSURE STATEMENT
(BORROWER)
(As required by the Business and Professions Code §10241
and Title 10, California Administrative Code, §2840)

_____
(Name of Broker/Arranger of Credit)

_____
(Business Address of Broker)

I. SUMMARY OF LOAN TERMS

A. PRINCIPAL AMOUNT . . . . $ _____

B. ESTIMATED DEDUCTIONS FROM PRINCIPAL AMOUNT

   1. Costs and Expenses (See Paragraph III-A) . . . . $ _____

   *2. Broker Commission/Organization Fee (See Paragraph III-B) . . . . $ _____

   3. Lender Origination Fee/Discounts (See Paragraph III-B) . . . . $ _____

   4. Additional compensation will/may be received from lender not deducted from loan proceeds.

      ☐ YES $ _____ (if known) or ☐ NO

   5. Amount to be Paid on Authorization of Borrower (See Paragraph III) . . . . $ _____

C. ESTIMATED CASH PAYABLE TO BORROWER (A less B) . . . . $ _____

II. GENERAL INFORMATION ABOUT LOAN

A. If this loan is made, Borrower will be required to pay the principal and interest at _____% per year, payable
as follows: _____ payments of $ _____
         (number of payments)   (monthly/quarterly/annually)
and a **FINAL/BALLOON** payment of $ _____ to pay off the loan in full.

NOTICE TO BORROWER: IF YOU DO NOT HAVE THE FUNDS TO PAY THE BALLOON PAYMENT WHEN IT COMES DUE, YOU MAY HAVE TO OBTAIN A NEW LOAN AGAINST YOUR PROPERTY TO MAKE THE BALLOON PAYMENT. IN THAT CASE, YOU MAY AGAIN HAVE TO PAY COMMISSIONS, FEES AND EXPENSES FOR THE ARRANGING OF THE NEW LOAN. IN ADDITION, IF YOU ARE UNABLE TO MAKE THE MONTHLY PAYMENTS OR THE BALLOON PAYMENT, YOU MAY LOSE THE PROPERTY AND ALL OF YOUR EQUITY THROUGH FORECLOSURE. KEEP THIS IN MIND IN DECIDING UPON THE AMOUNT AND TERMS OF THIS LOAN.

B. This loan will be evidenced by a promissory note and secured by a deed of trust on property identified as (street address or legal description):

_____
_____

C. 1. Liens presently against this property (do not include loan being applied for):

Nature of Lien	Priority	Lienholder's Name	Amount Owing
_____	_____	_____	_____
_____	_____	_____	_____
_____	_____	_____	_____

   2. Liens that will remain against this property after the loan being applied for is made or arranged (include loan being applied for):

Nature of Lien	Priority	Lienholder's Name	Amount Owing
_____	_____	_____	_____
_____	_____	_____	_____
_____	_____	_____	_____

NOTICE TO BORROWER: Be sure that you state the amount of all liens as accurately as possible. If you contract with the broker to arrange this loan, but it cannot be arranged because you did not state these liens correctly, you may be liable to pay commissions, fees and expenses even though you do not obtain the loan.

MS REVISED 10/2000 (PAGE 1 OF 3) Print Date

Borrower acknowledges receipt of copy of this page.

Borrower's Initials (_____)(_____)

Reviewed by _____ Date _____

EQUAL HOUSING
OPPORTUNITY

MORTGAGE LOAN DISCLOSURE STATEMENT (MS PAGE 1 OF 3)

Property Address: _____ Date: _____

D. If Borrower pays all or part of the loan principal before it is due, a PREPAYMENT PENALTY computed as follows may be charged:

_____
_____
_____

E. Late Charges: ☐ YES, see loan documents   or   ☐ NO
F. The purchase of credit life or credit disability insurance by a borrower is not required as a condition of making this loan.
G. Is the real property which will secure the requested loan an "owner-occupied dwelling?" ☐ YES____ or ☐ NO____
   (Borrower initial opposite YES or NO)

An "owner-occupied dwelling" means a single dwelling unit in a condominium or cooperative or residential building of four or fewer separate dwelling units, one of which will be owned and occupied by a signatory to the mortgage or deed of trust for this loan within 90 days of the signing of the mortgage or deed of trust.

III. DEDUCTIONS FROM LOAN PROCEEDS

A. Estimated Maximum Costs and Expenses of Arranging the Loan to be Paid Out of Loan Principal:

	PAYABLE TO	
	Broker	Others
1. Appraisal fee	_____	_____
2. Escrow fee	_____	_____
3. Title insurance policy	_____	_____
4. Notary fees	_____	_____
5. Recording fees	_____	_____
6. Credit investigation fees	_____	_____
7. Other costs and expenses:		

_____
_____
_____

Total Costs and Expenses . . . . $ _____

*B. Compensation . . . . $ _____
   1. Brokerage Commission/Origination Fee . . . . $ _____
   2. Lender Origination Fee/Discounts . . . . . . $ _____
C. Estimated Payment to be Made out of Loan Principal on Authorization of Borrower

	PAYABLE TO	
	Broker	Others
1. Fire or other hazard insurance premiums	_____	_____
2. Credit life or disability insurance premiums (see Paragraph II-F)	_____	_____
3. Beneficiary statement fees	_____	_____
4. Reconveyance and similar fees	_____	_____
5. Discharge of existing liens against property:		

_____
_____
_____

6. Other:

_____
_____
_____

Total to be Paid on Authorization of Borrower . . . . $ _____

If this loan is secured by a first deed of trust on dwellings in a principal amount of less than $30,000 or secured by a junior lien on dwellings in a principal amount of less than $20,000, the undersigned licensee certifies that the loan will be made in compliance with Article 7 of Chapter 3 of the Real Estate Law.

*This loan **may / will / will not** (delete two) be made wholly or in part from broker-controlled funds as defined in Section 10241(j) of the Business and Professions Code.

MS REVISED 10/2000 (PAGE 2 OF 3) Print Date

Borrower acknowledges receipt of copy of this page.

Borrower's Initials (_____)(_____)

| Reviewed by _____ Date _____ |

EQUAL HOUSING OPPORTUNITY

MORTGAGE LOAN DISCLOSURE STATEMENT (MS PAGE 2 OF 3)

Property Address: _____ Date: _____

*NOTICE TO BORROWER: This disclosure statement may be used if the Broker is acting as an agent in arranging the loan by a third person or if the loan will be made with funds owned or controlled by the broker. If the Broker indicates in the above statement that the loan "may" be made out of Broker-controlled funds, the Broker must notify the borrower prior to the close of escrow if the funds to be received by the Borrower are in fact Broker-controlled funds.

_____   _____
Name of Broker   Broker Representative

_____   _____
License Number   License Number

_____ OR _____
Signature of Broker   Signature

The Department of Real Estate License Information phone number is _____.

NOTICE TO BORROWER:

DO NOT SIGN THIS STATEMENT UNTIL YOU HAVE READ AND UNDERSTAND ALL OF THE INFORMATION IN IT. ALL PARTS OF THE FORM MUST BE COMPLETED BEFORE YOU SIGN.

Borrower hereby acknowledges the receipt of a copy of this statement.

DATED _____   _____
                                                                      (Borrower)

                                                                 _____
                                                                      (Borrower)

<u>Broker Review</u>: Signature of Real Estate Broker after review of this statement.

DATED _____   _____
                                                                 Real Estate Broker or Assistant Pursuant to Section 2725

Published and Distributed by:
REAL ESTATE BUSINESS SERVICES, INC.
a subsidiary of the California Association of REALTORS®
525 South Virgil Avenue, Los Angeles, California 90020

MS REVISED 10/2000 (PAGE 3 OF 3) Print Date

| Reviewed by _____ Date _____ |

MORTGAGE LOAN DISCLOSURE STATEMENT (MS PAGE 3 OF 3)

Since this time, there have been changes to the regulations; but it is important for you as a real estate professional to be aware of how this program works and the different changes made to the administration over time. Mortgage brokers will be a good resource for you to learn more about current changes.

The lender's investment remains protected in a FHA insured loan, due to the Mutual Mortgage Insurance policy. The borrower is charged a fee for this policy, insuring the investment will be sound. The FHA is able to fund its program through premiums on the Mutual Mortgage Insurance. Borrowers have an option to pay for the insurance in cash, or the amount of the premium may be financed in the loan. This premium must be paid at the close of escrow. A secondary premium is collected each month, if the property is a single-family residence.

The FHA also offers a graduated payment mortgage (GPM). The GPM is ideal for those borrowers who anticipate an increase in their income, but may not currently have the money for a down payment, or can only budget a limited payment. For the first five years, the borrower will pay only a percent of the interest. The remaining interest will be added to the principal. After five years, the loan will be recalculated and the payments adjusted accordingly. After the fifth year, and recalculation of the payment, the payments will remain the same until the note is paid in full.

Consumers wishing to apply for an FHA loan apply directly to an approved lender, rather than the Federal Housing Administration. The lender is then responsible for processing the application and submitting it to the FHA directly. Any borrower may apply for an FHA loan; and there are no restrictions or caps on qualifications

Overview:
- FHA insures loans
- Borrowers apply directly to approved lenders, who process the application and submit it to the FHA
- Borrowers pay Mutual Mortgage Insurance
- FHA offers the Graduated Payment Mortgage for clients anticipating an increase in income, but who currently have budget restrictions.

Department of Veteran Affairs
The department of Veteran Affairs started out as the Servicemen's Readjustment Act of 1944, and helped enlisted service men and women transition back to civilian life. As time went by, the act was expanded to include service men and women from later wars, their spouses and widows of service men and women, provided they remained unmarried. Today, the Department of Veteran Affairs (simply called the VA) authorizes first and second trust deeds for up to 25% of a property's value. The VA will guarantee payment of the remaining value of the mortgage debt, up to a certain maximum amount. This program does not cost the borrower any money. What the VA guarantees the lender is that they will pay the lender's net loss up to the amount of money guaranteed. This value will decrease over time, as the loan value is repaid.

People eligible for the VA guaranteed loan are service men and women who have served in the military and were not dishonorably discharged. The spouses of these men and women as well as members of the Army Reserve or the National Guard (as long as they have served for six years or more) are also eligible for the VA-guaranteed loan.

The lender will screen applicants, verify their veteran status and process the loan if the candidate meets all qualifications. The Department of Veteran Affairs does not need to approve any applications. Interested candidates request a Certificate of Eligibility from their VA office before filling out the loan application. This certificate will indicate the amount of loan guarantee or their veteran's entitlement.

VA loans may be used for the purchase of property, construction, repairs to a property or improvements to a property. The loan must be used for property consisting of one to four units, or a condominium. Residential complexes with more than four units will not qualify for a VA-guaranteed loan.

The loan guarantee amount is based on the size of the loan. The maximum guarantee is 60% of the loan (or $50,750, whichever is the lesser amount). A veteran is only able to use this loan once in his or her lifetime. If a veteran only uses a portion of their entitlement, they may use the remaining portion on a separate loan at a later date. There are, however, certain exceptions to this rule. For example: if a veteran has sold the property, and the VA-guaranteed loan is paid in full; if the Department of Veteran's Affairs is released from the original loan; if any losses suffered by the Department of Veteran's Affairs is paid in full; or, if the property is transferred to another veteran with loan guarantee benefits. In these cases, the veteran is entitled to increase the loan guarantee amount to its full amount.

If a veteran decides to sell his or her home, the VA requires a release from personal liability to the government to be signed prior to the sale of the home. If this release is not completed, the veteran will remain responsible for the property. Additionally, the release should be included as a condition of the sale. The VA can release the veteran from liability in the event of a foreclosure, provided there has been no fraud or bad faith by the veteran.

The VA must issue a certificate of reasonable value to the purchaser before signing the contract of sale. Otherwise, there should be a clause in the sale contract stating that: if the certificate of reasonable values is less than the purchase price, the buyer may either proceed with the purchasing property, or withdraw the offer. The certificate of reasonable value amount is determined by VA-recommended appraisers.

There are several different loan types available to veterans wishing to utilize a VA-guaranteed loan. The loans available are: fixed-term; adjustable rate mortgage; growing equity mortgage, and graduated payment mortgage.

VA – guaranteed loan types:
- Fixed-term
- Adjustable-rate mortgage
- Growing equity mortgage
- Graduated payment mortgage

Fixed term loans are fully amortized to no more than 30 years and 32 days.

Adjustable-rate mortgages (ARM) are adjusted based on the Treasury's securities index. This causes the loan payment amount to fluctuate, depending on the volatility of interest rates. Today, this loan is not available to veterans; however, any veteran who obtained this type of loan before 1995 may still be utilizing an ARM loan.

Growing equity mortgage (GEM) is connected to an index that increases the amount of payments. The increase of the payment goes directly toward the principal balance. The GEM is a way to pay off a mortgage early, while building equity in a home more quickly.

Graduated payment mortgage (GPM) allows the borrower to make a lower monthly payment for the first five years (or the equivalent of only 7% interest), regardless of interest rates. After five years, the payment will go up and shall remain at the same level for the life of the loan. Any interest not being covered in the first five years will automatically be added to the principal balance of the loan.

Interest rates are not negotiable on VA-guaranteed loans. If the payment is too large for the borrower to make, the lender may suggest a graduated payment mortgage, to allow for lower payments in the beginning of the note.

Mobile homes fall under a separate category. A mobile home must measure at least 400 square feet to qualify as a property for purchase with a VA-guaranteed loan. Single-wide mobile homes have a maximum financing term of 15 years and 32 days. Double-wide mobile homes have a maximum financing term of 20 years and 32 days.

VA-guaranteed loans do not require a down payment, provided that the estimate of reasonable value does not exceed the VA loan guarantee. The lender, on the other hand, may require a down payment of his or her own. This is negotiated directly with the lender. If the purchase price of a property is more than the reasonable value, a VA guaranteed loan may still be used, as long as the buyer pays the difference between the reasonable value and the purchase price in cash at closing.

In the event that a veteran has a difficult time paying the loan, and defaults for a period of three months, a notice of default is given to the Department of Veteran Affairs, alerting them to the situation. The VA will then aid the veteran in making the necessary payments, and counsel him or her on how to keep on track with future payments.

Overview:
- VA loans provide a guarantee to the lender that they will receive the loan guarantee amount based on the selling price of the home
- Lenders fill out all applications and submit them to the Department of Veteran's Affairs
- An approved VA appraiser must be used to arrive at the amount of the certificate of reasonable value
- There are 4 different loan types that may be used: fixed-term loans; adjustable-rate mortgage; growing equity mortgage, and graduated payment mortgage
- VA guaranteed loans for property consisting of 1-4 units (or con-dominiums) may be financed for up to 30 years and 32 days
- Single-wide mobile homes may be financed for up to 15 years and 32 days, while double-wide mobile homes may be financed for up to 20 years and 32 days
- There is no down payment required for a VA-guaranteed loan

California Veterans Farm and Home Purchase Program

California Veterans Farm and Home Purchase Program, or Cal-Vet (www.ns.net/cadva.) is a full service lender for veterans. Cal-Vet authorizes, processes, funds and services all loans they administer. The program was developed in 1921, to assist veterans in purchasing both homes and farms. There are no outside funds involved in the Cal-Vet programs; all the money that is used for these loans come from voter-approved bonds, issued by the legislature.

The California Department of Veteran Affairs will buy a property from its seller, and sell the property to an interested, qualified veteran. The title will remain with the California Department of Veteran Affairs until the note has been paid in full, though the borrower may take possession of the property immediately. Veterans may use the Cal-Vet program to purchase an existing home or farm, finance a land purchase to build a new home, remodel a home purchased as-is or make home improvements.

Veterans eligible for the Cal-Vet program must be purchasing a property in California, and must also be a California resident. They may not have taken a previous benefit from another state and must have served at least 90 days active service duty. Those veterans not serving at least 90 days on active duty must have been honorably discharged in order to qualify. In addition to the above criteria, each veteran must have served at lease one day in one of the following periods:

World War I	April 6, 1917 through November 11, 1918
World War II	December 7, 1941 through December 31, 1946
Korean Conflict	June 27, 1950 through January 31, 1955
Vietnam War	August 5, 1964 through May 7, 1975
Persian Gulf War	August 2, 1990 through present

Unmarried spouses of those veterans who were killed, or who have died by other means, are also eligible for benefits. The Cal-Vet system occasionally experiences shortages of funds for all applicants. In this event, there is a hierarchy of preference given to applicants, which is as follows:

1. Wounded or disabled veterans

2. Former prisoners of war and unmarried spouses of prisoners or war or those missing in action

3. Vietnam War veterans and Native American veterans applying for loans on reservation or trust land

4. All other eligible candidates

There is a maximum amount of money available to each applicant for a VA-guaranteed loan. The maximum amount of money available to purchase a home is $250,000, with a $70,000 lending limit for a mobile home and a $300,000 lending limit for the purchase of a farm. These loans require a down payment of 5% of the selling price. All applicants wishing to participate in a Cal-Vet loan must have applied for the loan before the purchase of property was made.

Overview:
- Cal-Vet loans are funded, serviced, processed and authorized in-house
- Eligibility requirements state that veterans must have served active duty for 90 days (or have been honorably discharged), and have also served at least one day during an active war or conflict
- Maximum loan amount for a home is $250,000, with a $70,000 lending limit for a mobile home and $300,000 lending limit for a farm

	FHA	VA	Cal-Vet
Type of Property	Dwellings consisting of one to four units	Dwellings consisting of one to four units	One-unit dwellings or farms
Borrower Eligibility Maximum Loan Amount	All U.S. Residents $121,296 - $219,849	U.S. Veterans None, but a loan based on maximum entitlement would be $203,000, including the funding fee.	California Veterans $70,000 – Mobile home $250,000 – home $300,000 - Farm
Maximum Purchase Price	None	None	None
Down Payment	At least 3% of acquisition cost	At the discretion of the lender	5%
Discount points	Yes	Yes	No
Type of loan	Variety of fixed and variable-rate loans	Fixed rate; GEM; GPM	Variable rate; others possible
Interest Rate	Negotiated	Negotiated	Set by Cal-Vet; can change annually
Maximum Loan Term	30 years; 35 years for new construction; less for mobile homes	30 years; less for mobile homes	30 years
Prepayment Penalty	None	None	None
Secondary Financing	Not at time of sale	Not at time of sale	Yes

In addition to the loans we have already discussed, there are a number of other loans available to persons wishing to purchase property.
These loans include:

- Open-ended loan
- Swing loan
- Blanket loan
- Package loan
- Wrap around loan
- Unsecured loan
- Fixed-rate loan
- Piggyback loan
- Adjustable-rate mortgage
- Rollover loan

An **open-ended loan** is structured in such a way that additional funds may be borrowed against the first trust deed, without any additional trust deeds needed. This is commonly used by developers of property who purchase land first, and then build houses, condominiums or apartments on that same land. The open-ended loan is an important one, because the original loan is always preserved as the priority claim in the event of foreclosure. A subordination clause is not necessary for lenders to ensure their loan gets paid first when the same loan stays open for additional funds.

Sometimes people will opt for a swing loan, also called a gap loan, to withdraw money against the equity of a home they are trying to sell. This happens when another home is purchased as a replacement for the home being sold but the original home is not yet sold. The homeowner may take out a temporary loan against the equity in the home to be sold, use that money to purchase another home, and then pay back the loan upon sale of the old, or original house.

While developers might choose an open-ended loan when purchasing property and then building homes on it, they may also wish to utilize a blanket loan. The blanket loan encompasses more than one parcel of property. Builders might be attracted to this loan when building a new development of condominiums or homes to be sold to consumers at a later date. The blanket loan will usually contain a release clause releasing individual houses or properties one at a time upon their sale, so that they are no longer covered under the blanket loan.

Loans are secured by the property themselves, ensuring repayment to the lender by the borrower. Usually, the property itself is sufficient to secure the loan; but, sometimes, more than property is required to secure a loan. Loans of this type are called **package loans**. The package loan utilizes not only the property or buildings as collateral, but also the fixtures attached to the property and/or any personal property (such as a vehicle) necessary to secure the loan.

Wrap around loans are another way to finance property. Sometimes these loans are called an all-inclusive trust deed (AITD). A wrap around loan usually consists of both the existing note held by the seller, and the new loan secured by the buyer. The new loan "wraps around" the existing loan, and one payment is made to cover both loans. One loan consumes all the present encumbrances of the property plus the amount of the new loan.

Because this is not a blanket loan or open-ended loan, there is a hierarchy which makes the AITD subordinate to any previously recorded trust deed on the property. If the property should be foreclosed, any previous trust deeds must be paid first (even though the wrap-around loan is making the payments for these loans). One difference regarding the AITD loan versus other financing is that, with an AITD loan, the buyer receives the title to the property at closing. Usually an AITD is utilized when a seller and buyer are both financing a property. In a traditional loan assumption or when the seller carries back a note on the property, the buyer takes a loan to cover the cost of the existing loan plus the difference in the sale price of the home. The seller benefits from this situation, because he or she receives the full price for the home. The buyer generally benefits through a lower down payment, and also does not have to endure the traditional qualifying process to obtain the loan.

The AITD includes the unpaid principal balance of the existing loan plus the amount of the new loan being made by the seller to the buyer. The seller continues to make payments on the loan they have taken out from their financial institution, while the buyer makes payments to the seller for the AITD. Of course payment from the buyer will be enough to cover the original loan plus a higher interest rate to the seller. This is in concert with the additional money borrowed from the seller to cover the difference between the original trust deed and the selling price of the property.

While this type of loan seems like a great idea for a buyer, there are situations when it simply does not work out as well. If a seller needs to cash out of a loan for the purchase of another property, or for any other reason, they are not able to do so with an AITD loan. The seller is obligated to repay the entire original note to the lender that is wrapped around by the loan they have provided to the buyer. Some loans contain a **due on sale** clause, meaning the seller would not be able to wrap around a loan to the existing loan, as the original loan must be paid off when the home is sold. If there is no due on sale clause, the lender may have to approve the wrap around loan, and there are some cases when the buyer may not qualify (for example, because of their credit score or debt to asset ratio). In a market with high interest rates, an AITD may not be the best choice, because the buyer ends up paying a much higher rate than the current market demands for the wrap around loan. This higher rate is, however, financially attractive to the seller.

The buyer typically does not make payments directly to the seller, although in theory that is what is happening. Instead, the buyer will usually make payments to a collection company, which will then distribute the money to the appropriate parties. The original lender will receive a monthly payment, while the seller will receive the amount predetermined by the contract. This is done to protect the buyer from mismanagement on the seller's behalf and to ensure that the original note is being paid according to the promissory note's terms and conditions. This protects all parties involved, and ensures that this type of financing remains feasible and functional.

Wrap around loan / All-inclusive trust deed:
- Seller finances the buyer, by providing a loan encompassing all payments to the first or subsequent trust deeds
- Buyer's payment to the seller includes the payment on the original loan, plus the higher interest rate, as well as the difference between the principal owed on the first note and the amount of the sale price of the home
- Wrap around loan is subordinate to the original loan
- Buyer takes the title to the home
- Buyer makes payments to a collection company ensuring that all funds are distributed to the appropriate parties

Fixed-rate loan, as its name suggests, is a loan where the interest rate is fixed for a given period of time. These are used for long-term amortized loans. Lenders generally don't like using this type of loan, and will usually opt for a loan with a shorter maturity and a variable interest rate.

Piggyback loans act as if they are two separate loans, but it is not. Think of it as a first trust deed and a second trust deed wrapped into one loan. Usually one lender will take one portion of the loan, while a second lender will take the other portion. The "first trust deed" portion of the loan is considered to be more secure as that lender will be the first person paid in the event of default, while the "second trust deed" portion of the loan comes with greater risk.

Adjustable-rate mortgage (ARM) is a loan where the interest rate will change based on current economic conditions. The ARM generally is easier for a person to qualify for because the interest rate is usually lower in the first year or first term of the loan. This allows a person to obtain the loan, buy a home and as his or her income increases they will be able to make a larger payment, assuming the interest rate increases. It is also good because a consumer can usually qualify for a larger loan when going with an ARM.

Rollover loans are partially amortized loans with a maturity of five or seven years. Once the loan is due, the borrower can refinance. These loans have payments as if they were structured on a 30-year mortgage, but don't have fixed interest rates. The term rollover comes to play when the five to seven period is over, the note is due in full and the borrower can refinance the note to continue paying on the current principal.

I N T E R E S T   R A T E S

Interest rates refer to the cost of borrowing money. Payments on a trust deed will be higher with higher interest rates, and lower when interest rates are lower. The interest rates will help determine who can afford to borrow money, and the amount of money they might qualify. At lower interest rates, more people will qualify to borrow higher amounts of money, with higher interest rates less people will qualify for large loans.

With more qualified buyers comes a seller's market. This means that more people will be bidding on the same amount of property, allowing homeowner's to ask higher prices for the same property. The inverse of this is true when interest rates are high. With less qualified buyers, there will be fewer buyers for the same amount of inventory, dictating a buyer's market. Prices tend to fall during a buyer's market.

You can see there is a direct correlation between interest rates, the number of qualified buyers, home prices and sales rates. It is an inverse relationship, when interest rates are high; prices tend to be lower with fewer buyers, with the opposite true when interest rates are low.

Remember
Sales are inversely related to interest rates. As interest rates increase, sales will decline and vice versa.

F I N A N C I N G

Before showing property, it is standard practice to pre-qualify the client. If you do not do this, you could end up wasting your time and theirs. By pre-qualifying you know the

265

price range of property the person will be able to afford, and will not show a more expensive property. After you pre-qualify the buyer, and have found a home he or she wants to make an offer, you then need to make sure the buyer obtains the necessary financing to close the deal. Once the financing process is underway, there are 5 steps most lenders go through. These steps are qualifying the buyer, qualifying the property, process the loan, close the loan and finally a lender needs to service the loan they originate.

Qualifying the buyer involves analyzing his or her character and capacity. When a lender analyzes the borrowers character and capacity both attitude and tangible aspects of the likelihood of repayment will be analyzed. This means a credit score is looked at. Current income, past income, and the debt to income ratio will be analyzed to see if the candidate will be able to make a specific payment. A borrower's credit history will be looked at to see how responsible they are with making payments on time and earning potential from bonuses, overtime or other sources if income will be taken into account. If a potential borrower shows he or she can take on a financial responsibility of this magnitude, the lender will approve the loan. If there are questions to the person's ability to repay the note he or she might be denied financing.

Qualifying the property includes analyzing it to make sure it is worth the amount of the loan. When a person obtains a trust deed to purchase property, they are pledging that property in the event they default on the note. This property must be worth enough to pay off the note at the very least. This is one reason for appraisals. Appraisals are helpful in finding out the value of the home when determining how much to ask when listing a property, but also what the market value of that home will be to the bank or lending institution. If the seller is asking much more than the home is worth, finds a buyer and that buyer defaults, the bank or lending institution will not be able to resell the property for the amount owed against it. Qualifying the property will keep the financial institution's investment.

Processing the loan is when all papers are generated regarding all aspects of the loan. The loan papers are created, disclosures are provided whenever necessary and escrow instructions are drawn up. Once all the paper can be generated, checked and distributed to the necessary parties, the loan can then be closed.

Closing the loan and closing of escrow are two different things. Closing the loan happens when all documents have been signed. Closing escrow is when all funds have been disbursed.

Finally a lender needs to service the loan after it has been made and closed. Servicing the loan involves making sure lenders are paying the minimum correct amount of money on time.

F I N A N C E   R E G U L A T I O N

Real Estate Settlement Procedures Act – RESPA
The Real Estate Settlement Procedures Act (RESPA) requires that lenders make certain disclosures to borrowers utilizing a federal mortgage loan or loan program. Any sale of property using these loans, with property that consists of one to four units must supply the appropriate disclosures. The federal mortgage loan or loan program includes the following:

- A loan made by a lender insured by FDIC or another federal agency
- A loan financed through a federal agency such as the Federal Housing Administration (FHA) or through the Department of Veteran's Affairs (VA)

266

- Sold in the secondary mortgage market to Fannie Mae, Ginnie Mae or Freddie Mac

Lenders are required to supply every applicant with all disclosures and material. If there is more than one person applying for a loan, each applicant must receive his or her own copy of all disclosures. The lender must send the applicants all material no later than three days after the application has been received. The following information must be supplied to the applicants:

- A copy of the special information booklet
- A good-faith estimate of the closing costs

A copy of the real estate settlement statement must also be supplied to the borrower no later than one day after closing on the property. The settlement statement lists all charges to the buyer and seller, and accompanied by the real estate transaction. Real estate settlement statements were covered in the escrow chapter.

Regulation Z – the Truth in Lending Act

The Federal Reserve Board created the Truth in Lending Act (simply called Regulation Z), which requires creditors to disclose various credit terms to the borrower. This allows the borrower to make an informed decision between the different creditors and/or sources of available credit.

Creditors are those who extend credit or make loans to borrowers (more than 25 times each year for non-secured loans; five times each year for those loans requiring real property as security for the loan). A written arrangement, outlining payment amount, timing and other terms of the loan is required. A creditor is allowed to charge interest on the loan, provided that the interest on the loan is payable in four installments and that there is written agreement to these terms. It is important to note that the person arranging credit is not the creditor. Rather, the institution, or actual person making the loan, is the creditor. For example, a loan officer at Wells Fargo Bank is not a creditor; Wells Fargo Bank is the creditor.

There are certain transactions that are exempt from the Truth in Lending Act. These transactions are commercial, agricultural or business loans. Loans made for more than $25,000 are exempt from Regulation Z, unless it is a purchase money loan (where the loan must be secured by real or personal property) and the borrower plans to use the property as his or her primary place of residence. Any loans made to purchase, maintain or improve a rental property fall under different regulations and rules. If this rental property will be owner-occupied within one year the following rules apply:

- Loans made to acquire rental property consisting of one or more units are considered business loans, and are regulated as such
- Loans made to improve or maintain a property consisting of four or more units are also considered business loans and are regulated as such

Any loans acquired for the purpose of purchasing, maintaining or improving a rental property, which will not be owner occupied will always, be considered a business loan. Customers who have decided not to go ahead with the purchase of a property may cancel the loan. This is known as the right to rescind. A borrower has three days to cancel any loan involving a security interest in the borrower's principal residence. The three-day period will end at midnight on the third business day. The following events must occur for the borrower to rescind:

- Use of the transaction

- Borrower has received the truth in lending disclosure statement

- Borrower has received notice of the right to rescind

The right to rescind does not apply to the following situations:

- Refinancing a loan secured by property which is not occupied by the owner

- Residential purchase money, first mortgage, or trust deed loans

- Borrower refinances a loan, and no new funds are advanced to the borrower

In emergency situations the right to rescind may be waived so that the lender can fund the borrower's loan as fast as possible. Such situations may occur when closing needs to happen at a specific time for the purchase contract to be accepted.

There are certain disclosures required by Regulation Z. All disclosures must be grouped together, with the information set off by a box apart from the rest of the information on the loan. A different type style, bold type, or a different color background is also required, so that the disclosures will clearly stand out. These disclosures must be made before the transaction is completed (which is generally before closing). Usually, this disclosure statement will be delivered to the borrower at the same time as the loan commitment information is sent. This is normally after the loan has been approved, but before the loan has been funded.

The required disclosures pertain to financial information. It is necessary to state: the name of the creditor; the description of the security interest; the amount of money to be financed; the finance charge associated with the loan; the annual percentage rate; the total amount of the payments, and the total sales price. The borrower must be informed of any prepayment penalties, rebates or late payment charges, so that there are no surprise charges associated with an early payoff or a late payment. When insurance is not a requirement of the loan, and the borrower wishes to obtain insurance on the item to be purchased, the borrower must sign a request for insurance. When a signature is not required, the borrower's initials must be placed on the document.

Five most important disclosures:
- Amount to be financed
- Finance charge
- Annual percentage rate
- Total amount of the payments
- Total sales price (for any credit sales)

As we learned in another chapter, loans may be assumable when the borrower wishes to sell the property to another buyer. A borrower in a residential mortgage transaction must be informed of whether or not this is possible with their loan. This should be included in the disclosure statement.

Regulation Z also governs the types of advertisements that may be made for loans. In any advertisement, the ad must state the annual percentage rate of the loan, along with its payment terms. Specific information regarding the different forms of adjustable rate loans must also be included in the advertisement.

Equal Credit Opportunity Act

The Equal Credit Opportunity Act (www.lawdog.com/equal2/ec1.htm) protects people from discrimination when applying for a loan. Under this act, no person may be discriminated based on his or her sex, religion, race, color, age, marital status, national origin or on the grounds of receiving public funds from welfare. Every buyer is assured that they will be treated fairly, without discrimination, when going through the loan application process for a home or for other credit.

Equal Opportunity Credit Act Guidelines:

- Borrowers are not required to answer questions regarding birth control practices or methods or whether they plan on starting a family

- Borrowers may be asked if they are married; however a lender is not allowed to ask if a borrower is divorced or widowed

- Borrowers must be notified within 30 days if they qualify for the loan for which they applied. If the borrower is denied for the loan, the lender must supply the reason(s) for the denial of the loan

- Borrowers are not required to reveal any information regarding receipt of child support or alimony. Those borrowers who must pay child support or alimony may be asked about it, as it pertains directly to the borrower's income versus obligations. Such obligations may be a determining factor in whether a borrower can make the necessary payment on a loan

- Borowers who have a poor credit rating due to sharing a joint account with another person may provide information showing that the delinquent account is through the fault of another person, and not their own

Personal Property Secured Transactions

You will remember that personal property is distinctly separated from real property. Personal property are things of value that may be moved. Examples include: jewelry, cars, money, boats and other such valuable items. Often, to purchase such items, a loan is necessary. When a consumer does not have enough money to purchase their dream car, or take a European cruise, they must secure a loan - just as if they were purchasing a home. When purchasing a home, the trust deed secures the home. When purchasing a high dollar item of personal property, the security agreement secures the loan for the car, boat or other desired good.

When placing an item of personal property as the security agreement to secure a loan to purchase another item, people usually attach a financing statement to the security agreement. This protects the item that is placed as security for the loan. The reason for doing this is so the item securing the loan will not be sold in the event that the loan defaults. A security interest is "perfected" (protected) when it is has been attached to a financing statement and recorded in the office of the Secretary of State in Sacramento. The financing statement is the only form used to record a debt. It will contain all details of the agreement, as well as all obligations. Once the security agreement is protected, or perfected, the security interest is protected from other creditors to whom the debtor may owe money.

Uniform Residential Loan Application

This application is designed to be completed by the applicant(s) with the Lender's assistance. Applicants should complete this form as "Borrower" or "Co-Borrower," as applicable. Co-Borrower information must also be provided (and the appropriate box checked) when ☐ the income or assets of a person other than the Borrower (including the Borrower's spouse) will be used as a basis for loan qualification or ☐ the income or assets of the Borrower's spouse or other person who has community property rights pursuant to state law will not be used as a basis for loan qualification, but his or her liabilities must be considered because the spouse or other person has community property rights pursuant to applicable law and Borrower resides in a community property state, the security property is located in a community property state, or the Borrower is relying on other property located in a community property state as a basis for repayment of the loan.

If this is an application for joint credit, Borrower and Co-Borrower each agree that we intend to apply for joint credit (sign below):

Borrower _____   Co-Borrower _____

I. TYPE OF MORTGAGE AND TERMS OF LOAN

Mortgage Applied for:	☐ VA ☐ FHA	☐ Conventional ☐ USDA/Rural Housing Service	☐ Other (explain):	Agency Case Number	Lender Case Number
Amount $	Interest Rate %	No. of Months	Amortization Type:	☐ Fixed Rate ☐ GPM	☐ Other (explain): ☐ ARM (type):

II. PROPERTY INFORMATION AND PURPOSE OF LOAN

Subject Property Address (street, city, state & ZIP)	No. of Units
Legal Description of Subject Property (attach description if necessary)	Year Built

Purpose of Loan	☐ Purchase ☐ Construction ☐ Other (explain): ☐ Refinance ☐ Construction-Permanent	Property will be: ☐ Primary Residence ☐ Secondary Residence ☐ Investment

Complete this line if construction or construction-permanent loan.

Year Lot Acquired	Original Cost $	Amount Existing Liens $	(a) Present Value of Lot $	(b) Cost of Improvements $	Total (a + b) $

Complete this line if this is a refinance loan.

Year Acquired	Original Cost $	Amount Existing Liens $	Purpose of Refinance	Describe Improvements ☐ made ☐ to be made Cost: $

Title will be held in what Name(s)	Manner in which Title will be held	Estate will be held in: ☐ Fee Simple ☐ Leasehold (show expiration date)

Source of Down Payment, Settlement Charges, and/or Subordinate Financing (explain)

III. BORROWER INFORMATION

Borrower	Co-Borrower
Borrower's Name (include Jr. or Sr. if applicable)	Co-Borrower's Name (include Jr. or Sr. if applicable)

Social Security Number	Home Phone (incl. area code)	DOB (mm/dd/yyyy)	Yrs. School	Social Security Number	Home Phone (incl. area code)	DOB (mm/dd/yyyy)	Yrs. School

☐ Married ☐ Unmarried (include ☐ Separated single, divorced, widowed)	Dependents (not listed by Co-Borrower) no. ages	☐ Married ☐ Unmarried (include ☐ Separated single, divorced, widowed)	Dependents (not listed by Borrower) no. ages

Present Address (street, city, state, ZIP) ☐ Own ☐ Rent ___ No. Yrs.	Present Address (street, city, state, ZIP) ☐ Own ☐ Rent ___ No. Yrs.
Mailing Address, if different from Present Address	Mailing Address, if different from Present Address

If residing at present address for less than two years, complete the following:

Former Address (street, city, state, ZIP) ☐ Own ☐ Rent ___ No. Yrs.	Former Address (street, city, state, ZIP) ☐ Own ☐ Rent ___ No. Yrs.

IV. EMPLOYMENT INFORMATION

Borrower	Co-Borrower

Name & Address of Employer	☐ Self Employed	Yrs. on this job	Name & Address of Employer	☐ Self Employed	Yrs. on this job
		Yrs. employed in this line of work/profession			Yrs. employed in this line of work/profession
Position/Title/Type of Business	Business Phone (incl. area code)		Position/Title/Type of Business	Business Phone (incl. area code)	

If employed in current position for less than two years or if currently employed in more than one position, complete the following:

Name & Address of Employer	☐ Self Employed	Dates (from – to)	Name & Address of Employer	☐ Self Employed	Dates (from – to)
		Monthly Income $			Monthly Income $
Position/Title/Type of Business		Business Phone (incl. area code)	Position/Title/Type of Business		Business Phone (incl. area code)
Name & Address of Employer	☐ Self Employed	Dates (from – to)	Name & Address of Employer	☐ Self Employed	Dates (from – to)
		Monthly Income $			Monthly Income $
Position/Title/Type of Business		Business Phone (incl. area code)	Position/Title/Type of Business		Business Phone (incl. area code)

V. MONTHLY INCOME AND COMBINED HOUSING EXPENSE INFORMATION

Gross Monthly Income	Borrower	Co-Borrower	Total	Combined Monthly Housing Expense	Present	Proposed
Base Empl. Income*	$	$	$	Rent	$	
Overtime				First Mortgage (P&I)		$
Bonuses				Other Financing (P&I)		
Commissions				Hazard Insurance		
Dividends/Interest				Real Estate Taxes		
Net Rental Income				Mortgage Insurance		
Other (before completing, see the notice in "describe other income," below)				Homeowner Assn. Dues		
				Other:		
Total	$	$	$	Total	$	$

*   Self Employed Borrower(s) may be required to provide additional documentation such as tax returns and financial statements.

Describe Other Income   *Notice:* **Alimony, child support, or separate maintenance income need not be revealed if the Borrower (B) or Co-Borrower (C) does not choose to have it considered for repaying this loan.**

B/C		Monthly Amount
		$

VI. ASSETS AND LIABILITIES

This Statement and any applicable supporting schedules may be completed jointly by both married and unmarried Co-Borrowers if their assets and liabilities are sufficiently joined so that the Statement can be meaningfully and fairly presented on a combined basis; otherwise, separate Statements and Schedules are required. If the Co-Borrower section was completed about a non-applicant spouse or other person, this Statement and supporting schedules must be completed about that spouse or other person also.

Completed ☐ Jointly ☐ Not Jointly

ASSETS Description	Cash or Market Value	Liabilities and Pledged Assets. List the creditor's name, address, and account number for all outstanding debts, including automobile loans, revolving charge accounts, real estate loans, alimony, child support, stock pledges, etc. Use continuation sheet, if necessary. Indicate by (*) those liabilities, which will be satisfied upon sale of real estate owned or upon refinancing of the subject property.		
Cash deposit toward purchase held by:	$			
List checking and savings accounts below		LIABILITIES	Monthly Payment & Months Left to Pay	Unpaid Balance
Name and address of Bank, S&L, or Credit Union		Name and address of Company	$ Payment/Months	$
Acct. no.	$	Acct. no.		
Name and address of Bank, S&L, or Credit Union		Name and address of Company	$ Payment/Months	$
Acct. no.	$	Acct. no.		
Name and address of Bank, S&L, or Credit Union		Name and address of Company	$ Payment/Months	$
Acct. no.	$	Acct. no.		

Name and address of Bank, S&L, or Credit Union		Name and address of Company	$ Payment/Months	$
Acct. no.	$	Acct. no.		
Stocks & Bonds (Company name/ number & description)	$	Name and address of Company	$ Payment/Months	$
		Acct. no.		
Life insurance net cash value	$	Name and address of Company	$ Payment/Months	$
Face amount: $				
Subtotal Liquid Assets	$			
Real estate owned (enter market value from schedule of real estate owned)	$			
Vested interest in retirement fund	$			
Net worth of business(es) owned (attach financial statement)	$	Acct. no.		
Automobiles owned (make and year)	$	Alimony/Child Support/Separate Maintenance Payments Owed to:	$	
Other Assets (itemize)	$	Job-Related Expense (child care, union dues, etc.)	$	
		Total Monthly Payments	$	
Total Assets a.	$	**Net Worth** (a minus b) ▶	$	**Total Liabilities b.**	$

Schedule of Real Estate Owned (If additional properties are owned, use continuation sheet.)

Property Address (enter S if sold, PS if pending sale or R if rental being held for income) ▼	Type of Property	Present Market Value	Amount of Mortgages & Liens	Gross Rental Income	Mortgage Payments	Insurance, Maintenance, Taxes & Misc.	Net Rental Income
		$	$	$	$	$	$
Totals		$	$	$	$	$	$

List any additional names under which credit has previously been received and indicate appropriate creditor name(s) and account number(s):

Alternate Name	Creditor Name	Account Number

VII. DETAILS OF TRANSACTION		VIII. DECLARATIONS					
		If you answer "Yes" to any questions a through i, please use continuation sheet for explanation.	Borrower		Co-Borrower		
			Yes	No	Yes	No	
a. Purchase price	$	a. Are there any outstanding judgments against you?	☐	☐	☐	☐	
b. Alterations, improvements, repairs		b. Have you been declared bankrupt within the past 7 years?	☐	☐	☐	☐	
c. Land (if acquired separately)		c. Have you had property foreclosed upon or given title or deed in lieu thereof in the last 7 years?	☐	☐	☐	☐	
d. Refinance (incl. debts to be paid off)		d. Are you a party to a lawsuit?	☐	☐	☐	☐	
e. Estimated prepaid items		e. Have you directly or indirectly been obligated on any loan which resulted in foreclosure, transfer of title in lieu of foreclosure, or judgment?	☐	☐	☐	☐	
f. Estimated closing costs		(This would include such loans as home mortgage loans, SBA loans, home improvement loans, educational loans, manufactured (mobile) home loans, any mortgage, financial obligation, bond, or loan guarantee. If "Yes," provide details, including date, name, and address of Lender, FHA or VA case number, if any, and reasons for the action.)					
g. PMI, MIP, Funding Fee							
h. Discount (if Borrower will pay)							
i. Total costs (add items a through h)							

	VII. DETAILS OF TRANSACTION		VIII. DECLARATIONS	Borrower		Co-Borrower	
			If you answer "Yes" to any questions a through i, please use continuation sheet for explanation.	Yes	No	Yes	No
j.	Subordinate financing						
k.	Borrower's closing costs paid by Seller		f. Are you presently delinquent or in default on any Federal debt or any other loan, mortgage, financial obligation, bond, or loan guarantee? If "Yes," give details as described in the preceding question.	☐	☐	☐	☐
l.	Other Credits (explain)		g. Are you obligated to pay alimony, child support, or separate maintenance?	☐	☐	☐	☐
			h. Is any part of the down payment borrowed?	☐	☐	☐	☐
m.	Loan amount (exclude PMI, MIP, Funding Fee financed)		i. Are you a co-maker or endorser on a note?	☐	☐	☐	☐
			j. Are you a U.S. citizen?	☐	☐	☐	☐
			k. Are you a permanent resident alien?	☐	☐	☐	☐
n.	PMI, MIP, Funding Fee financed		l. **Do you intend to occupy the property as your primary residence?** If "Yes," complete question m below.	☐	☐	☐	☐
o.	Loan amount (add m & n)		m. Have you had an ownership interest in a property in the last three years?	☐	☐	☐	☐
p.	Cash from/to Borrower (subtract j, k, l & o from i)		(1) What type of property did you own—principal residence (PR), second home (SH), or investment property (IP)? (2) How did you hold title to the home—solely by yourself (S), jointly with your spouse (SP), or jointly with another person (O)?	_____ _____		_____ _____	

IX. ACKNOWLEDGEMENT AND AGREEMENT

Each of the undersigned specifically represents to Lender and to Lender's actual or potential agents, brokers, processors, attorneys, insurers, servicers, successors and assigns and agrees and acknowledges that: (1) the information provided in this application is true and correct as of the date set forth opposite my signature and that any intentional or negligent misrepresentation of this information contained in this application may result in civil liability, including monetary damages, to any person who may suffer any loss due to reliance upon any misrepresentation that I have made on this application, and/or criminal penalties including, but not limited to, fine or imprisonment or both under the provisions of Title 18, United States Code, Sec. 1001, et seq.; (2) the loan requested pursuant to this application (the "Loan") will be secured by a mortgage or deed of trust on the property described in this application; (3) the property will not be used for any illegal or prohibited purpose or use; (4) all statements made in this application are made for the purpose of obtaining a residential mortgage loan; (5) the property will be occupied as indicated in this application; (6) the Lender, its servicers, successors or assigns may retain the original and/or an electronic record of this application, whether or not the Loan is approved; (7) the Lender and its agents, brokers, insurers, servicers, successors, and assigns may continuously rely on the information contained in the application, and I am obligated to amend and/or supplement the information provided in this application if any of the material facts that I have represented herein should change prior to closing of the Loan; (8) in the event that my payments on the Loan become delinquent, the Lender, its servicers, successors or assigns may, in addition to any other rights and remedies that it may have relating to such delinquency, report my name and account information to one or more consumer reporting agencies; (9) ownership of the Loan and/or administration of the Loan account may be transferred with such notice as may be required by law; (10) neither Lender nor its agents, brokers, insurers, servicers, successors or assigns has made any representation or warranty, express or implied, to me regarding the property or the condition or value of the property; and (11) my transmission of this application as an "electronic record" containing my "electronic signature," as those terms are defined in applicable federal and/or state laws (excluding audio and video recordings), or my facsimile transmission of this application containing a facsimile of my signature, shall be as effective, enforceable and valid as if a paper version of this application were delivered containing my original written signature.

Acknowledgement. Each of the undersigned hereby acknowledges that any owner of the Loan, its servicers, successors and assigns, may verify or reverify any information contained in this application or obtain any information or data relating to the Loan, for any legitimate business purpose through any source, including a source named in this application or a consumer reporting agency.

Borrower's Signature	Date	Co-Borrower's Signature	Date
X		X	

X. INFORMATION FOR GOVERNMENT MONITORING PURPOSES

The following information is requested by the Federal Government for certain types of loans related to a dwelling in order to monitor the lender's compliance with equal credit opportunity, fair housing and home mortgage disclosure laws. You are not required to furnish this information, but are encouraged to do so. The law provides that a lender may not discriminate either on the basis of this information, or on whether you choose to furnish it. If you furnish the information, please provide both ethnicity and race. For race, you may check more than one designation. If you do not furnish ethnicity, race, or sex, under Federal regulations, this lender is required to note the information on the basis of visual observation and surname if you have made this application in person. If you do not wish to furnish the information, please check the box below. (Lender must review the above material to assure that the disclosures satisfy all requirements to which the lender is subject under applicable state law for the particular type of loan applied for.)

BORROWER ☐ I do not wish to furnish this information	CO-BORROWER ☐ I do not wish to furnish this information
Ethnicity: ☐ Hispanic or Latino ☐ Not Hispanic or Latino	**Ethnicity:** ☐ Hispanic or Latino ☐ Not Hispanic or Latino
Race: ☐ American Indian or Alaska Native ☐ Asian ☐ Black or African American ☐ Native Hawaiian or Other Pacific Islander ☐ White	**Race:** ☐ American Indian or Alaska Native ☐ Asian ☐ Black or African American ☐ Native Hawaiian or Other Pacific Islander ☐ White
Sex: ☐ Female ☐ Male	**Sex:** ☐ Female ☐ Male

To be Completed by Interviewer This application was taken by: ☐ Face-to-face interview ☐ Mail ☐ Telephone ☐ Internet	Interviewer's Name (print or type)	Name and Address of Interviewer's Employer
	Interviewer's Signature Date	
	Interviewer's Phone Number (incl. area code)	

Use this continuation sheet if you need more space to complete the Residential Loan Application. Mark **B** f or Borrower or **C** for Co-Borrower.	Borrower:	Agency Case Number:
	Co-Borrower:	Lender Case Number:

I/We fully understand that it is a Federal crime punishable by fine or imprisonment, or both, to knowingly make any false statements concerning any of the above facts as applicable under the provisions of Title 18, United States Code, Section 1001, et seq.

Borrower's Signature	Date	Co-Borrower's Signature	Date
X		X	

> **Security interest "attaches" when:**
> - An agreement between two parties has been reached
> - The item has been given value
> - The debtor has acquired rights in the form of collateral

S U M M A R Y

As we have seen in this chapter, homeownership is feasible for more people nowadays, due to the different financing options available. Homes may be purchased by making a promissory note to a lender, securing the note by using the property as collateral (as evidenced by the trust deed or mortgage). By assuming a trust deed or mortgage, the lender is assured of recouping its initial investment through monthly payments on the loan, or by selling the property to cover the debt against it.

There are special clauses in financing which describe the hierarchy (or importance) of trust deeds or by requiring action on a loan in the event ownership changes. Additionally, junior trust deeds may be used to secure additional funding, in the event that the first trust deed and down payment are not sufficient to cover the selling price of the home.

Alternative financing is intended for those people who may have special situations or circumstances that make a traditional real estate loan impossible or unattractive. These loan programs allow rates, payments and terms of the loan to fluctuate with the needs of the borrower.

How to qualify the buyer and the steps in closing and servicing the loan were examined in depth. It is important for you to understand this process, as your clients will most likely have many questions regarding the process, how long it might take and the different steps or functions they may have to perform before being approved. You, as the agent, are the most logical first person to ask, and should be able to aid your client with all of his or her needs.

Finally, finance regulation was discussed and what rights the consumer has. These are also important to know, and will usually come out in the disclosure process.

Real estate finance is very in-depth and by no means does this chapter cover everything there is to know. For further understanding of a complicated, yet very important concept, it is in your best interest to take a real estate finance course.

T E R M S   A N D   P H R A S E S

Adjustable Rate Mortgage (ARM) – A loan with a flexible interest rate that increases or decreases with market interest rate changes.

Collateral – An object of value that is pledged as security for the purchase of another object of value. In real estate, collateral is the property that is pledged as security for the note, as evidenced by the trust deed.

Conforming Loan - Conventional loans that meet the underwriting standards for purchase by Fannie Mae or Freddie Mac

Default – Failure by the trustor to pay the monthly or installment payments on the promissory note for the property purchased.

Equity – The value in a property (or the appreciated value of the property over what is owed on the loan) after all the debts have been paid off.

Foreclosure – The procedure a lender may take to legally sell property in default (done through court action or by a trustee's sale).

Hard Money Loan – A type of trust deed or loan given in exchange for cash. The borrower can utilize the money for any purpose; it need not be used to purchase property.

Interest – The cost a lender will charge when lending money to a borrower.

Junior Trust Deed – A trust deed that is recorded after the first trust deed. The junior trust deed is considered less important (or of lesser priority) than the trust deed that was recorded first.

Mortgage – Legal document pledging property as security for a debt.

Mortgagee- The lender loaning the money for the purchase of real estate.

Mortgagor – The borrower requesting a loan to purchase real estate.

Prepayment Clause –A clause in a loan that penalizes a borrower for paying the loan back early. In the event the loan is paid off early, a percentage of the loan may be collected as penalty.

Primary Financing – Financing referring to a first trust deed.

Principal – The amount of a loan, not including the interest.

Promissory Note – The written promise a borrower makes to a lender pledging to pay back the loan. This promissory note is the evidence of debt.

Purchase Money Loan – A loan made specifically for the purchase of real estate.

Reconveyance Deed –The deed used to transfer property from a lender back to the borrower, once the loan is paid in full.

Secondary Financing – Financing referring to a second trust deed.

Second Trust Deed – A junior trust deed, or evidence of a debt that is recorded after the original trust deed.

Security – The collateral used to secure a loan.

Trust Deed – A document where the title to property (bare legal title) will pass to a third party (called a trustee) as security for the debt.

Trustee – Holds bare legal title to property where there is a deed of trust.

Trustor – The borrower in a trust deed.

Usury – The act of lending money and charging an interest rate greater than is allowed by law.

Wrap-Around Loan – A financing option in which a new loan is placed in a secondary position. The new loan includes both the unpaid principal balance of the first loan as well as whatever new sums are loaned by the lender. Wrap-around loans are sometimes called all-inclusive trust deeds.

C H A P T E R   Q U I Z

1. A loan generated from the Government National Mortgage Association (GNMA) or Ginnie Mae is considered to be:
     a. Primary financing
     b. Secondary financing
     c. First trust deed
     d. None of the above

2. Primary financing refers to:
     a. First trust deeds
     b. Junior trust deeds
     c. Any trust deed created from a financial institution
     d. Any trust deed created by a government agency

3. Money for mortgages and trust deeds come from two primary money market sources. These sources are:
     a. Directly from an individual or institutions that have accumulated private funds they are willing to lend.
     b. Indirectly from a financial institution that uses the deposits of its clients to lend money to other people for the purpose of buying a home.
     c. The government.
     d. Both A and B

4. Which of the following statements are true?
     a. The money market is stable and unchanging; it will be the same today as it was 10 years ago, as it will be 10 years into the future.
     b. The money market is unstable and changes constantly. The supply of money today may not be the same as tomorrow.
     c. The money market is changing, but slowly and changes generally take years to make.
     d. The money market can change, but is unlikely to change unless a major event occurs affecting our economy.

5. Conforming loans:
     a. Meet all Fannie Mae or Freddie Mac underwriting standards
     b. Are not assumable
     c. May be written for 15 or 30 years
     d. All of the above are correct

6. Which of the following is not a government originated and controlled loan program?
     a. Farmer Mac
     b. Ginnie Mae
     c. Freddie Mac
     d. All of the above are correct

7. Lenders can be classified into which of the following groups?
   a. Institutional and commercial
   b. Commercial and non-institutional
   c. Institutional and non-institutional
   d. Commercial and residential

8. Commercial banks, savings associations, and life insurance companies are examples of which type of lender?
   a. Institutional lenders
   b. Commercial lenders
   c. Residential lenders
   d. Non-institutional lenders

9. Mortgage companies make loans based on:
   a. Capital they borrow from commercial banks
   b. Their own capital
   c. Capital they borrow from clients
   d. None of the above

10. Seller carryback financing is available in which of the following situations?
    a. Only when the seller owns the home, free and clear of any loans or trust deeds.
    b. When the seller's trust deed or loan is transferable to another individual or individuals.
    c. When the buyer can only obtain primary financing, the seller can hold secondary financing.
    d. All of the above are correct.

11. What is the maximum commission a loan broker could make on a 5-year first trust deed, under $30,000?
    a. 3%
    b. 5%
    c. 10%
    d. 15%

12. What is the maximum commission a loan broker could make on a 10-year second trust deed worth $45,000?
    a. 15%
    b. 10%
    c. 5%
    d. There is no maximum.

13. A cash loan, not an extension of credit, is known as:
    a. Hard money loan
    b. Secondary financing
    c. Seller carryback
    d. None of the above

14. Shorter processing time, less red tape and more flexibility describes which type of loan?
    a. Government backed loan
    b. Conventional loan
    c. Commercial loan
    d. Institutional loan

15. Interest rates have what type of relationship to home sales? (A)
   a. Inverse relationship: when one increases, the other generally decreases
   b. Direct correlation: both increase or decrease at the same time
   c. There is no relationship; they are unrelated to each other.
   d. None of the above.

16. Lenders usually require what to secure the loan?
   a. Down payment
   b. Collateral
   c. Purchase contract or deposit receipt.
   d. All of the above.

17. A loan where the interest rate changes periodically, usually in relation to an index, with payments going up or down accordingly, is called:
   a. Fixed rate.
   b. All inclusive trust deed
   c. Adjustable rate mortgage
   d. Piggyback note

18. Which of the following is not a step in the financing process?
   a. Servicing the loan
   b. Approving and processing the loan
   c. Qualifying the borrower
   d. Qualifying the seller

19. Qualifying the borrower usually involves the three "C's". Which of the following is correct?
   a. Character
   b. Capacity
   c. Collateral
   d. All of the above are correct

20. Servicing the loan refers to:
   a. Closing escrow
   b. Transferring all appropriate funds to all parties as specified in the loan
   c. Record keeping of payments and loan status
   d. None of the above.

CHAPTER

TAXES

What you will learn in this Chapter

- Real Property Taxes

- Income Taxes

- Installment Sales

- Estate, Inheritance and Gift Taxes

- Foreign Investment in Real Property Tax Act

- California Withholding

- Tax Shelter

Test Your Knowledge

1. Ad valorem means:
   a. Full cash value
   b. Property taxes
   c. According to value
   d. Percentage

2. The difference between the seller's valuation on the sale of property and the new valuation based on the sales price of the property for tax purposes is covered in what?
   a. Supplemental tax bill
   b. Ad valorem
   c. Escrow
   d. Prorated value to be paid at the end of escrow

3. Proposition 60 allows for what persons to transfer the factored base year value of their current residence to a new residence within the same county?
   a. Persons 55 years or older.
   b. Taxpayers who are severely or permanently disabled
   c. A married couple where at least one spouse is 55 years or older.
   d. All of the above.

4. The "original basis" of property refers to:
   a. One-time closing costs, or buying expenses
   b. Purchase price
   c. Original base year value
   d. Both A and B

5. Under the like-kind rule:
   a. Real property may be exchanged for personal property but personal property may not be exchanged for real property
   b. Personal property may be exchanged for real property, but real property may not be exchanged for personal property
   c. Only real property may be exchanged for real property, and personal property exchanged for personal property
   d. Any type of property may be exchanged for any other type of property with no limits or regulations.

6. A single person occupying his or her residence for at least two years may exclude how much money from any taxable gain upon sale?
   a. $100,000
   b. $250,000
   c. $500,000
   d. $650,000

7. All of the following are considered home improvements except:
   a. Carpeting
   b. Room additions
   c. Pools
   d. Landscaping

One of the biggest headaches when buying or selling property is determining what taxes must be paid on the property, when those taxes will be due, and how to acquire the appropriate amount of money to pay those taxes on time. No doubt, property taxes are among the biggest hurdles for people buying property, and they may mean the difference between being able to afford the monthly mortgage and not being able to buy the property at all. In this chapter, we will look at the different taxes on personal and real property. We will also examine the tax rates applied to different types of property, the payment schedule for these taxes, and the withholdings, if any, that people must set aside. We will also look at exemptions, for those who qualify, and how to best use a tax exemption.

In addition to federal and state tax issues, we will examine the different requirements for foreign and domestic investors (from states outside of California). We will note the differences in withholding and any exceptions to the withholding rules for which an individual may qualify.

We will learn how taxes are assessed and also examine any special taxes people are required to pay. To wrap up the chapter, we will explore taxes on gifts or inheritances and any exemptions on such gifts.

The concept of taxation may be difficult to grasp, but it is very important for you, as a real estate professional, to protect both yourself and your client. You should also be able to aid your client in understanding the different steps required when buying or selling a home. Additionally, providing your client with information regarding the amount of property taxes required, as well as any special assessments or other issues of which they must be aware, will make the buying process easier for the client and allow him or her to gain confidence in you, as well.

R E A L   P R O P E R T Y   T A X E S

All real estate investments are taxed on three different levels. The first is the federal level, which includes income tax, estate tax and gift tax. These taxes are generally applied when the real estate has been conveyed to another person through sale or gifting.

The next level of taxation is the state level. The state will tax a homeowner on income made from the sale of his or her home (income tax). Just as with federal taxes, the state taxes from real estate profit are applied when the home is sold.

Finally, there are local government taxes on real estate. These taxes are based on the property's value (sometimes referred to as ad valorem). Taxes assessed at the local government level are property taxes, special assessments and transfer taxes.

Ad Valorem
- A term meaning "according to value". Real estate taxation at the local government level is based on a property's value.

Should a taxpayer not pay his or her taxes on time, or at all, they may lose their home in a process called foreclosure. Foreclosure can happen for many reasons, but in a tax situation it is to satisfy the unpaid tax debt on the property.

Taxes have a direct correlation to sales. There are many financial factors that go into buying a home. If a buyer is looking at a condominium he or she must analyze not only the monthly payment, but also the homeowners association dues, any special assessments and the tax responsibility. What may seem like a reasonable, or easy monthly payment now may become out of reach for the buyer. Taxes being one component to this equation may deter people from purchasing. When taxes are higher, sales will be lower, and the opposite is true when taxes are low.

California Tax Calendar
It is important for you to know the critical tax dates for the state of California. The following calendar will help you visualize these important dates. Your clients must be made aware of these dates so they can be made aware of when the tax obligations will be when purchasing the purchasing the home. Additionally, it is important for your client to understand that taxes will be prorated between the buyer and seller.

Real Property Tax Calendar

January	February	March
Jan 1: Delinquent taxes become a lien.	**Feb 1**: Payment due for the second tax installment.	
April	**May**	**June**
April 10: Unpaid second tax installment becomes delinquent at 5:00 P.M.		**June 8**: A list of all delinquent tax payers ispublished **June 30**: A book sale may be held **June 30**: Calif. tax year ends
July	**August**	**September**
July 1: California's tax year begins		**Sept 1**: Yearly tax rates are set
October	**November**	**December**
	Nov 1: Payment due for the first tax insatallment	**Dec 10**: First installment of taxes becomes delinquent at 5:00 P.M.

Billing
Depending on if a property owner pays taxes directly or if he or she utilizes a lending agency will determine how tax bills are sent, and what they might look like. If the owner is paying taxes separate from a lending agency one bill is sent out, the original, directly to the property owner. By contrast, if the property owner utilizes a lending agency, the lending agency will receive the original bill statement for payment. The owner will receive a copy of this tax bill, which will clearly say for information only. An

impound account is a trust account established by the lender to pay property taxes and hazard insurance.

Since taxes are due at the same time each year, it is the property owner's responsibility to make sure these taxes are paid on time. With knowledge of the tax calendar, property owners need to make sure they have either paid these bills, or that the lending agency normally paying the bill has received the original statement, and that it was paid in full. Not receiving a tax bill is not considered a valid reason for not paying taxes on time. Should the due date for taxes fall on a holiday or weekend, the due date is extended to the next business day.

Supplemental Tax Bill

Supplemental tax bills serve to "catch up" the new owner's tax responsibility on property. This statement may confuse you. The supplemental tax bill is in addition to the regular tax bill. The first tax bill received on property will be based on the assessed value of the property when the seller lived there. The new owner must pay this bill, and then pay the supplemental bill, which reflects the tax obligation on the property after the new assessment has been completed. In time, a third tax bill will be sent to the property owner with the correct value for him or her to pay. So you may think of the first two bills as the obligation for the first tax installment on the property, the third tax bill satisfies the second tax installment.

California Tax Bill

Each California tax bill will contain very specific information helping the property owner, bor lending agency easily identify it as the correct bill for the intended property. The bill will have identifying material listing an accurate description and parcel number. The bill will list the full cash value of the property. This value will reflect the full-assessed value of a home purchased after 1975, or the assessment as of 1975 for any home purchased before that date. All tax bills will have a breakdown of any special assessments from bonds and land assessments from improvement assessments. Finally, the full amount of the tax itemized into first and second installments will be on the bill. Again, just as it is the property owner's responsibility to make sure he or she pays the tax obligation on time, it is also their responsibility to make sure the tax bill is accurate.

Tax Year

The tax year runs from July 1 – June 30. Property taxes are payable in two installments, with one due on November 1 and the second due on February 1. For property owners who don't pay their installments at these set intervals, payment becomes delinquent as of December 10 (for the November installment) and April 10 (for the February installment). Those who make delinquent payments are charged a 10% penalty fee, which is added directly to the installment payment.

For those taxpayers who have not paid their taxes by the end of the tax year (June 30), a book sale or delinquent property sale will take place. The property owner will not lose possession or title to the property, but he or she has only 5 years to pay the delinquent balance. If a property owner does not pay these taxes within the 5-year grace period, the state may hold a public auction to sell the property to pay for all back taxes. The highest bidder will be the new owner of the property, provided he or she is able to pay for the bid in cash. The highest bidder also receives a tax deed to the property.

Remember

- The tax year runs from July 1 – June 30.
- Installment payments are due November 1 and February 1, respectively.
- Installment payments become delinquent after December 15 and April 15, respectively.
- A book sale allows the property owner to remain on the property, but gives him or her only 5 years to pay all delinquent taxes.
- An auction to sell the property occurs if the property owner does not pay his or her delinquent taxes within 5 years.
- The highest bidder receives a tax deed to the property.

There are a few exceptions to the tax schedule. For example, those persons 62 years of age or older, with at least 20% equity in their home and with total income less than $24,000 per year, may postpone taxes or defer them. When a person takes this option, a lien is placed on the property. There is no time limit on the postponement. The state will receive its money when the home is sold, when the claimant no longer qualifies for the postponement (if his or her annual income rises above $24,000) or when the claimant no longer occupies the property. In addition to those persons 62 years or older, those who are disabled or blind may also take advantage of postponement of taxes, creating a lien on their property to the state. For more information regarding the postponement of taxes, please visit www.soo.ca.gov.

Special Assessments

Special assessments are imposed on property when a community needs to raise money for a specific purpose, such as street repairs. Special assessments will appear on the tax bill as a separate entry. Just as property taxes are based on **ad valorem**, so too are the special assessments. Special assessments are not simply charged without the approval of the taxpayer. As long as a taxpayer exercises his or her right to vote, he or she will be aware of the assessment, as all special assessments must pass with a two-thirds voter majority. Special assessments may be paid in one payment, or may be spread out over several years.

Special assessments are exempt from any limitations that Proposition 13 places on property taxes. The city can sell municipal bonds and include these on the property tax bill. Additionally, any buyer who may receive a special assessment in a new development (as you will read below) must be told about the assessment. Buyers must also be made aware that their property taxes, when paid alone, will be less than when they are included with the special assessment. Any agents who fail to disclose a special assessment when selling property may be disciplined by their real estate commission.

The Street Improvement Act of 1911 raises money in a special assessment to repair underground utilities, sewers and streets. The special assessment for the Street Improvement Act of 1911 is placed on the properties it directly affects, with payments made during the regular tax installment intervals. The Street Improvement Act of 1911 is a very specific tax, designed for special projects or repairs.

The Mello-Roos Community Facilities Act finances projects and structures such as parks, fire stations, streets, sewers, schools and other services or recreational areas found in a new development. Each lot or parcel of land in the development will have a special assessment placed on it to pay for these services. A lien is placed on the property by the developer of the property, as the developer is responsible for payment of municipal bonds for these services. The developer is responsible for payments on this municipal bond(s) until the properties are sold and special assessments are paid. Mello-Roos is a specific type of special assessment for this purpose and does not charge its improvements to property taxes.

Proposition 13

In 1978, Proposition 13 was approved. It set a maximum annual tax on real property of no more than 1 percent of the property's base year value - i.e., its purchase price. Each year following this, the base year value may be increased by an inflation factor of no more than 2 percent. Each time a property is transferred from one owner to a new one, the base year value is reset for the new owner at the new selling price, and tax is reassessed at 1 percent of the new base year value.

Homeowners who make improvements to their properties, such as adding on a new room or putting in a pool, will have their properties reassessed to include the value of these improvements. However, those property owners who do not make any changes, improvements or remodels to their properties will continue to see only a maximum 2 percent increase per year over the original base year value. A base year value that has been increased by inflation factor adjustments is sometimes called the Factored Base Year Value (FBYV).

There are some special exceptions to the transfer of property and the assessment of the new base year value for property. Under Proposition 13, a property transfer between a husband and wife will not result in a new assessment of base year value. Additionally, any principal residence transferred from a parent to a child, or the first $1 million of other real property, will be exempt from reassessment of the base year value. In these two exemptions, spouses and children will continue to pay taxes on the factored base year value that applied at the time of the transfer.

Remember
- Proposition 13 took effect in 1978.
- Tax on property is limited to 1 percent of a property's original purchase price, or base year value.
- A maximum 2 percent increase in the base year value is allowed per year.
- When property is transferred from one owner to another, the sales price becomes the new base year value, and tax is assessed at 1 percent of this new amount.
- Spouses and children are exempt from having the base year value of property reset when there is a transfer of a principal residence or other real property worth one million dollars or less.

Proposition 58

Any property transfer between spouses is exempt from a reassessment. Additionally property transfer between parents and children is exempt from a reassessment provided it is a principal residence. Any property that is not a principle residence transferred between a parent and child will be exempt from reassessment for the first $1,000,000. Any amount past that will be subject to reassessment.

Proposition 60

Homeowners 55 years of age or older may sell their home and transfer their current base year value to their new property. There are, however, a few limitations on this base year value transfer. The newly purchased home must be of equal or lesser value than the home being sold, based on the current sales price of the old home, not its original purchase price. So, homeowners in this age bracket will greatly benefit from this type of tax incentive, because their new home will usually have a taxable value that is much lower than its current purchase price. The new property must be located in the same county as the property sold, and Proposition 60 must be recognized in that particular area, as well.

The way Proposition 60 works is that the base year value of the home being sold, which can be transferred and used as the base year value for the new home, is set at the old home's value as of March 1, 1975, or the year the property was purchased if it was after this date, plus the maximum 2 percent annual inflation adjustments. Rather than being taxed on the new home based on its purchase price, the buyer will be taxed on the base year value of the old home. An example will demonstrate this principle more clearly.

Example:

Andrew and Tammy purchased a home in 1978 for $100,000. The home was large enough for their 4 children who eventually left home. When their last child moved away, Andrew and Tammy decided they wanted a smaller home. Over the years, their home had appreciated to $300,000. The factored base year value on the home they were selling was $117,500 at the time of the sale. Andrew and Tammy were allowed to carry this over to the new property, due to Proposition 60. The new property they purchased cost $295,000.

Tax assessed on base year value carried over from sold property = $1,175 ($117,500 x 1%)

Tax that would have been assessed on the new property with no carryover = $2,950 ($295,000 x 1%)

By taking advantage of Proposition 60, Andrew and Tammy will save $1,776 in taxes.

Remember

- Proposition 60 took effect as of March 1, 1975
- Persons 55 years or older are allowed to transfer the base year value from one residence to another, provided the new property is currently worth the same or less than the fair market value of the property being sold.
- A maximum 2 percent increase in the base year value may continue to be assessed each year.

Proposition 90

Proposition 90 is similar to Proposition 60. In Proposition 60 homeowners are restricted to purchasing a replacement home in the same county as the one they are selling. Proposition 90 now allows homeowners who are selling a home in one county to purchase a home in another county in California. People in the market looking to buy property under Proposition 90 must be careful, however. Not every county in California accepts Proposition 90, so it is up to you as the agent to make sure your client can conduct the transaction under these terms.

Change-in-Ownership Statement

In all property transfers, the new buyer must notify the county assessor or recorder of the acquisition for local taxation purposes. The new owner must note the transaction within 45 days of recording the trust deed to the property.

Exemptions

In general, all real and personal property is taxable, although there are a few exemptions from taxation. These exemptions are:

- An individual's personal property and home furnishings

- Property owned by non-profit organizations (such as a private school)

- Stocks and promissory notes

- Government property

- Property owned by or used for religious groups, hospitals or charitable purposes

- Some boats or ocean vessels

- Agricultural crops, fruit-bearing trees less than five years old, and grape vines less than three years old

Homeowner's Exemption

The homeowner's exemption allows the owner to be exempt from taxes on the first $7,000 of the property's full cash value. This exemption is only allowed for primary residences, which may include townhouses, condominiums and residences. It is not available for vacation properties or income properties that are not the primary residence. The homeowner must obtain a form from the county tax assessor, and submit it by February 15 of the current tax year, to be eligible for the $7,000 exemption.

Veterans qualify for an additional exemption of $4,000 on property not already filed for exemption under the homeowner's exemption rule. So, any vacation properties or other properties not eligible for the homeowner's exemption may qualify for the veteran's exemption. There are, however, rules about which properties qualify. For example, property worth only $5,000, or property owned by a husband and wife that is worth $10,000 or less, is ineligible for the homeowner's exemption.

Unmarried spouses as well as a pensioned father or mother of a qualified deceased veteran are eligible to receive the veteran's exemption. Completely disabled veterans may be eligible for an exemption of up to $100,000. This exemption may also be extended to a disabled veteran's spouse, provided the spouse remains unmarried.

Senior Citizen's Property Tax Postponement

Senior citizens over the age of 62 and people who are disabled or blind may be eligible to forego paying property taxes. Eligibility requirements include age (as of January 1), income or disability. Some people may qualify for a partial tax postponement, while others may be relieved of paying all property taxes.

INCOME TAXES

Federal income taxes are based on a person's total earnings for the year. The amount of money a person made in that year will determine their tax bracket. The more money a person earns, the higher the percentage they will pay on that money. The same is true for those persons earning less money (i.e., less money = lower percentage of taxes).

To obtain a tax shelter or tax relief, people often buy real estate. Though real estate is taxed with property taxes, there are legal reductions in tax liability for those persons who own real estate. Real estate used as the person's primary residence as well as income properties will allow a person to qualify for these tax shelters. Specific rules for the property type must be followed in order to take full advantage of these legal reductions.

Personal Residence

In the past, California allowed its residents the option to rollover some or all gains earned from the sale of a primary residence, provided the sale of the primary residence was used to purchase a new primary residence. There was a four-year grace period given to the seller to find a replacement for the primary residence. In addition to the rollover allowance, homeowners 55 years of age or over were given a once-in-a-lifetime $125,000 exemption for the sale of their principal residence.

In May 6, 1997 the old exclusions and rollover allowances were replaced by new exclusion rules for homeowners selling their primary residence. There are, however, certain circumstances where the homeowner may elect to take the old exclusions rather than the new ones. The new rules now allow a homeowner, regardless of age, to exclude up to $250,000 of taxable income from the sale of a primary residence, while married couples may exclude up to $500,000. In order to qualify for this exemption, the homeowner must have lived in the home for the past two years. This includes the sale of property by a married couple. Both spouses must have lived in the property for at least two years to qualify for the exemption. If the woman lived in the home for three years, but the husband was only there for 21 months, the $500,000 tax exemption will not be realized. A $250,000 exemption will be granted as the woman qualifies for that portion of the exemption. Because of this time requirement, homeowners are generally allowed to take this exemption only once every two years. There are, however, certain circumstances, which allow a homeowner to take advantage of this exemption, even if they have not lived in the home for this two-year period. Persons who are transferred due to a job change or relocation, persons selling their home due to health reasons, or those transferring as a result of unforeseen tragedies may take advantage of this exemption. The two-year period does not have to be continuous.

Example:

Mark purchased a home in 2000. He lived in the home for 6 months, and then decided to rent it out due to financial reasons. The lease to his home expired in January 2004, and rather than release the home to the tenant, Mark decided to move back in. He then lived in the home an additional 18 months, then decided to sell. Because Mark lived in his residence for a total of 2 years combined, he is allowed to take the $250,000 tax exemption.

In addition to the exemption, homeowners may take certain deductions on their home. Interest on mortgage and property taxes is deductible for both primary and secondary homes. Unfortunately, a homeowner cannot deduct improvements or depreciation on the property, though improvements may be added to the cost basis when the home is sold. This aids the homeowner because the amount of taxable gain from the property at the close of sale will not be as high when the original cost basis of the home increases. If a person purchased their home for $300,000, made $75,000 of improvements, and then sold the home for $600,000, their capital gains tax will be based on a $225,000 profit. The cost of the improvements will be added to the original cost of the home, providing a break to the homeowner when they sell the property. Assuming our homeowners have been living on the property for more than 2 years, and given that the gain on the home is less than the allowable $250,000 exception, this homeowner will not have to pay capital gains taxes if they follow all necessary rules and steps when filing their taxes.

Original Purchase Price   *$300,000*
Improvements to the home   *$75,000*
Adjusted cost basis of the home   *$375,000*

Selling Price – Adjusted Cost Basis = Taxable Gain
$600,000 - $375,000 = $225,000

In order to fully understand the above example, you must understand what different terms mean. Basis is the original purchase price of the residence. For example, a home purchased 9 years ago for $300,000 is now worth $650,000. The basis of this home is $300,000. Adjusted cost basis is an adjustment to the original purchase price to take account improvements made to the property. For example, a home with $75,000 of improvements would now have a basis (adjusted basis) of $375,000. This is very important to understand, as it will save your client money in taxable gains. Capital gains is the profit realized by a person when they sell property. This money is subject to be taxed. Generally speaking, any money realized as a capital gain will be taxed at a maximum rate of 15 percent for property that has been owned for at least 12 months or more. This figure will change depending on what income bracket your client is in, so make sure to check the current laws and figures for your clients' situation.

Income Property
We know that by owning a primary residence, there are exemptions for which a homeowner may qualify if they live in the home that is being sold or certain tax deductions can be made, based on ownership of property. Income properties also have exceptions and tax benefits, though they are different from primary residence exemptions. Investors in income property can take a depreciation allowance on the property. This means that the owner of the income property can claim depreciation on the property

and deduct it from the annual tax bill. As you will recall, the owner of a primary residence does not have this option.

A deduction based on depreciation may not be a physical depreciation of the structure (such as the condition of the exterior paint, or the age of the furnace). Instead, the deduction is based on the economic or useful life of the property. After a certain number of years, the building will no longer be capable of generating income, and the property owner is allowed to take a yearly depreciation on the property. Depreciation on a property such as this is generally figured using straight line depreciation, or figuring up the number of years for which a property will be useful and dividing its purchase price into this figure. The resulting number is the amount yearly deductible from taxes, less the cost of land.

> *Example:*
>
> *The economic life of a property is 37 years. The value of the property is $500,000, while the land value is worth $200,000. The actual value of the structure is $300,000.*
>
> *$300,000 / 27 years = $10,000*
>
> *This investor is allowed an $11,111 tax deduction per year based on the structure's depreciation.*

Generally speaking, all real property must use the straight-line method of depreciation. Straight-line depreciation is figured by depreciating an equal amount of money over the life of the improvement or structure. For residential property, the useful life of an improvement is 27.5 years, while nonresidential property has a useful life of 39 years.

Occasionally the term depreciable basis may be used. This basis may be considered to be the original basis or property less its land value. Taking the original basis of the property and multiplying the percentage of improvements to the land can also figure it.

Other tax benefits extended to an investor include: deduction of the mortgage interest; deduction of maintenance and utilities; deduction of any loss on a sale of the property over the original or adjusted cost basis; insurance premium deduction, management fee deductions, and property tax deductions. Any profits made on the sale of an income property are deferrable (paid at a later time). This benefit is not given to owners of primary residences, however all gain (regardless of how much or how little) on the sale of an income property is taxable.

Capital gains taxes are calculated in the same way on an income property as it is on a primary residence. There are a few additional steps to be taken when figuring the income property. The income property will begin with the purchase price, plus any improvements. Any depreciation claimed is subtracted from the amount to arrive at the adjusted cost basis. Any expenses incurred during the sale of the property, such as realtor's commission, is deducted from the sale price to arrive at the adjusted selling price.

> *Original Purchase Price + Improvements – Depreciation Claimed = Adjusted Cost Basis*
>
> *Selling Price – Sale Expenses (Commissions) = Adjusted Selling Price*
>
> *Adjusted Selling Price – Adjusted Cost Basis = Taxable Gain or Loss*
>
> *(The loss is not taxable. In fact, in investor may take a tax deduction on this loss)*

292

Installment Sale

Installment sales are used to help spread out capital gains on a property for a period of more than one year. This is done by taking several, smaller payments for the sale of property instead of one large chunk of money. A seller may also take back a note, allowing the tax payments to be deferred. When a seller takes the option of a wrap-around loan, or an all-inclusive trust deed, he or she accepts monthly payments from the buyer. The seller will only be taxed on the gain earned in one year's time, which will be spread out over the term of the trust deed.

Besides the obvious advantage, an additional advantage of doing an installment sale is paying tax on current money in the future. This is an advantage because by paying tax on current money in the future you end up paying less money due to inflated dollars. One dollar today will be worth less than one dollar in five years due to inflation.

Tax-Deferred Exchanges

A tax-deferred exchange, also called a 1031 Exchange, occurs when an investor exchanges property for a like property of another property of equal value, and defers any taxes until the property being exchanged is sold.

Properties must be of equal value, at least on paper. Property must also be like kind property. Like kind property means the properties being exchanged are the same. Real property cannot be exchanged for personal property because those two types of property are not alike. A business may be exchanged for another, even if they manufacture different products; it is still a business for a business, or like kind.

When properties are not of equal value, cash or non-like property must be added to the exchange and given to the disadvantaged property owner, to make the exchange of the two properties equal in value. This exchange is called a boot exchange. Personal residences are not allowed as inclusions in a tax-deferred exchange. Only properties such as apartment buildings, commercial buildings or land are eligible. Like kind dictates property must be similar in nature, equal value dictates that an exchange must be of equal monetary value.

When the properties are sold, the cost basis of the original property being exchanged becomes the cost basis of the newly-purchased property, provided the two properties are equal. If there is a boot exchange to create equality, the cost basis will change. Ultimately, the capital gain or loss is figured in the same way as it is for other income property.

Example:

Property 1

Value	*$700,000*
Encumbrances	*$125,000*
Equity	*$575,000*

Property 2

Value	*$650,000*
Encumbrances	*$100,000*
Equity	*$550,000*

In order to qualify for a tax-deferred exchange, the person owning property 2 needs to add a boot worth $25,000 to make the two properties equal. The owner of property 1 will be taxed on the $25,000 boot he or she will receive in the exchange, while the owner of property 2 will not have any taxes.

A person may qualify for a complete tax-deferred exchange if he or she trades up to a property that is equal or greater in value than the property they currently have. This is usually referred to as the buy-up rule. All equity must be absorbed into the new property to be completely tax-deferred. If any money is taken out during the exchange, this money is subject to taxation, nullifying the complete tax-deferred exchange, making a partial tax-deferred exchange.

When conducting any type of exchange, property ownership must stay the same. This means if an individual owns property and is interested in an exchange, the new property must be individually owned. Similarly, if a corporation owns property and does an exchange, the new property will have to be owned by the corporation. There are three ways to hold property: as an individual, corporation, or partnership.

There may also be a reverse exchange. A reverse exchange is when a person finds a replacement property before exchanging his or her property. In this event, an exchange accommodation titleholder will take title to the new property until the sale of the exchange property is final. The sale of the old property, or the property to be exchanged, must happen within 180 days.

State Income Taxes
State income taxes and their brackets are different from the federal income taxes. Each person is required to file a return for both state and federal taxes.

Persons living in California for the entire year must file a tax return if they are either single or the head of a household making over $6,000 per year. They must also file if they are married with a combined income of over $12,000. All other persons who don't meet the one-year residency requirement are required to file a non-resident tax return.

Sale-Leaseback
When a person sells his or her home, he or she can gain a tax advantage by continuing to live in the sold property, assuming the buyer agrees to this. This is called a sale-leaseback. The property owner will sell the home, and then continue living there in a lease situation.

The person releasing the property that he or she just sold will realize several tax advantages. First, they can write off all payment of rent, as it is tax deductible. Second, it would improve the person's debt to asset ratio, making them more attractive to a lender in the event he or she wants to borrow money. Third, it frees up working capital. When the person owned the home, he or she had a lot of profit tied up in the home. By selling the house, and continuing to live there, the seller/renter now has quite a chunk of money freed up for other investing or other purposes.

The buyer will also realize advantages in the sale-leaseback program. First, they will be acquiring an investment property virtually free as someone else is paying the mortgage. The property will most likely appreciate in value, thus creating equity, with a minimal personal investment. Once the lease payments pay off the property, the lessor will receive title to the property with little out of pocket expense on their own behalf. Additionally, the yield on a sale-leaseback will typically be higher than on a traditional mortgage.

Principal residence real estate also receives special tax treatment. Taxpayers may only have one principal residence at any one time, as this is the residence he or she will reside in. If the taxpayer does not reside on the property, it cannot be considered a principal or primary residence. A principal residence does not have to be a single-family home, it can also be any other type of property used as a dwelling. Condominiums, mobile homes or any other form of housing used as a primary residence will qualify. The land that the home sits upon is also considered part of the primary residence. Any other residence not considered the primary residence would be referred to as the secondary residence. Generally a secondary residence, such as a vacation condominium or cabin, will typically receive favorable income tax treatment.

There are different ways to acquire a home, each one with unique tax implications. Take for example, buying a home. There will be closing costs associated with this purchase, which may or may not be written off. The property taxes and interest paid on the note will be deductible. Other closing costs may be written off, such as impound account fees or certain fees paid to acquire an FHA loan. These write-offs and costs are unique when buying a home, and are not incurred when acquiring property by any other method. Other methods in acquiring property are inheritance, building, or as a gift.

The basis for each of these methods of acquiring property will be of particular note as well. When, or if the home is ever resold, this original cost basis is important. The higher the cost basis, the less capital gains the seller will realize, thus less taxes will have to be paid. The original cost basis of the purchased home is its purchase price plus any buying expenses. The original cost basis for a home that is constructed, or built, is the cost of labor, materials, land, permits, professional services such as architecture and any other cost associated with building the property. For those people who inherit property, the original basis for this inheritance will be the market value of the home at the time the decedent passes away.

In terms of tax benefits, homeowners can write-off the real estate taxes incurred by the property. In addition to this write-off, homeowners can deduct mortgage interest. This is assuming they have a note on the property. Those homeowners who own their home outright will not have the deduction of mortgage interest. Not all properties will qualify for the mortgage interest deduction, however. Only the primary residence and one second home will qualify for this tax advantage. All other secondary properties or homes will not be eligible for a mortgage interest deduction.

A homeowner is more than likely in debt. The obvious debt a homeowner incurs is with the loan secured by a trust deed, with the home itself as collateral. This type of debt is called acquisition indebtedness. The total amount owed on a home is the acquisition indebtedness. Each time a payment is made, this debt goes down, until it is finally at zero. The other form of debt a homeowner can incur is in the form of equity. How can equity be a debt? As homeowners build equity in a home, they can use this equity to borrow against, pledging the property itself as collateral. The amount that can be borrowed is generally the current value of the home less the amount owed on the home loan, or the equity of the home. This type of debt is called equity indebtedness. The interest on a loan taken from equity is deductible.

The amount of gain realized by the seller, will determine how much tax there will be on the sale of property. Non-tax deductions are considered sales expenses, and the seller is allowed to add these expenses to the basis of the property, reducing gain. Some examples are documentary stamps, commission, inspection reports, title insurance and others. These will all be added up as sales expenses and then added to the original cost basis of the home, to arrive at the final adjusted cost basis. The adjusted cost basis less the sales price of the property is the realized gain.

Gain = Adjusted cost basis − Selling price

There are different types of gain. While a gain means the profit from the sale of the home, as you will see it is not always taxable, or even a profit. The different types of gain are realized, deferred, recognized and excluded.

Realized gain is the actual realized profit from the sale of a home. In some circumstances, which are rare, the realized gain might be a loss. If a home has to be sold for less than is owed then the gain is actually a loss. A realized gain may or may not be taxable.

Deferred gain is a profit made from the sale of a home. This profit is subject to taxation, but the tax obligation is deferred until a later time. The tax will eventually have to be paid, but not immediately.

Recognized gain is a profit that is taxable. This tax obligation is expected to be paid immediately, with no deferral.

Excluded gain is a profit that is not taxable. This gain is protected by the tax exclusion rules allowing a single person, $250,000, and a married couple, $500,000. This type of gain is only allowed every two years, after living in a primary residence for at least two years.

By adding all three types of gain, deferred, recognized and excluded, you come up with realized gain. As stated before, realized gain may or may not be positive, and may be subject to taxation. If the realized gain is more than allowable tax exemptions, it will be taxed, if it is less, it will not be taxed. It is possible for part of a large gain to be taxed, or recognized, while the rest is not taxable or excluded gain. Gain is very simple to calculate, and an easy concept to grasp if you think if it in terms of simple addition.

Example:
Mary and Todd are a married couple. They recently sold their home in San Diego for $800,000. They had been living in the home for the pasta 15 years. Over the past 15 years, Mary and Todd made $50,000 worth of improvements to the property. The closing costs totaled $17,000 while they originally paid $250,000 for the property. What is the realized gain? Is this gain taxable or not?

Original cost basis = $250,000
Improvements = $50,000
Selling costs = $17,000
Realized gain = $473,000

Original cost basis + selling costs + improvements = Adjusted Cost basis
Selling price – Adjusted cost basis = Realized gain

$800,000 - $250,000 + $17,000 + $50,000 = $473,000
This gain will not be taxable because it is less than the $500,000 exemption that the couple is eligible to take.

Remember
There are three different types of gain used to figure realized gain:
- Deferred gain
- Recognized gain
- Excluded gain

As we saw in the above example, the adjusted cost basis can greatly affect gain. Had the couple not kept track of their improvements over the years, they would have ended up with a gain over $500,000, and thus had to pay taxes on $27,000. It is important for you to understand the items or activities classified as home improvements.

The following is a partial listing of things that are considered improvements:

- roof
- patios
- floors
- walls
- sprinkler systems
- electrical wiring
- pipes and drainage
- fencing
- room additions
- pools

The following is a partial listing of things NOT considered improvements to a home:

- carpeting
- painting
- replacement of built-in appliances or furniture
- drapes

It is important for you to contact the IRS for a complete listing of allowable improvements before giving advice to your client. And always remember, it is best to have your client consult a tax professional for all matters pertaining to tax and taxation.

Excluded gain, or non-taxable gain, comes with a set of rules that must be met before the tax on a gain will be waived. We understand that a homeowner(s) must live in his or her home for at least two years to qualify. In some circumstances, however, a person may have to sell his or her home before they can qualify for the excluded gain. An example of this may be if the person is transferred to another state for a job. If he or she does have to leave before they can achieve the time requirement to waive their tax responsibility on any gain, they may be entitled to a partial exclusion. Again, it is important to consult the IRS regarding this before giving any advice to your client.

DOCUMENTARY TRANSFER TAX

A documentary transfer tax is a tax on the transfer of property from one person to another. This tax is payable to the jurisdiction in which the property is located (either the city or the county). Evidence of the tax is stated on the face of the deed or on an accompanying piece of paper.

The documentary transfer tax in California is 55 cents per $500, or $1.10 per every $1,000, of the purchase price of the property. Transactions in which the buyer is paying the full sale price of the property through a cash exchange, new loan or other method will see a documentary transfer tax on the entire purchase price. In an the seller's principal residence, or if the seller signs an affidavit of nonforeign status and the buyer signs an affidavit of residency for California.

> **Remember:**
> - Foreign or out-of-state property sellers must withhold 3.5% of the sales price for the state tax board.
> - Properties under $100,000 are exempt from withholding.
> - Properties being sold which was the seller's principal residence are exempt.
> - Persons who sign the seller's affidavit of nonforeign status or the buyer's affidavit of nonresidency for California are exempt from the withholding.

Example: A foreign investor is selling his personal residence in California to buy a new home of more value. Considering that this transaction is not taxable, does the buyer of the old property need to withhold?

Yes. The investor does not want the buyer to withhold; he will have to file for a withholding certificate from the IRS.

How is the buyer to know if the seller is a foreign person? The burden falls on the buyer, and there are only a few measures that will relieve the buyer of the obligation to withhold. In one such case the seller must provide the buyer with an affidavit of nonforeign status. The seller also must provide a U.S. taxpayer identification number and state, under penalty of perjury, that he or she is not a foreign person.

CALIFORNIA WITHHOLDING

As of January 2003, all people buying California real estate must withhold 3 1/3 percent of the sales price and send it to the Franchise Tax Board.

For real estate sales closing after December 31, 2002, the new law, Assembly Bill 2065, requires buyers of California real estate to withhold income taxes and send them to the Franchise Tax Board. The penalty for not complying is the greater of $500 or 10 percent of the withholding amount.

There are some exceptions to the law. Withholding is not required if the total sales price is $100,000 or less, or for principal residences, sales resulting in a taxable loss, like kind exchanges, and some involuntary conversions. Also exempted are sales where the seller is tax exempt or a California corporation or partnership. These exemptions are explained in detail later in this section.

Previous to January 2003 real estate withholding laws only apply to sales by nonresident sellers of California real estate. The new law expands to include all individuals–residents and nonresidents. Unlike the current law, the Franchise Tax Board will not grant individuals a waiver or reduced rate of withholding for sales with small taxable gains.

Tax withholding is a prepayment of state taxes that sellers who profit from their real estate sales will owe. Any exemptions to a realized gain will not be taxed, but all other gains will be taxed.

exchange where the buyer is assuming a current loan, and will make an additional down payment in cash to cover the selling price, the documentary transfer tax only applies to the amount of cash paid above what is owed on the assumed loan.

Example:
Amy and Sergio are purchasing a home by assuming an existing loan and paying the remaining balance of the transfer in cash. The home they are purchasing is $450,000, and they will assume an existing trust deed of $300,000. They plan on paying $150,000 in cash to cover the remaining amount of the sales price. The documentary transfer tax assessed on the transfer is:

$450,000 selling price - $300,000 existing trust deed = $150,000 taxable amount. $150,000 / 500 = $300 documentary transfer tax.

When the documentary transfer tax has been paid, the county recorder will place a stamp on the document indicating payment. These stamps are often referred to as "doc stamps."

Remember
A documentary transfer tax is imposed on the actual amount of money a person pays for a property. It is not applied when a buyer assumes an existing trust deed.

Some cities in California have imposed their own rate for the documentary transfer tax. Those cities and their rates are as follows:

- Culver City $4.50
- Los Angeles $4.50
- Pomona $2.20
- Redondo Beach $2.20
- Santa Monica $3.00

ESTATE, INHERITANCE AND GIFT TAXES

California currently does not have a state tax on inheritances and gifts, as these taxes were repealed by voters on June 8, 1982. There is, however, an estate tax, which follows federal rules regarding when the tax may be assessed. These rules state that the estate tax may be assessed when the estate is worth more than $850,000. The amount will increase in the next subsequent years to $950,000 in 2005, and $1,000,000 in 2006. If an estate qualifies for the tax, the total tax amount must be paid within nine months after the death of the property owner.

Federal gift taxes are paid by persons who make more than one gift of property worth $10,000 or more in a calendar year. If a married couple wishes to make a gift, the taxable gift must be worth more than $20,000 before taxes will apply (i.e., $10,000 x 2). There are restrictions on what constitutes a gift. Tuition payments or medical care cost coverage for another individual are not considered gifts, regardless of dollar amount. Any gift tax returns must be filed by April 15 of the year following the gift.

The person making the gift is called the donor. The person receiving the gift is referred to as the donee. A gift may be either real or personal property.

FOREIGN INVESTMENT IN REAL PROPERTY TAX ACT – FIRPTA

When people outside the United States wish to invest money in property located in California, there are different federal and state tax laws that apply. The Foreign Investment in Real Property Tax Act (FIRPTA) outlines the differences in the laws, as well as the requirements for the buyer. When a foreign investor wishes to make an investment, he or she is responsible for making property disclosures to the seller, so that all the necessary funds have been set aside. It is important for all real estate professionals to pay close attention to this type of transaction so that the escrow instructions are clear about the amount of funds that must be set aside for the additional taxes.

Federal income tax requirements for foreign investments require a seller who is either a non-resident of the United States or a legal alien to hold 10% of the sales price of the property, to pay any taxes from capital gains. Any property selling for less than $300,000 is exempt from this 10% requirement, and also exempt from the disclosure requirements.

Property sellers who are citizens of the United States are required to fill out a seller's affidavit of nonforeign status. This affidavit states that the seller is a citizen of the United States. A buyer must also sign a buyer's affidavit of residency, which indicates whether he or she is a citizen or legal resident. The buyer's affidavit also requires the person signing the statement to agree that the sale price of the property did not exceed $300,000 and that the property will be used as a residence. As long as the buyer is a resident, is purchasing the property for under $300,000, and will be living in the property as his or her primary residence, he or she will be exempt from the withholding requirement.

Remember:
- Foreign investors must set aside 10% of the sale price of a home (with the exception of homes under $300,000, which are exempt) for any capital gains.
- Sellers must sign a seller's affidavit of nonforeign status, stating they are a citizen or legal resident of the U.S.
- Buyers must sign a buyer's affidavit of residency stating they are a citizen or legal resident of the U.S. and that the property was | purchased for less than $300,000. They must also indicate whether the property will be used for a primary residence.

The state of California has its own tax rules and regulations regarding foreign investors and investors from other states. A seller of property who is not a legal resident of the United States or California must withhold 3.5% of the sales price for the Franchise Tax Board (state tax board). Buyers and real estate agents are also responsible for ensuring that this sum is withheld in the escrow instructions. There are, however, exceptions to this withholding. Any foreign investor or investor from another state is not required to withhold the 3.5% if the sales price of the property is $100,000 or less, if the home is

Sellers subject to withholding

The new law expands real estate withholding to include all individuals (residents and nonresidents). It continues to apply to non-individuals with a last known street address outside California.

Certifiable exceptions

Individuals will no longer have an exemption for being a resident. However, individuals can be exempt from withholding if they certify that they are:

- Selling the property for $100,000 or less,

- Selling their principal residence,

- Selling the property at a loss for California income tax purposes,

- Selling the property as part of an Internal Revenue Code Section 1031 exchange, or

- Selling the property because of an involuntary conversion and will replace the property within the provisions of Internal Revenue Code Section 1033

Waivers and reduced withholding
Individuals

There is no waiver process for individuals. The full amount of withholding is required unless the sellers can certify that they meet one of the exceptions or the buyer agrees to withhold on each payment of an installment sale.

Multiple sellers
Individuals

For individual sellers, withhold according to the seller's interest in the property

Loss on sale
Individuals

There is no withholding on individual sellers if they can certify that the sale will result in a loss. The law no longer allows individuals to request a withholding waiver.

Small gain
Individuals

Full withholding is required unless the individual has a loss on the sale for California income tax purposes. The Franchise Tax Board cannot allow reduced withholding for individual sellers.

Exchanges
Individuals

Individuals can certify that the sale is part of an Internal Revenue Code Section 1031 exchange and

1. if it is a simultaneous exchange, only the proceeds (boot) going to the seller will be withheld upon in escrow, or

2. if it is a deferred exchange, the proceeds will go to an intermediary who will withhold, if necessary.

CALIFORNIA ASSOCIATION OF REALTORS®

BUYER'S AFFIDAVIT
That Buyer is acquiring property for use as a residence
and that sales price does not exceed $300,000.
(FOREIGN INVESTMENT IN REAL PROPERTY TAX ACT)

1. I am the transferee (buyer) of real property located at _____
_____.

2. The sales price (total of all consideration in the sale) does not exceed $300,000.

3. I am acquiring the real property for use as a residence. I have definite plans that I or a member of my family will reside in it for at least 50 percent of the number of days it will be in use during each of the first two 12 month periods following the transfer of the property to me. I understand that the members of my family that are included in the last sentence are my brothers, sisters, ancestors, descendents, or spouse.

4. I am making this affidavit in order to establish an exemption from withholding a portion of the sales price of the property under Internal Revenue Code §1445.

5. I understand that if the information in this affidavit is not correct, I may be liable to the Internal Revenue Service for up to 10 percent of the sales price of the property, plus interest and penalties.

Under penalties of perjury, I declare that the statements above are true, correct and complete.

Date _____   Signature _____

                                 Typed or Printed Name _____

Date _____   Signature _____

                                 Typed or Printed Name _____

IMPORTANT NOTICE: An affidavit should be signed by each individual transferee to whom it applies. Before you sign, any questions relating to the legal sufficiency of this form, or to whether it applies to a particular transaction, or to the definition of any of the terms used, should be referred to an attorney, certified public accountant, other professional tax advisor, or the Internal Revenue Service.

Published and Distributed by:
REAL ESTATE BUSINESS SERVICES, INC.
a subsidiary of the CALIFORNIA ASSOCIATION OF REALTORS®
525 South Virgil Avenue, Los Angeles, California 90020

PRINT DATE

OFFICE USE ONLY
Reviewed by Broker
or Designee _____
Date _____

EQUAL HOUSING OPPORTUNITY

FORM AB-11 REVISED 2/91

SELLER'S AFFIDAVIT OF NONFOREIGN STATUS AND/OR CALIFORNIA WITHHOLDING EXEMPTION

FOREIGN INVESTMENT IN REAL PROPERTY TAX ACT (FIRPTA)
AND CALIFORNIA WITHHOLDING LAW
(Use a separate form for each Transferor)
(C.A.R. Form AS, Revised 1/03)

Internal Revenue Code ("IRC") Section 1445 provides that a transferee of a U.S. real property interest must withhold tax if the transferor is a "foreign person." California Revenue and Taxation Code Section 18662 provides that a transferee of a California real property interest must withhold tax if the transferor: **(i)** is an individual (unless certain exemptions apply); or **(ii)** is any entity other than an individual ("Entity") if the transferor's proceeds will be disbursed to a financial intermediary of the transferor, or to the transferor with a last known street address outside of California. California Revenue and Taxation Code Section 18662 includes additional provisions for corporations.

I understand that this affidavit may be disclosed to the Internal Revenue Service and to the California Franchise Tax Board by the transferee, and that any false statement I have made herein (if an Entity Transferor, on behalf of the Transferor) may result in a fine, imprisonment or both.

1. **PROPERTY ADDRESS** (the address of the property being transferred):
_____

2. **TRANSFEROR'S INFORMATION:**
   Full Name _____
   Telephone No. _____
   Address _____
   (Use HOME address for individual transferors. Use OFFICE address for Entities: corporations, partnerships, limited liability companies, trusts and estates.)
   Social Security No., Federal Employer Identification No., or California Corporation No. _____

3. **AUTHORITY TO SIGN:** If this document is signed on behalf of an Entity Transferor, THE UNDERSIGNED INDIVIDUAL DECLARES THAT HE/SHE HAS AUTHORITY TO SIGN THIS DOCUMENT ON BEHALF OF THE TRANSFEROR.

4. **FEDERAL LAW:** I, the undersigned individual, declare under penalty of perjury that, for the reason checked below, if any, I am exempt (or if signed on behalf of an Entity Transferor, the Entity is exempt) from the federal withholding law (FIRPTA):
   ☐ (For individual Transferors) I am not a nonresident alien for purposes of U.S. income taxation.
   ☐ (For corporation, partnership, limited liability company, trust and estate Transferors) The Transferor is not a foreign corporation, foreign partnership, foreign limited liability company, foreign trust, or foreign estate, as those term are defined in the Internal Revenue Code and Income Tax Regulations.

5. **CALIFORNIA LAW:** I, the undersigned individual, declare under penalty of perjury that, for the reason checked below, if any, I am exempt (or if signed on behalf of an Entity Transferor, the Entity is exempt) from the California withholding law:
   ☐ The total sale price for the property is $100,000 or less.
   For individual or revocable/grantor trust Transferors only:
   ☐ The property being transferred is in California and was my principal residence within the meaning of IRC Section 121.
   ☐ The property is being, or will be, exchanged for property of like kind within the meaning of IRC Section 1031.
   ☐ The property has been compulsorily or involuntarily converted (within the meaning of IRC 1033) and I intend to acquire property similar or related in service or use to be eligible for non-recognition of gain for California income tax purposes under IRC Section 1033.
   ☐ The transaction will result in a loss for California income tax purposes.
   For Entity Transferors only:
   ☐ (For corporation Transferors) The Transferor is a corporation qualified to do business in California, or has a permanent place of business in California at the address shown in paragraph 2 ("Transferor's Information").
   ☐ (For limited liability company ("LLC") or partnership Transferors) The Transferor is an LLC or partnership and recorded title to the property being transferred is in the name of the LLC or partnership and the LLC or partnership will file a California tax return to report the sale and withhold on foreign and domestic nonresident partners as required.
   ☐ (For irrevocable trust Transferors) The Transferor is an irrevocable trust with at least one trustee who is a California resident and the trust will file a California tax return to report the sale and withhold when distributing California source taxable income to nonresident beneficiaries as required.
   ☐ (For estate Transferors) The Transferor is an estate of a decedent who was a California resident at the time of his/her death and the estate will file a California tax return to report the sale and withhold when distributing California source taxable income to nonresident beneficiaries as required.
   ☐ (For tax-exempt Entity and nonprofit organization Transferors) The Transferor is exempt from tax under California or federal law.

By_____ Date _____
(Transferor's Signature) (Indicate if you are signing as the grantor of a revocable/grantor trust.)

_____   _____
Typed or printed name   Title (If signed on behalf of entity Transferor)

SURE TRAC
The System for Success™

Published by the
California Association of REALTORS®

Reviewed by _____ Date _____

EQUAL HOUSING
OPPORTUNITY

AS REVISED 1/03 (PAGE 1 OF 1) Print Date

Non-individuals

Non-individuals must still request a waiver from the Franchise Tax Board to eliminate or reduce withholding in escrow.

Due dates

Withholding must be sent to the Franchise Tax Board by the 20th day of the month following the month escrow closes.

T A X   S H E L T E R

There are times when a profit may have been realized in a real estate transaction, but because of tax shelter laws, no taxes had to be paid. Depreciation is shown as an expense. If the depreciation is great enough, it may lower the tax liability for the investor. In some cases, this liability may even appear to be negative on paper. This is perfectly legal, and a good way to shift assets and liabilities to avoid paying taxes on investments. Another way property may provide a tax shelter is when there is an operating loss on the property. The operating loss may be used to offset other non-real estate income.

S U M M A R Y

All real estate investments are taxed on three different levels. The first is the federal level, which includes income tax, estate tax and gift tax. These taxes are generally applied when the real estate has been conveyed to another person through sale or gifting.

The next level of taxation is the state level. The state will tax a homeowner on income made from the sale of his or her home (income tax). Just as with federal taxes, the state taxes from real estate profit are applied when the home is sold.

Finally, there are local government taxes on real estate. These taxes are based on the property's value (sometimes referred to as ad valorem). Taxes assessed at the local government level are property taxes, special assessments and transfer taxes.

The tax year in California begins on July 1 and ends on June 30. Property owners will receive two bills each year, breaking up the tax obligation in half. People buying new property will often receive a supplemental tax bill making up the difference between the old assessment and new tax obligation.

Propositions 13, 58, 60 and 90 serve to give tax relief to property owners. Some relieve the tax requirement partially or completely while others allow a property owner to transfer a current tax basis on one property to a new property, with a minimal increase. Disability, age or other requirements apply. The homeowner's exemption in the state is $7,000 of the assessed value for all properties.

The original basis is what a homeowner originally paid for the property; the adjusted cost basis is the original property price plus improvements and sales costs. These figures are used when figuring gain. Realized gain may or may not be taxable depending on if the homeowner meets the tax exemption rule of $250,000 for a single person, $500,000 for a married couple. Any realized gain over these exemptions, will be taxed. A taxpayer must live in the property for at least two years to qualify for an exemption, or qualify under a special circumstance.

Depreciation is tax deductible, and calculated on improvements. Generally residential property can use 27.5 years whole nonresidential property uses a 39-year life for depreciation. The amount of depreciation is equal over the life of the improvement.

Taxpayers can use a 1031 exchange to defer gains on the sale of business or investment property. Property being exchanged must be like kind and of equal value. If the value is not equal, there must be a boot used to create an equal amount.

Acquisition indebtedness is the debt incurred by a property owner when he or she purchases a home, whole equity indebtedness is the equity used from the home, secured by the home itself.

When property is sold, an installment sale may be used to relieve taxes on a large gain. Taxes can be spread out over a period of time, taxing the income little by little allowing a smaller tax bill than if paying all at once.

A sale-leaseback is when a seller sells property to an investor, but is then allowed to stay on the property, under a lease contract. This is generally ideal to both parties allowing the seller to free up capital for other investments, and the buyer to obtain an investment property where someone else (the seller, now lessee) pays the mortgage.

Federal income tax requirements for foreign investments require a seller who is either a non-resident of the United States or a legal alien to hold 10% of the sales price of the property, to pay any taxes from capital gains. Any property selling for less than $300,000 is exempt from this 10% requirement, and also exempt from the disclosure requirements.

As of January 2003, all people buying California real estate must withhold 3 1/3 percent of the sales price and send it to the Franchise Tax Board. Property transferred for less than $100,000 is exempt from withholding.

T E R M S   A N D   P H R A S E S

Ad Valorem – A term meaning "according to value". Real estate property taxes are based on the concept of ad valorem (taxes are assessed on the value of the home).

Adjusted Cost Basis – The original cost of the structure, plus any improvements made to the structure during ownership, minus its depreciation.

Adjusted Gross Income – The total amount of income a person receives from all sources, less any depreciation, tax deductions or other allowable deductions.

Assessed Value – The value a county assessor places on a property or structure to determine its tax basis.

Assessment Roll – The establishment of a tax base for an area or community by listing all taxable properties and showing the assessed value of each one.

Basis – Also referred to as "cost basis," it is the dollar value assigned to a property at the time of purchase. The Internal Revenue Service uses this basis to determine any gain or loss the seller may incur by selling the property to another person. The basis is also used in calculating the depreciation for income tax paid on the sale of the property.

Basis is the price of the home before making an adjusted cost basis, which takes into account the addition of any improvements, and deduction of all depreciation factors.

Benefit Assessment – The total amount of property owned and enhanced by any renovations, improvements or new construction.

Book Sale – The sale of real property to the state, in name only, when the property owner is delinquent on his or her property taxes.

Boot – In a property exchange, when properties are not equal, the owner or transferee of the lesser property must make up the difference by using money or offering additional property to the buyer (called cash boot), or assuming a mortgage larger than the one that is conveyed (called mortgage boot), to maintain an equal exchange.

Capital Asset – Any permanently owned asset used for producing income. Examples are machinery, land, structures or industrial equipment. Capital assets are distinctly different from inventory, as inventory is generally for sale and not permanent.

Capital Gain – The amount of money earned over the amount of the adjusted cost basis for any item for sale.

Capital Improvements – Any improvements made to property.

Certificate of Redemption – A certificate issued by the county tax collector to a property owner when all monies from past due taxes have been collected.

County Assessor – An elected official who determines the tax basis for each property under his or her jurisdiction.

Cost Basis – The original amount paid for property.

Deductions – Any amount of money that can be subtracted from the tax basis.

Depreciation – A decrease in value of an asset, which is used in computing property value for tax purposes; or, the decrease in value of an asset due to use or other factors causing it to be worth less.

Documentary Transfer Tax – A tax on all property transfers, as stated on the deed, or any separate papers accompanying the deed.

Donee – A person receiving a gift.

Donor – A person making a gift.

Economic Life – The life over which improvements to property will yield a return on the investment that is greater than returns based on land only.

Estate Tax – A tax applied to estates worth more than $600,000.

Franchise Tax – California's tax on corporations.

Fiscal Year – A year used for business or accounting purposes; the fiscal year may have different start and end dates from the calendar year.

Gift – A voluntary transfer of property from one person to another. There usually is no consideration given or taken for the transfer.

Homeowner's Exemption – California allows homeowners a $7,000 tax exemption on their principal home (not extended to vacation properties or homes).

Ordinary Income – Any income that does not qualify for capital gains tax.

Reassessment Event – An occurrence such as the sale of a property or an addition, improvement or renovation causing a re-evaluation of the property's value for tax purposes.

Recovery Property – A property that can be depreciated for income tax purposes, with the cost of the property deducted from the income over a stated period.

Special Assessment – Appropriation, in the form of a tax, on property that is enhanced by the renovation or addition of improvements (such as a new train line or other community improvement or service).

Tax Deed – The type of deed a successful bidder will receive for property gained at a tax auction.

Taxable Income – Income that is taxable from all sources, less certain payments or donations deemed untaxable (such as income placed into a retirement plan).

C H A P T E R   Q U I Z

1. Ad valorem means:
      a. Full cash value
      b. Property taxes
      c. According to value
      d. Percentage

2. When are property taxes due if the due date falls on a holiday or weekend?
      a. Property taxes are due on the same day, no matter if it is a holiday or weekend
      b. They are due the day before the holiday or weekend
      c. They are due on the next business day after the holiday or weekend
      d. Either B or C

3. The difference between the seller's valuation on the sale of property and the new valuation based on the sales price of the property for tax purposes is covered in what?
      a. Supplemental tax bill
      b. Ad valorem
      c. Escrow
      d. Prorated value to be paid at the end of escrow

4. A typical California tax bill would include which of the following items?
      a. A breakdown between land assessments and improvement assessments.
      b. Separate payment cards with the full tax value separated into two installments.
      c. Identifying parcel number
      d. All of the above would appear on a tax bill.

5. Proposition 60 allows for what persons to transfer the current factored base year value to a new residence within the same county?
  a. Persons 55 years or older.
  b. Taxpayers who are severely or permanently disabled
  c. A married couple where at least one spouse is 55 years or older.
  d. All of the above.

6. Proposition 90:)
  a. Is basically the same as proposition 60
  b. Allows for a transfer of the current factored base year value of property from one property to another in a different county
  c. Allows for persons under 55 to transfer the current factored base year value of property to another property
  d. Allows for corporations to transfer current factored base year value of property to another property.

7. Proposition 13 allows the tax rate to be increased by what percentage each year?
  a. 1%
  b. 2%
  c. 3%
  d. 4%

8. The "original basis" of property refers to:
  a. One time closing costs, or buying expenses
  b. Purchase price
  c. Original base year value
  d. Both A and B

9. The depreciable basis:
  a. Is based on the original purchase price
  b. Is based on the improvements made to the property
  c. Is based on the original purchase price minus the land value
  d. None of the above

10. A 1031 exchange allows a homeowner to:
  a. Defer tax liability
  b. Have more money to invest in a new property
  c. Avoid paying high income taxes on the sale of property
  d. All of the above

11. Under the like-kind rule:
  a. Real property may be exchanged for personal property, but personal property may not be exchanged for real property
  b. Personal property may be exchanged for real property, but real property may not be exchanged for personal property
  c. Only real property may be exchanged for real property, and personal property exchanged for personal property
  d. Any type of property may be exchanged for any other type of property with no limits or regulations.

12. Balancing of equities, or cash boot, may be which of the following?
  a. Cash
  b. Notes or trust deeds
  c. Jewelry
  d. All of the above.

13. Spreading the tax gain on property over two or more years is called:
    a. Boot
    b. Installment sale
    c. Exchange
    d. None of the above

14. A primary residence is considered to be:
    a. A single-family home
    b. Motor home
    c. Trailer
    d. Any of the above

15. A single person occupying his or her residence for at least two years may exclude how much money from any tax gain?
    a. $100,000
    b. $250,000
    c. $500,000
    d. $650,000

16. A taxpayer may acquire a home through which of the following methods?
    a. Gift
    b. Inheritance
    c. Purchasing an existing home or building a new home
    d. All of the above

17. For tax purposes, a homeowner may write off which of the following expenses?
    a. Real estate taxes
    b. Mortgage interest
    c. Money paid into impound accounts
    d. Both A and B

18. All of the following are considered home improvements except:
    a. Carpeting
    b. Room additions
    c. Pools
    d. Landscaping

19. A capital gain that a taxpayer may postpone paying is called:
    a. Realized gain
    b. Deferred gain
    c. Recognized gain
    d. Excluded gain

20. All of the following are exempt from withholding except:
    a. Property sold for less than $100,000
    b. Property sold at a loss
    c. Foreclosure sale
    d. All the above are exempt from withholding.

10

TITLE INSURANCE AND ESCROW

What you will learn in this Chapter

- Title Insurance
- Rebate Law
- Preliminary Title Report
- Escrow Rules
- Escrow Procedures
- Termination of Escrow
- Rights and Obligations of Each Party to an Escrow
- Relationship of the Escrow Holder and Real Estate Agent
- Real Estate Settlement Procedures Act (RESPA)
- Designating the Escrow Holder
- Terms
- Prorations
- Closing Statements

Test Your Knowledge

1. Several steps must be made to close escrow; which of the following is not a step taken at the close of escrow?
    a. The buyer will move into the property.
    b. The escrow agent sends an original copy of the title policy to the buyer.
    c. The escrow officer sends the deed and deed of trust to the recorder's office to be recorded.
    d. The escrow agent sends the seller and buyer closing statements showing all disbursement of funds.

2. Which of the following closing costs is not the responsibility of the buyer?
    a. Drawing up the deed
    b. Loan origination fee
    c. Appraisal fee
    d. Notary fees

3. Closing costs include all of the following except:
    a. Title insurance
    b. Broker's commission
    c. Transfer tax
    d. Recording documents

4. In the event escrow instructions have to be changed, what must happen?
    a. A completely new set of escrow instructions must be written.
    b. Any changes in the current document may be initialed by both parties.
    c. An oral agreement must be made between both parties.
    d. None of the above.

5. Legally, the escrow agent may not do which of the following?
    a. Hold money deposited by the either party until disbursed
    b. Renegotiate any part of the escrow separately with only one party to the escrow
    c. Act as a neutral party
    d. Make sure escrow does not close with an unverified check

6. Which of the following is not a party to the escrow?
    a. Broker
    b. Lender
    c. Buyer
    d. Seller

7. The extended title insurance policy covers all of the items covered in the standard policy, plus which additional items?
    a. Defects known to the buyer
    b. Changes in land use brought about by zoning ordinances
    c. Unrecorded liens not known of by the policy holder
    d. Defects and liens listed in the policy

INTRODUCTION

In this chapter, we will learn about escrow. California utilizes escrow agents in the transfer of property from one individual to another, to ensure that contracts are upheld and executed exactly as intended. The escrow agent acts as a third party between the buyer and seller and performs a series of actions to complete a transaction to its close.

Additionally, we will learn about title insurance. Buyers investing in real estate will usually want to take title insurance to protect their investment against unforeseen liens, defects or other items not apparent to the buyer. Title insurance guarantees a clear title, or the buyer is not responsible for any issues or problems associated with the title. We will learn about the two different insurance policies a buyer or lender can take, and what they cover.

TITLE INSURANCE

Title insurance is used to guarantee a marketable title against risk. Properties maintain value as long as they are capable of being sold. When the property cannot be sold due to a cloud on the title, the value of the property decreases.

Due to the high demand for property and the value associated with it, land or property may be bought and sold several times during the documented periods. Marriage rights associated with community property, joint tenancy and property legally willed to an heir create complications in freely selling or buying property. How are we to be sure the property being sold is being sold by its rightful owner?

Records are kept regarding change of ownership for each piece of property in a given county. Any interested person can search the chain of title (researching all owners of a specific property) for as long a the time as records have been kept. This chain of title search reveals the abstract of title, (a record of each time a property has changed ownership), as well as prior owners. Abstract of title is used (along with an attorney's opinion of title) to determine any claims of ownership on a property. Although it is a very good way of ensuring there is a marketable title, the process can be very time consuming.

The chain of title, abstract of title and an attorney's opinion of title are good resources in determining who is the lawful owner of a property. In some cases, however, they may be faulty methods, as in cases of fraud or forgery. In cases such as this, a marketable title may be contested. The last thing a new property owner wants to worry about is whether or not the title to his or her property will be contested. Title insurance companies help guard against recorded and unrecorded risks that may affect the marketable title to property.

There are two different types of title insurance: the standard policy and the extended policy.

Two Types of Title Insurance
- Standard Policy
- Extended Policy

A **standard policy** of title insurance protects against matters of record already on file with the county recorders office. It also protects against matters that would not be on record, such as forgery, fraud, impersonation or the failure of a competent party to create or enter into a contract. In addition, a standard policy will protect against federal tax liens and any expenses incurred in legally defending the title to a property. The standard policy will cover:

- Defects found in public records
- Forged documents
- Incomplete grantors
- Incorrect marital statements
- Improperly delivered deeds

The California Land Title Association (CLTA) is an association of California title companies that provides all members with a standard form for insurance. Note that this form is only used by those who choose to take out a standard policy. Those individuals who choose extended coverage will fill out a different form.

For an additional cost, most risks not covered in a standard policy can be covered in an extended policy. The American Land Title Association (ALTA) offers a policy known as the A.L.T.A. Owner's Policy, which covers the same items as in the standard policy. In addition, the policy protects the insured against the claims of people who may be in physical possession of the property, but have no recorded interest, marketability of title, water rights, mining claims, recorded easements and liens, rights or claims discovered from a proper survey and reservations in patents. Lenders, as well as property owners, usually take out this type of policy to protect their investment.

The A.L.T.A. policy protects against the following:

- Title defects either known to the policyholder at the time of insurance or shown in a survey
- Rights or claims of people in physical possession of the property, even those rights or claims that would not show up in public record
- Easements and liens not shown in public record
- Changes in land use dictated by zoning laws
- Water rights
- Mining claims
- Reservations
- Unrecorded liens

Neither the standard nor the extended policy will cover defects and liens listed in the policy, defects that are known to the buyer at the time of the purchase and changes in land because of zoning ordinances. These things are considered to be apparent and obvious to the buyer when he or she is making a decision to purchase the property.

In addition to the CLTA and ALTA, there are other, special insurance policies, which may be issued. In transfers not as simple as the transfer of a primary residence, such as a business property or investment property, these special insurance policies will be of significant importance to keep the investment as a whole safe. For example, if you were working with a client purchasing an apartment building, what was currently occupied, you would want to make sure the leasehold interest(s) were covered. Or if you were transferring property with natural resources such as oil, you would want to make sure the interests for these resources remained with the appropriate party as agreed upon in the purchase contract. Should there be a question regarding an issue on the title insurance policy that is unclear, generally it is resolved against the insurer.

REBATE LAW

Under no circumstances is it allowable for a title insurer to extend a rebate to a client for using their services. The rebate law specifically states that title insurers and escrow agents must charge brokers the same price as they would charge any other customer for their services. Any licensee found to have taken a rebate from either a title insurer or escrow company is subject to up to one year in prison and a fine of $10,000 for each rebate taken.

PRELIMINARY TITLE REPORT

A preliminary title report is typically issued on a property. This happens before the title insurance policy is issued to make sure there are no defects to the title, or claims to the property, which would prevent the property transfer to occur. Title to the land, encumbrances, defects, liens, restrictions and any interest a second party might have in the property will be listed in the preliminary title report. The preliminary title report not only is used to make sure the property will be able to be transferred from one party to another, but will determine what kind of title insurance coverage will be required. Upon receiving the preliminary title report, the information should be shared with your client. Certain items may have to be removed from the final report in order for the property transfer to take place. If you have any questions regarding this process, it is good to consult an escrow professional.

It is important to note that the preliminary title report will not necessarily show the condition of title. It is simply one of the precautions taken to eliminate risk in a property transaction. The preliminary title report, along with title records, underwriting standards of insurance companies and a careful examination of all recorded items to a property will help give the licensee, title insurer and escrow professional a clear picture of important items such as current vesting or items that will not need title insurance coverage.

ESCROW

Escrow is the "in-between" time, beginning when a purchase agreement is accepted and signed, and ending when the buyer takes possession of the property. During escrow, all documents that need to be collected, processed or distributed (as well as the necessary disbursement of funds) will be completed. The person or company assigned to carry out all instructions provided to them by the principals (outlined in the purchase contract) is called the escrow holder.

Escrow may involve more than just the sale of real property. Escrow agents are typically used in situations such as leasing of real property, sale of personal property, securities, loans or mobile homes. As in the sale of real property, the escrow agent must follow the instructions as laid out by the principals.

The escrow agent must follow instructions outlined in the purchase contract. Once escrow is opened, both parties must agree to any changes made. In other words, the buyer or seller alone cannot change escrow instructions without the approval of the other party. The two parties involved in the transaction are usually, but not always, a buyer and a seller.

California does not require escrow agents or that escrow be utilized in a real estate transaction. The decision to use an escrow agent is completely up to the principals involved in the transaction. It is advisable to go into escrow, however, because any mistakes, whether innocent or intentional, regarding the terms of the contract could be costly to one or both parties, as they may need to initiate litigation or challenges to the property transfer.

The main job of the escrow agent is to provide a line of communication between all parties involved in a sale. An escrow agent's duties go far beyond just communication between the buyer and the seller. The escrow agent must communicate with all of the brokers and sales agents involved in the transaction, the lender, and any service companies called in (such as inspectors, plumbers, appraisers and pest control companies). Thus, it is important that the escrow agent be a neutral third party who is not otherwise involved in the transaction.

Escrow Agent's Main Duties:
- Disburse funds as outlined in the purchase contract
- Communicate between all parties involved in the transaction

In order for an escrow to be valid it must include the following:

- Binding contract
- Conditional delivery

A **binding contract** is the first step of an escrow opening. This contract can be created in a number of different forms, though a purchase contract is the usual type. The following are all examples of a binding contract, capable of opening escrow:

1. Purchase contract

2. Agreement of sale

3. An option

4. An exchange agreement

5. Any legally binding document

The California Association of Realtors has created a single form, thus combining both the escrow instructions and the purchase agreement into one contract. This form creates a uniform contract for all realtors across California, making this process easier and less redundant than it might be otherwise.

The second step for escrow is **conditional delivery** of instruments of transfer to the escrow agent. These instruments include:

1. Money

2. Loan Documents

3. Deed transferring title

4. Other required paperwork

This 4-step process is called a conditional delivery, as all terms of the contract or additional escrow instructions, must still be carried out. These contract items include the disbursement of all necessary funds, the signing and delivery of the trust deed to the escrow agent to hold until close of escrow, and the signing of the note by the buyer, as well as any other terms requested by either party. Shortly before the closing of escrow, a buyer will receive the grant deed to the property, while the seller will receive any monies from the purchase.

LEGAL REQUIREMENTS FOR ESCROW OFFICERS

Officers Must:

- Act according to issued written instructions.

- Act as a neutral party at all times.

- Hold monies deposited by parties until disbursed.

- Follow escrow instructions in every detail unless instructions are in violation of the law.

- Give to parties only that information that concerns them.

- Make sure that escrow does not close with an unverified check.

Officers May Not:

- Make a transaction for another officer.

- Negotiate with the parties separately.

- Suggest that terms or provisions be inserted in the escrow.

- Act as collection agencies to persuade a client to furnish funds.

- Notify parties that they have not ordered a certain document that may be necessary to close an escrow.

ESCROW RULES

As mentioned earlier in this chapter, the only parties allowed to make changes to escrow instructions are the principals – the buyer and seller. The escrow agent must follow the instructions or any changes made in the purchase contract by the principals to the letter. Just as the escrow agent has no authority to make any changes to an escrow, neither does the broker. In addition, no changes may be made by one principal without the agreement and acknowledgement of the other.

> **Remember**
> An escrow agent is a neutral third party; thus, he or she may not make changes to the escrow instructions at any time.

All escrow agents must observe the following rules:

1. All actions of the escrow agent must be under the direction or approval of the principals. This means and requires that the principals must fully under stand both the purchase contract and all its binding obligations. The purchase contract will serve as the instructions for the escrow agent.

2. An escrow agent must not function as a mediator between the principals in the event of a disagreement between the principals. It is the escrow agent's responsibility to voice any concerns or objections of any one principal, while remaining a neutral party.

3. Escrow agents may not give legal advice regarding matters which would require an attorney.

4. An escrow agent must remain a neutral third party, as he or she is a dual agent to both principals. This means that no favoritism may be given to one principal over another. The agent is only allowed to abide by the instructions contained in the purchase contract or escrow instructions.

5. Escrow is open when both parties sign the purchase contract (or escrow instructions). Upon signature, these instructions are delivered to the escrow agent.

6. Escrow instructions must instruct the agent regarding which funds or documents may be accepted as payment in the transaction.

7. An escrow agent may not have a negative balance in the trust account.

8. If there are discrepancies between the escrow instructions and the purchase agreement, the signed escrow instructions will take precedence over the purchase agreement.

9. The escrow agent must remain neutral at all times and in all dealings during an open escrow.

10. Documents must be recorded in a timely manner and copies of each document distributed to all parties.

11. An escrow agent must be trustworthy.

12. The escrow agent must hold all information regarding the escrow in confidence (unless the principals give written permission to release that information to outside interested parties).

13. Escrow records must be maintained on a daily basis.

14. All information previously undisclosed to the principals by any broker, sales agent or other party must be disclosed by the escrow agent. Both principals must sign any changes this may create in the purchase agreement.

15. Any exchange of funds in the form of a check must have already been approved by a bank before the exchange of money is considered official.

16. A careful audit is required of all funds before the close of escrow is allowed.

17. Escrow must close in a timely manner.

ESCROW PROCEDURES

Once a purchase agreement is signed to indicate agreement to its terms, escrow may be opened. Escrow begins when the selling agent deposits the earnest money into an escrow account, which must occur within three days of the purchase agreement being signed. The escrow agent must also receive the signed purchase contract to begin escrow.

Some details of the purchase contract, or questions on which parties must come to agreement, include: Have all inspections been made? Who will pay for these inspections? Have all disclosures been made? If the broker is making a commission, has the amount of commission been made clear? Is the seller going to pay for this entire commission? It is a good idea to use a checklist to make sure all points have been considered, discussed and agreed upon.

Each party in an escrow has a responsibility. The parties involved in an escrow are the buyer, the seller and the escrow company or agent. The real estate broker is not considered a party to the escrow, although he or she will have a responsibility toward all other parties in the escrow. Each party must understand their responsibilities, which include:

Buyer's Responsibilities:

- Sign escrow instructions or purchase agreement
- Analyze the bill of sale (to understand which items of personal property will be conveyed separate of the purchase agreement)
- Acquire hazard insurance
- Review the preliminary report of the property and its encumbrances, if any, that appear on record
- Deposit all necessary funds to cover any deposits or other costs associated with the transaction (such as the earnest money deposit)
- Review the property inspection reports (to which an approval must be given by the buyer to move forward towards closing)
- Produce all copies of any documents that might affect the escrow
- Review all loan documents

Seller's Responsibilities:

- Sign escrow instructions
- Provide a release on any mortgage or encumbrance to be paid
- Include seller's deed, title insurance policy or any other document affecting title
- Produce copies of any document that might affect the escrow
- Provide the present loan status on the property
- Produce executed deed on the property
- Produce any existing insurance policies, which may be assumed by the buyer
- Provide any subordination agreements as required by the contract
- Provide any current tenant information (if the property being purchased is a rental)
- Provide any additional documentation necessary for escrow to close
- Produce bill of sale for all personal property items not included in the purchase agreement

Real Estate Broker's Responsibilities:

- Deliver signed copies of the purchase agreement to all parties in the escrow.
- Deliver and explain all escrow instructions to all parties.
- Review preliminary report and explain it, in detail, to the buyer.
- Provide escrow officer with necessary seller's payment coupons. (for current loans against the property), the grant deed or any additional documents required for escrow.
- Provide all disclosure reports.
- Suggest to the buyer that he or she consult an attorney to figure out how to take title of the property.
- Advise the seller to maintain the property as agreed in the purchase agreement, as well as continue to make all loan payments.
- Assist buyer in obtaining all property inspection reports.
- Assist the seller in finding the necessary companies to conduct all pest reports, and then ensure all necessary corrections are made.
- Make sure each party delivers the required money into escrow. (as detailed in the escrow instructions)
- Assist buyer in obtaining loans.
- Provide any assistance needed by all parties to help close escrow.

Most of the closing costs between buyer and seller are negotiable. Typically the buyer will pay for the following: credit report, loan origination, note and deed of trust, appraisal, lender's title insurance, applicable assumption fees, notary, recording, new hazard insurance premiums, FHA mortgage insurance, and prorated expenses agreed upon in the purchase contract. Sellers generally pay for: pest inspections, repairs, VA transaction charges, taxes, prorated items, notary fees for documents prepared for the seller only, loan payoff, prepayment penalties if applicable, and the beneficiary statement. Again, these costs are all negotiable. The purchase agreement or escrow instructions will direct the escrow agent as to the party from whom to collect fees to cover these costs.

Escrow instructions, once prepared, will be computer-generated. Each party must sign the instructions, with the seller's instructions containing information regarding the broker's commission. The instructions will most likely contain the following information and instructions:

1. Purchase price

2. Terms – whether the transaction will be in cash, loan assumption or new loan, as well as other agreements regarding the financial transaction

3. Vesting or title

4. Recorded issues (such as who will be responsible for any encumbrance at the time of sale)

5. Closing or time of escrow

6. Inspections

7. Prorations (all fees that may be prorated are based on a 30-day month, 360-day year)

8. Possession – the date the buyer moves in is not always considered the close of escrow. In some transactions the buyer will remain on the property after selling it, and rent from the new owner.

9. Documents

10. Disbursement – a final distribution of all necessary funds at the end of escrow.

The escrow officer will request a preliminary report, or title search of all records regarding the property in escrow. This information includes all previous owners and any liens or encumbrances the property may have against it. If the title search reveals no liens or encumbrances, escrow may be closed. Any existing liens or encumbrances must be paid before the title may be transferred from the seller to the buyer. The buyer, upon inspecting the document, must sign the preliminary report.

It is not uncommon for property to be conveyed before the trust deed or mortgage is paid in full. When this happens, the escrow agent must contact the existing lending institution to receive a **beneficiary statement**, which reflects the current payoff. This is necessary for closing, as the lender will receive a disbursement from the transaction to pay the current note on the property.

Lenders require a fire insurance policy on all property, including property currently in escrow. It is the escrow agent's responsibility, as well as the buyer's, to have a fire insurance policy in effect or to see that the seller's old policy is transferred. The escrow agent will hold and deliver the necessary policy during escrow.

In California, the escrow agent receives all loan documents regarding the property and completes them as necessary. The buyer then reviews the documents and signs them for the escrow agent, who delivers them back to the lending institution. The escrow agent takes care of these documents, because he or she is in charge of disbursement of the funds before closing.

Reports regarding pest control, structural condition or other issues whose disclosure is required in the transaction are held in escrow. These documents may need review by the buyer or seller. As a result, they are held in escrow until needed. The reports will be held in escrow until close, when the escrow agent may be required to deliver a report to a particular party.

One of the most important jobs of the escrow agent is the **audit** of any files upon close of escrow. Each file in the transaction must be audited to ensure that the accounting is accurate and that all funds have been disbursed in accordance with the escrow instructions. A cash reconciliation statement accompanies these closing statements. This statement will show the debits and credits to both the buyer and seller, additionally showing where the money from the transaction is going.

Escrow instructions will contain instructions about **prorations** decided upon by the buyer and seller. Most often, the prorated items are property taxes, interest on the note, fire insurance premiums and rental income. Prorations are based on a 30-day month, and a 360-day year. The escrow agent will determine the debits and credits of both the buyer and seller as directed by each. After this, the buyer will be required to make the down payment (plus all closing costs) to the escrow officer. At this time, the buyer will also sign the loan, sending the appropriate funds to escrow for disbursement. Escrow can now be closed.

Items that may be prorated:
- Property taxes
- Interest
- Fire insurance premiums
- Rental income

The escrow agent upon doing a final check of title can record all documents. First, there is a preliminary report to inspect the title on the property, followed by a final check on the title. Once the title check is finished, the escrow agent may record all necessary documents, including the trust deed, the grant deed or the option.

Finally, escrow may close. **Closing** occurs when the closing statement is delivered to both the buyer and the seller. Additionally, all monies will now be disbursed to the appropriate parties, along with any recorded documents. The seller of the property will receive his or her check, less any commissions, fees, payoffs or other costs required to be deducted from the amount due.

Completing the closing occurs when the buyer receives a grant deed to the property. As mentioned before, closing does not necessarily mean the seller vacates the property or that the buyer is moving into the property. For example, the seller may choose to rent the property from the buyer for a certain amount of time, thus preventing the buyer from moving into the property right at closing. So, closing simply means that the transaction is complete. These details would be worked out in the purchase agreement and escrow instructions.

TERMINATION OF ESCROW

Escrow can be terminated in one of two ways. The first way escrow is terminated is by carrying out all instructions, disbursing all funds, and recording and delivering all documents to the involved parties. This is called **full performance of escrow.** The second way escrow can be terminated is by mutual agreement between the principals. One principal may not decide to terminate escrow without the consent of the other, with the mutual decision made in writing.

Ways to terminate escrow:
1. Full performance
2. Mutual decision between both principals in writing

RIGHTS AND OBLIGATIONS OF EACH PARTY TO AN ESCROW

The parties involved in an escrow include the buyer, seller and escrow agent. Real estate agents are not a party to the escrow process unless they are making a personal purchase and thus representing themselves as a private agent. Real estate agents will not receive their commission until escrow has closed. It is important to point out again that the escrow agent is a neutral third party, and thus may not favor one principal over another. Additionally it is important to note that the escrow agent can only act as directed by the principals.

Parties involved in an escrow:
- Buyer
- Seller
- Escrow Agent

An escrow agent or company may be: a real estate broker; bank; savings and loan institution; escrow company; title insurance company or an attorney. Real estate agents may only act as escrow agents if they are the buyer or seller's broker.

The escrow agent holds **limited agency**, in that he or she must act as agent to both the buyer and seller. We say the agency is limited because the escrow agent does not hold any authority or power outside of the instructions provided by his or her principals. Escrow agents must treat both principles equally, showing no partiality, and should keep this in mind during the entire escrow period.

Each year, the escrow company must submit a report to the real estate commissioner outlining the escrow company's operation. A CPA must prepare this report. In addition to this report, an additional audit must be prepared for the Commissioner of Corporations.

The Commission of Corporations must license all escrow companies. Corporations are the only entities that are eligible to be licensed. Individuals cannot hold license as an escrow company. There are, however, exemptions to licensure by the Commission of Corporations. Real estate brokers, banks, savings and loan institutions, attorney's and title insurance companies are exempt from licensure. All escrow companies must be bonded, to protect against loss of escrow funds.

Each party signing the escrow instructions or purchase agreement must be given a copy of the document. Additionally, only those involved in the escrow may be given information regarding the escrow. Blank escrow documents (to be filled in after-the-fact) are not legally allowable documents. All parties involved must initial any changes or alterations to the escrow.

RELATIONSHIP OF THE ESCROW HOLDER AND REAL ESTATE AGENT

A real estate broker is not considered a party to the escrow, but that does not mean that he or she is not an important part of the process. It is necessary for the broker and escrow agent to keep the lines of communication open to ensure all agreements made in the escrow instructions are carried out correctly. An escrow agent should check with the broker on a routine basis to ensure all information is correct and then report the progress of the escrow to the broker. This allows the broker to keep his or her clients informed about the process.

REAL ESTATE SETTLEMENT PROCEDURES ACT (RESPA)

The Real Estate Settlement Procedures Act (RESPA) requires that lenders providing certain federal mortgage loans make certain disclosures. The act pertains only to private homes consisting of 1-4 units. Loans that fall under this type of jurisdiction are: loans made by a lender who is FDIC insured, any federal agencies such as the FHA (Federal Housing Authority) or VA (Department of Veteran Affairs), or loans made in the secondary mortgage market (such as Ginnie Mae).

Lenders are required to supply each applicant with a special information booklet, prepared by the Department of Housing and Urban Development, along with an estimate of closing costs. If more than one applicant is applying for a loan, only one set of materials is required. By law, lenders must send out the special information booklet within 3 days from receipt of a loan application. Almost all lenders fall under RESPA. Private parties will be exempt from these rules and regulations. Violators of RESPA may be fined up to $10,000 and face imprisonment for one year.

Remember:
- Almost all lenders fall under RESPA, with the exception of private party lenders.

DESIGNATING THE ESCROW HOLDER

There are no laws governing who must act as the escrow holder in California. The buyer and seller are given the power to determine, between the two parties, who will be the escrow company for the property transfer. The buyer and seller will decide what individual or agency will be the escrow holder after all terms to the purchase agreement have been agreed to, and the contract signed. The contract the buyer and seller sign will become the escrow instructions. If the buyer and seller don't have any escrow professional in mind, you as a licensee may make a suggestion as to a reliable company you have worked with in the past, but there is to be no commissions or kickbacks given to the licensee from the escrow agent.

SUMMARY

To complete a transaction, an escrow officer is usually used to carry out the escrow instructions (which can also be the purchase agreement, if applicable). The escrow agent must be a neutral third party, who is following the instructions as agreed upon by both the buyer and the seller. These instructions may be altered only if both the buyer and seller mutually agree and sign off on the changes. An escrow agent cannot make any changes to the instructions, or favor one party over another. Each party in an escrow knows what is required of him or her, and the escrow officer can carry out the escrow procedures based on these responsibilities. After all instructions have been carried out, and money has been disbursed, escrow can close.

Abstract of Title - A full summary of all consecutive grants, conveyances, wills, records and judicial proceedings affecting title to a specific parcel of real estate.

A.L.T.A. (American Land Title Association) Owner's Policy - a policy of extended title insurance, which can be purchased by either a lender or buyer.

Beneficiary Statement – A statement from the lender showing the exact balance left on a loan for property. Typically these statements are issued when a seller is selling a home so escrow knows how much money will need to go the lender to pay off the note.

Binding Contract – A document that legally binds two parties to carry out specific actions or agreements.

California Land Title Association - A trade organization consisting of the state's title companies.

Chain of Title - The recorded history of matters such as conveyances, liens and encumbrances affecting title to a parcel of real estate.

Closing Costs – Money that must be paid at the closing of a property transfer beyond the actual purchase price for the property. Some costs include escrow services, recording of documents, broker's commission and other such costs. Typically the party who pays these costs will be agreed upon between the buyer and seller.

Closing Statement – Statements of issues to the buyer and seller indicating all credits and debits that each party incurred during the transaction.

Closing Escrow – The portion of the escrow period when delivery of documents and disbursement of all funds is done – making the escrow complete.

Escrow – The process by which a neutral third party will carry out all instructions of the purchase agreement or escrow instructions between the time an offer is made and the buyer's taking possession of the property. Escrow occurs when all necessary documents are processed and transmitted and funds are disbursed.

Escrow Agent – The neutral third party who carries out the instructions of an escrow, or holds money and other items of value in trust during the transfer of real property or other goods.

Escrow Instructions – The purchase agreement or written set of instructions signed by the principals, and which the escrow agent must follow, outlining all processes necessary for the real property exchange, transfer or purchase to close.

Extended Policy - An extended title insurance policy.

Guarantee of Title - An assurance that a title to property is clear.

Impound Account – A special trust fund set up for recurring costs. A property owner can put funds into this account to pay for items such as taxes or insurance. Upon the sale of the property, any money left over in the account will be returned to the seller.

Instrument – A document in real estate.

Insurance – A protective policy that will guard against personal losses in the event of a catastrophe. Insurance is offered for earthquakes, fires, floods and a policy simply called homeowners policy covering personal belongings in addition to the home.

Interest – The cost for borrowing money. When a loan is granted there will be a percentage of loan charged for the use of the money, stated in percentage points.

Lien - A claim on the property of another for payment of a debt.

Property Taxes – The tax a property owner must pay on his or her property annually. This amount is divided into two equal payments. The tax calendar year in California runs from July 1 – June 30.

Prorations – Monthly, quarterly or annual bills that are to be split or divided between the buyer and seller. The bill is prorated to the individual's actual use before or after the purchase of a home.

Reconveyance – The transfer of property. When a buyer purchases property from a seller, and does not assume an existing loan, the loan is paid off and a deed of reconveyance is given to the buyer.

Recurring Costs – Bills and payments a property owner will have to make more than once. Taxes and insurance are an example of these costs.

Rents – The consideration generally given for the use of a leased property. Rents are prorated in the transfer of property from one owner to another, making sure the rightful owner of the property collects the rent money.

Settlement Statement – A document provided to both the buyer and seller in a real estate transaction that indicates all profit or expenses of the transaction.

Standard Policy - A policy of title insurance covering only matters of record.

C H A P T E R Q U I Z

1. Title insurance protects the buyer from:
        a. Encumbrances
        b. The seller
        c. The lender
        d. None of the above

2. A standard title insurance policy covers which of the following?
        a. Forgery
        b. Defects found in public records
        c. Improperly delivered deeds
        d. All of the above

3. The extended title insurance policy covers all of the items covered in the standard policy, plus which additional items?
        a. Defects known to the buyer
        b. Changes in land use brought about by zoning ordinances

c. Unrecorded liens not known of by the policy holder

d. Defects and liens listed in the policy

4. What is required before a title insurance policy will be issued?
    a. Preliminary title report
    b. Official title report
    c. Zoning report
    d. Subdivision report

5. The purpose of the escrow agent is to:
    a. Distribute documents
    b. Disburse money
    c. Distribute
    d. All of the above

6. Who may be the escrow agent?
    a. Real estate broker
    b. Attorney
    c. Buyer or seller
    d. Both A and B

7. Which of the following is not a party to the escrow?
    a. Broker
    b. Lender
    c. Buyer
    d. Seller

8. What is a broker's function during the escrow?
    a. Nothing, the broker is not a party to the escrow and serves no function during this process.
    b. Explain escrow procedures to the client
    c. Monitor the escrow process to make sure there are no delays
    d. Both B and C

9. Legally, the escrow agent may not do which of the following?
    a. Hold money deposited by the either party until disbursed
    b. Renegotiate any part of the escrow separately with only one party to the escrow
    c. Act as a neutral party
    d. Make sure escrow does not close with an unverified check

10. What governs the escrow agency relationship?
    a. Escrow agent
    b. Broker
    c. Purchase agreement / escrow instructions
    d. State of California

11. In the event escrow instructions have to be changed, what must happen?
    a. A completely new set of escrow instructions must be written.
    b. Any changes in the current document may be initialed by both parties.
    c. An oral agreement must be made between both parties.
    d. None of the above.

12. Which of the following is not required in order to be a licensed escrow officer?
    a. Be financially solvent
    b. Set up a trust fund for all money deposited into the escrow

c. Be a member of the California Escrow Association
d. Furnish a surety bond for $10,000

13. Escrow is closed when:
    a. The remainder of the purchase price has been produced
    b. Deed has been signed
    c. Broker authorizes the transaction
    d. Both A and B

14. When are all funds in the escrow disbursed?
    a. On the day the deed is recorded
    b. At the close of escrow
    c. When all forms of payment have been verified
    d. When the escrow officer releases the funds

15. Closing costs include all of the following except:
    a. Title insurance
    b. Broker's commission
    c. Transfer tax
    d. Recording documents

16. Which of the following closing costs is not the responsibility of the seller?
    a. Owners title policy
    b. Recording the deed
    c. Obtaining the reconveyance deed
    d. Notary fees

17. Which of the following closing costs is not the responsibility of the buyer?
    a. Drawing up the deed
    b. Loan origination fee
    c. Appraisal fee
    d. Notary fees

18. What is the property tax year in California?
    a. January 1 – December 31
    b. March 1 – February 28
    c. July 1 – June 30
    d. November 1 – October 31

19. Certain fees and costs will be prorated during escrow. Which of the following is not a prorated fee or cost?
    a. Property taxes
    b. Insurance
    c. Rents
    d. Utility bills

20. Several steps must be made to close escrow; which of the following is not a step taken at the close of escrow?
    a. The buyer will move into the property.
    b. The escrow agent sends an original copy of the title policy to the buyer.
    c. The escrow officer sends the deed and deed of trust to the recorder's office to be recorded.
    d. The escrow agent sends the seller and buyer closing statements showing all disbursement of funds.

11

PROPERTY MANAGEMENT

What you will learn in this Chapter

- Property Management
- Basic Responsibilities
- Types of Properties Managed
- Management Contract
- Accounting Records
- Residential Leasing
- Termination of the Lease

Test Your Knowledge

1. Which of the following is not a step in an unlawful detainer?
    a. Tenant is given a verbal notice of past rent that is due
    b. Tenant is served a three-day notice to quit the premises or pay rent
    c. Landlord files an unlawful detainer against the tenant in a court of law
    d. The sheriff sends the tenant an eviction notice

2. The maximum security deposit a landlord may collect from a tenant for an unfurnished unit is:
    a. One month's rent
    b. Two months' rent
    c. Three months' rent
    d. Four months' rent

3. Which of the following is a valid reason to refuse a potential tenant's application for residency?
    a. On the basis of age
    b. On the basis of sex
    c. On the basis of national origin
    d. On the basis of credit history

4. A percentage lease would commonly be used with:
    a. A business or retail complex
    b. A residential complex
    c. An industrial complex
    d. Any of the above

5. A property manager specializing in park development, maintenance of public amenities and approval of lease assignments on the sale of different units would most likely be a manager in a:
    a. Mobile-home park
    b. Office park
    c. Condominium complex
    d. None of the above

6. An analysis of the character of the immediate neighborhood, trends in population growth, economic level of neighborhood residents, condition of the housing market, and current vacancy factors is used when:
    a. Establishing rent schedules
    b. Deciding to use a property manager for a small property
    c. Determining the basic responsibilities of a property manager
    d. Deciding contract terms for renters

7. Which of the following is not a type of property manager?
    a. Residential manager
    b. Estate manager
    c. Individual property manager
    d. Licensee / property manager

Property management is a specialized area of real estate that has been around for a remarkable period of time. Looking back in history, we can trace the roots of property management back for hundreds and hundreds of years.

In this chapter you will learn what a property manager does, and be introduced to all the specializations that make up the field. You will be introduced to professional organizations in which property managers can participate. Additionally, we will look at the different qualifications that a person must possess in order to become a property manager.

After learning about specific property management duties, we will then look at the different types of leasehold estates that a person may enter into. In this section we will discuss the rights and responsibilities of all parties in a lease, as well as the process of transferring and terminating a lease.

Property management is much more than collecting rents and showing apartments to prospective tenants; it is a highly skilled and technical side of real estate.

P R O P E R T Y   M A N A G E M E N T

The concept of property management is by no means new or limited to the past 100 years. If we look at history, we can track property management or managers back hundreds or even thousands of years. In the past, property managers were sometimes called "overseers," or managers hired by chartered owners of property to watch over the property and its functions. An example of this is the Virginia Company in the seventeenth century, employing managers to run its operation in Colonial America on behalf of the stockholders back in England.

Today, property management has grown significantly. This growth has been attributed to two historical events: the Great Depression and the invention of the electric elevator. During the Great Depression, many people lost everything they had, including their homes. Because of the high rate of foreclosures, lenders began to accumulate a large inventory of property. Property managers were needed to make sure these properties were being kept up in good condition rather than deteriorate and become un-sellable.

The electric elevator allowed buildings to begin to be constructed higher and higher. With more square footage in one single building, and companies swallowing up entire floors, owners had to hire building managers to make sure everything was functioning as it should. Think about your office building, or a large urban building; there is usually a property manager to oversee the janitorial staff, hire out repair work when necessary, show vacant office space and complete all other behind-the-scenes functions most of us take for granted.

T Y P E S   O F   P R O P E R T Y   M A N A G E R S

There are three different types of property managers: residential, outside and institutional managers.

A residential manager is a property manager who lives in the building or complex that is managed. Think of an apartment manager. He or she shows vacant units, manages the janitorial staff, collects rents and reports directly to the person who owns the building or to a larger management agency contracted to manage the property. The state of California requires a residential manager in apartments containing 16 or more units and mobile home parks with 50 or more units. If a residential manager wishes to manage more than just the property he or she lives in, then a real estate brokers license is necessary. However, if the manager strictly takes care of the one property, no license is necessary.

Outside managers usually work for a property-management firm and represent many different properties. Outside managers must possess a real estate brokers license. Usually the outside manager will replace the owner in the daily management duties of a property, and can sometimes be referred to as the general manager of property.

Institutional managers are sometimes referred to as building supervisors. They do not need a real estate license as they generally work for a real estate management firm, government agency or some other agency where a license is not required. These managers will work for a direct salary, no commissions are given.

Remember:
The three kinds of property managers include
- Residential manager
- Outside manager
- Institutional manager

Professional Organizations

Just like real estate salespeople and brokers have professional organizations such as National Association of REALTORS (NAR), property managers also have organizations they can take part in. The most notable of these groups is the Institute of Real Estate Management, or IREM for short. IREM is a division of NAR. IREM was founded by a group of Realtors during the Depression to help facilitate the growth and professionalism of the property management field, when it was a relatively new industry.

IREM has a code of ethics similar to that of NAR. All Realtors applying to be part of the Institute of Real Estate Management must adhere to these ethical standards in order to become a member. One of the advantages to joining IREM and agreeing to the ethical standards is to become a CPM, or certified property manager. All members of the IREM are allowed to use this designation after their name. CPM's are considered individuals while AMO's are entities or firms. AMO stands for Accredited Management Organization. In order for a firm to be designated as AMO, at least one member must be a certified property manager.

Remember:
- IREM stands for Institute of Real Estate Managers, started by Realtors associated with NAR
- CPM stands for Certified Property Managers, a designation only given to individuals
- AMO stands for Accredited Management Organization, a title given to firms specializing in property management

Types of Leasehold Estates

There are different types of leaseholds. These are estate for years, estate from period to period, estate at will and estate at sufferance. The main difference between these types of leaseholds is the duration of the tenancy. If the duration of the tenancy is over one year, a lease in writing is required. For tenancy duration of less than one year, either a written or verbal agreement may be used.

Types of Leaseholds:
- Estate for years
- Estate from period to period
- Estate at will
- Estate at sufferance

Estate for Years

An "estate for years" is a lease created between a landlord and tenant and is valid only for a specific amount of time. This type of lease may last for several years, as its name indicates. However, an estate for years may also last only months, weeks or even days. Because both the landlord and tenant know when the lease expires, no notice is required at the end of the lease period.

This type of lease is attractive to tenants who are looking for long-term housing or rental space, because the rental price will usually stay the same for the specific duration of the lease. Landlords like this type of lease, because they can find tenants who will occupy the space for an extended period of time. This prevents the landlord from having to continually fill vacancies.

Additionally, when this lease is up, there are no automatic extensions or renewals of the lease. If the tenant and landlord mutually agree to renew the tenancy, another estate for years is formed. Some contracts or leases will have an option for the tenant to form a month-to-month contract. Such a contract is not considered an estate for years; rather, it is an estate from period to period.

Estate from Period to Period

An "estate from period to period" is also referred to as a periodic tenancy. This type of tenancy occurs when a tenant pays his or her rent at the end of a lease, and the landlord accepts the payment. The lease is automatically extended for the period of time for which the tenant paid. As long as the landlord accepts payment, the lease is renewed. To terminate this type of rental agreement, a notice must be given by one party to the other. If the tenant plans to vacate the space, he or she must notify the landlord prior to leaving. If the landlord does not wish to renew the tenant's contract, the landlord must give notice to the tenant that the lease will not be renewed.

Periodic Tenancy

Periodic tenancy is generally a month-to-month contract. Because most leases require the tenant to pay rent once each month, each time the rent is paid, the contract will be extended for that month. Periodic tenancies are not always month-to-month leases, although that is the most common form.

Estate at Will

An estate at will requires no rental agreement or contract between the landlord and tenant. Either party may terminate the contract at will without the other's consent. However, if the contract if terminated, a 30-day notice must be given by the party who chooses to terminate the contract. This type of tenancy is uncommon in California.

Estate at Sufferance

An estate at sufferance is created when a tenant does not vacate a property at the end of a lease agreement, and so remains in possession of the property. The tenant will remain in control of the property without the consent of the landlord. Additionally, if a tenant gives notice to vacate, but does not leave and does not pay rent, an estate at sufferance is created. The landlord may give notice of termination of the lease at any time. This type of instability makes the estate at sufferance the least desirable type or lowest form of tenancy. If the tenant pays rent, and the landlord accepts the payment, it is no longer an estate at sufferance. Rather, it is a periodic tenancy.

Types of Leases

There are four different types of leases:

1. Gross lease
2. Net lease
3. Graduated lease
4. Percentage lease

In a **gross lease**, a tenant pays a landlord a fixed amount of money per month. The landlord will use this amount to pay utility bills, taxes, mortgages or other expenses incurred by the building or property. Generally a landlord will consider these costs before setting the price of rent, to ensure all rental expenses are covered.

The net lease is similar to the gross lease, with the exception that the tenant pays expenses incurred by the landlord. A set monthly rent is agreed upon, and each month the tenant must pay for additional expenses (such as repairs, taxes or other costs that may be billed monthly, or a single occurrence during the duration of the tenancy).

In a **graduated lease** the base rent or monthly charge varies from month to month, unlike the fixed amount of monthly rent associated with gross and net leases. One factor causing fluctuations in a graduated lease may be the time of year for which the lease is in place and the corresponding energy costs associated with that season. For example, utility bills go up in winter, due to the cooler weather and cost of heating the unit.

A **percentage lease** might be used by a landlord who owns commercial space that is rented to a retail business. In a percentage lease, rent is based on a percentage of the tenant's gross profits.

Landlords must take into account several different factors when determining rent they will charge for a specific piece of property. Landlords, of course, need to cover all of their costs of maintenance, repairs, utilities, taxes and any additional mortgage payment if applicable. The landlord also wants to ensure some extra income for him or herself. After all, most people invest in an income property to make money. The amount of money a landlord asks in rent from a tenant is usually called the contract rent. Contract rent is not the same as economic rent (which is how much rent a specific property could bring).

For example, let's say you have been living in the same apartment building for 10 years. Your rent has most likely increased while you have lived there. However, you are most likely not paying what your new neighbor across the hall is paying. Your rent is contract rent, kept low due to a few different factors (such as rent control). Your neighbor's rent is closer to economic rent (if not right at economic rent), as they are new to the building.

> **Remember:**
> **Contract Rent** is the amount of rent a landlord is currently charging or receiving for a property, **Economic Rent** is the amount of rent a landlord could charge for a specific property in an open market.

Types of property managed

There are many different types of property a manager might have to be hired to oversee. Some are more obvious than others, but when you think about it, almost any type of property lends itself to the necessity of a property manager. Perhaps the most obvious are apartments. We can group apartments into the property type of residential, which will also include single-family homes, duplexes, triplexes, condominiums, mobile home parks and public housing. Besides residential property, managers are also needed to oversee office buildings, retail stores, hotels, industrial parks, and even medical buildings and complexes.

Residential Properties

Residential properties are not only the most obvious property lending itself to the necessity of a manager, it is also the most numerous of all properties.

Perhaps the single most important area for property managers to be very well familiar with are fair housing laws and the Real Estate Commissioner's Regulations dealing with fair housing. Specifically the California Fair Employment and Housing Act, or Rumford Act, and the Unruh Civil Rights Act and Federal Civil Rights Acts. These laws and regulations are in place to protect applicants from discrimination or unfair treatment. Any manager found to be in violation of these laws may be held liable for damages caused due to his or her actions.

It is important for all residential property managers to be aware of all local codes, restrictions, laws and ordinances governing rental properties and rental practices. For example some cities have rent control allowing rents to go up only a certain percentage a year. Generally this increase is equal to yearly inflation.

Condominiums

Many urban areas are now constructing high-rise luxury condominiums to maximize space and builders profits. Because of the boom in condominium development in the past 25 years a demand for managers has been on the rise. Condominiums will obviously be different from apartment complexes because units will be privately owned, so rental issues will not apply here. Individuals will own their private units, and a share of the common areas of the building. It is these common areas where the management would most be concerned. The need here is to have a manager work directly with the HOA, or Home Owners Associations to keep the complex in good shape.

Mobile-Home Parks

Like all managers of property, managers of mobile-home parks must juggle many different tasks. A mobile-home park manger must be well versed in not only sales of units but also lease assignments. He or she must enforce park rules, manage and maintain all amenities and participate in park development. As you can see there are aspects of sales as well as management. In certain mobile-home parks, a manager's duties are similar to that of a manager in a condominium association. This happens when the individuals own their home and lot.

Remember:
Property managers in mobile-home parks must specialize in:
- Park development
- Enforcement of all park rules
- Maintenance of park amenities
- Approval of lease assignments on the sale of units

Multifamily Units (Duplexes and Triplexes)

Multifamily units are common in all parts of California. Individuals will sometimes build a duplex or triplex and live in one of the units, while renting out the other unit(s) to help with the mortgage. When the individual lives on the premises, the owner is generally the manager. Sometimes, investors will build a series of duplexes or triplexes and not live in any of the units. Property managers are then used to oversee the property, and take care of renting the units out.

Single-family Homes

Some people own vacation homes in resort areas, or cabins in remote areas of the state. When they are not using their property, they often will rent them out to help cover the mortgage payments. Property managers are usually used to handling the logistics of renting out the property, collecting the rent money, general maintenance and cleaning.

Public Housing

Government housing, or federal programs in housing, have a need for managers just the same as private owners. In addition to public housing authorities, cooperative apartments, real estate investment trusts and townhouses are also grouped under this type of management.

Office Buildings

Office buildings and corporate parks are all over. Usually the developer who owns these properties will have a completely hands off approach to the management of the building(s) and relies heavily on property managers, and management companies. A manager will be responsible for every aspect of the building from space rental, to maintenance and cleaning, safety and preventative measures.

Industrial Management

Just like all other types of management, industrial managers must be very well versed and skilled in the area of industrial property, the rules and regulations associated with all aspects of industrial property and special restrictions or requirements. Examples of restrictions or requirements are load capacities per floor or loading dock requirements.

Each type of property requires a different set of duties for the property manager. It would be difficult to summarize general duties all property managers. Below is a partial list of duties that are applicable to most management situations, but keep in mind, not all duties apply to every manager.

1. Collects rents and handles eviction proceedings if necessary

2. Manages trust fund accounts for specific functions, such as maintenance and repairs

3. Completes reports for the owner/management firm on the status of all duties. The frequency of reports may vary on the specific task.

4. Supervise maintenance and cleaning of the building

5. Manages personnel

6. Preparation of budgets

7. Plan rent schedules

8. Rental of units

9. Inspection of vacant units to keep them in good rental condition

10. Prepare rental documents

11. Credit check and qualification of potential renters

12. Payment of taxes

13. Keep the property safe and free of hazards

MANAGEMENT CONTRACT

Contracts between the owner of property and the property manager or management firm should be in writing. This contract should clearly define the specific duties the manager is expected to complete for the property. Additionally it should specify the rights and benefits available to the manager. There are pre-printed forms that may be used between owners and managers. These forms may be taken at face value, or altered to fit the exact management situation. A pre-printed form is not required, owners and managers may draw up a new contract, separate from existing forms. It is important to use a lawyer when doing so to make sure all aspects of the contract are clear and not open to interpretation.

Compensation
Managers may be compensated in a number of different ways. Some managers are paid on a straight salary. Some, such as apartment managers, will have living arrangements paid for. Other compensation methods are a percentage basis and commission.

A straight salary is simple to understand, and requires little explanation. Many apartment managers will receive both the salary and have an apartment to live in rent-free. Managers who are paid on a percentage basis give the manager higher motivation to work hard to keep all available rental units rented. The percentage is based on gross

_____ ("Owner"), and
_____ ("Broker"), agree as follows:

1. **APPOINTMENT OF BROKER:** Owner hereby appoints and grants Broker the exclusive right to rent, lease, operate and manage the property(ies) known as _____
_____ and any additional property that may later be added to this Agreement ("Property"), upon the terms below, for the period beginning (date) _____ and ending (date) _____, at 11:59 PM.
(If checked:) ☐ Either party may terminate this Property Management Agreement ("Agreement") on at least 30 days written notice _____ months after the original commencement date of this Agreement. After the exclusive term expires, this Agreement shall continue as a non-exclusive agreement that either party may terminate by giving at least 30 days written notice to the other.

2. **BROKER ACCEPTANCE:** Broker accepts the appointment and grant, and agrees to:
   A. Use due diligence in the performance of this Agreement.
   B. Furnish the services of its firm for the rental, leasing, operation and management of the Property.

3. **AUTHORITY AND POWERS:** Owner grants Broker the authority and power, at Owner's expense, to:
   A. **ADVERTISING:** Display FOR RENT/LEASE and similar signs on the Property and advertise the availability of the Property, or any part thereof, for rental or lease.
   B. **RENTAL;LEASING:** Initiate, sign, renew, modify or cancel rental agreements and leases for the Property, or any part thereof; collect and give receipts for rents, other fees, charges and security deposits. Any lease or rental agreement executed by Broker for Owner shall not exceed _____ year(s) or ☐ shall be month-to-month. Unless Owner authorizes a lower amount, rent shall be at market rate; OR ☐ a minimum of $ _____ per _____;
   OR ☐ see attachment.
   C. **TENANCY TERMINATION:** Sign and serve in Owner's name notices that are required or appropriate; commence and prosecute actions to evict tenants; recover possession of the Property in Owner's name; recover rents and other sums due; and, when expedient, settle, compromise and release claims, actions and suits and/or reinstate tenancies.
   D. **REPAIR;MAINTENANCE:** Make, cause to be made, and/or supervise repairs, improvements, alterations and decorations to the Property; purchase, and pay bills for services and supplies. Broker shall obtain prior approval of Owner for all expenditures over $ _____ for any one item. Prior approval shall not be required for monthly or recurring operating charges or, if in Broker's opinion, emergency expenditures over the maximum are needed to protect the Property or other property(ies) from damage, prevent injury to persons, avoid suspension of necessary services, avoid penalties or fines, or suspension of services to tenants required by a lease or rental agreement or by law, including, but not limited to, maintaining the Property in a condition fit for human habitation as required by Civil Code §§ 1941 and 1941.1 and Health and Safety Code §§ 17920.3 and 17920.10.
   E. **REPORTS, NOTICES AND SIGNS:** Comply with federal, state or local law requiring delivery of reports or notices and/or posting of signs or notices.
   F. **CONTRACTS;SERVICES:** Contract, hire, supervise and/or discharge firms and persons, including utilities, required for the operation and maintenance of the Property. Broker may perform any of Broker's duties through attorneys, agents, employees, or independent contractors and, except for persons working in Broker's firm, shall not be responsible for their acts, omissions, defaults, negligence and/or costs of same.
   G. **EXPENSE PAYMENTS:** Pay expenses and costs for the Property from Owner's funds held by Broker, unless otherwise directed by Owner. Expenses and costs may include, but are not limited to, property management compensation, fees and charges, expenses for goods and services, property taxes and other taxes, Owner's Association dues, assessments, loan payments and insurance premiums.
   H. **SECURITY DEPOSITS:** Receive security deposits from tenants, which deposits shall be ☐ given to Owner, or ☐ placed in Broker's trust account and, if held in Broker's trust account, pay from Owner's funds all interest on tenants' security deposits if required by local law or ordinance. Owner shall be responsible to tenants for return of security deposits and all interest due on security deposits held by Owner.
   I. **TRUST FUNDS:** Deposit all receipts collected for Owner, less any sums properly deducted or disbursed, in a financial institution whose deposits are insured by an agency of the United States government. The funds shall be held in a trust account separate from Broker's personal accounts. Broker shall not be liable in event of bankruptcy or failure of a financial institution.
   J. **RESERVES:** Maintain a reserve in Broker's trust account of $ _____.
   K. **DISBURSEMENTS:** Disburse Owner's funds held in Broker's trust account in the following order:
      (1) Compensation due Broker under paragraph 6.
      (2) All other operating expenses, costs and disbursements payable from Owner's funds held by Broker.
      (3) Reserves and security deposits held by Broker.
      (4) Balance to Owner.
   L. **OWNER DISTRIBUTION:** Remit funds, if any are available, monthly (or ☐ _____), to Owner.
   M. **OWNER STATEMENTS:** Render monthly (or ☐ _____) statements of receipts, expenses and charges for each Property.
   N. **BROKER FUNDS:** Broker shall not advance Broker's own funds in connection with the Property or this Agreement.
   O. ☐ (If checked) Owner authorizes the use of a keysafe/lockbox to allow entry into the Property and agrees to sign a keysafe/lockbox addendum (C.A.R. Form KLA).

Owner's Initials (_____)(_____)
Broker's Initials (_____)(_____)

Reviewed by _____ Date _____

Owner Name: _____ Date: _____

4. **OWNER RESPONSIBILITIES:** Owner shall:
   A. Provide all documentation, records and disclosures as required by law or required by Broker to manage and operate the Property, and immediately notify Broker if Owner becomes aware of any change in such documentation, records or disclosures, or any matter affecting the habitability of the Property.
   B. Indemnify, defend and hold harmless Broker, and all persons in Broker's firm, regardless of responsibility, from all costs, expenses, suits, liabilities, damages, attorney fees and claims of every type, including but not limited to those arising out of injury or death of any person, or damage to any real or personal property of any person, including Owner, for: (i) any repairs performed by Owner or by others hired directly by Owner; or (ii) those relating to the management, leasing, rental, security deposits, or operation of the Property by Broker, or any person in Broker's firm, or the performance or exercise of any of the duties, powers or authorities granted to Broker.
   C. Maintain the Property in a condition fit for human habitation as required by Civil Code §§ 1941 and 1941.1 and Health and Safety Code §§ 17920.3 and 17920.10 and other applicable law.
   D. Pay all interest on tenants' security deposits if required by local law or ordinance.
   E. Carry and pay for: (i) public and premises liability insurance in an amount of no less than $1,000,000; and (ii) property damage and worker's compensation insurance adequate to protect the interests of Owner and Broker. Broker shall be, and Owner authorizes Broker to be named as an additional insured party on Owner's policies.
   F. Pay any late charges, penalties and/or interest imposed by lenders or other parties for failure to make payment to those parties, if the failure is due to insufficient funds in Broker's trust account available for such payment.
   G. Immediately replace any funds required if there are insufficient funds in Broker's trust account to cover Owner's responsibilities.

5. **LEAD-BASED PAINT DISCLOSURE:**
   A. ☐   The Property was constructed on or after January 1, 1978.
   OR B. ☐   The Property was constructed prior to 1978.
      (1) Owner has no knowledge of lead-based paint or lead-based paint hazards in the housing except: _____
      _____
      (2) Owner has no reports or records pertaining to lead-based paint or lead-based paint hazards in the housing, except the following, which Owner shall provide to Broker: _____

6. **COMPENSATION:**
   A. Owner agrees to pay Broker fees in the amounts indicated below for:
      (1) Management: _____.
      (2) Renting or Leasing: _____.
      (3) Evictions: _____.
      (4) Preparing Property for rental or lease: _____.
      (5) Managing Property during extended periods of vacancy: _____.
      (6) An overhead and service fee added to the cost of all work performed by, or at the direction of, Broker: _____.
      (7) Other: _____.
   B. This Agreement does not include providing on-site management services, property sales, refinancing, preparing Property for sale or refinancing, modernization, fire or major damage restoration, rehabilitation, obtaining income tax, accounting or legal advice, representation before public agencies, advising on proposed new construction, debt collection, counseling, attending Owner's Association meetings or _____
      _____
      If Owner requests Broker to perform services not included in this Agreement, a fee shall be agreed upon before these services are performed.
   C. Broker may divide compensation, fees and charges due under this Agreement in any manner acceptable to Broker.
   D. Owner further agrees that:
      (1) Broker may receive and keep fees and charges from tenants for: (i) requesting an assignment of lease or sublease of the Property; (ii) processing credit applications; (iii) any returned checks and/or (☐ if checked) late payments; and (iv) any other services that are not in conflict with this Agreement.
      (2) Broker may perform any of Broker's duties, and obtain necessary products and services, through affiliated companies or organizations in which Broker may own an interest. Broker may receive fees, commissions and/or profits from these affiliated companies or organizations. Broker has an ownership interest in the following affiliated companies or organizations: _____
      _____
      Broker shall disclose to Owner any other such relationships as they occur. Broker shall not receive any fees, commissions or profits from unaffiliated companies or organizations in the performance of this Agreement, without prior disclosure to Owner.
      (3) Other: _____

7. **AGENCY RELATIONSHIPS:** Broker shall act, and Owner hereby consents to Broker acting, as dual agent for Owner and tenant(s) in any resulting transaction. If the Property includes residential property with one-to-four dwelling units and this Agreement permits a tenancy in excess of one year, Owner acknowledges receipt of the "Disclosure Regarding Agency Relationships" (C.A.R. Form AD). Owner understands that Broker may have or obtain property management agreements on other property, and that potential tenants may consider, make offers on, or lease through Broker, property the same as or similar to Owner's Property. Owner consents to Broker's representation of other owners' properties before, during and after the expiration of this Agreement.

8. **NOTICES:** Any written notice to Owner or Broker required under this Agreement shall be served by sending such notice by first class mail or other agreed-to delivery method to that party at the address below, or at any different address the parties may later designate for this purpose. Notice shall be deemed received three (3) calendar days after deposit into the United States mail OR ☐ _____.

Owner's Initials (_____)(_____)
Broker's Initials (_____)(_____)

Reviewed by _____ Date _____

PMA REVISED 4/03 (PAGE 2 OF 3)

PROPERTY MANAGEMENT AGREEMENT (PMA PAGE 2 OF 3)

Owner Name: _____ Date: _____

9. **DISPUTE RESOLUTION**
   A. **MEDIATION:** Owner and Broker agree to mediate any dispute or claim arising between them out of this Agreement, or any resulting transaction before resorting to arbitration or court action, subject to paragraph 9B(2) below. Paragraph 9B(2) below applies whether or not the arbitration provision is initialed. Mediation fees, if any, shall be divided equally among the parties involved. If, for any dispute or claim to which this paragraph applies, any party commences an action based on a dispute or claim to which this paragraph applies, without first attempting to resolve the matter through mediation, or refuses to mediate after a request has been made, then that party shall not be entitled to recover attorney fees, even if they would otherwise be available to that party in any such action. THIS MEDIATION PROVISION APPLIES WHETHER OR NOT THE ARBITRATION PROVISION IS INITIALED.
   B. **ARBITRATION OF DISPUTES:** Owner and Broker agree that any dispute or claim in law or equity arising between them regarding the obligation to pay compensation under this agreement, which is not settled through mediation, shall be decided by neutral, binding arbitration, including and subject to paragraph 9B(2) below. The arbitrator shall be a retired judge or justice, or an attorney with at least 5 years of residential real estate law experience, unless the parties mutually agree to a different arbitrator, who shall render an award in accordance with substantive California Law. The parties shall have the right to discovery in accordance with Code of Civil Procedure § 1283.05. In all other respects, the arbitration shall be conducted in accordance with Title 9 of Part III of the California Code of Civil Procedure. Judgment upon the award of the arbitrator(s) may be entered in any court having jurisdiction. Interpretation of this agreement to arbitrate shall be governed by the Federal Arbitration Act.
   (2) **EXCLUSIONS FROM MEDIATION AND ARBITRATION:** The following matters are excluded from mediation and arbitration hereunder: (i) a judicial or non-judicial foreclosure or other action or proceeding to enforce a deed of trust, mortgage, or installment land sale contract as defined in Civil Code § 2985; (ii) an unlawful detainer action; (iii) the filing or enforcement of a mechanic's lien; and (iv) any matter that is within the jurisdiction of a probate, small claims, or bankruptcy court. The filing of a court action to enable the recording of a notice of pending action, for order of attachment, receivership, injunction, or other provisional remedies, shall not constitute a waiver of the mediation and arbitration provisions.
   "NOTICE: BY INITIALING IN THE SPACE BELOW YOU ARE AGREEING TO HAVE ANY DISPUTE ARISING OUT OF THE MATTERS INCLUDED IN THE 'ARBITRATION OF DISPUTES' PROVISION DECIDED BY NEUTRAL ARBITRATION AS PROVIDED BY CALIFORNIA LAW AND YOU ARE GIVING UP ANY RIGHTS YOU MIGHT POSSESS TO HAVE THE DISPUTE LITIGATED IN A COURT OR JURY TRIAL. BY INITIALING IN THE SPACE BELOW YOU ARE GIVING UP YOUR JUDICIAL RIGHTS TO DISCOVERY AND APPEAL, UNLESS THOSE RIGHTS ARE SPECIFICALLY INCLUDED IN THE 'ARBITRATION OF DISPUTES' PROVISION. IF YOU REFUSE TO SUBMIT TO ARBITRATION AFTER AGREEING TO THIS PROVISION, YOU MAY BE COMPELLED TO ARBITRATE UNDER THE AUTHORITY OF THE CALIFORNIA CODE OF CIVIL PROCEDURE. YOUR AGREEMENT TO THIS ARBITRATION PROVISION IS VOLUNTARY."
   "WE HAVE READ AND UNDERSTAND THE FOREGOING AND AGREE TO SUBMIT DISPUTES ARISING OUT OF THE MATTERS INCLUDED IN THE 'ARBITRATION OF DISPUTES' PROVISION TO NEUTRAL ARBITRATION."

   Owner's Initials _____ / _____   Broker's Initials _____ / _____

10. **EQUAL HOUSING OPPORTUNITY:** The Property is offered in compliance with federal, state and local anti-discrimination laws.
11. **ATTORNEY FEES:** In any action, proceeding or arbitration between Owner and Broker regarding the obligation to pay compensation under this Agreement, the prevailing Owner or Broker shall be entitled to reasonable attorney fees and costs from the non-prevailing Owner or Broker, except as provided in paragraph 9A.
12. **ADDITIONAL TERMS:** ☐ Keysafe/Lockbox Addendum (C.A.R. Form KLA) ☐ Lead-Based Paint and Lead-Based Paint Hazards Disclosure (C.A.R. Form FLD) _____

13. **TIME OF ESSENCE; ENTIRE CONTRACT; CHANGES:** Time is of the essence. All understandings between the parties are incorporated in this Agreement. Its terms are intended by the parties as a final, complete and exclusive expression of their Agreement with respect to its subject matter, and may not be contradicted by evidence of any prior agreement or contemporaneous oral agreement. If any provision of this Agreement is held to be ineffective or invalid, the remaining provisions will nevertheless be given full force and effect. Neither this Agreement nor any provision in it may be extended, amended, modified, altered or changed except in writing. This Agreement and any supplement, addendum or modification, including any copy, may be signed in two or more counterparts, all of which shall constitute one and the same writing.

Owner warrants that Owner is the owner of the Property or has the authority to execute this contract. Owner acknowledges Owner has read, understands, accepts and has received a copy of the Agreement.

Owner _____ Date _____
Owner _____
    Print Name   Social Security/Tax ID # (for tax reporting purposes
Address _____ City _____ State _____ Zip _____
Telephone _____ Fax _____ E-mail _____

Owner _____ Date _____
Owner _____
    Print Name   Social Security/Tax ID # (for tax reporting purposes
Address _____ City _____ State _____ Zip _____
Telephone _____ Fax _____ E-mail _____

Real Estate Broker (Firm) _____ Date _____
By (Agent) _____
Address _____ City _____ State _____ Zip _____
Telephone _____ Fax _____ E-mail _____

SURE TRAC The System for Success™   Published by the
California Association of REALTORS®

PMA REVISED 4/03 (PAGE 3 OF 3)   Reviewed by _____ Date _____

PROPERTY MANAGEMENT AGREEMENT (PMA PAGE 3 OF 3)

revenues taken in on a monthly basis. Generally the percentage is anywhere between 6.5 – 15 percent. Some managers are given a commission based on each unit rented. These commissions are generally between 2-15 percent. The percent earned in a commission or percent basis usually corresponds directly with the size of the property being managed. In addition to regular compensation, many managers will receive bonuses based on their performance.

ACCOUNTING RECORDS

The accounting requirements to be carried out by the manager will be determined by the size of the property being managed. Regardless of the size of property, it is solely the manager's responsibility to make sure he or she has very detailed records regarding trust funds and allocation of money to different resources. Budgetary record keeping is also very important so the manager knows how much money is allotted to different functions, and how much of that budget is left. It is always good practice to have a tax professional or accountant audit all records to make sure everything is in order.

There are many different reasons for keeping detailed and accurate records. The following seven reasons are essential for every licensee in property management to keep accurate records and protect him or herself from potential problems that may arise from accounting mistakes or issues.

Reasons for accounting:
- Statutory requirements mandate separate records for each property managed must be kept
- Fiduciary responsibilities to the owner of the building
- Required by the contract between the owner and manager
- Control, and clear knowledge of all resources coming in and going out
- Records for income tax filing
- Satisfy any requirements of interested third parties to the property
- To keep accurate records in the broker's files

Fortunate for today's property managers, computers can lend tremendous help. Data can be accessed at the stroke of a few keys, and paperwork is minimized. Laptop computers and portable data devices can greatly aid managers dealing with multiple properties, reducing the amount of files or papers that must be transferred from one office to another.

Trust Ledger
Section 2830 of the commissioner's regulations requires each property manager to keep a trust ledger for property management accounts. All money coming in and going out must be clearly recorded in this ledger. This ledger aids in carrying out the fiduciary responsibility a manager owes the owner. When an owner has questions regarding what resources are being spent where, the manager can access this ledger and quickly and accurately account for all income or expense activity.

The majority of rentals in California are residential. It is important for the manager to be very thorough when choosing tenants to make sure they will make payments on time, will not be destructive to the property and respect the other tenants in the building. Sometimes managers will require a list of references to verify the renter's good history and past performance as a tenant. Managers will usually run a credit report on the tenant to make sure he or she has a good history of paying creditors on time. It is in the owner's best interests for the manager to find a good tenant. A bad tenant is typically seen as more problematic than a vacant unit.

Rental Application

The agreement between the landlord (or lessor) and tenant (or lessee) is called a lease. The lease will outline all terms of the tenancy, including: the rent amount; beginning and ending dates of the tenancy; and any restrictions or rules a tenant must observe.

In California, any lease for a period of more than one year must be made in writing. This lease must be signed by the landlord, but does not have to be signed by the tenant. When a tenant takes possession of the property, he or she is acknowledging the terms of the lease, and is therefore not required to sign the contract. Although the tenant is not required to sign the lease, it is a good idea for both parties to carefully read the lease, to understand all its terms. It is also wise for both parties to sign the lease regardless, to avoid any misunderstanding which may arise in the future. The right of the landlord to reclaim the property being leased is called reversionary right.

All leases must contain: the name of the parties; description of the property involved; period of time or duration the lease will last; and the required, monthly rent or consideration. An easy way to remember these requirements is with the four P's:

> **Lease Requirements (or, the Four P's):**
> - Parties
> - Property
> - Period (of time)
> - Payment (rent)

All leases should clearly identify the landlord, the tenant and any additional persons occupying the property. These people are known as the parties, though leases will usually use the terms lessee and lessor to identify the parties involved in the tenancy.

Leases must clearly describe the property that will be occupied as well as any restrictions or allowable uses the tenant must observe in leasing the property.

Every lease will specify a time period during which the lease will be valid. This should indicate the start and end date of the lease. If there is no duration mentioned in the lease, the consideration or payment is used to indicate the length of time for which the lease is considered valid. For example, if rent has been paid for three months, the lease is considered to be valid for three months.

There are a few limitations to the duration of time for which a lease can be offered. For instance, a property located within a city may only be leased for a maximum for 99 years. Property outside of a city or town (for instance, agricultural land) may only be leased for 51 years.

Each lease must specify the consideration or payment (also called rent) required for a lessee to take and retain possession of a property. The rent (as well as the schedule for payment of rent) will be specified in the lease. For example, if a tenant moves into an apartment building in the middle of a month, rent may be due on that date each month. Alternatively, the first and last months of rent may be prorated, with rent due on the first day of each month. Advance payments, penalties for late payments, and other issues regarding consideration will also be covered in this part of the lease.

Leases may be altered or changed as long as both parties acknowledge the change. If the lease is for less then one year in duration, and is made orally, the contract may be altered orally. If the lease is for more than one year in duration, the lease must be made in writing, and any changes to this contract must also be made in writing. It is important to remember that leases are legal, binding contracts, and all persons entering into the lease must be legally competent for such a contract to be valid. As we have seen with the "four P's," each lease must specify the terms of the contract.

Cleaning and Security Deposits

Landlords will usually require a security deposit to be paid at the beginning of the lease, to be held until the tenant vacates the property. This security deposit may be used to cover any damage caused by the tenant, as well as any routine costs and repairs needed after the tenant vacates the unit. Such costs include repainting or cleaning. While not every landlord requires a security deposit, (nor is there a minimum deposit a landlord must accept), the state has set maximums on the amount of security deposit a landlord is allowed to collect from a tenant. For unfurnished properties, a landlord may lawfully collect up to two months' rent; for furnished properties, a landlord can collect up to three months' rent.

Tenants are entitled to a refunded deposit, less repairs and routine maintenance, within three weeks of vacating a property. The landlord must include an itemized list of all work performed, as well as the cost of each of the services, and provide a check for the remaining balance of the renter's deposit. Any landlord who does not provide this documentation to the tenant, or who keeps any amount of the deposit in bad faith, is subject to a $600 fine and is also liable for any loss suffered by the tenant. Landlords must prove that all claims made to the security deposit are valid and must defend them if challenged. The law will accept a tenant's challenge and award the full security deposit to the tenant if the landlord cannot prove the validity of each claim.

Tenants should always inspect property before they move in or occupy the space. They should document any defects or damages to the property before taking possession. By inspecting the property before moving in and filling out the statement of property condition, a tenant will protect his or her security deposit from being used to fix prior damage to the unit or property. The statement of property condition also helps avoid disputes between the tenant and landlord upon termination of the contract. The statement will outline which damages were already present when the tenant moved in, as well as any damages for which the tenant will be held financially responsible.

If a landlord sells a rental property during a tenant's lease term, any security deposit made by the renter will be transferred to the new owner. The new owner must be aware of each tenant's security deposit, so that the necessary accounting and documentation may be prepared for any existing tenants upon the termination of their leases.

Nonresidential property has different rules governing security deposits. There are no limits or restrictions on how much money a landlord may collect as security deposit on this type of property. As a result, a landlord may collect as much as he or she considers necessary to protect his or her own interest in the property. When a tenant vacates a property, the landlord may take up to 60 days to return the tenant's security deposit, less any charges made against it for repairs or routine maintenance. Landlords of nonresidential property are not required to provide a written statement of charges made against the security deposit.

Security Deposit Quick Guideline:
Residential:
- Landlord must return a tenant's deposit within three weeks of the tenant's vacating the property
- Landlord must supply a written statement of damages or routine maintenance costs deducted from the security deposit
- Landlord may only collect a security deposit equal to: two months' rent for unfurnished units; three months' rent for furnished units

Nonresidential:
- Landlord may collect any amount of security deposit
- Landlord must return security deposit to the tenant within 60 days of tenant's vacating the property
- Landlord is not required to provide a written statement of damages or routine maintenance paid for with the security deposit upon returning the remainder to the tenant

Lease-Option Arrangement
Sometimes, property can be leased to a tenant, with the intention of purchasing the property at a later date. This is ideal for people without a down payment or with little or no credit. Lease-options will usually allot a portion of the rent to go toward the purchase price. This can be an ideal situation for a first-time homebuyer who does not want to spend money in rent, when it could be put toward equity in a home.

Responsibilities and Rights of a Tenant
In a lease, a tenant is expected to perform certain tasks, and is guaranteed certain rights in return. Provided that tenants obey all guidelines as outlined in the contract, and remain in good standing regarding the payment of rent, tenants are entitled to "peaceful enjoyment and possession" of the property. The right of possession by the tenant is guaranteed by the covenant of quiet enjoyment, implied by law and granted by the landlord. "Quiet enjoyment" refers to the tenant's right not to be interfered with by the landlord. That is, a landlord may not enter the property and disrupt a tenant's possessions or use of the property, unless eviction proceedings against that tenant have begun.

In addition to quiet enjoyment, a tenant has the right to live in a safe, healthy environment. If there is something that threatens this environment, the landlord must make any necessary repairs to rectify the threat. If the landlord does not make the necessary repairs, the tenant may use up to one months' rent to make the necessary repairs, subtracting that cost from the next payment of rent. Tenants are allowed by law to make these repairs and deduct said expenses from rent only twice in a 12-month period, with no retaliation from the landlord. Landlords may not retaliate by raising the rent to offset the cost of the repair for a period of 180 days. Additionally, a landlord may not evict a tenant who uses rent to make necessary repairs to a rental property.

Responsibilities of a Tenant:
- Pay rent on time
- Provide a 30-day notice before ending a periodic tenancy
- Do not interfere with the rights of other tenants.

A tenant must pay his or her rent on time. If the tenant does not do so, a landlord may begin the eviction process. Rent is usually due at the beginning of each month, unless stated differently in the rental agreement. In some cases, a partial month of tenancy may result in the proration of rent.

In a periodic tenancy, tenants are required to provide the landlord with a 30-day notice before terminating the tenancy. Usually periodic tenancies are month-to-month situations, in which the tenant gives a one-month notice to vacate. This allows the landlord time to find a replacement tenant to occupy the space currently held by the vacating tenant, so the landlord can avoid losing any income the property would otherwise generate.

Tenants are not allowed to interfere with the rights of other tenants. For example, they may not create an excessive amount of noise late in the evening, keeping neighbors awake. Apartment complexes often have rules or set hours for use of common recreational rooms or areas such as pool or Jacuzzi, as well as restricted hours when onsite laundry facilities may be used. These rules are intended to keep noise levels low in the evening, for the benefit of all tenants.

Improvements made by tenants, sometimes called tenant improvements, must be approved by the landlord before a tenant alters a unit. Many times, a landlord will agree to these improvements, but require the tenant to change the unit back to its original condition upon vacating. For example, if a tenant wants to repaint an apartment in a new color, he or she can usually do so, but then must restore the unit to its original color before moving out, or pay to have it repainted.

Rights and Responsibilities of a Landlord
Just as a tenant has certain rights and responsibilities, so too does the landlord. The landlord makes a promise to the tenant to allow the quiet enjoyment of the property in exchange for rent. The landlord also agrees to give up possessory rights to the property during the tenancy, with a few exceptions. For example, the landlord may enter the property under the following circumstances:

1. An emergency
2. Pursuance of a court order
3. To perform necessary or agreed-upon repairs
4. To show the property to prospective new tenants
5. When the property has been abandoned

345

In the event that the landlord must enter the property, he or she must give the tenant sufficient notice, except in emergencies. A 24-hour notice is usually considered adequate, though each rental agreement may contain different time requirements for notification.

In addition to granting the tenant quiet enjoyment of the property, a landlord also guarantees to the tenant that all health and safety codes are being met. This means not only within the unit itself, but also in the hallways, common areas of the building and any recreational areas. It is the landlord's responsibility to adequately maintain and repair such areas in the appropriate manner.

Landlords must be very careful not to discriminate when renting their property to an individual. Both state and federal law prevent discrimination based on race, color, religion, creed, national origin, sex, marital status, presence or absence of children, or physical handicap.

Landlords must provide a tenant with a 30-day notice when terminating a month-to-month periodic tenancy, just as the tenant must do if vacating the property. If the termination of the tenancy is unjust, the tenant may have legal recourse.

Security deposits, as mentioned earlier in this chapter, must be refunded within three weeks of the tenant's vacating a property. This refund check must be accompanied by an itemized list of all deductions made from the security deposit. Any landlord who does not refund a tenant's deposit within the 3-week period will be subject to a $600 fine, and may also be held liable for any damages which that may have occurred.

Landlords are bound to all established building standards and requirements. These established standards, also referred to as codes, insure the safety of the tenants. Even if a contract does not directly state this, such a standard is implied under the "warranty of habitability." This warranty prevents rental property from being rented if it is considered untenable. An untenable dwelling is one that has any of the following characteristics:

- Damaged floors, railings or stairways
- Inadequate or dirty trash collection areas
- Damaged or missing hot and cold water fixtures or lack of proper sewage disposal
- Inadequate weatherproofing
- Damaged or inadequate heating system
- Dirty conditions or pest infestation at the inception of the lease
- Inadequate or non-functional plumbing or gas lines
- Wiring that is not up to code

As mentioned earlier, landlords are not allowed to penalize tenants for complaining about inadequate living conditions, nor may they penalize them for remedying such a situation. Unjust eviction or imposing increased rents as a result of a tenant's fixing any of the problems with the unit (especially those that make the unit untenantable) is strictly prohibited.

Responsibilities of a landlord:
- Protect the health and safety of tenants by ensuring the unit is tenable
- Give 24 hours notice before entering the property for any non-emergency reason
- Return deposits within 21 days
- Give a 30-day notice when terminating a month-to-month tenancy
- Must not engage in discriminatory renting practices against any parties

Transferring a Lease

Jennifer is a young professional just graduating from UCLA. She had signed a year-long lease during her last year of school, and had planned on finding a job in Los Angeles upon completing her schooling. Two weeks before graduation ceremonies, she receives a job offer in Sacramento that she cannot turn down. She accepts the position, to begin one month following her graduation.

What happens to Jennifer's lease? She agreed to an entire year, but she has only been there for half the time period to which she committed. Is she allowed to break the lease, or must she tell her new employer that she is not able to accept the job based on her lease agreement?

As you can see from the above example, there are situations when we need to exit a lease early. But, is this possible? The answer is "yes", and there are two different ways to do so. A tenant may transfer his or her interest in a lease by assignment or subleasing.

Remember:
There are two ways to transfer a lease
- Assignment
- Subleasing

In assignment of a lease, the current tenant of a property transfers his or her entire interest in a lease to another tenant. The original tenant is no longer responsible to the landlord, and can walk away from the lease in good standing. The new tenant is completely responsible to the landlord and will occupy the property for the duration of the original lease. Assignment of a lease is the best option for someone like Jennifer. She plans on moving away from Los Angeles and not returning. So, she needs to transfer her complete interest in the lease to another person for the duration of the lease.

In subleasing, the current tenant transfers only some interest in the lease. The original tenant is still responsible to the landlord, and the subleasing tenant is responsible to the original tenant. Subleasing would be ideal for those people who are leaving for a short while, but plan on returning to the property, and want to keep their interest in the lease.

Andrew lives in a very desirable beachfront apartment and enjoys rent control. He has lived there for several years, and pays rent that is well under what the apartment could bring on the open market. He decides to take a short-term job in New York City, which would take him away from California for five months. Realizing that he cannot afford to pay rent in two places, but not willing to give up his beachfront apartment, he decides to sublease his California apartment to his friend Tammy. Tammy is now responsible to Andrew, and must pay him the monthly rent, which Andrew will, in turn, pay to the landlord. When Andrew returns to California from New York City, Tammy will have to vacate the property, and the sublease will be terminated.

TERMINATION OF A LEASE

A lease may be terminated for a number of reasons. The duration of the lease may have expired, and the tenant can choose to sign a new lease, be on a periodic tenancy month to month, or choose to find a new place to rent. A lease may also be terminated because one party did not meet one or more of the contractual obligations of the lease.

A lease can be set up for a number of different time frames, but the majority of us are most familiar with a year lease agreement to rent an apartment. Once that year is over, the lease is expired. The lease will state a termination date that meets the expectations of both parties. For example, a 30-day notice might be expected if the tenant does not plan on extending the lease. Termination of a lease by expiration is considered "bilateral termination," because both parties are aware of and agree to the termination.

Additionally, both parties are aware of all options available upon termination (such as periodic tenancy, a new lease or complete termination of a lessee/lessor relationship).

Leases may also be unilaterally terminated. This happens when one party violates the terms of the contract and the other party decides to terminate the lease, whether the lease is due to expire or not. The party who terminates the lease does not have to obtain the other party's permission to terminate.

Tenants may terminate a lease when:
- The landlord has violated the duty to repair a unit, or has failed to keep the unit habitable
- The landlord has violated the tenant's right to quiet enjoyment
- The landlord violates a condition of the lease
- The landlord has evicted the tenant
- The property has been destroyed
- The government has exercised the power of eminent domain and taken the property

Landlords may terminate a lease when:
- Tenants use the unit for purposes unauthorized by the lease agreement
- The tenant breaches the contract of the lease
- The tenant abandons the property
- The property has been destroyed

Abandonment happens when a tenant simply vacates a property with no notice. If the tenant has been away from the property, rent has been delinquent for at least 14 days, and/or the landlord believes that the tenant is not going to return to the property, the landlord may establish abandonment by giving written notice. The tenant must respond to the notice within 18 days of receipt, to deny that he or she intends to abandon the property. If the tenant fails to respond, abandonment has been established, and the landlord may reclaim the property.

Eviction happens when the landlord legally removes the tenant from the premises for violating one or more terms of the contract or lease agreement. Eviction commonly happens when rent is not paid for a certain period of time while the tenant remains in possession of the property. If the tenant fails to pay rent, the landlord may begin eviction proceedings by giving the tenant a three-day notice in writing. This notice is called the "three-day notice to pay rent or quit," where the tenant is given the option to either pay the rent or move out within three days.

If the tenant fails to respond to the three-day notice, the landlord may file an unlawful detainer in a municipal court. The unlawful detainer is a document, listing all charges against the tenant, to which the tenant must respond within five days. If the tenant fails to respond to the unlawful detainer, a hearing will be set. The landlord may choose to sue the tenant for all rent owed. Alternatively, the landlord can request an order of eviction from the court. If the landlord sues the tenant, this does not constitute an eviction, and the tenant may retain possession of the unit currently being rented.

Even if a landlord has filed an unlawful detainer, the tenant still has rights. A tenant may defeat the unlawful detainer if:

- The landlord's facts are not true
- The landlord filed the unlawful detainer in retaliation for a tenant's improvements or corrections to a unit that have been charged to the landlord
- The landlord's action is arbitrary
- Proper notice was not given
- Other violations occurred in the process of the eviction procedures

If the tenant does not answer the lawsuit brought by the landlord, or the court finds in favor of the landlord, a **writ of possession** is granted. A writ of possession authorizes the sheriff of the county where the property is located to serve an eviction notice to the tenant. After five days have passed from delivery of the eviction notice, the landlord may physically move the tenant's possessions into a storage locker, with the tenant paying for the cost of storage. After 30 days have passed, a public auction to sell the tenant's stored belongings may be held. Any profits made from this auction may be used to pay for the storage of the belongings, as well as any sale costs. Any remaining amount is returned to the tenant.

S U M M A R Y

Property management began to make a big wave in the real estate profession during the Great Depression when banks were taking in large amounts of properties on foreclosures, and had to have some way of maintaining them. As the industry began to grow, professional organizations began to surface such as IREM.

Include Form LRA application to rent and deposit receipt form here

CALIFORNIA ASSOCIATION OF REALTORS®

APPLICATION TO RENT/SCREENING FEE
(C.A.R. Form LRA, Revised 4/03)

I. APPLICATION TO RENT

THIS SECTION TO BE COMPLETED BY APPLICANT. A SEPARATE APPLICATION TO RENT IS REQUIRED FOR EACH OCCUPANT 18 YEARS OF AGE OR OVER, OR AN EMANCIPATED MINOR.

Applicant is completing Application as a (check one) ☐ tenant, ☐ tenant with co-tenant(s) or ☐ guarantor/co-signor.
Total number of applicants _____

PREMISES INFORMATION

Application to rent property at _____ ("Premises")
Rent: $_____ per _____ Proposed move-in date _____

PERSONAL INFORMATION

FULL NAME OF APPLICANT _____
Social security No. _____ Driver's License No. _____ State _____ Expires _____
Phone number: Home _____ Work _____ Other _____
Email _____
Name(s) of all other proposed occupant(s) and relationship to applicant _____

Pet(s) or service animals (number and type) _____
Auto: Make _____ Model _____ Year _____ License No. _____ State _____ Color _____
Other vehicle(s): _____
In case of emergency, person to notify _____ Relationship _____
Address _____ Phone _____
Does applicant or any proposed occupant plan to use liquid filled furniture? ☐ No ☐ Yes Type _____
Has applicant been a party to an unlawful detainer action or filed bankruptcy within the last seven years?   ☐ No   ☐ Yes
If yes, explain _____
Has applicant or any proposed occupant ever been convicted of or pleaded no contest to a felony?   ☐ No   ☐ Yes
If yes, explain _____
Has applicant or any proposed occupant ever been asked to move out of a residence?   ☐ No   ☐ Yes
If yes, explain _____

RESIDENCE HISTORY

Current address _____	Previous address _____
City/State/Zip _____	City/State/Zip _____
From _____ to _____	From _____ to _____
Name of Landlord/Manager _____	Name of Landlord/Manager _____
Landlord/Manager's phone _____	Landlord/Manager's phone _____
Do you own this property? ☐ No ☐ Yes	Did you own this property? ☐ No ☐ Yes
Reason for leaving current address _____	Reason for leaving this address _____

EMPLOYMENT AND INCOME HISTORY

Current employer _____	Supervisor _____ From _____ To _____
Employer's address _____	Supervisor's phone _____
Position or title _____	Phone number to verify employment _____
Employment gross income $_____ per _____	Other $_____ per _____ Source _____
Previous employer _____	Supervisor _____ From _____ To _____
Employer's address _____	Supervisor's phone _____
Position or title _____	Employment gross income $_____ per _____

LRA REVISED 4/03 (PAGE 1 OF 2) Print Date

Applicant's Initials (_____)(_____)
Reviewed by _____ Date _____

APPLICATION TO RENT/SCREENING FEE (LRA PAGE 1 OF 2)

Property Address: _____ Date: _____

CREDIT INFORMATION

Name of creditor	Account number	Monthly payment	Balance due

Name of bank/branch	Account number	Type of account	Account balance

PERSONAL REFERENCES

Name _____ Address _____

Phone _____ Length of acquaintance _____ Occupation _____

Name _____ Address _____

Phone _____ Length of acquaintance _____ Occupation _____

NEAREST RELATIVE(S)

Name _____ Address _____

Phone _____ Relationship _____

Name _____ Address _____

Phone _____ Relationship _____

Applicant understands and agrees: **(i)** this is an application to rent only and does not guarantee that applicant will be offered the Premises; and **(ii)** Landlord or Manager or Agent may accept more than one application for the Premises and, at using their sole discretion, will select the best qualified applicant.

Applicant represents the above information to be true and complete, and hereby authorizes Landlord or Manager or Agent to: **(i)** verify the information provided; and **(ii)** obtain credit report on applicant.

If application is not fully completed, or received without the screening fee, **(i)** the application will not be processed, and **(ii)** the application and any screening fee will be returned.

Applicant _____ Date _____ Time _____

Return your completed application and any applicable fee not already paid to: _____

Address _____ City _____ State _____ Zip _____

II. SCREENING FEE

THIS SECTION TO BE COMPLETED BY LANDLORD, MANAGER OR AGENT.

Applicant has paid a **nonrefundable** screening fee of $ _____, applied as follows (the screening fee may not exceed $30.00 (adjusted annually from 1-1-98 commensurate with the increase in the Consumer Price Index).

$ _____ for credit reports prepared by _____ ;

$ _____ for _____ (other out-of-pocket expenses); and

$ _____ for processing.

The undersigned has read the foregoing and acknowledges receipt of a copy.

_____ _____
Applicant Signature   Date

The undersigned has received the screening fee indicated above.

_____ _____
Landlord or Manager or Agent Signature   Date

SURE TRAC The System for Success™

Published by the
California Association of REALTORS®

LRA REVISED 4/03 (PAGE 2 OF 2)

Reviewed by _____ Date _____

EQUAL HOUSING OPPORTUNITY

APPLICATION TO RENT/SCREENING FEE (LRA PAGE 2 OF 2)

CALIFORNIA
ASSOCIATION
OF REALTORS®

RESIDENTIAL LEASE OR
MONTH-TO-MONTH RENTAL AGREEMENT
(C.A.R. Form LR, Revised 10/04)

_____ ("Landlord") and
_____ ("Tenant") agree as follows:

1. **PROPERTY:**
   A. Landlord rents to Tenant and Tenant rents from Landlord, the real property and improvements described as: _____
      _____ ("Premises").
   B. The Premises are for the sole use as a personal residence by the following named person(s) **only:** _____
      _____.
   C. The following personal property, maintained pursuant to paragraph 11, is included: _____
      _____ or ☐ (if checked) the personal property on the attached addendum.

2. **TERM:** The term begins on (date)_____ ("Commencement Date"), **(Check A or B):**
   ☐ A. **Month-to-Month:** and continues as a month-to-month tenancy. Tenant may terminate the tenancy by giving written notice
      at least 30 days prior to the intended termination date. Landlord may terminate the tenancy by giving written notice as
      provided by law. Such notices may be given on any date.
   ☐ B. **Lease:** and shall terminate on (date) _____ at _____ ☐ AM/☐ PM.
      Tenant shall vacate the Premises upon termination of the Agreement, unless: **(i)** Landlord and Tenant have extended this
      agreement in writing or signed a new agreement; **(ii)** mandated by local rent control law; or **(iii)** Landlord accepts Rent from
      Tenant (other than past due Rent), in which case a month-to-month tenancy shall be created which either party may
      terminate as specified in paragraph 2A. Rent shall be at a rate agreed to by Landlord and Tenant, or as allowed by law. All
      other terms and conditions of this Agreement shall remain in full force and effect.

3. **RENT:** "Rent" shall mean all monetary obligations of Tenant to Landlord under the terms of the Agreement, except security deposit.
   A. Tenant agrees to pay $ _____ per month for the term of the Agreement.
   B. Rent is payable in advance on the **1st (or ☐** _____**) day** of each calendar month, and is delinquent on the next day.
   C. If Commencement Date falls on any day other than the day Rent is payable under paragraph 3B, and Tenant has paid one full
      month's Rent in advance of Commencement Date, Rent for the second calendar month shall be prorated based on a 30-day
      period.
   D. **PAYMENT:** Rent shall be paid by ☐ personal check, ☐ money order, ☐ cashier's check, or ☐ other _____, to (name)
      _____ (phone) _____ at (address)
      _____, (or at any other location
      subsequently specified by Landlord in writing to Tenant) between the hours of _____ and _____ on the following days
      _____. If any payment is returned for non-sufficient funds ("NSF") or
      because tenant stops payment, then, after that: (i) Landlord may, in writing, require Tenant to pay Rent in cash for three months
      and (ii) all future Rent shall be paid by ☐ money order, or ☐ cashier's check.

4. **SECURITY DEPOSIT:**
   A. Tenant agrees to pay $ _____ as a security deposit. Security deposit will be
      ☐ transferred to and held by the Owner of the Premises, or ☐ held in Owner's Broker's trust account.
   B. All or any portion of the security deposit may be used, as reasonably necessary, to: **(i)** cure Tenant's default in payment of Rent (which
      includes Late Charges, NSF fees or other sums due); **(ii)** repair damage, excluding ordinary wear and tear, caused by Tenant or by a
      guest or licensee of Tenant; **(iii)** clean Premises, if necessary, upon termination of the tenancy; and **(iv)** replace or return personal
      property or appurtenances. **SECURITY DEPOSIT SHALL NOT BE USED BY TENANT IN LIEU OF PAYMENT OF LAST
      MONTH'S RENT.** If all or any portion of the security deposit is used during the tenancy, Tenant agrees to reinstate the total security
      deposit within five days after written notice is delivered to Tenant. Within 21 days after Tenant vacates the Premises, Landlord shall:
      (1) furnish Tenant an itemized statement indicating the amount of any security deposit received and the basis for its
      disposition and supporting documentation as required by California Civil Code § 1950.5(g); and **(2)** return any remaining
      portion of the security deposit to Tenant.
   C. **Security deposit will not be returned until all Tenants have vacated the Premises. Any security deposit returned by
      check shall be made out to all Tenants named on this Agreement, or as subsequently modified.**
   D. No interest will be paid on security deposit unless required by local law.
   E. If the security deposit is held by Owner, Tenant agrees not to hold Broker responsible for its return. If the security deposit is held
      in Owner's Broker's trust account, **and** Broker's authority is terminated before expiration of this Agreement, **and** security deposit
      is released to someone other than Tenant, **then** Broker shall notify Tenant, in writing, where and to whom security deposit has
      been released. Once Tenant has been provided such notice, Tenant agrees not to hold Broker responsible for the security
      deposit.

5. **MOVE-IN COSTS RECEIVED/DUE:** Move-in funds made payable to _____
   shall be paid by ☐ personal check, ☐ money order, or ☐ cashier's check.

Category	Total Due	Payment Received	Balance Due	Date Due
Rent from _____ to _____ (date)				
*Security Deposit				
Other _____				
Other _____				
Total				

*The maximum amount Landlord may receive as security deposit, however designated, cannot exceed two months' Rent for
unfurnished premises, or three months' Rent for furnished premises.

LR REVISED 10/04 (PAGE 1 OF 6) Print Date

Tenant's Initials (_____)(_____)
Landlord's Initials (_____)(_____)

Reviewed by _____ Date _____

EQUAL HOUSING
OPPORTUNITY

RESIDENTIAL LEASE OR MONTH-TO-MONTH RENTAL AGREEMENT (LR PAGE 1 OF 6)

Premises: _____ Date: _____

6. **LATE CHARGE; RETURNED CHECKS:**
   A. Tenant acknowledges either late payment of Rent or issuance of a returned check may cause Landlord to incur costs and expenses, the exact amounts of which are extremely difficult and impractical to determine. These costs may include, but are not limited to, processing, enforcement and accounting expenses, and late charges imposed on Landlord. If any installment of Rent due from Tenant is not received by Landlord within **5 (or ☐ _____) calendar days** after the date due, or if a check is returned, Tenant shall pay to Landlord, respectively, an additional sum of $ _____ or _____% of the Rent due as a Late Charge and $25.00 as a NSF fee for the first returned check and $35.00 as a NSF fee for each additional returned check, either or both of which shall be deemed additional Rent.
   B. Landlord and Tenant agree that these charges represent a fair and reasonable estimate of the costs Landlord may incur by reason of Tenant's late or NSF payment. Any Late Charge or NSF fee due shall be paid with the current installment of Rent. Landlord's acceptance of any Late Charge or NSF fee shall not constitute a waiver as to any default of Tenant. Landlord's right to collect a Late Charge or NSF fee shall not be deemed an extension of the date Rent is due under paragraph 3 or prevent Landlord from exercising any other rights and remedies under this Agreement and as provided by law.

7. **PARKING: (Check A or B)**
   ☐ A. Parking is permitted as follows: _____
   _____
   The right to parking ☐ is ☐ is not included in the Rent charged pursuant to paragraph 3. If not included in the Rent, the parking rental fee shall be an additional $ _____ per month. Parking space(s) are to be used for parking properly licensed and operable motor vehicles, except for trailers, boats, campers, buses or trucks (other than pick-up trucks). Tenant shall park in assigned space(s) only. Parking space(s) are to be kept clean. Vehicles leaking oil, gas or other motor vehicle fluids shall not be parked on the Premises. Mechanical work or storage of inoperable vehicles is not permitted in parking space(s) or elsewhere on the Premises.
   OR ☐ B. Parking is not permitted on the Premises.

8. **STORAGE: (Check A or B)**
   ☐ A. Storage is permitted as follows: _____
   The right to storage space ☐ is, ☐ is not, included in the Rent charged pursuant to paragraph 3. If not included in the Rent, storage space fee shall be an additional $ _____ per month. Tenant shall store only personal property Tenant owns, and shall not store property claimed by another or in which another has any right, title or interest. Tenant shall not store any improperly packaged food or perishable goods, flammable materials, explosives, hazardous waste or other inherently dangerous material, or illegal substances.
   OR ☐ B. Storage is not permitted on the Premises.

9. **UTILITIES:** Tenant agrees to pay for all utilities and services, and the following charges: _____
   except _____, which shall be paid for by Landlord. If any utilities are not separately metered, Tenant shall pay Tenant's proportional share, as reasonably determined and directed by Landlord. If utilities are separately metered, Tenant shall place utilities in Tenant's name as of the Commencement Date. Landlord is only responsible for installing and maintaining one usable telephone jack and one telephone line to the Premises. Tenant shall pay any cost for conversion from existing utilities service provider.

10. **CONDITION OF PREMISES:** Tenant has examined Premises and, if any, all furniture, furnishings, appliances, landscaping and fixtures, including smoke detector(s).
    (Check all that apply:)
    ☐ A. Tenant acknowledges these items are clean and in operable condition, with the following exceptions: _____
    _____.
    ☐ B. Tenant's acknowledgment of the condition of these items is contained in an attached statement of condition (C.A.R. Form MIMO).
    ☐ C. Tenant will provide Landlord a list of items that are damaged or not in operable condition within **3 (or ☐ _____) days** after Commencement Date, not as a contingency of this Agreement but rather as an acknowledgment of the condition of the Premises.
    ☐ D. Other: _____.

11. **MAINTENANCE:**
    A. Tenant shall properly use, operate and safeguard Premises, including if applicable, any landscaping, furniture, furnishings and appliances, and all mechanical, electrical, gas and plumbing fixtures, and keep them and the Premises clean, sanitary and well ventilated. Tenant shall be responsible for checking and maintaining all smoke detectors and any additional phone lines beyond the one line and jack that Landlord shall provide and maintain. Tenant shall immediately notify Landlord, in writing, of any problem, malfunction or damage. Tenant shall be charged for all repairs or replacements caused by Tenant, pets, guests or licensees of Tenant, excluding ordinary wear and tear. Tenant shall be charged for all damage to Premises as a result of failure to report a problem in a timely manner. Tenant shall be charged for repair of drain blockages or stoppages, unless caused by defective plumbing parts or tree roots invading sewer lines.
    B. ☐ Landlord ☐ Tenant shall water the garden, landscaping, trees and shrubs, except: _____
    _____.
    C. ☐ Landlord ☐ Tenant shall maintain the garden, landscaping, trees and shrubs, except: _____
    _____.
    D. ☐ Landlord ☐ Tenant shall maintain _____.
    E. Tenant's failure to maintain any item for which Tenant is responsible shall give Landlord the right to hire someone to perform such maintenance and charge Tenant to cover the cost of such maintenance.
    F. The following items of personal property are included in the Premises without warranty and Landlord will not maintain, repair or replace them: _____.

Tenant's Initials (_____)(_____)
Landlord's Initials (_____)(_____)

Reviewed by _____ Date _____

RESIDENTIAL LEASE OR MONTH-TO-MONTH RENTAL AGREEMENT (LR PAGE 2 OF 6)

12. **NEIGHBORHOOD CONDITIONS:** Tenant is advised to satisfy him or herself as to neighborhood or area conditions, including schools, proximity and adequacy of law enforcement, crime statistics, proximity of registered felons or offenders, fire protection, other governmental services, availability, adequacy and cost of any speed-wired, wireless internet connections or other telecommunications or other technology services and installations, proximity to commercial, industrial or agricultural activities, existing and proposed transportation, construction and development that may affect noise, view, or traffic, airport noise, noise or odor from any source, wild and domestic animals, other nuisances, hazards, or circumstances, cemeteries, facilities and condition of common areas, conditions and influences of significance to certain cultures and/or religions, and personal needs, requirements and preferences of Tenant.

13. **PETS:** Unless otherwise provided in California Civil Code § 54.2, no animal or pet shall be kept on or about the Premises without Landlord's prior written consent, except: _____.

14. **RULES/REGULATIONS:**
    A. Tenant agrees to comply with all Landlord rules and regulations that are at any time posted on the Premises or delivered to Tenant. Tenant shall not, and shall ensure that guests and licensees of Tenant shall not, disturb, annoy, endanger or interfere with other tenants of the building or neighbors, or use the Premises for any unlawful purposes, including, but not limited to, using, manufacturing, selling, storing or transporting illicit drugs or other contraband, or violate any law or ordinance, or commit a waste or nuisance on or about the Premises.
    B. **(If applicable, check one)**
        ☐ 1. Landlord shall provide Tenant with a copy of the rules and regulations within _____ days or _____.
        OR ☐ 2. Tenant has been provided with, and acknowledges receipt of, a copy of the rules and regulations.

15. ☐ **(If checked) CONDOMINIUM; PLANNED UNIT DEVELOPMENT:**
    A. The Premises is a unit in a condominium, planned unit development, common interest subdivision or other development governed by a homeowners' association ("HOA"). The name of the HOA is _____. Tenant agrees to comply with all HOA covenants, conditions and restrictions, bylaws, rules and regulations and decisions. Landlord shall provide Tenant copies of rules and regulations, if any. Tenant shall reimburse Landlord for any fines or charges imposed by HOA or other authorities, due to any violation by Tenant, or the guests or licensees of Tenant.
    B. **(Check one)**
        ☐ 1. Landlord shall provide Tenant with a copy of the HOA rules and regulations within _____ days or _____.
        OR ☐ 2. Tenant has been provided with, and acknowledges receipt of, a copy of the HOA rules and regulations.

16. **ALTERATIONS; REPAIRS:** Unless otherwise specified by law or paragraph 27C, without Landlord's prior written consent, **(i)** Tenant shall not make any repairs, alterations or improvements in or about the Premises including: painting, wallpapering, adding or changing locks, installing antenna or satellite dish(es), placing signs, displays or exhibits, or using screws, fastening devices, large nails or adhesive materials; **(ii)** Landlord shall not be responsible for the costs of alterations or repairs made by Tenant; **(iii)** Tenant shall not deduct from Rent the costs of any repairs, alterations or improvements; and **(iv)** any deduction made by Tenant shall be considered unpaid Rent.

17. **KEYS; LOCKS:**
    A. Tenant acknowledges receipt of (or Tenant will receive ☐ prior to the Commencement Date, or ☐ _____):
        ☐ _____ key(s) to Premises,   ☐ _____ remote control device(s) for garage door/gate opener(s),
        ☐ _____ key(s) to mailbox,   ☐ _____,
        ☐ _____ key(s) to common area(s),   ☐ _____.
    B. Tenant acknowledges that locks to the Premises ☐ have, ☐ have not, been re-keyed.
    C. If Tenant re-keys existing locks or opening devices, Tenant shall immediately deliver copies of all keys to Landlord. Tenant shall pay all costs and charges related to loss of any keys or opening devices. Tenant may not remove locks, even if installed by Tenant.

18. **ENTRY:**
    A. Tenant shall make Premises available to Landlord or Landlord's representative for the purpose of entering to make necessary or agreed repairs, decorations, alterations, or improvements, or to supply necessary or agreed services, or to show Premises to prospective or actual purchasers, tenants, mortgagees, lenders, appraisers, or contractors.
    B. Landlord and Tenant agree that 24-hour written notice shall be reasonable and sufficient notice, except as follows. 48-hour written notice is required to conduct an inspection of the Premises prior to the Tenant moving out, unless the Tenant waives the right to such notice. Notice may be given orally to show the Premises to actual or prospective purchasers provided Tenant has been notified in writing within 120 days preceding the oral notice that the Premises are for sale and that oral notice may be given to show the Premises. No notice is required: **(i)** to enter in case of an emergency; **(ii)** if the Tenant is present and consents at the time of entry or **(iii)** if the Tenant has abandoned or surrendered the Premises. No written notice is required if Landlord and Tenant orally agree to an entry for agreed services or repairs if the date and time of entry are within one week of the oral agreement.
    C. ☐ (If checked) Tenant authorizes the use of a keysafe/lockbox to allow entry into the Premises and agrees to sign a keysafe/lockbox addendum (C.A.R. Form KLA).

19. **SIGNS:** Tenant authorizes Landlord to place FOR SALE/LEASE signs on the Premises.

20. **ASSIGNMENT; SUBLETTING:** Tenant shall not sublet all or any part of Premises, or assign or transfer this Agreement or any interest in it, without Landlord's prior written consent. Unless such consent is obtained, any assignment, transfer or subletting of Premises or this Agreement or tenancy, by voluntary act of Tenant, operation of law or otherwise, shall, at the option of Landlord, terminate this Agreement. Any proposed assignee, transferee or sublessee shall submit to Landlord an application and credit information for Landlord's approval and, if approved, sign a separate written agreement with Landlord and Tenant. Landlord's consent to any one assignment, transfer or sublease, shall not be construed as consent to any subsequent assignment, transfer or sublease and does not release Tenant of Tenant's obligations under this Agreement.

21. **JOINT AND INDIVIDUAL OBLIGATIONS:** If there is more than one Tenant, each one shall be individually and completely responsible for the performance of all obligations of Tenant under this Agreement, jointly with every other Tenant, and individually, whether or not in possession.

LR REVISED 10/04 (PAGE 3 OF 6)

Tenant's Initials (_____)(_____)
Landlord's Initials (_____)(_____)

| Reviewed by _____ Date _____ |

EQUAL HOUSING OPPORTUNITY

RESIDENTIAL LEASE OR MONTH-TO-MONTH RENTAL AGREEMENT (LR PAGE 3 OF 6)

22. ☐ **LEAD-BASED PAINT (If checked):** Premises was constructed prior to 1978. In accordance with federal law, Landlord gives and Tenant acknowledges receipt of the disclosures on the attached form (C.A.R. Form FLD) and a federally approved lead pamphlet.

23. ☐ **MILITARY ORDNANCE DISCLOSURE:** (If applicable and known to Landlord) Premises is located within one mile of an area once used for military training, and may contain potentially explosive munitions.

24. ☐ **PERIODIC PEST CONTROL:** Landlord has entered into a contract for periodic pest control treatment of the Premises and shall give Tenant a copy of the notice originally given to Landlord by the pest control company.

25. DATABASE DISCLOSURE: NOTICE: The California Department of Justice, sheriff's departments, police departments serving jurisdictions of 200,000 or more, and many other local law enforcement authorities maintain for public access a database of the locations of persons required to register pursuant to paragraph (1) of subdivision (a) of Section 290.4 of the Penal Code. The data base is updated on a quarterly basis and a source of information about the presence of these individuals in any neighborhood. The Department of Justice also maintains a Sex Offender Identification Line through which inquiries about individuals may be made. This is a "900" telephone service. Callers must have specific information about individuals they are checking. Information regarding neighborhoods is not available through the "900" telephone service.

26. POSSESSION:
   A. Tenant is not in possession of the premises. If Landlord is unable to deliver possession of Premises on Commencement Date, such Date shall be extended to the date on which possession is made available to Tenant. If Landlord is unable to deliver possession within **5 (or ☐ _____) calendar days** after agreed Commencement Date, Tenant may terminate this Agreement by giving written notice to Landlord, and shall be refunded all Rent and security deposit paid. Possession is deemed terminated when Tenant has returned all keys to the Premises to Landlord.
   B. ☐ Tenant is already in possession of the Premises.

27. TENANT'S OBLIGATIONS UPON VACATING PREMISES:
   A. Upon termination of the Agreement, Tenant shall: **(i)** give Landlord all copies of all keys or opening devices to Premises, including any common areas; **(ii)** vacate and surrender Premises to Landlord, empty of all persons; **(iii)** vacate any/all parking and/or storage space; **(iv)** clean and deliver Premises, as specified in paragraph C below, to Landlord in the same condition as referenced in paragraph 10; **(v)** remove all debris; **(vi)** give written notice to Landlord of Tenant's forwarding address; and **(vii)** _____.
   B. All alterations/improvements made by or caused to be made by Tenant, with or without Landlord's consent, become the property of Landlord upon termination. Landlord may charge Tenant for restoration of the Premises to the condition it was in prior to any alterations/improvements.
   C. **Right to Pre-Move-Out Inspection and Repairs as follows: (i)** After giving or receiving notice of termination of a tenancy (C.A.R. Form NTT), or before the end of a lease, Tenant has the right to request that an inspection of the Premises take place prior to termination of the lease or rental (C.A.R. Form NRI). If Tenant requests such an inspection, Tenant shall be given an opportunity to remedy identified deficiencies prior to termination, consistent with the terms of this Agreement. **(ii)** Any repairs or alterations made to the Premises as a result of this inspection (collectively, "Repairs") shall be made at Tenant's expense. Repairs may be performed by Tenant or through others, who have adequate insurance and licenses and are approved by Landlord. The work shall comply with applicable law, including governmental permit, inspection and approval requirements. Repairs shall be performed in a good, skillful manner with materials of quality and appearance comparable to existing materials. It is understood that exact restoration of appearance or cosmetic items following all Repairs may not be possible. **(iii)** Tenant shall: **(a)** obtain receipts for Repairs performed by others; **(b)** prepare a written statement indicating the Repairs performed by Tenant and the date of such Repairs; and **(c)** provide copies of receipts and statements to Landlord prior to termination. Paragraph 27C does not apply when the tenancy is terminated pursuant to California Code of Civil Procedure § 1161(2), (3) or (4).

28. BREACH OF CONTRACT; EARLY TERMINATION: In addition to any obligations established by paragraph 27, in the event of termination by Tenant prior to completion of the original term of the Agreement, Tenant shall also be responsible for lost Rent, rental commissions, advertising expenses and painting costs necessary to ready Premises for re-rental. Landlord may withhold any such amounts from Tenant's security deposit.

29. TEMPORARY RELOCATION: Subject to local law, Tenant agrees, upon demand of Landlord, to temporarily vacate Premises for a reasonable period, to allow for fumigation (or other methods) to control wood destroying pests or organisms, or other repairs to Premises. Tenant agrees to comply with all instructions and requirements necessary to prepare Premises to accommodate pest control, fumigation or other work, including bagging or storage of food and medicine, and removal of perishables and valuables. Tenant shall only be entitled to a credit of Rent equal to the per diem Rent for the period of time Tenant is required to vacate Premises.

30. DAMAGE TO PREMISES: If, by no fault of Tenant, Premises are totally or partially damaged or destroyed by fire, earthquake, accident or other casualty that render Premises totally or partially uninhabitable, either Landlord or Tenant may terminate this Agreement by giving the other written notice. Rent shall be abated as of the date Premises become totally or partially uninhabitable. The abated amount shall be the current monthly Rent prorated on a 30-day period. If the Agreement is not terminated, Landlord shall promptly repair the damage, and Rent shall be reduced based on the extent to which the damage interferes with Tenant's reasonable use of Premises. If damage occurs as a result of an act of Tenant or Tenant's guests, only Landlord shall have the right of termination, and no reduction in Rent shall be made.

31. INSURANCE: Tenant's or guest's personal property and vehicles are not insured by Landlord, manager or, if applicable, HOA, against loss or damage due to fire, theft, vandalism, rain, water, criminal or negligent acts of others, or any other cause. **Tenant is advised to carry Tenant's own insurance (renter's insurance) to protect Tenant from any such loss or damage.** Tenant shall comply with any requirement imposed on Tenant by Landlord's insurer to avoid: **(i)** an increase in Landlord's insurance premium (or Tenant shall pay for the increase in premium); or **(ii)** loss of insurance.

32. WATERBEDS: Tenant shall not use or have waterbeds on the Premises unless: **(i)** Tenant obtains a valid waterbed insurance policy; **(ii)** Tenant increases the security deposit in an amount equal to one-half of one month's Rent; and **(iii)** the bed conforms to the floor load capacity of Premises.

Tenant's Initials (_____)(_____)
Landlord's Initials (_____)(_____)
Reviewed by _____ Date _____

EQUAL HOUSING OPPORTUNITY

RESIDENTIAL LEASE OR MONTH-TO-MONTH RENTAL AGREEMENT (LR PAGE 4 OF 6)

Premises: _____ Date: _____

33. **WAIVER:** The waiver of any breach shall not be construed as a continuing waiver of the same or any subsequent breach.

34. **NOTICE:** Notices may be served at the following address, or at any other location subsequently designated:
Landlord: _____ Tenant: _____
_____ _____
_____ _____
_____ _____

35. **TENANT ESTOPPEL CERTIFICATE:** Tenant shall execute and return a tenant estoppel certificate delivered to Tenant by Landlord or Landlord's agent within 3 days after its receipt. Failure to comply with this requirement shall be deemed Tenant's acknowledgment that the tenant estoppel certificate is true and correct, and may be relied upon by a lender or purchaser.

36. **TENANT REPRESENTATIONS; CREDIT:** Tenant warrants that all statements in Tenant's rental application are accurate. Tenant authorizes Landlord and Broker(s) to obtain Tenant's credit report periodically during the tenancy in connection with the modification or enforcement of this Agreement. Landlord may cancel this Agreement: **(i)** before occupancy begins; **(ii)** upon disapproval of the credit report(s); or **(iii)** at any time, upon discovering that information in Tenant's application is false. A negative credit report reflecting on Tenant's record may be submitted to a credit reporting agency if Tenant fails to fulfill the terms of payment and other obligations under this Agreement.

37. **MEDIATION:**
   A. Consistent with paragraphs B and C below, Landlord and Tenant agree to mediate any dispute or claim arising between them out of this Agreement, or any resulting transaction, before resorting to court action. Mediation fees, if any, shall be divided equally among the parties involved. If, for any dispute or claim to which this paragraph applies, any party commences an action without first attempting to resolve the matter through mediation, or refuses to mediate after a request has been made, then that party shall not be entitled to recover attorney fees, even if they would otherwise be available to that party in any such action.
   B. The following matters are excluded from mediation: **(i)** an unlawful detainer action; **(ii)** the filing or enforcement of a mechanic's lien; and **(iii)** any matter within the jurisdiction of a probate, small claims or bankruptcy court. The filing of a court action to enable the recording of a notice of pending action, for order of attachment, receivership, injunction, or other provisional remedies, shall not constitute a waiver of the mediation provision.
   C. Landlord and Tenant agree to mediate disputes or claims involving Listing Agent, Leasing Agent or property manager ("Broker"), provided Broker shall have agreed to such mediation prior to, or within a reasonable time after, the dispute or claim is presented to such Broker. Any election by Broker to participate in mediation shall not result in Broker being deemed a party to this Agreement.

38. **ATTORNEY FEES:** In any action or proceeding arising out of this Agreement, the prevailing party between Landlord and Tenant shall be entitled to reasonable attorney fees and costs, except as provided in paragraph 37A.

39. **C.A.R. FORM:** C.A.R. Form means the specific form referenced or another comparable from agreed to by the parties.

40. **OTHER TERMS AND CONDITIONS; SUPPLEMENTS:** _____
_____

The following ATTACHED supplements are incorporated in this Agreement: ☐ Keysafe/Lockbox Addendum (C.A.R. Form KLA);
☐ Interpreter/Translator Agreement (C.A.R. Form ITA); ☐ Lead-Based Paint and Lead-Based Paint Hazards Disclosure (C.A.R. Form FLD)

41. **TIME OF ESSENCE; ENTIRE CONTRACT; CHANGES:** Time is of the essence. All understandings between the parties are incorporated in this Agreement. Its terms are intended by the parties as a final, complete and exclusive expression of their Agreement with respect to its subject matter, and may not be contradicted by evidence of any prior agreement or contemporaneous oral agreement. If any provision of this Agreement is held to be ineffective or invalid, the remaining provisions will nevertheless be given full force and effect. Neither this Agreement nor any provision in it may be extended, amended, modified, altered or changed except in writing. This Agreement is subject to California landlord-tenant law and shall incorporate all changes required by amendment or successors to such law. This Agreement and any supplement, addendum or modification, including any copy, may be signed in two or more counterparts, all of which shall constitute one and the same writing.

42. **AGENCY:**
   A. **CONFIRMATION:** The following agency relationship(s) are hereby confirmed for this transaction:
   Listing Agent: (Print firm name) _____ is the
   agent of (check one): ☐ the Landlord exclusively; or ☐ both the Landlord and Tenant.
   Leasing Agent: (Print firm name) _____ (if not
   same as Listing Agent) is the agent of (check one): ☐ the Tenant exclusively; or ☐ the Landlord exclusively; or ☐ both the Tenant and Landlord.
   B. **DISCLOSURE:** ☐ (If checked): The term of this lease exceeds one year. A disclosure regarding real estate agency relationships (C.A.R. Form AD) has been provided to Landlord and Tenant, who each acknowledge its receipt.

43. ☐ **TENANT COMPENSATION TO BROKER:** Upon execution of this Agreement, Tenant agrees to pay compensation to Broker as specified in a separate written agreement between Tenant and Broker.

44. ☐ **INTERPRETER/TRANSLATOR:** The terms of this Agreement have been interpreted for Tenant into the following language: _____. Landlord and Tenant acknowledge receipt of the attached interpretor/translator agreement (C.A.R. Form ITA).

45. **FOREIGN LANGUAGE NEGOTIATION:** If this Agreement has been negotiated by Landlord and Tenant primarily in Spanish, Chinese, Tagalog, Korean or Vietnamese. Pursuant to the California Civil Code Tenant shall be provided a translation of this Agreement in the language used for the negotiation.

Tenant's Initials (_____)(_____)
Landlord's Initials (_____)(_____)

| Reviewed by _____ Date _____ |

RESIDENTIAL LEASE OR MONTH-TO-MONTH RENTAL AGREEMENT (LR PAGE 5 OF 6)

Premises: _____ Date: _____

> Landlord and Tenant acknowledge and agree Brokers: **(a)** do not guarantee the condition of the Premises; **(b)** cannot verify representations made by others; **(c)** cannot provide legal or tax advice; **(d)** will not provide other advice or information that exceeds the knowledge, education or experience required to obtain a real estate license. Furthermore, if Brokers are not also acting as Landlord in this Agreement, Brokers: **(e)** do not decide what rental rate a Tenant should pay or Landlord should accept; and **(f)** do not decide upon the length or other terms of tenancy. Landlord and Tenant agree that they will seek legal, tax, insurance and other desired assistance from appropriate professionals.

Tenant   Date
Address _____ City _____ State _____ Zip _____
Telephone _____ Fax _____ E-mail_____
Tenant _____ Date _____
Address _____ City _____ State _____ Zip _____
Telephone _____ Fax _____ E-mail_____

46. ☐ **GUARANTEE:** In consideration of the execution of the Agreement by and between Landlord and Tenant and for valuable consideration, receipt of which is hereby acknowledged, the undersigned ("Guarantor") does hereby: **(i)** guarantee unconditionally to Landlord and Landlord's agents, successors and assigns, the prompt payment of Rent or other sums that become due pursuant to this Agreement, including any and all court costs and attorney fees included in enforcing the Agreement; **(ii)** consent to any changes, modifications or alterations of any term in this Agreement agreed to by Landlord and Tenant; and **(iii)** waive any right to require Landlord and/or Landlord's agents to proceed against Tenant for any default occurring under this Agreement before seeking to enforce this Guarantee.

Guarantor (Print Name) _____
Guarantor _____ Date _____
Address _____ City _____ State _____ Zip _____
Telephone _____ Fax _____ E-mail_____

47. **OWNER COMPENSATION TO BROKER:** Upon execution of this Agreement, Owner agrees to pay compensation to Broker as specified in a separate written agreement between Owner and Broker (C.A.R. Form LCA).

48. **RECEIPT:** If specified in paragraph 5, Landlord or Broker acknowledges receipt of move-in funds.

Landlord _____ Date _____
(Owner or Agent with authority to enter into this Agreement)
Landlord _____ Date _____
(Owner or Agent with authority to enter into this Agreement)
Landlord Address _____ City _____ State _____ Zip _____
Telephone _____ Fax _____ E-mail_____

> **REAL ESTATE BROKERS:**
> **A.** Real estate brokers who are not also Landlord under the Agreement are not parties to the Agreement between Landlord and Tenant.
> **B.** Agency relationships are confirmed in paragraph 42.
> **C.** **COOPERATING BROKER COMPENSATION:** Listing Broker agrees to pay Cooperating Broker (Leasing Firm) and Cooperating Broker agrees to accept: **(i)** the amount specified in the MLS, provided Cooperating Broker is a Participant of the MLS in which the Property is offered for sale or a reciprocal MLS; or **(ii)** ☐ (if checked) the amount specified in a separate written agreement between Listing Broker and Cooperating Broker.

Real Estate Broker (Leasing Firm) _____
By (Agent) _____ Date _____
Address _____ City _____ State _____ Zip _____
Telephone _____ Fax _____ E-mail_____

Real Estate Broker (Leasing Firm) _____
By (Agent) _____ Date _____
Address _____ City _____ State _____ Zip _____
Telephone _____ Fax _____ E-mail_____

SURE TRAC
The System for Success®

Published and Distributed by:
REAL ESTATE BUSINESS SERVICES, INC.
a subsidiary of the California Association of REALTORS®
525 South Virgil Avenue, Los Angeles, California 90020

Reviewed by _____ Date _____

LR REVISED 10/04 (PAGE 6 OF 6)

RESIDENTIAL LEASE OR MONTH-TO-MONTH RENTAL AGREEMENT (LR PAGE 6 OF 6)

CALIFORNIA
ASSOCIATION
OF REALTORS®

MOVE IN / MOVE OUT INSPECTION
(C.A.R. Form MIMO, Revised 4/03)

Property Address _____ Unit No. _____
Inspection: Move In _____ (Date) Move Out _____ (Date)
Tenant(s) _____

When completing this form, check the Premises carefully and be specific in all items noted. Check the appropriate box:
N – NEW   S – SATISFACTORY/CLEAN   O – OTHER   D – DEPOSIT DEDUCTION

	MOVE IN				MOVE OUT			
	N	S	O	Comments	S	O	D	Comments
Front Yard/Exterior								
Landscaping	☐	☐	☐	_____	☐	☐	☐	_____
Fences/Gates	☐	☐	☐	_____	☐	☐	☐	_____
Sprinklers/Timers	☐	☐	☐	_____	☐	☐	☐	_____
Walks/Driveway	☐	☐	☐	_____	☐	☐	☐	_____
Porches/Stairs	☐	☐	☐	_____	☐	☐	☐	_____
Mailbox	☐	☐	☐	_____	☐	☐	☐	_____
Light Fixtures	☐	☐	☐	_____	☐	☐	☐	_____
Building Exterior	☐	☐	☐	_____	☐	☐	☐	_____
Entry								
Security/Screen Doors	☐	☐	☐	_____	☐	☐	☐	_____
Doors/Knobs/Locks	☐	☐	☐	_____	☐	☐	☐	_____
Flooring/Baseboards	☐	☐	☐	_____	☐	☐	☐	_____
Walls/ Ceilings	☐	☐	☐	_____	☐	☐	☐	_____
Light Fixtures/Fans	☐	☐	☐	_____	☐	☐	☐	_____
Switches/Outlets	☐	☐	☐	_____	☐	☐	☐	_____
Living Room								
Doors/Knobs/Locks	☐	☐	☐	_____	☐	☐	☐	_____
Flooring/Baseboards	☐	☐	☐	_____	☐	☐	☐	_____
Walls/Ceilings	☐	☐	☐	_____	☐	☐	☐	_____
Window Coverings	☐	☐	☐	_____	☐	☐	☐	_____
Windows/Locks/Screens	☐	☐	☐	_____	☐	☐	☐	_____
Light Fixtures/Fans	☐	☐	☐	_____	☐	☐	☐	_____
Switches/Outlets	☐	☐	☐	_____	☐	☐	☐	_____
Fireplace/Equipment	☐	☐	☐	_____	☐	☐	☐	_____
Dining Room								
Flooring/Baseboards	☐	☐	☐	_____	☐	☐	☐	_____
Walls/Ceilings	☐	☐	☐	_____	☐	☐	☐	_____
Window Coverings	☐	☐	☐	_____	☐	☐	☐	_____
Windows/Locks/Screens	☐	☐	☐	_____	☐	☐	☐	_____
Light Fixtures/Fans	☐	☐	☐	_____	☐	☐	☐	_____
Switches/Outlets	☐	☐	☐	_____	☐	☐	☐	_____

Tenant's Initials (_____)(_____)   Tenant's Initials (_____)(_____)

MIMO REVISED 4/03 (PAGE 1 OF 5) Print Date BDC Mar 04

Reviewed by _____ Date _____

EQUAL HOUSING
OPPORTUNITY

Property Address: _____ Date: _____

	MOVE IN				MOVE OUT			
	N	S	O	Comments	S	O	D	Comments

Other Room _____

	N	S	O	Comments	S	O	D	Comments
Doors/Knobs/Locks	☐	☐	☐	_____	☐	☐	☐	_____
Flooring/Baseboards	☐	☐	☐	_____	☐	☐	☐	_____
Walls/Ceilings	☐	☐	☐	_____	☐	☐	☐	_____
Window Coverings	☐	☐	☐	_____	☐	☐	☐	_____
Windows/Locks/Screens	☐	☐	☐	_____	☐	☐	☐	_____
Light Fixtures/Fans	☐	☐	☐	_____	☐	☐	☐	_____
Switches/Outlets	☐	☐	☐	_____	☐	☐	☐	_____

Bedroom # _____

	N	S	O	Comments	S	O	D	Comments
Doors/Knobs/Locks	☐	☐	☐	_____	☐	☐	☐	_____
Flooring/Baseboards	☐	☐	☐	_____	☐	☐	☐	_____
Walls/Ceilings	☐	☐	☐	_____	☐	☐	☐	_____
Window Coverings	☐	☐	☐	_____	☐	☐	☐	_____
Windows/Locks/Screens	☐	☐	☐	_____	☐	☐	☐	_____
Light Fixtures/Fans	☐	☐	☐	_____	☐	☐	☐	_____
Switches/Outlets	☐	☐	☐	_____	☐	☐	☐	_____
Closets/Doors/Tracks	☐	☐	☐	_____	☐	☐	☐	_____

Bedroom # _____

	N	S	O	Comments	S	O	D	Comments
Doors/Knobs/Locks	☐	☐	☐	_____	☐	☐	☐	_____
Flooring/Baseboards	☐	☐	☐	_____	☐	☐	☐	_____
Walls/Ceilings	☐	☐	☐	_____	☐	☐	☐	_____
Window Coverings	☐	☐	☐	_____	☐	☐	☐	_____
Windows/Locks/Screens	☐	☐	☐	_____	☐	☐	☐	_____
Light Fixtures/Fans	☐	☐	☐	_____	☐	☐	☐	_____
Switches/Outlets	☐	☐	☐	_____	☐	☐	☐	_____
Closets/Doors/Tracks	☐	☐	☐	_____	☐	☐	☐	_____

Bedroom # _____

	N	S	O	Comments	S	O	D	Comments
Doors/Knobs/Locks	☐	☐	☐	_____	☐	☐	☐	_____
Flooring/Baseboards	☐	☐	☐	_____	☐	☐	☐	_____
Walls/Ceilings	☐	☐	☐	_____	☐	☐	☐	_____
Window Coverings	☐	☐	☐	_____	☐	☐	☐	_____
Windows/Locks/Screens	☐	☐	☐	_____	☐	☐	☐	_____
Light Fixtures/Fans	☐	☐	☐	_____	☐	☐	☐	_____
Switches/Outlets	☐	☐	☐	_____	☐	☐	☐	_____
Closets/Doors/Tracks	☐	☐	☐	_____	☐	☐	☐	_____

Bedroom # _____

	N	S	O	Comments	S	O	D	Comments
Doors/Knobs/Locks	☐	☐	☐	_____	☐	☐	☐	_____
Flooring/Baseboards	☐	☐	☐	_____	☐	☐	☐	_____
Walls/Ceilings	☐	☐	☐	_____	☐	☐	☐	_____
Window Coverings	☐	☐	☐	_____	☐	☐	☐	_____
Windows/Locks/Screens	☐	☐	☐	_____	☐	☐	☐	_____
Light Fixtures/Fans	☐	☐	☐	_____	☐	☐	☐	_____
Switches/Outlets	☐	☐	☐	_____	☐	☐	☐	_____
Closets/Doors/Tracks	☐	☐	☐	_____	☐	☐	☐	_____

Tenant's Initials (_____)(_____)   Tenant's Initials (_____)(_____)

MIMO REVISED 4/03 (PAGE 2 OF 5)

Reviewed by _____ Date _____

EQUAL HOUSING OPPORTUNITY

Property Address: _____ Date: _____

| | **MOVE IN** | | | | **MOVE OUT** | | | |
| | **N** | **S** | **O** | **Comments** | **S** | **O** | **D** | **Comments** |

Bath #_____

	N	S	O	Comments	S	O	D	Comments
Doors/Knobs/Locks	☐	☐	☐	_____	☐	☐	☐	_____
Flooring/Baseboards	☐	☐	☐	_____	☐	☐	☐	_____
Walls/Ceilings	☐	☐	☐	_____	☐	☐	☐	_____
Window Coverings	☐	☐	☐	_____	☐	☐	☐	_____
Windows/Locks/Screens	☐	☐	☐	_____	☐	☐	☐	_____
Light Fixtures	☐	☐	☐	_____	☐	☐	☐	_____
Switches/Outlets	☐	☐	☐	_____	☐	☐	☐	_____
Toilet	☐	☐	☐	_____	☐	☐	☐	_____
Tub/Shower	☐	☐	☐	_____	☐	☐	☐	_____
Shower Door/Rail/Curtain	☐	☐	☐	_____	☐	☐	☐	_____
Sink/Faucets	☐	☐	☐	_____	☐	☐	☐	_____
Plumbing/Drains	☐	☐	☐	_____	☐	☐	☐	_____
Exhaust Fan	☐	☐	☐	_____	☐	☐	☐	_____
Towel Rack(s)	☐	☐	☐	_____	☐	☐	☐	_____
Toilet Paper Holder	☐	☐	☐	_____	☐	☐	☐	_____
Cabinets/Counters	☐	☐	☐	_____	☐	☐	☐	_____

Bath #_____

	N	S	O	Comments	S	O	D	Comments
Doors/Knobs/Locks	☐	☐	☐	_____	☐	☐	☐	_____
Flooring/Baseboards	☐	☐	☐	_____	☐	☐	☐	_____
Walls/Ceilings	☐	☐	☐	_____	☐	☐	☐	_____
Window Coverings	☐	☐	☐	_____	☐	☐	☐	_____
Windows/Locks/Screens	☐	☐	☐	_____	☐	☐	☐	_____
Light Fixtures	☐	☐	☐	_____	☐	☐	☐	_____
Switches/Outlets	☐	☐	☐	_____	☐	☐	☐	_____
Toilet	☐	☐	☐	_____	☐	☐	☐	_____
Tub/Shower	☐	☐	☐	_____	☐	☐	☐	_____
Shower Door/Rail/Curtain	☐	☐	☐	_____	☐	☐	☐	_____
Sink/Faucets	☐	☐	☐	_____	☐	☐	☐	_____
Plumbing/Drains	☐	☐	☐	_____	☐	☐	☐	_____
Exhaust Fan	☐	☐	☐	_____	☐	☐	☐	_____
Towel Rack(s)	☐	☐	☐	_____	☐	☐	☐	_____
Toilet Paper Holder	☐	☐	☐	_____	☐	☐	☐	_____
Cabinets/Counters	☐	☐	☐	_____	☐	☐	☐	_____

Bath #_____

	N	S	O	Comments	S	O	D	Comments
Doors/Knobs/Locks	☐	☐	☐	_____	☐	☐	☐	_____
Flooring/Baseboards	☐	☐	☐	_____	☐	☐	☐	_____
Walls/Ceilings	☐	☐	☐	_____	☐	☐	☐	_____
Window Coverings	☐	☐	☐	_____	☐	☐	☐	_____
Windows/Locks/Screens	☐	☐	☐	_____	☐	☐	☐	_____
Light Fixtures	☐	☐	☐	_____	☐	☐	☐	_____
Switches/Outlets	☐	☐	☐	_____	☐	☐	☐	_____
Toilet	☐	☐	☐	_____	☐	☐	☐	_____
Tub/Shower	☐	☐	☐	_____	☐	☐	☐	_____
Shower Door/Rail/Curtain	☐	☐	☐	_____	☐	☐	☐	_____
Sink/Faucets	☐	☐	☐	_____	☐	☐	☐	_____
Plumbing/Drains	☐	☐	☐	_____	☐	☐	☐	_____
Exhaust Fan	☐	☐	☐	_____	☐	☐	☐	_____
Towel Rack(s)	☐	☐	☐	_____	☐	☐	☐	_____
Toilet Paper Holder	☐	☐	☐	_____	☐	☐	☐	_____
Cabinets/Counters	☐	☐	☐	_____	☐	☐	☐	_____

Tenant's Initials (_____)(_____)   Tenant's Initials (_____)(_____)

MIMO REVISED 4/03 (PAGE 3 OF 5)

Reviewed by _____ Date _____

EQUAL HOUSING OPPORTUNITY

Property Address: _____ Date: _____

	MOVE IN N S O	Comments	MOVE OUT S O D	Comments

Kitchen
Flooring/Baseboards	☐ ☐ ☐	_____	☐ ☐ ☐	_____
Walls/Ceilings	☐ ☐ ☐	_____	☐ ☐ ☐	_____
Window Coverings	☐ ☐ ☐	_____	☐ ☐ ☐	_____
Windows/Locks/Screens	☐ ☐ ☐	_____	☐ ☐ ☐	_____
Light Fixtures	☐ ☐ ☐	_____	☐ ☐ ☐	_____
Switches/Outlets	☐ ☐ ☐	_____	☐ ☐ ☐	_____
Range/Fan/Hood	☐ ☐ ☐	_____	☐ ☐ ☐	_____
Oven(s)/Microwave	☐ ☐ ☐	_____	☐ ☐ ☐	_____
Refrigerator	☐ ☐ ☐	_____	☐ ☐ ☐	_____
Dishwasher	☐ ☐ ☐	_____	☐ ☐ ☐	_____
Sink/Disposal	☐ ☐ ☐	_____	☐ ☐ ☐	_____
Faucet(s)/Plumbing	☐ ☐ ☐	_____	☐ ☐ ☐	_____
Cabinets	☐ ☐ ☐	_____	☐ ☐ ☐	_____
Counters	☐ ☐ ☐	_____	☐ ☐ ☐	_____

Hall/Stairs
Flooring/Baseboards	☐ ☐ ☐	_____	☐ ☐ ☐	_____
Walls/Ceilings	☐ ☐ ☐	_____	☐ ☐ ☐	_____
Light Fixtures	☐ ☐ ☐	_____	☐ ☐ ☐	_____
Switches/Outlets	☐ ☐ ☐	_____	☐ ☐ ☐	_____
Closets/Cabinets	☐ ☐ ☐	_____	☐ ☐ ☐	_____
Railings/Banisters	☐ ☐ ☐	_____	☐ ☐ ☐	_____

Laundry _____
Faucets/Valves	☐ ☐ ☐	_____	☐ ☐ ☐	_____
Plumbing/Drains	☐ ☐ ☐	_____	☐ ☐ ☐	_____
Cabinets/Counters	☐ ☐ ☐	_____	☐ ☐ ☐	_____

Systems
Furnace/Thermostat	☐ ☐ ☐	_____	☐ ☐ ☐	_____
Air Conditioning	☐ ☐ ☐	_____	☐ ☐ ☐	_____
Water Heater	☐ ☐ ☐	_____	☐ ☐ ☐	_____
Water Softener	☐ ☐ ☐	_____	☐ ☐ ☐	_____

Other _____

_____

Tenant's Initials (_____)(_____)   Tenant's Initials (_____)(_____)

MIMO REVISED 4/03 (PAGE 4 OF 5)

Reviewed by _____ Date _____   EQUAL HOUSING OPPORTUNITY

Property Address: _____ Date: _____

	MOVE IN				MOVE OUT			
	N	S	O	Comments	S	O	D	Comments
Garage/Parking								
Garage Door	☐	☐	☐	_____	☐	☐	☐	_____
Other Door(s)	☐	☐	☐	_____	☐	☐	☐	_____
Driveway/Floor	☐	☐	☐	_____	☐	☐	☐	_____
Cabinets/Counters	☐	☐	☐	_____	☐	☐	☐	_____
Light Fixtures	☐	☐	☐	_____	☐	☐	☐	_____
Switches/Outlets	☐	☐	☐	_____	☐	☐	☐	_____
Electrical/Exposed Wiring	☐	☐	☐	_____	☐	☐	☐	_____
Window(s)	☐	☐	☐	_____	☐	☐	☐	_____
Other Storage/Shelving	☐	☐	☐	_____	☐	☐	☐	_____
Back/Side/Yard								
Patio/Deck/Balcony	☐	☐	☐	_____	☐	☐	☐	_____
Patio Cover(s)	☐	☐	☐	_____	☐	☐	☐	_____
Landscaping	☐	☐	☐	_____	☐	☐	☐	_____
Sprinklers/Timers	☐	☐	☐	_____	☐	☐	☐	_____
Pool/Heater/Equipment	☐	☐	☐	_____	☐	☐	☐	_____
Spa/Cover/Equipment	☐	☐	☐	_____	☐	☐	☐	_____
Fences/Gates	☐	☐	☐	_____	☐	☐	☐	_____
Safety/Security								
Smoke/CO Detector(s)	☐	☐	☐	_____	☐	☐	☐	_____
Security System	☐	☐	☐	_____	☐	☐	☐	_____
Security Window Bars	☐	☐	☐	_____	☐	☐	☐	_____

Personal Property
_____

Keys/Remotes/Devices
Keys _____
Remotes/Devices _____

☐ **Attached Supplement(s)** _____

THIS SECTION TO BE COMPLETED AT MOVE IN: Receipt of a copy of this form is acknowledged by:
Tenant _____ Date _____
Tenant _____ Date _____
New Phone Service Established? ☐ Yes ☐ No   New Phone Number _____
Landlord (Owner or Agent) _____ Date _____
Landlord _____
(Print Name)

THIS SECTION TO BE COMPLETED AT MOVE OUT: Receipt of a copy of this form is acknowledged by:
Tenant _____ Date _____
Tenant _____ Date _____
Tenant Forwarding Address _____

Landlord (Owner or Agent) _____ Date _____
Landlord _____
(Print Name)

SURE TRAC
The System for Success®

Published and Distributed by:
REAL ESTATE BUSINESS SERVICES, INC.
a subsidiary of the California Association of REALTORS®
525 South Virgil Avenue, Los Angeles, California 90020

MIMO REVISED 4/03 (PAGE 5 OF 5)

EQUAL HOUSING OPPORTUNITY

Reviewed by _____ Date _____

There are three different types of property managers: residential, outside and institutional managers. These managers oversee residential, commercial, industrial, retail and other types of property. Each property type dictates the duties and licensure requirements of the manager.

Managers may be compensated in a number of different ways. Some managers are paid on a straight salary. Some, such as apartment managers, will have living arrangements paid for. Other compensation methods are a percentage basis and commission.

All leases must contain: the name of the parties; description of the property involved; period of time or duration the lease will last; and the required, monthly rent or consideration.

In assignment of a lease, the current tenant of a property transfers his or her entire interest in a lease to another tenant. The original tenant is no longer responsible to the landlord, and can walk away from the lease in good standing. The new tenant is completely responsible to the landlord and will occupy the property for the duration of the original lease.

A lease may be terminated for a number of reasons. The duration of the lease may have expired, and the tenant can choose to sign a new lease, be on a periodic tenancy month to month, or choose to find a new place to rent. A lease may also be terminated because one party did not meet one or more of the contractual obligations of the lease.

T E R M S   A N D   P H R A S E S

Abandonment – Forfeiting property through non-use (generally acknowledged by the tenant removing his or her belongings from the premises.)

Assignee – Person or party to whom a lease is assigned or, in some cases, transferred.

Assignment – To transfer the entire interest in a lease from the original lessee to a new lessee (who is sometimes called the assignee).

Chattel real – Another name for personal property (leases are considered such personal property, or chattel real)

Contract rent – The amount of rental income a landlord will receive from a tenant's rent as agreed upon in the rental contract.

Constructive eviction – The interference of a landlord with a tenant's agreed-upon use of property by entering property and making unwarranted alterations or changes to the property, thus preventing the intended use.

Covenant of quiet enjoyment – The promise a landlord makes to a tenant, implied by law, not to interfere in the possession or use of leased property.

Covenant to repair – Legally implied responsibility of the landlord to make necessary repairs to leased properties

Demise – The conveyance of real estate to a person for use during a set period of time. A lease will demise property to the tenant for the duration of the contract.

Economic rent – The amount of rent which a property could bring in the current market if the property were vacant and available to be rented.

Escalator clause – Provisions in a lease which allow for increases in rent based on increases in the consumer price index.

Estate at sufferance – Tenancy created when the lessee is in wrongful possession of property (even if the initial possession was lawful).

Estate at will – Tenancy where the lease may be ended unilaterally by either party. There is no official termination of the estate; however, one party must give the other party 30-days notice of termination.

Estate for years – Tenancy with a definite end date (must be renegotiated upon its termination).

Estate from period to period – Tenancy that will automatically be renewed at the end of each period by the landlord's acceptance of rent. This type of tenancy does not require renegotiation at the end of the term, and is usually called a month-to-month tenancy, or periodic tenancy.

Eviction –The process by which a landlord legally removes a tenant from a property for some breach in the contract or lease agreement.

Fair Employment and Housing Act (FEHA) – A California civil code preventing discrimination against tenants based on marital status, race, color, religion, sex, national origin or ancestry .

Fair Housing Amendments Act of 1988 - A federal law preventing landlords from discriminating against physical handicap, familial status and age of tenants.

Graduated payment lease – Lease requiring periodic increase in rent.

Gross lease – A lease in which the landlord pays for the operating expenses on a property (which may include taxes, maintenance and repairs).

Holdover tenancy – A tenancy where the tenant remains in possession of the property after the lease term has ended.

Landlord – The lessor or property owner who rents property to another individual.

Lease – An agreement between the landlord and tenant (lessor and lessee) allowing the tenant possession of property for a specific amount of time. The lease may be written or verbal depending on the duration of the contract.

Lease assignment – The action wherein a tenant transfers his or her interest in the leasehold to another tenant. The transfer of lease is permanent, and the original tenant has no further responsibilities to the landlord after the transfer.

Lease option – A lease wherein the landlord gives the current tenant the option to purchase the property within a certain time period.

Lessee – The tenant or person leasing property from another individual.

Lessor – The landlord or person leasing property to another individual.

Less-than-freehold – Another name for a lease or the interest a lessee has in property when leasing from another.

Net lease – A lease where the tenant will pay all expenses (such as taxes, maintenance and repairs) in addition to monthly rent.

Notice to pay or quit – The notice a landlord will supply to a tenant who has not paid the rent, giving them three days to pay rent or vacate the premises.

Percentage lease – A lease where the tenant will pay the landlord a percentage of gross sales as rental consideration.

Periodic tenancy – The same as a tenancy from period to period. This type of tenancy is valid for a set time period, but is automatically renewed upon the landlord's acceptance of rent.

Rent – The consideration a tenant will pay the landlord for use of a property.

Rent control – Laws passed by local government to control the rents that landlords may charge for rental property.

Residential rental property – Property where 80% or more of the profits come from residential units.

Retaliatory eviction – The process by which a landlord will either evict a tenant for making unauthorized repairs made to keep the unit within health or safety codes or evict a tenant as a response to complaints made by the tenant.

Reversionary right – The right of possession in which rental property returns to the landlord upon termination of a lease.

Right of entry – The right of a landlord to enter into the rental property to make necessary repairs or to check on the safety and well-being of a tenant.

Sandwich lease – A lease created when a tenant subleases his or her interest to another tenant for a short period of time. The original lessee is responsible to the landlord, and the new tenant is responsible to the original lessee. Thus, the original lessee is "sandwiched" between the new lessee and the landlord.

Security deposit – The amount a tenant pays a landlord at the beginning of the tenancy. This money is to be held in an account to make necessary or routine repairs once the tenant vacates the property. If the entire deposit is not used in repairs, the landlord must return any remaining amount to the tenant within 21 days of the tenant's vacating the premises, accompanied by an itemized statement of how the deposit was utilized.

Sublease – The process by which a lessee transfers his or her interest to another lessee. The new lessee is responsible to the original lessee, while the original lessee is responsible to the landlord.

Surrender – The process by which a tenant voluntarily gives up control of a property.

Tenant – The person leasing property from a landlord (also called a lessee).

Unlawful detainer –The papers filed in a court of law against a tenant in unlawful possession of a property.

Unruh Civil Rights Act – California civil code making it unlawful to discriminate against tenants based on sex, race, color, religion, ancestry or national origin.

Untenable dwelling – Property lacking necessary utilities, or one that is in poor condition, causing it to fall under the minimum property standards and making it uninhabitable for tenants.

Warranty of habitability – A legal implication whereby landlords must maintain certain standards of minimal housing to keep buildings up to code.

Writ of possession – Court order directing the sheriff to physically remove a tenant from the premises.

C H A P T E R   Q U I Z

1. Which of the following is not a type of property manager?
    a. Residential manager
    b. Estate manager
    c. Individual property manager
    d. Licensee/property manager

2. A successful residential manager will have all of the following skills except:
    a. Ability to select residents based on their credit references and economic capability
    b. Ability to show apartments, contact prospective tenants and close the rental of a unit
    c. "Hands-off" managerial skills when dealing with maintenance and housekeeping, to let them accomplish all tasks as they see fit
    d. Awareness of and sensitivity to all events occurring on the property

3. A property manager's primary duty is:
    a. Collecting rents
    b. Purchasing supplies and equipment and paying for repairs
    c. Keeping property records and preparing necessary reports
    d. All of the above

4. An analysis of the character of the immediate neighborhood, trends in population growth, economic level of neighborhood residents, condition of the housing market and current vacancy factors is used when:
    a. Establishing rent schedules
    b. Deciding to use a property manager for a small property
    c. Determining the basic responsibilities of a property manager
    d. Deciding contract terms for renters

5. Which of the following is not a type of property typically managed by a professional manager?
    a. Airport
    b. Apartment building
    c. Private single-family home
    d. Office building

6. Which of the following properties are the most common of the properties subject to professional management?
    a. Commercial properties
    b. Residential properties
    c. Mobile-home parks
    d. Restaurants

7. A property manager specializing in park development, maintenance of public amenities, and approval of lease assignments on the sale of different units would most likely be a manager in a:
    a. Mobile-home park
    b. Office park
    c. Condominium complex
    d. None of the above

8. Which of the following tasks should not be done by computer?
    a. Rent increase calendar
    b. Rent receipts
    c. Check writing
    d. Reading blueprints

9. Which of the following is a leasehold estate?
    a. Freehold estate
    b. Joint tenancy
    c. Tenancy-in-common
    d. Estate from period to period

10. A lease where the tenant pays utilities, real estate taxes, maintenance, repairs and other special assessments in addition to the normal rent is called:
    a. Gross lease
    b. Net lease
    c. Percentage lease
    d. Either A or B

11. A percentage lease would commonly be used with:
    a. A business or retail complex
    b. A residential complex
    c. An industrial complex
    d. Any of the above

12. A lease where the tenant takes possession of the unit legally, but remains on the property after the lease has expired without the owner's permission, is called:
    a. Estate from period to period
    b. Estate at will
    c. Estate at sufferance
    d. Estate for years

13. Which type of estate has no specified time limit?
    a. Estate for years
    b. Estate at will
    c. Estate at sufferance
    d. Estate from period to period

14. Which of the following is a valid reason to refuse a potential tenant's application for residency?
    a. On the basis of age
    b. On the basis of sex
    c. On the basis of national origin
    d. On the basis of credit history

15. Which of the following is not specifically mentioned in the lease agreement?
    a. Date the lease is valid
    b. Inspection (by the tenant)
    c. Age requirements
    d. Pets

16. The maximum security deposit a landlord may collect from a tenant for an unfurnished unit is:
    a. One month's rent
    b. Two months' rent
    c. Three months' rent
    d. Four months' rent

17. Cleaning deposits are:
    a. Commonly collected to make sure the unit will be cleaned when it is vacated
    b. Illegal
    c. Included in the security deposit
    d. None of the above

18. A landlord may enter the property in all of the following circumstances except:
    a. To retrieve tools left there by the maintenance staff
    b. In an emergency situation
    c. If the tenant has abandoned the premises
    d. Under a court order

19. Under the California Civil Code, a tenant is obligated to:
    a. Keep the living unit clean and sanitary
    b. Pay rent on time
    c. Avoid defacing or damaging property
    d. All of the above

20. Which of the following is not a step in an unlawful detainer?
    a. Tenant is given a verbal notice of past rent that is due
    b. Tenant is served a three-day notice to quit the premises or pay rent
    c. Landlord files an unlawful detainer against the tenant in a court of law
    d. The sheriff sends the tenant an eviction notice

12

ETHICS

What you will learn in this Chapter

- Ethics

- Violations

- Trade and Professionalism

- NAR Code of Ethics

- Special Disclosures

- Complaints and Disputes

- Code of Ethics

- Fair Housing

- Federal Laws

- The California Business and Professions Code

- Trust Funds

Test Your Knowledge

1. Ethics are based on:
    a. Laws
    b. Minimum standards
    c. The golden rule
    d. Acceptable behaviors

2. Which of the following is true?
    a. Ethics change to accommodate current attitudes and perceptions.
    b. Laws change to accommodate current attitudes and perceptions.
    c. Both ethics and laws change to accommodate current attitudes and perceptions.
    d. Neither ethics nor laws change to accommodate current attitudes and perceptions.

3. The "Suggestions for Professional Conduct in Sale, Lease, and Exchange Transactions" and "Suggestions for Professional Conduct When Negotiating or Arranging Loans Secured by Real Property or Sale of a Promissory Note Secured by Real Property" are enforced by:
    a. The Real Estate Commissioner
    b. The Department of Real Estate
    c. The California judicial system
    d. None of the above

4. Civil rights acts and the Thirteenth and Fourteenth Amendments to the Constitution are considered:
    a. Laws
    b. Wording to promote fair treatment of all people
    c. Ethical
    d. All of the above

5. Which of the following words or phrases are considered acceptable by HUD?
    a. Caucasian only
    b. Kosher meals
    c. No children
    d. No women

6. Which of the following is not a protected class under the Civil Rights Act of 1968?
    a. Sexual Orientation
    b. National Origin
    c. Race
    d. Religion

7. The Americans with Disabilities Act applies to all businesses employing:
    a. Any number of employees
    b. 10 or more employees
    c. 15 or more employees
    d. 20 or more employees

Many people think that if they are following the law, they are acting ethically, and by breaking the law their actions are unethical. While logically this makes sense, it is not always true. Ethical, legal and moral actions are not always one in the same, although they do go hand in hand on many occasions.

Where the law ends, ethics can usually be interpreted further. Ethics generally holds professionals to a higher standard compared to that of law. Ethics can be thought of as a system of standards that govern the conduct of a specific group of people. The National Association of Realtors, for example, has the NAR Code of Ethics all realtors are expected to follow. Simply stated, ethics are attitudes and conduct considered socially appropriate and acceptable.

ETHICS AND PROFESSIONALISM

As a real estate agent, it is challenging to stay on top of all the law changes, specific requirements of clients, disclosures for each property, and other rules and regulations you must follow as an agent. Being able to juggle several tasks at once, stay on top of all such projects and educate yourself to any changes made in your office and industry, as well as specific requirements of each one of your properties will keep you very busy. Sometimes, it is easy to get caught up in certain aspects of your job, while allowing others to slide.

Your number one responsibility is to your client. However, you must also work hard, and ethically. It seems easy to assume you will make all the right, ethical decisions every time; but, when dealing with difficult clients, it is sometimes easy to forget about a disclosure. You may also become so focused on your task that you simply forget some rules and regulations.

Full disclosure is one of the most important duties for you to always remember. Your broker or firm will provide you with all the necessary forms for disclosure, but it is your responsibility to remain in compliance with the law at all times. Each disclosure may require a different compliance with the law. It is also your job to fully explain what each disclosure means to your client, so that your client understands all of the disclosures they must read and sign. All of the most important disclosures will be included in the deposit receipt; but that does not necessarily mean that your client understands what they mean. Real estate is perhaps one of the largest investments a person will make in their lifetime; so, it is important for you to be very informative and patient. Disclosures will be covered in detail later in this section.

Because of unethical business practices in real estate, professional associations were formed. The National Association of REALTORS (NAR) was created in 1908. NAR was one of the first business associations to write, and enforce a code of ethics, which was written in 1913. This code of ethics helped to lay the foundation for many of the original state licensing laws. Additionally, states began regulating the sale of property. In 1917, California became the first state to pass a real estate license law. The law was determined unconstitutional and rewritten to become the Real Estate Act of 1919. The purpose of this law was to protect public interest in terms of real estate. The question may rise which set of rules to do you follow, the California Real Estate Rules and Regulations or the NAR Code of Ethics? The answer is simple; every licensee in California must follow the Real Estate Law and Commissioner's Regulations.

Additionally every REALTOR must follow the NAR Code of Ethics. The basis of NAR's Code of Ethics is taken from the golden rule, "or do unto others as you would like them to do to you." The golden rule is also referred to as the Ethic of Reciprocity. This ethic states that each person should treat others in a decent manner. By following these rules of ethics and regulations set forth by regulatory commissions or associations you will be operating at a high standard, encouraging referrals and repeat business.

VIOLATIONS OF REAL ESTATE LAW

When a real estate agent does not comply with the law, they must be prepared for civil or criminal punishment. They must also face the Real Estate Commission, where monetary penalties as well as the possibility of having their license suspended or revoked may occur. Accountability is the key. If a real estate agent fails to follow the law, a court will hold them accountable. Unfortunately, as our society becomes more and more litigious, real estate agents must become better at their job, especially regarding what to disclose, when to disclose it and to whom.

Remember!
Realtors found in violation of Real Estate Law may face:
- Criminal punishment
- Civil punishment
- Sanctions or punishment from the Real Estate Commission

Real Estate Law is found in the Business and Professional Code of the California Code of Regulations. Policing of these laws lies in the hands of the state Real Estate Commissioner. He or she may adopt regulations to enforce the Real Estate Law, or may use the court for more serious violations. Real estate professionals need to be well-versed with the Commissioner's Regulations, as they will be held accountable for them. They should also be familiar with the code of ethics to which realtors will be held accountable.

Because of the importance of the Commissioners Regulations, the following articles are included below. These article deal with disciplinary action and other sections you, as a licensee, should be concerned with most.

Business and Professions Code – a partial list
10137. It is unlawful for any licensed real estate broker to employ or compensate, directly or indirectly, any person for performing any of the acts within the scope of this chapter who is not a licensed real estate broker, or a real estate salesman licensed under the broker employing or compensating him; provided, however, that a licensed real estate broker may pay a commission to a broker of another State.

No real estate salesman shall be employed by or accept compensation from any person other than the broker under whom he is at the time licensed.

It is unlawful for any licensed real estate salesman to pay any compensation for performing any of the acts within the scope of this chapter to any real estate licensee except through the broker under whom he is at the time licensed.

For a violation of any of the provisions of this section, the commissioner may temporarily suspend or permanently revoke the license of the real estate licensee, in accordance with the provisions of this part relating to hearings.

10137.1. Nothing contained in this division shall preclude a partnership from performing acts for which a real estate broker license is required, provided every partner through whom the partnership so acts is a licensed real estate broker.

10138. It is a misdemeanor, punishable by a fine of not exceeding one hundred dollars ($100) for each offense, for any person, whether obligor, escrow holder or otherwise, to pay or deliver to anyone a compensation for performing any of the acts within the scope of this chapter, who is not known to be or who does not present evidence to such payor that he is a regularly licensed real estate broker at the time such compensation is earned.

For a violation of any of the provisions of this section, the commissioner may temporarily suspend or permanently revoke the license of the real estate licensee in accordance with the provisions of this part relating to hearings.

10140. Every officer, agent or employee of any company, and every other person who knowingly authorizes, directs or aids in the publication, advertisement, distribution or circularization of any false statement or representation concerning any land or subdivision thereof, as defined in Chapter 1 (commencing at Section 11000) of Part 2 of this division, offered for sale or lease, or, if the land is owned by the State or Federal Government, which such person offers to assist another or others to file an application for the purchase or lease of, or to locate or enter upon, and every person who, with knowledge that any advertisement, pamphlet, prospectus or letter concerning any said land or subdivision, as defined in Chapter 1 (commencing at Section 11000) of Part 2 of this division, contains any written statement that is false or fraudulent, issues, circulates, publishes or distributes the same, or causes the same to be issued, circulated, published or distributed, or who, in any other respect, willfully violates or fails to comply with any of the provisions of this section, or who in any other respect willfully violates or fails, omits or neglects to obey, observe or comply with any order, permit, decision, demand or requirement of the commissioner under this section, is guilty of a public offense, and shall be punished by a fine not exceeding one thousand dollars ($1,000), or by imprisonment in a county jail not exceeding one year, or by both such fine and imprisonment, and, if a real estate licensee, he shall be held to trial by the commissioner for a suspension or revocation of his license, as provided in the provisions of this part relating to hearings. The district attorney of each county in this State shall prosecute all violations of the provisions of this section in respective counties in which the violations occur.

10140.5. Each advertisement or other statement which is published by a real estate broker or salesman offering to assist persons to file applications for the purchase or lease of, or to locate or enter upon, lands owned by the State or Federal Government shall, when published, indicate the name of the broker for whom it is published and state that he is licensed as a real estate broker by the State of California.

10140.6. A real estate licensee shall not publish, circulate, distribute, nor cause to be published, circulated, or distributed in any newspaper or periodical, or by mail any matter pertaining to any activity for which a real estate license is required which does not contain a designation disclosing that he is performing acts for which a real estate license is required.

The provisions of this section shall not apply to classified rental advertisements reciting the telephone number at the premises of the property offered for rent or the address of the property offered for rent.

10141. Within one month after the closing of a transaction in which title to real property or in the sale of a business when real or personal property is conveyed from a seller to a purchaser through a licensed real estate broker, such broker shall inform or cause the information to be given to the seller and purchaser in writing of the selling price thereof and in event an exchange of real property or a business opportunity is involved, such information shall include a description of said property and amount of added money consideration, if any. If the transaction is closed through escrow and the escrow holder renders a closing statement, which reveals such information that shall be deemed compliance with this section on the part of the broker.

10141.5. Within one week after the closing of a transaction negotiated by a real estate broker in which title to real property is conveyed from a seller to a purchaser and a deed of trust secured by real property is executed, such broker shall cause such deed of trust to be recorded with the county recorder of the county in which the real property is located, or cause it to be delivered to the beneficiary with a written recommendation that it be recorded forthwith, unless written instructions not to record are received from the beneficiary. If the transaction is closed through escrow and the deed of trust is delivered to the escrow holder within the time prescribed by this section that shall be deemed compliance with this section on the part of the broker. Nothing in this section shall affect the validity of a transfer of title to real property.

10142. When a licensee prepares or has prepared an agreement authorizing or employing such licensee to perform any of the acts for which he is required to hold a license, or when such licensee secures the signature of any person to any contract pertaining to such services or transaction, he shall deliver a copy of the agreement to the person signing it at the time the signature is obtained.

10148. (a) A licensed real estate broker shall retain for three years copies of all listings, deposit receipts, canceled checks, trust records, and other documents executed by him or her or obtained by him or her in connection with any transactions for which a real estate broker license is required. The retention period shall run from the date of the closing of the transaction or from the date of the listing if the transaction is not consummated. After notice, the books, accounts, and records shall be made available for examination, inspection, and copying by the commissioner or his or her designated representative during regular business hours; and shall, upon the appearance of sufficient cause, be subject to audit without further notice, except that the audit shall not be harassing in nature.

(b) The commissioner shall charge a real estate broker for the cost of any audit, if the commissioner has found, in a final desist and refrain order issued under Section 10086 or in a final decision following a disciplinary hearing held in accordance with Chapter 5 (commencing with Section 11500) of Part 1 of Division 3 of Title 2 of the Government Code that the broker has violated Section 10145 or a regulation or rule of the commissioner interpreting Section 10145.

(c) If a broker fails to pay for the cost of an audit as described in subdivision (b) within 60 days of mailing a notice of billing, the commissioner may suspend or revoke the broker's license or deny renewal of the broker's license. The suspension or denial shall remain in effect until the cost is paid or until the broker's right to renew a license has expired.

The commissioner may maintain an action for the recovery of the cost in any court of competent jurisdiction. In determining the cost incurred by the commissioner for an audit, the commissioner may use the estimated average hourly cost for all persons performing audits of real estate brokers.

10175. Upon grounds provided in this article and the other articles of this chapter, the license of any real estate licensee may be revoked or suspended in accordance with the provisions of this part relating to hearings.

10175.2. (a) If the Real Estate Commissioner determines that the public interest and public welfare will be adequately served by permitting a real estate licensee to pay a monetary penalty to the department in lieu of an actual license suspension, the commissioner may, on the petition of the licensee, stay the execution of all or some part of the suspension on the condition that the licensee pay a monetary penalty and the further condition that the licensee incur no other cause for disciplinary action within a period of time specified by the commissioner.

(b) The commissioner may exercise the discretion granted under subdivision (a) either with respect to a suspension ordered by a decision after a contested hearing on an accusation against the licensee or by stipulation with the licensee after the filing of an accusation, but prior to the rendering of a decision based upon the accusation. In either case, the terms and conditions of the disciplinary action against the licensee shall be made part of a formal decision of the commissioner.

(c) If a licensee fails to pay the monetary penalty in accordance with the terms and conditions of the decision of the commissioner, the commissioner may, without a hearing, order the immediate execution of all or any part of the stayed suspension in which event the licensee shall not be entitled to any repayment nor credit, prorated or otherwise, for money paid to the department under the terms of the decision.

(d) The amount of the monetary penalty payable under this section shall not exceed two hundred fifty dollars ($250) for each day of suspension stayed nor a total of ten thousand dollars ($10,000) per decision regardless of the number of days of suspension stayed under the decision.

(e) Any monetary penalty received by the department pursuant to this section shall be credited to the Recovery Account of the Real Estate Fund.

10176. The commissioner may, upon his or her own motion, and shall, upon the verified complaint in writing of any person, investigate the actions of any person engaged in the business or acting in the capacity of a real estate licensee within this state, and he or she may temporarily suspend or permanently revoke a real estate license at any time where the licensee, while a real estate licensee, in performing or attempting to perform any of the acts within the scope of this chapter has been guilty of any of the following:

(a) Making any substantial misrepresentation.

(b) Making any false promises of a character likely to influence, persuade or induce.

(c) A continued and flagrant course of misrepresentation or making of false promises through real estate agents or salespersons.

(d) Acting for more than one party in a transaction without the knowledge or consent of all parties thereto.

(e) Commingling with his or her own money or property the money or other property of others, which is received and held by him or her.

(f) Claiming, demanding, or receiving a fee, compensation or commission under any exclusive agreement authorizing or employing a licensee to perform any acts set forth in Section 10131 for compensation or commission where the agreement does not contain a definite, specified date of final and complete termination.

(g) The claiming or taking by a licensee of any secret or undisclosed amount of compensation, commission or profit or the failure of a licensee to reveal to the employer of the licensee the full amount of the licensee's compensation, commission or profit under any agreement authorizing or employing the licensee to do any acts for which a license is required under this chapter for compensation or commission prior to or coincident with the signing of an agreement evidencing the meeting of the minds of the contracting parties, regardless of the form of the agreement, whether evidenced by documents in an escrow or by any other or different procedure.

(h) The use by a licensee of any provision allowing the licensee an option to purchase in an agreement authorizing or employing the licensee to sell, buy, or exchange real estate or a business opportunity for compensation or commission, except when the licensee prior to or coincident with election to exercise the option to purchase reveals in writing to the employer the full amount of licensee's profit and obtains the written consent of the employer approving the amount of the profit.

(i) Any other conduct, whether of the same or a different character than specified in this section, which constitutes fraud or dishonest dealing.

(j) Obtaining the signature of a prospective purchaser to an agreement which provides that the prospective purchaser shall either transact the purchasing, leasing, renting or exchanging of a business opportunity property through the broker obtaining the signature, or pay a compensation to the broker if the property is purchased, leased, rented or exchanged without the broker first having obtained the written authorization of the owner of the property concerned to offer the property for sale, lease, exchange or rent.

(k) Failing to disburse funds in accordance with a commitment to make a mortgage loan that is accepted by the applicant when the real estate broker represents to the applicant that the broker is either of the following:

(1) The lender.

(2) Authorized to issue the commitment on behalf of the lender or lenders in the mortgage loan transaction.

(l) Intentionally delaying the closing of a mortgage loan for the sole purpose of increasing interest, costs, fees, or charges payable by the borrower.

10176.1. (a) (1) Whenever the commissioner takes any enforcement or disciplinary action against a licensee, and the enforcement or disciplinary action is related to escrow services provided pursuant to paragraph (4) of subdivision (a) of Section 17006 of the Financial Code, upon the action becoming final the commissioner shall notify the Insurance Commissioner and the Commissioner of Corporations of the action or actions taken. The purpose of this notification is to alert the departments that enforcement or disciplinary action has been taken, if the licensee seeks or obtains employment with entities regulated by the departments.

(2) The commissioner shall provide the Insurance Commissioner and the Commissioner of Corporations, in addition to the notification of the action taken, with a copy of the written accusation, statement of issues, or order issued or filed in the matter and, at the request of the Insurance Commissioner or the Commissioner of Corporations, with any underlying factual material relevant to the enforcement or disciplinary action. Any confidential information provided by the commissioner to the Insurance Commissioner or the Commissioner of Corporations shall not be made public pursuant to this section. Notwithstanding any other provision of law, the disclosure of any underlying factual material to the Insurance Commissioner or the Commissioner of Corporations shall not operate as a waiver of confidentiality or any privilege that the commissioner may assert.

(b) The commissioner shall establish and maintain, on the Web site maintained by the Department of Real Estate, a database of its licensees, including those who have been subject to any enforcement or disciplinary action that triggers the notification requirements of this section. The database shall also contain a direct link to the databases, described in Section 17423.1 of the Financial Code and Section 12414.31 of the Insurance Code and required to be maintained on the Web sites of the Department of Corporations and the Department of Insurance, respectively, of persons who have been subject to enforcement or disciplinary action for malfeasance or misconduct related to the escrow industry by the Insurance Commissioner and the Commissioner of Corporations.

(c) There shall be no liability on the part of, and no cause of action of any nature shall arise against, the State of California, the Department of Real Estate, the Real Estate Commissioner, any other state agency, or any officer, agent, employee, consultant, or contractor of the state, for the release of any false or unauthorized information pursuant to this section, unless the release of that information was done with knowledge and malice, or for the failure to release any information pursuant to this section.

10176.5. (a) The commissioner may, upon his or her own motion, and shall upon receiving a verified complaint in writing from any person, investigate an alleged violation of Article 1.5 (commencing with Section 1102) of Chapter 2 of Title 4 of Part 4 of Division 2 of the Civil Code by any real estate licensee within this state. The commissioner may suspend or revoke a licensee's license if the licensee acting under the license has willfully or repeatedly violated any of the provisions of Article 1.5 (commencing with Section 1102) of Chapter 2 of Title 4 of Part 4 of Division 2 of the Civil Code.

(b) Notwithstanding any other provision of Article 1.5 (commencing with Section 1102) of Chapter 2 of Title 4 of Part 4 of Division 2 of the Civil Code, and in lieu of any other civil remedy, subdivision

(a) Of this section is the only remedy available for violations of Section 1102.6b of the Civil Code by any real estate licensee within this state.

10177. The commissioner may suspend or revoke the license of a real estate licensee, or may deny the issuance of a license to an applicant, who has done any of the following, or may suspend or revoke the license of a corporation, or deny the issuance of a license to a corporation, if an officer, director, or person owning or controlling 10 percent or more of the corporation's stock has done any of the following:

(a) Procured, or attempted to procure, a real estate license or license renewal, for himself or herself or any salesperson, by fraud, misrepresentation, or deceit, or by making any material misstatement of fact in an application for a real estate license, license renewal, or reinstatement.

(b) Entered a plea of guilty or nolo contendere to, or been found guilty of, or been convicted of, a felony or a crime involving moral turpitude, and the time for appeal has elapsed or the judgment of conviction has been affirmed on appeal, irrespective of an order granting probation following that conviction, suspending the imposition of sentence, or of a subsequent order under Section 1203.4 of the Penal Code allowing that licensee to withdraw his or her plea of guilty and to enter a plea of not guilty, or dismissing the accusation or information.

(c) Knowingly authorized, directed, connived at, or aided in the publication, advertisement, distribution, or circulation of any material false statement or representation concerning his or her business, or any business opportunity or any land or subdivision (as defined in Chapter 1 (commencing with Section 11000) of Part 2) offered for sale.

(d) Willfully disregarded or violated the Real Estate Law (Part 1 commencing with Section 10000)) or Chapter 1 (commencing with Section 11000) of Part 2 or the rules and regulations of the commissioner for the administration and enforcement of the Real Estate Law and Chapter 1 (commencing with Section 11000) of Part 2.

(e) Willfully used the term "realtor" or any trade name or insignia of membership in any real estate organization of which the licensee is not a member.

(f) Acted or conducted himself or herself in a manner that would have warranted the denial of his or her application for a real estate license, or has either had a license denied or had a license issued by another agency of this state, another state, or the federal government revoked or suspended for acts that, if done by a real estate licensee, would be grounds for the suspension or revocation of a California real estate license, if the action of denial, revocation, or suspension by the other agency or entity was taken only after giving the licensee or applicant fair notice of the charges, an opportunity for a hearing, and other due process protections comparable to the Administrative Procedure Act (Chapter 3.5 (commencing with Section 11340), Chapter 4 (commencing with Section 11370), and Chapter 5 (commencing with Section 11500) of Part 1 of Division 3 of Title 2 of the Government Code), and only upon an express finding of a violation of law by the agency or entity.

(g) Demonstrated negligence or incompetence in performing any act for which he or she is required to hold a license.

(h) As a broker licensee, failed to exercise reasonable supervision over the activities of his or her salespersons, or, as the officer designated by a corporate broker licensee, failed to exercise reasonable supervision and control of the activities of the corporation for which a real estate license is required.

(i) Has used his or her employment by a governmental agency in a capacity giving access to records, other than public records, in a manner that violates the confidential nature of the records.

(j) Engaged in any other conduct, whether of the same or a different character than specified in this section, which constitutes fraud or dishonest dealing.

(k) Violated any of the terms, conditions, restrictions, and limitations contained in any order granting a restricted license.

(l) Solicited or induced the sale, lease, or listing for sale or lease of residential property on the ground, wholly or in part, of loss of value, increase in crime, or decline of the quality of the schools due to the present or prospective entry into the neighborhood of a person or persons of another race, color, religion, ancestry, or national origin.

(m) Violated the Franchise Investment Law (Division 5 (commencing with Section 31000) of Title 4 of the Corporations Code) or regulations of the Commissioner of Corporations pertaining thereto.

(n) Violated the Corporate Securities Law of 1968 (Division 1 (commencing with Section 25000) of Title 4 of the Corporations Code) or the regulations of the Commissioner of Corporations pertaining thereto.

(o) Failed to disclose to the buyer of real property, in a transaction in which the licensee is an agent for the buyer, the nature and extent of a licensee's direct or indirect ownership interest in that real property. The direct or indirect ownership interest in the property by a person related to the licensee by blood or marriage, by an entity in which the licensee has an ownership interest, or by any other person with whom the licensee has a special relationship shall be disclosed to the buyer.

(p) Violated Article 6 (commencing with Section 10237). If a real estate broker that is a corporation has not done any of the foregoing acts, either directly or through its employees, agents, officers, directors, or persons owning or controlling 10 percent or more of the corporation's stock, the commissioner may not deny the issuance of a real estate license to, or suspend or revoke the real estate license of, the corporation, provided that any offending officer, director, or stockholder, who has done any of the foregoing acts individually and not on behalf of the corporation, has been completely disassociated from any affiliation or ownership in the corporation.

10177.1. The commissioner may, without a hearing, suspend the license of any person who procured the issuance of the license to himself by fraud, misrepresentation, deceit, or by the making of any material misstatement of fact in his application for such license.

The power of the commissioner under this section to order a suspension of a license shall expire 90 days after the date of issuance of said license and the suspension itself shall remain in effect only until the effective date of a decision of the commissioner after a hearing conducted pursuant to Section 10100 and the provisions of this section.

A statement of issues as defined in Section 11504 of the Government Code shall be filed and served upon the respondent with the order of suspension. Service by certified or registered mail directed to the respondent's current address of record on file with the commissioner shall be effective service.

The respondent shall have 30 days after service of the order of suspension and statement of issues in which to file with the commissioner a written request for hearing on the statement of issues filed against him. The commissioner shall hold a hearing within 30 days after receipt of the request therefore unless the respondent shall request or agree to a continuance thereof. If a hearing is not commenced within 30 days after receipt of the request for hearing or on the date to which continued with the agreement of respondent, or if the decision of the commissioner is not rendered within 30 days after completion of the hearing, the order of suspension shall be vacated and set aside.

A hearing conducted under this section shall in all respects, except as otherwise expressly provided herein, conform to the substantive and procedural provisions of Chapter 5 (commencing with Section 11500) of Part 1 of Division 3 of Title 2 of the Government Code applicable to a hearing on a statement of issues.

10177.2. The commissioner may, upon his or her own motion, and shall, upon the verified complaint in writing of any person, investigate the actions of any licensee, and he or she may suspend or revoke a real estate license at any time where the licensee in performing or attempting to perform any of the acts within the scope of Section 10131.6 has been guilty of any of the following acts:

(a) Has used a false or fictitious name, knowingly made any false statement, or knowingly concealed any material fact, in any application for the registration of a mobile home, or otherwise committed a fraud in that application.

(b) Failed to provide for the delivery of a properly endorsed certificate of ownership or certificate of title of a mobile home from the seller to the buyer thereof.

(c) Has knowingly participated in the purchase, sale, or other acquisition or disposal of a stolen mobile home.

(d) Has submitted a check, draft, or money order to the Department of Housing and Community Development for any obligation or fee due the state and it is thereafter dishonored or refused payment upon presentation.

10177.4. (a) Notwithstanding any other provision of law, the commissioner may, after hearing in accordance with this part relating to hearings, suspend or revoke the license of a real estate licensee who claims, demands, or receives a commission, fee, or other consideration, as compensation or inducement, for referral of customers to any escrow agent, structural pest control firm, home protection company, title insurer, controlled escrow company, or underwritten title company. A licensee may not be disciplined under any provision of this part for reporting to the commissioner violations of this section by another licensee, unless the licensee making the report had guilty knowledge of, or committed or participated in, the violation of this section.

(b) The term "other consideration" as used in this section does not include any of the following:

(1) Bona fide payments for goods or facilities actually furnished by a licensee or for services actually performed by a licensee, provided these payments are reasonably related to the value of the goods, facilities, or services furnished.

(2) Furnishing of documents, services, information, advertising, educational materials, or items of a like nature that are customary in the real estate business and that relate to the product or services of the furnisher and that are available on a similar and essentially equal basis to all customers or the agents of the customers of the furnisher.

(3) Moderate expenses for food, meals, beverages, and similar items furnished to individual licensees or groups or associations of licensees within a context of customary business, educational, or promotional practices pertaining to the business of the furnisher.

(4) Items of a character and magnitude similar to those in paragraphs (2) and (3) that are promotional of the furnisher's business customary in the real estate business, and available on a similar and essentially equal basis to all customers, or the agents of the customers, of the furnisher.

(c) Nothing in this section shall relieve any licensee of the obligation of disclosure otherwise required by this part.

10177.5. When a final judgment is obtained in a civil action against any real estate licensee upon grounds of fraud, misrepresentation, or deceit with reference to any transaction for which a license is required under this division, the commissioner may, after hearing in accordance with the provisions of this part relating to hearings, suspend or revoke the license of such real estate licensee.

10178. When any real estate salesman is discharged by his employer for a violation of any of the provisions of this article prescribing a ground for disciplinary action, a certified written statement of the facts with reference thereto shall be filed forthwith with the commissioner by the employer and if the employer fails to notify the commissioner as required by this section, the commissioner may temporarily suspend or permanently revoke the real estate license of the employer, in accordance with the provisions of this part relating to hearings.

10179. No violation of any of the provisions of this part relating to real estate or of Chapter 1 of Part 2 by any real estate salesman or employee of any licensed real estate broker shall cause the revocation or suspension of the license of the employer of the salesman or employee unless it appears upon a hearing by the commissioner that the employer had guilty knowledge of such violation.

10180. The commissioner may deny, suspend or revoke the real estate license of a corporation as to any officer or agent acting under its license without revoking the license of the corporation.

10182. As a condition to the reinstatement of a revoked or suspended license, the commissioner may require the applicant to take and pass a qualifying examination.

10185. Any person, including officers, directors, agents or employees of corporations, who willfully violates or knowingly participates in the violation of this division shall be guilty of a misdemeanor punishable by a fine not exceeding ten thousand dollars ($10,000), or by imprisonment in the county jail not exceeding six months, or by a fine and imprisonment.

TRADE AND PROFESSIONAL ORGANIZATIONS

Trade associations are voluntary, nonprofit organizations of independent and competing businesses participating in the same industry. These professional organizations have been formed to promote the industry, solve internal and external problems, and enhance the service provided by members. Examples of trade organizations in real estate are the California Association of REALTORS (CAR) and the National Association of REALTORS (NAR).

In contrast to trade associations are real estate boards. These boards (sometimes also called real estate associations, not to be confused with trade associations) are made up of members who share an interest in the real estate business. Generally speaking, if a real estate agent joins a local real estate board, he or she will also automatically become a member of CAR and NAR. Real estate boards serve a similar function to that of trade associations. They are intended to bring people together to encourage professional conduct and protect the public from irresponsible licensees.

NAR CODE OF ETHICS

Every real estate agent belonging to NAR or CAR is referred to as a REALTOR. Only those licensees belonging to these professional associations are referred to as such, any other licensee not belonging to one of these professional associations are not REALTORS. Every licensee must follow real estate law regardless of affiliation with a trade association while REALTORS must follow real estate law as well as the code of ethics found in NAR and CAR. CAR serves the same function as NAR, but is practiced at a state level while NAR is national.

The code of ethics focuses on three primary populations. It serves to protect clients, the public and REALTORS in that order. Even with real estate laws, and the code of ethics, the Department of Real Estate still deals with complaints. The most common complaints received deal with misrepresentation, mishandling of trust funds, agency and advertising. It is very important for you as a licensee to be very well versed in these topics to avoid any problems or misunderstandings with clients.

Misrepresentation

Misrepresentation is the act of making false statements or hiding material facts known to be true. There are three different types of misrepresentations: innocent misrepresentations, negligent misrepresentations and fraudulent misrepresentations.

Innocent misrepresentation is when an agent provides wrong information unknowingly. While no dishonesty is involved, the party who feels misled or who may have suffered damage due to the misrepresentation may still revoke the contract. The broker would not be held liable for any damages due to the hold harmless clause. This states that statements made that were unknown to be untrue carry no legal liability. The only action that may be taken would be the cancellation of the contract.

Negligent misrepresentations are statements made without facts to back them up. The agent is not aware that the statements are untrue at the time, but can be held liable for any damages. An agent making statement unknown to be true or not is puffing. Puffing is making statements with no factual information to back them up. Agents use puffing as a way to close a sale. If the agent convinces the client that the statements are true, and then discovered later that they are false, the client may hold the agent liable for the damages.

Fraudulent misrepresentations are false statements made by an agent known to be false. An agent may be held liable for damages caused by these statements.

Trust Funds

One of the job requirements you will face is collecting funds from clients for deposits or other purposes. This money is usually presented in the form of a check, to be used later in the transaction, during the disbursement process of escrow. The money you receive is called a trust fund, and real estate law is very specific on how this money should be treated. Those agents who do not perform the appropriate transaction may have their license suspended or revoked. Agents who mismanage these funds may be held financially responsible for any damages caused by such negligent actions. In certain conditions, criminal actions may be filed against the agent.

The first step in appropriately handing your client's money is identifying what is considered 'trust fund money'. Trust fund money is money collected by a real estate professional on behalf of their principal and used for a transaction in which a license is required. This kind of money is generally cash or a personal check that will be used as a deposit for the purchase of a home or a note made payable to the seller of property. Trust funds may also be items of value other than money. There is other money that an agent may collect from a principal such as commissions, which is not considered trust fund money. These funds do not belong to a third party. Thus, they are not considered trust funds. The money that does not belong to a broker (trust funds) has been given to the broker with the trust that it will be used for its intended purpose, that of purchasing property. This money MUST be accounted for separately. Accurate records are required for this money to show that all actions have been lawful, and that all accounting is up to date with the trust funds.

Once a broker or salesperson receives trust fund money from a principal, the transaction has begun. These trust funds must be placed into a trust fund account, separate from all other accounts under the broker's control. The broker or salesperson must place this money in the trust fund within three business days following the receipt of funds. An exception to the three-day rule is trust fund money received as a deposit for the offer to purchase property. This money may be held until the offer has been accepted, even if it is more than three days from receipt of the money. Once the offer has been accepted by the seller (or offeree), the check is held (and not deposited) only with written permission from the seller. Unless otherwise stated, the check must be deposited in a trust account within three days after the acceptance. Before the seller accepts the funds, the buyer (or offeror) is the rightful owner of the funds. However, as soon as the offer is accepted, the seller is the owner of these funds.

A broker's trust fund account must be set up as a trust account in the name of the broker, who is the trustee of the account. All broker's trust fund accounts must be set up in the state of California with a recognized depository or bank for all transactions. Any withdrawals from this account may only be made with a signature of one or more approved persons who have access to the account. Trust fund accounts are generally not interest-bearing accounts, where written notice must be given for withdrawals. However, they can be in certain circumstances.

Agency

The relationship between an agent and principal is called agency. An agency consists of three parties: the agent, the principal and a third party. The broker is the agent, the seller is the principal and the third party is the person with whom the principal and agent negotiate.

The agent has a responsibility to act in the best interest of the principal. The agent, while remaining fair and truthful with all third parties, gives fiduciary responsibility and loyalty to the principle. These basic responsibilities are defined in the laws of agency and bind the agent, principal and third party in a legal relationship.

A real estate agent under contract with a seller may establish agency with a buyer as well. This is referred to as dual agency. Dual agency may be created when the agent is an actual agent of both the buyer and seller, or the agent of the seller and ostensible or implied agent of the buyer. Legally an agent may be a dual agent, but must have the informed consent from both the buyer and the seller. It is important to remember, as an agent of both parties, you must not share information with one party that will harm the other party.

The most important thing to remember is that acting as a dual agent is legal. A dual agency becomes illegal when the agency is not disclosed, and written consent is not attained from all parties. A real estate licensee may have his or her license suspended or revoked for not complying with all disclosure laws.

Real Estate Advertising
Real estate advertising is governed by Section 804 of the Federal Fair Housing Law, which prohibits advertising from discriminating against race, color, religion, sex, handicap, familial status, or national origin. Advertising with key phrases or words which may discourage a specific group from moving into the area, or viewing the property for sale, is strictly prohibited.

All residential real estate advertisements must contain the equal opportunity logo and slogan, large enough to be read, and clearly understood. The logo features a photo of people of multiple ethnicities. When it is unclear that each of the people are of different descent, the logo is considered too small.

Advertisers of real estate need to be very careful about the images, models, photographs or drawings they use in advertisements. If the images seem exclusive, members of certain groups may feel excluded from that property or neighborhood. Images must clearly define a reasonable cross-section of all majority and minority groups, in equal social situations, using both sexes and showing families with children. The advertisements should indicate to every person that the open property is inviting to all interested buyers, and does not exclude any person based on sex, age, color, national origin, religion, race, handicap or familial status.

Word usage should not imply a preference or limitation to any group of people, based on any demographic. Catch phrases or words to be avoided are:

- Adult building
- No children
- Asian area
- Near mosque
- Ideal for physically fit
- Prefer smart, healthy person
- Restrictive
- Lutheran Church nearby
- Russian businesses in area
- Male or Female only
- Single people only
- Racially-integrated neighborhood

Words or phrases, which are acceptable, include:
- Gated
- Parks nearby
- Houses of worship nearby
- Quiet, residential area
- Close to schools

One of the most important aspects of real estate is the concept of full disclosure. What used to be a relatively easy process has turned into a complex, drawn-out one. A disclosure is a statement revealing some fact regarding the real estate transaction. It could turn out that the plumbing has a leak in the guest bathroom, and that the owner is aware of it; however, the owner does not plan to make any repairs. A disclosure could also be made to a financing company, regarding the buyer and seller agreement to do a wrap around loan. Agents must disclose to clients if they have a personal interest in the property, such as if they are the buyer or seller. What is important is that the agent guides the client through all the necessary disclosures, receives all the necessary signed statements to show that the disclosure has been made, and ensured all statements made are true. If all of this is taken care of, there will be no problems. Any disclosures that go unattended may result in the loss of the sale, penalties or even criminal prosecution against the parties withholding information.

The following pages will go over all the necessary disclosures that must be made in a real estate transaction. Some have been covered in previous chapters, but this list will give you a more thorough look at these disclosures that you must cover.

Real Estate Transfer Disclosure Statement
There are many physical features or issues of a property, which a seller must disclose to a buyer. If there are too many defects in a property, a buyer may not be interested in the property, but should be made aware of these problems before making an offer. Not making these disclosures is against real estate law, as the buyer has the right to rescind out of the offer with no penalty. Any seller of a one-to-four unit home or dwelling must deliver a disclosure to potential buyers regarding the property's structure and condition. This requirement is extended to the transfer of property by sale, exchange, installment land sale contract, lease with an option to purchase, and other option to purchase, or ground lease coupled with improvements. There may be Local Opinion Transfer Disclosure Statements required or provided for neighborhoods, city or counties that would disclose special local facts regarding the property. The following are required facts that must be disclosed to a buyer of property by the seller or the seller's agent:

- The age, condition or any defects, malfunctions or problems with the structural component of the home. This includes plumbing, electrical, heating and other mechanical components or systems of the home.

- Easements, common drives, walks or fences shared with neighbors.

- Additional rooms added to the property after it was originally built, and whether or not these rooms have the necessary building permits for construction.

- Flooding drainage or soil problems on, near or in any way affecting the property.

- Major damage to the structure or property caused from fire, earthquake or landslide.

- Whether or not the property is located within a known earthquake fault line or zone.

- Citations against the property, lawsuits against the owner affecting the transferability of the property, or other legal issues with the current owners and property.

- Homeowner's association dues and deed restrictions or common area problems, which may result in a special assessment.
- Zoning violations, such as nonconforming uses or insufficient setbacks.

Certain groups are exempt from the requirement to provide a Transfer Disclosure Statement.

- When property is transferred from one co-owner to another
- Sale by the state controller for unclaimed property
- The first sale of a residential property within a subdivision, where a copy of a public report is delivered to the buyer or where such a report is not required.
- In a foreclosure sale
- Selling to or buying from any government entity
- A court-ordered transfer by a fiduciary in the administration of a probate estate or a testamentary trust.
- Selling property to a spouse or to another related person, resulting from a judgment of dissolution of a marriage, or a legal separation, or in a property settlement agreement.
- Sale of property due to failure to pay taxes.

If a buyer does not receive the necessary disclosure document on a property in the allotted time, he or she may terminate the offer to purchase the property. The intention to terminate must be made either 3 days in person or 5 days after a deposit has been given to United States Postal Services. A written notice of termination must reach the seller or the seller's agent. The time the Transfer Disclosure Statement must be delivered varies depending on the type of transfer. If the transfer is a regular sale, then the Transfer Disclosure Statement must be delivered before the transfer of title. If the transaction was a lease option or a ground lease with improvements, the Transfer Disclosure Statement must be delivered before execution of the contract.

The seller, the seller's agent or any agent working in cooperation with the seller's agent is responsible for preparing the Transfer Disclosure Statement. This same person is in charge of delivering the disclosure to the buyer. In the event that there are multiple agents working with the seller, the agent who obtained the offer will be responsible for creating and delivering the Transfer Disclosure Statement.

Inspections may limit the liability of the seller and his or her agents. Inspections such as a land survey, pest inspection, roof inspection, plumbing inspection, geologic inspection or general contractor's opinion of the structure will give the buyer a better idea of the condition of the property. The seller's liability is limited, because any problems with the structure will be discovered in these inspections, and the buyer will not run into any surprises with the property. If there has been a violation of the law regarding the structure, it will not invalidate the property transfer. However, the seller will most likely be held responsible for fixing the problem, or may be held liable for any damages suffered by the buyer.

Transfer Disclosure Statement!
- Disclosed facts and information regarding the physical structure of the property, which is important to the potential buyer.
- Statement must be prepared and delivered by the seller, seller's agent or any agent working for the seller's agent.
- Buyers have the right to terminate any offer made if a Transfer Disclosure Statement is not received in the allotted amount of time after an offer is made.
- There are certain exemptions for which this statement does not have to be prepared.

Mello-Roos Disclosure

The Mello-Roos Community Facilities Act of 1982 authorizes communities to form facilities districts, issue bonds and levy special taxes, which finance public facilities or other services for the benefit of the public. As of July 1, 1993, the seller of a property consisting of one-to-four units, subject to the lien of a Mello-Roos community facilities district, must make a good faith effort to obtain from the district a disclosure notice concerning the special tax or levy and give the notice to a prospective buyer. Prospective buyers must be made aware of any special tax or levy that might be applied to their property so that they are aware of any additional taxes for which they might be responsible, beyond real estate taxes. Exemptions from this disclosure are listed in the Transfer Disclosure Statement.

Disclosure Regarding Lead-Based Paint Hazards

Homes that were built before 1978 fall under this disclosure. The Residential Lead-Based Paint Hazard Reduction Act of 1992, which became effective in 1996, requires owners of property with four or fewer units to offer the lead-based paint and lead-based paint hazard disclosures in a property transfer. The seller, landlord and real estate agent involved in the transfer have certain requirements under the new law. All agents must comply with the law, even if the landlord or seller fails to do so. Agents are not responsible for any information an owner or landlord conceals. The specified group must make the following list of requirements:

Seller and Landlord Responsibilities:

- Include standard warning language as an attachment to the contract or lease.
- Give the buyers or tenants a pamphlet called "Protect Your Family From Lead in Your Home"
- For sale transactions only, sellers must give buyers a 10-day opportunity to test the home for lead.
- Disclose all known lead-based and lead-based paint hazards in the dwelling and provide the buyer or tenant with any available reports.
- Retain the signed acknowledgment for three years.
- Complete and sign statements verifying completion of requirements.

An agent must ensure that:

- Sellers and landlords are aware of their responsibilities

- Leases and sales contracts include the proper disclosure language and appropriate signatures.

- Seller and landlords disclose property information to buyers and tenants.

- Sellers give buyers the opportunity to conduct an inspection for 10 days or another mutually agreed-upon time period.

Smoke Detector Statement of Compliance

California state law requires that each living structure have a smoke detector installed in a centrally-located spot outside of the bedrooms. For two story homes with bedrooms on both floors, there are two smoke detectors required. When a property is sold, the seller must provide the buyer with a written statement, which states that the property is in compliance with this law.

New construction, whether of a completely new home or an addition onto an existing home, and improvements or remodels valued at over $1,000 have different rules. In these situations, there must be one smoke detector in each bedroom, as well as a smoke detector in a central location outside of the bedrooms. New construction requires that these smoke detectors be hardwired into the home itself, with a battery backup. In existing structures, a battery-operated smoke detector is required.

Disclosure Regarding State Responsibility Areas

State Responsibility Areas describe property that is located in a rural portion of the state, not protected at the city or federal level for fire. In these areas, if there is a large-scale wildfire, the state will be in charge of extinguishing the blaze. Whether it is a state crew fighting the fires, or just state-funded firefighters, all responsibility lies with the state. Maps of these State Responsibility Areas are generated every five years, as the boundaries often change with the influx of people into or out of an area. If a seller knows that his or her property is in this State Responsibility Zone, he or she is required to disclose this information, along with the possibility of substantial fire risk at the property. In addition to these disclosures, the seller must disclose to the buyer that the land is subject to certain preventative measures.

To further blur the line of responsibility, with either the department's consent or by ordinance, a county may assume all responsibility for fires in state responsibility areas. In this situation, the seller must disclose to the buyer that the state is no longer responsible for fires in the area, but that the county, city or other district will be providing all fire protection.

Delivery of Structural Pest Control Inspection and Certification Reports

California does not require a structural pest control inspection in the transfer of real property. Financing firms or buyers, on the other hand, might require that a pest control inspection be completed before a loan can be financed, or as a condition to purchase the home. If a pest inspection is required, it must be made as soon as possible after learning that it is required. Before the title is transferred or before execution of the sales contract, the buyer must receive a copy of the pest report. The person conducting the report must also state in writing whether or not wood-destroying termites were visible. A licensed or registered structural pest-control company must prepare this report and written statement.

The pest inspection must be divided into two portions. The first portion will outline any existing damage or infestation, while the second portion of the report will outline the probability of other damage or infestation unseen by the inspector. The real estate agent who obtained the offer on the property is also responsible for obtaining the report and delivering it to the buyer. This occurs unless the seller has given written directions regarding the delivery of the report to another agent (such as the buyer's agent). The report may be delivered to the buyer in person or by mail, and the agent who obtains the report must keep it in his or her files for three years.

Disclosure of Geological Hazards and Special Studies Zones
The earth is a dynamic medium on which we live. Each day, there are geological changes to the surface of the earth, as well as changes happening within its core. Some of these geological changes require disclosures, while others do not. These geological changes that require disclosures are those that pose a potential, major hazard from phenomena, such as earthquakes, flooding, landslides, erosion and expansive soils. One specific condition requiring a disclosure is fault creep, or stress to the land caused by the shaking of an earthquake. Soil plays a major factor in fault creep. Softer soils or sediments, which are looser, tend to magnify an earthquake. Harder sediment, such as rock, will mask an earthquake. It is important for a new homebuyer to understand the type of soil their home sits on and the possible repercussions of this soil type during an earthquake. Also, proximity to the fault line will also play a big part in what happens during an earthquake. The closer a property is to the fault line, the more severe an earthquake will be to the property. Again, this is something that must be disclosed to a homebuyer.

The State Division of Mines and Geology offers maps that show areas of the state more susceptible to fault creep. These maps may also show areas that have had landslides in the past and possibly forecast future landslides. For disclosure purposes, sellers and the agents working with them usually rely on maps offered by the state Division of Mines and Geology as the basis for the necessity of disclosure. For new construction, however, most structures designed for inhabitation are subject to the findings and recommendations of a geologic report. A geologist or soils engineer registered in, or licensed by, the state of California prepares this report.

Under the Alquist-Priolo Special Studies Zones Act, a seller who sells real estate, the seller's real estate agent, or any other cooperating agents must disclose the fact that a home sits in a special studies zone. This disclosure must be made on the Transfer Disclosure Statement, the Local Option Real Estate Transfer Disclosure Statement, or in the purchase agreement.

There are certain situations in which property is excluded from the requirements of the special studies zone. These circumstances are:

- Alterations worth under 50% of the total value of the structure

- Structures in existence prior to May 4, 1975

- Single-family, wood-frame or steel structures not over two stories high, provided the dwelling is not part of a development consisting of four or more dwellings.

- Single-family, wood-frame or steel-frame structures, for which geologic reports have been approved, to be built in subdivisions authorized by the Subdivision Map Act.

- Conversions of existing apartments into condominiums. It must be disclosed that the property is located within a delineated special-studies zone.

An additional piece of literature for potential buyers is the Homeowner's Guide to Earthquake Safety, distributed by the Seismic Safety Commission. This is not so much a disclosure as a public brochure to encourage awareness of geologic and seismic hazards throughout the entire state of California. It outlines the related structural and nonstructural hazards, as well as recommendations for mitigating the hazards of an earthquake. The guide states that safety and damage prevention cannot be guaranteed with respect to major earthquakes; only precautions (such as retrofitting) can be undertaken to reduce the risk of damage. If a buyer of real property receives a copy of the Homeowner's guide, the seller is not required to provide any additional information regarding geologic and seismic hazards. Sellers and real estate agents must, however, disclose that the property is in a special studies zone and that there are known hazards in the area.

The delivery of the Homeowner's Guide to Earthquake Safety is required in transactions where there is a transfer of real property, those involving a residential dwelling built before January 1, 1960, and those consisting of one-to-four units (any of which are conventional, light-frame construction). It is also required in real estate transfers of any masonry building with wood-frame floors or roofs built before January 1, 1975. Exemptions to these rules apply to the same of those of the Real Estate Transfer Disclosure Statement.

The bottom line is that full disclosure is required for all material facts regarding a special studies zone, local ordinances or known structural deficiencies affecting the property. Buyers or agents may be responsible for further inquires of appropriate governmental agencies. The obligation of the buyer or the buyer's agent to make additional inquiries does not eliminate the duty of the seller's agent to make a diligent inquiry to identify the location of the real property in relationship to a defined special studies zone.

Natural Hazard Disclosure Statement
California passed the Natural Hazard Disclosure Law in 1998, which served to simplify and standardize the natural hazard disclosure requirements. As we can see from the previous disclosure requirement, there are times when disclosure is required, and times when it is not. Now, with this law, the state requires all sellers, as well as the seller's agents, to determine and disclose to prospective purchasers, whether a lot is in certain, officially-mapped natural hazard zones. It is the seller's and their agent's responsibility to do the research on this and make any necessary disclosure to the buyer.

The new law requires six disclosures in addition to informing the buyer of any other hazards of which he or she are aware. The six disclosures required by this law are: whether the property is located in a seismic hazard zone; flood hazard are, earthquake fault zone; a state responsibility fire area; if the property is in a flood zone due to the possibility of dam failure; or, a high fire hazard severity zone. These disclosures must be made before the transfer of title, unless the purchase contract specifies that they be made earlier. If the buyer does not approve of the location of the property (due to its geographic location in a hazard zone), the buyer may rescind the offer within three days of a hand-delivered disclosure statement, or within five days of receiving the disclosure statement in the mail.

Natural Hazard Disclosure Statement requires six disclosures to be made.

- Seismic hazard zone
- Flood hazard area
- Earthquake fault zone
- State responsibility fire area
- Flood zone, due to the possibility of dam failure
- Extreme fire hazard severity zone

Secured Water Heater Law

One of the largest hazards in an earthquake is the damage to mechanical components or utilities that use electricity or gas. By damaging these lines or wires, fire is possible, which can create an even worse situation. Local requirements dictate how water heaters should be attached, strapped or anchored to the ground, so that they do not tip over in the event of an earthquake. Besides a possible fire hazard from damage to the water heater, there is the possibility of water damage to the area around the water heater. A suggested disclosure form can be found in the Homeowner's Guide to Earthquake Safety.

Disclosure of Ordnance Location

Military bases or training facilities were once scattered throughout the state, where live ammunition may still be buried. State law requires sellers of property located within one mile of these training sites to disclose to buyers that this hazard exists. The disclosure must be made to the buyer before the transfer of title. Disclosure is required only if the current seller is aware of the hazard. If the seller is not aware of the ordnance, or military supplies, the disclosure is not required.

Environmental Hazard Disclosure

Sellers of property who are aware of chemical or environmental hazards are responsible to disclose this fact to a prospective buyer, under the California Real Estate Transfer Disclosure Statement. It also requires sellers to disclose the presence of asbestos, formaldehyde, radon gas, lead-based paint, fuel or chemical storage tanks, contaminated soil, water, mold or any other hazardous substances. A landlord or owner of nonresidential property must also disclose any of these hazards to tenants or a person who leases space in the building. Sellers and property owners who do not give proper disclosures will be held liable (perhaps in the form of civil penalties) for any damages caused by these hazards.

Proposition 65 states that certain businesses may not knowingly and intentionally expose any individual to a cancer-causing agent, chemical or reproductive toxin without first giving clear warning to any person present in or using the space. You will recall warning signs at filling station regarding one or more chemicals present in gas or at the filling station that may cause cancer. These signs are required to be posted by law, giving consumers proper warning to proceed at their own risk. Recent laws have also included asbestos disclosure requirements for owners of commercial buildings built before 1979.

In addition to posted signs in commercial spaces, the Department of Real Estate, in conjunction with the Office of Environmental Health Hazard Assessment, has developed a booklet to help educate and inform consumers about environmental hazards that may affect real property. The booklet explains common environmental hazards and describes the risks involved with each of the hazards. The hazards discussed in the booklet cover asbestos, radon gas, lead and formaldehyde. If a buyer has been given this booklet, the seller and the seller's agents are not required to provide any further information on such hazards. If the seller is aware that one or more of these hazardous agents are present at the time of sale, this must be disclosed.

Energy Conservation Retrofit and Thermal Insulation Disclosure

Energy conservation is a present concern for the growing population of California, due to its limited resources. State law requires a minimum energy conservation standard for all new construction. If these minimum standards are not met, a building may not receive the building permit needed to go forward with construction. Besides the state standard, local standards are imposed for further energy conservation measures on new and existing homes. By retrofitting homes before selling them, these conservation goals can be met. A seller of property must disclose to buyers the existence of state and local requirements of energy conservation. In addition to this disclosure, federal law requires sellers of new homes to disclose the type, thickness and R-value of the insulation, which has been, or will be used in each part of the house.

Special Flood Hazard Area Disclosure and Responsibilities of the Federal Emergency Management Agency (FEMA)

The Federal Emergency Management Agency (FEMA) creates flood hazard boundary maps, which identify general flood hazard zones in a community. These maps show areas of minimal risk, or areas that face risk of flooding every 500 years. There are also areas of moderate flood hazard, which has a possibility of flooding every 100 – 500 years. Special flood zones are labeled for those areas, which have the possibility of flooding every 100 years. This flood information is very useful for insurance companies when determining where more probable flood zones are located.

A seller of property within a special flood zone (or a flood hazard zone) must disclose this information to the buyer, because federal law requires the buyer to obtain flood insurance in order to secure financing for a property. The cost of flood insurance will vary, depending on the flood zone in which the property is located. So, it is important for the buyer to contact the insurance company, to determine what kind of policy is necessary for financing.

Local Requirements Resulting from City and County Ordinances

Each city, county or community has their own ordinances for land use, zoning requirements, building codes, fire, health and other safety codes and regulations. These ordinances or requirements on how to remain in compliance with the laws, as well as whom these laws will affect, must be disclosed by the seller and the seller's agents to any prospective buyer of the property. Buyers may be deterred from purchasing property if its use is restricted. This is imperative for the buyer to know before the transaction is complete.

Foreign Investment in Real Property Tax

Under federal law, if a buyer purchases property from a foreign seller, the buyer must withhold and send the Internal Revenue Service (IRS) 10% of the gross sales price. As with most other disclosures, there are exemptions to this rule, as well. To be sure you are following the law correctly, it is advisable to contact the IRS and consult them regarding the transaction. Further assistance may be sought from a CPA, attorney or tax advisor.

The following exemptions are given for people investing in property sold by foreign sellers:

- Seller's non-foreign affidavit and U.S. taxpayer I.D. number

- A qualifying statement obtained through the IRS, stating that arrangements have been made for the collection of, or exemption from, the tax.

- Sales price does not exceed $300,000.

- Buyer intends to reside on the property as his or her main residence.

Notice Regarding the Advisability of Title Insurance

In the event there is no title insurance being issued in an escrow, the buyer is required to sign the following notice as a separate document to the escrow:

Important: In a purchase or exchange of real property, it may be advisable to obtain title insurance, in connection with the close of escrow, where there may be prior recorded liens and encumbrances which affect your interest in the property being acquired. A new policy of title insurance should be obtained, in order to insure your interest in the property that you are acquiring.

The escrow holder is usually the person who will deliver this statement to the buyer, though there is no person specifically called out to do so by law. If the real estate agent is the escrow holder, the agent will be responsible for this notice.

Furnishing Controlling Documents and a Financial Statement

Any person selling a common interest development property (condominium, community apartment project, planned development or stock cooperative) must provide all prospective buyers with the following, required disclosures:

- Information on any approved change in the assessments or fees not yet due and payable as of the disclosure date (or a future date)

- A copy of the governing documents of the development such as homeowner's association rules and guidelines

- A copy of the homeowner's association's most recent financial statement

- If there is an age restriction that is not allowable by law, there must be a statement that the age restriction is only enforceable to the extent permitted by law; as well as applicable provisions of the law. This is restrictions outside of the age exemption made for seniors

- A written statement from the association specifying the amount of current regular and special assessments, as well as any unpaid assessment, late charges, interest and costs of collection which are, or may become, a lien against the property

Notice and Disclosure to Buyer of State Tax Withholding on Disposition of California Real Property

In some transactions, the State Franchise Tax Board requires the buyer to withhold 3 1/2% of the total sales price as state income tax. The escrow holder is required to notify the buyer of this responsibility. Any buyer who does not withhold this amount may be assessed a penalty; any escrow holder not informing the buyer of this obligation will see penalties assessed against the escrow holder. The following transactions are subject to this law:

- The seller shows an out-of-state address, or sales proceeds are to be disbursed to the seller's financial intermediary.

- The seller does not certify that he or she is a California resident, or that the property being conveyed is his or her personal residence.

- The sale price exceeds $100,000

COMPLAINTS AND DISPUTES

Avoiding disputes and complaints by acting very ethically and meticulously when dealing with a client is the best business practice. Unfortunately, problems can and do arise. The best way to handle disputes is to be very patient with your client and listen to their concerns. Once you have heard them out, talk about the problem and try to arrive at an agreed-upon solution.

If discussing the problem does not resolve the dispute, the local board or association can help. They have procedures in place to help resolve disputes. These local associations usually do arbitration to resolve money issues between REALTORS. An ethics complaint usually implies that a REALTOR has violated one or more Articles of the Code of Ethics.

Any arbitration request or ethics complaint is submitted to the Grievance Committee of the local board or association. This committee will be the first to review the complaint. If this complaint meets all standards it is then forwarded on to the Professional Standards Committee for a hearing. The Professional Standards Committee is the final decision-making committee.

The local board or association does not have any jurisdiction over California Real Estate law or other law. Legal matters of this caliber are handled by the Department of Real Estate. Additionally the local board or association cannot suspend or revoke a licensee's license. The local board or association only has jurisdiction over violations of member's duties and the Code of Ethics.

The local board or association can discipline a REALTOR in an ethical complaint by issuing a letter of warning or reprimand, require attendance at an ethics refresher course or other training class, fine not to exceed $5,000, place the member on probation or suspend his or her membership in the association and/or expel the member. If a local board or association is in an arbitration over a monetary issue, the amount awarded cannot exceed the amount of money in dispute.

CODE OF ETHICS

**Code of Ethics and Standards of Practice
of the NATIONAL ASSOCIATION OF REALTORS®**

To view the National Association of Realtor's Code of Ethics, please visit the National Association of Realtor's home page at www.realtor.org.

It is illegal to discriminate against persons renting, buying or leasing property. Any licensee found giving preferential treatment or discriminating against a person based on race, sex, color, religion, physical disability, marital status, national origin, ancestry, age or familial status can be prosecuted for breaking the law. Fair housing laws are very clear and specific, it is in your best interest as a licensee to fully understand these laws so you are operating within the full letter of the law at all times.

Real Estate Commissioner's Suggestions for Professional Conduct:

(a) Suggestions for Professional Conduct in Sale, Lease, and Exchange Transactions. In order to maintain a high level of ethics and professionalism in their business practices, real estate licensees are encouraged to adhere to the following suggestions in conducting their business activities:

(1) Aspire to give a high level of competent, ethical and quality service to buyers and sellers in real estate transactions.

(2) Stay in close communication with clients or customers to ensure that questions are promptly answered and all significant events or problems in a transaction are conveyed in a timely manner.

(3) Cooperate with the California Department of Real Estate's enforcement of, and report to that Department evident violations of, the Real Estate Law.

(4) Use care in the preparation of any advertisement to present an accurate picture or message to the reader, viewer, or listener.

(5) Submit all written offers in a prompt and timely manner.

(6) Keep oneself informed and current on factors affecting the real estate market in which the licensee operates as an agent.

(7) Make a full, open, and sincere effort to cooperate with other licensees, unless the principal has instructed the licensee to the contrary.

(8) Attempt to settle disputes with other licensees through mediation or arbitration.

(9) Advertise or claim to be an expert in an area of specialization in real estate brokerage activity, e.g., appraisal, property management, mortgage loan, etc., only if the licensee has had special training, preparation, or experience in such areas.

(10) Strive to provide equal opportunity for quality housing and a high level of service to all persons regardless of race, color, sex, religion, ancestry, physical handicap, marital status, or national origin.

(11) Base opinions of value, whether for the purpose of advertising or promoting real estate brokerage business, upon documented objective data.

(12) Make every attempt to comply with these Suggestions for Professional Conduct and the Code of Ethics of any organized real estate industry group of which the licensee is a member.

(b) Suggestions for Professional Conduct When Negotiating or Arranging Loans Secured by Real Property or Sale of a Promissory Note Secured by Real Property. In order to maintain a high level of ethics and professionalism in their business practices when performing acts within the meaning of subdivision (d) and (e) of Section 10131 and Sections 10131.1 and 10131.2 of the Business and Professions Code, real estate licensees are encouraged to adhere to the following suggestions, in addition to any applicable provisions of subdivision (a), in conducting their business activities:

(1) Aspire to give a high level of competent, ethical and quality service to borrowers and lenders in loan transactions secured by real estate.

(2) Stay in close communication with borrowers and lenders to ensure that reasonable questions are promptly answered and all significant events or problems in a loan transaction are conveyed in a timely manner.

(3) Keep oneself informed and current on factors affecting the real estate loan market in which the licensee acts as an agent.

(4) Advertise or claim to be an expert in an area of specialization in real estate mortgage loan transactions only if the licensee has had special training, preparation, or experience in such area.

(5) Strive to provide equal opportunity for quality mortgage loan services and a high level of service to all borrowers or lenders regardless of race, color, sex, religion, ancestry, physical handicap, marital status, or national origin.

(6) Base opinions of value in a loan transaction, whether for the purpose of advertising or promoting real estate mortgage loan brokerage business, on documented objective data.

(7) Respond to reasonable inquiries of a principal as to the status or extent of efforts to negotiate the sale of an existing loan.

(8) Respond to reasonable inquiries of a borrower regarding the net proceeds available from a loan arranged by the licensee.

(9) Make every attempt to comply with the standards of professional conduct and the code of ethics of any organized mortgage loan industry group of which the licensee is a member.

FEDERAL LAWS

There have been a series of Federal laws passed in since the Civil War intended on protecting all people. While these laws had good intentions, they did not seem to be enough to protect all people equally. Since then, numerous Civil Rights Acts have been passed, making it illegal to discriminate against any one person based on certain criteria or circumstances.

Civil Rights Acts of 1866 and 1870
The first of these laws was the Civil Rights Act of 1866, granting people of any color to make, enter into and enforce contracts. A segment of the Act that best describes it is "…all persons within the jurisdiction of the United States have the same right in every

State and Territory to make and enforce contracts...and to the full and equal benefit of laws and proceedings for the security of persons and property as is enjoyed by white citizens..."

The Civil Rights Act of 1870 granted individuals of all color the right to buy, sell or inherit property. It reads "All citizens of the United States shall have the same right, in every State and Territory, as is enjoyed by white citizens thereof to inherit, purchase, lease, sell, hold, and convey real and personal property."

Federal Fair Housing Act

Almost 100 years later, it became clear that the Civil Rights Acts in law were not enough to prevent discrimination prompting the Federal Fair Housing Act in 1968. This Act states "...it shall be unlawful to refuse to sell or rent after the making of a bona fide offer, or to refuse to negotiate for the sale or rental of, or otherwise make unavailable or deny, a dwelling to any person based of race, color, religion, sex, familial status, or national origin." This act also made it illegal for realtors to suggest to a client a neighborhood he or she thinks the person should live based on discrimination. This practice is called steering.

Brokers now had to not only be very careful with what they told potential clients, and their actions toward these people, but they also had to take into consideration the type of advertising they put out for property. To exclude a person based on race, color, religion, sex, familial status or national origin or make an advertisement look less favorable based on any of these criteria is illegal.

Again in 1988 the Federal Fair Housing Act was updated to protect against discrimination against people based on familial status, or if a person or couple had children, and handicapped persons.

The Federal Fair Housing Act was not only enforced on licensees, but also on those lenders making loans. Should a person find a property they wish to purchase, draw up a valid purchase agreement the law also protects them against discrimination based on race, color, religion, sex, familial status, national origin and handicapped status during the financing portion of the process.

There are exemptions to the Federal Fair Housing Act. Religious organizations, the non-profit sectors of the religious organization and private clubs are exempt from the Federal Fair Housing Act. Religious groups are allowed to sell or rent dwellings which they own or operate to persons of the same religion, or to give preference to persons of the same religion, providing that membership in the religion is not restricted based on race, color, religion, sex, handicap, familial status or national origin. Private clubs may limit membership or enrollment and give preference to its members as long as they too are not violating restrictions based on all the afore mentioned criteria.

Special communities may also be exempt from the Federal Fair Housing Act when providing housing to senior citizens. A community, or housing complex intended for seniors will be able to lawfully keep out families with children. As long as a percentage of the residents are over a target age, this type of restriction is allowed.

Any person feeling as if a licensee or financial institution has discriminated them against may report a complaint to the Department of Housing and Urban Development (HUD). Should HUD determine illegal action has taken place, they may initiate judicial action against the violator. Damages awarded in the case of discrimination may be as high as $50,000 in a first offense, and up to $100,000 for any subsequent offense.

Americans with Disabilities Act (ADA)
The ADA applies to equal access to employment, public services, public accommodations, public transportation and telecommunications.

The Unruh Civil Rights Act
The Unruh Act prohibits discrimination in business. Under the Unruh law, it is illegal for anyone to deny services to any person based on age, sex, race, ancestry, religion or national origin. This applies to real estate brokerage as well, as it is considered a service. Steering, redlining or block busting are all considered discriminatory actions on the part of real estate professionals. Steering is when a realtor only shows clients properties in certain areas, and not in others. Redlining is the act of using a property's location to ensure a client is denied financing. Block busting is a tactic used to create sales by other neighbors by telling them that an undesirable group of people are interested in other homes in the area. This causes property values to slide in that area. All of these actions are strictly prohibited.

The California Fair Employment and Housing Act (formerly called the Rumford Act)
The California Fair Employment and Housing Act prohibits discrimination in the sale or rental of property. This law also covers discrimination in financing homes. Discrimination in sale, rental or financing based on race, color, marital status, ancestry, religion, sex or national origin is strictly prohibited, and any grievances must be reported directly to the state Department of Fair Employment and Housing.

Housing Financial Discrimination Act (or the Holden Act)
The Housing Financial Discrimination Act prohibits lenders from discriminating against a loan applicant based on the location, neighborhood or other characteristic of the property to be financed. Redlining applies here, as it prohibits a lender from denying a loan based on the aforementioned factors. The exception is if it is proven that the loan is a risky one that the bank or lender would refuse anyway. Any violations based on the Housing Financial Discrimination Act should be reported directly to the state's Secretary for Business and Transportation.

THE CALIFORNIA BUSINESS AND PROFESSIONS CODE

Section 125.6: Disciplinary Provisions for Discriminatory Acts
Under Section 125.6, every person who holds a license under the provisions of the code is subject to disciplinary action if he or she refuses to perform the licensed activity or makes any discrimination or restriction in the performance of the licensed activity because of an applicant's race, color, sex, religion, ancestry, physical handicap, or national origin.

Section 10177(l): Further Grounds for Disciplinary Action
Discrimination occurs if a licensee "solicited or induced the sale, lease, or the listing for sale or lease, of residential property on the ground, wholly or in part, of loss of value, increase in crime, or decline of the quality of the schools, due to the presence or prospective entry into the neighborhood of a person or persons of another race, color, religion, ancestry, or national origin."

Section 2780: Discriminatory Conduct
Prohibited discriminatory conduct by real estate licensees based on race, color, sex, religion, physical handicap or national origin. This includes:

a. refusing to negotiate for the sale, rental or financing;

b. refusing or failing to show, rent, sell, or finance;

c. discriminating against any person in the sale or purchase, collection of payments, performance of services;

d. discriminating in the conditions or privileges/of sale rental or financing;

e. discriminating in processing applications or referrals, or assigning licenses;

f. representing real property as not available for inspection;

g. processing an application more slowly;

h. making any effort to encourage discrimination;

i. refusing to assist another licensee;

j. making an effort to obstruct, retard, or discourage a purchase;

k. expressing or implying a limitation, preference, or discrimination;

l. coercing, intimidating, threatening, or interfering;

m. soliciting restrictively;

n. maintaining restrictive waiting lists;

o. seeking to discourage or prevent transactions;

p. representing alleged community opposition;

q. representing desirability of particular properties;

r. refusing to accept listings;

s. agreeing not to show property;

t. advertising in a manner that indicates discrimination;

u. using wording that indicates preferential treatment;

v. advertising selectively;

w. maintaining selective pricing, rent, cleaning, or security deposits;

x. financing in a discriminatory manner;

y. discriminating in pricing;

z. discriminating in services;

aa. discriminating against owners, occupants, or guests, or making an effort to
     encourage discrimination;

ab. implementing discriminatory rules in multiple listings and other services; and

ac. assisting one who intends to discriminate

Section 2781: Panic Selling
Section 2781 prohibits discriminatory conduct that creates fear or alarm to induce sale
or lease because of the entry into an area of persons of another race, color, sex, religion, ancestry, or national origin.

Section 2782: Duty to Supervise
A broker shall take reasonable steps to be familiar with, and to familiarize his or her
salespersons with, the federal and state laws pertaining to prohibition of discriminatory
process.

TRUST FUNDS

One of the job requirements you will face is collecting funds from clients for deposits or
other purposes. This money is usually presented in the form of a check, to be used
later in the transaction, during the disbursement process of escrow. The money you
receive is called a trust fund, and real estate law is very specific on how this money
should be treated. It is imperative that you be well-versed with the laws regarding how
to handle these funds, as a fiduciary duty has been formed between you and the rightful owner of the money (your client). Those agents who do not perform the appropriate
transactions may have their license suspended or revoked. Agents who mismanage
these funds may be held financially responsible for any damages caused by such negligent actions. In certain conditions, criminal actions may be filed against the agent.

The first step in appropriately handing your client's money is identifying what is considered "trust fund money." Trust fund money is money collected by a real estate professional on behalf of their principal and used for a transaction in which a license is
required. This kind of money is generally cash or a personal check that will be used as
a deposit for the purchase of a home, or a note made payable to the seller of property.
Trust funds may also be items of value other than money. There is other money that
an agent may collect from a principal such as commissions, which are not considered
trust fund money, because they do not belong to a third party. The money that does not
belong to a broker (trust funds) has been given to the broker with the trust that it will be
used for its intended purpose, that of purchasing property. This money MUST be
accounted for separately. Accurate records are required for this money, to show that all
actions have been lawful, and that all trust fun accounting is up-to-date.

Once a broker or salesperson receives trust fund money from a principal, the transaction has begun. These trust funds must be placed into the escrow depository, or into a
trust fund account that is separate from all other accounts under the broker's control.
This money must be placed in the trust fund within three business days following the
receipt of funds by the broker or salesperson. An exception to the three-day rule is
trust fund money received as a deposit for the offer to purchase property. This money
may be held until the offer has been accepted, even if it is more than three days from
receipt of the money.

Once the offer has been accepted by the seller (or offeree), the check can only continue to be held and not deposited if there is written permission from the seller. Unless

otherwise stated, the check must be deposited into escrow or in a trust account within three days after the acceptance. If deposited into escrow, it is deposited into a neutral depository, or into an account held by a licensed escrow holder. Before the seller accepts the funds, the buyer (or offeror) is the rightful owner of the funds. However, as soon as the offer is accepted, the seller is the owner of these funds. The funds will then be handled according to the escrow instructions (the agreed-upon instructions by both the buyer and the seller).

Trust Fund Accounts

A broker's trust fund account must be set up as a trust account in the name of the broker, who is the trustee of the account. In the state of California, all broker's trust fund accounts must be set up with a recognized depository or bank. Any withdrawals from this account may only be made with a signature of one or more approved persons who have access to the account. Trust fund accounts are generally not interest-bearing accounts, where written notice must be given for withdrawals. However, they can be in certain circumstances.

Anyone authorized to take money out of the account is able to make withdrawals from it. The people with this authorization are the broker (in whose name the account is maintained), any designated broker-officer (if the trust account happens to be in the name of a corporate broker) or any individuals who are authorized in writing by the broker. This person may be another broker in the firm or a salesperson working for the broker. Additionally, unlicensed employees of the broker, so long as permission is given in writing, may make withdrawals. Any authorized unlicensed employees must also be covered by a fidelity bond.

Commingling

Commingling is defined as the mixing of trust funds with personal funds, and is strictly prohibited by real estate law. Any broker found to be commingling funds may be punished with suspension or revocation of his or her license. Brokers may, however, keep up to $200 of personal money in a trust account, to pay for any charges the bank may issue against the account. Commingling happens whenever any personal or company money is deposited into the trust fund bank account. The opposite is also true: if any trust money is deposited into a personal account, commingling has occurred. If any commissions paid on the transaction are due from the trust account, the money must be withdrawn within 30 days. Commissions left in the account for more than 30 days are considered commingling.

S U M M A R Y

As we have seen in this chapter, ethics and law are not always the same. Sometimes ethics can supercede the law, or sometimes by acting in an illegal manner it could be interpreted as ethical. It is important for you to understand the division between the two, and have a good understanding not only of real estate law and regulations, but also the Code of Ethics.

T E R M S   A N D   P H R A S E S

Blockbusting – Influencing people to move out of a neighborhood because another group of people are moving in, causing a perception of lower home values.

Commingling – The mixing of a broker's private funds (over $200) with other people's money, specifically clients' money in the form of trust funds.

Neutral Depository – An escrow business conducted by someone who is a licensed escrow holder.

Redlining – The act of denying financing to people based on the location or neighborhood of the property being purchased (done by financing firms).

Steering – Discriminatory action a realtor can take by showing properties located in only one area to a prospective client.

Trust Funds – Money received by a real estate broker or salesperson on behalf of the client.

C H A P T E R   Q U I Z

1. The word "ethics" derives from words meaning:
    a. "Moral" and "character"
    b. "Character" and "truth"
    c. "Moral" and "truth"
    d. All of the above

2. Ethics are based on:
    a. Laws
    b. Minimum standards
    c. The golden rule
    d. Acceptable behaviors

3. Which of the following is true?
    a. Ethics change to accommodate current attitudes and perceptions.
    b. Laws change to accommodate current attitudes and perceptions.
    c. Both ethics and laws change to accommodate current attitudes and perceptions.
    d. Neither ethics nor laws change to accommodate current attitudes and perceptions.

4. What sometimes determines whether behavior is ethical?
    a. Action
    b. Reaction
    c. Motive
    d. All of the above

5. An ethical agent can measure his or her success in:
    a. Referrals
    b. Loyal clients
    c. Dollars
    d. Both A and B

6. Which of the following is the most ethical statement?
    a. The end justifies the means
    b. Do unto others as you would like them to do unto you
    c. What will it do for me now
    d. I'll do whatever it takes to make you happy

7. A legal act is always ethical while performing an illegal act will always be unethical.
    a. True
    b. False

8. The "Suggestions for Professional Conduct in Sale, Lease, and Exchange Transactions" and "Suggestions for Professional Conduct When Negotiating or Arranging Loans Secured by Real Property or Sale of a Promissory Note Secured by Real Property" are enforced by:
    a. The Real Estate Commissioner
    b. The Department of Real Estate
    c. The California judicial system
    d. None of the above

9. The United States Constitution is to law as ethics is to:
    a. Declaration of Independence
    b. State Constitutions
    c. Bill of Rights
    d. None of the above

10. Civil rights acts and the Thirteenth and Fourteenth Amendments to the Constitution are considered:
    a. Laws
    b. Wording to promote fair treatment of all people
    c. Ethical
    d. All of the above

11. Which of the following is not a protected class under the Civil Rights Act of 1968?
    a. Sexual Orientation
    b. National Origin
    c. Race
    d. Religion

12. Which of the following words or phrases are considered acceptable by HUD?
    a. Caucasian only
    b. Kosher meals
    c. No children
    d. No women

13. Which of the following is considered an exemption to the Civil Rights Act of 1968?
    a. Owners of one to four residential units who occupy a unit and rent out the other three units without the help of an agent may discriminate on who they allow into their complex.
    b. Private clubs can discriminate preference to members when selling or leasing houses for noncommercial purposes.
    c. Religious groups can discriminate in providing nonprofit housing providing the religion is open to all groups of people.
    d. All of the above

14. The Fair Housing Amendment in 1988 protected which classification or group of people?
    a. Sexual orientation
    b. Educational level
    c. Familial status
    d. Income status

15 The Americans with Disabilities Act applies to all businesses employing:
   a. Any number of employees
   b. 10 or more employees
   c. 15 or more employees
   d. 20 or more employees

16. Under the Americans with Disabilities Act, a "place of public accommodation" refers to:
   a. Shops
   b. Offices
   c. Commercial facilities
   d. All of the above

17. The Fair Housing Act is also known as:
   a. The Unruh Act
   b. ADA
   c. The Rumford Act
   d. None of the above

18. The California Business and Professional Code is:
   a. Legally enforced
   b. Not legally enforced, but a suggestion on how agents should act
   c. Considered ethical
   d. Both A and C

19. The Real Estate Commissioner's Rules and Regulations are enforced by:
   a. The Real Estate Commissioner
   b. The Department of Real Estate
   c. The California judicial system
   d. None of the above

20. Sexual harassment is defined by:
   a. Law
   b. Your intent
   c. How others view your actions
   d. None of the above

CHAPTER

REAL
ESTATE
INVESTMENT

What you will learn in this Chapter

- Investing in Real Estate
- Investment Factors
- Benefits of Investing
- Arguments Against Investing
- Financing Income Properties
- Prospecting and Marketing
- Investing, Planning and Counseling
- Property Analysis
- Determining Taxable Income
- Valuation
- Analyzing the Rental Market
- Study Area Characteristics
- Characteristics of the Rental Market
- Syndication
- Forms of Legal Organization
- Advantages of the Limited Partner Format
- Brokerage Opportunities
- Steps in Setting up a Syndicate
- Estate Planning and Real Estate
- Real Estate Investment by Foreigners

Test Your Knowledge

1. Any person purchasing property in the United States from a foreign seller must withhold what percent of the price?
    a. 5%
    b. 10%
    c. 15%
    d. 20%

2. "An association of individuals, formed for the purpose of conducting and carrying out some particular business transaction, ordinarily of a financial character, in which the members are mutually interested, formed for some temporary purpose, such as the organization of a real estate trust and the sale of shares to the public," describes what concept?
    a. Syndication
    b. Limited partnership
    c. Corporation
    d. Brokerage

3. As the capitalization rate increases, that happens to the value of property?
    a. Increases
    b. Decreases
    c. Stays the same
    d. The capitalization rate does not have an effect on property value

4. Total Return refers to:
    a. Adjusted gross spendable income
    b. Principal payments for the entire year
    c. Both A and B
    d. Neither A nor B

5. The amount of income an owner will receive from rents before deductions for expenses and debt is referred to as:
    a. Gross operating income
    b. Net operating income
    c. Profit
    d. Net profit

6. Which of the following is not a source of financing for an income property?
    a. Commercial banks
    b. Life insurance companies
    c. Credit unions
    d. Savings and loan associations

7. Which of the following is not a benefit of investing in property?
    a. Tax shelter
    b. Hedge against inflation
    c. Strength of the dollar
    d. Interim use

In this chapter we will cover investing in real estate from two different viewpoints. We will examine investing from both the investor's point of view and then from the real estate professional's point of view. We will look at different investment factors that should be considered when deciding to invest. Some of these factors are benefits, risks, arguments against investing, financing income properties and the roles played by licensees. We will then analyze the rental market and the opportunities and risks associated with it. Finally we will discuss estate planning.

I N V E S T I N G   I N   R E A L   E S T A T E

People invest in real property for many reasons. Generally speaking, these reasons can be placed into three main categories: to meet their personal goals and objectives, to have the capacity to meet their financial commitments, and because of the economic soundness of real property when viewed in light of the investor's objectives and capacity.

> **Remember:**
> There are three primary reasons for people to invest in real property:
> - Meet their personal goals and objectives
> - To have the capacity to meet their financial commitments
> - Economic soundness

Objectives
What are the objectives of real estate investors? What does an investor hope to accomplish from his or her investment? Different investors will certainly have different objectives for their investments. Some may be seeking income and choose to invest in a more secure, tangible asset such as property. Some investors may need tax shelters to invest money instead of losing it in taxes. Still others may be investing in retirement or vacation properties, trying to diversify their portfolios, gaining prestige and recognition, or creating an estate. It is important to prioritize the main objectives for investing before selecting the best-suited property.

Capacity
Financially, investors need to be able to bear the burdens of investing. Some burdens include debt service and taxes and the need to retain a cash reserve for emergencies. It may even be argued that the investor must be psychologically able to live with the fact that the large sums required for investment result in price increases. Prices continue to escalate with the continued rise in inflation and appreciation, so the costs of investing continue to go up.

Soundness
Not only is it important to analyze the objectives and financial capacity of an investor, but also to analyze the potential of the chosen property to produce long-term income. Does the surrounding area continue to grow and develop in a positive direction? What does the city have planned for zoning adjacent to the property? Does the income of residents in the surrounding area continue to grow? Not only should projections for the costs of and competition for investment funds be taken into consideration, but the general economic picture must be considered as well. This will create an accurate picture of the viability of the investment.

From an economic point of view, the investment should be sound; that is, investors should carefully examine projected figures. Ultimately, these figures should reflect reality by including market and economic analysis. For instance, one might trade off risk for growth, cash flow and initial investment, as will be explained later. Also, the market for the property should be properly and objectively analyzed. This means there should be a real need for the services the property is expected to provide. Oftentimes only income tax consequences are considered.

INVESTMENT FACTORS

Generally speaking, the income tax factor is perhaps the most common consideration when investing in real estate. However, the most visible force for the investor in real property is the prospect for growth through appreciation. There are numerous other reasons for buying, but the factors common to all investments, which every potential investor should consider, can be reduced to the following nine. They are listed alphabetically, since the order of importance will depend upon the objectives of each individual investor.

Appreciation
Appreciation is the increase in value over the original investment amount. In other words, it is the amount of increase in the property value from the original purchase price. This gain results from many factors, but mainly from the pressures of a changing society where increasing needs and expanding use create higher demands.

Cash Flow
Net income generated by a property before depreciation and other non-cash expenses is called its "cash flow." Not all investors share the same cash needs; persons with high incomes may be seeking tax shelters or growth, or both, more than immediate cash. As will be illustrated later, it is possible to achieve growth, a tax shelter and cash flow at the same time.

Leverage
Leverage is the ratio of debt to current value. Maximizing leverage utilizes the principle of maximizing the use of borrowed funds, providing a large percentage of return on a relatively small cash outlay. The term "leverage" is used because this is similar to lifting a large weight with a lever when there is a small distance between the object and the fulcrum. High leverage is not always advantageous, however. The retired person, who is on a fixed income, or the investor with large cash resources but low income, may prefer to buy with a large down payment, reducing the leverage faster because of uncertainties in meeting future obligations. After all, high leverage usually has a multiplier effect; that is, when losses occur they are compounded in much the same way as gains.

Liquidity
Liquidity is the ability to generate cash in a hurry. There are two types of liquidity that can be gained from property. One originates from the sale of the property, while the other stems from hypothecation, or pledging the property as collateral to secure a loan. How readily can the investment be reconverted into cash in the event it is needed? More than that, will the asset be marketed at its current value, bringing an expected profit, or will it suffer loss due to the distress circumstances under which it may need to be sold? Financing terms, pricing, and other factors will affect the answers to these crucial questions.

Management and Administration

Management and administration require time and effort to oversee the investment, and skill and expertise to promote its productivity and appreciation. A novice should consider using the professional services of others. If this is done, will the expense of employing professional managers be recovered through increased benefits so that management becomes a completely recoverable cost? Costs of professional management are recoverable through three possible areas: 1) increased efficiency; that is, lower costs, less turnover, and higher rents; 2) income tax benefits from increased write-offs; and 3) psychological benefits; that is, transferring to the stresses of dealing with tenants, worrying over vacancies, rent collection, repairs, and so forth to professional managers.

Quality and Stability

Quality and stability have to do with the soundness and durability of income properties. How sound is the investment in terms of the economic ups and downs of the market? This leads to other questions. How stable is the economy? The property itself? What is the competitive area like, in terms of the rental market? What about the tenants, as measured by the tenancy turnover ratio?

Safety

Safety is frequently considered to be on the opposite end of the spectrum that contains risk. The safety/risk spectrum overlaps those considerations of liquidity, stability and return. How speculative is the investment? Is the investor willing to risk loss of part or all of the capital invested? Government bonds and insured savings accounts provide a certain level of safety of principal, but the returns are fixed and relatively low. Is the investor's objective to seek out high risk with the opportunity for a high return, or to seek out safe outlets where the principal is virtually secured? Since risk is the price one pays for yield, cash flow, and other benefits, investors set out to reach their objectives at the lowest possible risk. At a certain point the risk becomes unacceptable. Of course, that point of unacceptable risk varies from person to person.

Tax Shelters

Tax shelters provide additional tax benefits by allowing investors to legally avoid or reduce their tax liability. Tax laws allow special consideration for the real estate investor who desires to take advantage of allowable depreciation schedules, capital gains privileges, tax-deferred exchanges, and other benefits.

Yield

Yield is the amount the investor makes on the capital invested during the time the investment is held. If high risk is involved, there should be an opportunity for exceptionally high gain if conditions develop as originally projected. With relatively low risk, the return will usually be correspondingly less.

Investment factors in real estate:
- Appreciation
- Cash flow
- Leverage
- Liquidity
- Management and administration
- Quality and stability
- Safety
- Tax shelter
- Yield

Some of the rewards of investing in real estate are implicit in the list above. Whether investment factors are beneficial, of course, depends on the degree to which they meet or exceed the investor's specific objectives. Of necessity, some of the investment factors listed above will be repeated in the following discussions, as we show how investment rewards compare with the disadvantages of investing.

Tax Shelter

For those in high income tax brackets, part of their ordinary income could be "sheltered," or preserved, through wise estate planning, selection, and operation of an income-producing property. Depreciation allowances on both the real and personal property may account for a substantial portion of the cash flow generated from the operation of the property, particularly in the earlier years of the investment. This occurs through accelerated depreciation, as will be demonstrated later. The level of income subject to ordinary tax rates can be reduced through proper deductions for operating expenses from the rental income generated from the investment. Many investors seek ways to preserve all of their income from taxation, but more than that, they seek to save on taxes for which they will be liable on their regular income from wages, salary, and so on.

Other Tax Benefits

Gains can also be deferred through one of several devices. Some of those include a tax-free exchange, a deferred sale or an installment sale. As a side benefit, the proceeds from a profitable sale could be reinvested into another profitable venture.

Appreciation Potential

One of the special features of real estate, particularly urban, is the possibility to project its growth potential. Growth is the effect of economic conditions: demand calling for more supply, population spreading to specific areas, and the lack of other resources or options. The value of property is related to its usefulness (inherent or anticipated), and as the usefulness increases, the value does, too.

Hedge against Inflation

For the past thirty years, the purchasing power of the dollar has been losing ground to varying degrees. Real estate tends to follow this trend, more or less, as is evident from the sometimes spectacular rise in prices of real estate that has taken place during this period. This is especially true in California, where superlatives have been used to describe the very rapid growth of many areas since the 1970's.

Income

One of the main objectives of investing in property is to achieve an annuity. This income may be used for daily expenses or saved for retirement funds. How much an investment will yield depends on a number of factors, including the size of the investment and the amount of debt involved. For example, a well-managed shopping center with many tenants will most likely provide the investor with a very high monthly income, as long as the debt of the investment is low. A smaller property with a large loan will provide little, if any, positive cash flow. Proper debt structure and management can increase the income a property will yield.

Interim Use
Ownership of a property such as a farm, ranch, vacation retreat or other such investment, gives the investor the opportunity to use the property while waiting for the property to increase in value.

Stability
The investors in certain types of real estate, particularly commercial and industrial properties, enjoy long-term leases with tenants (businesses) having top financial credit. This can produce a dependable, stable income for twenty years or more. In terms of residential properties, especially apartments, the same kind of effect can be produced by using strong neighborhood patterns, based on favorable shopping conveniences, transportation routes, zoning and community planning, and other ingredients that can assure long term performance of the highest level.

Basic value trends are capable of being charted in many instances, and this can further beneficially influence the initial decision to invest. These trends require careful analysis and the assistance of well-informed brokers and other trained individuals.

Flexibility and Control
Investors have the opportunity to thoroughly study the environment and economic background of their investments with an eye toward analyzing them for tax shelter and other tax benefits, inflation hedges, financing opportunities, income and cash flow, and stability. All of these can be altered from time to time to serve the goal of improving the investment. This action might take different forms, such as the rezoning of a property to allow its highest and best use, which may strongly affect its immediate value and opportunities for appreciation, or introducing a new leasing pattern to different lessees, at a higher rental, which can produce dramatic results in terms of improving the gross income picture and its ability to be financed.

Refinancing
As an example of the flexibility of real estate, let's take a look at an investment property with a large equity amount. It could be raw land or land developed to its highest and best use. If the owner decides to refinance the property and take on a second trust deed in order to purchase more income property, four things will be accomplished. First, the proceeds secured through refinancing are tax free since the equity is not being sold, but merely collateralized. Second, the interest paid on the new debt is fully deductible. Third, the investor is acquiring another investment that will add to the benefits already enjoyed. Finally, the "trade-in" of part of the first property's equity for the 2nd trust deed may more than pay for the second property. In effect, the equity is being swapped for an income-producing asset, resulting in the investor owning not one, but two properties.

Amenities
Other benefits which accrue to the investor include pride of ownership, security, status, achievement, estate building, opportunity to improve the profit over that initially contemplated, and the uniqueness of the property as a local, fixed, tangible product capable of accomplishing any number of unique objectives sought by the investor.

Benefits of investing in real estate:
- Tax shelter / tax benefits
- Appreciation
- Hedge against inflation
- Income
- Interim use
- Stability
- Flexibility and control
- Refinancing
- Amenities

ARGUMENTS AGAINST INVESTING

Wherever there are benefits to investing in real estate, inevitably there will be drawbacks that provide challenges. Some of the factors that may work to encourage the decision NOT to invest in real estate include the following:

Size of Capital
The amount of money that must be placed as a down payment when investing in real estate is considerably larger than when investing in another venture outside of real estate. Large down payments may be required if the investment is to payoff immediately. For example, if an investor wishes to invest in an apartment complex but only comes up with the minimum down payment the monthly payment on the complex may exceed the amount of income generated by the property. This would not be a very smart investment in the beginning stages.

Lack of Liquidity
Investors wishing to liquidate their investment and use that money in alternative investing may find it is difficult to sell certain properties. There are many different factors that may cause this problem; a slow real estate market, a highly specialized or unique property, high interest rates or other factors causing other investors to shy away from the property. Should this happen, it might cause the investor to be forced to keep a property he or she wishes to liquidate.

Management Care
Real estate investments will tend to be management intensive. This means that the investor should make great efforts to have a hands-on approach to the investment knowing exactly what is going on at all times, making crucial decisions and making sure the rate of return will be maximized. Those investors who do not have the time or skill to take an active role in management need to hire skilled managers who can create this environment for the investor.

Financing
The amount and terms of financing that will meet the goals and objectives of the investor may not be available. For example, where the purchaser requires a relatively large cash flow, the financing market may be such that only high-interest and comparatively short-term loans are obtainable, resulting in a high annual constant debt obligation. The financing terms might also be onerous and restrictive, containing such burdens as acceleration in the event of disposition, lock-in provisions, interest escalation clauses, prepayment penalties, and other disadvantages.

Diminished Capacity

Emotional attachment to property may cause an investor to hold onto property longer than it is capable of producing a return, or spend more money on improvements than the property is worth. Diminished capacity refers to properties ability to no longer produce the optimum rate of return, causing a loss or lower earnings than if it were sold and to reinvest the money into another investment.

Miscellaneous Factors

Other factors that may be seen as a disadvantage to investing in property may include taxation, immobility, restrictions to property use or zoning laws and changes, poor management, depreciation, softening real estate market and obsolescence. Most of these factors are out of the investors' control, but must be anticipated when deciding to invest in property. Pitfalls inherent in group investments via syndication (where promoters may misstate the facts) include the possibility of losing status as a limited partner due to too much involvement in decision making and the risk of being treated as a dealer instead of an investor.

Arguments against investing:

- Size of capital needed
- Lack of liquidity
- Management care
- Financing
- Diminished capacity
- Miscellaneous

FINANCING INCOME PROPERTIES

Among the outstanding advantages of real estate is the special financing and refinancing opportunities available to the investor. The spectrum of lenders available and eager to lend is broad indeed, and this often makes the kind of leverage sought by the investor possible to obtain.

The amount of financing available depends upon the source. High debt ratio financing can be achieved from some sources, while financing using a relatively low ratio is obtained from others. In any event, how much is attainable is dependent upon the property to be collateralized, the credit of the individual, market conditions, the relationship between the borrower and the lender, and other variables.

The sources can be summarized in four broad categories:

Four financing categories:

- Savings and loan associations
- Commercial banks
- Life insurance companies
- Miscellaneous

Savings and loan associations are largely concerned with housing, particularly with single-family residences. However, they are increasingly expanding into the apartment market. Savings and loan associations are also active in land financing, where they may lend up to 5 percent of their assets. They are not active in special purpose properties, such as marinas and religious facilities.

Commercial banks are very active in take out loans, or interim financing and working with FHA or VA programs in financing single-family homes.

State-chartered banks are interested in land loans, where firm plans and permanent financing are demonstrated by the investor/developer. Legal restrictions, having to do with the percentage of loan to appraisal and maturities of the loan, are imposed by regulatory agencies. Many will lend to the developer at a pre-set loan-to-value ratio for from six to 18 months, but only after they are satisfied that the developer will be able to build or develop during this time period, and that the project is subject to approval of permanent financing and the developer purchases a completion bond.

Banks prefer to specialize in interim financing, soliciting relationships with reputable developers and people of proven credit for the purpose of supplying interim financing on tract homes and select income properties. They will also loan for special purpose properties and projects, but again, the relationship with the borrower and the strength of the security of the lessee are paramount.

Commercial bank participation in the real estate market is generally governed by the traditional bank-customer relationship and by the bank's role as a supplier of short-term credit. The bank strives to build long-standing relationships with each of its customers by providing all needed banking and financial services for their business activities.

Life insurance companies make loans to customers who live a long distance away from their firm or office. Life insurance companies are not restricted by legislation in their acquisition of loans, or ability to fund loans and thus are able to participate in a much larger geographic region. Typically life insurance companies will utilize mortgage bankers to act as a local representative to a given region

Miscellaneous sources of funds for investment properties include syndicates and trusts (to be discussed in a separate section), real estate bonds and debentures, bank-administered pension trust funds, sellers under purchase, money transactions and land contracts, and a variety of others to a lesser degree. Real estate syndicates and REIT's (real estate investment trusts) have proven to be useful devices for higher-income investors as well as small investors, who can pool their resources to develop and operate residential income and commercial properties.

Seller carryback purchase money trust deeds and contracts of sales are perhaps the most important sources of financing for raw land and many special purpose projects. In particular, during tight money periods they frequently become the only available source of financing, wherein the seller effectively operates as a bank, actually supplying the financing which the buyer agrees to replace when and if he or she can secure outside financing.

PROSPECTING AND MARKETING

Prospecting for income property is similar to prospecting for single-family residences. There will be an emotional appeal that will be different between investment prospecting and single-family prospecting. Most residential prospecting will appeal to an emotional feeling, while investment prospecting will appeal to a business or investment drive. The sources for both will be similar.

For instance, we have seen previously that two of the benefits of real estate investing are to provide supplemental income and to build one's estate. Why not, then, approach the seller of a home with the idea that they can replace that home with a fourplex, occupy one of the units and rent out the other three? This could well be the start of a happy broker-client relationship, one in which repeat business might be expected as the clients add to their investments in an active quest for building a real estate portfolio.

In addition to the exhaustive list of prospect sources discussed earlier, we should add any other sources that the broker might consider likely (and even not so likely). Few, if any, on the list would be removed; more importantly, some will be emphasized to a greater extent than others, where one source is more likely to help find a buyer than another on the list.

For example, suppose that you were the listing agent on a ten-unit apartment building. You would advertise in the newspapers, send a direct mailing to the prospect list you maintain, place the listing on multiple listing services so that other brokers will become aware of the new offering, and so on. Whether you get permission to place a "for sale" sign on the property would depend upon your ability to persuade the owner that the tenants would not leave en masse, a fear not without merit. Occasionally occupants will terminate their tenancy because of the uncertainty surrounding impending change. They may fear a rise in rents, a less concerned owner-landlord, loss of a smooth relationship they might have experienced under the old owner, and even fear that the new owners may oust them. On the other side of the fence, there could be tenants who, seeing that the property is going to be sold anyway, may take advantage of the changeover by withholding one or more rent payments or perhaps even leave before the new management has had a chance to catch up with them.

Whether or not you are persuasive in your arguments, one frequently overlooked source of prospecting is always close to home: the tenants themselves. After all, they very likely are satisfied with the property, location and so on, or they would not be living there. Many have no children or have spouses who also work, and therefore may have saved more than their counterparts who have added financial obligations because of house and family. Tenants may consequently need more tax shelter, and are in many ways logical candidates for owning the property and taking advantage of the benefits it will bring them. It might be noted that commercial tenants are even more likely prospects than residential tenants. The alert broker may send a letter to the tenants that might be framed as follows:

> We wish to inform you that the property in which you reside is being offered for sale.

> It occurred to us that you might be seeking an investment in order to obtain some of the many advantages which buyers of such properties are accorded.

> CBA Realtors specializes in all types of real estate. Should you wish to learn about the many benefits of this or any other properties, we are happy to be of service. Simply dial 789 -1225 or write to us at the above address. There is no obligation, of course.

To assist the broker in qualifying prospects, certain information should be obtained. A "Confidential Client Personal Data Worksheet" might be used for such purposes. The worksheet would contain the names and ages of family members, occupations and income, sources of other income, assets and encumbrances, investment needs, and additional remarks. The knowledgeable broker will know how to assess the prospect's ability to buy and will be able to determine what kind of property to purchase and how much he or she should invest. The process of qualifying the purchaser of investment property is not much different from that of qualifying the homebuyer except that the agent should understand financial analysis better and be able to take into account and weigh the investment objectives of the prospects.

Listing an apartment building is not unlike listing a house. The agent meets the owners, asks searching questions, comes prepared with valuation data, creates opportunities for the principals by showing them how the proceeds can be reinvested, and so on. Greater emphasis is placed on financial benefits in these discussions than on sentimental attachments. In gathering information, more detailed facts are sought, needed repairs are noted, as is the condition of units, the quality of the tenants, rent schedules and lease terms, vacancy factors, and an evaluation of income and expenses are compiled. Showing the owners how they can improve their estate or income through selling and buying, or exchanging for more profitable property, will help the agent secure a saleable listing. For example, pointing out how a fully depreciated property or one that has a low book value no longer meets the objectives of the owners, may promote a listing at a price that will sell.

INVESTING, PLANNING AND COUNSELING

Investment planning may be thought of as the integration of a number of steps, starting with a thorough analysis of the client's investment objectives. Remember, those objectives include any combination of the following: income, appreciation, retirement, estate buildup, resale or exchange, tax shelter, diversification, leverage liquidity, and funding of future obligations, i.e. college education, retirement income, a trip around the world, etc. Conferring with the client's attorney, accountant, or business advisor may be advisable somewhere along the way.

The second step in investment planning is the researching and selecting of properties that meet the objectives of the client. A decision to buy a particular property is then made. The broker negotiates its acquisition, followed by the title search and opening of escrow. Management of the property is next, to safeguard the investment, minimize expenses and maximize profits. Along every step of the way, the broker must be cognizant of change, offering suggestions and making recommendations as the circumstances dictate. More about this subject will be covered in section five of this chapter, "Estate Planning and Real Estate."

Remember:
An effective broker will keep an exhaustive, confidential folder on each client, updating records whenever appropriate. Brokers who keep detailed records will be able to secure additional sales by understanding the client's needs.

Residential Income Properties

The factors to be considered in embarking upon residential income property investment and the advantages and disadvantages of such ventures are the same factors as in any real property investment, and these were discussed at length earlier. In this section then, we will explain the following in detail as they pertain to residential income property investments: analysis, valuation, management and the rental market.

PROPERTY ANALYSIS

The preparation of a comprehensive income and expense analysis on any given income property project is a complicated and difficult process. The income and expense analysis should be directed toward the full operating history of the property. Most income properties are held for long-term investment, and the third year, the seventh year, and the tenth year can all be as important to the investor as the first year. Below are definitions of terms that are associated with income and expense analysis.

Price is the asking price. Loans include all forms of financing. Down payment is the initial amount of money a buyer plans to put towards the purchase price of the property, not to be financed. Scheduled income is the amount of income generated through rent when all units are occupied.

Vacancy factor refers to vacancies and uncollectible rents. It is natural for a property to have open units. The vacancy factor will give an allowance for a certain percentage of units to remain unoccupied while maximizing the return on the investment. There are different factors that determine the vacancy factor, depending on the type, size or location of the investment, but generally a three percent vacancy factor is used for analysis then making the investment.

Vacancies are calculated in three different ways. First is the actual vacancy for any given time. Second is an average for the property given a historical vacancy rate on the property over time. Lastly is gathering vacancy data on other properties in the area and using a comparative number in line with these properties.

Gross operating income is the scheduled gross income, adjusted for vacancy. It is often referred to as the **effective gross income** and represents the amount of money the owner will receive from rent collections before deductions for expenses and debts.

Operating expenses include fixed and variable expenses, as detailed in the bottom half of the Income Property Statement. Many real estate licensees remember the largest of these expenditures (which are inevitably found in every statement) by an acronym MITUM. The initials stand for Maintenance, Insurance (not interest), Taxes (not trust deed), Utilities, and Management (not mortgage). These are items that are operational in nature and are encountered whether the property is fully encumbered or free and clear. Therefore, loan payments are not included nor are depreciation allowances, reserves, or provision for income taxes.

Earns on sales price ratio is a fraction, the numerator of which is the net operating income and the denominator is the sales price. Dividing one by the other shows the earnings ratio on the selling price and is referred to as the **capitalization (or cap) rate**.

Net operating income is what is left from the adjusted gross income after deducting the operating expenses, but before loan payments, reserves for replacements, depreciation allowances, and income tax liability from any taxable income are subtracted. In many ways it is the single most important figure in the entire income-expense statement, for it is this item that is used by lenders, appraisers, and investors to determine the value of the property. Such valuation is calculated by use of the capitalization rate, which the net operating income determines, as will be explained in the valuation section later.

The **loan payments** entry represents the annual payments for principal and interest on the loans shown in the loans segment at the top of the statement. While only the interest portion will be deductible for tax purposes, the entire loan payment is subtracted in order to calculate **spendable income**, or **gross cash flow**, as it is sometimes called.

Gross spendable is the amount of cash remaining after all out-of-pocket expenditures have been subtracted. It is gross spendable income, and not net spendable income, because it has not yet taken into account reserves for replacement of personal property, such as furniture, carpets, and drapes, nor any allowance for replacing certain items classified as fixtures, such as garbage disposal units, water heaters, and others.

Furniture reserve and **carpet reserve** are, as implied in the titles, reserves or allowances for ultimate replacement of furniture and carpeting. The amount set aside is determined on an annual basis and is readily computed by dividing the replacement cost by the asset's useful life. Such useful life is at best estimated and will vary from two to seven years, depending on the quality, use, tenant demands and financial feasibility (and ability) to replace each on a profitable (or at least break-even) basis. **Adjusted gross spendable income** is the amount of money left over after replacement reserves have been subtracted from gross spendable income. It represents the cash that the investor can reasonably expect, at least for the first year shown, without having to dig into the receipts for additional expenditures. It is an item that is especially important to the investor who is seeking cash flow, or income, and is frequently referred to as "**net cash flow.**" Technically, it is the unadjusted spendable cash flow, since no allowance has yet been made for income tax liabilities (which will decrease the flow of income) or tax savings (which will increase the cash flow).

Paid on principal represents the amount of money paid on principal, or amortization. Because it is a reduction of principal balance and thus increasing the equity portion of the investment, it is frequently referred to as **equity buildup**. It does not include the interest portion of the loan payments, which in the filled-in form represents about 84 percent of total payments.

Total return is the adjusted gross spendable income plus the principal payments for the year. It is not the same as taxable income, since no allowance for depreciation has been deducted and the reserves set aside for replacement are not an allowable deduction even if the money is physically put aside. As will be shown later, however, if such replacements actually equal depreciation allowance on the personal property items, then only depreciation on the improvements needs to be computed to arrive at taxable income. In other words, total return represents the net cash flow plus equity buildup and is occasionally cited as the return of cash invested, return of capital invested, or return of equity invested.

Spendable on down payment is also a ratio formula, the numerator representing the adjusted gross spendable income, which is divided by down payment (the lower half of the fraction). It expresses the cash flow plus equity buildup as a percentage of the initial equity, i.e. the down payment. Each year, the amortization payments are added to the original down payment to arrive at a new equity base, so that the ratio will, of course, change correspondingly. The numerator, or spendable portion, will increase as amortization increases, while the denominator will increase by the same amortization amount, resulting in a proportionately larger spendable ratio.

Earns on down payment is also a ratio, with the numerator representing total return and the denominator again being the down payment. The end result is cash flow plus equity buildup expressed as a percentage of down payment, another important criterion in the investor's selection process.

Times gross is the "gross multiplier" used, or rather abused, by many real estate practitioners. It is simply the proposed selling price divided by the scheduled income, the multiple used as a ballpark figure to weigh the prospective value of the investment. It is somewhat like the price-earnings (P/E) ratio in the stock market, used by investors to help decide the worth of a company, except that in the stock market, potential stock investors use net income instead of gross income. While times gross is a useful tool to screen out properties, it measures only the quantity of income and therefore should always be considered along with other tests to determine whether the property is an acceptable investment. All too often, however, brokers misuse it by ignoring other factors that measure the quality and durability of the income, which is to a large extent revealed in the preceding ratios, shown as formulas 1, 2, and 3 in the upper right-hand side of the Income Property Listing Work-sheet.

Residential property investment analysis factors include:
- Price
- Operating history of the property
- Financing
- Down payment
- Anticipated or scheduled income
- Vacancy factors
- Gross operating income
- Operating expenses
- Furniture / carpet expense
- Gross spendable income
- Paid on principal
- Spendable on down payment
- Earns on down payment
- Gross multiplier

DETERMINING TAXABLE INCOME

Since the two income property forms deal with listings of income-producing assets, no provision is made for computation of taxable income. We implied above that total return was the nearest thing to taxable income, since it represented net operating income less interest and personal property reserves for replacements. This last item may or may not equal the depreciation allowance for the personal property items.

To show how taxable income is derived, we will use some of the same data from the filled-in forms and show them side by side with the analysis of spendable income. For the **depreciation allowance**, we will use the maximum permitted by law for residential rental property, 27+ years, which translates to 3.63% per year. The bottom of the Income Property Statement breaks down the ratios of land, improvements and personal property as 20 percent, 79 percent, and 1 percent respectively.

We derived the ratios of land, improvements, and personal property from the assessed values as shown on the local tax bill. From this it is reasonable to conclude that if a buyer were to purchase the property for its listed price of $156,000, then the 20 percent attributable to land equals $31,200, 79 percent (attributable to improvements) is $123,240 and the remaining 1 percent attributable to personal property is $1,560. Using straight-line depreciation at 3.63% will produce a first year write-off for $4,474 on the building and $312 on the personal property — for a total first year depreciation deduction of $4,786.

The amount that the taxpayer will pay on the net taxable income will depend upon other income. The data shown under the second column (Taxable Income) is summarized in Schedule D of the taxpayer's return and will be subject to the rules governing capital gains transactions. In this case, since there is a negative taxable income, the taxpayer would actually receive a rebate ($1,564 times the tax bracket rate of the taxpayer). However, the sellers may elect to report the purchase money second trust deed on the installment sale if it will improve their tax position.

V A L U A T I O N

As you know, the three principal approaches to valuation of real estate are the market or comparison approach, the cost approach, and the income or capitalization approach. The real estate professional who is to take a saleable listing must know how to price it correctly. While the comparative approach is emphasized in connection with listings of houses, the most valid approach to the valuation of income-producing properties is the income approach or, more precisely, the **capitalization** of **net income** technique.

Remember:
The three approaches to valuation are:
- Market / comparison approach
- Cost approach
- Capitalization approach

Capitalization of Net Income
All of the different methods to determine the capitalization of net income use the same formula:

Net Operating Income = Capitalization Rate x Value

The value (or sale price) of an income property may be obtained by dividing net operating income by an appropriate capitalization rate, which is basically the rate of return that the owner of the property would like to receive. As a simple example, let's go back to the property we listed at $156,000. Suppose its net operating income (NOI) is $14,206. Since we know the price of the property ($156,000) and the annual net operating income ($14,206), we can solve for the capitalization rate, or return on investment:

NOI   =   Cap Rate x Value

$14,206 = Cap Rate times $156,000

$14,206 divided by $156,000 = 0.091, which when read as a percentage, is 9.1% (0.091 x 100).

Stated differently, if four-unit residential rental properties of this grade and quality attract investors only if they offer a 9.1 percent rate of return, we say that such investment properties are capitalized at 9.1 percent - that is, the cap rate or yield is 9.1 percent. Thus, if records reveal that a certain income property is producing a net operating income of $14,206 and the prospective purchaser demands at least a 9.1 percent return on his or her total investment, he or she will not pay more than $156,500, the capitalized value as indicated by the net income, computed as follows:

NOI   =   Cap Rate x Value

$14,506 =   9.1% x Value

$14,506 divided by 9.1% = $156,407

Substitution of other numbers for those representing NOI will reveal larger or smaller amounts of value, assuming the purchaser requires at least a 9.1 percent return. For instance, if the NOI was $91,000, the capitalized value ($91,000 ÷ 9.1%) would indicate a value of $1 million. In contrast, if the income after allowance for all operating expenses was, say, $18,200, then the investor could expect to pay only $200,000 ($18,200 ÷ 9.1%) and still get a return of 9.1 percent.

From the foregoing it can readily be seen that by modifying the income where the cap rate remains constant, the capitalized value can vary considerably. Similarly, if the net operating income remains the same but the cap rate changes, the results will correspondingly change: an increase in the rate will decrease the capitalized value, while a decrease in the rate will increase the capitalized value.

For instance, if the rate of return demanded by investors for this type of property was 14.2 percent, the property will show a valuation of only $100,000, computed by dividing $14,206 by 14.2 percent. In other words, if the investor paid more than $100,000 for a property netting $14,206 after operating expenses, he would not receive the desired 14.2 percent return. On the other hand, if an investor is willing to settle for only a 7.1 percent return, he could theoretically afford to pay as much as $200,000 for the property ($14,206 ÷ 7.1%).

The math may be appear easy to understand up to this point, but what about the obvious question that may be gnawing at you by this time: how does one arrive at a realistic capitalization rate? Values can change by thousands of dollars when there is even a slight variation in the cap rate - a difference of one percent in the rate increases or decreases the indicated value by varying amounts.

Summation Method

This approach of determining the capitalization rate adds four components to formulate one overall rate. The first factor is the **safety rate**, or current rate of return on highly safe liquid investments such as government bonds. This is added to the **risk rate**, which provides a reasonable yield to compensate for the element of hazard involved in the exposure of the invested capital. The third component is the **management rate**, which represents the burden of managing the property. The fourth component is the **non-liquidity rate**, which is a "penalty" applied to real estate investments because of the length of time ordinarily required to realize cash from the disposition of the property, i.e. sell the property to receive the cash. All forms of real estate require more time to sell than competitive investments such as stocks, bonds, trust deed and mortgage notes, and other assets. Because real estate investments are in competition with other investment outlets, this method of calculating the capitalization rate is frequently referred to as the **competitive rate**. Because it is a composite of several components, it is also popularly called the **component rate**.

Each of the components used in the summation method varies with market conditions, availability of financing, use and quality of the property, and other considerations. The result of this method may depend on the following conditions: the loan constant involved in amortizing the loan; the investor's tax protection; the property's specific location, price and terms of the offering; and so on.

As an example of its application, the following overall rate might be developed:

Safe Rate	4.0%
Risk Rate	2.0%
Management Rate	2.5%
Non-liquidity Rate	2.5%
Composite Rate	11.0%

Using this composite rate as the cap rate, in our example of a property that produced a net operating income of $14,206, its indicated value is approximately $130,000 ($14,206 ÷ 11.0%).

Band of Investment Theory

This method of using net income to determine value is based on a weighted average for rates charged on the trust deed loans and the equity position. Going back to our $156,000 property example, suppose it was shown that a first loan was obtainable for $109,000, at 7.5 percent interest. This represents a loan-to-value ratio (LTV) of 70 percent. The seller has agreed to finance $16,000, or about 10 percent of the purchase price, by taking back a purchase money second at 8.5 percent interest per year. The balance, $31,000, is the down payment - approximately 20 percent. If investors in such properties demand a 10 percent return to induce them to invest a 20 percent equity stake, the cap rate would be calculated as follows:

	Ratio of Loan to Value x	Nominal Rate =	Band Rate
First Trust Deed	70%	7.5%	5.25%
Second Trust Deed	1 0%	8.5%	0.85%
Down Payment (Equity)	20%	10.0%	2.00%
Weighted Average Rate	100%		8.10%

By weighing the rates charged on the two loans and then adding the return demanded for the 20 percent equity position, the overall (composite) rate is 8.1 percent. The table shows that the indicated value of a property generating a $14,206 net income is approximately $175,380 ($14,206 divided by 8.1%). This method of capitalizing net income accounts for changes in interest rates, loan terms, and cash flow requirements for equity. It also reflects financing potential and leverage.

Direct Comparison

Selecting a cap rate through this method is done by comparing interest rates in the marketplace and then adding the rate of recapture through depreciation. Such a combined rate provides for both a return on capital and a return of capital. To illustrate, let's take our $156,000 property and for purposes of simplification assume the building value is $100,000 and that it has a true economic life of 25 years. The cap rate is computed as follows:

Sales Price	$156,000
Less: Land Value	56,000
Building Value	100,000

Net annual operating income, before depreciation $14,206

Economic life of the building is 25 years. To calculate the depreciation recapture rate, we need to divide 100% (the full recapture rate) by the economic life of the building, which is 25 years. So,

100%

$25 = 4\%$ annual depreciation recapture;

$4\% \times \$100,000 = 4,000$

Net annual income from land and building $ 10,206

Interest rate = $10,206 ÷ $156,000 sale price, or	6.5%
Plus: Depreciation recapture rate	4.0%
Overall capitalization rate	10.5%

What we did is add an interest rate extracted from the total return on the investment minus the return of the building value through the annual depreciation write-off. The result is a pure interest rate of return, attributable to the property's productivity, which we added the recapture on the 80 percent of the property's building value.

This method is called the direct comparison approach because the appraiser or investor checks out a number of properties offered for sale in the open market and compares the indicated rates to established rates that are acceptable to typical investors for various types of properties. Regardless of whether there is sufficient market data available, many investors use the prime interest rate charged by lenders as the minimum interest portion of the overall rate. Then they add the depreciation rate, computed on a straight-line basis over the building's life.

Other Methods

There are many other techniques used by investors, appraisers, and lenders to arrive at reasonable capitalization rates, some of which are variations of those just discussed. There is a rate selected from the gross rent multiplier, especially useful when reliable expense figures are not available. A rate can also be selected by comparison of quality attributes, which is determined on the basis of the "ideal investment" as measured by the reliability, validity, and quality of income, expense, and other attributes. Another approach is the split rate method, which computes separate interests in property (fee, leaseholds, etc.) at different rates. The mortgage-equity method, an extension of the band of investment theory, produces an overall cap rate allowing for debt financing, term of ownership, and increase or decrease in value. It utilizes the Ellwood tables widely used by appraisers of investment properties.

The cash flow method is yet another technique for determining value of income-producing property. It takes into account the leverage factor, maximizing reduction in income tax and forgoing maximization of current income. The Inwood method is based on an internal rate of return and assumes that the value of income property is equivalent to the present value of future rents, with a portion of the investment returned each year. As stated earlier, should you be so inclined, you may explore these and other approaches to value in the many publications available through the American Institute of Real Estate Appraisers and other professional societies and associations.

REAL ESTATE INVESTMENT BY FOREIGNERS

Any person purchasing real property located in the United States (buyer) from a foreigner (seller) is required to deduct and withhold a tax equal to 10% of the amount realized by the transferor on the sale, unless one of the following six rules is satisfied:

1. The seller furnishes the buyer with a certificate, executed under penalty of perjury, stating the seller's U.S. taxpayer identification number and affirming that the seller is not a foreign person.

2. The seller furnishes the buyer a qualifying statement from the U.S. Treasury indicating that the seller is exempt from tax.

3. The sale or exchange involves a property acquired for use as a residence by the buyer or a member of buyer's family and the amount realized by the seller on the sale does not exceed $300,000.

4. Pursuant to any nonrecognition provision of the Internal Revenue Code, such as the tax-free exchange under section 1031, the seller is not required to recognize any gain or loss.

5. The transfer involves the sale or exchange of a class of stock of a domestic corporation that is regularly traded on an established securities market.
6. The sale or exchange involves the sale of an interest in a domestic corporation, and the seller furnishes the buyer with a statement issued by the domestic corporation certifying that the interest in the domestic corporation is not a U.S. real property interest.

After withholding, the buyer is required to remit the tax by the tenth day after the transfer and file forms 8288 and 8288A with the IRS. If a buyer fails to withhold, he or she is still liable for the tax and may also be subject to criminal penalties. If the amount withheld is less than the seller's tax liability, the amount withheld is treated as an estimated payment. If the amount withheld exceeds the seller's tax liability, the seller may obtain a refund.

A good market analysis will help an investor decide:
- When and how to purchase property
- Features of the property such as size, number of units, furnishings, location, room layout, and local population concentrations.

SYNDICATION

There is no precise legal definition of "syndication." Black's Law Dictionary describes it as "An association of individuals, formed for the purpose of conducting and carrying out some particular business transaction, ordinarily of a financial character, in which the members are mutually interested, formed for some temporary purpose, such as the organization of a real estate trust and the sale of shares to the public."

Loosely then, a syndication can be thought of as an association of two or more people who combine their financial resources for the purpose of achieving one or more investment objectives. It is the process of pooling or combining investment capital, as in a mutual fund, for the purpose of acquiring real estate which ordinarily could not be bought by individuals alone. The rights and responsibilities, and the benefits and obligations, of the syndicator or promoter of the investment group, and of the investors toward each other, are determined and governed by the legal form of business organization adopted by the participants, whether it be a limited liability company, limited partnership or a corporation.

FORMS OF LEGAL ORGANIZATION

Syndications can assume a number of different forms of business organizations, the ultimate choice being dependent upon the specific objectives of the individual participants. Since the limited partnership is the most often used form, we will discuss it first.

Limited partnerships are a safe investment partnership for its investors because each individual investor is limited to loosing just his or her initial capital investment. Debts or obligations of the limited partnership are separated from individual partners. Only the general partner stands to loose more than his or her initial investment. This is because the general partner also has the responsibilities of managing the limited partnership, which could lead to losses or debts, thus making this individual responsible. The limited partners participation will be limited to voting for issues affecting the limited partnership and hiring or firing the general partner. They will also be allowed to inspect the books to make sure all funds are accounted for and will obviously share in profits or losses (loss responsibility up to their own initial capital investment).

Interests of general partners are not assignable, but those of limited partners are generally assignable without affecting the continuity of the partnership. Ordinarily the l.p. agreement grants the right of first refusal to the general partner(s), with the substituted limited partner assuming the same rights as those of his or her assignor. Thus, it is

425

possible for the general partner to also acquire an interest as a limited partner as well, to the extent of any fractional interests purchased.

General partnerships differ from a limited partnership because each co-owner has unlimited personal liability for any debt incurred by the partnership. General partnerships are similar to limited partnerships in that they are made up of two or more people for profit. General partnerships are the simplest partnership to create. There is no general partner, and every partner has an equal management of the organization.

Corporations are separate from the people who set them up. Interests in a corporation are in the form of stock. Ownership lends itself to having a board of directors made up of officers. These people will decide all important decisions the corporation might face. Any investor in a corporation is similar to that of a limited partner in a limited partnership. He or she is limited in any management or decision-making power and has only a financial liability of any initial financial investment he or she makes in the corporation.

A disadvantage of a corporation is that there is the possibility of double taxation. A members may be taxed on any income realized from being a part of the corporation, and may also be taxed on the corporations earnings. Additionally owners are not allowed to take any deductions based on depreciation, only the corporation as a whole can realize the depreciation deduction.

Under certain conditions where there are fewer than eleven stockholders and where no more than 20 percent of the corporate income is derived from rents, interest, and dividends, the investors may elect to have their corporation taxed as a **subchapter S corporation**. This is a small business form of corporation which is taxed like the partnership forms of ownership, thus avoiding double taxation.

Real estate investment trusts, popularly referred to as REITs, were created by Congress as an incentive to investors to entice them to increase investments in real estate and in mortgages. REITs are publicly traded and ownership in a REIT is evidenced by "shares of equity" which may be purchased on the stock market, as with any public company. Because of very stringent tests that must be met to qualify for the trust's favored tax status, this form of organization is rarely used by the typical syndication.

REITs are commonly used to raise mortgage funds and when this is its primary purpose, are sometimes referred to as a real estate mortgage trust (REMT) or a mortgage REIT. If it is used for investments in both mortgages and real property, it would be labeled a "hybrid" REIT, however the term "REIT" has been generally used to refer to all of these types of real estate-based trusts.

The requirements that need to be met to establish this form of unincorporated trust or association are stipulated by law and include the following: the number of shareholders allowed, management, receipt and distribution of income, tax consequences, transferability of interests, sources of revenue, and other factors. The main advantage of this form of ownership is that the qualified trust itself pays no income taxes and passes the tax benefit onto its members (shareholders). Since at least 90 percent of its income must be distributed to the members (subject to some exemption), the tax is imposed on the individual recipients to the extent of the distributions, as in a partnership, and double taxation is eliminated.

Additionally, because shares may be bought on the open market either individually or through mutual funds, they provide the most liquid way to invest in real estate. This should not be overlooked, as this advantage offers real estate investors the opportunity for both high yields and high convertibility.

Other forms of ownership include tenancy in common, which has the advantage of separate depreciation schedules that may be selected by each co-tenant; joint tenancy, which might be held by related investors due to the incidence of survivorship; joint venture; and others that are virtually never used in California.

ADVANTAGES OF LIMITED PARTNERSHIPS

Limited partnerships are the most common form corporate ownership in California. It is more popular than the other forms of ownership because of limited partnership characteristics. Each limited partner is considered separate from all other partners and taxed as such, thus avoiding any double taxation. Each individual partner has the ability to transfer or sell his or her interest in the limited partnership without affecting the limited partnership as a whole, nor will the death or retirement of an individual cause the dissolution of the group. With limited partnership comes limited liability. Should a limited partnership fail, each individual will only loose his or her individual capital contribution made to the limited partnership and no more. Limited partnerships have majority rule. Lastly, limited partnerships give its members a greater purchasing power by pooling their resources, with the ability to do more investing then if trying to do so as an individual.

Remember:
When buying property in California from a foreign investor or seller, you must withhold 10% of the gain for taxes, unless the transaction is exempt.

STEPS IN SETTING UP A SYNDICATE

Organizing a syndication is a twelve-step process:

1. Research and analyze the area and the specific property to be syndicated.

2. Execute an option to purchase, allowing sufficient time to meet the statutory requirements and to attract the required capital.

3. Study the financing necessary on the property to determine the desired yield to the investors and establish whether any existing loans can and should be assumed or refinanced.

4. Make a formal appraisal to determine fair market value.

5. Project anticipated income and expenses, amortization payoff schedules, and calculate the number of shares (limited partnership interests), the number of syndicated units, and the size and terms of the interests to be offered.

6. Prepare a prospectus, a subscription agreement, and supporting docu-

ments, which are to be filed with the Department of Corporations (California's regulatory agency having jurisdiction over the proposed offering), and which ultimately will be furnished to each prospective purchaser.

7. File an application with the appropriate regulatory agency. Generally, the syndicator must file and secure permission from the Department of Corporation's commissioner. If interstate offerings are made, the promoter must apply with the Securities and Exchange Commission and file necessary registration statements, subject to certain specified exemptions. If exempted, however, the syndicator is still required to go through the Department of Corporations.

8. After any required changes in the prospectus and subscription agreement are made and approval has been obtained, print the forms and documents in their approved form for distribution to prospective investors.

9. Assign the option to purchase the property to the syndicate, i.e. the limited partnership to be formed, under an appropriately selected DBA ("doing business as" name). At this point the only partners would be the promoter and a few associates, perhaps an attorney and an accountant.

10. Negotiate the purchase of the property according to the price and terms projected and outlined in the prospectus and offering circular. This may be done at the very outset or at any intermediate step along the way, as per the terms of the option. Of course, if the purchase option is not carefully drafted, the promoter who is unable to market the shares may end up buying the property him or herself.

11. Solicit investors and open escrow to receive the funds until the sale is ready to close.

12. After all subscriptions are sold, file the Limited Partnership Agreement or other appropriate completed form. The general partner now assumes the managerial functions as provided for in the agreement.

Remember:
A syndication is an association of people, formed for the purpose of conducting and carrying out some particular business transaction where each member has mutual interest.

ESTATE PLANNING AND REAL ESTATE

Real estate investments can be the foundation on which a person builds an accumulation of wealth. But acquiring assets and meeting objectives are not necessarily the same thing, just as acquiring property is not the same as conserving it. The purpose of estate planning is to secure to the owner maximum benefits in the possession and use of his or her property, and to enable him or her to pass it on to family or other beneficiaries with the least amount of diminution or shrinkage of the estate.

Proper estate planning is concerned with five broad considerations:

1. Conservation of the assets, or "corpus," of the estate;

2. Orderly transfer of the estate through trusts and/or by a carefully thoughtout and effectively drafted will to beneficiaries;

3. Minimization of federal and state income taxes;

4. Minimization of estate and inheritance taxes; and

5. Abatement of probate costs.

Without proper planning, tremendous liquidity and tax problems could ensue. Many legal and economic factors must be considered and thoroughly thought through. This requires a coordinated estate planning team, consisting of, if necessary, an attorney, certified public accountant (CPA), certified financial planner (CFP), life underwriter, real estate specialist, business manager, trust company, executor or executrix, and of course, the principal actors, the testators themselves. In deciding whether to dispose of property by gift during life or by will at death, the interplay of tax laws with legal and economic considerations is critical, requiring the combined talents of the specialists mentioned above.

Estate planning involves making provisions for the conservation of one's assets, both real and personal property. Conservation devices include the following techniques:

1) Providing for liquidation at favorable times and under favorable circumstances;

2) Minimizing estate taxes through gifts and inter vivos (living) trusts;

3) Establishing a testamentary (by will) trust to avoid the double tax that occurs when community property is left to one spouse and subsequently transferred to the children;

4) Setting up the method of title ownership that will minimize expenses and fees, delays in transfer, and estate and inheritance taxes;

5) Creating an irrevocable trust that will avoid federal estate taxes and shift income to reduce income tax liabilities;

6) Retaining a life estate upon transfer of real property as a gift, in order to reduce gift taxes;

7) Giving away other assets, including securities, while living instead of at death, to reduce taxes;

8) Transferring property to a minor under the California Uniform Transfers to Minors Act;

9) Designating a named payee in life insurance contracts to avoid taxation; and

10) Other strategies.

There is an adage that says that creating an estate is easier than preserving it. Statistical evidence confirms that a good number of people have accumulated moderate to large estates, only to have them depleted after death; sometimes, even before. The subject of estate planning is such a vast one and we have only introduced it here briefly but urge the reader to consult with competent counsel and other specialists as noted above to "team up" for finding the your optimum solutions. The fees paid to these specialists can often be the best insurance policy a person can buy to protect an estate.

S U M M A R Y

We looked at the factors that go into the decision to invest in real property, and then we analyzed why people invest their money. From the decision about whether to invest, we then looked at the financial side of investing, to see how potential investors can plan to finance investment properties.

We also returned to the subject of prospecting and marketing. We analyzed prospecting and marketing in great depth at the beginning of this book; prospecting can help not only brokers seeking new clients looking for single family dwellings, but also investors looking to put their money into a rental property, business or undeveloped land.

Valuation was discussed; we learned how to arrive at the appropriate figures to determine whether the investment will make financial sense, or to see what kind of potential return on an investment that an investor might be able to expect. We revisited the same valuation methods discussed earlier in this book: cost, market and capitalization methods. We then looked at analyzing the rental market and outlined how to determine its health.

We briefly touched on the tax withholding requirements of buyers who purchase property from a foreign seller.

Syndication, or the meeting of potential investors for a mutual investment, was explained, highlighting the different types of legal organizations that may be used to form this partnership and the advantages and disadvantages of each. Brokerage opportunities relating to syndication were also discussed.

Finally, we briefly introduced estate planning, and how best to preserve the value of an estate and pass property from the owner to the beneficiaries of the owner's choosing.

T E R M S   A N D   P H R A S E S

Adjusted Gross Income – Gross Income minus allowable adjustments.

Appreciation – The increase in value over the original investment.

Cash Flow - Net income generated by a property before depreciation and other non-cash expenses.

Diminished Capacity – A state of mind that causes an imbalance between the perceived value of the real property investment and actual return on investment of the real property investment. Usually this happens when a property purchase is made impulsively and not carefully thought out; i.e., the investor "fell in love" with the property.

Leverage - The ratio of debt to current value.

Liquidity – The ability to generate cash from an investment in a hurry.

Replacement Reserves – The portion of the annual income set aside for the replacement of wasting assets, such as mechanical and electrical equipment, roofing, carpeting, paint and other impermanent building components.

Syndication - An association of people, formed for the purpose of conducting and carrying out some particular business transaction where each member has mutual interest.

Tax Shelter - A special consideration provided for by the tax code to the real estate investor who de-sires to take advantage of allowable depreciation schedules, capital gains privileges, tax-deferred exchanges and other benefits. Commonly used to refer to the real property that has provided the tax consideration and not actually the tax consideration itself.

Yield - The amount the investor makes on the capital invested during the time the investment is held.

C H A P T E R   Q U I Z

1. The ratio of debt to current value is called:
   a. Leverage
   b. Cash flow
   c. Liquidity
   d. Appreciation

2. Which of the following is not a benefit of investing in property?
   a. Tax shelter
   b. Hedge against inflation
   c. Strength of the dollar
   d. Interim use

3. The amount the investor makes on the capital invested during the time the investment is held is called:
   a. Cash flow
   b. Yield
   c. Appreciation
   d. Leverage

4. Which of the following factors promote stability in real estate?
   a. Favorable zoning
   b. Proximity to shopping venues
   c. Length of lease
   d. All of the above

5. Which of the following would be considered a disadvantage of investing in real estate?
   a. Flexibility and control
   b. Refinancing
   c. Amenities
   d. Management care

6. Which of the following is not a source of financing for an income property?
    a. Commercial banks
    b. Life insurance companies
    c. Credit unions
    d. Savings and loan associations

7. One-fourth of the entire debt of the United Sates is located in what region of the country?
    a. Midwest
    b. Pacific Coast
    c. East Coast
    d. South

8. The amount of financing available to an investor depends ultimately on what factor?
    a. The source of financing
    b. The investor's debt to asset ratio
    c. The investor's down payment
    d. All of the above

9. REIT stands for:
    a. Real Estate Investment Theory
    b. Real Estate Investment Time
    c. Real Estate Investment Transfer
    d. Real Estate Investment Trust

10. The amount of income an owner will receive from rents, before deductions for expenses and debt, is referred to as:
    a. Gross operating income
    b. Net operating income
    c. Profit
    d. Net profit

11. Which of the following is not an operational expense?
    a. Taxes
    b. Interest
    c. Insurance
    d. Management

12. Total Return refers to:
    a. Adjusted gross spendable income
    b. Principal payments for the entire year
    c. Both A and B
    d. Neither A nor B

13. Which of the following is not a valuation approach?
    a. Market
    b. Cost
    c. Income
    d. All are valuation approaches

14. A capitalization rate is used in which valuation approach?
    a. Income
    b. Cost
    c. Market
    d. Both A and C

15. As the capitalization rate increases, that happens to the value of property?
- a. Increases
- b. Decreases
- c. Stays the same
- d. The capitalization rate does not have an effect on property value

16. All of the following are characteristics of the rental market except:
- a. Current vacancy rates
- b. Income characteristics
- c. Diminished capacity
- d. Rent-income relationships

17. Which of the following is an example of syndication?
- a. Limited partnership
- b. Joint tenancy
- c. Corporation
- d. All are forms of syndication

18. "An association of individuals, formed for the purpose of conducting and carrying out some particular business transaction, ordinarily of a financial character, in which the members are mutually interested, formed for some temporary purpose, such as the organization of a real estate trust and the sale of shares to the public," describes what concept?
- a. Syndication
- b. Limited partnership
- c. Corporation
- d. Brokerage

19. Any person purchasing property in the United States from a foreign seller must withhold what percent of the price?
- a. 5%
- b. 10%
- c. 15%
- d. 20%

20. Which of the following is not an advantage of a limited partnership?
- a. Partners are taxed as individuals
- b. A majority vote can assign or remove the general partner
- c. More leverage
- d. All are advantages of a partnership

EXCHANGES
AND
TRADE-IN
PROGRAMS

What you will learn in this Chapter

- Definition and Qualifications for an Exchange
- Reasons for Exchanging
- 1031 Exchanges
- Adjusted Cost Basis
- Analysis of the Exchange Agreement
- Multiple Exchanges
- Home Trade-In Sales
- Types of Trade-In Programs
- Steps in a Trade-In Program
- Brokerage Opportunities in Exchanges

Test Your Knowledge

1. To qualify for a tax-free exchange:
   a. Boot may be used to make the values of the two properties equal
   b. The exchange must be even; no other exchange is allowed to create equality in the transfer
   c. Cash may be used to make the values of the two properties equal
   d. Net mortgage relief may be received by the taxpayer claiming tax-free status.

2. Which of the following is a reason to do a tax-free exchange?
   a. To acquire property without using cash
   b. Avoid depreciation recapture for pre-1987 transactions
   c. Allow taxpayers to dispose of an unwanted property and immediately acquire a new one
   d. All of the above

3. Which type(s) of property qualify for the tax-free exchange?
   a. Investment
   b. Rental
   c. Dealer
   d. Both A and B

4. The adjusted basis for property received in an exchange can be found by adding which of the following items to the original basis?
   a. Cash received
   b. Depreciation allowance
   c. Amortization and depletion taken
   d. Special assessments

5. Different rules apply for different exchanges; however, every exchange requires the parties to answer four basic questions. Which of the following is not a question to be answered in a tax-free exchange?
   a. Questions dealing with realized gain
   b. Questions dealing with the new basis of property acquired
   c. Questions dealing with amortization
   d. Questions dealing with postponed portion of gain

6. A broker will act as a principal in what type of program?
   a. Tax-free exchange
   b. Trade-in
   c. Both A and B
   d. Neither A nor B

7. Which of the following is a trade-in program?
   a. Straight trade
   b. Guaranteed trade
   c. Tax-deferred trade
   d. Both A and B

INTRODUCTION

One way to defer payment of taxes on the sale of real property is to enter into a qualified tax-free exchange. The sale of the property, which will be illustrated in a comprehensive example reflect a sizable taxable gain, including the recognition of a substantial portion as ordinary income through depreciation recapture. We now discuss how part or all of that gain could be deferred by means of an exchange.

DEFINITION

An exchange involves the transfer of like kind property. The exchange of a business for a business, or investment property for investment property is considered a like kind trade. In addition to the exchange of real property, a leasehold lasting 30 years or longer could be exchanged for fee simple interest. Exchanges are tax-free, but must qualify in before the exchange is permitted.

There are five qualities that must be met before an interested party can do a tax-free exchange. First, the property must be exchanged for another property of like kind. Again, this means the properties being exchanged must be used for the same purpose – such as income properties. Second, the properties must be of equal value. No boot, cash or net mortgage relief may be received by the taxpayer wishing to claim tax-free status. Should the properties not be equal, the boot or cash will be taxed normally, and not deferred. Third and exchange cannot happen between relatives directly related by blood or marriage. Forth none of the properties involved in the exchange can be held as stock in trade, dealer property, or property held primarily for sale or resale. Lastly property to be acquired must be clearly identified within 45 days of the disposition of the original property, and close within 180 days.

In the event all five qualities of a tax-free exchange are met, the property will be exempt from taxation until it is sold, or disposed of. The term tax-free exchange may be a little misleading. The property is not actually tax-free, the taxes are simply delayed until the property is sold before they are due. Should there be a gain, this gain is taxed at the final sale of the property. If there is a gain, but the property owner passes away before the property is sold, the property will indeed be tax-free as the new basis is stepped up for the person inheriting the property.

Remember:
- A tax-free exchange may take place as long as property is exchanged for like kind property.
- Tax liability on gain is not forgiven, merely postponed.

REASONS FOR EXCHANGING

You may be wondering when a person might elect to do a tax free exchange. There are several reasons when and why a person may wish to exchange property rather than selling it and paying taxes on the gain immediately.

One reason is that an exchange will allow a taxpayer to get rid of unwanted property and acquire a new one immediately. Should a person with an investment property have a new property he or she wanted to acquire, and was not able to do so until the old property was sold, a faster route is to exchange the two properties between owners. Whatever the reason may be, exchanging will allow a transaction to happen immediately without waiting on a sale.

Deferring all or part of the gain on property is another good reason to exchange property. This could be of benefit to the person exchanging property in a rising market to avoid paying tax on a large gain immediately. Should the market come back down, and the investor sell the property the tax would be considerably less than if all the tax was paid for in the original exchange.

An exchange allows the person to trade property without using cash. This is good for those people who are ready to acquire a different property, but may not have a lot of free cash to exchange on a property. Additionally it does not require the property owner to enter into a trust deed on the property.

Exchanging property will allow the tax-payer to avoid paying recapture depreciation on transactions prior to 1987.

An exchange may allow the tax-payer to dispose of a hard-to-sell property that might sit on the open market for some time if sold on a conventional sale. Should it be attractive to another tax-payer as part of an exchange deal, it will be a quick transaction avoiding a long sales / escrow period.

One final reason a tax-payer might choose to do an exchange is to get rid of one large property for several smaller properties, or diversification of his or her assets. Now not all of the tax-payers money will be tied up in one investment, but several that may be sold off at a later date, one at a time. The converse is true as well, a person with several smaller properties may choose to consolidate into one large property through an exchange.

1 0 3 1   E X C H A N G E S

A 1031 Exchange occurs when an investor exchanges property for a like property of another property of equal value, and defers any taxes until the property being exchanged is sold.

Properties must be of equal value, at least on paper. Property must also be like kind property. Like kind property means the properties being exchanged are the same. Real property cannot be exchanged for personal property because those two types of property are not alike. A business may be exchanged for another, even if they manufacture different products; it is still a business for a business, or like kind.

When properties are not of equal value, cash or non-like property must be added to the exchange and given to the disadvantaged property owner, to make the exchange of the two properties equal in value. This exchange is called a boot exchange. Personal residences are not allowed as inclusions in a tax-deferred exchange. Only properties such as apartment buildings, commercial buildings or land are eligible. Like kind dictates property must be similar in nature, equal value dictates that an exchange must be of equal monetary value.

Property can be classified under five categories: principal residence, dealer, trade or business, rental, and investment. Trade or business, rental and investment properties are the only types that qualify for a tax-free exchange under Section 1031. As long as property is neither personal use property, like a primary residence, nor property held for sale to customers like a lot in a subdivision for sale by a dealer, it is considered like kind and qualifies for the exchange.

Remember:
Property can be classified into five categories:
- Principal residence
- Dealer
- Trade or business
- Rental
- Investment

The category property falls under is strictly up to how the owner uses the property. For example, if A owns a townhouse and rents it out, this is considered an income property. Should A exchange a property with B, who uses her townhouse as a personal residence it would not negate the exchange as long as A uses the new townhouse as an investment property still. So, like kind means the intention of the use. Even if the other party uses a similar property for a completely different purpose will not negate the exchange. Additionally income-producing properties may be exchanged for investment properties, or that investment properties may be traded for properties used in one's trade or business, or in any other combination of the three categories that fall under the rules of Section 1031.

When the properties are sold, the cost basis of the original property being exchanged becomes the cost basis of the newly-purchased property, provided the two properties are equal. If there is a boot exchange to create equality, the cost basis will change. Ultimately, the capital gain or loss is figured in the same way as it is for other income property.

A person may qualify for a complete tax-deferred exchange if he or she trades up to a property that is equal or greater in value than the property they currently have. This is usually referred to as the buy-up rule. All equity must be absorbed into the new property to be completely tax-deferred. If any money is taken out during the exchange, this money is subject to taxation, nullifying the complete tax-deferred exchange, making a partial tax-deferred exchange.

When conducting any type of exchange, property ownership must stay the same. This means if an individual owns property and is interested in an exchange, the new property must be individually owned. Similarly, if a corporation owns property and does an exchange, the new property will have to be owned by the corporation. There are three ways to hold property: as an individual, corporation, or partnership.

There may also be a reverse exchange. A reverse exchange is when a person finds a replacement property before exchanging his or her property. In this event, an exchange accommodation titleholder will take title to the new property until the sale of the exchange property is final. The sale of the old property, or the property to be exchanged, must happen within 180 days.

A D J U S T E D   C O S T   B A S I S

To calculate the adjusted cost basis for a property acquired by way of an exchange the new property will equal to the basis of the old property adding or subtracting any adjustments that must be made. Items added to the original basis are cash or other property paid (boot), assumed trust deeds, recognized gain, capital additions or special

439

assessments. Items subtracted from the original basis are any remaining trust deed loans, cash or property received (boot), amortization or depletion taken, depreciation and reimbursed casualty loss. Upon making the necessary additions and subtractions from the original basis of the property exchanged, you will arrive at the new basis for the property received in the exchange.

> **Remember:**
> • Adjusted cost basis is the basis for property after all additions and subtractions have been made from the original basis.

ANALYSIS OF THE EXCHANGE AGREEMENT FORM

Exchange agreements are a three-page document. They leave plenty of space for the user to fill in all necessary terms to the contract. This form is not all that different from a traditional Purchase Agreement and Receipt for Deposit, making it somewhat familiar to the user. Make sure, however, to use the exchange agreement form and not a deposit receipt form as the exchange agreement must be very carefully filled out to qualify for a tax-free exchange. It is a good idea to have a tax advisor look over the forms to make sure they will pass IRS audits.

The following is an analysis of the exchange agreement form:

Page 1 of the Exchange Agreement

The first line of the first page is where the names of the offering party (offeror) will go. The properties involved are described by numbers, eliminating the necessity for names or repetitive property descriptions.

After the names comes a description of the properties and encumbrances. Estimated market value, loans and equities for both properties are listed in the terms and conditions clause of the contract.

A warning appears at the bottom of page 1 telling the real estate agent he or she should not to give legal and tax advice, suggesting that the parties obtain competent advice from other professionals in areas outside the expertise of the agent.

Page 2 of the Exchange Agreement

Page 2 contains all the numbered items and conditions. It is allowable to change or delete one or more of the clauses if necessary. If there is an inconsistency between a specific provision, the written information, and a general provision, the typed information, the specific provision will take precedence.

Page 3 of the Exchange Agreement

The last page contains the acceptance as well as the agreement to pay a commission to the broker for his or her services. The broker will receive this commission as soon as the deed is recorded or in the event of a land contract, when it is delivered. Should there be a disagreement over who pays the fee and a court case is necessary, the prevailing party is entitled to reasonable attorneys' fees and costs.

The offeror and broker must sign the offer and agree to the fee agreement. All parties will receive a copy of the agreement upon signing.

MULTIPLE EXCHANGES

It is not often that two owners will wish to exchange property with the other. Usually a third party has be included in the exchange. Multiple exchanges or a two-party exchange with a cash buyer added, are more realistic.

Example:
Alex wants to trade his 10–unit apartment for Jennifer's 15-unit apartment complex. Jennifer does not want Alex's apartment and prefers cash. Alex can enter into an exchange with Jennifer as long as there is a third party ready to buy his 10-unit apartment complex.

Remember:
- Exchanges don't always happen between two people. There can be multiple parties involved in an exchange.

HOME TRADE-IN SALE

Benefits to the Broker
The home trade-in program involves an agent as the principle, not the middleman to a transaction. This means that the broker will put up the capital for the trade. It operates very similar to how a car might be traded at a dealership. The broker will take the property in exchange for a new one. The broker will put up the money, and momentarily take title to the property until it is sold to another buyer. Please don't confuse this with the broker taking a listing to property, it is completely different.

Remember:
- Trade-ins are different from exchanges. In an exchange, the broker acts as a middleman in the transfer of property for another. In a trade-in, the broker acts as a principal, furnish ing capital, specialized knowledge and time to the transaction.

The broker who is engaged in the increasingly popular activity of trade-ins will profit in a variety of ways. First, it might attract more buyers and sellers into his or her office as well as gain more referrals from cooperating brokers. Second the broker will make a double commission on the sale, one on the sale of the old property and a sales commission on the replacement home. Third, the property traded will increase the broker's inventory. This will be helpful with additional interested buyers attracted to the brokerage. A fourth reason a broker might engage in trade-ins is to expand his or her practice and reputation in the industry. Finally, the broker will be given an opportunity to work with builders with trade-in programs by taking an old house for a newly constructed one.

Personal Data Worksheet.

Personal Data

Name _____ Age ___ Address _____ Phone _____ Date _____

Wife _____ Children _____ Ages _____ Prepared by _____

OCCUPATION _____ ANNUAL INCOME _____

1. Annual income last year _____

2. Projected income next year _____

3. Wife's occupation _____ Annual income _____

4. Wife's annual income last year _____

5. Wife's projected income next year _____

6. Other occupational income _____

OTHER INCOME

1. Interest _____ etc.

2. Dividends _____

3. Annuities _____

4. Capital Gains _____

5. Real Estate _____

ASSETS

Life Insurance: Face Value _____ Cash Value _____

Savings _____ Other cash available for investment _____

Notes receivable _____

Savings Bonds _____ Other Bonds _____

IRA's _____ Other _____

Stocks

_____

_____

_____

_____

Real Estate:

Address _____ Value _____ Encumbrance

Address _____ Value _____ Encumbrance

Address _____ Value _____ Encumbrance

INVESTMENT NEEDS

1. Additional income now _____ Amount _____

2. Growth _____

3. Need monthly income for retirement _____ How much?

REMARKS

_____

_____

_____

_____

_____

When to Trade

An owner will find it advantageous to trade under a variety of circumstances. First, size requirements might be a reason to trade. If a growing family needs more space, or if a all the children in another family have grown up and moved away, a smaller house might be more convenient. Location of property might be another reason to trade. Finding a residence closer to work, or closer to family may cause a property owner to trade. Third, if an investment property has dropped below a pre-determined rate of return, the owner may wish to trade that property for a different one. Length of time at the same residence may be another reason to trade. Some people may wish to make a change not based on location, space or any other tangible reason, but more of an emotional reason. Finally a trade may happen when a homeowner's current property has a substantial amount of equity.

TYPES OF HOME TRADE-IN PROGRAMS

There are three kinds of trade-in programs, guaranteed trade, time-limit trade and straight trade. The program selected will depend on the resources available to the broker and the type of need displayed by the client.

Guaranteed Trade

In a guaranteed trade, the broker agrees to buy the house at a preset number, referred to as the "turnover" or "upset" price. This price is usually about 80—85 percent of estimated market value, based on the commission allowance, expenses of sale, holding and operating costs, and a small reserve for contingencies. Typically brokers make a charge of 1 percent or more of the guaranteed price for the guarantee privilege, with the proviso that it will be waived if the house sells within the allotted listing period. The broker underwrites the owner's equity, agreeing to buy only if a sale is not made within a prescribed period of time.

Time-Limit Trade

A time-limit trade will happen only if the present house can sell. Should the house not sell within the deadline date, there is no enforceable contract. No guarantee is made, and the broker is relieved of the responsibility of providing the requisite capital to purchase a property, which may tie up his or her funds in an idle venture. Time-limit trades are usually used when the seller is unwilling to list at the upset price as determined by the broker. Agreements to sell under a conditional plan are sometimes made in the form of an option for a limited period of time.

Highly capitalized firms may offer loan plans to borrowers dealing directly with the firm. This allows the company to pick up additional listings and sales through making "purchase funds" available to owners who do not have sufficient assets to purchase another house without first selling their present homes.

Straight Trade

A straight trade is an outright exchange of properties. This is very similar to the way as an old car is traded outright for a new. A broker will take equity from an old house, and let the buyer apply this equity toward the new house. Straight trades may also be direct trades between two owners, without the services of a broker.

> **Remember:**
> The different types of home trade-in programs include:
> - Guaranteed title
> - Time-limit trade
> - Straight trade

SELLER'S INTENT TO EXCHANGE SUPPLEMENT
(C.A.R. Form SES, Revised 10/01)
(For use with a seperate purchase agreement)

The following terms and conditions are hereby incorporated in and made a part of the agreement, dated _____,
on property known as _____ ("Property"), in which
_____ is referred to as Buyer,
and _____ is referred to as Seller.
All other provisions of the existing agreement shall remain in full force.

1. **SELLER'S INTENT TO EXCHANGE:** It is the intent of Seller to utilize this transaction as part of an exchange of like-kind property under Internal Revenue Code §1031 and the regulations promulgated thereunder. Buyer and Seller agree to cooperate in effecting such an exchange, as follows:
   A. Seller intends to use the Property as part of an exchange for "Other Property":
      (Check One Only)
      ☐ Described as _____.
      OR ☐ To be located and designated by Seller, who shall take all steps necessary to enter into a contract to sell and transfer such Other Property.
   B. Seller shall indemnify, defend and hold harmless all other parties to this transaction from all liabilities and any additional costs arising from or connected in any way with the exchange.
   C. If Seller is unable to locate, designate, enter into a contract to acquire, or complete acquisition of such Other Property:
      (Check One Only)
      ☐ This transaction shall close escrow as a sale, without extension of time for closing.
      OR ☐ The close of escrow for this transaction shall be extended by a maximum of _____ **Days** to enable Seller to complete such arrangements.
      OR ☐ This transaction shall be canceled and all parties shall be released from further obligation.
      OR ☐ Other: _____
   D. Buyer in this transaction shall not be required to take title to Other Property for any period of time, as an accommodation to Seller, unless agreed to in writing.
   E. All parties agree to take such actions and execute or consent to such additional documents and transactions as may be reasonably requested by Seller, provided that all other conditions of this agreement are met.

2. **ADDITIONAL TERMS:** _____
   _____
   _____
   _____
   _____
   _____

3. **TAX AND LEGAL CONSEQUENCES OF AN EXCHANGE:** Locating and designating properties pursuant to this Agreement, if applicable, are the responsibility of the party requesting the exchange ("Exchangor"), and will not occur automatically as a result of this Agreement. If the exchange will be non-simultaneous, under federal tax law: (i) the property to be acquired by Exchangor must be identified within 45 days after transfer of Exchangor's current property; (ii) the acquisition generally must be completed within 180 days after transfer of Exchangor's current property; and (iii) the 180 day period may be shorter under some circumstances. The manner of structuring an exchange transaction will have significant tax and legal consequences. Parties should consult their legal and/or tax advisors regarding this important matter.

By signing below, the parties acknowledge that they have read, understand, accept and have received a copy of this agreement.

Buyer _____ Seller _____

Date _____ Date _____

Buyer _____ Seller _____

Date _____ Date _____

Published and Distributed by:
REAL ESTATE BUSINESS SERVICES, INC.
a subsidiary of the CALIFORNIA ASSOCIATION OF REALTORS®
525 South Virgil Avenue, Los Angeles, California 90020

Reviewed by _____
Broker or Designee _____ Date _____

EQUAL HOUSING
OPPORTUNITY

SES-11 REVISED 10/01 (PAGE 1 OF 1) Print Date RBS JAN 02

The steps in a trade-in program may be as follows:

1. List the property on an exclusive basis.

2. Shop the market for an acceptable replacement house if the seller has not already selected one.

3. Submit a purchase offer that will be contingent upon the execution of a satisfactory guaranteed sales agreement on the present dwelling within a specified time, such as five days. If necessary, the broker may advance the down payment or a deposit as earnest money.

4. Appraise the property to determine its probable market value, using the market and cost approaches.

5. Break down the expenses, holding and operating costs, encumbrances, and reserves for risks; arrive at a reasonably close net equity position to determine the feasibility of a trade.

6. Prepare a guarantee agreement and other documentation for owners' approval.

7. After obtaining the required signatures, open escrow.

8. Market the owner's present home during the listing period. Barring a sale within the allotted time, the broker buys it at the predetermined turnover price. Thereafter, he or she sells it through his or her normal brokerage activities; he or she retains the listing commission, and the sales commission is paid to the salesperson producing the sale.

BROKERAGE OPPORTUNITIES IN EXCHANGES

There are abundant opportunities to become an exchange broker. When doing exchange work, there are more opportunities to express creativity in putting transactions together. Usually financing is not an issue as exchanging properties involves trading of equities. So, even in a depressed money market, built-in financing provides a convenient marketing vehicle.

Commissions are pooled and then split by the brokers representing the respective parties. Exchange brokers usually have higher earnings when compared to other brokers. This is based both transactional and over a period of time.

One of the reasons exchange brokers make more money over time is because inventory for exchanges stays constant, it does not change with housing market supply fluctuations. Many owners are "don't-wanters" – people who simply desire to unload properties, for whatever reason. Traditional selling of a house requires that the broker know his or her clients and their situation in every way, however exchanging properties involve less direct personal involvement, with the result that the clientele tends to be less fussy and more likely to be satisfied.

Exchange brokers will have lower overhead costs. They don't need a large office keeping rental costs down. The location of the brokerage is not important so the prestige of an upscale address is not necessary. Most exchange brokers will spend most of their time in a mobile office. Large sales forces are not necessary either, eliminating the need to pay salaries to multiple people. Most exchange brokers can get by with an assistant handling administrative matters. Advertising costs are minimal, generally relying on word of mouth more than any other source.

Finding prospects will be the most important activity for an exchange broker. For a broker to succeed in the exchange field, he or she needs to be alert to the methods of finding prospects, of arousing their interest, of stimulating their desire, and of developing the exchange even if one participant wants only cash.

Remember:
- Commissions realized in an exchange are typically pooled by the brokers involved, and then split evenly.
- Exchange brokers do not need a large support staff, if any at all, nor do they need a large office.

S U M M A R Y

In this chapter we examined exchanges and trade-ins, and learned the differences between them and the qualifications for each program. First, the exchange was carefully explained, looking at two-way exchanges and multiple exchanges. A sample exchange agreement was shown, and then analyzed for further understanding of the process and paperwork that goes into the exchange. In understanding exchanges, the cost basis and adjusted cost basis were presented, and calculating these was explained.

Trade-ins were then analyzed, to see the process, the types of programs available and the role of a broker in a trade compared to the role of a broker in an exchange. You can see that the broker has quite a different role in the trade than in an exchange. To further your personal understanding of trade-ins, a step-by-step program was provided from the beginning of the trade to the end.

Finally, brokerage opportunities in exchanges were discussed. In this section, you could see how a brokerage office dealing in exchanges would be markedly different from a brokerage office dealing strictly in real estate sales. The size of the office, staff and location of an exchange broker's office are all different from a real estate broker's office.

T E R M S   A N D   P H R A S E S

Adjusted Cost Basis – For tax purposes, it is the cost of the property plus improvements and minus depreciation, amortization, and depletion.

Exchange - A transfer of property in return for other property or services.

Like-kind property – Property that is alike based on the nature or class of property.

Net mortgage relief - The difference between loan values. A person may take a lesser loan value, or a greater loan value that the one he or she is giving up.

1. In order to exchange property, the two properties must be:
   a. Of equal value
   b. In the same business, such as a hardware store exchanged for a hardware store
   c. Like for like, meaning one productive use exchanged for another, such as an apartment building exchanged for a hardware store
   d. Both A and C

2. To qualify for a tax-free exchange:
   a. Boot may be used to make the values of the two properties equal
   b. The exchange must be even; no other exchange is allowed to create equality in the transfer
   c. Cash may be used to make the values of the two properties equal
   d. Net mortgage relief may be received by the taxpayer claiming tax-free status.

3. The two parties in the exchange:
   a. Must be related by blood or marriage
   b. Cannot be related by blood or marriage
   c. May be any persons, with equal property
   d. May be any persons, with equal property, where both properties are located in the same county

4. In a tax-free exchange:
   a. There is no tax on gains
   b. Gains are taxed immediately
   c. Gain is not taxed until the sale is final
   d. None of the above

5. Which of the following is a reason to do a tax-free exchange?
   a. To acquire property without using cash
   b. Avoid depreciation recapture for pre-1987 transactions
   c. Allow taxpayers to dispose of unwanted property and immediately acquire a new one
   d. All of the above

6. The provisions for non-recognition of gains or losses are set out in:
   a. The Commissioner's Code
   b. Internal Revenue Code
   c. Internal Revenue Service Code
   d. All of the above

7. Which of the following is not a classification of property?
   a. Commercial
   b. Principal residence
   c. Dealer
   d. Trade or business

8. Which type(s) of property qualify for the tax-free exchange?
   a. Investment
   b. Rental
   c. Dealer
   d. Both A and B

9. True or false: an apartment building may be classified as "like kind" and exchanged for vacant land for building a shopping center.
    a. True
    b. False

10. True or false: real property cannot be exchanged for personal property.
    a. True
    b. False

11. Personal property may be exchanged for personal property as long as:
    a. The exchange is for less than $5,000
    b. The exchange is for more than $5000
    c. The properties are of similar nature or class
    d. Personal property is not a commodity allowed to be traded under a tax-free exchange

12. Net mortgage relief is:
    a. Another term for a tax-free exchange
    b. The difference between the loan given up and the new loan acquired
    c. Taxable
    d. None of the above

13. The adjusted basis for property received in an exchange can be found by adding which of the following items to the original basis?
    a. Cash received
    b. Depreciation allowance
    c. Amortization and depletion taken
    d. Special assessments

14. Different rules apply for different exchanges; however, every exchange requires the parties to answer four basic questions. Which of the following is not a question to be answered in a tax-free exchange?
    a. Questions dealing with realized gain
    b. Questions dealing with the new basis of property acquired
    c. Questions dealing with amortization
    d. Questions dealing with postponed portion of gain

15. True or false: encumbrances or liens are listed on the exchange agreement form.
    a. True
    b. False

16. The adjusted basis for property received in an exchange can be found by subtracting which of the following items from the original basis?
    a. Special assessments
    b. Other property or boot paid
    c. Reimbursed casualty loss
    d. All of the above

17. A broker will act as a principal in what type of program?
    a. Tax-free exchange
    b. Trade-in
    c. Both A and B
    d. Neither A nor B

18. Which of the following is not a benefit for a broker participating in trade-ins?
    a. Single commissions
    b. Attract more sellers and buyers into the office
    c. Affords the broker an opportunity to work with builders
    d. Increases inventory

19. Which of the following is a trade-in program?
    a. Straight trade
    b. Guaranteed trade
    c. Tax-deferred trade
    d. Both A and B

20. An "outright exchange of properties" describes:
    a. A straight trade
    b. Guaranteed trade
    c. Time-limit trade
    d. None of the above

BUSINESS SALES AND OTHER BROKERAGE ACTIVITIES

What you will learn in this Chapter

- Selling a Business
- Alcoholic Beverage Control Act
- Valuation of Business Opportunities
- Real Property Securities Dealers
- Insurance
- Notary Public Services
- Escrow
- Loan Brokerage Activities
- State of California Sales Opportunities
- Subdivision Sales Opportunities
- Mobile Home Brokerage

Test Your Knowledge

1. A broker may sell a mobile home if:
    a. He or she is registered with the Department of Motor Vehicles for at least one year
    b. The unit is greater than 8 feet wide and 40 feet long
    c. Both A and B
    d. Neither A nor B, the broker requires a separate license

2. All of the following are a function of a notary public except:
    a. Applying and affixing his or her official signature and seal to insure as fully as possible that the original agreement cannot be altered in any way
    b. Determining if the parties are truly who they claim to be
    c. Certifying that all documents have been accurately filled out
    d. Obtaining the acknowledgement of the parties that they have signed the agreement or taking oath that they are aware of the contents of the agreement

3. Who issues or oversees the regulations governing insurance licensees?
    a. Real Estate Commissioner
    b. Insurance Commissioner
    c. Department of Business and Transportation
    d. Both B and C

4. Goodwill is valued using which of the following methods of valuation?
    a. Length of time the business has been in existence
    b. Vehicle/customer traffic count
    c. Present and future anticipated competition
    d. All of the above

5. When a seller engages in a business where sales of personal property at retail are made, he or she must secure a seller's permit obtained from:
    a. State Board of Equalization
    b. Real Estate Commissioner
    c. Any broker
    d. County Recorder's office

6. Article 6 of the Uniform Commercial Code requires the transferee to give public notice to all creditors regarding the sale of a business at least:
    a. 10 days prior to the sale
    b. 12 days prior to the sale
    c. 15 days prior to the sale
    d. 17 days prior to the sale

7. What is the final step in the sale of a business?
    a. Closing statements and documents are delivered to the parties at the close of escrow
    b. A bill of sale for all personal property is issued to the buyers
    c. The lease is transferred to the new owners
    d. A clearance receipt, Certificate of Payment of Sales and Tax Use, and a seller's permit for the new owner must be secured from the state Board of Equalization

Brokers can engage in a variety of activities that complement the basic real estate brokerage operation. This chapter will expose you to the many different opportunities that a broker can tap into. Each of these activities can not only supplement income from real estate sales, but can also provide the broker with additional sources of prospects, which can of course lead to sales. Happy clients, who have purchased or sold with the broker, may become clients again through one of the broker's other business activities.

Clients who have developed a relationship of trust with a broker may purchase a security interest such as a trust deed note or a mineral, oil and gas lease through the same broker. The client may ask for the broker's counsel on hazard insurance for property, seek out the broker for notary services, or consult the broker for exchange services. This relationship of trust can lead to the client regarding the broker as his or her financial advisor.

All of these topics will be discussed in this chapter, introducing you to the many opportunities a broker has at his or her fingertips.

S E L L I N G   A   B U S I N E S S

Under Section 10030 of the Real Estate Law a business opportunity is defined as a "sale or lease of the business and goodwill of an existing business enterprise or opportunity." In addition to the sale of real property, usually when a business is sold, inventory is sold with the business, meaning personal property. The laws and rules governing the sale of personal property will apply to the sale of the business as well as real property laws.

Business transactions generally involve few assets. The assets that are transferred are inventory, fixtures, stock-in-trade (if any) and goodwill. Goodwill is defined as the existing good name of the business, along with the customer loyalty currently enjoyed by the current owners. It is not a tangible asset like inventory, but more of an attitude people have of the current business. Usually real property is not transferred in the sale of a business, but an existing lease is transferred to the buyer.

Remember:
* When a business is sold, the goodwill, or existing customer base and good name, is sold with the business.

Steps in the Sale
The steps n the sale of a business opportunity are similar to the steps in the sale of real property. It is important, however, for the broker to be aware of the additional steps and legal issues he or she must keep in mind or do extra when selling a business.

The main differences from a regular real property transaction are that the prospective purchaser must sign a take-out agreement. A Notice of Intention to Sell or a Notice to Creditors of Bulk Transfer is recorded with the county recorder in the county in which the business resides. A notice of sale is then published in the local paper. A Financing statement is filed with the secretary of state, if the sale of the business is not a cash purchase. The State Board of Equalization must issue a Certificate of Payment of Sales and Tax Use and a sellers permit for the new owner of the property. If the current business has an alcohol license, this must be transferred to the new owners by obtaining approval from the Department of Alcoholic Beverage Control. Should any employees be involved in the sale of the business, clearance must be obtained by the state Department of Employment Development. This is to make sure all unemployment insurance taxes are current as well a making any necessary adjustments on benefits, time off or sick pay. Next a bill of sale is prepared for any personal property issued to the buyers. This step may also be used in a regular real property transaction if there the seller is selling personal property to the buyer, but most notably used in a business transaction. Finally the lease is transferred to the new owners. All other parts of the transaction will be the same as real property.

Each sale of a business will be different and unique and require special knowledge from the real estate professional handling the transaction. While no two transactions are alike, there are different steps that must be taken. The following is a general list of a typical business opportunity sale. Again, please remember this is not an exclusive list; merely an idea of the process, and a good place to begin when dealing with a business opportunity transaction.

1. The business is listed for sale.

2. A business opportunity deposit receipt or offer is completed when a buyer is found to purchase the property.

3. The offer is presented to the seller by the broker or agent for the seller's approval.

4. Escrow is opened upon the acceptance of the offer.

5. All creditors of the current business are notified of the sale and a notice of intended bulk sale is published, according to the requirements of the Bulk Sales Act.

6. To fulfill the requirements of the Uniform Commercial Code (UCC) a financing statements is filed with the Secretary of State or the recorder's office. The financing statement is a written notice of a creditor's interests in per sonal property.

7. All necessary forms are filed with the Department of Alcoholic Beverage Control, if there is a liquor license involved in the transaction.

8. The landlord is contacted to reassign the lease to the buyer.

9. Copies of the seller's permit and clearance receipt are collected from the Board of Equalization to protect the buyer from any liability resulting from the unpaid sales tax that the previous owner owed.

10. Information regarding the current employee's salaries, benefits and unemployment insurance tax is noted.

11. Inventory is taken of all stock, fixtures and other personal property to be transferred in the sale of the business.

12. A bill of sale is executed, transferring ownership of all elements of the business.

13. Buyer and seller receive closing statements at the close of escrow.

Remember:
- Selling a business is very similar to selling real estate. There must be a licensed agent, the property is advertised, and a buyer is found. Once a buyer is found, a purchase contract is agreed upon, and escrow is opened.

Listing Agreement

Each individual broker draws up listing agreements for the sale of a business. There are no standardized forms like in the sale of real property. Once this listing agreement is drawn up, an agency agreement between the seller and broker is formed.

Legal Requirements for the Sale of a Business

In every sale of a business, there are certain legal requirements that must be met before the transaction can go through. The requirements of the Bulk Transfer Act, Alcoholic Beverage Control Act, Uniform Commercial Code and the California sales and use tax regulations must be met for a successful sale of the business.

Bulk Transfer Act

When a business is sold, the majority of its inventory is usually sold with the business. The Uniform Commercial Code (UCC), which you will read about in the next few paragraphs, regulates the sale of this aspect of a business. The purpose of the Bulk Transfer Act is to protect the creditors from a business being sold. When a business is sold, public notice is given, so that all creditors are aware of the transfer. This is regulated under Division 6 of the UCC.

When a business is sold, the transfer and a notice of sale must be filed with the county recorder after 12 days have passes. Additionally a notice must be printed in the local newspaper where the business is being sold, as well as notice given to the county tax collector in the same twelve days before the transfer of property.

The notice to creditors will give anyone fair notice of the transfer of property, in the event the seller owes any creditors for current inventory. If a business is up for sale and a seller owes a creditor, the creditor should make sure they are paid for any services or goods provided before the transfer. If the business is sold without complying with the requirements of the bulk transfer law, the sale is valid between the buyer and the seller, but is considered fraudulent and void with regard to any creditors. In the event that the creditors are not notified, they may take recourse against the seller for any debt owed them, as the business was sold without the debt having been satisfied; nor was the creditor made aware of the transfer.

ALCOHOLIC BEVERAGE CONTROL ACT

When a business with the issue of an alcohol license is sold ,the buyer must not assume that the license will be transferred with the sale of the business. In the event that a bar, restaurant or any other establishment is sold where the buyer is interested in the alcohol license, that buyer must apply to the Department of Alcoholic Beverage Control to have the license transferred to their name. A buyer may be turned down for this license, or may be faced with a price of up to $12,000.00 for the license. Any seller who has had a license for more than two years may negotiate the price for the license between the buyer and seller in the sale of the business. However, if the license is sold for any time period before those two years, the buyer is subject to the price the Department of Alcoholic Beverage Control will charge for the license.

Remember:
- The transfer of a business where an alcohol license is required by the Department of Alcohol and Beverage Control for businesses less than two years old charging up to $12,000 for the license, or for businesses over two years old a price agreed upon by the buyer and seller.

Uniform Commercial Code

Most likely, when a business is being sold, the buyer will borrow money to purchase the business and all personal belongings to that business. In this situation, the Uniform Commercial Code, Division 9 sets the requirements for the transfer of the business and any personal property being transferred. A financing statement must be filed with the Secretary of State or the county recorder's office, giving the public notice of any security interest being created by the debt.

When a person borrows money for a real estate loan, a promissory note must be signed. The same is true for a note in the transfer of a business. A note is signed, showing the evidence of debt for the business transfer. The buyer then executes a security agreement, giving the lender an interest in the personal property and the financing statement, which will be recorded. When the financing statement is recorded, public notice is given and all parties are made aware of any interests in the property. This is much the same as a recoded trust deed, which gives public notice of a debt against real property.

Remember:
- The purpose of the Security Agreement and Financing Statement is to keep innocent purchasers from encumbrances not disclosed by the seller.

Accurate completion of the form "Notice to Creditors" assures that the specific requirements of the UCC are met. These requirements include:

1. Information that a bulk transfer is to be made;

2. Location and general description of the property to be transferred;

3. The name and business address of the transferor, and all other names and addresses used by him within the previous three years, so far as is known to the intended transferee; and

4. The place and date on or after which the bulk transfer is to be consummated.

Should a seller not comply with the notice requirements the transfer becomes fraudulent and void against those creditors of the transferor whose claims are based on credit transactions prior to the bulk transfer. With compliance, on the other hand, the creditors' recourse is against sellers only, not against the business or buyers.

Tax Return Form.

STATE OF CALIFORNIA
BOARD OF EQUALIZATION—Department of Business Taxes
STATE, LOCAL and DISTRICT SALES and USE TAX RETURN

	PERIOD	YEAR
FOR		
PARTIAL PERIOD		

DUE ON OR BEFORE	_____

Mail to:

STATE BOARD OF EQUALIZATION
P.O. BOX 942879
SACRAMENTO, CA   94279-0001

BUSINESS CODE	AREA CODE	ACCOUNT NUMBER

NAME	
	WORK COPY
BUSINESS ADDRESS	
	Not acceptable as a Return by the
CITY	STATE ZIP CODE REPORTING BASIS
	State Board of Equalization

READ INSTRUCTIONS BEFORE PREPARING

STATE SALES AND USE TAX

1. TOTAL (GROSS) SALES........ IF YOU INCLUDE TAX CHARGED—SEE LINE 9 $
2. ADD—Purchase price of tangible personal property purchased without California sales or use tax and used for some purpose other than resale ENTER "NONE" IF YOU HAVE NOTHING TO REPORT
3. TOTAL (Line 1 plus Line 2) .... ENTER "NONE" IF YOU HAVE NOTHING TO REPORT $
   DEDUCT EXEMPT TRANSACTIONS (See Instructions) $
4. Sales to other retailers for purposes of resale ....
5. Nontaxable Sales of Food Products ....
6. Nontaxable Labor (Repair and Installation) ....
7. Sales to the United States Government ....
8. Sales in interstate or foreign commerce to out-of-state consumers ..
9. Amount of sales tax (if any) included in Line 1 ....
10. Other exempt transactions ....
    (Clearly Explain)..
11. TOTAL TRANSACTIONS EXEMPT FROM STATE & COUNTY SALES & USE TAX (Lines 4 thru 10) $
12. Amount on which STATE & COUNTY Sales and Use Tax applies (Line 3 minus Line 11) ..... $
13. AMOUNT OF TAX......5% (4¾% State, ¼% County) (Multiply amount on Line 12 by .05) ... $

UNIFORM LOCAL SALES AND USE TAX

14. Amount on which State Tax applies (Enter amount from Line 12) .... $
15. Adjustments (See Instruction 15) .... $
16. Amount on which LOCAL Tax applies (Line 14 plus or minus Line 15) ... $
17. AMOUNT OF LOCAL TAX 1% (Multiply amount on Line 16 by .01) .... $

DISTRICT SALES AND USE TAX

Enter Amount of Transit/Traffic Authority/Transportation Commission Tax (From Line A14, Schedule A)

A	BAY AREA RAPID TRANSIT .001	C	SANTA CLARA COUNTY TRAFFIC AUTHORITY .006	E	SANTA CRUZ METRO. TRANSIT .004
B	SAN MATEO COUNTY TRANSIT .002	D	TRANSIT DISTRICT .003	F	LOS ANGELES CO. TRANS. COMM. .005

18. TOTAL OF BLOCKS A, B, C, D, E and F............................ $

TOTAL TAX

19. TOTAL STATE, COUNTY, LOCAL & DISTRICT TAX (Total of Lines 13, 17 and 18)   TOTAL TAX $
20. Deduct amount of sales or use tax or reimbursement therefor imposed by other states and paid by you on the purchase of tangible personal property. Purchase price must be included in Line 2 (See Instruction 20)
21. NET STATE, COUNTY, LOCAL AND DISTRICT TAX (Line 19 minus Line 20) .... $
22. LESS—Tax Prepayments | 1ST PREPAYMENT | 2ND PREPAYMENT | Total ▶ Prepayments |
23. REMAINING STATE, COUNTY, LOCAL AND DISTRICT TAX (Line 21 minus Line 22) .... $
24. Penalty of 10% (.10) if payment is made after the due date shown above ....   Penalty
25. Interest is due on tax for each month or fraction of a month that payment is delayed after the due date; refer to Notice of Interest Rate Change, Form BT-581, for current rate   Interest
26. TOTAL AMOUNT DUE AND PAYABLE (Line 23 plus Lines 24 & 25) .... $

I hereby certify that this return, including any accompanying schedules and statements, has been examined by me and to the best of my knowledge and belief is a true, correct and complete return.

SIGNATURE AND TITLE ....   (   )
MAKE CHECK OR MONEY ORDER PAYABLE TO STATE BOARD OF EQUALIZATION   PHONE NUMBER
Always Write Your Account Number on Your Check or Money Order

457

Certificate of Payment.

CERTIFICATE OF PAYMENT

[　] Sections 6811, 6812 and 6813　　　[　] Sections 9012, 9022 and 9023

Please refer to account number(s) in all correspondence.

Name ....　Account No.(s) ....

....　...........................

Address ....

....

Period of Operation—From .... to ....
(Both dates inclusive)

The State Board of Equalization does hereby certify that its records disclose as of this date, that no taxes, interest, or penalties accruing under the provisions of Part 1, Division 2, or, where applicable, Part 1.5 and 1.6, Division 2, Revenue and Taxation Code or Part 3, Division 2, Revenue and Taxation Code are due from the above-named seller for the period of operation set forth above; and that there is no requirement that any buyer or buyers withhold any amount for payment of such taxes, interest, or penalties from the purchase price paid or to be paid to said seller for his business or stock of goods.

This certificate is given solely for the protection of the purchaser or purchasers of the business or stock of goods and does not release the seller from any taxes, interest, or penalties.

Dated at ....

this .... day of .... 19 ....

STATE BOARD OF EQUALIZATION

By ....

For District ....

☐ Purchaser (See Reverse)
☐ Seller
☐ Escrow Holder
☐ Hq. Central Files

Remember:
- The Uniform Commercial Code is a body of laws adopted throughout the United States standardizing business and commerce practices. Specifically covered are bulk transfers, mitigation of fraudulent practices and notice to creditors when the business is to be sold.

California Sales and Use Tax

In the event that a business is sold, and the previous owner did not pay the necessary taxes to the state, the California Sales and Use Tax will protect the buyer from any debt owed to the State Equalization Board by the seller. All unpaid sales tax will be forgiven as far as the buyer is concerned, with the seller responsible for any dollar amount not paid to the board.

The owner of a business may obtain a seller's permit, allowing him or her to purchase goods at wholesale prices and not pay sales taxes on these products or goods. The business owner must then collect sales tax from the customers when the products are sold and give this money to the State Board of Equalization. A copy of the seller's permit and clearance receipt (stating that the business is current on sales taxes), from the State Board of Equalization should be requested by a buyer before assuming ownership of the business.

Remember:
- The sale of a business is subject to a sales tax, or taxes on personal property items. Goodwill, patents, or other items are not subject to this tax.
- Escrow is required to withhold money to cover any liability of unpaid taxes, offering additional protection for the buyer.

Bill of Sale

A bill of sale will transfer personal property the same way that a grant deed transfers real property.

Assignment of Lease

In a typical business opportunity, title to the land and improvements to that land is usually not transferred. For this reason, we are concerned with the transfer of the lease to the property. The seller of the business must make sure this lease is transferred to the new owner.

VALUATION OF BUSINESS OPPORTUNITIES

It is important for all licensees dealing with business opportunities to understand how to determine fair market value of the business. There are many variables taken into account in addition to pre-determined values based on tables. Variables include items such as age, inventory value, furnishings (including age of, value and usefulness to the new owner), location of the business, appearance of all improvements to the business and terms of the lease. Keep in mind personal property such as furniture will depreciate.

Office furniture being sold with the business that is 10 years old will bring less money than furniture that is 2 years old.

The most difficult thing to measure is goodwill. Goodwill is very intangible and subjective. Some qualifiers can be measured to determine goodwill such as the age of the business, location, competition, customer and vehicular traffic in the area, and consumer habits. With favorable conditions it is reasonable to assume the goodwill will be high, and in good standing. With unfavorable conditions it is reasonable to assume the goodwill will not be as favorable.

Remember:
- The value of a business is based on inventory, age of the business, appearance and usefulness of any furnishings, fixtures, equipment, exterior and interior physical appearance or improvements of the structure, location, terms and conditions of the lease, goodwill, and net multipliers.

Guidelines have been set on how to determine the value for a business based on net multipliers. These net multipliers are based on the businesses annual net income multiplied on some standardized number. The net multipliers may be based on a number of different factors. Annual net income before depreciation, owner's salary or withdrawals and interest are some of these factors.

REAL PROPERTY SECURITIES DEALER

Real property securities dealers are regulated under Chapter 3, Article 6 of Real Estate Law. A real property security dealer and real property loan broker are actually very similar with the difference being real property securities dealers will be dealing in the secondary mortgage market, whiled real property loan brokers are dealing in the primary mortgage market. The statutes that regulate this area of real estate activity cover bulk transactions in trust deeds and real property sales contracts and investment plans dealing with them.

All real property securities dealer must have a real estate broker's license. A broker can simply request an endorsement from the real estate commissioner. Sending a written application as well as a corporate surety bond totaling $5,000 does this.

Section 10237.1 defines a real properties security dealer as "any person, acting as principal or agent, who engages in the business of: (A) Selling real property securities to the public ... (b) Offering to accept or accepting funds for continual reinvestment in real property securities, or from placement in an account, plan, or program whereby the dealer implies that a return will be derived from a specific real property sales contract or promissory note secured directly or collaterally by a lien on real property which is not specifically stated to be based upon the contractual payments thereon." To simplify this definition, you can think of a real property securities dealer as a person who holds deeds of trust sold under an investment contract where the dealer guarantees the deed of trust in any one of several ways, or makes advances to or on behalf of the investor.

Each broker wishing to sell real property securities to the public must obtain a license from the Real Estate Commissioner. This permit is valid for not only selling existing securities but also it will allow the broker to acquire and sell securities under a proposed plan or program. Should the permit be used to acquire and sell securities under a proposed plan or program, the permit must be acquired before any activity happens.

BROKERAGE OPPORTUNITIES IN PROBATE SALES

A probate sale is the court-approved sale of any property of a person who is deceased. Even property that is inherited may be subject of a court's approval. All estates in California worth $60,000 or more must be approved by the probate court.

Probate courts make sure that any creditors of the estate or deceased are paid prior to the heirs inheriting the property. Once all of the creditors have been paid, and any other debts have been settled, the property may be distributed to the proper heirs or persons named in the deceased's will.

The department of the superior court presides over a probate sale. Certain procedures are followed in a probate court hearing. The following is a brief list of these procedures:

- Any offer to purchase the property must be at least 90% of the appraised value of the property.

- All buyers must petition the court for an approved sale. When the court has set a hearing to approve the sale, other persons may make bids.

- Any additional bids must be 10% of the first $10,000 of the property's value and 5% of anything over that amount.

- The court will determine which bid to accept, then confirms the sale of the property.

- At the time of sale, the court will set the amount of commission a real estate agent will receive, if there is a real estate agent involved in the transfer of the property. This amount is usually not negotiable, and is set by the court.

Once the court decides which offer it will accept, a normal escrow is opened, as defined on the terms handed down from the court.

Remember:
When taking offers for probate property:
- The first offer must be at least 90% of the inheritance tax appraisal value
- Any additional offer must be at least 10% of the first $10,000, and 5% of the remaining portion of the original bid.
- Any estate worth $60,000 or more is subject to probate court approval before assets can be disbursed to living heirs or according to the deceased will.

Many real estate brokers also choose to be insurance brokers. Given the associative nature between insurance requirements and real property, it seems natural for a broker to participate in this industry. When the broker acts as in insurance agent, he or she will be considered an agent of the underwriter, not the person taking out the insurance policy. Should the broker both sell a property and insure that property, he or she must be very careful to secure adequate coverage in order to cover the loan balance on the home. The broker must be very careful not to violate any fiduciary responsibilities to the client in making insurance suggestions, and offer a policy that would be fair in the open market.

Categories

There are five categories of insurance: fire and casualty, life and disability, title insurance and mortgage guarantee, surety and fidelity, and government. A real estate broker will usually find opportunities to work with fire and casualty and life and disability insurance. Just the same as a there are different licensure designations for a licensee in real estate (broker and salesperson) the same is true for licensure in insurance. An individual may be a broker, agent or solicitor. The broker has the power to independently work for him or herself, while the work for a company or broker.

Remember:
There are five broad categories of insurance:
- Fire and casualty
- Life and disability
- Title insurance and mortgage guarantee
- Surety and fidelity
- Government

Types of Property Insurance

The different types of property insurance include fire, homeowners, public liability and business coverage. If a broker chooses to also be in insurance, it is important for him or her to have a very thorough understanding of insurance to be able to provide the necessary coverage, but also maintain fiduciary responsibility to the client. The broker's level of insurance knowledge should mirror his or her level of real estate knowledge.

Remember:
The different types of property insurance include:
- Fire
- Homeowners
- Public liability
- Business coverage

Fire Insurance

The standard form of fire insurance used in California covers all direct loss by fire or lightning. Not only the damage itself is covered, but effects as well, including the cost of removing debris, smoke damage, and water used in fighting the fire. There are special forms of fire insurance for single-family and multifamily dwellings, office buildings, loft buildings, manufacturing plants, and other special-purpose properties.

Coverage for other hazards, such as windstorm and hail, earthquake, vandalism and malicious mischief, sprinkler leakage, glass breakage, explosion, riot and civil commotion, flood damage, and landslides, can be added by endorsement to the basic policy.

While many insurers offer to extend the coverage to the full replacement cost of the improvements without regard to depreciation, the insured must usually meet two tests. He or she must repair or replace the damage or loss, and he or she must carry insurance for at least 80 percent of the improvement portion of the current property value.

Homeowner's Insurance

Because of so many different types of insurance are available to protect property, a homeowners insurance policy was developed to provide multiple-coverage wrapped up into one policy. This A homeowner's policy also will help reduce the cost of insurance. Some of the items covered are fire, wind, theft, bodily injury, burglary, property damage, vandalism and malicious mischief

Public Liability

Public liability insurance protects the homeowner and any person who may be on his or her property. Should an accident occur, the injured person would be covered under this policy. Slippery floors, falling objects, structural defects, exposed wiring, poor lighting, and an array of other hazards confront the owner. To meet the needs and demands of owners, insurers have introduced a number of contracts to protect against most of these hazards: the comprehensive personal liability policy; the owner's, landlords, and tenant's public liability policy; the manufacturer's public liability policy; and the owner's and contractor's protective public liability coverage. Such policies cover the policyholder for bodily injury, property damage, and the cost of investigating claims and defending the insured in case of suit.

Business Coverage

Just as it is very important for a private residence to carry the appropriate amount of insurance for not only the structure, but also the protection of all people on the property the same is true of a business. A number of commercial forms of coverage guard against direct losses to businesses, such as fire and destruction, as well as indirect losses or consequential losses. The latter include insurance for business interruption, rental loss, leasehold, loss of profits and commissions, extra expense, and so on.

In addition to physical losses, a business insurance policy will also cover workers' compensation. Under the California Workers' Compensation Act, all employers are required to carry insurance for their employees against job-connected injuries. Unlimited medical benefits are included in the policy, together with payment for loss of earnings during the disability period.

NOTARY PUBLIC SERVICES

An individual designated as a notary public authenticates written documents, confirming all signing parties involved in a given contract are indeed who they claim to be. Notary publics can perform several functions depending on the type of contract needing to be authenticated. A licensee may use his or her notary public license to acknowledge a deed. The notarization itself is a written statement or certification in which the notary public has affixed his or her official signature, seal, title, jurisdiction, commission, expiration date, and address.

By signing and sealing a document, the notary public has acknowledged that the contents inside are filled out completely and accurately. All parties have agreed to and signed the contract. Once this is done, changes cannot be made to the document. After the notary has signed and sealed the document, he or she will then make an entry into a written record of the notarial function. After a notary has signed a document, the notarized document may then be recorded with the county recorder's office.

Official Seal of Notary

All public notaries use an official seal. This seal identifies the notary by name, the state seal, "Notary Public," the county where the notary public is located and the date the notary public's commission expires. This seal must be able to be reproduced accurately when photographed. Each seal is limited to 1" x 2_" or two inches in diameter if circular. Each seal must also have a serrated edge and may be either a rubber stamp or a metal seal. Once affixed to a document, this seal may not be altered in any way. A seal that is not clear, or that cannot be reproduced will not be accepted as an official notarized document.

Remember:
- The seal of a public notary may not be larger than 1" x 2 _ or over two inches in diameter if the seal happens to be a circular shape.

ESCROW ACTIVITIES

Escrow is the "inbetween" time, beginning when a purchase agreement is accepted and signed, and ending when the buyer takes possession of the property. During escrow, all documents that need to be collected, processed or distributed (as well as the necessary disbursement of funds) will be completed. The person or company assigned to carry out all instructions provided to them by the principals (outlined in the purchase contract) is called the escrow holder. Under the Real Estate Law, an individual cannot be licensed as an escrow company; however, a broker may act as an escrow agent in those transactions in which he or she represents the buyer or seller or both. Any real estate licensee who acts as an escrow agent (or escrow holder) must maintain all escrow funds in a trust account subject to inspection by the Real Estate Commissioner, and keep proper records.

Escrow may involve more than just the sale of real property. Escrow agents are typically used in situations such as leasing of real property, sale of personal property, securities, loans or mobile homes. As in the sale of real property, the escrow agent must follow the instructions as laid out by the principals.

The escrow agent must follow instructions outlined in the purchase contract. Once escrow is opened, both parties must agree to any changes made. In other words, the buyer or seller alone cannot change escrow instructions without the approval of the other party. The two parties involved in the transaction are usually, but not always, a buyer and a seller.

The escrow holder is the agent for both parties in the transaction, and should not favor one party over the other. When the conditions are performed, he or she usually becomes the agent of each of the parties; that is, of the grantor to deliver the deed and of the grantee to pay over the purchase money. The agency, however, is considered a limited one, and the only obligations to be fulfilled by the escrow holder are those set forth in the instructions.

California does not require escrow agents or that escrow be utilized in a real estate transaction. The decision to use an escrow agent is completely up to the principals involved in the transaction. It is advisable to go into escrow, however, because any mistakes – whether innocent or intentional regarding the terms of the contract – could be costly to one or both parties, as they initiate litigation or challenges to the property transfer.

The main job of the escrow agent is to provide a line of communication between all parties involved in a sale. An escrow agent's duties go far beyond just communication between the buyer and the seller, however. The escrow agent must communicate with both of the brokers and sales agents involved in the transaction, the lender, and any service companies called in (such as inspectors, plumbers, appraisers and pest control companies). Thus, it is important that the escrow agent be a neutral third party who is not otherwise involved in the transaction.

Escrow Agent's Main Duties:
- Disburse funds as outlined in the purchase contract
- Communicate between all parties involved in the transaction

LOAN BROKERAGE ACTIVITIES

A very natural fit for a real estate broker is to participate in financing of real estate, or loan origination. Clients may not have financing lined up, and if the broker can assist in making that happen at the same time as finding the property, it can increase the speed of the transaction, as well as be a lucrative sidelight for the broker.

The broker may find him or herself originating new loans, or negotiating between the seller and buyer in the event the seller is able to finance the buyer directly. This is advantageous to the broker as he or she might be able to get a buyer financed with alternative methods where the buyer may not have qualified with a traditional trust deed. By doing this, the broker is assured his or her transaction will go through and a commission will be earned.

Some brokers choose to set up a completely separate division of his or her brokerage devoted to financing. This will allow the broker to be a more full service mortgage out-let for clients, not only taking applications and passing them along to the appropriate source of funding, but becoming a direct representative of a lending institution matching up buyers with available financing. So, in this capacity the broker may simply aid a client in filling out applications or associate with a mortgage lending institution and be a full representative.

_____

(Name of Firm)

_____

(Address of Firm)

1. **Property Owner:**
   a) Name and Address of Fee Owner _____
   b) Purchaser under a Real Property Sales Contract (if any) _____
   c) Credit information relative to maker or obligor:
      1) Employed by _____
      2) Years employed _____ 3) Monthly salary $ _____
      4) *Other Assets* _____
      5) List financial obligations and amount of monthly payments:
         _____ $ _____
         _____ $ _____
         _____ $ _____

2. **Securing Property:**
   a) Street Address and/or Legal Description _____
      _____
   b) If improved, describe type of improvement (Indicate if none) _____
      _____
   c) Which of the following have been installed on or adjacent to property:
      1) ☐ Sewers ☐ Streets ☐ Water Mains ☐ Curbs and Gutters ☐ Other
      2) If improvements have not been paid, list balance due: $ _____
   d) If security is a note, complete the following:
      1) Date of last sale of property _____
      2) Purchase price _____
      3) Cash down payment (if other, explain) _____
   e) If an appraisal has been made, complete the following:
      1) Appraised value $ _____
      2) Date of Appraisal _____
      3) Name of Appraiser _____
   f) Dealer's opinion of current fair market value of property _____ $ _____
   NOTE: If an Appraisal Has Not Been Made, the Purchaser Must Complete the Following Certification:

   I hereby certify that I do not wish an appraisal made by the real property securities dealer or an independent appraiser and that I will obtain my own appraisal.

                                    _____
                                            Purchaser

3. Terms and amounts of prior assessments, including taxes and improvement bonds:
   a) _____ $ _____
   b) _____ $ _____
   c) _____ $ _____

4. Terms and conditions of all prior recorded deeds of trust and other encumbrances, other than above, which constitute liens upon the property:
   a) _____
      Status of payments _____ Principal Balance $ _____
   b) _____
      Status of payments _____ Principal Balance $ _____
   c) _____
      Status of payments _____ Principal Balance $ _____
      Principal Balance of Outstanding Prior Encumbrances _____ $ _____
      Owner's Estimated Equity _____ $ _____

5. Terms and conditions of note or contract:
   a) Present balance _____ $ _____
   b) Original amount _____ $ _____
   c) Date of note or contract _____ Interest rate _____
   d) Maturity date _____
   e) Amount of monthly payment (if other, explain) _____
   f) Status of payments (if not current, explain) _____
   g) Will request for notice of default be recorded _____
   h) Terms and conditions of subordination agreement, if any _____
   i) In both words and figures, state balance due at maturity, if any. (If none, so state) _____ $ _____
      _____ Dollars

   The undersigned certifies that this transaction is in compliance with California Real Estate Law, that he is acting as principal ☐ or Agent ☐ and that the information set forth herein is true and correct.

   _____ _____ _____
   (Date)   (Dealer)   License No.

   The undersigned purchaser acknowledges receipt of a copy of this statement and certifies that he has read the same and has approved the purchase of the contract or note and deed of trust.

   _____ _____
   (Date)   Name

Listing of Probate Properties.

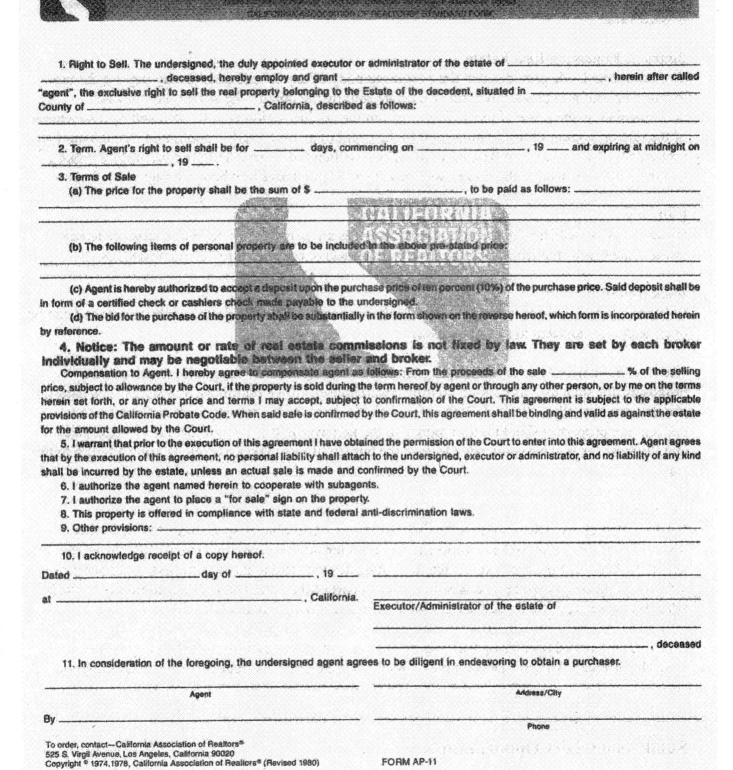

EXCLUSIVE AUTHORIZATION AND RIGHT TO SELL

CALIFORNIA ASSOCIATION OF REALTORS STANDARD FORM

1. **Right to Sell.** The undersigned, the duly appointed executor or administrator of the estate of _____
_____, deceased, hereby employ and grant _____, herein after called "agent", the exclusive right to sell the real property belonging to the Estate of the decedent, situated in _____
County of _____, California, described as follows:
_____
_____

2. **Term.** Agent's right to sell shall be for _____ days, commencing on _____, 19 ____ and expiring at midnight on
_____, 19 ____ .

3. **Terms of Sale**
   (a) The price for the property shall be the sum of $ _____, to be paid as follows: _____
_____
_____

   (b) The following items of personal property are to be included in the above pre-stated price:
_____
_____

   (c) Agent is hereby authorized to accept a deposit upon the purchase price of ten percent (10%) of the purchase price. Said deposit shall be in form of a certified check or cashiers check made payable to the undersigned.

   (d) The bid for the purchase of the property shall be substantially in the form shown on the reverse hereof, which form is incorporated herein by reference.

4. **Notice: The amount or rate of real estate commissions is not fixed by law. They are set by each broker individually and may be negotiable between the seller and broker.**
   Compensation to Agent. I hereby agree to compensate agent as follows: From the proceeds of the sale _____ % of the selling price, subject to allowance by the Court, if the property is sold during the term hereof by agent or through any other person, or by me on the terms herein set forth, or any other price and terms I may accept, subject to confirmation of the Court. This agreement is subject to the applicable provisions of the California Probate Code. When said sale is confirmed by the Court, this agreement shall be binding and valid as against the estate for the amount allowed by the Court.

5. I warrant that prior to the execution of this agreement I have obtained the permission of the Court to enter into this agreement. Agent agrees that by the execution of this agreement, no personal liability shall attach to the undersigned, executor or administrator, and no liability of any kind shall be incurred by the estate, unless an actual sale is made and confirmed by the Court.

6. I authorize the agent named herein to cooperate with subagents.

7. I authorize the agent to place a "for sale" sign on the property.

8. This property is offered in compliance with state and federal anti-discrimination laws.

9. Other provisions: _____
_____

10. I acknowledge receipt of a copy hereof.

Dated _____ day of _____, 19 ____   _____

at _____, California.   _____
Executor/Administrator of the estate of

_____

_____, deceased

11. In consideration of the foregoing, the undersigned agent agrees to be diligent in endeavoring to obtain a purchaser.

_____   _____
Agent   Address/City

By _____   _____
Phone

To order, contact—California Association of Realtors®
525 S. Virgil Avenue, Los Angeles, California 90020
Copyright © 1974, 1978, California Association of Realtors® (Revised 1980)   FORM AP-11

467

There will sometimes be opportunities for brokers to dispose of state owned land. An example of when this might happen is when government owned land intended on being used for an easement is no longer being used, and thus will be sold. Real estate owned by schools may be sold, and a commission given to a broker as well as leasing airspace next to a state highway.

Board of Education Real Estate
Just as in a traditional property transfer, the broker who was the procuring cause of sale will receive a commission. Offers to purchase property owned by a school should be submitted as a sealed bid. These bids will include the name of the broker who is procuring the deal and the rate of commission.

Caltrans
Brokers are able to lease airspace in and around California's highway system. Commissions will be received for negotiating signed contracts. The airspace may be adjacent to, over or under a state highway.

The State Highway District maintains a listing of all available airspace sites that a broker may review. Upon finding a person to lease this airspace, the state will then pay the broker a commission. A Brokers Commission Agreement will obligate the commission to the broker. The broker will receive his or her commission once the person leasing the airspace begins paying the state.

SUBDIVISION SALES OPPORTUNITIES

Intrastate Sales
Subdivision is the act of dividing land into smaller parcels or lots, in an effort to sell, develop or further that division at a later time. Technically, a subdivision occurs when one larger lot of land is divided into five or more lots. Most have been subdivided at one time or another, with the possible exception of agricultural, ranch and remote, rural areas. There was a need for some type of control in the division and sale of the land to ensure that the quality of life that people were seeking was preserved; not lost through development or division. All land sold in subdivisions are governed by the Subdivision Map and Subdivided Lands Acts. Regulation is oversaw by the Real Estate Commissioner as well as the county authorities responsible for the review of maps in a new subdivision where there will be property for sale.

There are two basic laws, which control subdivisions in California; the Subdivided Lands Act and the Subdivision Map Act. These two laws were adopted to protect consumers by interpreting subdivision and its laws in two separate ways, both beneficial. The basic areas of jurisdiction covered by these laws are design, planning, site preparation, construction of structures, and sale of the land.

Laws controlling subdivisions:
- Subdivided Lands Act
- Subdivided Map Act

The Subdivided Lands Act governs several developments and transactions between buyer and seller. First, the law outlines the different forms of ownership allowed for land that is divided up into five or more parcels, as well as land areas 160 acres or less. Lots with land masses over 160 acres are exempt from the Subdivided Lands Act, which also governs the marketing and financing of subdivisions.

The Subdivision Map Act is concerned with the appearance of a subdivision. The specific design of the buildings, layout of the streets, size of the lots, drainage and sewage systems and impact on the environment are some specific elements looked at by city and county authorities when a developer wishes to create a subdivision. The act will also define the rules for filing maps. Whereas the Subdivided Lands Act is overseen by the Real Estate Commissioner, city and county authorities will govern the Subdivision Map Act. Specific guidelines are set, with any future improvements reviewed and approved by the same city or county board that approved the original development. The Subdivision Map Act is an enabling act, as it gives the authorization to cities and counties to establish local requirements based on local government.

New Construction

Most buyers will wish to improve the property by building. If a buyer buys a vacant property, it would only be logical that he or she will be interested in constructing a home. It is important for you to not only sell the lot, but also know who to direct the buyer to so they can get approved for a construction loan.

Interstate Sales

Buyers of property not only come from inside the state, but also from outside of California. Licensees must be aware of the responsibilities accompanied with selling land to out-of-state buyers. Full disclosure is required as mandated by the Interstate Land Sales full Disclosure Act of 1968. This will help prevent fraud or promotions abuse when advertising land to out-of-state buyers. Should a developer already complied with California's Subdivided Lands Act, he or she will only have to file a copy of the subdivision questionnaire with the Department of Real Estate to be in compliance with the Interstate Land Sales Full Disclosure Act.

M O B I L E H O M E B R O K E R A G E

A mobile home is one of the few pieces of property a person can own that may be considered either real or personal property, depending on the terms of ownership. A mobile home is a manufactured home, built on a chassis and wheels. If the home remains on the chassis and wheels, it is moveable. Thus, it is considered personal property. If the mobile home is permanently attached to the ground, it is considered real property.

Remember!
- Mobile homes still attached to their chassis and wheels are moveable, and so are considered personal property.
- Mobile homes that are permanently attached to a foundation are considered real property

A mobile home is commonly referred to as a trailer. Many communities have special lots that people can buy to permanently attach their home to a foundation. This creates not only a real property interest in the home, but also a community where other mobile homes can be established on lots appropriate to the size of the home. Because the housing market in California is relatively high prices, affordable housing is highly sought after. Manufactured homes are one solution to the rapidly-booming housing market and its prices.

Mobile homes are built in several widths, which defines the general size of the home. The lengths can vary as well and they may be as long as 60 feet. Standard widths are 8, 10 and 12 feet. Obviously, an object of this size is not easy to move, and so most are attached permanently to foundations once they are manufactured, and then moved to their desired location. Sometimes, two units are placed side-by-side, creating a double-wide or extra large residence. This creates a structure that is practically the same size as a traditional home, but at a much lower cost.

Simply attaching a manufactured home to a foundation will not create real property; there are four steps that must be followed. Once the structure is attached, all requirements are met for it to become real property; though the home may be moved again, if necessary. There are steps required in moving the property, as well. The four steps required to create real property from a manufactured home are:

- The manufactured home must be placed on a permanent foundation

- The residents must obtain a building permit to place the home on the foundation

- The residents must obtain a certificate of occupancy before inhabiting the home

- A document must be recorded, stating that the manufactured home has been placed on a permanent foundation.

Once a manufactured home becomes real property, it is taxable as such, and no longer requires registration from the Department of Motor Vehicles. Instead, it is registered with the county recorder as real property.

If an owner wants to move the mobile home to another community, or simply to another lot, he or she can do this. The required steps for moving a mobile home are:

- Notify the Department of Housing and Community Development 30 days before moving the mobile home

- Notify any person with interest in the property

- Notify the local tax assessor

- Obtain a new registration from the Department of Motor Vehicles or a transportation permit from the Department of Housing and Community Development.

Real estate agents may sell mobile homes as long as they are considered real property. Those manufactured homes that have been permanently attached to a foundation and sold in the current lot are under the jurisdiction of a real estate agent. A real estate agent who sells a mobile home must report the sale to the Department of Housing and Community Development within 10 calendar days from the sale of the home. Those mobile homes that are sitting on a chassis and wheels (i.e., not yet permanently attached to a foundation) can only be sold by a licensed mobile home dealer.

As with any sale of real property, the licensees involved have certain rights and actions they can perform and others they cannot. The following is a list of approved activities for licensees who are dealing with the transfer of a mobile home:

- A real estate agent may only sell manufactured homes that have been permanently attached to a foundation. In the event of attachment, the home may be listed and sold in the same manner as all other real property.

- Real estate agents must notify the Department of Housing and Community Development within 10 business days from when a mobile home has been sold.

- Used mobile homes not considered real property, but if they are at least 8 feet wide and 30 feet long they may be sold by a real estate agent who has been licensed for at least one year.

- Sales of new mobile homes may only be made by a licensed mobile home dealer.

Buyers of a mobile home are qualified for the same financing as a traditional, built-in place structure. Additionally, loans are available through government participating programs such as FHA, VA and Cal-Vet.

The Department of Housing and Community Development is the agency responsible for licensing mobile homes. Anyone acquiring or releasing an interest in a mobile home must notify the department within 20 days of a sale, so that the necessary registration card may be provided to all lien holders. A certificate of title must be signed by both the buyer and the seller. All mobile homes considered to be real property must have a tax liability clearance waver signed by the county tax collector.

Just as a condominium complex has homeowner's association rules and regulations, so too does a mobile home park. Agents must be aware of all the rules and regulations of the mobile home park before selling a home in the community, as the buyer must be informed of all rules which may result in a sale or lack of sale, depending on qualifications and rules.

Generally, in a mobile home park, the buyer of a mobile home will rent the lot from the park's owner. The homeowner will own the house itself, but not the lot to which it is attached. The buyer of the home must be approved by the owner of the mobile home park before the sale can commence. Additionally, the buyer of the home must agree to all rules and regulations of the mobile home park. A real estate agent will obtain a copy of these rules and regulations when showing a prospective buyer a home in a mobile home park, so that he or she is aware of all rules and regulations required to live there. An example of some of the rules a person might find in a mobile home park are pet policies, minimum age requirements to live there, or other rules to govern a small community.

Remember:
Mobile homes are available in two different size classifications:
- Singlewide
- Multi-sectional

In order to be classified as a mobile home, the home must be:
- At least 8 feet wide
- At least 32 feet long

EXCLUSIVE AUTHORIZATION AND RIGHT TO SELL

(MOBILEHOME registered at least one year under Vehicle Code Div. 3 or Part 2 of Division 13 of Health and Safety Code)
THIS IS INTENDED TO BE A LEGALLY BINDING AGREEMENT. READ IT CAREFULLY.

CALIFORNIA ASSOCIATION OF REALTORS® STANDARD FORM

1. RIGHT TO SELL. I hereby employ and grant _____
hereafter called "Agent", the exclusive and irrevocable right commencing on _____
19 _____ , and expiring at midnight on _____
19 _____ , to sell or exchange the mobilehome situated at _____
_____ County, California in _____ Mobilehome Park.
Space # _____ described as follows: Make _____ Model _____ Year _____
Net Length _____ Expando _____ Width _____ Class _____
Type _____ Bedrooms _____ Baths _____ Exterior _____ Roof _____ Skirting _____

Serial #'s:		CAL. HCD #'s:	HUD #'s:	19 _____ License #'s:
_____	U (A)	_____	_____	_____
_____	X (B)	_____	_____	_____
_____	XX (C)	_____	_____	_____
_____	XXX (D)	_____	_____	_____

together with all built in appliances, heating units and water heater and the following equipment:
Refrigerator _____ Range _____ Oven _____ Washer _____ Dryer _____
Disposal _____ Dishwasher _____ Air Conditioner—Serial #—Tonnage _____
Carport Awning _____ Patio Awning _____ Porch _____ Screen Rm. _____
Wheels _____ Tires _____ Other _____

Park Information

Type _____ Clubhouse _____ Swimming Pool _____ Space Rental _____
Gas _____ Electricity _____ Guests _____ Children _____ Pets _____ Cable TV _____
Name of Manager _____ Phone No. _____ Sign _____ Caravan _____
Has seller obtained written agreement from Park Management permitting overage mobilehome to remain? _____ Yes _____ No

2. TERMS OF SALE. The purchase price shall be $ _____ , to be paid on the following terms:
_____
_____
_____

(a) The following items of personal property are to be included in the above-stated price:
_____
_____
_____

(b) Agent is hereby authorized to accept and hold on my behalf a deposit upon the purchase price. (c) I agree to deliver the above described mobilehome and personal property, if any is included, free of liens, encumbrances, recorded, filed or registered, or known to me. (d) Evidence of title shall be in form of a duly endorsed, dated and delivered Certificate of Ownership or mobilehome and delivery of current Registration Certificate, as required by the Vehicle Code. (e) I warrant that I am the owner of the mobilehome or have authority to execute this agreement. I warrant that the above described mobilehome complies with equipment requirements of Division 12 (commencing with section 24000) of the Vehicle Code. (f) I warrant that the above described mobilehome conforms to the requirements of the Health and Safety Code and the regulations of the Department of Housing and Community Development, HUD Regulations, and any applicable local ordinances and is either 1) located within an established mobilehome park as defined in Section 18214 of the Health and Safety Code and that advertising or offering for its sale is not contrary to any items of any contract between myself and the mobilehome park owner, or 2) located pursuant to a local zoning ordinance or permit, on a lot where its presence has been authorized or its continued presence and such use would be authorized for a total and uninterrupted period of at least one year. (g) I agree to deliver as soon as possible to Agent for submission to buyer a copy of my lease or rental agreement and all current park rules and regulations and inform agent of any changes occurring during the term hereof.

3. **Notice: The amount or rate of real estate commissions is not fixed by law. They are set by each broker individually and may be negotiable between the seller and broker.**

COMPENSATION OF AGENT. I hereby agree to compensate Agent as follows: (a) _____ % of the selling price if the mobilehome is sold during the term hereof, or any extension thereof, by Agent, on the terms herein set forth or any other price and terms I may accept, or through any other person, or by me, or _____ % of the price shown in 2), if said mobilehome is withdrawn from sale, transferred, or leased without the consent of Agent, or made unmarketable by my voluntary act during the term hereof or any extension thereof. (b) The compensation provided for in subparagraph a) above if the mobilehome is sold or otherwise transferred within _____ days after the termination of this authority or any extension thereof to anyone with whom Agent has had negotiations prior to final termination, provided I have received notice in writing, including the names of the prospective purchasers, before or upon termination of this agreement or any extension thereof.

4. If action be instituted to enforce this agreement, the prevailing party shall receive reasonable attorney's fees and costs.

5. I authorize the Agent named herein to cooperate with sub-agents.

6. The mobilehome is offered in compliance with state and federal Anti-Discrimination Laws.

7. In the event of an exchange, permission is hereby given Agent to represent all parties and collect compensation or commissions from them, provided there is full disclosure to all principals of such agency. Agent is authorized to divide with other agents such compensation or commissions in any manner acceptable to them.

8. I agree to hold Agent harmless from any liability arising from any incorrect information supplied by me, or from any material fact known by me concerning the mobilehome, the park or other location in which it is located, which I fail to disclose.

9. Other provisions: _____

10. I acknowledge that I have read and understand this Agreement, and that I have received a copy hereof.
DATED: _____ , 19 _____ _____ , California
Owner _____ Owner _____
Address _____ City, State, Phone _____

11. In consideration of the above, Agent agrees to use diligence in procuring a purchaser.
Agent _____ Address, City _____
By _____ Phone, Date _____

NO REPRESENTATION IS MADE AS TO THE LEGAL VALIDITY OF ANY PROVISION OR THE ADEQUACY OF ANY PROVISION IN ANY SPECIFIC TRANSACTION.

To order, contact—California Association of Realtors®
525 S. Virgil Avenue, Los Angeles, California 90020
(Revised 1982)

FORM MHL-14

Chattel – Another name for real property.

Encumbrance – Liens, easements or any other restriction placed on property.

Escrow - An impartial third party whose functions are to 1) act as a depository of funds and documents placed with it; 2) prorate those charges and expenses between the parties to the escrow as instructed under the terms of the agreement for the sale and purchase; and 3) act as a clearinghouse for the exchange of monies and documents when the escrow is ready to close, that is, at the time when all the terms and conditions have been met.

Goodwill – The customer base and good name of a business that will also be sold with the physical inventory and other aspects of a business.

Insurance - A contract for indemnity.

Mobile Home - A home that can be moved. Like a vehicle, the mo-bile home is built on a steel chassis and equipped with wheels so that it can be pulled by truck from the factory to a dealer's lot and then to a site in a park or on private land.

Notary Public– A person who is authorized to authenticate contracts, acknowledge deeds, take affidavits, and perform other official activities.

Uniform Commercial Code - A body of law adopted throughout the United States that standardizes a number of practices commonly found in commerce and business.

C H A P T E R   Q U I Z

1. The sale of a business primarily involves the sale of:
    a. Real property
    b. Personal property
    c. Goodwill
    d. Both B and C

2. What is the final step in the sale of a business?
    a. Closing statements and documents are delivered to the parties at the close of escrow
    b. A bill of sale for all personal property is issued to the buyers
    c. The lease is transferred to the new owners
    d. A clearance receipt, Certificate of Payment of Sales and Tax Use, and a seller's permit for the new owner must be secured from the state Board of Equalization

3. The standardized CAR listing agreement form used by brokers in the sale of a business is form:
    a. SB-14
    b. CA-14
    c. BUS-14
    d. There isn't such a form.

4. Bulk transfers are covered in what document?
   a. Commissioner's Code
   b. Uniform Commercial Code
   c. Individual state legislation
   d. None of the above

5. Bulk transfer laws protect:
   a. The seller of the business
   b. The buyer of the business
   c. The creditors of the seller
   d. Both A and C

6. Article 6 of the Uniform Commercial Code requires the transferee to give public notice to all creditors regarding the sale of a business at least:
   a. 10 days prior to the sale
   b. 12 days prior to the sale
   c. 15 days prior to the sale
   d. 17 days prior to the sale

7. When a seller engages in a business where sales of personal property at retail are made, he or she must secure a seller's permit obtained from:
   a. State Board of Equalization
   b. Real Estate Commissioner
   c. Any broker
   d. County Recorder's office

8. All businesses must pay a 6% sales tax on all gross receipts. This amount is remitted to state and local agencies:
   a. Quarterly
   b. Bi-yearly
   c. Once a year
   d. None of the above

9. When selling a business, what is the most difficult item of value to measure?
   a. Personal property
   b. Fixtures
   c. Goodwill
   d. Used furniture

10. Goodwill is valued using which of the following methods of valuation?
    a. Length of time the business has been in existence
    b. Vehicle/customer traffic count
    c. Present and future anticipated competition
    d. All of the above

11. Which of the following is not a category of insurance?
    a. Fire and casualty
    b. Life and disability
    c. Government
    d. Personal property

12. Who issues or oversees the regulations governing insurance licensees?
    a. Real estate commissioner
    b. Insurance commissioner
    c. Department of Business and Transportation
    d. Both B and C

13. All of the following are aspects of government insurance except:
    a. Federal Deposit Insurance Corporation
    b. Federal Housing Administration
    c. Social Security
    d. Federal Emergency Aid

14. Which of the following is not a type of property insurance?
    a. Public liability
    b. Wind insurance
    c. Fire insurance
    d. Home owners insurance

15. All of the following are a function of a notary public except:
    a. Applying and affixing his or her official signature and seal to insure as fully
       as possible that the original agreement cannot be altered in any way
    b. Determining if the parties are truly who they claim to be
    c. Certify that all documents have been accurately filled out
    d. Obtaining the acknowledgement of the parties that they have signed the agree-
       ment or taking oath that they are aware of the contents of the agreement

16. What are the qualifications to become a public notary in California?
    a. Be a California resident for at least 12 months prior to applying
    b. Achieve a 75% on the notarial law exam, included in the application.
    c. Be a United States citizen
    d. All of the above

17. A real estate broker may not:
    a. Be licensed as an escrow company
    b. Be a licensed insurance agent
    c. Be a property manager
    d. All of the above

18. True or false, a real estate broker who wishes to be a loan broker must obtain a
    separate license?
    a. True
    b. False

19. A broker may sell a mobile home if:
    a. He or she is registered with the Department of Motor Vehicles for at least one year
    b. If the unit is greater than 8 feet wide and 40 feet long
    c. Both A and B
    d. Neither A nor B, the broker requires a separate license

20. According to Manufactured Housing Industry statistics, how many people live in a
    mobile home?
    a. 7 million
    b. 10 million
    c. 12 million
    d. 15 million

ABATEMENT OF JUDGMENT - A document containing a condensation of the essential provisions of a court judgment.

ABATEMENT OF NUISANCE - The act of ending or terminating a nuisance; a type of legal action brought to end a nuisance.

ABSTRACT OF JUDGMENT - A summary of money judgment. The summary is usually prepared so that it may be recorded, thereby creating a (judgment) lien on real estate owned by the judgment debtor.

ABSTRACT OF TITLE - A summary of the instruments affecting title to a parcel of real property as shown by the public records.

ACCELERATE - To make a note all due and payable at one time.

ACCELERATION CLAUSE - A clause in a deed of trust or mortgage giving the lender the right to call all sums owing him or her to be immediately due and payable upon the occurrence of a certain event. It is also a clause that permits a debtor to pay off a loan before the due date.

ACCELERATION CLAUSE - A clause in a promissory note, deed of trust, or mortgage that provides that upon default of a payment or some other stated event, the entire unpaid balance becomes immediately due and payable.

ACCEPTANCE - An essential element of every contract, it is the consent to be bound by the offer. In deeds, it is the consent to accept a grant of real property.

ACCESS RIGHT - The right of an owner to go into and out of his or her property.

ACCOMMODATION PARTY - A person who, without receiving value, signs a promissory note to help another person borrow money or get credit.

ACCORD AND SATISFACTION - The discharge of an existing contract by accepting the performance under a substitute contract. Generally, consideration under the new contract is different from and of lesser value than under the original contract, and satisfaction is the performance of that contract; the combination discharges the original contract.

ACCRETION - A gradual addition to land from natural causes; for example, from gradual action of ocean or river waters.

ACCRUED DEPRECIATION
1. The difference between the cost of replacement new as of the date of the appraisal and the present appraised value.
2. The accumulated loss in value that has affected the improvements on real property

ACKNOWLEDGEMENT - A formal declaration before an officer duly authorized as a notary public by a person who has executed an instrument, stating that the execution is his or her act and deed. A formal statement (usually before a notary public) by the person signing a deed or document that the instrument was actually and freely signed.

ACOUSTICAL TILE - Blocks of fiber, mineral, or metal with small holes or a rough-textured surface to absorb sound, used as covering for interior walls and ceilings.

ACQUISITION - The act or process by which a person procures property. ACRE A measure of land equaling 160 square rods, 4840 square yards, 43,560 square feet, or a tract about 208.71 feet square.

AD VALOREM - According to value.

ADA - Refers to the Americans With Disabilities Act. The ADA applies to equal access to employment, public services, public accommodations, public transportation and telecommunications. ADA Refers to the Americans With Disabilities Act. The ADA applies to equal access to employment, public services, public accommodations, public transportation and telecommunications.

ADJACENT - Located next to or near an object or parcel of property.

ADJOINING - Located so as to touch an object or share a common property line.

ADJUSTED COST BASIS - For tax purposes it is the cost of the property plus improvements and minus depreciation, amortization, and depletion.

ADMINISTRATOR - A person appointed by the probate court to administer the estate of a deceased person. His or her duties include making an inventory of the assets, managing the property, paying the debts and expenses, filing necessary reports and tax returns, and distributing the assets as ordered by the probate court.

ADULT - Any person 18 years of age and older.

ADVERSE POSSESSION - A method of acquiring property based on open and notorious possession, under a claim of right, color of title, continuous use for five years, and the payment of taxes. A method of acquiring property through continuous use of that property while paying taxes on it.

AFFIDAVIT - A statement or declaration reduced to writing, sworn to or affirmed before some officer who has authority to administer an oath or affirmation, such as a notary public or a commanding officer in the service.

AFFIRM - To confirm, swear, ratifying, verity.

AGENCY RELATIONSHIP - A special relationship of trust by which one person (agent) is authorized to conduct business, sign papers, or otherwise act on behalf of another person (principal). This relationship may be created by expressed agreement, ratification, or estoppel.

AGENT - One who represents another called a principal and has authority to act for the principal in dealing with third parties. The relationship is referred to as an agency. Someone authorized to act for another (called the principal) in business matters.

AGREEMENT - A mutual understanding or compact between parties. Although often used a synonymous with contract, technically it denotes mutual promises that fail as a contract for lack of consideration.

AGREEMENT OF SALE - 1. A written contract between a buyer and seller setting out the terms of sale. 2. An installment sales contract covering real property, especially a long-term contract

AIDS - The seller of real property, his agents or his sub agents do not have to disclose that somebody died of AIDS or had AIDS in said property.

ALIENATION - The transferring of property to another. Conveyance or transfer of title to real estate from one person to another person.

ALIENATION CLAUSE - In a deed of trust or mortgage, a provision that if the secured property is sold or transferred, the lender has the option of accelerating the loan and declaring the entire unpaid balance immediately due and payable. Also called a "due-on-sale" clause.

ALLIGATOR - Purchasing lower priced properties will limit the appetite of the alligator. The alligator is an expensive piece of property that gobbles up all the profits. Negative cash flow on a keeper property is referred to as an alligator.

ALL-INCLUSIVE DEED OF TRUST - A financing device whereby a lender makes payments on the existing trust deeds of a borrower and takes from the borrower a junior trust deed with a face value in an amount equal to the amount outstanding on the old trust deeds and the additional amount of money borrowed.

ALLUVION (ALLUVIUM) - Soil that has been deposited by accretion on the shore of a river or body of water and that increases the real property.

ALTA POLICY - The title insurance policy issued to institutional lenders. The initials stand for American Land Title Association, an organization that regulates and standardizes the provisions within title policies.

ALTER EGO - A doctrine, which holds that a corporation is really owned by shareholders as their own property, and therefore it should not be considered as a separate entity. Usually used to try to hold shareholders liable for corporate debts.

AMBULATORY - Capable of being changed or revoked. In wills, it refers to the concept that a will may be revoked or modified at any time up to the testator's death.

AMELIORATING WASTE - Improvements to property that, while not damaging the value of the property, technically qualify as waste. For example, an apartment building constructed on property designated only for single-family structures is considered ameliorating waste.

AMENITIES - As used in the real estate business, the features that make a piece of real property, especially a home, enjoyable.

AMORTIZATION
1. The liquidation of a financial obligation on an installment basis, which includes both principal and interest.
2. Recovery of cost or value over a period of time. The method or plan for the payment of a debt, bond, deed of trust, etc., by installments or sinking fund.

ANNUAL PERCENTAGE RATE (APR) - The cost of credit as determined in accordance with Regulation Z of the Board of Governors of the Federal Reserve System for implementing the Federal Truth in Lending Act.

ANNUITY- A sum of money received or paid yearly or at other fixed periods.

ANTICIPATION- Affirms that value is created by the anticipated benefits to be derived in the future.

ANTICIPATORY BREACH- Advance notice of intention to violate the terms of a contract.

APPEAL- The review or rehearing by a higher court of a low (inferior) court's decision.

APPELLANT- The party appealing a court decision. Either party may appeal; hence, the appellant could have been either the plaintiff or the defendant in the trial court.

APPRAISAL- An estimate and opinion of value. An opinion or estimate of the fair market value of a property.

APPRAISER - One qualified by education, training, and experience, who is hired to estimate the value of real and personal property on the basis of experience, judgment, facts, and use of formal appraisal processes.

APURTENANT- Attached to or considered part of land, because of being considered necessary and incidental to the use of that land. Commonly applied to easements that are considered part of property.

ASSESSED VALUE- Value placed on property as a basis for taxation. A value used by the tax assessor before July 1978. It represented 25 percent of the assessor's fair market value. After deducting any exemptions from assessed value, one applied the tax rate to the net figure to determine annual property taxes.

ASSESSMENT- The valuation of property for the purpose of levying a tax, or the amount of tax levied.

ASSESSOR- The official who has the responsibility of determining the assessed values.

ASSIGNEE- One to whom property is assigned or transferred.

ASSIGNMENT- A transfer to another of any property or right. The transfer of one's entire interest in property. Generally, the term is limited to intangible personal property (that is, stocks, bonds, promissory notes) and to leasehold estates.

ASSIGNMENT OF RENTS CLAUSE- A clause in a deed of trust or mortgage, providing that in the event of default, all rents and income from the secured property will be paid to the lender to help reduce the outstanding loan balance.

ASSIGNMENT OF RENTS - An assignment of future rents form property as security for a debt.

ASSIGNOR- One who assigns or transfers property.

ASSUMPTION- Acceptance of personal liability for another's debt or obligation. In the case of the sale of real estate, the buyer personally accepts and promises to pay off the existing deed of trust.

ASSUMPTION OF AGREEMENT - A contract by which a person agrees to pay a debt or obligation owed by someone else.

ASSUMPTION OF MORTGAGE OR DEED OF TRUST - The taking of title to property by a grantee in which he or she assumes liability for payment of existing note secured by a mortgage or deed of trust against the property.

ATTACHMENT - Seizure of property by court order before judgment, usually done to have it available in the event a judgment is obtained in a pending law suit. The actual or constructive seizure of property by court order during a lawsuit. The usual purpose is to hold the assets as security for the satisfaction of a judgment.

ATTACHMENT LIEN - A lien on property arising because of an attachment of that property.

ATTEST
1. To affirm to be true or genuine.
2. An official act establishing authenticity.

ATTORNEY-IN-FACT - An agent authorized to perform certain acts for another under a power of attorney. (See Power of Attorney.)

AVULSION - The sudden tearing away or removal of land by the action of water flowing over or through it.

BACKFILL - The replacement of excavated earth in a hole or against the side of a structure.

BALANCE SHEET - A financial statement showing a person's assets, liabilities, and net worth.

BALLOON PAYMENT - When the final payment on a note is greater than the preceding normal installments, the final installment is termed a balloon payment. An installment promissory note providing for the last payment to be much larger than any previous payment. By statute, any payment more than twice the smallest payment is a balloon payment, although in practice generally the term refers only to the last payment.

BANKRUPTCY - Will not eliminate all loans secured by real property.

BASE AND MERIDIAN - Imaginary lines used by surveyors from which they find, measure, and describe the location of lands.

BASE MOLDING - Molding used at the top of the baseboard.

BASE SHOW - Molding used at junction of baseboard and floor, sometimes called a carpet strip.

BASEBOARD - A board that goes around the room against the wall and next to the floor.

BATTEN - Narrow strips of wood or metal used to cover joints on the interior or exterior of a building; they are also used for decorative effect.

BLOCKBUSTING- The illegal practice of trying to lower property values.

BEAM- A horizontal structural member supporting a load.

BEARING WALL OR PARTITION- A wall or partition that supports any vertical load, in addition to its own weight.

BENCH MARKS- A location indicated on a permanent marker by surveyors.

BENEFICIARY
1. One entitled to benefit from a trust.
2. The lender on the security of a note and deed of trust. The creditor (lender) under a deed of trust

BENEFICIARY STATEMENT- (See Offset Statement.)

BEQUEATH- To leave by will.

BEQUEST- Personal property that is given by the terms of a will. A gift of personal property by will.

BETTERMENT- An improvement on real property that increases the value and is considered a capital asset.

BILATERAL CONTRACT- A contract in which the consideration given by each party is a promise: that is, a promise for a promise.

BILL OF SALE- A written instrument given by the seller to the buyer to pass title to personal property.

BINDER- A written statement that binds the parties to an agreement until formal contracts can be drawn; an agreement to cover a down payment as evidence of good faith.

BLACKTOP- Asphalt paving used in streets and driveways.

BLANKET DEED OF TRUST- A deed of trust binding more than one parcel of property as security. It is frequently encountered in subdivisions, where every lot in the subdivision is bound by the same deed of trust. As the lots are sold, they are released from the deed of trust by a partial release provision.

BLANKET MORTGAGE- One mortgage or deed of trust that covers more than one piece of real property.

BLIGHTED AREA- An area in which real property is declining in value because of destructive economic forces.

BOARD FOOT- A unit of measurement for lumber: one foot wide, one foot long, one inch thick (144 cubic inches).

BONA FIDE- Good faith.

BONA FIDE PURCHASER (BFP)- A purchaser who pays fair value for property in good faith, and without notice of adverse claims.

BOND - An obligation under seal. Real estate bonds are issued on the security of a mortgage or deed of trust. A certificate representing a contract for the payment of money, often used to repay certain loans or held as security to ensure the performance of a stated act.

BOOK VALUE - An accounting term, which is the difference between cost and the total amount of depreciation that has been taken.

BRACING - Frame lumber nailed at an angle in order to provide stability to the structure.

BREACH - The breaking of or failure of duty, either by an act or omission. The violation of or failure to perform an obligation.

BREEZEWAY - A covered porch or passage, open on two ends, that connects the house and garage, or two parts of the house.

BRIDGING - Wood or metal pieces used to brace floor joists.

BROKER - An agent who earns income by arranging sales and other contracts. A real estate broker is an individual licensed by the state of California to arrange the sale or transfer of interests in real property for compensation.

BROKER'S TRUST FUND ACCOUNT - Withdrawals from this account may be made only by the broker.

BTU - British Thermal Unit; the quantity of heat required to raise the temperature of one pound of water one degree Fahrenheit.

BUILDING LINE - Often called a setback line, a building line is a line running a certain distance from the street, in front of which an owner cannot build. These lines are set by law.

BUILDING PAPER - A heavy waterproofed paper used as sheathing in exterior walls, or in roof construction as insulation and protection against moisture.

BUILT-INS - Cabinets and other features built in as a part of the house.

BUSINESS AND PROFESSIONS CODE - One of the 25 California codes containing the laws passed by the state legislature. It contains the statutes regulating the conduct of real estate brokers and establishes the Department of Real Estate.

BUSINESS OPPORTUNITY - A term used to describe a business including its stock-in-trade, fixtures, and goodwill.

C.A.R. - Abbreviation for the California Association of Realtors.

C.C. & R. - Abbreviation for covenants, conditions, and restrictions. Often used synonymously with general plan restrictions on a subdivision.

CAL-VET LOAN (CALIFORNIA VETERANS) - A program administered by the State Department of Veterans LOAN) Affairs for the direct financing of farms and homes for veterans who qualify. The funds for these loans come from the sale of state bonds.

CAPITAL ASSESTS- Assets of a permanent nature used in the production of income. Examples would include land, buildings, and equipment.

CAPITAL GAIN- The gain recognized for federal and state income tax purposes when a taxpayer disposes of a capital asset.

CAPITALIZATION- In appraising, a method of determining value of property by considering net income and a reasonable percentage of return on the investment.

CAPITALIZATION RATE- The percentage rate or rate of interest considered a reasonable return on the investment. It is used in the capitalization method of determining value based upon net return.

CARET- California Association of Real Estate Teachers; a division of the California Association of Realtors.

CARPET STRIP- (See Base Shoe.)

CASEMENT WINDOW- Windows set in frames of wood or metal that swing outward.

CASH FLOW- The new amount of cash a property produces when all cash income and other cash generated are added together and all cash expenses and other cash payments are deducted.

CAUSE OF ACTION- A legal right; facts giving rise to an enforceable claim.

CAVEAT EMPTOR- A Latin phrase meaning " let the buyer beware"; the legal maxim stating that the buyer must examine the goods or property and buy at his or her own risk.

CERTIFICATE OF REASONABLE VALUE- The Veterans Administration's written appraisal of the value (CRV) of a property.

CERTIORARI- The Supreme Court order indicating that the court has decided to exercise its discretion and accept a case offered on appeal. The court reviews only those select cases that it deems worthy of review.

CHAIN OF TITLE- A series of conveyances, encumbrances, and other instruments affecting the title from the time original patent was granted, or as far back as records are available. A history of the recorded ownership of real estate and claims against title to real estate.

CHATTEL- The old name for personal property.

CHATTEL MORTGAGE- A personal-property mortgage. (See Security Agreement.)

CHATTEL REAL- In real estate, an estate less than a freehold estate, such as a lease.

CHATTELS
1. Personal property.
2. This term is sometimes used in a law to describe any interest in real or personal property other than a freehold.

CIRCUIT BREAKER- An electrical device that automatically interrupts an electrical circuit when an overload occurs. Circuit breakers can be reset and today are used instead of fuses.

CIVIL CODE - One of the 25 California codes containing the statutes passed by the state legislature. The most important code relating to contracts and real estate, the Civil Code defines the nature and requirements for contracts and real estate transactions, among its many other provisions.

CIVIL LAW - A system of jurisprudence, sometimes called Roman law, wherein all the laws are set forth in advance to regulate conduct (as opposed to common law, where the principles of law develop on a case-by-case basis). In California the term also refers to the law relating to and between individuals, as opposed to criminal law.

CLAPBOARD - Boards that are used for siding and that are usually thicker at one edge.

CLIENT - A person represented by a broker or an attorney.

CLOUD ON TITLE - A claim or document that affects title to real estate. The actual cloud may ultimately prove invalid, but its existence mars the title.

CLTA POLICY - The title insurance policy issued to homeowners and non-institutional lenders. The initials stand for the California Land Title Association, an organization that regulates and standardizes the provisions within title policies.

CODE OF CIVIL PROCEDURE - One of the 25 California codes that contain the statutes passed by the state legislature. It contains most of the procedural requirements for enforcing rights granted by other codes, including the procedures for evictions, foreclosures, and lawsuits.

CODICIL - An amendment to a will.

COLLAR BEAM - A beam that connects the pairs of opposite roof rafters above the attic floor.

COLLATERAL - Property subject to a security interest; property used as security for a debt. (See Security Agreement.)

COLLATERAL SECURITY - The transfer of property of other valuables to ensure the performance of a principal agreement; an obligation attached to a contract to guarantee its performance.

COLLUSION- A secret agreement between two or more persons wishing to defraud another for a wrongful purpose or to obtain an object forbidden by law.

COLOR OR TITLE - That which appears to be a good title but, in fact, is not; for example, a forged deed. A document that appears to convey title, but in fact is ineffective, conveying no title at all. It is one of the requirements for adverse possession and easement by prescription.

COMBED PLAYWOOD - A grooved building material used primarily for interior finish.

COMMERCIAL ACRE - A term applied to the remainder of an acre of land after the area devoted to streets, sidewalks, curbs, and so on has been deducted from the acre.

COMMERCIAL PAPER- Negotiable instruments used in business.

COMMINGLING- The mixing of different funds so that they can no longer be distinguished. In domestic law it refers to the combination of separate property and community property, so that the separate property and community funds can no longer be distinguished; in such cases all property is considered community property. For brokers it refers to the mixing o clients' money with the broker's separate bank accounts.

COMMISSION- An agent's compensation for performing the duties of his or her agency agreement. In the real estate business, it is usually a percentage of the selling price or a percentage of the lease or rents, for example. Reduction of a real estate commission for a listing contract is considered to be unethical.

COMMISSION- A real estate broker may receive a commission from both parties.

COMMITMENT- A pledge or a promise; a firm agreement.

COMMON LAW- The body of law that grew from customs and practices developed and used in England. A body of unwritten law that developed in England from the general customs and usage. It was adopted in the United States and exercised by court decisions following the ancient English principles and the recorded law of a state.

COMMUNITY PROPERTY- All property acquired by a husband and wife living together, except separate property. (See Separate Property.) Property owned in common by a husband and wife as a kind of marital partnership.

COMPACTION- Packing or consolidation of soil. When soil is added to a lot to fill in low places or to raise the level of the lot, it is often too loose to sustain the weight of buildings. Therefore, it is necessary to compact the added soil so that it will carry the weight of the building without danger of settling or cracking.

COMPARATIVE MARKET ANALYSIS- One of three methods in the appraisal process. A means of comparing similar type properties, which have recently sold, to the subject property.

COMPETENT- Legally qualified or capable.

COMPOUND INTEREST- Interest paid on the original principal and also on the accrued and unpaid interest that has accumulated as the debt matures.

CONCLUSIVE PRESUMPTION- A legal assumption that cannot be rebutted, and is therefore accepted as true and binding on the courts.

CONDEMNATION
1. The act of taking private property for public use by a political subdivision.
2. A declaration by proper governmental authorities that a structure is unfit for use. The taking of private property for public use through the exercise of the power of eminent domain.

CONDITION
A provision in a contract stating that the contract will not go into effect or that it will terminate upon the occurrence of some specified future event.
1. A restriction added to a conveyance that, upon the occurrence or non-occurrence of some act or event, causes the estate to be defeated.

2. A contractual provision that upon the occurrence or nonoccurrence of a stated act or event, an obligation is created, destroyed, or defeated

CONDITION PRECEDENT - A condition that must occur before an estate is created or enlarged, or before some other right or obligation occurs.

CONDITION SUBSEQUENT - A condition that, upon its failure or nonperformance, causes the defeat or extinguishment of an estate, right, or obligation.

CONDITIONAL COMMITMENT - A loan commitment for a definite amount under certain terms and conditions. It is subject to an unknown purchaser's satisfactory credit rating.

CONDITIONAL SALE CONTRACT - A contract for the sale of property whereby the seller retains legal title until the conditions of the contract have been fulfilled. The buyer has an equitable interest in the property. (See Security Agreement.) A contract for the sale of property by which possession is delivered to the buyer, but title remains with the seller until full payment or the satisfaction of other stated conditions.

CONDITIONAL USE PERMIT- An exception to or relief from the application of a zoning ordinance, because of special authorization granted by the zoning authorities. The issuance rests on public policy benefits and prior authorization in the zoning ordinance.

CONDOMINUM - A system of individual ownership of units in a multifamily structure, combined with joint ownership of common areas of the structure and the land. The ownership of an individual unit in a multi-unit structure, combined with joint ownership of common walkways, land, and other portions of the property.

CONDUIT - Usually a metal pipe in which electrical wiring is installed.

CONFESSION OF JUDGMENT - Any entry of judgment upon the debtor's voluntary admission or confession.

CONFIRMATION OF SALE - A court approval of the sale of property by an executor, administrator, guardian, or conservator.

CONSIDERATION- Anything of value, or that is legally sufficient, given to induce some-one to enter into a contract. The inducement for entering into a contract; usually money, services, or a promise, although it may consist of a legal benefit to the promisor or any legal detriment to the promisee.

CONSTRUCTION - The interpretation of an ambiguous term or provision in a statute or agreement.

CONSTRUCTIVE - A fiction imputed by law.

CONSTRUCTIVE EVICTION - A breach of the landlord's warranty of quiet enjoyment. Any acts by the landlord that substantially interferes with the tenant's use and enjoyment of the premises.

CONSTRUCTIVE NOTICE - Notice given by the public records; that which is considered equivalent to actual notice even though there is not actual notice.
1. Notice given by a recorded document.
2. Notice imputed by a law because a person could have discovered certain facts upon reasonable investigation, and a "reasonable man" in the same situation would have

conducted such an investigation.

CONSUMER CREDIT PROTECTION ACT- A federal law that includes the truth-in-Leading Law.

CONSUMER GOODS- Goods sold or purchased primarily for personal, family, or household purposes.

CONTINGENT- Conditional, uncertain, conditioned upon the occurrence or nonoccurrence of some uncertain future event.

CONTINUATION STATEMENT- A statement filed to extend the time limit on a financing statement that had been filed earlier.

CONTRACT OF SALE- (See Conditional Sale Contract.)

CONVENANT- An agreement or a promise to do or not to do a particular act. Covenant: A contractual agreement whereby one of the parties promises to perform or to refrain from doing certain acts.

CONVENTIONAL LOAN- A loan that is made that is not federally insured or guaranteed.

CONVERSION- Is the misappropriation or misuse of trust funds.

CONVERTIBLE ADJUSTABLE RATE- Allows the borrower to adjust to a fixed interest rate.

MORTGAGE CONVERTIBLE ADJUSTABLE RATE- Allows the borrower to adjust to a fixed interest rate.

MORTGAGE CONVEYANCE
1. The transfer of the title of real property from one to another.
2. An instrument that transfers an interest in real property from one person to another. The transfer of title to real estate from one person to another.

COOPERATIVE APARTMENT- A form of ownership in which each individual apartment owner shares in a cooperative venture that entitles the owner to use, rent, or sell a specific apartment unit.

CORPORATION- A group or a body of persons recognized by law as an individual person with rights and liabilities distinct from those of the persons comprising it. Since the corporation is created by law, it may continue for any length of time that the law prescribes. An artificial entity given authority to conduct business and possess many of the rights of natural persons. One of the key characteristics is that of perpetual existence.

COST BASIS- See Adjusted Cost Basis.

CO-TENANCY- Any form of joint ownership.

COUNTERFLASHING- Flashing used on chimneys at roofline to cover shingle flashing and prevent moisture entry.

COUNTER-OFFER- The rejection of an offer by the submission of another offer, different in terms from the original offer. Any purported acceptance of an offer that introduces new terms is a rejection of that offer, and amounts to a counter-offer.

COVERSION - The wrongful appropriation of another's goods to one's own use; to change from one character or use to another.
1. In tort, an unauthorized claim of ownership over another's personal property.
2. In property, the change of character of property from real to personal, or vice versa.

CPM - Certified Property Manager; a member of the Institute of Real Estate Property management of the National Association of Realtors.

CRAWL HOLE - Exterior or interior opening permitting access underneath a building, as building codes may require.

CREDIT UNIONS - A growing source of funds for real estate loans.

CRV - These initials mean Certificate of Reasonable Value.

CURTAIL SCHEDULE - A list of the due dates and amounts by which the principal sum of an obligation will be reduced by partial payments.

DAMAGES - The indemnity recoverable by a person who has sustained an injury to either his or her person, property, or rights through the act or default of another. Compensation ordered by the courts for the loss of or injury to one's person or property.

DEALER - A person who holds property primarily for sale to his or her customers in the ordinary course of his or her business.

DEBT SERVICE - The sum of money needed each payment period to amortize the loan or loans.

DEBTOR
1. A party who "owns" the property that is subject to a security interest.
2. A person who owes a debt

DECK - Usually an open porch on the roof or another part of the structure.

DECLARATORY RELIEF - A court's decision on the rights of the parties in a question of law, without ordering anything to be done.

DEDICATION- An appropriation of land by its owner for some public use and accepted for such use by authorized public officials on behalf of the public. A gift of privately owned land to the public or for public use. It may be voluntary or involuntary.

DEED - A written instrument that when properly executed and delivered conveys title.

DEED OF TRUST - A security instrument transferring title to property to a third person (trustee) as security for a debt or other obligation.

DEFAULT
1. Failure to fulfill a duty or promise or to discharge an obligation.
2. Omission or failure to perform any act. Failure to perform a legal duty or to discharge a promise

DEFAULT JUDGMENT- A judgment obtained because the defendant failed to appear and defend his case.

DEFEASANCE CLAUSE- The clause in a mortgage or deed of trust that gives the borrower the right to redeem his or her property upon the payment of his or her property upon the payment of his or her obligations to the lender.

DEFEASIBLE- Capable of being defeated. A defeasible estate is one that has a condition attached to the title, which if broken causes the termination of that estate.

DEFENDANT- The party being sued in a lawsuit; the party against whom an action is filed.

DEFERRED MAINTENANCE- Maintenance and accumulated repairs that have been postponed.

DEFICIENCY JUDGEMENT- A judgment given for the unpaid balance of a debt remaining after the surety is sold. A court decree holding a debtor personally liable for the shortage or insufficiency realized on the sale of secured property. The debtor owes the difference between the sale price of the property and the amount of the secured debt.

DELIVERY (OF A DEED)- The unconditional, irrevocable intent of a grantor immediately to divest (give up) an interest in real estate by a deed or other instrument.

DEPOSIT- Money given to another as security to ensure the performance of a contract. The money is usually intended to be applied toward the purchase price of property, or forfeited on failure to complete the contract.

DEPOSIT RECEIPT- A contract used in the he real estate business that includes the terms of the contract and acts as a receipt for "earnest money" to bind an offer for property by the prospective purchaser. The name given to most real estate contracts containing the terms of the sale of real estate, and receipt for earnest money (deposited).

DEPRECIATION- A loss in value from any cause. This loss in value to real property may be caused by age or physical deterioration, or by functional or economic obsolescence.

DESIST AND REFRAIN ORDER- An order that the Real Estate Commissioner is empowered by law and refrain from committing an act in violation of the Real Estate Law.

DETERIORATION- The process of gradual worsening or depreciation.

DEVISE- A gift of real property by deed.

DEVISEE- One who receives real property under a will.

DICTUM- A written observation, remark, or opinion by a judge to illustrate or suggest an argument or rule of law not incidental to the case at hand, and which, therefore, although persuasive, is not binding on the judge.

DIRECTIONAL GROWTH- The direction in which the residential sections of a city seem destined or determined to grow.

DISCLOSURE STATEMENT - A statement that the Truth-in-Lending Law requires a creditor to give a debtor showing the finance charge, annual percentage rate, and other required information.

DISCOUNT - To sell a promissory note before maturity at a price less than the outstanding principal balance of the note at the time of sale. It may also be the amount deducted in advance by the lender from the face of the note.

DISCOUNT POINTS - A fee charged by the lender when making an FHA or VA loan to offset the lower interest rate the lender will receive compared with conventional loan interest rates. One point is equal to 1 percent.

DISCOUNT RATE - The interest rate that is charged on money borrowed by banks from the Federal Reserve System.

DISCOUNTED TRUST DEED - An investment in this kind of deed can be a perfect investment.

DISCRIMINATORY CONDUCT - The DRE Regulations state that discriminatory conduct is a basis for disciplinary action.

DISSOLUTION OF MARRIAGE - A divorce.

DISTRICT COURT - The main trial court in the federal court system and the lowest federal court. It has jurisdiction in civil cases where the plaintiffs and defendants are from different states (diversity of citizenship) and the amount in controversy is over $10,000, and in cases involving a federal question.

DIVESTMENT - The elimination or removal of a right or title, usually applied to the cancellation of an estate in land.

DOMICILE - A person's permanent residence.

DOMINANT TENEMENT - The tenement obtaining the benefit of an easement appurtenant. That parcel of land that benefits from an easement across another parcel of property (servient tenement).

DONEE - The person to whom a gift is made.

DONOR - The person who makes a gift.

DOUBLE ESCROW - An escrow that will close only upon the condition that a prior escrow is consummated. The second escrow is contingent upon and tied to the first escrow. While double escrow is not illegal, unless there is full and fair disclosure of the second escrow, there may be a possibility of fraud or other actionable conduct by the parties.

DOWER - The right that a wife has in her husband's estate at his death. Dower has been abolished in California.

DUE PROCESS OF LAW - A constitutional guarantee that the government will not interfere with a person's private property rights without following procedural safeguards prescribed by law.

DUE-ON-ENCUMBRANCE CLAUSE- A clause in a deed of trust or mortgage that provides that upon the execration of additional deeds of trust or other encumbrances against a secured parcel of property, the lender may declare the entire unpaid balance of principal and interest due and owing.

DUE-ON-SALE CLAUSE- An acceleration clause that grants the lender the right to demand full payment of the mortgage or deed of trust upon sale of the property. A clause in a deed of trust or mortgage that provides that if the secured property is sold or transferred, the lender may declare the entire unpaid balance immediately due and payable. Its use has been severely limited by recent court decisions. Also called an alienation clause.

DURESS- Unlawful constraint by force or fear. E.I.R. Abbreviation for Environmental Impact Report.

EARNEST MONEY DEPOSIT - A deposit of money paid by a buyer for real property as evidence of good faith. Cannot be given back to the buyer unless he obtains written permission from the seller.

EASEMENT- A right, privilege, or interest that one party has to use the land of another. Example: A right of way. A legal right to use another's land for one's benefit or the benefit of one's property (right-of-way).

EASEMENT APPURTENANT- An easement created for the benefit of a particular parcel of property. There is both a dominant and a servient estate. The easement is annexed to and part of the dominant property.

EASEMENT IN GROSS- An easement that benefits a particular individual, not a parcel of property. Involves only a servient estate. A public utility easement is an example.

EASY QUALIFIER MORTGAGE- This may be referred to as "low doc" or "no doc" loan.

EAVES- The lower projecting edge of a roof over the wall.

ECONOMIC LIFE- The remaining useful life of an improvement or structure; that period during which an improvement will yield a return on the investment.

ECONOMIC OBSOLESCENCE- The loss in value to property due to external causes such as zoning or a deteriorating neighborhood. It is also referred to as social obsolescence.

EFFECTIVE GROSS INCOME- The amount of net income that remains after the deduction from gross income of vacancy and credit losses.

EGRESS- Exit; the act or avenue or leaving property.

EMBLEMENTS- Things that grow on the land require annual planting and cultivation.

EMINENT DOMAIN- The right of the government and certain others, such as public utilities, to acquire property for public or quasi-public use by condemnation, upon payment of just compensation to the owner. The constitutional or inherent right of a government to take private property for public good upon the payment of just compensation.

ENCROACHMENT - The projection of a structure onto the land of an adjoining owner. A structure or natural object that unlawfully extends into another's property.

ENCUMBRANCE - Any claim, interest, or right improperly possessed by another that may diminish the true owner's rights or value in the estate. Examples include mortgages, easements, or restrictions of any kind. A claim, lien, or charge on property.

ENDORSEMENT - See Indorsement.

ENVIRONMENTAL IMPACT REPORT- A report that must be prepared whenever any agency or individual considers a project that may have a significant impact on the environment, as directed by the California Environmental Quality Act.

EQUAL CREDIT OPPORTUNITY ACT - Prohibits discrimination amongst lenders.

EQUAL HOUSING OPPORTUNITY - Prohibits discrimination in the listing, sale, lease, rental or financing of real property due to race, creed, religion, sex, marital status or handicap. Should apply exactly the same in all real estate

EQUAL PROTECTION - The Fourteenth Amendment to the U.S. Constitution and similar provisions in the California Constitution require each citizen to receive equal protection of the laws. There are no minimum standards of protection; all equally situated individuals must simply be treated equally. (The due process clause of the Constitution imposes certain minimum standards of protection.)

EQUITY
1. The interest or value that on owner has in real property over and above the liens against it.
2. A part of our justice system by which courts seek to supplement the strict terms of the law to fairness under the circumstances, rather than on fixed legal principles or statutes.
3. Ownership in property, determined by calculating the fair market value less the amount of liens and encumbrances.

EQUITY BUILD-UP - The increase of the owner's equity due to mortgage principal reduction and value appreciation.

EQUITY OF REDEMPTION - The right to redeem property during the foreclosure period. In California the mortgagor has the right to redeem within 12 months after the foreclosure sale.

EROSION - The wearing away of the surface of the land by the action of wind, water, and glaciers, for example.

ESCALATOR CLAUSE - A clause in a contract that provides for the upward or downward adjustment of certain items to cover the specific contingencies set forth. A clause in a promissory note, lease, or other document that provides that upon the passage of a specified time or the happening of a stated event, the interest rate shall increase.

ESCHEAT - The reversion of property to the state when there are no devisees or heirs capable of inheritance. Reversion of property to the state upon the death of an owner who has no heirs able to inherit.

ESCROW - The deposit of instruments and funds with a third neutral party with instructions to carry out the provisions of an agreement or contract. A complete or perfect escrow is one in which everything has been deposited to enable carrying out the instructions. The neutral third party (stakeholder) who holds deeds or other documents pursuant to instructions for delivery upon completion or occurrence of certain conditions.

ESTATE- The degree, quantity, nature, and extent of the interest that a person has in real property.
1. Ownership interest in real estate.
2. The quality and quantity of rights in property

ESTATE AT WILL- The occupation of real property by a tenant for an indefinite period. One or both parties may terminate it at will. A leasehold tenancy, which at common law could be terminated by either party at any time, without advance notice. Thirty days' notice is now required to terminate this type of estate in California.

ESTATE FOR LIFE- A freehold estate whose duration is measured by and limited to the life or lives of one or more persons.

ESTATE FOR PERIOD TO PERIOD- A leasehold tenancy that continues indefinitely for successive periods of time, until terminated by proper notice. When the periods are one month in duration, it is often called a month-to-month tenancy.

ESTATE FOR YEARS- A lease that will expire at a definite time or date. A leasehold tenancy of a fixed duration, being a definite and ascertainable period of a year or any fraction of multiple thereof. It has a definite beginning and ending date, and hence a known and definite duration.

ESTATE OF INHERITANCE- An estate that may go to the heirs of the deceased. All freehold estates are estates of inheritance, except life estates.

ESTOP- To ban, stop, or impede.

ESTOPPEL- A doctrine whereby one is forbidden to contradict or deny his or her own previous statement, act, or position. The doctrine that prevents a person from exercising a legal right, because that person previously acted in an inconsistent manner, so that a third person detrimentally relied on the earlier acts. An agency is created this way when an individual knowingly allows another individual to act as their agent without authorizing such acts.

ET AL- Abbreviation meaning and others (other person).

ET UX- Abbreviation meaning and wife.

ETHICS- A standard of conduct that all members of a given profession owe to the public, clients or patrons, and to other members of that profession. Refers to a branch of philosophy that deals with moral science and moral principles. It is a debatable subject and cannot be legislated. It is based on what each individual feels is good or bad.

ETHNIC- The seller of a property is not allowed to ask the buyer their ethnic background.

EVICTION- Dispossession by legal process, as in the termination of a tenant's right to possession through re-entry or other legal proceedings.

EVIDENCE - All relevant information, facts, and exhibits admissible in a trial.

EX PARTE - By only one party or side. For example, an injunction obtained by evidence presented by only one side, without notice to the other parties.

EXCEPTION - (See Reservation.)

EXCHANGE - A reciprocal transfer of properties between two or more parties.

EXCLUSIVE AGENCY - A contract hiring the broker as the exclusive agent for the seller. If anyone, except the seller, finds a buyer, the broker has earned the commission.

EXCLUSIVE AGENCY LISTING - A written agreement giving one agent the exclusive right to sell property for a specified period of time, but reserving the right of the owner to sell the property himself or herself without liability for the payment of a commission.

EXCLUSIVE RIGHT TO SELL AGENCY - A contract hiring the broker as the only person authorized to sell property. If anyone, including the seller, finds a buyer, the broker earns the commissions.

EXCLUSIVE-RIGHT-TO-SELL LISTING - A written agreement giving one agent the exclusive right to sell property for a specified period of time. The agent may collect a commission if the property is sold by anyone, including the owner, during the term of the listing agreement.

EXCULPATORY CLAUSE - A provision in leases and other instruments seeking to relieve one party of liability for his negligence and other acts. In residential leases such clauses are invalid, and in other leases the courts have limited the landlord's ability to escape liability for intentional acts, and for acts of affirmative negligence.

EXECUTE - To complete, make, perform, do or to follow out. To sign a document, intending to make it a binding instrument. The term is also used to indicate the performance of a contract.

EXECUTION LIEN - A lien arising because of an execution on property. A judgment is not self-executing; however, when a writ of execution has been obtained, the sheriff will levy (seize) property, which creates a lien on the property.

EXECUTOR - A person named by the testator of a will to carry out its provisions as to the disposition of the estate. A personal representative appointed in a will to administer a decedent's estate.

EXPANSIBLE HOUSE- A home designed for expansion and additions in the future.

EXPANSION JOINT - A fiber strip used to separate units of concrete to prevent cracking due to expansion as a result of temperature changes.

FACADE - The face of a building, especially the front face.

FAIR MARKET VALUE - The amount of money that would be paid for a property offered on the open market for a reasonable length of time with both the buyer and the seller knowing all uses to which the property could be put and with neither party being under pressure to buy or sell. See market Value.

FALSE PROMISE- A statement used to influence or persuade.

FANNY MAE- The Federal National Mortgage Association (FNMA).

FARM- It is a specific geographical location in which an agent walks every month in order to obtain listings.

FEDERAL DEPOSIT INSURANCE- A federal corporation that insures deposits in commercial CORPORATION banks (FDIC).

FEDERAL FAIR HOUSING ACT- Was established under Title VIII of the United States Civil Rights Act of 1969. It was amended in 1988. It was created to provide fair housing through out the United States.

FEDERAL HOME LOAN BANK (FHLB)- A district bank of the Federal Home Loan Bank System that lends only to savings and loan associations who are members.

FEDERAL HOME LOAN MORTGAGE CORPORATION (FHLMC)- A federal corporation that provides savings and loan associations with a secondary mortgage money market for loans. It is also known as Freddy Mac.

FEDERAL HOUSING ADMINISTRATION- An agency of the federal government that insures mortgage (FHA) loans.

FEDERAL NATIONAL MORTGAGE ASSOCIATION (FNMA)- A federal corporation that provides lenders with a secondary mortgage money market.

FEDERAL RESERVE SYSTEM- The federal banking system of the United States under the control of a central board of governors (Federal Reserve Board). It involves a central bank in each of 12 geographical districts, with broad powers in controlling credit and the amount of money in circulation.

FEDERAL SAVINGS AND LOAN INSURANCE CORPORATION (FSLIC)- A federal corporation that insures deposits in savings and loan associations.

FEE- An estate of inheritance in real property for life.

FEE SIMPLE- An estate in real property by which the owner has the greatest possible power over the title. In modern use it expressly establishes the title of real property with the owner without limitation or end. He or she may dispose of it by sale, trade, or will, as he or she chooses. In modern estates the terms "Fee" and "Fee Simple" are substantially synonymous.

FEE SIMPLE ABSOLUTE- The highest estate known at law. A freehold estate of indefinite duration, incapable of being defeated by conditions or limitations. Sometimes simply called fee or fee estate.

FEE SIMPLE DEFEASIBLE- A fee simple estate to which certain conditions or limitations attach, such that the estate may be defeated or terminated upon the happening of an act or event. Also called a fee simple subject to condition subsequent estates.

FEE SIMPLE SUBJECT TO A CONDITION SUBSEQUENT- A fee simple defeasible estate that requires the holder of the future interest to act promptly to terminate the present interest, in order for that interest to be terminated.

FHA - The FHA does not loan money. The FHA loan may be paid off at any time without a penalty. The buyer or the seller may pay discount points on a FHA loan. The down payment on a FHA loan is usually LESS than the down payment on a conventional loan.

FIDUCIARY - A person in a position of trust and confidence, as between principal and broker. A fiduciary may not make a profit from his or her position without first disclosing it to the beneficiary.

FINANCIAL FREEDOM - The freedom to make purchases with no restraint.

FINANCING STATEMENT - The instrument filed to perfect the security agreement and give constructive notice of the security interest, thereby protecting the interest of the secured parties. (See Security Agreement; Security Interest; and Secured Party.) The security interest in personal property. It is analogous to a mortgage on real property, except that it secures personal property. Under the U.C.C., it may be filed in Sacramento with the secretary of state.

FINDER'S FEE- Money paid to a person for finding someone interested in selling or buying property. To conduct any negotiations of sale terms, the finder must be a licensed broker or he violates the law.

FINISH FLOOR - The final covering on the floor, such as wood, linoleum, cork, or carpet.

FIRE STOP - A solid, tight closure of a concealed space placed to prevent the spread of fire and smoke through the space.

FIRST AMENDMENT - The constitutional amendment guaranteeing freedom of speech, press, assembly, and religion.

FIXTURE - An item of personal property that has been so attached to real property as to be considered part of that real property.

FIXTURES - Items that were originally personal property but that have become part of the real property, usually because they are attached to the real property more or less permanently. Examples: Store fixtures built into the property and plumbing fixtures.

FLASHING - Sheet metal or similar material used to protect a building from water seepage.

FLIPPER PROPERTY - Any property bought for immediate resale and profit.

FOOTING- The base or bottom of a foundation wall, pier or column.

FORCIBLE DETAINER - Wrongful retention of property by actual or constructive force.

FORCIBLE ENTRY - Entry into property without the consent of the owner, by acts that constitute more than mere trespass.

FORECLOSURE - A legal proceeding to enforce a lien on such as a mortgage or deed of trust. The process by which secured property is seized and sold to satisfy a debt. A mortgage or involuntary lien must be sold by a court-ordered sale; a sale under a deed of trust may be either by court action or through a private trustee's sale.

FOREFEITURE- Loss of a legal right, interest, or title by default.

FORMAL WILL- A will signed by the testator in the presence of two or more witnesses, who must themselves sign the will.

FOUNDATION- That part of a structure or wall wholly or partly below the surface of the ground that is the base or support, including the footings.

FOURTEENTH AMENDMENT- The constitutional amendment that directs that no state can deprive a person of life, liberty, or property without due process or equal protection of the law.

FRAUD- Deception that deprives another person of his her rights or injures him or her. False representation or concealment of material facts that induces another justifiably to rely on it to his detriment.

FREEHOLD- An estate of fee. An estate in real property that is either a life estate or an estate in fee.

FRONT FOOT- Property measurement for sale or valuation purposes. The property measurement is along the street line, and each front foot extends to the depth of the lot. It is usually used in connection with commercial property.

FROSTLINE- The depth of frost penetration in the soil.

FRUCTUS- Fruits, crops, and other plants. If the vegetation is produced by human labor, such as crops, it is called fructus industrials; vegetation growing naturally is called fructus naturales.

FURRING- Strips of wood or metal fastened to wall to even it, form air space, or to give the wall greater thickness.

FUTURE ADVANCES- Future (additional) loans made by a lender and secured under the original deed of trust. The advances may be either optional or obligatory, but the deed of trust or mortgage must provide in the security instrument that it will cover any such future advances.

FUTURE INTEREST- An estate that does not or may entitle one to possession or enjoyment until a future time.

GABLE ROOF - Pitched roof with sloping sides.

GAMBREL ROOF- A curb roof, having a steep lower slope with a flatter upper slope above.

GARNISHMENT- A legal process to seize a debtor's property or money in the possession of a third party.

GAURANTEED NOTE- A permit must be received from the real estate commissioner before being allowed to sell a guaranteed note.

GENERAL PLAN RESTRICTIONS - Covenants, conditions, and restrictions placed on a subdivision or other large tract of land, designed to benefit and burden each lot in the tract.

GIFT - A voluntary transfer of property without consideration.

GIFT DEED - A deed for which there is no material consideration.

GIRDER - A beam used to support other beams, joists, and partitions.

GOVERNMENT NATIONAL MORTGAGE - A federal corporation that assists in financing special ASSOCIATION (GNMA) assistance programs for federally aided housing. The corporation is also known as Ginny Mae.

GRADE - Ground level at the foundation.

GRADUATED LEASE - Usually a long-term lease that provides for adjustments in the rental rate on the basis of some future determination. For example, the rent may be based upon the result of appraisals to be made at predetermined times in the future.

GRANT
1. To transfer.
2. A deed.
3. When used in a deed, a technical term implying certain warranties. A transfer or conveyance of real estate.

GRANT DEED - In California, a deed in which the word grant is used as a work of conveyance and therefore by law implies certain warranties deed used to transfer property in California. By statute it impliedly contains only two limited warranties.

GRANTEE - The buyer; a person to whom a grant is made.

GRANTOR - The seller; one who signs a deed. The seller or person who executes a grant.

GRID - A chart used in rating the borrower, property, and neighborhood.

GROSS INCOME - Total income before expenses are deducted.

GROSS RENT MUTIPLIER - A number that reflects the ratio between the sales price of a property and its gross monthly rents. It is used in the income approach of appraising property.

GROUND LEASE - An agreement leasing land only, without improvements, ordinarily with the understanding that improvements will be placed on the land by the tenant.

GROUND RENT
1. Earnings from the ground only.
2. Earnings of improved property after an allowance are made for earnings of improvements.
3. A perpetual rent that a grantor in some states may reserve to himself or herself and his or her heirs when he or she conveys real property.

GROWTH EQUITY MORTGAGE - This type of mortgage will be paid back faster than the typical 30 year fully amortized mortgage.

HANDICAP - Includes but is not limited to a physical or mental impairment that substantially limits one or more of a person's major life activities.

HAZARD INSURANCE- Insurance that protects the owner and lender against physical hazards to property such as fire and windstorm damage.

HEADER- A beam placed perpendicularly to joists and to which joists are nailed in the framing of openings such as windows, doors, and stairways.

HEIRS- Persons who succeed to the estate of someone who dies intestate (without a will). It sometimes indicates anyone who is entitled to inherit a decedent's property.

HEREDITAMENT- A term usually referring to real estate and all that goes with it as being incidental.

HIGHEST AND BEST USE- An appraisal phrase that means that use of real property that is most likely to produce the greatest net return on land or buildings, or both, over a given period of time.

HIP ROOF- A pitched roof with sloping sides and ends.

HOLDEN ACT- Specifically states that "redlining" is illegal in California.

HOLDER IN DUE COURSE- One who has taken a negotiable note, check, or bill of exchange in due course
1. before it was past due;
2. in good faith;
3. without knowledge that it has been previously dishonored and without notice of any defect at the time it was negotiated to him or her;
4. for value. Someone who acquires a negotiable instrument in good faith and without any actual or constructive notice of defect. The acquisition must occur before the note's maturity. Such a holder takes the note free from any personal defenses (such as failure of consideration, fraud in the inducement) that may be available against the maker

HOLOGRAPHIC WILL- A will that is entirely written, dated, and signed by the testator in the testator's handwriting. No witnesses are needed.

HOMEOWNER'S EXEMPTION- An exemption or reduction in real property taxes available to those who reside on their property as of March 1. The current amount is $70 off the normal tax bill otherwise due.

HOMESTEAD
1. A home upon which the owner or owners have recorded a Declaration of Homestead, as provided by California statutes, that protects the home against judgments up to a specified amount.
2. A probate homestead is a similarly protected home property set aside by a California probate court for a widow or minor children. A special, limited exemption against certain judgments available to qualified homeowners.

HUNDRED PERCENT LOCATION- A retail business location considered the best available for attracting business.

ILLUSORY CONTRACT - An agreement that gives the appearance of a contract, but in fact is not a contract because it lacks one of the essential elements.

IMPLIED - Not expressed by words, but presumed from facts, acts, or circumstances.

IMPOUND ACCOUNT - A trust account established by the lender to pay property taxes and hazard insurance.

INCOME APPROACH - An appraisal technique used on income producing properties. Also known as the capitalization approach.

INCOME TAX - The cost to remodel vacant property may be deducted from the income tax.

INCOMPETENT - Someone incapable of managing his or her own affairs by reason of age, disease, weakness of mind, or any other cause.

INCREMENT - Any increase.
1. A term frequently used to refer to the increased value of land because of population growth and increased wealth in the community.
2. "Unearned increment" is used in this connection since the values increased without effort on the part of the owner.

INDEBTEDNESS - A debt or obligation.

INDEMNIFICATION - Compensation to a person who has already sustained a loss. For example, insurance payment for a loss under policy.

INDIRECT LIGHTING - A method of illumination in which the light is reflected from the ceiling or other object outside the fixture.

INDORSEMENT
1. The act of signing one's name on the back of a check or a note, with or without further qualification.
2. The signature described above.

INFATIONARY HEDGE - Real estate is considered to be the best bet against inflation.

INFLATION - This is not an easy condition to eliminate.

INFLATIONARY HEDGE - Real estate is considered to be the best bet against inflation.

INGRESS - The act of or avenue for entering property.

INHERIT - To take property through a deceased's estate.

INJUNCTION - An order issued by a court to restrain one or more parties to a suit or proceeding from performing an act deemed inequitable or unjust in regard to the rights of some other party or parties in the suit or proceeding.

INJUNCTION - A court order prohibiting certain acts, or ordering specific acts.

INSTALLMENT - A partial payment of a debt due in a series of payments.

INSTALLMENT NOTE - A note that provides that payments of a certain sum or amount be paid in more than one payment on the dates specified in the instrument.

INSTALLMENT SALES CONTRACT- Also known as an agreement of sale or a land contract.

INSTALLMENT-SALE METHOD- A method of reporting capital gains by installments for successive tax years to minimize the impact of capital gains tax in the year of the sale.

INSTITUTIONAL LENDER- Lenders who make a substantial number of real estate loans, such as banks, savings and loan associations, and insurance companies.

INSTRUMENT- A written legal document created to affect the rights of the parties.

INTEREST- The charge or cost for the use of money.

INTEREST RATE- The percentage of a sum of money charged for its use.

INTEREST RATE CAP- The majority of all the mortgages do contain an interest rate cap.

INTERPLEADER- A court proceeding initiated by a stakeholder, such as a broker or escrow agent. This decides the ownership or disposition of trust funds.

INTESTATE- A person who dies without a will.

INTREST DEDUCTION- The amount of a home equity loan that qualifies for an interest deduction cannot exceed $100,000.00.

INVESTOR- A person who holds property primarily for future appreciation in value for federal and state income tax purposes.

INVITEE- A person who enters another's land because of an express or implied social invitation, such as a social guest. The term also covers certain government workers who enter someone's land, such as police officers and firefighters. Classification of such status was revoked by a recent court case.

INVOLUNTARY CONVERSION- The loss of real property due to destruction, seizure, condemnation, foreclosure sale, or tax sale.

INVOLUNTARY LIEN- Any lien imposed on property without the consent of the owner. **IRREVOCABLE** Incapable of being recalled or revoked; unchangeable.

IRRIGATION DISTRICTS- Quasi-political districts created under special laws to provide for water services to property-owners in the district.

JALOUSIE - A screen or shutter consisting of overlapping horizontal slats that is used on the exterior to keep out sun and rain while admitting light and air.

JAMB- The side post or lining of a doorway, window, or other opening.

JOINT- The space between the adjacent surfaces of two components joined and held together by nails, glue, or cement, for example.

JOINT NOTE- A note signed by two or more persons who have equal liability for payment.

JOINT TENANCY - Joint ownership by two or more persons with right of survivorship. Four unities must be present: time, title, interest, and possession. Property held by two or more people with right of survivorship.

JOINT VENTURE - In legal effect it is a partnership for a limited, specific business project.

JOISTS - One of a series of parallel beams to which the boards of floor and ceiling laths or plaster boards are nailed and supported in turn by larger beams, girders, or bearing walls.

JUDGMENT - A court of competent jurisdiction's final determination of a matter presented to it. The final decision by a court in a lawsuit, motion, or other matter.

JUDGMENT AFFIRMED - A decision by an appellate court reaffirming, approving, and agreeing with an inferior court's decision.

JUDGMENT DEBTOR - A person who has an unsatisfied money judgment levied against him or her.

JUDGMENT LIEN - A money judgment that, because it has been recorded, has become a lien against the judgment debtor's real property.

JUDGMENT REVERSED - A decision by an appellate court disagreeing with an inferior court's decision and modifying the decision to conform with its findings.

JUNIOR LIEN - A lien lower in priority or rank than another or other liens.

JUNIOR MORTGAGE - A mortgage second in lien to a previous mortgage.

JURISDICTION - The authority of a court to hear and decide a particular type of case. The power of a court to hear and decide a case or issue.

LACHES - Unreasonable delay in asserting one's legal rights.

LAND CONTRACT - A contract used in the sale of real property when the seller wishes to retain legal title until all or a certain part of the purchase price is paid by the buyer. It is also referred to as an installment sales contract or an agreement of sale.

LAND SALES CONTRACT - A contract for the sale of property, by which possession is delivered to the buyer, but title remains with the seller until full payment or the satisfaction of other stated conditions.

LANDLOCKED - Property totally surrounded by other property with no means of ingress or egress.

LANDLORD - The person who leases property; the owner of the property.

LANDS, TENEMENTS, AND HEREDITAMENT - Inheritable lands or interest.

LATE CHARGE - A charge made by a lender against a borrower who fails to make loan installments when due.

LATE SUPPORT- The support that the soil of an adjoining owner gives to his or her neighbor's land.

LATH- A building material of wood, metal gypsum, or insulating board fastened to the frame of a building to act as a plaster base.

LEASE- A contract between owner and tenant, setting forth conditions upon which the tenant may occupy and use the property and the term of the occupancy.

LEASEHOLD ESTATE- The estate of a tenant under a lease. (See Estate for Years.)

LEGACY- A gift of money by will.

LEGAL DESCRIPTION- A description recognized by law; a description by which property can be definitely located by reference to government surveys or approved recorded maps.

LENDER GUIDELINES- Most lenders use Fannie Mae and Freddie Mac underwriting guidelines.

LESSEE- A tenant; the person who is entitled to possession of property under a lease.

LESSOR- A landlord; the property owner who executes a lease.

LETTER OF INTENT- An expression of intent to invest, develop, or purchase without creating any firm legal obligation to do so.

LEVY- To execute upon; to seize and sell property to obtain money to satisfy a judgment.

LIABILITIES- Debts or claims that creditors have against assets.

LICENSE- Personal, non-assignable authorization to enter and perform certain acts on another's land.

LICENSEE- Under the law before 1968, which classified persons who entered upon others' land, a licensee was someone who entered upon land with the owner's express or implied permission for a business purpose.

LIEN- A lien makes the debtor's property security for the payment of a dept or the discharge of an obligation. A charge or claim against property as security for payment of a debt or obligation.

LIFE ESTATE- An estate in real property that continues for the life of a particular person. The "life" involved may be that of the owner or that of some other person. An estate in property whose duration is limited to and measured by the life of a natural person or persons.

LIGHT COLORS- Light colors make a room look larger.

LIMITED PARTNERSHIP- A partnership composed of some partners whose contribution and liability are limited. There must always be one or more general partners with unlimited liability and one or more limited partners with limited liability. A special partnership composed of limited and general partners. The general partners have unlimited liability and total management, whereas the limited partners have to voice in the management and their only financial exposure is to the extent of their investment. In some ways the limited partners' interest is similar to that of stockholders in a corporation.

LINTEL - A horizontal board that supports the load over an opening such as a door or window.

LIQUIDATED DAMAGES CLAUSE - An agreement between the parties that in the event of a breach, the amount of damages shall be liquidated (set or fixed). The amount is set before the breach, usually at the time of making the contract, on the assumption that the exact amount of damages is difficult to determine because of the nature of the contract.

LIS PENDENS - A notice of pending litigation recorded to give constructive notice of a suit that has been filed. A recorded notice that a lawsuit is pending, the outcome of which may affect title to property.

LISTING - An employment contract between a broker and his principal (client). A listing is automatically canceled upon the death of the agent (real estate broker) or the principal (owner). Another real estate broker must negotiate a new listing with the owner upon the death of the real estate broker.

LISTING AGREEMENT - An employment contract authorizing a broker to sell, lease, or exchange an owner's property.

LITIGATION - A civil lawsuit; a judicial controversy.

LOAN COMMITTEE - The committee in a lending institution that reviews and approves or disapproves the loan applications recommended by a loan officer.

LOAN CORRESPONDENT - A loan agent usually used by distant lenders to help the lender make real estate loans.

LOAN PACKAGE - A group of documents prepared along with a loan application to give the prospective lender complete details about the proposed loan.

LOAN TRUST FUND ACOUNT - (See Impound Account.)

LOAN VALUE - The lender's appraised value of the property.

LOUVER - An opening with a series of horizontal slats set at an angle to permit ventilation without admitting rain, sunlight, or vision.

LTV - These initials mean "loan to valuation"

MAI - A term that designates a person who is a member of the American Institute of Appraisers of the National Association of Realtors.

MANDAMUS - A court decree ordering a lower court judge, public official, or corporate officer to perform an act acquired of that office.

MARGIN OF SECURITY - The difference between the amount of secured loan(s) on a property and its appraised value.

MARGINAL LAND- Land which barely pays the cost of working or using it.

MARKET DATA APPROACH- (See Comparative Market Analysis.)

MARKET PRICE- The price paid regardless of pressures, motives, or intelligence.

MARKET VALUE
1. The price at which a willing seller would sell and a willing buyer would buy, neither being under abnormal pressure.
2. As defined by the courts, it is the highest price estimated in terms of money that a property would bring if exposed for sale in the open market, allowing a reasonable time to find a purchaser with knowledge of the property's use and capabilities for use.

MARKETABLE TITLE- Title free and clear of reasonable objections and doubts; also called merchantable title.

MATERIAL FACT- A fact that would be likely to affect a person's decision in determining whether to enter into a particular transaction. Any information that will influence the judgment or decision of the customer.

MECHANIC'S LIEN- A lien given by statute to persons supplying labor, materials, or other services to improve real property. Whenever a contractor, laborer, or materialman provides labor or materials to improve real property and is not paid, that person is enti-tled to a lien against the property as a means of securing payment. Certain statutory steps must be taken to file, record, and foreclose the lien. Memo to set: A document filed in a lawsuit which asks to be placed on the waiting list ("docket") for the next avail-able court date.

MENACE- A threat to use duress. (See Duress.)

MERCHANTABLE TITLE- (See Marketable Title.)

MERGER OF TITLE- The combination of two estates. Also refers to the joining of one estate burdened by an encumbrance and another estate benefited by the encum-brance. Whenever a benefit and a burden are merged, the encumbrance is extin-guished.

MERIDIANS- Imaginary north-south lines that intersect base lines to form a starting point for the measurement of land.

METES AND BOUNDS- Terms used to describe the boundary lines of land, setting forth all the boundary lines together with their terminal points and angles. Metes means measurements Bounds means boundaries.

MILLIONARES- Ninety percent of all millionaires become that way from owning proper-ty.

MINOR
1. A person under the age of majority.

2. In California all persons under eighteen years of age - the age of majority in California. Someone under age 18.

MINUS CASH FLOW- An event that takes place when there is not enough cash to cover expenses and service the mortgage debt.

MISREPRESENTATION - An intentional or negligent suggestion or statement of a material fact in a false manner with the intent of deceiving someone into taking a course of action he would not otherwise normally pursue. A licensee may be disciplined for misrepresentation even though the misrepresentation did not result in a loss to the principal.

MITIGATION - Facts or circumstances that tend to justify or excuse an act or course of conduct.

MOBILE HOME - A stationary, non-motorized vehicle designed and equipped for human habitation. It may be transported to a home site by special equipment.

MOLDING - Usually patterned strips used to provide ornamental variation of outline or contour, such as cornices, bases, window and doorjambs.

MONEY TO MAKE MONEY - It takes money to make money in real estate is the general belief.

MONTH-TO-MONTH TENANCY - A lease of property for a month at a time, under a periodic tenancy that continues for successive months until terminated by proper notice, usually 30 days.

MONUMENT - A fixed object and point established by surveyors or others to establish land locations.

MORATORIUM - The temporary suspension, usually by stature, of the enforcement of liability for debt.

MORTGAGE - An instrument by which property is hypothecated to secure the payment of a debt or obligation.

MORTGAGE - A contract by which property is hypothecated (pledged without delivery) for the repayment of a loan.

MORTGAGE GUARANTY INSURANCE - Insurance against financial loss available to mortgage lenders from the Mortgage Guaranty Insurance Corporation, a private company organized in 1956.

MORTGAGE LOAN BROKER - Is required to have a real estate license.

MORTGAGEE - One to whom a mortgagor gives a mortgage to secure a loan or performance of an obligation: the lender under a mortgage. (See Secured Party.) A creditor (lender) under a mortgage.

MORTGAGOR - One who gives a mortgage on his or her property to secure a loan or assure performance of an obligation; the borrower under a mortgage. (See Debtor.) A borrower (property owner) of money under a mortgage.

MULTIPLE LISTING - A listing, usually an exclusive-right-to-sell, taken by a member of an organization composed of real estate brokers with the provisions that all members will have the opportunity to find an interested client; a cooperative listing. A listing taken by a broker and shared with other brokers through a specialized distribution service, usually provided by the local real estate board. Generally, such listings are exclusive right to sell listings.

MUNICIPAL COURT- An inferior trial court having jurisdiction in cases involving up to $15,000 in money damages and in unlawful detainer actions in which the rental value is under $1,000 per month.

MUTUAL ASSENT- An agreement between the parties in a contract. The offer and acceptance of a contract.

MUTUAL WATER COMPANY- A water company organized by or for water-users in a given district, with the object of securing an ample water supply at a reasonable rate. Stock is issued to users.

NAR- National Association of Realtors.

NAREB- National Association of Real Estate Boards. This trade organization is now known as the National Association of Realtors.

NEGATIVE AMORTIZATION- Occurs when normal payments on a loan are insufficient to cover all interest then due, so that unpaid interest is added to principal. Thus, even though payments are timely made, the principal grows with each payment.

NEGATIVE AMORTIZATION- Occurs when the debt service is not sufficient to cover the interest amount of the loan. This note should only be used in area that is appreciating in value.

NEGATIVE AMORTIZATION- Occurs when the debt service is not sufficient to cover the interest amount of the loan.

NEGLIGENCE- Either the failure to act as a reasonable, prudent person, or the performance of an act that would not be done by a reasonable, prudent person.

NEGOTIABLE INSTRUMENT- A check or promissory note that meets specified statutory requirements and is therefore easily transferable in somewhat the same manner as money. The negotiable instrument can be passed by endorsement and delivery (or in some cases by mere delivery), and the transferee takes title free of certain real defenses (such as failure of consideration, fraud in the inducement) that might exist against the original maker of the negotiable instrument.

NEPA- Abbreviation for the National Environmental Protection Act, a federal statute requiring all federal agencies to prepare an Environmental Impact Statement and meet other requirements whenever a major federal action is anticipated that could significantly affect the environment.

NET LISTING- listing that provides that the agent may retain as compensation for his or her services all sums received over and above a stated net price to the owner. An employment agreement that entitles the broker to a commission only in the amount, if any that the sales price of the property exceeds the listing price.

NONFREEHOLD ESTATE- A lease tenancy. (See under Estates for the four types of leasehold estates.)

NONJUDICIAL FORECLOSURE- Foreclosure and sale of property without resort to court action, by private sale. For deeds of trust the foreclosure provisions are outlined by the statutes and the requirements in the security instrument, which include a notice of default, right to reinstate, publication of sale, and trustee's sale.

NOTARY PUBLIC - An individual licensed by the state to charge a fee for acknowledging signatures on instruments.

NOTE - A signed written instrument promising payment of a stated sum of money. Shortened name for a promissory note.

NOTICE OF COMPLETION - A notice recorded after termination of work on improvements, limiting the time in which mechanic's liens can be filed against the property.

NOTICE OF DEFAULT - A notice that is recorded in the county recorder's office stating that a trust deed is in default and that the holder has chosen to have the property sold. The trustor (property owner) has three months after the date of recording to reinstate the loan. Recorded notice that a trustor has defaulted on his secured debt.

NOTICE OF NONRESPONSIBILITY - A notice provided by law designed to relieve a property owner from responsibility for the cost of work done on the property or materials furnished for it when the work or materials were ordered by a person in possession. Notice relieving an owner from possession. Notice relieving an owner from mechanic's liens for work on property not ordered by that owner.

NOTICE TO QUIT - A notice to a tenant to vacate rented property. Also called a three-day notice. Notice given to a tenant in default of his lease terms or on his rent, which directs him either to cure the default or to vacate the premises.

NOVATION - The acceptance of a new contract in substitution for the old contract, with the intent that the new contract will extinguish the original contract. Sometimes encountered in transfers of deeds of trust, where the new owner assumes the debt and the lender, through novation, releases the former owner from any liability under the original promissory note and deed of trust.

NUISANCE - Anything that is injurious to health or indecent or offensive to the senses, or any obstruction to the free use of property so as to interfere with the comfortable enjoyment of life or property or unlawfully obstructs the free passage or use, in the customary manner, of any navigable lake or river, bay, stream, canal, or basin, or any public park, square, street, or highway. A legal wrong arising from acts or use of one's property in a way that unreasonably interferes with another's use of hid property.

OBLIGEE - A promisor; a person to whom another is bound by a promise or another obligation.

OBSOLESCENCE - Loss in value due to reduced desirability and usefulness of a structure because its design and construction become obsolete; loss because of becoming old-fashioned and not in keeping with modern needs.

OFFER - A proposal to create a contract, which signifies the present intent of the offer-or to be legally bound by his proposal.

OFFEREE - A person to whom an offer is made.

OFFEROR - A person who makes an offer.

OFFSET STATEMENT- Statement by owner of a deed of trust or mortgage against the property, setting forth the present status of the debt and lien. Also called a beneficiary statement.

OPEN HOUSE- Is an opportunity for a licensee to meet potential buyers and sellers, and therefore is considered to be in the best interest of the licensee and not the seller. This is NOT the most effective way to method to advertise a piece of rental property.

OPEN LISTING- An authorization given by a property-owner to a real estate agent in which the agent is given the nonexclusive right to secure a purchaser. Open listings may be given to any number of agents without liability to compensate any except the one who first secures a buyer ready, willing, and able to meet the terms of the listing or who secures the acceptance by the seller of a satisfactory offer.

OPEN-END MORTGAGE OR DEED OF TRUST- A mortgage containing a clause that permits the mortgagor or trustor to borrow additional money without rewriting the mortgage or deed of trust.

OPTION- A right to have an act performed in the future; a right given for a consideration to purchase or lease a property upon specified terms within a specified time; a contract to keep an offer open for a particular period of time. The right of a person to buy or lease property at a set price at any time during the life of a contract.

OPTION LISTING- A listing that also includes an option, permitting the broker to buy the property at the stated price at any time during the listing period.

ORAL CONTRACT- A verbal agreement, one not reduced to writing.

ORDINANCE- A law passed by a political subdivision of the state (such as a town, city, or county).

ORIENTATION- Placement of a house on its lot with regard to its exposure to the rays of the sun, prevailing winds, privacy from the street, and protection from outside noises.

OR-MORE CLAUSE- A simple prepayment clause that permits the borrower to make a normal payment or any larger amount, up to and including the entire outstanding balance, without a prepayment penalty.

OSTENSIBLE AGENCY- An agency implied by law because the principal intentionally or inadvertently caused a third person to believe someone to be his agent, and that third person acted as if that other person was in fact the principal's agent.

OVER IMPROVEMENT- An improvement that is not the highest and best use for the site on which it is placed, by reason of excessive size or cost.

OVERAGES IN TRUST ACCOUNT- Any unexplained overages in the trust account must be held in trust by the licensee and must be maintained in a separate record.

OVERHANG- The part of the roof that extends beyond the walls and that shades buildings and covers walks.

OWNERSHIP- The right of a person to use and possess property to the exclusion of others.

PARITY WALL - A wall erected on the line between two adjoining properties that are under different ownership for the use of both owners.

PAROL - Oral or verbal.

PAROL EVIDENCE RULE - A rule of courtroom evidence that once the parties make a written contract, they may not then introduce oral agreements or statements to modify the terms of that written agreement. An exception exists for fraud or mistake, which will permit the parties to offer evidence to vary the terms of the writing.

PARQUET FLOOR - Hardwood flooring laid in squares or patterns.

PART TIME STATUS - Many real estate agents have other full-time jobs. . A part time agent cannot devote a full time effort to represent a client; therefore the failure to disclose a part time status is considered unethical real estate practice.

PARTIAL RECONVEYANCE - In a deed of trust or mortgage, a clause that permits release of a parcel or part of a parcel from the effects and lien of that security instrument. The release usually occurs upon the payment of a specified sum of money.

PARTITION ACTION - A legal action by which co-owners seek to sever their joint ownership. The physical division of property between co-owners, usually through court action.

PARTNERSHIP - An association of two or more persons to unite their property, labor or skill, or any one or combination thereof, in prosecution of some joint business, and to share the profits in certain proportions. An agreement of two or more individuals jointly to undertake a business enterprise. If it is a general partnership, all partners have unlimited liability and, absent other agreements, share equally in the management and profits of the business.

PATENT - Conveyance of title to government land.

PAYMENT CLAUSE - A provision in a promissory note, deed of trust, or mortgage, permitting the debtor to pay off the obligation before maturity.

PENNY - The term, as applied to nails, that serves as a measure of nail length and is abbreviated by the letter d.

PERCENTAGE LEASE - A lease on property, the rental for which is determined by the amount of business done by the tenant, usually a percentage of gross receipts from the business, with provision for a minimum rental.

PERIMETER HEATING - Baseboard heating or any system in which the heat registers are located along the outside walls of a room, especially under the windows.

PERIODIC TENANCY - A leasehold estate that continues indefinitely for successive periods of time, until terminated by proper notice. When the periods are one month in duration, it is often called a month-to-month lease.

PERSONAL INJURY - A term commonly used in tort (e.g. negligence cases) indicating an injury to one's being or body (for example, cuts or broken bones) as opposed to injury to his property.

PERSONAL PROPERTY - Any property that is not real property. (See Real Property.) Property that is movable, as opposed to real property, which is immovable; also includes intangible property and leasehold estates.

PETITIONER- A person who petitions the court on a special proceeding or a motion.

PIER- A column of masonry used to support other structural members.

PITCH- The incline or rise of a roof.

PLAINTIFF- The party who initiates a lawsuit; the person who sues another.

PLATE- A horizontal board placed on a wall or supported on posts or studs to carry the trusses of a roof or rafters directly; a shoe or base member, as of a partition or other frame; a small flat board placed on or in a wall to support girders and rafters, for example.

PLEDGE- Deposition of personal property by a debtor with a creditor as security for a debt or engagement.

PLEDGEE- One who is given a pledge as security. (See Security Party)

PLEDGOR- One who gives a pledge as security. (See Debtor)

PLOTTAGE INCREMENT- The appreciation in unit value created by joining smaller ownerships into one large single ownership.

PLYWOOD
1. Laminated wood made up in panels.
2. Several thickness of wood glued together with grains at different angles for strength.

POCKET LISTING- When a real estate licensee convinces a seller that he can procure a buyer for the property and wants to withhold the information from the multiple listing services. This is considered unethical.

POINTS- Points paid for refinancing must be spread out over the life of the loan to be deductible on a person's income tax.

POLICE POWER- The right of the state to enact laws and regulations and its right to enforce them for the order, safety, health, morals, and general welfare of the public. The power of the state to prohibit acts that adversely affect the public health, welfare, safety, or morals. (Zoning and building codes are examples of exercise of the police power.)

POWER OF ATTORNEY- An instrument authorizing a person to act as the agent of the person granting it. A special power of attorney limits the agent to a particular or specific act, as a landowner may grant an agent special power of attorney to convey a single and specific parcel of property. Under a general power of attorney, the agent may do almost anything for the principal that the principal could do himself or herself. A document authorizing a person (an attorney-in-fact) to act as an agent.

POWER OF TERMINATION- The future interest created whenever there is a grant of a fee simple subject to a condition subsequent estate. The future interest matures into a present interest estate only if the holder timely and properly exercises his right upon a breach by the current holder of the fee estate.

PREFABRICATED HOUSE - A house manufactured, and sometimes partly assembled, before delivery to the building site.

PREJUDGEMENT ATTACHMENT - An attachment of property made before the trial, with the intent of holding that property as security, to have an asset to sell if the court judgment is favorable to the attaching party.

PREPAYMENT PENALTY - Penalty for the payment of a note before it actually becomes due. A fee or charge imposed upon a debtor who desires to pay off his loan before its maturity. Not all prepayment clauses provide for a penalty, and in many real estate transactions the law regulates the amount of penalty that may be changed.

PRESCRIPTION - Securing of an easement by open, notorious, and uninterrupted use, adverse to the owner of the land for the period required by statute, which, in California, is five years. A method of obtaining an easement by adverse use over a prescribed period of time.

PRESENT INTEREST - An estate in land that gives the owner the right to occupy his property immediately; as opposed to a future interest, which grants only the right to occupy the premises at some future date.

PRESUMPTION - That which may be assumed without proof. A conclusion or assumption that is binding in the absence of sufficient proof to the contrary.

PRIMA FACIE
1. Presumptive on its face.
2. Assumed correct until overcome by further proof. Facts, evidence, or documents that are taken at face value and presumed to be as they appear (unless proven otherwise).

PRINCIPAL- The (client) employer of an agent. Someone who hires an agent to act on his behalf. The term also refers to the amount of an outstanding loan (exclusive of interest).

PRIORITY - That which comes first in point of time or right. Superior, higher, or preferred rank or position.

PRIVITY - Closeness or mutuality of a contractual relationship.

PROBATE - Court supervision of the collection and distribution of a deceased person's estate. This takes place in Superior Court within the county where the property is located.

PROCEDURAL LAW - The law of how to present and proceed with legal rights (for example, laws of evidence, enforcement of judgments). It is the opposite of substantative law.

PROCURING CAUSE - That event originating from another series of events that, without a break in continuity, results in an agent's producing a final buyer. Proximate cause. A broker is the procuring cause of a sale if his or her efforts set in motion an unbroken chain of events that resulted in the sale.

PROFIT A PRENDRE - An easement coupled with a power to consume resources on the burdened property.

PROMISSORY NOTE- A written promise to pay a designated sum of money at a future date.

PROPERTY- Anything that may be owned. Anything of value in which the law permits ownership.

PRORATION OF TAXES- Division of the taxes equally or proportionately between buyer and seller on the basis of time of ownership.

PUFFING- Putting things in their best perspective is not subject to disciplinary action.

PUNITIVE DAMAGES- Money awarded by the court for the sole purpose of punishing the wrongdoer, and not designed to compensate the injured party for his damages.

PURCHASE MONEY INSTRUMENT- A mortgage or deed of trust that does not permit a deficiency judgment in the event of foreclosure and sale of the secured property for less than the amount due on the promissory note. It is called purchase money since the deed of trust and mortgage was used to buy all or part of the property.

PURCHASE-MONEY MORTGAGE OR PURCHASE-MONEY DEED OF TRUST- A mortgage or deed of trust given as part or all of the consideration for the purchase of property or given as security for a loan to obtain money for all or part of the purchase price.

QUARTER ROUND - A molding whose profile resembles a quarter of a circle.

QUASI- Almost as if it were.

QUASI-CONTRACT- A contract implied by law; that is, the law will imply and consider certain relationships as if they were a contract.

QUIET ENJOYMENT- The right of an owner to the use of property without interference with his or her possession or use.

QUIET TITLE ACTION- A lawsuit designed to remove any clouds on a title to property. It forces the claimant of an adverse interest in property to prove his right to title; otherwise he will be forever barred from asserting it.

QUITCLAIM DEED- A deed to relinquish any interest in property that the grantor may have, but implying no warranties. A deed that transfers only whatever right, title, or interest, if any, the grantor owns, without implying any warranties.

QUITE TITLE- A court action brought to establish title and to remove a cloud from the title.

RADIANT HEATING - A method of heating, usually consisting of coils or pipes placed in the floor, wall, or ceiling.

RAFTER- One of a series of boards of a roof designed to support roof loads.

RANGE- A strip of land six miles wide, determined by a government survey, running in a north-south direction.

RATIFICATION - The adoption or approval of an act performed on behalf of a person without previous authorization. Approval and confirmation of a prior act performed on one's behalf by another person without previous authority.

READY, WILLING, AND ABLE BUYER - A purchaser of property, who is willing to buy on terms acceptable to the seller, and who further possesses the financial ability to consummate the sale. Producing such a buyer sometimes earns the broker a commission, even though a sale is not forthcoming.

REAL ESATE LICENSEE- Can be a good source to find first trust deeds that can be purchased at a discount.

REAL ESTATE BOARD - An organization whose members consist primarily of real estate brokers and salespersons.

REAL ESTATE INVESTMENT TRUST - A specialized form of holding title to property that enables investors to pool their resources and purchase property, while still receiving considerable tax advantages, without being taxed as a corporation. Also known as REIT.

REAL ESTATE TRUST - A special arrangement under federal and state law whereby investors may pool funds for investments in real estate and mortgages and yet escape corporation taxes.

REAL PROPERTY - Land and anything affixed, incidental, or appurtenant to it, and anything considered immovable under the law. Land, buildings, and other immovable property permanently attached thereto.

REALTOR - A real estate broker holding active membership in a real estate board affiliated with the National Association of Realtors.

REBUTTABLE PRESUMPTION - A presumption that is not conclusive and that may be contradicted by evidence. A presumption that applies unless proven inapplicable by the introduction of contradictory evidence.

RECAPTURE
1. The rate of interest necessary to provide for the return of an investment.
2. A provision in tax laws that reduces certain benefits from claiming depreciation.

RECEIVER - A neutral third party, appointed by the court to collect the rents and profits from property, and distribute them as ordered by the court. Often used as a remedy when mere damages are inadequate.

RECONVEYANCE - A conveyance to the landowner of the legal title held by a trustee under a deed of trust. The transfer of property back from a lender who holds an interest as security for the payment of a debt. In a deed of trust, the beneficiary reconveys property upon satisfaction of the promissory note.

RECORDATION - Filing of instruments for record in the office of the county recorder. The act of having a document filed for record in the county recorder's office. Once recorded, the instrument gives constructive notice to the world.

REDEMPTION - Buying back one's property after a judicial sale. The repurchasing of one's property after a judicial sale.

REFORMATION- A legal action to correct a mistake in a deed or other document.

REINSTATEMENT- A right available to anyone under an accelerated promissory note secured by a deed of trust or mortgage on property. If a deed of trust is foreclosed by trustee's sale, the debtor may have up to three months from the recording of the notice of default to pay the amount in arrears plus interest and costs, thereby completely curing the default (reinstating) without penalty.

REJECTION- Refusal to accept an offer. Repudiation of an offer automatically terminates the offer.

RELEASE- To give up or abandon a right. The release of rights may be voluntary, as when one voluntarily discharges an obligation under a contract. The release may be involuntary, by operation of the law; for example, one's wrongful conduct may bar him from asserting his rights. In deeds of trust a partial release clause frees certain property from the security of the deed of trust upon the payment of specified sums of money.

RELEASE CLAUSE- A stipulation in a deed of trust or mortgage that upon the payment of a specific sum of money to the holder of the deed of trust or mortgage, a particular lot or area shall be removed from the blanket lien on the whole area involved.

RELICTION- The gradual lowering of water from the usual watermark.

REMAINDER- An estate that vests after the termination of the prior estate, such as after a life estate. Example: A life estate may be granted to Adams, with the remainder granted to Baker. Most commonly, an estate (future interest) that arises in favor of a third person after a life estate.

REMAND- To send back to a lower court for further action.

REMEDY- The means by which a right is enforced, preserved, or compensated. Some of the more common remedies are damages, injunctions, rescission, and specific performance.

RENT- The consideration paid by a tenant for possession of property under a lease.

RENTAL PROPERTY- Renting property to the first person that comes along can be a costly mistake.

RENTAL PROPERTY- Rental income from a smaller property may show a higher rate of profit than from a more expensive property.

RENUNCIATION- Is the cancellation of an agency relationship by the real estate agent requires written notice to the principal.

RESCISSION- The unmaking of a contract, and the restoring of each party to the same position each held before the contract arose.

RESCISSION OF CONTRACT- The canceling of a contract by either mutual consent of the parties or legal action.

RESERVATION- A right or interest retained by a grantor when conveying property; also called an exception.

RESIDUE - That portion of a person's estate that has not been specifically devised.

RESPA - Prohibits the giving and receiving of kickbacks and unearned fees.

RESPONDEAT SUPERIOR - This Latin phrase, "let the master answer," means that an employer is liable for the tortuous acts of an employee, and a principal is liable for the acts of an agent. To be liable, the acts must be within the "course and scope" of the agency or employment. For example, an employer would not be liable for the acts of an employee while at home and not doing work for the employer.

RESPONDENT - The person against whom an appeal is taken; the opposite of an appellant.

RESTRICTION - A limitation on the use of real property arising from a contract or a recorded instrument. An encumbrance on property that limits the use of it; usually a covenant or condition.

RETALIATORY EVICTION - A landlord's attempt to evict a tenant from a lease because the tenant has used the remedies available under the warranty of habitability.

REVERSION - The right a grantor keeps when he or she grants someone an estate that will or may end in the future. Examples: The interest remaining with a landlord after he or she grants a lease, or the interest an owner of land has after he or she grants someone a life estate. Any future interest (estate) left in the grantor. The residue of an estate left in the grantor after the termination of a lesser estate.

REVOCATION - Withdrawal of an offer or other right, thereby voiding and destroying that offer or right. It is a recall with intent to rescind.

RIDGE - The horizontal line at the junction of the top edges of two sloping roof surfaces. (The rafters at both slopes are nailed at the ridge.)

RIDGE BOARD - The board placed on edge at the ridge of the roof to support the upper ends of the rafters; also called rooftree, ridge piece, ridge plate, or ridgepole.

RIGHT OF SURVIVORSHIP - The right to acquire the interest of a deceased joint-owner. It is the distinguishing feature of a joint tenancy.

RIGHT OF WAY - The right to pass over a piece of real property or to have pipes, electrical lines, or the like go across it. An easement granting a person the right to pass across another's property.

RIPARIAN RIGHTS - The right of a landowner with regard to a stream crossing or adjoining his or her property.

RISER
1. The upright board at the back of each step of a stairway.
2. In heating, a riser is a duct slanted upward to carry hot air from the furnace to the room above.

RULE AGAINST PERPETUITIES - A complex set of laws designed to prevent excessive restrictions on the transferability of property. The rule holds that "no interest is good unless it must vest, if at all, not later than 21 years after some life in being at the creation of the interest."

RUMFORD ACT- Prohibits discrimination in employment and housing. Is enforced by the Department of Fair Employment and Housing.

SAFETY CLAUSE - In a listing agreement, a provision that if anyone found by the broker during his listing period purchases the property within a specified time after the expiration of the listing, the broker receives his full commission.

SALE-LEASEBACK- A situation in which the owner of a piece of property sells it and retains occupancy be leasing it from the buyer.

SALES CONTRACT- A contract between buyer and seller setting out the terms of sale.

SALESPERSON- An individual licensed to sell property, but who must at all times be under the supervision and direction of a broker.

SANDWICH LEASE - A leasehold interest that lies between the primary lease and the operating lease. Example: A leases to B; B subleases to C; C subleases to D. C's lease is a sandwich lease.

SASH- A wood or metal frame containing one or more windowpanes.

SATISFACTION- Discharge of a mortgage or deed of trust lien from the records upon payment of the secured debt. Discharge of an obligation or indebtedness by paying what is due.

SAVINGS ACCOUNT- An investor should not place money in a savings account if he wants to have financial freedom.

SEAL- An impression mark or stamp made to attest to the execution of an instrument.

SECONDARY FINANCING- A loan secured by a second mortgage or a second deed of trust.

SECONDARY MONEY MARKET- Where loans are purchased and sold.

SECTION- A square mile of land, as established by government survey, containing 640 acres.

SECURED DEBT- An obligation that includes property held as security for the payment of that debt; upon default, the property may be sold to satisfy the debt.

SECURED PARTY- The party having the security interest in personal property. The mortgagee, conditional seller, or pledgee is referred to as the secured party.

SECURITY AGREEMENT- An agreement between the secured party and the debtor that creates a security interest in personal property. It replaced such terms as chattel mortgage, pledge, trust receipt, chattel trust, equipment trust, conditional sale, and inventory lien.

SECURITY DEPOSIT- A deposit made to assure performance of an obligation, usually by a tenant. A sum of cash given as collateral to ensure faithful performance of specified obligations.

SECURITY INTEREST- A term designating the interest of a secured creditor in the personal property of the debtor.

SEIZIN - The possession of land under a claim of freehold.

SENIOR LIEN - A lien that is superior to or has priority over another lien. Also, the first deed of trust or lien on a property.

SEPARATE PROPERTY - Property that is owned by a husband or wife and that is not community property. It is property acquired by either spouse prior to marriage or by gift or inheritance after marriage; also, in California, it is the income from separate property after marriage. Property held by a married person that is not community property; it includes property owned before marriage and property acquired after marriage by gift or inheritance.

SEPTIC TANK- An underground tank in which sewage from the house is reduced to liquid by bacterial action and drained off.

SERVIENT ESTATE - That parcel of property, which is burdened by and encumbered with an easement.

SERVIENT TENEMENT - An estate burdened by an easement.

SET-BACK ORDINANCE - An ordinance prohibiting the erection of a building or structure between the curb and the set-back line. (see Building Line)

SEVERALTY - Sole ownership of property. Ownership by one person.

SEVERALTY OWNERSHIP - Ownership by only one person; sole ownership.

SHAKE - A hand-split shingle, usually edge-grained.

SHEATHING - Structural covering, such as boards, plywood, or wallboard, placed over the exterior studding or rafters of a house.

SHERIFF'S DEED - A deed given by court order in connection with the sale of property to satisfy a judgment.

SILL - The board or piece of metal forming the lower side of an opening, such as a doorsill or windowsill.

SINKING FUND
1. A fund set aside from the income from property that, with accrued interest, will eventually pay for replacement of the improvements.
2. A similar fund set aside to pay a debt.

SMALL CLAIMS COURT - A branch of the Municipal Court. The rules of this court forbid parties to be assisted by attorneys dispense with most formal rules of evidence, and have all trials heard by judges. The monetary limit of cases before the court is $1,500.

SOIL PIPE - Pipe carrying waste from the house to the main sewer line.

SOLD TO THE STATE - A bookkeeping entry on the county tax rolls indicating that the property taxes are delinquent. The entry begins the five-year redemption period, after which the property may be physically sold to the public for back taxes.

SOLE OR SOLE PLATE- A structural member, usually two-by-four, on which wall and partition studs rest.

SPAN- The distance between structural supports, such as walls, columns, piers, beams, and girders.

SPECIAL ASSESSMENT- Legal charge against real estate by a public authority to pay the cost of public improvement, as distinguished from taxes levied for the general support of government.

SPECIFIC PERFORMANCE- A legal action to compel performance of a contract; for example a contract for the sale of land. A contract remedy by which one party is ordered by the court to comply with the terms of the agreement.

SPOUSE- A person's husband or wife.

SQUARE FOOTAGE OF BUILDING- An appraiser always uses the exterior dimensions to calculate the square footage of a building.

SRA- The Society of Real Estate Appraisers.

STARE DECISIS- A fundamental principle of law, which holds that courts should follow prior decisions on a point of law. A proper decision is a binding precedent on equal or lower courts having the same facts in controversy.

STATUTE- A written law.

STATUTE OF FRAUDS- The state law that provides that certain contracts must be in writing in order to be enforceable in the courts. Examples: real property leased for more than one year or an agent's authorization to sell real estate. A law that requires certain contracts (including most real estate contracts) to be in writing to be enforceable.

STATUTE OF LIMITATIONS- A statute that requires lawsuits to be brought within a certain time to be enforceable. The basic periods are one year for personal injury, two years for oral contracts, three years for damages to real or personal property, four years for written contracts, and three years from date of discovery for fraud.

STEERING- An illegal procedure where individual buyers, who are usually minorities, are only shown properties in specific neighborhoods.

STEPPED-UP BASIS- A higher, increased tax value of property given as the result of most sales or taxable transfers. The tax basis is used in computing capital gains and losses on the transfer of property.

STOP NOTICE- A notice served on the owner of property or custodian of funds. It requests, with certain penalties for noncompliance, that any funds due to a general contractor be paid to the claimant, laborer, or materialman.

STRAIGHT MORTGAGE OR DEED OF TRUST- A mortgage or deed of trust in which there is no reduction of the principal during the term of the instrument. Payments to interest are usually made on an annual, semiannual, or quarterly basis.

STRAIGHT NOTE- A promissory note that is unamortized. The principal is paid at the end of the term of the note.

STRAIGHT-LINE DEPRECIATION- An accounting procedure that sets the rate of depreciation as a fixed percentage of the amount to be depreciated; the percentage stays the same each year.

STRING, STRINGER
1. A timber or other support for cross-members.
2. In stairs, the support on which the stair treads rest.

STUDS OR STUDDING - Vertical supporting timbers in walls and partitions.

SUBCHAPTER-S CORPORATION - A corporation that, for federal tax purposes only, is taxed similarly to a partnership. The corporate entity is disregarded for most federal tax purposes, and the shareholders are generally taxed as individual partners.

SUBJACENT SUPPORT - Support that the soil below the surface gives to the surface of the land.

SUBJECT TO
1. Burdened by and liable for an obligation.
2. A method of taking over a loan without becoming personally liable for its payment

"SUBJECT TO" MORTGAGE OR DEED OF TRUST - When a grantee takes a title to real property subject to a mortgage or deed of trust, he or she is not responsible to the holder of the promissory note for the payment of any portion of the amount due. The most that he or she can lose in the event of a foreclosure is his or her equity in the property. In neither case is the original maker of the note released from his or her responsibility. (See also Assumption of Mortgage or Deed of Trust.)

SUBLEASE - A lease given by a tenant.

SUBORDINATE - To make subject or junior to.

SUBORDINATION AGREEMENT- In a mortgage or deed of trust, a provision that a later lien shall have a priority interest over the existing lien. It makes the existing lien inferior to a later lien, in effect exchanging priorities with that later lien.

SUBORDINATION CLAUSE - Senior lien that makes it inferior to what would otherwise be a junior lien.

SUBROGATE - To substitute one person for another's legal rights to a claim or debt.

SUBROGATION - The substitution of another person in place of the creditor with regard to an obligation.

SUBSTANTATIVE LAW - The laws describing rights and duties. Differs from procedural law, which only describes how to enforce and protect rights.

SUCCESSION - The inheritance of property.

SUCCESSOR IN INTEREST - The next succeeding owner of an interest in property. The transferee or recipient of a property interest.

SUPERIOR COURT- The principal trial court of the state; a court of unlimited monetary and subject matter jurisdiction, and an appeal court for decisions of municipal courts and small claims courts.

SUPREME COURT- The highest court in the California and the federal court structure. This court is almost exclusively an appeals court, accepting (by certiorari) only those cases that, in the court's discretion, involve issues of significant magnitude and social importance.

SURETY- One who guarantees the performance by another, a guarantor.

SURVEY- The process by which a parcel of land is located on the ground and measured.

SWING LOAN- This is a short-term equity loan.

SYNDICATION- A group of individuals pooling their resources to purchase property through the holding vehicle of a partnership, corporation, or other association. Each individual owns share in the legal entity formed to acquire and hold title to the property. This is an alternative method to finance and purchase real estate. This allows an investment in real estate with out having to do any of the work.

TAX - A compulsory charge on property or individuals, the payment of which supports a government.

TAX BASIS- The tax value of property to the taxpayer. It is a figure used to compute capital gains and losses.

TAX DEED- Deed issued to the purchaser at a tax sale.

TAX SALE- Sale of property after a period of nonpayment of taxes.

TENANCY- A leasehold estate. (For specific types of leases see Estates.)

TENANCY-IN-COMMON- Ownership by two or more persons who hold an undivided interest in real property, without right of survivorship; the interests need not be equal.

TENANT- One who leases real property from the owner.

TENEMENTS- All rights in real property that pass with a conveyance of it.

TENTATIVE MAP- The Subdivision Map Act requires subdividers initially to submit a tentative map of their tract to the local planning commission for study. The approval or disapproval of the planning commission is noted on the map. Thereafter, the planning commission requests a final map of the tract embodying any changes.

TENURE IN LAND- The manner in which land is held.

TERMITE SHIELD- A shield, usually of non-corrodible metal, placed on top of the foundation wall or around pipes to prevent passage of termites.

TERMITES- Antlike insects that feed on wood.

TESTAMENT- The written declaration of one's last will.

TESTAMENTARY DISPOSITION - A gift passing by will.

TESTATE - Describes a person who dies leaving a will.

TESTATOR- A person who makes a will. Technically, a testator is a male and a testatrix is a female, although in common use testator refers to anyone who makes a will.

THE VOLUNTARY AFFIRMATIVE MARKETING AGREEMENT - Is a voluntary commitment by real estate licensees to promote fair housing by using methodology that is fairer than government regulations.

THIRTY-DAY NOTICE - A notice terminating a periodic tenancy without cause, by ending a tenancy thirty days from date of service.

THREE-DAY NOTICE - A notice giving a tenant three days in which to cure a default or quit the premises. It is the first step in an unlawful detainer action, as the means of terminating a lease for cause. When rent is delinquent, it is sometimes called a notice to quit or pay rent.

THRESHOLD - A strip of wood or metal beveled on each edge and used above the finished floor under outside doors.

"TIME IS OF THE ESSENCE" - These words, when placed in an agreement, make it necessary that all time limitations and requirements be strictly observed.

TITLE - Evidence of the owner's right or interest in property.

THE RIGHT OF OWNERSHIP - The evidence of a person's ownership or interest in property.

TITLE INSURANCE - Insurance written by a title company to protect a property-owner against loss if title is defective or not marketable. A special policy of insurance issued by a title company, insuring the owner against loss of or defects in title to the insured property. The policy may be either a CLTA policy, issued to the property owner and to non-institutional lenders, or an ALTA policy, issued to institutional lenders.

TOPOGRAPHY - Nature of the surface of the land. Topography may be level, rolling, or mountainous.

TORRENS TITLE - A title included in a state-insured title system no longer used in California.

TORT
1. A wrongful act.
2. A wrong or injury.
3. Violation of a legal right. A civil wrong, not arising from a breach of contract. Most torts lie in negligence, although they could also be intentional torts (such as assault and battery, trespass) or strict liability torts.

TORTFEASOR - A person who commits a tort.

TORTIOUS - Conduct which amounts to a tort.

TOWNSHIP - A territorial subdivision that is six miles long and six miles wide and that contains 36 sections, each one mile square.

TRADE FIXTURES - Articles of personal property that are annexed to real property but that are necessary to the carrying on of a trade and are removable by the owner. Fixtures installed to further one's trade, business, or profession. They are an exception to the general rule that fixtures are part of a building. Such fixtures installed by a tenant may be removed before the expiration of the tenancy.

TRADE-IN - Method of guaranteeing an owner a minimum amount of cash on the sale of his or her present property to permit him or her to purchase another. If the property is not sold within a specified time at the listed price, the broker agrees to arrange financing to purchase the property at an agreed-upon discount.

TRANSFER - Conveyance; passage of title.

TRANSFER DISCLOSURE STATEMENT - It is the responsibility of the seller (transfer-or) to issue the statement.

TRANSFEREE - The person to whom a transfer is made.

TRANSFEROR - The person who makes a transfer.

TREADS - Horizontal boards of a stairway.

TRESPASS - An invasion of an owner's rights in his or her property.
1. Unauthorized entry onto another's land.
2. Invasion of another's rights or property.

TRESPASSER - One who trespasses. The importance of this classification of individuals on property is created by the methods for removal and the liability of the property owner if the trespasser is injured on his property.

TRIM- The finish materials in a building, such as moldings applied around openings (window trim, door trim) or at the floor and ceiling (baseboard, cornice, picture molding).

TRUST- A right of property, real or personal, held by one party called the trustee for the benefit of another party called the beneficiary. Arrangement whereby one person holds property for the benefit of another under fiduciary (special confidential) relationship.

TRUST DEED- Deed given by a borrower to a trustee to be held pending fulfillment of an obligation, which is usually repayment of a loan to a beneficiary. A deed of trust. Foreclosure of this deed maybe at a foreclosure or at a trustee's sale. The lender in the trust deed is referred to as the beneficiary. Trust deed investments should be on improved property rather than on unimproved property.

TRUST FUNDS- Consists of money or property received by a real estate licensee on behalf of others. Cannot be given to the seller without the permission of the buyer. Must be in writing. These funds may not be commingled. It is against the law. Protects the money in case a legal action is taken against the broker. These records are subject to audit and examination by the D.R.E. All records and corresponding instruments must be kept for a period of (3) three years.

TRUSTEE - One who holds property in trust for another. The person who holds property in trust for another. In a deed of trust, the person who holds bare legal title in trust.

TRUSTEE'S DEED - The deed issued by the beneficiary after the foreclosure and sale under a deed of trust.

TRUSTEE'S SALE - The private sale of property held by a trustee under a deed of trust as part of the foreclosure proceedings.

TRUSTEE'S SALE - This sale must be conducted in approximately four months.

TRUSTOR
1. One who conveys his or her property to a trustee.
2. The borrower or debtor under a deed of trust.

TRUSTOR'S REINSTATEMENT RIGHTS - These rights continue for five business days prior to the date of the trustee's sale.

TRUTH IN LENDING LAW - A complex set of federal statutes designed to provide a borrower with a means of discovering and comparing the true costs of credit. Under Regulation Z of the act, certain borrowers of property have three days after accepting a loan to rescind without cost or liability.

UNDUE INFLUENCE - A compulsory charge on property or individuals, the payment of which supports a government.

UNDUE INFLUENCE - Taking any fraudulent or unfair advantage of another's necessity or weakness of mind. Using a position of trust and confidence improperly to persuade a person to take a course of action. By relying on the trusted confidant, the decision maker fails to exercise his free will and independent judgment.

UNEARNED INCREMENT- An increase in value of real estate due to no effort on the part of the owner, often due to an increase in population.

UNENFORCEABLE - Incapable of being enforced at law. An example of an unenforceable contract is an oral listing agreement to pay a broker a commission.

UNIFORM COMMERCIAL CODE - A group of statutes establishing a unified and comprehensive scheme for regulation of security transactions in personal property and other commercial matters, superseding the existing statutes on chattel mortgages conditional sales, trust receipts, assignment of accounts receivable, and other similar matters.

UNILATERAL - One-sided, ex parte.

UNJUST ENRICHMENT - A legal doctrine that prevents a person from inequitably benefiting from another's mistake, poor judgment, or loss. In a land sales contract the vender may no longer keep both the property and the buyer's excess payments (over his damages) in the event of breach, because to do so would unjustly enrich him at the buyer's expense.

UNLAWFUL DETAINER - An action to recover possession of real property. A lawsuit designed to evict a defaulting tenant, or anyone unlawfully in possession of property, from premises. It is summary in nature, entitled to a priority court trial, and litigates only the right to possession of property (and damages resulting there from).

UNLAWFULL- Illegal.

UNRUH CIVIL RIGHTS ACT- Deals with equal rights in business establishments, prohibits age limitations in housing, and sets age limitations necessary for senior housing. It states that all persons within California are free and equal no matter what their sex, race color, ancestry, national origin or disability, they are entitled to full and equal accommodations.

UNSECURED DEBT- A debt not backed by specific property to satisfy the indebtedness in case of default.

URBAN PROPERTY- City property; closely settled property.

USURY- Claiming a rate of interest greater that that permitted by law. Charging a greater rate of interest on loans than the rate allowed by law (10 percent in many cases).

VA LOAN - This loan does not contain a "due on sale " clause.

VALID
1. Legally sufficient and authorized by law.
2. Having force or binding force. Fully effective at law; legally sufficient.

VALLEY- The internal angle formed by the junction of two sloping sides of a roof.

VALUATION

1. Estimated worth or price.
2. The act of valuing by appraisal.

VARIABLE INTEREST RATE- An interest rate that fluctuates in a set proportion to changes in an economic index, such as the cost of money. Extensive regulations cover use of VIRs in loans on residential property.

VARIANCE- An exception or departure from the general rule. An exception granted to a property owner, relieving him from obeying certain aspects of a zoning ordinance. It's granting is discretionary with the zoning authorities and is based on undue hardship suffered by the property owner because of unique circumstances affecting his property.

VENDEE- Purchaser or buyer or real property.

VENDOR- Seller of real property.

VENEER- Thin sheets of wood placed over another material.

VENT- A pipe installed to provide a flow of air to or from a drainage system or to provide a circulation of air within such system to protect trap seals from siphonage and backpressure.

VENUE- The location in which a cause of action occurs; it determines the court having jurisdiction to hear and decide the case. For real estate, the court having proper venue is one in the county in which the property is located.

VERIFICATION- A sworn statement before a duly qualified officer as to the correctness of the contents of an instrument. Written certification under oath and/or penalty of perjury, confirming the truth of the facts in a document.

VERSUS - Against (abbreviated v. or vs.). Used in case names, with the plaintiff's name given first.

VESTED - Bestowed upon someone, such as title to property. Absolute, not contingent or subject to being defeated.

VETERAN'S EXEMPTION - A deduction from the annual property tax allowed to a qualified veteran residing on residential property. Since July 1978, it has amounted to $40 off the normal tax bill.

VOID - To have no legal force or effect; that which is unenforceable. Unenforceable, null, having no legal effect.

VOIDABLE - An instrument that appears to be valid and enforceable on its face but is, in fact, lacking some essential requirement. May be declared void, but is valid unless and until declared void.

VOLUNTARY LIEN - Any lien placed on property with the consent of the owner or as a result of the voluntary act of the owner.

WAIVE - To give up a right.

WAIVER - Giving up of certain rights or privileges. The relinquishment may be voluntary and knowing, or it may occur involuntarily through action of the parties. The action resulting in the waiver is unilateral, and requires no action or reliance by the other party.

WARRANTY - An absolute undertaking or promise that certain facts are as represented. Occasionally used interchangeably with guarantee.

WARRANTY DEED - A deed that is used to convey real property and that contains warranties of title and quiet possession; the grantor the lawful claims thus agrees to defend the premises against of third persons. It is commonly used in other states, but in California the grant deed has replaced it. Used predominantly in states that do not have title insurance companies. This deed contains six full warranties of protection to the buyer, including warranties that the seller owns the property, that it is unencumbered, and that the seller will defend title against any defects.

WARRANTY OF HABITABILITY - Implied warranty in residential leases. The landlord covenants by implication that the premises are suitable for human occupancy. The implied warranties are found in the statutes and implied by common law.

WASTE - The destruction, or material alteration of or injury to premises by a tenant-for-life, or tenant, or tenant-for-years. Example: a tenant cutting down trees or mining coal. The destruction, injury, material alteration, or abusive use of property by a person rightfully in possession, but who does not own the fee or entire estate (for example, by a lessee or life tenant).

WATER TABLE - Distance from the surface of the ground to a depth at which natural groundwater is found.

WILL - A document that directs the disposition of one's property after death.

WITNESSED WILL- A formal will, signed by the testator in the presence of two or more witnesses, each of whom must also sign the will.

WRAP AROUND MORTGAGE (DEED OF (See All-Inclusive Deed of Trust.) TRUST)

WRAP-AROUND DEED OF TRUST - A sophisticated financing package that permits the seller to sell his property without paying off the outstanding deed of trust. The buyer's larger loan, which is used to purchase the property, includes provisions for paying off the seller's existing loan.

WRIT - A process of the court under which property may be seized. An order from the court to the sheriff or other law enforcement officer directing and authorizing a specific act.

WRIT OF ATTACHMENT - A writ authorizing and directing the physical attachment (seizure) of property.

WRIT OF EXECUTION - An order directing the sheriff to seize property to satisfy a judgment.

WRIT OF IMMEDIATE POSSESSION - An order authorizing a landlord to obtain immediate possession of a tenant's premises, pending the outcome of an unlawful detainer action or other court proceeding.

ZONE - The area set off by the proper authorities in which the real property can be used for only specific purposes.

ZONING - Act of city or county authorities specifying the type of use to which property may be put in specific areas. A government's division of a city or other geographic area into districts, and the regulation of property uses within each district.

I N D E X

Commission:

    Right To 28, 59-60, 72, 92-93, 133, 144, 148, 165, 190, 200, 348

Commissioner's Regulations 200

Communication 3, 54-55, 63, 88, 90-91, 95, 116, 120, 129, 133

    Direct Contact 61

    Letter 37-38, 53, 90, 94, 317

    Telephone 32-33, 36, 38-39, 53, 60, 62-63, 103, 191

Compensation 15-17, 21, 24-25, 27-28, 70, 81-82, 92-93, 153, 462

Condominiums 146, 166, 170

Contract:

    Lease 6, 14-15, 24, 35, 52-54, 92, 133, 144, 153, 186, 329, 348-349

    413, 419, 434, 452, 465, 478-481, 486-488, 491, 493

    Management 3, 6, 14 23, 31, 60, 61, 62, 84, 90, 138, 167, 329, 425, 429, 462

Corporation 53, 191

County Recorder 138, 141

Covenants 147, 187

Credit Application 153, 170

D

Department of Housing and Urban Development 55, 62, 148

Department of Real Estate 22-24, 31, 127-128, 130, 145

Deposit Receipt 105-106, 126, 131, 168, 172-174, 183-191, 199-201, 206-209, 213, 222-223, 230-232

Depreciation 7, 85, 87, 92,

Direct Mail 31, 36, 45, 48, 60-61, 63-64

Disclosures 4, 62, 69, 73, 83, 116, 125, 127-129, 133, 146-147, 153, 165, 170, 184, 201, 209, 230-231, 233, 237, 312, 336, 341, 490

E

Equal Credit Opportunity Act 153, 170

Equal Housing Opportunity 57, 84

Estate Planning 7

Exclusive Right to Sell 93

F

Fair Housing 6, 22-23, 57, 369, 379,

Financing:

    Conventional 5-6, 245,

    Government 7, 10, 53-54, 60, 83, 127, 141, 283, 348

    Income Properties 7, 85-86, 91, 137

    Mobile Home 14, 27, 52-53

Fixtures 190, 208, 480

G

Gross operating Income 436

H

Hedge Against Inflation 428

Home Ownership 35, 49,
Home Trade-in Sales 8, 455, 462
Housing and Urban Development (HUD) 62

I

Income:

    Classification of 452

    Investment 5, 7, 24, 87, 117, 154, 281, 421, 425, 459, 452

Income Property 14, 27, 41, 44, 59, 87, 91

    Financing of 43

Income Tax 87, 109, 154, 344

Industrial Property 21

Inheritance 5, 281

Inspection 4, 51, 125, 141, 143, 154, 166-167, 169, 187, 209, 221, 232, 319-320

Internal Revenue Service 15, 27, 462

Investment Property 462

Irrevocable Order 183-184, 199, 207, 209

J

Joint Tenancy 119

L

Lease:

    Assignment of 82, 199

Leverage 88, 425

Licensing:

    Examination 25, 28

M

Mode of Acceptance Clause 465

Mortgage Loan Disclosure 147, 252

Mortgage-Equity Method 442

Multiple Exchanges 8, 455, 466, 472

Multiple Listing Service 14, 72, 85, 88, 93, 188

N

National Association of Real Estate Boards 550

Negative Amortization 149, 261, 265-266

Net Listing 68, 72-73, 93

Notary Public Services 8, 477, 499

O

Occupancy 186, 188, 223, 230, 304, 306, 309, 318, 344-345, 370, 410, 435

    Agreement for 81, 207, 239

Offer:

    Contract 358, 369, 371, 386-387, 389, 391, 393-395, 397, 460, 464-466, 470, 480-482, 489, 494, 496, 498

    Presenting 4, 115, 127, 171, 202-204, 209

Chapter 1

Test Your Knowledge: 1-D, 2-B, 3-A, 4-C, 5-C, 6-D, 7-DC
Chapter Quiz: 1-D, 2-B, 3-D, 4-C, 5-B, 6-A, 7-C, 8-D, 9-A, 10-C, 11-C, 12-A, 13-D, 14-B, 15-A, 16-C, 17-D, 18-C, 19-C, 20-B

Chapter 2

Test Your Knowledge: 1-B, 2-A, 3-D, 4-B, 5-D, 6-C, 7-C
Chapter Quiz: 1-B, 2-D, 3-B, 4-A, 5-C, 6-D, 7-C, 8-D, 9-D, 10-B, 11-D, 12-D, 13-C, 14-B, 15-C, 16-A, 17-C, 18-B, 19-D, 20-C

Chapter 3

Test Your Knowledge: 1-D, 2-C, 3-D, 4-A, 5-A, 6-B, 7-C
Chapter Quiz: 1-C, 2-D, 3-C, 4-C, 5-A, 6-B, 7-D, 8-B, 9-A, 10-C, 11-B, 12-D, 13-A, 14-C, 15-D, 16-D, 17-D, 18-B, 19-C, 20-C

Chapter 4

Test Your Knowledge: 1-C, 2-D, 3-D, 4-A, 5-D, 6-B, 7-C
Chapter Quiz: 1-C, 2-A, 3-B, 4-C, 5-D, 6-B, 7-D, 8-D, 9-A, 10-D, 11-C, 12-A, 13-B, 14-B, 15-D, 16-C, 17-B, 18-C, 19-A, 20-B

Chapter 5

Test Your Knowledge: 1-A, 2-B, 3-D, 4-D, 5-B, 6-D, 7-D
Chapter Quiz: 1-B, 2-A, 3-B, 4-C, 5-C, 6-C, 7-A, 8-D, 9-B, 10-D, 11-B, 12-C, 13-D, 14-B, 15-D, 16-C, 17-A, 18-D, 19-D, 20-D

Chapter 6

Test Your Knowledge: 1-D, 2-D, 3-C, 4-C, 5-C, 6-B, 7-D
Chapter Quiz: 1-D, 2-C, 3-C, 4-D, 5-B, 6-D, 7-A, 8-B, 9-C, 10-C, 11-A, 12-C, 13-C, 14-A, 15-B, 16-D, 17-B, 18-D, 19-A, 20-D

Chapter 7

Test Your Knowledge: 1-A, 2-C, 3-D, 4-B, 5-A, 6-B, 7-B
Chapter Quiz: 1-A, 2-C, 3-B, 4-D, 5-D, 6-C, 7-D, 8-B, 9-C, 10-D, 11-A, 12-A, 13-D, 14-C, 15-B, 16-C, 17-D, 18-D, 19-A, 20-B

Chapter 8

Test Your Knowledge: 1-B, 2-D, 3-A, 4-C, 5-B, 6-C, 7-D
Chapter Quiz: 1-B, 2-A, 3-D, 4-B, 5-D, 6-D, 7-C, 8-A, 9-B, 10-D, 11-C, 12-D, 13-A, 14-B, 15-A, 16-B, 17-C, 18-D, 19-D, 20-C

Chapter 9

Test Your Knowledge: 1-C, 2-A, 3-D, 4-D, 5-C, 6-B, 7-A
Chapter Quiz: 1-C, 2-C, 3-A, 4-D, 5-D, 6-B, 7-B, 8-D, 9-C, 10-D, 11-C, 12-D, 13-B, 14-D, 15-B, 16-D, 17-D, 18-A, 19-B, 20-D

Chapter 10

Test Your Knowledge: 1-A, 2-A, 3-B, 4-B, 5-B, 6-A, 7-C
Chapter Quiz: 1-A, 2-D, 3-C, 4-A, 5-D, 6-D, 7-A, 8-D, 9-B, 10-C, 11-B, 12-C, 13-D,
14-A, 15-B, 16-B, 17-A, 18-C, 19-D, 20-A

Chapter 11

Test Your Knowledge: 1-A, 2-B, 3-D, 4-A, 5-A, 6-A, 7-B
Chapter Quiz: 1-B, 2-C, 3-D, 4-A, 5-C, 6-B, 7-A, 8-D, 9-D, 10-B, 11-A, 12-C,
13-B, 14-D, 15-C, 16-B, 17-B, 18-A, 19-D, 20-A

Chapter 12

Test Your Knowledge: 1-C, 2-B, 3-D, 4-D, 5-B, 6-A, 7-C
Chapter Quiz: 1-A, 2-C, 3-B, 4-C, 5-D, 6-B, 7-B, 8-D, 9-A, 10-D, 11-A, 12-B, 13-D,
14-C, 15-C, 16-D, 17-C, 18-D, 19-A, 20-C

Chapter 13

Test Your Knowledge: 1-B, 2-A, 3-B, 4-C, 5-A, 6-C, 7-C
Chapter Quiz: 1-A, 2-C, 3-B, 4-D, 5-D, 6-C, 7-B, 8-A, 9-D, 10-A, 11-B, 12-C,
13-D, 14-A, 15-B, 16-C, 17-D, 18-A, 19-B, 20-D

Chapter 14

Test Your Knowledge: 1-B, 2-D, 3-D, 4-D, 5-C, 6-B, 7-D
Chapter Quiz: 1-D, 2-B, 3-B, 4-C, 5-D, 6-B, 7-A, 8-D, 9-A, 10-A, 11-C, 12-B,
13-D, 14-C, 15-A, 16-C, 17-B, 18-A, 19-D, 20-A

Chapter 15

Test Your Knowledge: 1-C, 2-C, 3-D, 4-D, 5-A, 6-B, 7-A
Chapter Quiz: 1-D, 2-A, 3-D, 4-B, 5-C, 6-B, 7-A, 8-A, 9-C, 10-D, 11-D, 12-D, 13-D,
14-B, 15-C, 16-D, 17-A, 18-B, 19-C, 20-C=